THE BHAGAVAD GĪTĀ

SUNY Series in Cultural Perspectives
Antonio T. de Nicolas, Editor

THE BHAGAVAD GĪTĀ

Translated by

author: WINTHROP SARGEANT

Revised Edition Edited by
CHRISTOPHER CHAPPLE

Foreword by
CHRISTOPHER CHAPPLE

STATE UNIVERSITY OF NEW YORK PRESS

Published by
State University of New York Press, Albany

Printed in the United States of America

For information, address State University of New York
Press, State University Plaza, Albany, N.Y., 12246

Library of Congress Cataloging in Publication Data

Bhagavadgītā. English & Sanskrit.
The Bhagavad Gītā.

I. Sargeant, Winthrop, 1903- II. Title.
BL1138.64.E5 1984 294.5′924 83-18287
ISBN 0-87395-831-4
ISBN 0-87395-830-6 (pbk.)

10 9 8

THE BHAGAVAD GĪTĀ

To my dear wife, Jane

CONTENTS

THE BHAGAVAD GĪTĀ

Foreword

The *Bhagavad Gītā* is one of the most studied and most translated texts in the history of world literature. Emerging from post-Vedic India, it has made its mark as a standard, almost universal work of the Hindu tradition. It also has intrigued and eluded interpreters outside India for over two centuries. Some are fascinated by its linguistic contribution; others are interested in sorting out the many philosophical and religious implications of the text. Part of the appeal of the *Gītā*, both at home in India and abroad, lies in its multivalent quality: it explicitly advances numerous teachings, some of them seemingly contradictory, and has been used in support of various others that have arisen since its composition. As Gerald Larson has noted, "The *Gītā* has been construed in all sorts of interpretive modalities, most of which can be argued to be more or less authentic and legitimate."[1] In this brief introduction, a sketch of the story line is given, followed by an assessment of how the many possible construals of the text in fact reflect the uniquely Hindu worldview that tolerates and in some cases requires holding together multiple positions simultaneously.

The *Bhagavad Gītā* tells a story of great crisis, a crisis that is solved through the interaction between Arjuna, a Pāṇḍava warrior hesitating before battle, and Krishna, his charioteer and teacher. The *Gītā* is included in the sixth book (*Bhīṣmaparvan*) of the *Mahābhārata* and documents one tiny event in a gargantuan epic tale. The main plot of the larger work involves a dispute between cousins over rulership of the Kurukṣetra kingdom in north central India. The kingdom had been lost by five brothers, the Pāṇḍavas, during a dice game and ceded to their cousins, the hundred sons of the blind king Dhṛtarāṣṭra. By prearranged agreement, the latter group was due to give back rulership to the five Pāṇḍava brothers, but refused to abide by the contract. The Pāṇḍavas are forced to wage war in order to regain their rightful territory. However, these two sets of cousins were raised together and shared the same

[1]Gerald James Larson, "The Song Celestial: Two Centuries of the *Bhagavad Gītā* in English" (*Philosophy East and West* 31:513-541).

teachers. The prospect of war between the two camps is especially repugnant because so many good friends and close relatives must be killed. Thus, we arrive at the opening of the *Bhagavad Gītā*, the moment just before the battle begins. Arjuna is thrust into crisis; he must face the anguish of killing his relatives and friends or allow himself to be killed.

The text begins with the blind king Dhṛtarāṣṭra asking his minister Saṃjaya to tell him what is happening on the field of the Kurus, the battlefield. Saṃjaya proceeds to list the principal warriors on the field and then directs his focus to Arjuna and his charioteer Krishna. Arjuna asks Krishna to place the chariot in the center of the field and then sees arrayed before him his teachers, uncles, brothers, sons, grandsons, and friends. The sight overwhelms him; it is clear that all will be slain. Thinking that if all is destroyed then kingdom and pleasure would be of no use, he throws down his bow, refusing to fight, his mind overcome with grief. In the chapters that follow, Krishna takes Arjuna on a philosophical journey, bringing into question Arjuna's attachment to both himself and others. The dialogue builds until Arjuna receives from Krishna a vision of totality that liberates him from his prior self-preoccupied identity. This experience prompts Arjuna to seek new answers from Krishna, answers that explain how to live with an understanding in which action becomes purposeful and liberating.

How does Krishna exact the transformation of Arjuna from a man filled with doubt to a man of great knowledge and resolve? He begins in chapter two by explaining the Yoga of Knowledge, recounting to Arjuna the insights to be gained from the Sāṃkhya philosophy. He reminds him that although contact with the objects of sense produces pleasure and pain, both are not lasting (II:14). He speaks of that which is beyond all change: weapons do not cut it; fire does not burn it; water does not wet it; winds do not dry it (II:23). He tells Arjuna that as a warrior his duty is to fight. If he wins, he gains the earth, if he loses, he gains heaven (II:37). Krishna urges Arjuna to ready himself for battle, to regard pleasure and pain, gain and loss, victory and failure as the same. Only when Arjuna has renounced interest in the fruits of his action can he find true peace.

These sage words, however, are not enough to prompt Arjuna into action. As will happen again and again over several more chapters, Arjuna asserts to Krishna that this teaching is not enough, that his mind is still confused, that he needs to hear a better path. Although the reasons provided by Krishna are certainly sufficient for Arjuna to move into battle, they remain empty theories; Arjuna is unable to act. So Krishna persists. In the third chapter, the Yoga of Action, Arjuna is advised to perform the action that has to be done, staying always free from attachment (III:19). Krishna points out that it was by action alone that Janaka, the philosopher-king, attained perfection and tells Arjuna that he should act, attending to the holding together of the world (*loka-saṃgraha*) (III:20). Bringing to mind the Sāṃkhya system, he reiterates that actions are done by the *guṇas of prakṛti* alone; it is only the deluded one who thinks "I am the doer" (III:27). By knowing that all this is only the *guṇas* acting on *guṇas*, one becomes free from attachment. When asked by Arjuna why a man is impelled to do evil, Krishna responds that desire and anger, born of passion (*rajas*), conceal true knowledge and fuel the senses. Only by subduing the senses and controlling the mind can desire be overcome.

In a discourse on the Yoga of Renunciation of Action in Knowledge in the fourth chapter, Krishna provides yet another teaching. He explains that one must see action in inaction and inaction in action; only then can one be free of compulsive desire. This is accomplished by renouncing the fruit of action (*karma-phala-asaṅga*), leading to constant satisfaction and independence. Such a one is said to do nothing, even though engaged in action (IV:20). Sacrifice is cited as the model for proper action; the sacrifice of knowledge (*jñāna-yajña*) is said to being the completion of all action (IV:33). In the fifth chapter, the Yoga of Renunciation, Krishna further articulates the need for the relinquishment of attachment, saying that the wise ones see a cow, an elephant, a dog, an outcaste, and even a learned and wise Brahmin as the same (V:18). He describes the sage intent on release as one whose senses, mind, and intelligence are controlled, who has overcome desire, fear and anger; such a one is forever liberated (V:28). The means to achieve this are described in yet another teaching, the Yoga of Meditation. To gain yoga, Krishna advises "Abandoning those desires whose origins lie in one's intention, all of them without exception, and completely restraining the multitude of senses with the mind; little by little he should come to rest, with the intelligence firmly grasped. His mind having been fixed in the self, he should not think of anything" (VI:Þł$_{7}$–25). Krishna assures Arjuna that even a small amount of practice will be beneficial.

As before, none of these teachings resolves Arjuna's crisis. Hence, Krishna continues. In the next four chapters, Krishna tells Arjuna of the highest self, attainable through Krishna himself. In the Yoga of Knowledge and Discrimination, Krishna distinguishes between the lower *prakṛti*, which is the world of the senses and the mind, and the higher *prakṛti*, from which all life emerges. Both are said to have their origin in Krishna, who is the "seed of all beings." He declares that even those who sacrifice to lesser gods in fact sacrifice to Krishna, but their fruit is of little consequence. "To the gods the god-worshipping go; My worshippers go surely to me" (VII:23). In the Yoga of Imperishable Brahman, Krishna explains *puruṣa* as the support of things, the vision to be attained, "within which all beings stand, by which all this universe is pervaded" (VIII:22). In knowing this, all fruits of action are transcended and peace is attained. In the Yoga of Royal Knowledge and of Royal Mystery, the ninth chapter, Krishna speaks of the *prakṛti* that he issues forth. Those who see the higher *prakṛti* through sacrifice and devotion make their offerings to Krishna: he is witness, the final shelter; the origin, dissolution, and foundation; immortality; existence and nonexistence; the enjoyer of all sacrifices. In chapter ten, the Yoga of Manifestation, Krishna explains the nature of his compassion: by appearing as so many gods, sages, trees, horses, weapons, demons, mantras, warriors, rivers, victories, Vedic hymns, and more, he has proven to be the manifestation of all that is worthy of worship, all that inspires ascension to the true self. At the end, he declares, "I support this entire universe constantly with a single fraction of Myself" (X:42).

Finally, after so much preparation and so many discourses, Arjuna asks Krishna in chapter eleven to reveal the form that is described as Lord and Highest Self. He asks for a direct experience, a showing (*darśana*): "If Thou thinkest it possible for me to see this, O Lord, Prince of Yoga, then to me cause to be seen Thyself, the Imperishable" (XI:4). In response, Krishna reveals to Arjuna the vision that he has requested. "If there should be in the sky a thousand suns risen all at once, such splendor would be of the splendor of that Great Being" (XI:12). The vision is without beginning or end; all worlds are pervaded by it. The gods stand in amazement, singing praise. Into Krishna's many mouths, studded with terrible tusks "glowing like the fires of universal destruction," are cast all the players on the battlefield: the sons of Dhṛtarāṣṭra, the sage Bhīṣma, the teacher Droṇa, and all the others. Having revealed what time will bring, Krishna tells Arjuna to stand up, to conquer his enemies. "By Me these have already been struck down; be the mere instrument" (XI:33). Overwhelmed by Krishna's powers, Arjuna praises him as the first of gods, the primal *puruṣa*, the knower and what is to be known. After expressing homage and obeisance, he asks Krishna to return to his human form, and the dialogue once more resumes, but with a difference.

Arjuna has now had direct experience of what has been so lavishly praised and described by Krishna. The true self is no longer a theoretical abstraction but has been revealed in embodied form.

From chapters twelve through eighteen, Arjuna no longer implores Krishna for definite answers about what he should or should not do. Rather than focusing on his own selfish concerns, Arjuna asks for further explanations on the nature of the devotion by which he has been given his vision. He asks Krishna to talk more about the difference between *puruṣa*, the knower of the field, and *prakṛti*, the field of change. He asks more about the three *guṇas* and how they function within *prakṛti*; he finds out how the yogins see the highest self through the eye of wisdom. Krishna elucidates the distinction between liberating and binding conditions and then, in the concluding chapter, explains the Yoga of Freedom by Renunciation. The contents of the chapter reflect concerns that Krishna has addressed consistently since the second chapter: sacrifice of the fruits of action, the distinctions of the *guṇas*, the cultivation of equanimity, the importance of nondoership.

The pivotal verse of the last chapter, indicating that Krishna's task as teacher has been completed, is as follows: "Thus to thee by Me has been expounded the knowledge that is more secret than secret. Having reflected on this fully, do as thou desirest" (XVIII:63). Until this point, even after receiving the vision of totality, Arjuna has regarded Krishna as his teacher and relied utterly on him for guidance and instruction. Krishna's command "Do as thou desirest!" signals that Arjuna's knowledge has now been fully embodied, that he has reached the point where he can in full conscience act without hesitation. His decisions become his own. Arjuna's final statement, notable for its firm resolve in contrast to his lack of nerve in the first chapter, is this: "Delusion is lost and wisdom gained, through Thy grace, by me, Unchanging One. I stand with doubt dispelled. I shall do as Thy command" (XVIII:73). Arjuna, at the conclusion of the *Gītā*, is free to act.

In our brief overview of the *Bhagavad Gītā*, we have encountered a multiplicity of teaching. Arjuna stated his anguish in chapter one and, for the next nine chapters, received plausible advice from Krishna. Considered separately, it might even seem that any one of the nine yogas prescribed in those chapters by Krishna would be sufficient for Arjuna to solve his dilemma. However, all these yogas as well as everything else are ultimately negated by the vision of the True Self provided in chapter eleven. In the final chapters, these teachings and in fact the world itself are resurrected in service of an enlightened way of detached action.

The unfolding of the *Gītā* may be summarized in four movements: the crisis of Arjuna in chapter one, his instruction by Krishna in chapters two through ten, the revelation of chapter eleven, and then continued instruction in chapters twelve through eighteen. It might be supposed that the enlightenment experience of chapter eleven would be for Arjuna an eschatological event, that his vision of Krishna as Lord would utterly transform his relationship with the world, thus putting an end to any need for further teaching. But this is simply not the case: the vision is followed by further affirmation of what Krishna has taught, a sequence of chapters "which show the 'rehabilitation' process of a man who has seen the emptiness beyond his own old structures of meaning and does not know yet how to proceed in the interpretation of the new."[2] Furthermore, if we look at the larger story of Arjuna as it unfolds in the great epic, even the autonomy that Arjuna achieves in chapter eighteen does not help him when he attempts to enter heaven; the lessons of the *Gītā* must be repeated again and again, as new circumstances, new worlds, arise and fall.

Herein lies one of the special contributions of the *Bhagavad Gītā*: the religious vision, like the Hindu conception of life itself, is a forever repeating experience. The instruction Arjuna received before his enlightening vision remains essential following this experience, and is also deemed helpful for all who heed it. This is illustrated in the final verse of the text, in which Saṃjaya poetically proclaims: "Wherever there is Krishna, Lord of Yoga, wherever there is the Son of Pṛthā, the archer (Arjuna), there, there will surely be splendor, victory, wealth, and righteousness; this is my thought" (XVIII:78).

Theologically, the approach presented in the *Gītā* differs from generally accepted notions about *mokṣa* as requiring the renunciation of the world and of *samādhi* as trance-like obliteration of all things and thoughts. The *Gītā* presents a view of religious practice at variance with the classical tradition as found in the *Dharmaśāstra*, a view that Madeleine Biardeau attributes to a more open conception of liberation characteristic of the later sections of the *Mahābhārata*. She writes that this new approach

> gave every svadharma (one's own duty) religious content and an access to ultimate salvation. The Brahmanic model was not lost sight of, but was generalized so as to fit all other categories of Hindu society, including Sudras, women, and all impure castes. Once the kṣatriya gained access to salvation through his . . . activities, the generalization became easy. . . . Nothing was

[2]Antonio T. de Nicolás, *Avatāra: The Humanization of Philosophy through the Bhagavad Gītā* (New York: Nicolas Hays, 19786), p. 273.

outside the realm of ultimate values, though at the same time the status of the Brahmans remains unimpaired.[3]

As Biardeau points out, it is no longer one path, the path leading from studentship to householding to renunciation to blessedness that enables one to lead a full religious life. In the model presented by the *Bhagavad Gītā*, every aspect of life is in fact a way of salvation. The Krishna tells Arjuna of innumerable ways to achieve peace of mind, to resolve his dilemma, and it is clear that the answers are provided not only for Arjuna but are paradigmatic for people of virtually any walk of life. The *Gītā* becomes a text appropriate to all persons of all castes or no caste; its message transcends the limits of classical Hinduism.

It is interesting to note that just as Krishna presented many perspectives to Arjuna, so have many scholars, both traditional and modern, held many perspectives on the *Bhagavad Gītā*. Robert N. Minor, whose own position is that "the *Gītā* proclaims as its highest message the lordship of Kṛṣṇa and the highest response of the human being to that lordship is devotion, *bhakti*,"[4] notes several different usages of the text. For Śaṁkara (A.D. 788-820), the message is the "end of the world and its accompanying activity." Madhusudana and Venkatanātha, while not rejecting Śaṁkara's view, place more emphasis on devotion, as does Jñāneśvara, the Marathi commentator. Bhaskara takes issue with Śaṁkara's interpretation, asserting that the world is a real aspect of Brahman. Rāmānuja used the *Gītā* in support of his position that "the true self is not divine and not one with the other selves, though in liberation it is identical in knowledge to those other selves." Nimbārka, a twelfth century thinker, prompted interpretations that see Krishna as teaching "innate nonidentity in identity." Madhva (1238-1317), the famous dualist, "radically reinterprets the text so that it asserts an eternal and complete distinction between the Supreme, the many souls, and matter and its divisions." Minor also cites modern interpretations by Bal Gangadhar Tilak and Mohandas K. Gandhi which used the text to help inspire the independence movement, and Sri Aurobindo, Sarvepalli Radhakrishnan, and Swami Vivekananda, who took a syncretistic approach to the text.[5]

[3]Madeleine Biardeau, "The Salvation of the King in the *Mahābhārata*" in *Way of Life: King, Householder, Renouncer. Essays in Honour of Louis Dumont*, ed. T.N. Madan (New Delhi: Vikas, 1982), p. 77.

[4]Robert N. Minor, *Bhagavad Gītā: An Exegetical Commentary* (New Delhi: Heritage Publisher, 1982), p. xvi.

[5]Ibid., pp. xvi-xix.

Few of the scholars cited above seem to agree on the meaning of the text, yet none of them can be said to be incorrect. It may be argued that this utter contextualization of the text causes it to fall into a fatal relativism; that the text, because it is open to so many interpretations and has been used to confirm opposing positions ranging from Śaṁkara's monism to Madhva's dualism, is trivial and perhaps meaningless. But how, then, could such a text survive? How can one account for or even describe a text that includes and is used to support a virtual cacophony of traditions and positions? Setting aside even the interpretations of later commentators mentioned above, how can the explicitly nontheistic Sāṃkhya appear alongside with the thoroughly theistic *bhakti* approach also taught by Krishna?

Max Mueller addressed a similar issue when trying to cope with the multiplicity of gods in the Ṛg Veda and invented a term to describe it:

> To identify Indra, Agni, and Varuna is one thing, it is syncretism; to address either Indra or Agni or Varuna, as for the time being the only god in existence with an entire forgetfulness of all other gods, is quite another; it was this phase, so fully developed in the hymns of the Ve'da which I wished to mark definitely by a name of its own, calling it henotheism.[6]

The Vedic method which extols different gods within the same text is similar to that employed in the *Bhagavad Gītā*, in which each time Arjuna asks Krishna for one truth, again and again Krishna offers Arjuna yet another perspective, another chapter, another yoga. Each view, whether that of a god being sacrificed to or a yogic discipline being practiced, is given life as long as it proves effective. Multiplicity is the rule, with one god, one perspective gaining and holding ascendancy as long as it, he, or she proves efficacious. That one is then swept from its elevated position as new situations, new questions emerge: and yet, if pressed, a Hindu will always admit, of course, Indra is best; of course, Agni is best; of course, Varuna is best; of course, Karma Yoga is best, of course, Bhakti Yoga is best.

Paul Hacker has referred to the accommodation of multiple teachings within one tradition as "inclusivism."[7] Antonio T. de Nicolás has explained this phenomenon philosophically as

[6]Max Mueller, *The Six Systems of Indian Philosophy* (London: Longmans, Green, and Co., 1928), p. 40.

[7]Gerhard Oberhammer, ed., *Inklusivismus: Eine Indische Denkform* (Vienna: Institute for Indology, University of Vienna, 1983).

> a systematic and methodic effort to save rationality in its plural manifestations through an activity of embodiment that emancipates man from any form of identification, allowing him the freedom to act efficiently in any one identifiable field in the social fabric.[8]

Just as the many gods of the Vedas are effective in different situations, so the many yogas are prescribed in the Gītā without compromising or subordinating one to another. Mutual paths are allowed to exist in complementarity.

In a sense, the *Gītā* is composed in the spirit of the Jaina approach to truth. The Jainas assert that every statement is an utterance of partial truth; all postulation is rendered senseless by the ultimate postulate that no words are ever totally adequate to experience (*avaktavya eva*). Similarly, Krishna painstakingly guides Arjuna through many yogas, yet, the entire problematic is obliterated when Krishna reveals his true form to Arjuna. All the words, all the individual personalities and collective armies are swallowed up by the gaping mouth of Krishna, the origin and dissolution of all things. The net result is that all possibilities are present for Arjuna when he gains the knowledge that all are impermanent.

The *Bhagavad Gītā* sets forth a multiplicity of possible paths. A panoply of perspectives is offered to the reader in a nonjudgmental way; the many positions proposed by Krishna do not necessarily compete with one another but rather complete one another. If one needs to act, one uses Karma Yoga; if one needs to meditate, one uses Dhyāna Yoga. This "henocretic" text is written with a gentle tolerance, allowing various practices and positions to be pursued.

In a manner true to the construction of the text itself, the present rendition by Winthrop Sargeant does the least violence to the original of all the translations of the *Gītā* with which I am familiar. He shows the reader the possibilities offered by the text, setting out in menu form variant English language samplings for each of the Sanskrit terms. His work makes a unique contribution, inviting the reader to consider the cooked translation he serves up, but also inviting the reader to experiment with creating his or her own delicacy.

It has been an honor working with this edition of the book. My sole contribution has been editing the grammatical analysis for consistency and completeness; any errors or omissions that occur are my own.

Christopher Chapple, Department of Theology
Loyola Marymount University, Los Angeles, California

[8]Antonio T. de Nicolás, *Avatāra*, p. 164.

THE BHAGAVAD GĪTĀ

TRANSLATOR'S PREFACE

Why add one more to the numerous English translations of the Bhagavad Gītā? It is said to have already been translated at least two hundred times, in both poetic and prose forms. My excuse is that, though many fine translations exist, none that I know of presents the original Sanskrit with an interlinear word-for-word arrangement that permits the reader to learn the sound as well as the meaning of each word. The arrangement also makes it possible for the reader to see the metrical formation of the poem's stanzas, and their grammatical structure. It should also enable the studious reader to savor something of the original language, which is elegant and extremely concise. As an added aid, a running vocabulary is provided, referring to the Sanskrit words on each page, along with their grammatical forms. Below each stanza will be found a readable English translation which I hope will give greater coherence to what is often awkwardly expressed in the literal word-for-word interlinear translation. The line of transliteration is designed to show the reader how the words are pronounced, so that, if he desires, he can appreciate the sound of the original language. In making the readable translation that appears at the bottom of each page, my object has been to stick as closely as possible to literal meaning rather than to attempt a masterpiece of English prose. Such grand poetic concepts as appear in the translation are inherent in the poem. I have added nothing, and what I have striven for is simple clarity along with a reproduction of something of the force and economy of the original.

I have consulted numerous previous translations, among them those of Franklin Edgerton, S. Radhakrishnan, Eliot Deutsch, Swami Prabhavananda and Christopher Isherwood, and Swami Chidbhavananda, Juan Mascaro and P. Lal. I have found them all worth reading, each, as I suppose is inevitable, showing a slightly different approach. To a poem such as this, many approaches are possible, and all are worth considering. I have tried in the vocabularies to indicate a considerable variety of possible meaning. In writing the introductory chapters on language, cosmology and psychology, and the setting of the poem as the principal didactic jewel of the great Hindu epic, the Mahābhārata, I have had recourse to numerous sources – Pratap Chandra Roy's translation of the Epic, Chakravarti Narasiṁhan's "The Mahābhārata," C. Rajagopalachari's condensed version, the account given under various headings in Benjamin Walker's "The Hindu World," and in connection with other matters I have consulted the admirable prefaces to Swami Nikhilananda's "The Upanishads" as well as his translations of these works, Surendranath Dasgupta's "History of Indian Philosophy," Sukumari Bhattacharji's "The Indian Theogony," Ralph T. H. Griffith's translation of the Ṛg Veda, Dr. J. A. B. van Buitenen's translation of Rāmānuja's commentary on the Bhagavad Gītā, as well as the recently published first volume of his translation of the Mahābhārata (University of Chicago Press) and countless works on Hindu religion and philosophy that I have read in the past, along with such useful staples of Sanskrit study as Whitney's Sanskrit Grammar, the Oxford Sanskrit Dictionary edited by Monier-Williams, and the abridged version of Böhtlingk and Roth's St. Petersburg Lexicon.

I am greatly indebted to Dr. J. A. B. van Buitenen, of the University of Chicago, who kindly offered to read the manuscript before publication, who made innumerable small corrections and many suggestions, nearly all of which I have followed, and who read the proofs. I would also like to express belated gratitude to the late Sarat Lahiri, a Bihari Brāhman, resident in New York, from whom I learned my first Sanskrit many years ago. I am also grateful to Alice Morris for much patient copying and to my old friend Louis Biancolli for encouragement.

As to my own qualifications, though I am known primarily as a magazine writer and music critic, my interest in the Sanskrit language has been of long duration, and I have spent a considerable amount of time in India as a journalist. As a Sanskrit scholar I am largely self taught, but am certainly competent for the task in hand. Moreover, the present translation has been read and approved by the highest authority. I have been acquainted for many years with the Bhagavad Gītā in translation, and have found many translations somewhat unsatisfactory because of deviations in meaning, and because few of them give any idea of the poem's structure, either metrical or grammatic. My aim has been to fill the gap by relating each word to the original, giving a grammatical commentary and a vocabulary from which various alternative meanings for each word may be picked – thus making it possible for the reader to make his own translation if he disagrees with mine. In the case of stanzas which are not entirely clear in translation, I have appended explanatory footnotes, many of them quoted from the commentary of Rāmānuja, the great eleventh-century south Indian religious philosopher, as translated by J. A. B. van Buitenen, Motilal Banarsidas, Delhi, Patna, Varanasi, 1968. I have translated the poem afresh, and I know many parts of it by heart in the original language. The work has been a labor of love. If it in any way clarifies the poem to the reader, or interests him in the language in which it was originally written, my aim will have been realized. In a project as complex as this one, a few errors are apt to occur, and for these I ask the reader's indulgence.

Winthrop Sargeant

THE LANGUAGE OF THE BHAGAVAD GĪTĀ

Sanskrit is a euphonious and very elegant language which has been spoken by upper-caste Indians, and the Vedic Aryans before them, for a longer time than any other known tongue. It is one of the ancient Indo-European languages, with many cognates in ancient Greek and Latin as well as in practically every modern major European language except Finnish and Hungarian. It is safe to say that it was spoken before 1,600 B.C. by the Aryans, and it is still spoken by a minority of brāhmans today. It also appears continually in modern India, in proper names, names of institutions and regions, and so on; and several modern Indian languages, including Hindi and Bengali, are derived from it. It has also influenced several languages of southeast Asia including that of Indonesia. There is, to be sure, considerable difference between Vedic Sanskrit (circa 1400–300 B.C.) and the Sanskrit of later times, but this difference is not as great as is sometimes supposed. The later language tends to join prefixes to the words they modify, whereas in Vedic they are usually separated. Also, an important feature of the Vedic language was the use of aorist forms which tend to disappear in the later language. There is also, as might be expected, considerable difference in vocabulary. Epic-Purāṇic Sanskrit succeeded the earlier Vedic language somewhere around 500 B.C., and was itself succeeded by so-called Classical Sanskrit during the Gupta Empire and the later Princely States (circa 400–1500 A.D.). Classical Sanskrit differs from Epic-Purāṇic mainly in the increased use of long compound words. The written, as opposed to the spoken language dates only from about 300 B.C., and even then very little was written down. Indians have always prided themselves on their memories, which have indeed been phenomenal when one considers that the whole literature of the Vedas, the Epics, the Upanishads, the Purāṇas, and much other material has been handed down by word of mouth. The bulk of Sanskrit literature was not written down until well into the Christian era. Even today there are some brāhmans who look down upon the printed word as a method of preserving the literature, and there exists in India a tremendously complicated method of mnemonics by which lengthy items of literature can be memorized. It is interesting to note that, owing to the detailed researches of Paṇini (350–250 B.C.?) and other great Hindu grammarians – researches that were not only linguistic but also concerned lingual and laryngeal anatomy – Sanskrit is the only ancient language the exact pronunciation of which is known today.

The Bhagavad Gītā is conceived in Epic-Purāṇic Sanskrit, the language of the Epics, Purāṇas and Upanishads, and it was probably first written down in the early centuries of the Christian era though like many other works which are embodied in written form, it undoubtedly dates from an earlier word-of-mouth version. Epic-Purāṇic Sanskrit is in many ways the simplest form of the language. An occasional aorist remains (there are eight or ten of them in the Bhagavad Gītā) and there is an occasional use of the prohibitive "mā" in place of the "na" ("not") of Classical Sanskrit. But the long compounds of Classical Sanskrit have not yet appeared. The Bhagavad Gītā, in its written form at any rate, is generally thought to date from the second or third century A.D., being considered a later interpolation in the long Epic, the Mahābhārata, most of which describes an India of an earlier period, possibly 800 B.C.

Sanskrit being one of the Indo-European group of languages, its general formation resembles that of Ancient Greek and Latin, being slightly more complex than that of the former and much more complex than that of the latter. Its verbal forms are derived from roots which also give birth to nouns and adjectives. Certain Sanskrit participial forms, such as the present participle in "ant" can still be found in French (German "end," English "ing"). The past passive participle ending "ta" survives in modern Italian, and there are fascinating resemblances among the personal pronouns to the "we" (*vayam*), "you" (*yūyam*) and "us" (*asmān*) of modern English, as well as prominent cognates to German such as the verb √*vṛt* which is close to "werden," and means "to exist," or "to become" among other things. There is also a marked similarity of the Sanskrit verbs √*bhū* and √*as*, both of which mean "be," and "is." Sanskrit verbs have a first person, second person and third person (singular and plural) similar in construction to Latin, with elements of the same *m* (*o*); *s*, *t*, *mas* (*mus*), *tas* (*tus*), *nt* endings that go with these persons in Latin. Sanskrit, however, has a dual form for both verbs and nouns (we two, you two, they two), and its verbs have two distinct conjugation systems, the active, or *parasmāipada*, and the middle, or *ātmanepada*, the former having our normal active meaning and the latter sometimes, but not always, having a more passive or reflexive character. In the simpler areas of conjugation the *parasmāipada* forms end in i and the *ātmanepada* forms in e.

Nouns in Sanskrit are declined as they are in Latin, except that Sanskrit has one more case. The cases in Sanskrit are as follows:

Nominative, used for the subject of a sentence.

Accusative, used for the direct object and also in the dative sense of "to."

Instrumental, used where English would use "by," "with," or "by means of."

Dative, used in the sense of "for," "to," or "toward."

Ablative, used in the senses of "of" and "from."

Genitive, used for the most part in the same sense of "of" as the ablative (in many words the ablative and genitive are identical).

Locative, used in the senses of "in" or "on," or occasionally "to," "toward," or "among."

Vocative, used as in Latin in direct address ("O Vishnu," etc.).

There are three genders of nouns and adjectives – masculine, feminine and neuter.

In the vocabularies of the following translation, the abbreviations nom., acc., inst., abl., gen., loc., and voc. are used to designate the above described cases, and sg. and pl. are used for singular and plural. In the matter of verbs, the root is given with the preceding sign √, and 1st sg., 2nd sg., etc., mean first person singular, second person singular and so on. Participial forms are indicated. The gerund form ending in "ya" or "tvā" is very common, having the approximate meaning of the English present participle in "ing," or of "having done," "having seen," etc. There is a gerundive form in "ya" indicating future action, "to be done," "to be known," etc. The infinitive ending in "tum" is standard in the Epic-Purāṇic language, and the perfect active participle in "tavant" or "navant" is common. There are some special verbal forms – the passive, intensive, desiderative and causative – whose applications are obvious and which are noted in the vocabularies. There are also the standard tenses for verbs – indicative, subjunctive (which does not appear in the Bhagavad Gītā except in its aorist form), the optative (usually conveying the meaning "should"), the imperative, imperfect, perfect, aorist (rare) and future; also a periphrastic future in which the nominative singular of a noun or of a *nomen agentis* type noun ending in *tṛ* combined with the verb √*ās*, "be," and a periphrastic perfect in which the perfect forms of the verbs √*as* and √*kṛ* (sometimes √*bhū*) are used as suffixes of an accusative derivative noun stem in *ām*. For further information, I recommend any standard Sanskrit grammar. I have used Whitney's Sanskrit Grammar (Harvard University Press; also Oxford University Press), a pioneer work which is still standard.

The Sanskrit alphabet is as follows:

अ a, pronounced as in but.
आ ā, " " " father.
इ i, " " " lily *or* it.
ई ī, " " " police.
उ *u*, " " " push, full.
ऊ ū, " " " prude *or* crude.
ऋ ṛ, " as a slightly trilled vowel r, having the sound of ir in "birth" or ur in "purpose." N.B. There is a long tradition involving the pronunciation ri for this vowel, and it is recommended by Monier-Williams on grounds of euphony. It is used by many Indians, and it survives in the ri of Sanskrit (*Saṁskṛta*). But the ri pronunciation has been abandoned by most present-day Sanskrit scholars in favor of a simple vowel ṛ such as appears in many Slavonic languages.
ॠ ṝ, the same pronunciation, more prolonged.
ऌ ḷ, pronounced by many Indians and the English as "lry" (as in reve*lry*), but probably originally a pure l vowel as in the "le" of "simple" (see Whitney 24). There is, theoretically, also a long ḹ vowel but it is practically never used.

ए e, pronounced as in bet or tempo.
ऐ āi, " " " aisle.
ओ o, " " " stone or pole.
औ āu, " " " German "Haus."

क्	k,	,,	,, ,, kill or meek.
ख्	kh,	,,	,, ,, inkhorn or bunkhouse.
ग्	g,	,,	,, ,, go, get or dog.
घ्	gh,	,,	,, ,, loghouse.
ङ्	ṅ,	,,	,, ,, sing or kink.
च्	c,	pronounced ch as in church.	
छ्	ch,	pronounced chh as in bir*ch h*ill.	
ज्	j,	pronounced as in judge or jump.	
झ्	jh,	,,	,, ,, hedgehog (he*jh*og).
ञ्	ñ,	,,	,, ,, French *bon*, or as in hinge (hi*n*ge).
ट्	ṭ,	,,	,, ,, true.
ठ्	ṭh,	,,	,, ,, an*th*ill.
ड्	ḍ,	,,	,, ,, drum.
ढ्	ḍh,	,,	,, ,, re*dh*ead.
ण्	ṇ,	,,	,, ,, no*n*e.
त्	t,	,,	,, ,, tone or tub.
थ्	th,	,,	,, ,, nu*th*atch.
द्	d,	,,	,, ,, dot (slightly toward the th sound).
ध्	dh,	,,	,, ,, a*dh*ere.
न्	n,	,,	,, ,, nut or thin.
प्	p,	,,	,, ,, pot or hip.
फ्	ph,	,,	,, ,, u*ph*ill or she*ph*erd.
ब्	b,	,,	,, ,, beer or rub.
भ्	bh,	,,	,, ,, a*bh*or.
म्	m,	,,	,, ,, man or ham.
य्	y,	,,	,, ,, young or royal.
र्	r,	,,	,, ,, red or shear.
ल्	l,	,,	,, ,, law or lead.
व्	v,	,,	like w in twine or wind.
श्	ś,	,,	as in sure.
ष्	ṣ,	,,	,, ,, shut or bush.
स्	s,	,,	,, ,, sin or hi*ss*.
ह्	h,	,,	,, ,, hero or hit.

When attached to consonants, vowel marks are as follows: ` above the line = e (as in ते te). ˆ above the line = āi (as in रै rāi). ो indicates o at the middle or end of a word (as in को ko). ौ indicates āu at the middle or end of a word (as in तौ tāu). ु below the line indicates u (as in तु tu). ू below the line indicates ū (as in भू bhū). र्‍ above the line indicates a consonant r (as in मर्त marta). Below the line it indicates a vowel ṛ (as in भृत् bhṛt). The short i at the middle or end of a word is indicated by a tie to the left (as in धृति dhṛti). The long ī is indicated by a similar tie to the right (as in भी bhī). Long ā is indicated by an extra downstroke ा (as in आत्मन् ātman). Otherwise every consonant is assumed to be followed by a short a. Most combined consonants are self explanatory, except for क्ष kṣa, श्च śca, ज्ञ jña, क्त kta and त्र tra (the diagonal stroke within the letter always indicates a consonant r). The *visarga* (" : " written at the end of a word in place of s or r, and transliterated as ḥ) is pronounced like the English aspirate h, but in Hindu usage it is followed by a short echo of the preceding vowel. The *anusvāra* (ṁ or ṅ) is a nasal sound like n in French "bon." A diagonal stroke to the right beneath a letter (म्, द् etc.) indicates that it is a final, and is not followed by an "a" as it otherwise would be.

Although accent in Sanskrit is supposed to be quantitative as it was in Ancient Greek, the practice for many centuries has been to use a stress accent somewhat milder than that used in English, meanwhile observing the difference between long and short syllables. (Theoretically at least, a long syllable is twice as long as a short syllable). This accent falls on the penultimate syllable, or, in the case of a word ending with two short syllables, on the antepenultimate, or, in the case of a word ending in three short syllables, on the fourth from the end. These rules apply only to Classical and Epic-Purāṇic Sanskrit. Vedic Sanskrit has a more complicated system of accentuation. A long syllable is one containing a long vowel, a diphthong, or followed by more than one consonant. All others are short.

There remains the complicated subject of *saṁdhi*, or the laws of euphonious combination, which are to be found at work in virtually every phrase of Sanskrit. The aim of these laws is to enhance the elegance of sound of the language. There are laws relating to internal (i.e. within a given word) euphonic combination, which I shall pass over, since their effects are to be found in the vocabularies. External *saṁdhi* is a much more noticeable and puzzling phenomenon. It occurs at the end of a word, and is determined by the beginning of the following word. The reader will probably notice it first in the peculiar behavior of *s* when it occurs at the end of a word. It may be converted into *ś* or *ṣ* or *r*, or : (visarga), or, in the case of final *as* into o, or, what is perhaps still more common, it may disappear altogether. Other letters behave somewhat similarly. Final *r* may also become : (visarga). Final *t* is interchangeable with *d*, and sometimes also even with *n*, *j*, *l*, *c* and several other letters, depending on the beginning of the following word. *i* and *y* are interchangeable, the latter being used before a vowel and losing its independence as a syllable. The same thing is true of *u* and *v*. *n* becomes *ṇ* under certain circumstances (e.g., when preceded in the same word by *s* or *r*, or when followed by more than one consonant) and *ñ* under others. Final *n* after a short vowel and before a succeeding vowel is doubled to *nn*. Vowels, as the above alphabet shows, come in short and in long (*ā*,*ī*,*ū*,*ṝ*) forms. The vowel ḷ, in practice, has only a short form. Diphthongs are *e*, *āi*, *o* and *āu*. In euphonic combination all types of *a* (long or short) combine to made *ā*, and all forms of *i* combine to make *ī*; all forms of *u* combine to make *ū*. *a* or *ā* combines with vowel *ṛ* to form *ar*. *a* or *ā* combine with *i* or *ī* to form *e*, *a* or *ā* combine with *u* or *ū* to form *o*, *a* or *ā* combine with *e* to form *āi*, and *a* or *ā* combine with *o* to form *āu*. An initial *a* after a final *e* or *o* is dropped and an apostrophe or *avagraha* is put in its place. Before a vowel *āu* becomes *āv*, *e* becomes *a* and *āi* becomes *ā*. And so on. For all the circumstances under which these changes and others occur, there is no recourse but a careful study of the subject as presented in Whitney's or some other grammar.

While most if not all the above changes will be found written out in the text, the *anusvāra* (*ṁ* or occasionally *ṅ*) is not always as easy to detect. It is very common, and its accurate rendering is vital to the proper pronunciation of Sanskrit. In the Sanskrit text it is indicated merely by a dot above the line. Its commonest occurrence is as a substitute for final *m* before a word beginning with a consonant or semivowel such as y, h or v. In transliteration it is written *ṁ*, or sometimes *ṅ*. Its pronunciation, as has been said, is approximately like the *n* in French "bon", thus a fairly indeterminate nasal sound with no closure either of the mouth or of the palate. It occurs also in such words and names as "saṁdhi," "Saṁjaya," "Jarāsaṁdha," etc. Proper pronunciation makes the transition to the following consonant as smooth as can be imagined. In other texts, especially where internal *saṁdhi* is concerned, the dot, in transliteration is often placed below the *ṃ* instead of above it, as is the practice I have followed, mainly for the sake of uniformity.

The metre of most of the stanzas of the Bhagavad Gītā is what is known as *śloka* metre, consisting of four lines of eight syllables each, and can be conveniently remembered by the English reader as the metre of Longfellow's "Hiawatha" (e.g. "by the shores of Gitchee Gumee" etc.). The verse is blank, i.e. there are no rhymes. There are, however, a number of stanzas, particularly at more dramatic moments, in which the *triṣṭubh* metre, consisting of four lines of eleven syllables each, is used. The *śloka* is the all-purpose metre of the Epics as well as much popular poetry. The *triṣṭubh* metre originated as the commonest metre of the Vedas, and is supposed to convey a warlike or powerful impression.

Regarding the page by page vocabularies in this edition, it might be remarked that Sanskrit is a very ambiguous language in which a single word may have scores of meanings, sometimes contradictory ones. Thus the common verb √dhā, according to Monier-Williams' dictionary, can mean put, place, take, bring, remove, direct, fix upon, resolve upon, destine for, bestow on, present, impart, appoint, establish, constitute, make, generate, produce, create, cause, effect, perform, execute, seize, take hold of, bear, support, wear, put on, accept, obtain, conceive, get, assume, have, possess, show, exhibit, incur, undergo, etc. In the vocabulary attached to each stanza I have included only the meanings that are close to the ones intended in the poem.

A concluding word about the transliteration and the literal English translation: as far as is possible I have placed the transliterated word, as well as the translated one, directly beneath its Sanskrit equivalent. I have taken the liberty, however, of introducing definite and indefinite articles (the former rarely used and the latter non-existent in Sanskrit) in order to make the meaning clearer. I have also placed the word "and" (Sanskrit "ca") before the last of the words it connects, instead of after a couple, or group, of connected words as is the Sanskrit usage (similar to the use of "que" in Latin).

THE SETTING OF THE BHAGAVAD GĪTĀ

The Mahābhārata, one of the two great Hindu epics (the other is the Rāmāyaṇa), and the one in which the Bhagavad Gītā appears at a climactic moment, is a creation of tremendous length. It has been estimated to be seven times as long as the Iliad and the Odyssey put together, or nearly three times as long as the Judaeo-Christian Bible. It is also a somewhat rambling work, containing many interpolated stories and moral treatises, and it is very Indian in its treatment of time, swinging backward and forward and not always sticking to a consistent chronology. What I have abstracted from it here, with the help of secondary sources, is merely a thin genealogical thread which leads up to the famous Battle of Kurukṣetra, along with a very much condensed narrative of that battle and its aftermath. The heroes of the battle, known as the Pāṇḍava Princes, are Arjuna (whose colloquy with the god Krishna forms the substance of the Bhagavad Gītā) and his half-brothers Yudhiṣthira, Bhīma, Nakula and Sahadeva. The villains are the hundred Sons of Dhṛtarāṣṭra, their cousins, otherwise known as the Kāurava (Sons of Kuru) Princes. The mythological ancestry and relationships between all these characters are complex, and the following condensation attempts to describe them. The battle itself is a tragic episode in which nearly all the kṣatriya, or warrior, race is destroyed, the villains being killed and the heroes, when not slain, dying on a long pilgrimage, eventually attaining heaven. The one exception, King Yudhiṣthira, reaches heaven by a more roundabout route.

Unlike the Hebrew and Christian conceptions of creation, the Indian allows for the infinity of time, and regards the universe as one of many that stretch, in cycles of creation and destruction, into the endless past, and that will stretch, in similar cycles, into the endless future. The mythology pertaining to this particular universe concerns a primaeval darkness, when all was water, until the eternal First Cause formed the *Hiraṇya-garbha*, the "golden foetus" or "golden egg," which floated on the cosmic waters, and, in later myth, became identified with the creator god Brahmā. The egg divided itself into two parts, one becoming the heavens, the other the earth.

Now, Brahmā, the creator god, had a spiritual son (a product of Brahmā's thumb, according to some sources) named Marīci, and Marīci's son in turn became the tremendously prolific sage-king Kaśyapa, sometimes referred to as Prajāpati, or "the Lord of Creatures." Kaśyapa married the twelve daughters of Dakṣa (who is also sometimes referred to as Prajāpati). Dakṣa was the son of Pracetas, an earlier being. It is perhaps significant that these early names are personifications, though names as personifications are common throughout the epic. Brahmā is thought to derive from the root $\sqrt{}$*bṛh* which means "grow" or "evolve." Dakṣa means "intelligence" or "mastery." (It is cognate with the English "dextrous" and its etymological ancestors.) And Pracetas means "clever" or "wise." In any case, Kaśyapa impregnated the daughters of Dakṣa, and they gave birth to the gods, demons, animals and many other types of being. One of these daughters, named Dākṣāyaṇī, or Savarṇā, gave birth to the sun god, Vivasvat (which means "shining forth"). The extraordinary scope of the Hindu imagination is illustrated by the fact that the great Indian commentator Rāmānuja. who lived in the eleventh century A.D., placed the date of Vivasvat's birth at twenty-eight mahāyugas (about 120 billion years) before his own time, a figure that is perhaps closer to modern scientific theories of the birth of the sun than the chronologically vague account in Genesis would place it.

Vivasvat, who is mentioned in the Bhagavad Gītā (IV, 1), became the father of Manu Vāivasvata (also mentioned in IV, 1), the Noah of Hindu mythology, who survived a great flood with the assistance of Vishnu (Vishnu had assumed the form of a fish for the purpose according to the Purāṇas). So ancient are the theoretical origins of this mythology that Manu Vāivasvata was merely the seventh in a long list of Manus belonging to previous universes. He became, after the flood, the progenitor of the human race. This he accomplished by holding a sacrifice during which a woman named Ilā was created. With Ilā's help he begot nine sons, among whom was Ikṣvāku (likewise mentioned in the Bhagavad Gītā, IV, 1), progenitor of the Solar Race to which the sage-king Janaka (mentioned in the Bhagavad Gītā, III, 20) belonged. Other early members of the Solar Race were King Sagara of Ayodhyā, Raghu Rāma, grandfather of Rāma, the hero of the Rāmāyaṇa, and Sudyumna, another son of Manu Vāivasvata, who became the progenitor of the Lunar Race with which we are concerned here.

Among the descendants of Sudyumna was one Purūravas who married an *apsarā*, or water nymph, named Urvaśī, and begot three sons – Āyu, whose descendants founded the Kāśi line of kings to which some of the warriors at the Battle of Kurukṣetra belonged; Amāvasu, with whom we need not be concerned here, and Nahuṣa, father of the great King Yayāti Nāhuṣa. Yayāti practically peopled the whole subcontinent of India, as well as some territory north of the Himālaya, doing for India what his ancestor Manu Vāivasvata had done for the known world. Yayāti had two wives, Devayānī and Śarmiṣṭhā. By the former he begot Yadu, who became the progenitor of the Yādava and Vṛṣṇi clans from which Krishna was descended. By the latter he begot Pūru, the ancestor of Bharata, progenitor of both the Pāṇḍava and Kāurava lines, from which most of the heroes of the Battle of Kurukṣetra were descended. (It is interesting to note that apparently the Pūru, or Pāurava family continued under its own name down to the time of Alexander's invasion of India, when a great king named "Poros" by the Greeks, was defeated in a memorable battle by Alexander, and later became his friend.) Among the early descendants of Bharata was King Hastin who founded the city of Hāstinapura where the Pāṇḍava and Kāurava princes were brought up. Among Hastin's descendants was one Saṁvaraṇa who married Tapatī, a daughter of the Sun god by Chāyā (which means "shade"), and they begot Kuru. At this point the Kāuravas (Sons of Kuru) and the Pāṇḍavas (Sons of Pāṇḍu) are not yet differentiated, and this is a bit confusing because the Pāṇḍavas were as much "sons of Kuru" as the Kāuravas were. Some way further down the genealogical line we meet Prince Pratīpa, who was a descendant of Bharata and Kuru, and here we are closer to the immediate ancestry of our principal characters. Prince Pratīpa was the father of King Śaṁtanu, who, in turn, was the father of the great warrior Bhīṣma, known in the Mahābhārata as "the Grandsire," actually an uncle of Pāṇḍu, and the great uncle, and teacher in the art of arms, of the Pāṇḍava Princes, Yudhiṣṭhira, Bhīma, Arjuna, Nakula and Sahadeva, as well as the villainous Duryodhana and the remaining ninety-nine sons of Dhṛtarāṣṭra. In the great battle the Pāṇḍava Princes are arrayed against their beloved teacher Bhīṣma, a circumstance which is one of the causes of Arjuna's agony of indecision at the beginning of the Bhagavad Gītā.

It is one of the universal rules of mythology that great heroes always have mysterious or divine births. Bhīṣma was the son of King Śaṁtanu by Gaṅgā, otherwise known as the River Ganges. By another wife, Satyavatī, Śaṁtanu begot Citrāṅgada and Vicitravīrya. Vyāsa (mentioned in the Bhagavad Gītā, X, 13) was also a son of Satyavatī, but his birth was premarital. He was a son of the hermit Parāśara. The birth of Vyāsa as a son of Satyavatī is one of those odd features of Hindu literature that defy chronological sense. Vyāsa is supposed to have compiled the Vedas, the earliest of which date from about a thousand years previously, as well as the Mahābhārata, in which he appears as an important character. The word vyāsa means "divider," "arranger" or "compiler." Perhaps there were more than one of these, or perhaps, according to the Hindu theory of reincarnation, a Vyāsa was born whenever compiling was to be done. He appears in the Mahābhārata as a respected sage.

Now, Bhīṣma was a man of great nobility. When his father, King Śaṁtanu, approached him noting that he was an only son (this was long before the birth of Citrāṅgada and Vicitravīrya), and that if anything happened to him the line would become extinct, Bhīṣma went to the house of a fisherman, whose daughter Satyavatī, mentioned above, the aging king had met and admired, and asked Satyavatī's father for her hand in marriage to *his* father. The fisherman agreed on one condition – that Satyavatī's sons should inherit Śaṁtanu's throne. Bhīṣma, Śaṁtanu's first-born and proper heir, met this condition by renouncing the throne and vowing to remain childless throughout his life, thus permitting the sons of Satyavatī the royal succession. Not only did Bhīṣma make this sacrifice (continence was, and is, an admired trait in India), he went to the court of the King of the Kāśi and took part in a trial of arms, defeating all opponents and winning the daughters of that king, Aṁbā, Aṁbikā and Aṁbālikā, as wives for his half-brother Vicitravīrya, son of Satyavatī. On the death of Śaṁtanu, Vicitravīrya, who was still a minor, reigned at Hāstinapura, with Bhīṣma as regent. Such was the extraordinary generosity of Bhīṣma, and he became, during his lifetime, the greatest warrior in the world, as well as the greatest teacher of the art of arms. But after marrying Aṁbikā and Aṁbalikā, King Vicitravīrya proved to be childless (the story of what happened to Aṁbā, the other sister, who refused marriage, must await its place), and his half-brother Vyāsa, the sage, lay with his wives, according to the custom of levirate, to beget sons for him. Aṁbikā then became the mother of Dhṛtarāṣṭra, the blind and vacillating king of the Kāuravas, and Aṁbālikā became the mother of Pāṇḍu, who later became formally though not actually the father of the Pāṇḍava (or

Sons of Pāṇḍu) Princes. Thus it will be seen that the Pāṇḍavas and the Kāuravas (Descendants of Kuru) were, barring a few supernatural interventions and a remarkable amount of substitute fatherhood, cousins, and that while the Kāuravas were very distant descendants of Kuru, the Pāṇḍavas were also descended from Kuru through their official, if not actual, father Pāṇḍu.

But before we get to the reasons why Yudhiṣṭhira, Bhīma, Arjuna, Nakula and Sahadeva were not the real sons of Pāṇḍu, we must relate what happened to Aṁbā. At the time Bhīṣma won her as a bride for his half-brother Vicitravīrya, Aṁbā was in love with a certain Śālva, King of Sāubha and one of the royal personages who had participated in the trial of arms in which Bhīṣma had defeated all adversaries. Among others, he had defeated Śālva, and then spared his life. (Such trials of arms were held traditionally whenever a princess reached marriagable age. Sometimes the victor carried her off, as was the case with Bhīṣma. Sometimes the event was what was called a *svayaṁvara*, or "own choice," at which the princess made her choice among the assembled warriors.) When Bhīṣma brought Aṁbā to Hāstinapura along with her sisters, Aṁbā refused to marry Vicitravīrya, and told those present that she had chosen Śālva as her future husband according to the rule of *svayaṁvara*. Bhīṣma obligingly sent her back to Śālva. But when she got there, Śālva, who felt humiliated by his defeat at the hands of Bhīṣma, refused to have anything to do with her. He sent her back to Bhīṣma, whom he felt had won her in honorable combat. Aṁbā, as might be expected, was rather upset. When she returned to Hāstinapura, things got even worse: Vicitravīrya refused to marry anyone whose heart was pledged to another. Aṁbā asked Bhīṣma to marry her, but this was out of the question because of Bhīṣma's vow of chastity. Aṁbā became overwhelmed with hatred for Bhīṣma, who had been the author of all her misfortunes. She approached Śālva again, but he refused her a second time. Then she sought champions among the princes at Hāstinapura who might fight and kill Bhīṣma. But none of them would volunteer. They not only respected the old warrior, they were afraid of him. Then Aṁbā undertook austerities in order to gain the favor of the god Vishnu, and Vishnu gave her a garland, saying that whoever wore it would become an enemy of Bhīṣma. Aṁbā then approached King Drupada of the Pāñcālas, offering him the garland. But even Drupada, who was a mighty warrior, declined to fight with Bhīṣma. Finally, on the advice of some ascetics, she went to see Paraśurāma ("Rāma of the Axe"), a famous brāhman who had taken up the un-brahmanical profession of arms, and had vowed to exterminate the kṣatriya, or warrior, caste. Paraśurāma also became an *avatār* of the god Vishnu in honor of whom she had previously performed austerities. He agreed to be her champion. But when the battle took place Paraśurāma was defeated by Bhīṣma. This was the last straw for Aṁbā. She went to the Himālaya where she practiced extreme austerities to gain the favor of the god Shiva. Shiva appeared before her, and promised that she would, in her next incarnation, become a man. Impatient for her next birth, she built a great fire and plunged into it to be burned to death. She was subsequently reborn as Śikhaṇḍin, son of King Drupada. In due time, she, or he, became one of the warriors at the Battle of Kurukṣetra, and, as Arjuna's charioteer, participated in the slaying of her old enemy Bhīṣma. In this combat Bhīṣma refused to defend himself against Śikhaṇḍin because he knew of his reincarnation and considered him to be a woman.

Now we come to the story of Pāṇḍu, officially the son of King Vicitravīrya but actually the son of Vicitravīrya's half brother Vyāsa by Aṁbālikā. Pāṇḍu was also a half brother of the blind King Dhṛtarāṣṭra, who was the son of Vyāsa by Aṁbikā. Dhṛtarāṣṭra had a hundred sons. Pāṇḍu reigned at Hāstinapura with Bhīṣma as advisor. Pāṇḍu had two wives – Kuntī, daughter of Śūra, a Yādava king (who was also the father of Vasudeva, Krishna's father, thus making Kuntī Krishna's aunt), and Mādrī, another princess. Once, while out hunting, Pāṇḍu had the misfortune to kill a deer which was copulating with its mate and which was really a sage in disguise. While dying, the sage levelled a curse at Pāṇḍu. He would die the instant he had intercourse with a woman. Thus Pāṇḍu was incapable of having children, and the stage was set for the sort of divine, or otherwise peculiar births that are mandatory for great heroes. All of the so-called Sons of Pāṇḍu had gods for fathers.

Kuntī, who had been adopted in childhood by her father's childless cousin Kuntibhoja, and had taken her name from him (it had originally been Pṛthā) had once received a *mantra*, or magical invocation, from the sage Durvāsas with which she could summon any god to be the father of her children. As a matter of fact, or properly speaking, legend, she had used it once before her marriage to Pāṇḍu. She had summoned the Sun god, and by him had had a child named Karṇa who was born with earrings and a complete suit of armor. Kuntī had been so embarrassed by this illegitimate, though divine, birth (it was also a virgin birth), that she had set the child afloat in a river, where he was picked up by a charioteer named Adhiratha, and brought up by him as his son. Karṇa was unaware of his miraculous birth until the Battle of Kurukṣetra, and thought of himself as the son of a humble charioteer. Just before the battle, however, Kuntī informed him of his divine lineage. But this happened after Karṇa had cast his lot with the Kāuravas, and was preparing to fight against his half brothers, the Pāṇḍava Princes. Kuntī told her legal husband Pāṇḍu about the *mantra*, and promptly went about becoming the mother of great heroes by various gods. By Dharma, the god of righteousness, she became the mother of the just and honorable Yudhiṣṭhira. By Vāyu, the god of the winds, she begot the powerful Bhīma, whose habit was to uproot trees to use as weapons, and who had the appetite of a wolf. By Indra, the chief of the Vedic gods, she begot Arjuna, the stainless knight who is the hero of the Bhagavad Gītā. In the meantime, Pāṇḍu's other wife, Mādrī, was busy along similar lines. She became the mother of the twins, Nakula and Sahadeva by the twin Aśvins, the heavenly horsemen who pull the chariot of the dawn. Thus, all the Pāṇḍava Princes, as befits heroes, were of divine birth. As to Pāṇḍu, he died suddenly in a moment of forgetfulness while having intercourse with Mādrī. Mādrī dutifully committed suttee (or satī as the Sanskrit has it), burning herself upon her husband's funeral pyre.

Meanwhile, at the court of King Śūra, of the Yādava line, his grandson Krishna was born. There had already been intimations of his divine role as the *avatār* of the god Vishnu. When his father, Vasudeva, was born there had been a rolling of heavenly drums because he was to become the parent of Vishnu's *avatār*. Vasudeva duly married Devakī, a niece of King Ugrasena of Mathurā. There were difficulties. Devakī's cousin, an evil tyrant named Kaṁsa who had imprisoned King Ugrasena and usurped the throne, arranged that all Devakī's children should die at birth (a sage had predicted that Kaṁsa would be slain by a son of Devakī). Six children thus perished. But Vasudeva magically inserted the seventh into the womb of Rohinī, another of his wives, and the child who was born was Balarāma, Krishna's older brother. Krishna himself was placed by Vasudeva into the hands of a cowherd named Nanda. Krishna was brought up by Nanda and his wife among cowherds and milkmaids. He was a sly child, and delighted in stealing milk, butter and fruit. But he also performed several heroic feats as a child. And he pursued the opposite sex, accumulating, according to some sources, as many as 16,108 wives including his chief wife Rukminī. The evil Kaṁsa continued to try to waylay Krishna and his brother Balarāma, seeking their death, but was always foiled by one stratagem or another. Finally, Kaṁsa invited Krishna and Balarāma to take part in an athletic contest in which he sent savage demons and wild beasts to fight them. Among these was Keśin, king of the savage horse-demons, whose death at Krishna's hands earned Krishna the epithet of Keśinisūdana (Slayer of Keśin) by which, among other nicknames, he is addressed in the Bhagavad Gītā. The demons and beasts being easily overcome by Krishna and Balarāma, Kaṁsa himself entered the arena and was killed, in fulfillment of the sage's prophecy, by Krishna. Kaṁsa's brother Sunāman then tried to avenge Kaṁsa's death, but was slain by Balarāma. The result was that the imprisoned King Ugrasena was freed and reigned again in his kingdom at Mathurā. Shortly afterward, Krishna descended into hell to bring back his six brothers whom Kaṁsa had caused to be slain at birth. The six then ascended to heaven with Krishna's help. Then Krishna changed his habits, left the milkmaids behind, underwent purification ceremonies and acknowledged Vasudeva and Devakī as his true parents. Along with his brother Balarāma, he received spiritual instruction, and instruction in the art of war, from Sāṁdīpani, a famous warrior-sage. During this period, Pañcajana, a marine demon who lived at the bottom of the sea in the form of a conch, kidnapped Sāṁdīpani's son. Krishna went to the rescue and slew Pañcajana, and thereafter used the conch shell Pāñcajanya (mentioned in the Bhagavad Gītā I, 15) as a trumpet.

Jarāsaṁdha, King of Māgadha, whose daughters had married Kaṁsa, heard of Kaṁsa's death at the hands of Krishna, and sent a great army against Mathurā, attacking the city eighteen times without decisive result. A "barbarian" (Greek) king named Kālayavana, "Black Greek" (Yavana, "Ionian," was the Indian term for Greeks, many of whom had settled in India at this time), joined his armies to Jarāsaṁdha's, and finally Krishna was forced to abandon the city. He moved his capital to a town in the Gujarat called Dvārakā ("the city of gates or doors") which then became one of India's sacred cities. Krishna's later exploits included battles with, and defeats of, the gods Indra, Varuṇa and Shiva, the conquest of a large number of tribes and kings, the abduction of a Gandhāra princess from her *svayaṁvara* and the defeat of the King of Niṣāda who had attacked Dvārakā. He became India's ideal of manhood and a god who is worshipped to this day.

Pāṇḍu and his half brother Dhṛtarāṣṭra seem to have divided the throne at Hāstinapura, Dhṛtarāṣṭra, disqualified because of his blindness, acting as regent until the death of Pāṇḍu, who, as has been said, died because of the sage's curse (he had by the time of his death taken up residence in the forest with his wives and children). Kuntī, his chief wife, remained to take care of the children while Mādrī, as has been related, committed suttee. The sages of the forest took Kuntī and the children back to Hāstinapura, entrusting them to the old warrior Bhīṣma. The children (the Pāṇḍava Princes Yudhiṣṭhira, Bhīma, Arjuna, Nakula and Sahadeva) grew up together with the hundred sons of Dhṛtarāṣṭra (the Kāurava princes) in typical boyish rivalry and general high spirits. But Bhīma was something of a bully. Much more powerfully built than the others, he delighted in grasping the Sons of Dhṛtarāṣṭra with his arms and holding them under water until their breaths gave out, and when they climbed trees he would shake the trunks until they fell out like ripe fruit. The Sons of Dhṛtarāṣṭra hated Bhīma from infancy. Chief among them was Duryodhana ("Dirty Fighter"), and he became an early enemy of the Pāṇḍava Princes, partly because of Bhīma's bullying but also because he was afraid that Pāṇḍu's eldest son, Yudhiṣṭhira, might succeed to the throne instead of himself. Duryodhana hatched a plot to wipe out the Sons of Pāṇḍu. He poisoned Bhīma's food, bound him, and threw him into a river to drown, and he planned to cast Arjuna and Yudhiṣṭhira into prison, and seize the throne himself. But the poison only strengthened Bhima, who burst his bonds and swam to shore. Meanwhile the sons of Pāṇḍu and the Sons of Dhṛtarāṣṭra were taught the arts of war by the older warriors Kṛpa, Droṇa and "the grandsire" Bhīṣma. It was Arjuna who grew up to be the most skillful warrior, while Bhīma, because of his superhuman strength, became the most powerful one.

During this time, the unacknowledged half-brother of the Pāṇḍava Princes, Karṇa, who had been born to Kuntī by the Sun god but had been brought up as the son of a humble charioteer, appeared at Hāstinapura. He challenged Arjuna to combat, much to the delight of Duryodhana. It is said that the father of both heroes, the god Indra and the Sun god, appeared in the sky to encourage their offspring. But there was some question as to whether Karṇa, allegedly the son of a charioteer, was of sufficient rank to fight with Arjuna, and the fight was called off. Duryodhana thereupon crowned Karṇa King of Añga, a kingdom some authorities identify with modern Bengal. But the encounter did not follow immediately, for Duryodhana carried Karṇa off in his chariot. Knowing that such an encounter was inevitable at some point, the god Indra, father of Arjuna, sought to weaken Karṇa. He appeared to Karṇa in the guise of a brāhman and begged from him his earrings and armor. Karṇa, who was famous for his generosity, gave them up, and Indra, astonished by this act, granted Karṇa in return the use of the Śakti, a magical weapon which was Indra's own and which had the power to kill even at a great distance. But Indra made a proviso. The weapon could be used by Karṇa only once, after which it would return to its godly owner. Karṇa went to the warlike brāhman Paraśurāma ("Rāma of the Axe") who hated all members of the kṣatriya, or warrior, caste. He represented himself to Paraśurāma as a brāhman, and Paraśurāma taught him the proper *mantra*, or magical invocation, to use with the Śakti. But one day while Karṇa slept, a stinging insect burrowed into his thigh, inflicting a painful and bloody wound. Karṇa bore the pain without flinching. Paraśurāma then knew immediately that Karṇa was not the brāhman he represented himself to be. Only a kṣatriya, or member of the warrior caste, could stand such pain without crying out. Karṇa had to confess that he was a kṣatriya, and Paraśurāma, outraged by the deception, pronounced a curse on Karṇa – he would be doomed to forget the *mantra* at the moment he needed it most. And so it turned out. But we are getting ahead of our story.

In the forest hermitage of the sage Bharadvāja, his own son, the great hero Droṇa was trained in archery along with Drupada, son of the king of the Pāñcālas. As has been said, mythology demands that all heroes be born in a peculiar manner, and the births of Droṇa and Drupada were peculiar indeed, for neither had a mother. Droṇa, whose name means "bucket," was born from a bucket into which his father's seed had fallen. Something similar had happened to Pṛṣata, the king of Pāñcāla. He was observing a beautiful nymph, named Menakā when his seed fell to the ground. Ashamed, he took a rapid (dru) step (pada) to stamp out the seed. But he did not succeed, and Drupada was born from it. Droṇa was a brāhman, but despite his birth became a renowned warrior. Drupada was a kṣatriya. During their childhood Drupada often spoke of giving half his kingdom to Droṇa. But when King Pṛṣata died and Drupada ascended the throne of Pāñcāla, he spurned his former friend, calling him a poor beggar. Droṇa, however, was selected by "the grandsire" Bhīṣma to train the five Sons of Pāṇḍu as well as the hundred sons of Dhṛtarāṣṭra in the arts of war. After their apprenticeship was over, Droṇa sent the Sons of Pāṇḍu on an expedition to defeat and capture Drupada. They defeated the Pāñcālas and took Drupada prisoner. Droṇa then forgave Drupada, but retained, as a pledge of future friendship, half the Pāñcāla kingdom, thus gaining by force what he had been promised and then denied. Drupada was angry, and hoped for a son who would slay Droṇa. He performed a great sacrifice to this end, in which, it is said, ten million cattle were killed. When the moment arrived, Drupada's wife was unprepared to receive his seed. But a son and a daughter sprang forth miraculously from the sacrificial fire. These were the twins Dhṛṣtadyumna ("He whose splendor is bold") and Draupadī ("Daughter of Drupada"), later the collective wife of the five Pāṇḍava Princes. Many years later, Dhṛṣtadyumna did indeed slay Droṇa.

Duryodhana, the evil elder son of the blind King Dhṛtarāṣṭra, became enraged at the popularity and success at arms of the Pāṇḍava Princes, and the possibility that Yudhiṣthira, instead of he, might succeed to the throne of Hāstinapura. With the connivance of Karṇa and Śakuni, the brother-in-law of Dhṛtarāṣṭra, he plotted to destroy the Sons of Pāṇḍu. At first, Dhṛtarāṣṭra, who was inclined to kindliness toward his nephews, the Sons of Pāṇḍu, would hear nothing of the plot. Later, owing to the wiles and insistent arguments of Duryodhana, he agreed to it, and mentioned to the Sons of Pāṇḍu that a great festival in honor of Shiva was to take place in the nearby city of Vāraṇāvata, and that the Pāṇḍavas owed it to themselves to attend, because the people of Vāraṇāvata were anxious to see them. Before the festival took place, Duryodhana, Karṇa and Śakuni sent a minister named Purocana to Vāraṇāvata to construct a palace for the Sons of Pāṇḍu to stay in during their visit. By prearrangement this palace was built of wax and other inflammable materials. The idea was to set fire to the palace while the Sons of Pāṇḍu were asleep, and thus destroy them. But Vidura, a younger brother of Pāṇḍu and Dhṛtarāṣṭra, who favored the Pāṇḍava Princes, warned Yudhiṣṭhira that something was afoot in Vāraṇāvata, and sent a miner to dig a subterranean exit from the wax palace. Pretending that they knew nothing of the plot, the Sons of Pāṇḍu took up residence in the palace, but kept a sharp lookout. At midnight the palace was set aflame, and the Sons of Pāṇḍu escaped through the subterranean tunnel. Dhṛtarāṣṭra and his sons exchanged their garments for funereal ones and performed impressive obsequies near a river for the supposedly dead Pāṇḍava Princes. Only Vidura was not overcome by apparent grief; he knew that the Pāṇḍavas had escaped.

The Sons of Pāṇḍu journeyed into the forest, often carried with their mother Kuntī on the broad shoulders and hips, or with the hands, of the powerful Bhīma. During this journey they met their grandfather the sage Vyāsa, who gave them good counsel and advised them to dress as brāhmans. Finally they arrived at a city called Ekacakra ("One Wheel," actually "the City of the One Wheel of Dominion"), whose king had fled, and which was being held in thrall by a terrible cannibalistic demon named Bakāsura ("Crane Demon"). A brāhman family gave them shelter, and when they learned about the demon and his insistence on tribute in the form of human flesh and other foods, Bhīma set out to destroy him. A terrific battle ensued in which the demon pulled up trees by the roots to belabor Bhīma with. But Bhīma, who was well aware of this tactic, finally threw him to the ground and broke his bones. He returned to the city, dragging the demon's body to the city gates, took a bath and then told the brāhman family of his deed.

While the Sons of Pāṇḍu were sojourning at Ekacakra, they heard about the *svayaṁvara* of Princess Drāupadī, daughter of King Drupada ("Rapid Step") of Pāñcāla who has already been mentioned in connection with his boyhood friend Droṇa. Drāupadī was a great beauty, and princes came from many distant kingdoms to compete for her hand. The Sons of Pāṇḍu were still disguised as humble brāhmans, and after a long march they arrived at Pāñcāla where they took up residence at the home of a potter. When the great day of the *svayaṁvara* arrived, even Krishna and his brother Balarāma had come to Pāñcāla to compete in the ceremony. King Drupada had caused a revolving ring to be placed on a pole at a great height, and had had a very large bow constructed which was difficult to bend. He who shot an arrow through the ring with this bow could claim Drāupadī as his wife. It would be a difficult feat, and the gods assembled in midair to witness the spectacle. One by one, the princes stepped up to try their skill. Some could not even bend the bow, and none succeeded in hitting the target. Then Arjuna stepped forward, took up the bow and shot five arrows straight through the ring. Both King Drupada and Princess Drāupadī were overjoyed, though there were murmurs of objection from some who were present – including Karṇa and Śalya, King of Madra – that a brāhman should win a prize reserved for warriors (Arjuna was still disguised as a brāhman).

When the Pāṇḍava Princes returned home, they agreed that Yudhiṣṭhira, the eldest of them, should marry Drāupadī. But as they saw their mother, Kuntī, they cried out "We have won a great prize today," and Kuntī said "Then share the prize between you." Kuntī's word being law, there was nothing to do but marry all five Sons of Pāṇḍu to Drāupadī. King Drupada objected to the marriage (polyandry was not a common practice among Hindus, though polygamy was), but he finally yielded. It was arranged that Drāupadī should stay two days at the house of each brother in turn, and that none of the others would see her during this time. She subsequently bore five sons, one by each of the brothers; Prativindhya by Yudhiṣṭhira, Sutasoma by Bhīma, Śrutakīrti by Arjuna, Śatānīka by Nakula and Śrutakarman by Sahadeva. Arjuna was her favorite husband, and when he afterward married a second wife, Subhadrā, a sister of Krishna whom he had carried off by force with Krishna's permission, Drāupadī was overcome with jealousy.*

Back in Hāstinapura, the capital of Dhṛtarāṣṭra's kingdom, the Sons of Kuru heard of the doings at Pāñcāla and realized for the first time that the Sons of Pāṇḍu had not perished in the burning of the wax palace. Vidura was happy at this news. His brother, the vacillating, blind King Dhṛtarāṣṭra, was at first relieved to hear the news, but later connived with his sons against the Pāṇḍavas. Duryodhana, eldest of the Sons of Dhṛtarāṣṭra, was infuriated, and so was his brother Duḥśāsana. They consulted with their uncle Śakuni, plotting the downfall of the Pāṇḍavas all over again. They considered setting the sons of Kuntī (Yudhiṣṭhira, Bhīma and Arjuna) and the sons of Mādrī (Nakula and Sahadeva) against each other. They considered bribing Drupada to join them against the Pāṇḍavas. They also considered fomenting jealousy among the Pāṇḍavas through experts in the art of erotics, and fomenting the jealousy of Drāupadī by catching the Pāṇḍavas *in flagrante delicto* with other women. By this time the Pāṇḍavas had been joined by Dhṛṣṭadyumna, son of Drupada, and also by Śikhaṇḍin, the male incarnation of Aṁbā, daughter of the King of the Kāśis, now a son of Drupada. In addition, they had been joined by Krishna and the Yādavas, Krishna's tribe. This was a formidable group to contend with, and the Sons of Dhṛtarāṣṭra were understandably fearful. The wise, aged and generous Bhīṣma counselled making peace with the Sons of Pāṇḍu and giving them half the kingdom. Droṇa agreed. The hotter-headed Duryodhana and Karṇa did not.

* There has been some speculation among historians as to the relative customs of the Pāṇḍavas and the Kāuravas. The Cambridge History of India holds that the polyandry of the Pāṇḍavas is an indication of their comparative primitiveness, that they were a northern tribe who went to war with the more civilized Kāuravas, and that the latter were an old settled people who preferred to gain their ends by guile and conspiracy rather than war – a point that seems to be borne out by the narrative.

But Vidura, their virtuous uncle, was sent to Drupada's court to make peace with the Pāṇḍavas and bring them back to Hāstinapura along with their mother and common wife. This being accomplished, the kingdom was divided in half, Yudhiṣṭhira was crowned king of the other half, and the Sons of Pāṇḍu took up residence in a new city (identified by some with modern Delhi). They named the city Indraprastha, and there they reigned justly for thirty-six years.

Meanwhile, Yudhiṣṭhira began to have dreams of empire, and sent for Krishna to advise him whether or not he might undertake the Rājasūya Sacrifice and name himself emperor. But Krishna pointed out that as long as his, Krishna's old enemy King Jarāsaṁdha, King of Magadha, reigned, held some eighty-six princes in prison, and planned to attack and imprison a full hundred, nobody else could proclaim himself emperor. Yudhiṣṭhira was inclined to give up his idea, but Bhīma did not like this spirit of complacence, which he thought unworthy of a king. Krishna proposed that he, Bhīma and Arjuna set out to kill Jarāsaṁdha and free his prisoners who would then become allies of the Pāṇḍavas. Arjuna was enthusiastic. The Sons of Pāṇḍu had too long refrained from heroic deeds. So they set out. Now, Jarāsaṁdha, like all the other warrior heroes in this epic, had had a strange birth. His father, one Bṛhadratha, had been childless, and had consulted a sage about his problem. At that moment a mango fell into the lap of the sage. The sage cut the mango into two halves and presented them to Bṛhadratha, who gave each half to one of his two wives. The result was that each wife gave birth to half a child, and that only on the intervention of a rākṣasī, or female demon named Jarā ("the Old One"), who tied the two halves together, was Jarāsaṁdha made into a complete human being (hence his name, "put together by Jarā"). He grew into a man of immense strength, and a very wicked one. When Krishna and the Pāṇḍava Princes arrived at Jarāsaṁdha's court, they were disguised as holy men, and Jarāsaṁdha welcomed them with courtesy. But soon they revealed themselves as warriors, and sought battle with him in single combat. Jarāsaṁdha chose Bhīma as his opponent, and they battled each other for thirteen days. On the thirteenth, Bhīma killed Jarāsaṁdha, the captive princes were released, Jarāsaṁdha's son was made king of Māgadha and Krishna and the Sons of Pāṇḍu returned to Indrapraṣṭha. Yudhiṣṭhira performed the Rājasūya Sacrifice, which was indispensable for one who sought imperial dominion, and proclaimed himself emperor. After the ceremony, however, the sage Vyāsa, his natural grandfather, who had been in attendance, cautioned Yudhiṣṭhira, and prophesied evil days to come for the kṣatriya race.

Duryodhana, who had also attended the ceremony, noted the prosperity that the Pāṇḍavas had brought to Indrapraṣṭha, and this inflamed his anger even further. He went to his uncle Śakuni with a proposal that the Sons of Dhṛtarāṣṭra should declare war against the Sons of Pāṇḍu, and take back the half of the kingdom they had been given. But the wily and evil Śakuni proposed that, on the contrary, they should invite Yudhiṣṭhira to a game of dice. He, Śakuni, was skilled in the tricks of dice playing. Yudhiṣṭhira was not. Śakuni could accomplish by peaceful means what Duryodhana wanted to gain by war. King Dhṛtarāṣṭra was reluctant to approve this idea, but as usual he vacillated and finally consented, causing a large hall of games to be built and sending his brother Vidura with an invitation to Yudhiṣṭhira. Vidura was not happy with his assignment, and he warned Yudhiṣṭhira that probably no good would come of the invitation. Nevertheless, partly out of courtesy, partly because he had a weakness for gambling, Yudhiṣṭhira accepted, and went with his retinue to Hāstinapura, where the Sons of Pāṇḍu were put up in regal fashion by the Sons of Dhṛtarāṣṭra. Next morning, a cloth having been spread in the hall of games, the game began. Yudhiṣṭhira was quite aware of Śakuni's reputation as an expert at the game, but he plunged ahead. He wagered jewels and gold, then chariots and horses. Śakuni won every throw. Intoxicated by the game, Yudhiṣṭhira went on to wager cattle, sheep, villages, citizens and all their possessions. Śakuni won them all. Then, in desperation, the foolish Yudhiṣṭhira began to wager his brothers Nakula, Sahadeva and finally Arjuna, Bhīma and himself. Śakuni won them all, and then asked Yudhiṣṭhira to wager their common wife Drāupadī. (This was technically against the rules. It was bad form for one side to suggest to the other what he should wager.) The elders, Droṇa, Kṛpa, Bhīṣma and Vidura, and even King Dhṛtarāṣṭra himself were outraged by this suggestion, but the evil Duryodhana, Karṇa and the remaining Sons of Dhṛtarāṣṭra shouted in exultation. Śakuni won again, and Drāupadī was sent for, to become the household servant of the Sons of Dhṛtarāṣṭra. Vidura was filled with forebodings. Duryodhana sent his brother Duḥśāsana to fetch Drāupadī. He caught her by the hair and dragged her before the assembly. The elders hung their heads in shame. Even Vikarṇa, one of Dhṛtarāṣṭra's sons, protested that the game had been rigged and that, contrary to the rules, it was Śakuni who had suggested the wager of Drāupadī. But Duryodhana was adamant, and his brother Duḥśāsana even went to the extreme of stripping the clothes from the Pāṇḍavas, including Drāupadī. In Drāupadī's case, however, a miracle occurred. As her robes were stripped away, new ones appeared in their place, and Duḥśāsana, having piled up a great heap of elegant garments, was finally forced to cease, from fatigue. At this point Bhīma swore a mighty oath, that one day he would rend the breast of Duḥśāsana and drink his blood. The howling of animals was suddenly heard from the forest. King Dhṛtarāṣṭra, foreseeing the destruction of his race, called Drāupadī and Yudhiṣṭhira to his side, asked them for forgiveness and restored their kingdom to them. (There had been a legal dilemma not only over Śakuni's right to suggest the wager of Drāupadī, but also as to whether Yudhiṣṭhira, who had wagered and lost himself, any longer had the right to wager Drāupadī who, at that point, was no longer his property. One of the reasons Dhṛtarāṣṭra set the Sons of Pāṇḍu free was the dubious legality of this wager.)

But when the Pāṇḍava Princes had left, Duryodhana, seeing his plans frustrated, upbraided his father, King Dhṛtarāṣṭra, and complained that by his generous action he had strengthened their enemies again. Dhṛtarāṣṭra, who was a doting father, gave in to Duryodhana's arguments and agreed once more to a game of dice. Yudhiṣṭhira was again summoned, and the crafty Śakuni again took up the dice. This time the stake was that the defeated party go with his brothers into exile for thirteen years, spending the last of the thirteen incognito. If they were recognized during the thirteenth year, they would agree to go into exile again for another twelve years. Needless to say, Yudhiṣṭhira lost again, and the Sons of Pāṇḍu took to the forest. Droṇa and Vidura were both apprehensive. They felt that, in retribution, the race of the Kāuravas (the Sons of Dhṛtarāṣṭra, along with Dhṛtarāṣṭra himself, Vidura and Śakuni) was doomed. But Duryodhana slapped his thighs in derision. Then Vidura pronounced a curse on Duryodhana to the effect that he would die, with both legs broken, on the battlefield at the hands of Bhīma if he proceeded with his evil plans. After that, Vidura left the court and cast his lot with the Sons of Pāṇḍu.

At this point, Krishna was busy lifting the siege of Dvārakā, which had been besieged in his absence by a certain King Śālva, whose friend, Śiśupāla, Krishna had slain. When he heard of the dice game at Hāstinapura he set out at once to find the Pāṇḍavas in the forest, and he brought along with him many men of the Bhoja and Vṛṣṇi tribes as well as Dhṛṣṭaketu, King of Cedi, and members of a warrior tribe known as the Kekayas who had been friends of the Pāṇḍavas. Krishna found the Pāṇḍavas, but stayed with them only long enough to express his sympathy, and then returned to Dvārakā with Subhadrā, the second wife of Arjuna, and their child Abhimanyu. As to Arjuna himself, he went on a pilgrimage to the Himālaya, where he practiced austerities. He was met by his father, the god Indra, who was disguised as a brāhman. Indra advised him to do penance to Shiva (a god who was rapidly displacing the old Vedic god Indra at this time). Arjuna did as he was told. But during his austerities he was charged by a wild boar. He shot it with an arrow, and another huntsman shot it at the same moment. This was Shiva himself, though Arjuna was unaware of the fact. Shiva suggested that they fight over the matter of who had killed the boar. Arjuna accepted, and the two battled. But Arjuna soon noticed that his opponent was unscathed while he himself was being wounded. Then he recognized Shiva, asked forgiveness, and Shiva healed his wounds, strengthening him a hundredfold. He was then taken in a chariot to Indra's realm, rested for a while in the kingdom of the gods and obtained divine weapons.

While Arjuna was away, Krishna and Balarāma again visited the Pāṇḍavas, and several sages told them stories to take their minds off their misfortunes. But Drāupadī never gave up lamenting her humiliation at the hands of the Sons of Dhṛtarāṣṭra. Drāupadī wanted revenge, and eventually she got it. Many things happened in the forest. A great army was collecting around the Pāṇḍavas, and was becoming a burden to support. They sent it away, telling those who were so inclined to go to the court of Dhṛtarāṣṭra, and the others to the court of Drupada. The Pāṇḍavas then went on a pilgrimage, during which Bhīma stumbled upon his half brother Hanumān (also a son of the wind god Vāyu), who had taken a heroic role in the Rāmāyaṇa, the other great Hindu epic. The encounter brought joy to both brothers, and Hanumān recounted the adventures he had had while assisting Rāma to bring back his beloved Sītā from captivity at the hands of the King of Lañkā (Ceylon). Meanwhile, against the advice of Dhṛtarāṣṭra, Duryodhana and the Kāuravas went to the forest to gloat over the misery of the Pāṇḍavas. There, they attacked a group of gandharvas (heavenly musicians) and were defeated after a great battle. They were rescued by the just and noble Yudhiṣṭhira, with whom the gandharvas refused to fight, and the rescue humiliated Duryodhana, Karṇa and the Sons of Dhṛtarāṣṭra. Miracles occurred, and adventures without number came the way of the Sons of Pāṇḍu. Arjuna returned from his pilgrimage. Finally, the thirteenth year of their exile arrived, and, in various disguises, they came to the court of Virāṭa, King of the Matsyas, where they took up domestic service. Yudhiṣṭhira became a courtier to the king; Bhīma served as a cook; Arjuna disguised himself as a eunuch to serve the ladies of the court; Nakula became a stable boy; Sahadeva became the king's cowherd, and Drāupadī became the attendant of the queen and the princesses of Virāṭa's court. But soon Drāupadī's beauty caught the eye of Kīcaka, the commander in chief of Virāṭa's armies, and he sought to seduce her. Her entreaties that she was merely a low-caste serving woman were of no avail. Kīcaka pursued her and tried to rape her. Careless of revealing the identities of the Sons of Pāṇḍu, she arranged for an assignation with Kīcaka, and persuaded Bhīma to go in her place. When Kīcaka appeared, Bhīma pounded him to a pulp, later going back to his kitchen, taking a bath and sleeping with satisfaction. Kīcaka's death made Drāupadī an object of fear at the court of King Virāṭa, and she was asked to leave. She requested one more month's stay (it was the last month of the thirteenth year of the exile of the Sons of Pāṇḍu, and they were obliged to preserve their incognito until it ended).

But rumors of the slaying of Kīcaka began to reach Hāstinapura, and, as everybody knew Kīcaka to be a man of great physical prowess, slayable only by the mighty Bhīma, a suspicion began to grow that the Pāṇḍavas were at Virāṭa's court. Duryodhana proposed invading Virāṭa's realm, and was enthusiastically supported by King Suśarman of Trigarta (which lay in the neighborhood of modern Lahore). Suśarman had long had an account to settle with Virāṭa, and now that the latter's chief of armies had been killed, he thought it a good time to strike. Karṇa agreed. Suśarman attacked the dominions of Virāṭa, laying waste the land. Virāṭa regretted the loss of his general, but Yudhiṣṭhira reassured him. Though he was a mere holy man, Yudhiṣṭhira said, he was also an expert in the art of war. If Virāṭa would permit him to arm the cook, the stable boy and the cowherd, they would protect him. These, of course, were Bhīma, Nakula and Sahadeva, and they set out, this time without Arjuna, to protect Virāṭa and defeat Suśarman and the Kāuravas. There was a big battle, and Virāṭa was taken captive for a time. Bhīma at one point wanted to uproot a tree to use as a weapon, but this was such a well-known habit of his that Yudhiṣṭhira cautioned him against it, lest the identity of the Pāṇḍava Princes be discovered. Bhīma took his place in a chariot, and the Pāṇḍavas threw back the armies of Suśarman, released Virāṭa and brought him back to his capital city, Matsya, in triumph. Meanwhile, Duryodhana had attacked Virāṭa's realm from the opposite side and was stealing the cattle that were part of Virāṭa's wealth. Virāṭa's son, Prince Uttara, was anxious to respond to this attack, and he had heard that Arjuna, though a eunuch (still disguised), had at one time been a charioteer. He asked Arjuna to serve him in this capacity, and the two of them went out alone to tackle the whole Kāurava army. It was Uttara's first battle, and when he saw the Kāuravas arrayed,

Arjuna was at some pains to keep him from fleeing the field. Finally, he made Uttara *his* charioteer, and, sending him to retrieve some weapons he had hidden in a tree, prepared for battle, sounding his conch horn Devadatta. Droṇa and Bhīṣma had already recognized him. But the period of thirteen years had expired. Droṇa advised the Kāuravas to let Duryodhana return to Hāstinapura with part of the army, and to leave another part to seize Virāṭa's cattle. Bhīṣma, Droṇa, Kṛpa, Aśvatthāman, son of Droṇa, and Karṇa would remain to give battle to Arjuna. But Arjuna pursued Duryodhana, and at the same time managed to put the cattle stealers to flight. Then he returned to fight with the Kāurava forces, defeating them all and finally using a magic weapon that made them fall down unconscious. He then stripped their clothes off, and they were forced to return to Hāstinapura in disgrace. Meanwhile, Arjuna sent word back to the court of Virāṭa, saying that the young Uttara had won a glorious victory. On the way back, he hid his arms in the tree again, and assumed his former effeminate garb as a eunuch.

When Virāṭa returned to his court after the victory over Suśarman, he noticed that his son, Uttara, was missing, but Uttara soon turned up. On being questioned, he gave all the credit for the victory to Arjuna, and the Pāṇḍava Princes immediately disclosed their true identity. No longer was it necessary for them to maintain their incognito. They left Virāṭa's capital and settled in the city of Upaplavya, another place in Virāṭa's realm. Here they summoned their friends and relatives. Krishna and Balarāma arrived with Arjuna's second wife Subhadrā and their son Abhimanyu, along with many Yādava warriors. Those who had briefly joined the Pāṇḍavas in the forest returned. The King of the Kāśis and Śāibya, King of the Śibis, arrived with their retinues. Drupada, King of the Pāñcālas, brought a considerable army, along with Śikhaṇḍin (the former Ambā) and his twin brother Dhṛṣṭadyumna. Sātyaki (otherwise known as Yuyudhāna, and a kinsman of Krishna) was present also. Led by Krishna, this mighty gathering of warriors thought of sending a last peace envoy to the Kāuravas. Balrāma was in favor of this move. But Sātyaki deplored the idea as unworthy of warriors, and Drupada agreed. A brāhman was nevertheless sent to Hāstinapura with proposals to Duryodhana for a peaceful settlement, the settlement being that the Sons of Dhṛtarāṣṭra agree to return the lands they had taken from the Sons of Pāṇḍu. The aged Bhīṣma was in favor of the settlement, but Karṇa was for war. Krishna and Balarāma regarded themselves as neutrals, friendly to both sides. Duryodhana approached Krishna asking for his help in the coming battle. Krishna offered Duryodhana and Arjuna each a choice between himself, unarmed, and his army, the Nārāyaṇa tribesmen. Arjuna chose Krishna, and Duryodhana the army. Krishna agreed to serve as Arjuna's charioteer. Balarāma decided to abstain from the battle.

Meanwhile a tremendous mobilization took place on both sides. Śalya, King of Madra Deśa, marched toward the Pāṇḍavas with a huge army, intending to join them, but Duryodhana extended exaggerated hospitality toward him and his troops, and when Śalya asked how he could repay it, Duryodhana asked him to join the side of the Kāuravas, which he did. Śalya was an uncle of Nakula and

Sahadeva, and thus he cast his lot against them just to keep a promise. His sympathies, however, remained with the Pāṇḍavas, and he promised Yudhiṣṭhira that if he were to become Karṇa's charioteer when Karṇa attacked Arjuna, he would hamper Karṇa's efforts. Ultimately, at their headquarters in Upaplavya, in Virāṭa's kingdom, the Pāṇḍavas mobilized a force of seven divisions. The Kāuravas, at Hāstinapura, mobilized a much larger force of eleven divisions. Each division consisted of 21,870 chariots, an equal number of elephants, three times as many horsemen and five times as many foot soldiers. Thus, tremendously large armies were prepared to fight. By count, the Pāṇḍavas had an army of 153,090 chariots, 153,090 elephants, 459,270 horsemen and 765,450 foot soldiers, while the Kāuravas, under the Sons of Dhṛtarāṣṭra, had an army of 240,570 chariots, 240,570 elephants, 721,710 horsemen and over a million foot soldiers. Even allowing for the exaggerations common in epics, these were armies of colossal dimensions, perhaps similar to the massive armies of contemporary Persia, and far exceeding in number those of the contemporary Greeks.

Two last minute efforts were made to avoid war. Dhṛtarāṣṭra, the blind and weak-minded king of the Kāuravas, sent his minister Saṁjaya to plead for peace with the Pāṇḍavas, but Saṁjaya was merely the personal envoy of a monarch who confessed he could not control his own sons. Drāupadī, the collective wife of the Pāṇḍavas, was prepared to sacrifice anything for revenge, and was very much for war. Krishna made a trip to see the Kāuravas without much hope, and, as he expected, was spurned by Duryodhana. There was no recourse but war. One more thing happened just before hostilities broke out. Kuntī, mother of the Pāṇḍava Princes, met Karṇa while he was at prayers near a river, and informed him that he was not the humble charioteer's son he thought he was, but her own son by the Sun god. This gratified Karṇa, but it was too late to withdraw from battle against his half brothers, Yudhiṣṭhira, Bhīma and Arjuna.

Now that we are on the eve of the great Battle of Kurukṣetra, it might be wise to review our cast of main characters.

First the Sons of Pāṇḍu, otherwise known as the Pāṇḍavas (the Good Guys):

Yudhiṣṭhira ("He who is steady in battle"), son of Pṛthā or Kuntī by the god Dharma ("Righteousness" or "Law"), the eldest of the Pāṇḍava Princes, known for his uprightness of character, rightful inheritor of the throne at Hāstinapura, king of Indraprastha, and, after the slaying of Jarāsaṁdha, emperor.

Arjuna, son of Pṛthā or Kuntī by the god Indra, and hero of the Bhagavad Gītā. (Because of his mother's two names, he is often referred to as Pārtha, "Son of Pṛthā," or Kāunteya, "Son of Kuntī".) He is a blameless knight (his name means "Silver White") and a powerful warrior noted particularly for his skill as an archer.

Bhīma, son of Pṛthā or Kuntī by the wind god Vāyu, and sometimes referred to as Vṛkodara ("the Wolf-bellied") because of his insatiable appetite. He is not the most intelligent, but he is by far the most powerful of the Pāṇḍava Princes, a man accustomed to uprooting trees to assail his enemies with. He is a great slayer of demons. He is also a half brother of Hanumān, the monkey god who assisted the great hero Rāma, of the epic The Rāmāyaṇa. During the final stages

of the Battle of Kurukṣetra, he tears apart the evil Kāurava, Duḥśāsana, and drinks his blood. "Bhīma" means "terrible" or "awful."

Nakula ("Color of the Mongoose"), son of Mādrī by one of the Aśvins, the divine horsemen who draw the chariot of the dawn. The Aśvins were Vedic gods of very early origin. Nakula led the Vatsa tribesmen in the great battle.

Sahadeva ("Accompanied by the gods"), son of Mādrī by the other of the Aśvins, and twin brother of Nakula.

Next, their allies:

Drupada ("Rapid Step"), King of Pāñcāla, father of Dhṛṣṭadyumna and of his twin Drāupadī, the collective wife of the Pāṇḍava Princes, thus their father-in-law.

Dhṛṣṭadyumna ("He whose Splendor is Bold"), son of Drupada, and commander in chief of the Pāṇḍava armies.

Śikhaṇḍin ("He who wears a Tuft of Hair"), son of Drupada, a reincarnation of Aṁbā, who had refused to marry Vicitravīrya – now a powerful warrior, though still regarded by Bhīṣma as female.

Abhimanyu ("Into Anger"), son of Arjuna by his second wife Subhadrā.

Sātyaki ("He whose Nature is Truth"), otherwise known as Yuyudhāna ("Anxious to Fight"), a kinsman of Krishna and King of the Vṛṣṇi tribe.

Virāṭa ("Ruling Widely"), King of Matsya, at whose court the Pāṇḍava Princes had taken refuge in disguise during the thirteenth year of their exile.

Uttara ("Superior"), son of Virāṭa, and brother-in-law of Abhimanyu.

Sahadeva ("Accompanied by the Gods"), son of the dead Jarāsaṁdha, King of Māgadha, not to be confused with the Pāṇḍava Prince of that name.

Śāibya ("Relating to the Śibis"), King of the Śibis.

Ghaṭotkaca ("Shining like a Jug" – a name derived from the fact that he was bald), son of Bhīma by a rākṣasī, and thus half rākṣasa, or demon.

Irāvat ("Comfortable"), son of Arjuna by a Nāga (Serpent-demon) princess.

The King of the Kāśis, father of Aṁbā, Aṁbikā and Aṁbālikā, the last two of whom married Vicitravīrya and, by Vyāsa, became grandmothers of the Pāṇḍava Princes.

Dhṛṣṭaketu ("He whose Brightness is Bold"), King of the Cedis.

Cekitāna ("Intelligent"), a prince, ally of the Pāṇḍavas.

Krishna ("Black" or "Dark"), theoretically a neutral, but acting as Arjuna's charioteer. He is the avatār of Vishnu, or the Supreme Spirit, and he speaks most of the lines of the Bhagavad Gītā. He is also related to the Pāṇḍavas by marriage, being the brother of Kuntī, mother of the Sons of Pāṇḍu, and hence their uncle.

Besides these notables, the Pāṇḍava army contained members of the Abhisāra tribe of West Kashmir, the Daśārnas, a people from south-east of Madhya Deśa, the Karūṣa, an outcaste tribe related to the Cedis, the Vatsas, inhabitants of a country of that name, and the Yādavas (members of Krishna's tribe). This army was mobilized at Upaplavya in the land of Matsya, ruled by Virāṭa.

Now, the Sons of Dhṛtarāṣṭra, otherwise known as the Kāuravas or the Sons of Kuru (the Bad Guys):

Duryodhana ("Dirty Fighter"), eldest son of Dhṛtarāṣṭra and instigator of the events that led up to the Battle of Kurukṣetra. His primary aim was to deny Yudhiṣṭhira the throne of Hāstinapura, and to rule in his place.

Śakuni ("Large Bird" or "Cock"), brother-in-law of King Dhṛtarāṣṭra and maternal uncle of the Kāurava Princes. A counsellor to Duryodhana.

Duḥśāsana ("Of Bad Commands"), a son of Dhṛtarāṣṭra and the warrior who dragged Drāupadī by the hair before the assembled Kāuravas after the first dice game.

Karṇa ("Ear" – a name perhaps derived from the fact that he was born wearing a pair of earrings), a son of Kuntī by the Sun god before her marriage to Pāṇḍu, and hence an unacknowledged half brother of the Pāṇḍava Princes. He was left afloat in a river as an infant and brought up by a charioteer. Until just before the battle, he was unaware of his true identity. A powerful warrior and great general.

Bhīṣma, aged warrior, teacher of the princes on both sides of the Battle of Kurukṣetra. He was the great uncle of both the Sons of Pāṇḍu and the Sons of Dhṛtarāṣṭra, and he was reluctant participant in the battle. However, because of his sagacity in matters of war, he was made generalissimo of the Kāurava forces until he was slain by Arjuna and his charioteer Śikhaṇḍin. His name, like Bhīma's means "terrible" or "awful."

Droṇa ("Bucket"), a great warrior and teacher of warriors. A brāhman by birth, and the father of Aśvatthāman.

Kṛpa (a name related to kṛpā, f. "pity"), warrior and teacher of warriors, adopted son of King Śaṁtanu, one of the elder warriors at Kurukṣetra, and at one point, general of the Kāurava forces.

Aśvatthāman ("He who has the Strength of a Horse"), son of Droṇa by Kṛpa's sister Kṛpī.

Vinda, a son of Dhṛtarāṣṭra.

Sudakṣiṇa ("Having a good Right Hand"), King of the Kambojas. The Kambojas of the Mahābhārata are located north of Kuruksetra.

Bhagadatta ("He who is Given by Bhaga," a god who bestows wealth), King of Prāgjyotiṣa (modern Assam), who led the Kirāṭa, a *mleccha*, or barbarian, tribe in the battle.

Śalya ("Spear"), King of Madra, brother of Pāṇḍu's second wife, Mādrī and thus a maternal uncle of the Pāṇḍava Princes Nakula and Sahadeva.

Śālva ("Son of the Śalvas"), King of the Śalva people.

Jayadratha ("He whose Chariot is Victorious"), King of Sindhu-Sāuvīra, a country near the Indus River.

Śūrasena ("He whose Army is Valiant"), King of Mathurā.

Kṛtavarman ("He whose Armor is Ready"), an allied warrior.

Bhūriśravas ("He whose Praise Abounds"), son of King Somadatta of the Bāhlikas (Bactrians).

Citrasena ("He whose Army is Excellent"), a son of Dhṛtarāṣṭra.

And along with these notables, the Kāurava army contained members of the Andhaka, Aṁbaṣṭha, Darada, Kṣudraka, Mālava, Kaliṅga, Kekaya, Muṇḍa, Niṣāda, Śalva, Śibi (which had members on both sides), Sindhu, Bāhlika

(Bactrian), Vañga (Bengal), Videha and Vidarbha tribes, along with some Yādavas.

The blind King Dhṛtarāṣṭra stood behind the Kāurava lines and listened while his minister Saṁjaya described the battle to him.

At the time of this legendary, and also probably historic, battle, northern India was divided into small, warlike kingdoms. It was the time of the later "Vedic" works, the Brāhmaṇas, the Upanishads and the Āraṇyakas, and, though the warriors at Kurukṣetra (with the exception of Krishna) were not particularly involved in intellectual pursuits, it was a time of enormous intellectual ferment among the brāhmans, who were engaged in interpreting, and adding to, the Vedas. The India portrayed in the Mahābhārata still retained some of the warlike traditions of the Aryans who had invaded the subcontinent less than a thousand years previously. It was also a country comprising a wide variety of races: Dravidians (the inhabitants at the time of the Aryan invasion), Persians, Scyths, Mongols, Greeks and many primitive tribes that may have originated in the pre-Dravidian races – the Australoids and paleolithic Negritos. And it also included what is now practically the whole of North India, plus some territory to the East and West. (N.B. Though the date of the Battle of Kurukṣetra has been tentatively placed by authorities at some point between 800 and 600 B.C., the Mahābhārata, of which it forms a part, is vague as to dates, and was probably in process of compilation from 400 B.C. to 300 A.D.).

The great battle was supposed to be fought according to certain rules of knightly etiquette, which were, in fact, adhered to in the very beginning. Fighting was to take place only in daylight. After sunset, everybody mixed in friendship. Single combats were supposed to be only among equals. Anyone leaving the field or sitting in Yoga posture was supposed to be immune from attack. Anyone who surrendered was to be spared. Anyone momentarily disengaged was prohibited from attacking one already engaged. Horsemen were prohibited from attacking foot soldiers. Mounted warriors could fight only with other mounted warriors. Warriors in chariots could fight only with other chariot-borne warriors. Anyone disarmed could not be attacked, and no attacks could be made on drummers, conch blowers or attendants, including charioteers. Animals were not to be killed unnecessarily or deliberately. As in all wars, however, these rules rapidly broke down as passions rose, and during the last days of the battle they were not observed at all.

Just as the first day of battle started, Arjuna, overcome with grief at the prospect of killing relatives, teachers and friends, asked Krishna, his charioteer, to draw up the chariot between the two armies, and the Bhagavad Gītā – all 2,800 lines of it – was spoken between Krishna and Arjuna. The great Yale Sanskritist Franklin Edgerton has called this a dramatic absurdity. With all due respect, I do not agree. When God speaks, it is not illogical for time to stand still while armies stand frozen in their places. In fact, I consider this frozen moment a dramatic triumph, and it is set at a point of climax in the epic where what follows is a foregone tragic conclusion.

Then the battle started. On the *first day* the Pāṇḍavas fared badly. Bhīṣma fought with Abhimanyu, Arjuna's son and his own great grand nephew, gallantly complimenting him on his technique. Abhimanyu became a great hero. When he was hard pressed by Bhīṣma, Virāṭa, Uttara (his son), Dhṛṣṭadyumna and Bhīma came to his assistance (this had been a fight between the oldest and the youngest warriors present). Uttara attacked Śalya, accidentally killing Śalya's horse, and Śalya promptly killed Uttara (first casualty). But Uttara's elephant continued to fight until it was killed. Śveta, a Pāṇḍava warrior, attacked Śalya, and for a time held off the whole Kāurava army single-handed, including Bhīṣma, but Bhīṣma finally killed him (second casualty) and went on to harass the Pāṇḍava army. The Pāṇḍavas were downcast as the sun set.

On the *second day* Dhṛṣṭadyumna, the Pāṇḍava commander in chief, arrayed his army very carefully. But Bhīṣma attacked it with fearful results. Arjuna said to Krishna, "The grandsire (Bhīṣma) must be slain." Arjuna attacked. The Kāuravas tried to protect Bhīṣma but Arjuna fought them off. The gods came down to witness the battle. Bhīṣma hit Krishna (Arjuna's charioteer) with an arrow. This angered Arjuna, but he did not succeed in killing Bhīṣma. At another point in the battlefield Droṇa was attacking Dhṛṣṭadyumna, the Pāṇḍava generalissimo. The latter was hard pressed, but Bhīma came to his aid and carried him off in his chariot. Duryodhana then sent the Kaliṅga army against Bhīma who slew great numbers. Bhīṣma supported the Kaliṅgas: Sātyaki and others supported Bhīma and Abhimanyu. Sātyaki killed Bhīṣma's charioteer (foul play) and Bhīṣma was forced to flee. The Kāuravas were routed.

On the *third day*, the Kāuravas attacked Arjuna. Śakuni attacked Sātyaki and Abhimanyu. Abhimanyu rescued Sātyaki, whose chariot had been destroyed. Droṇa and Bhīṣma attacked Yudhiṣṭhira. Bhīma and his son Ghaṭotkaca attacked Duryodhana with heroism. Duryodhana swooned in his chariot, hit by Bhīma's arrows, and was forced to retreat. Bhīma slew Kāuravas by the score. Then Bhīṣma and Droṇa regrouped the Kāuravas and Duryodhana returned to the field. Duryodhana criticized Bhīṣma for lack of zeal. Bhīṣma then made a tremendous attack on the Pāṇḍavas, and the Pāṇḍavas scattered. Krishna egged on Arjuna to attack Bhīṣma, but Arjuna's heart was not in it. Bhīṣma, with great gallantry, continually praised his opponents. The Kāuravas were turned back at the end of the day.

On the *fourth day* the Kāuravas advanced under Bhīṣma, Droṇa and Duryodhana. Aśvatthāman, Bhūriśravas, Śalya and Citrasena surrounded Abhimanyu and attacked him, but his father, Arjuna, came to his rescue, and Dhṛṣṭadyumna arrived with reinforcements. Then Bhīma appeared, and the Kāuravas sent a large force of elephants against him, He scattered them all and caused panic among the Kāuravas. Bhīma then attacked Duryodhana and nearly killed him. Bhīma's bow was shattered. He picked up a new one and cut Duryodhana's bow in two. Duryodhana smote Bhīma so heavily that he was forced to sit upon the ground. Bhīma's son Ghaṭotkaca came to his defense. Eight of Duryodhana's brothers were killed by Bhīma. By nightfall the Pāṇḍavas had won a victory, and the Kāuravas were downcast. Bhīṣma advised suing for peace, but Duryodhana wouldn't listen to him.

On the *fifth day* Bhīṣma attacked the Pāṇḍavas and caused considerable havoc. Arjuna then attacked Bhīṣma. Duryodhana complained to Droṇa about the weakness of the Kāurava attacks. Droṇa then attacked Sātyaki and Bhīma came to his defense. Droṇa, Bhīṣma and Śalya together attacked Bhīma, but Śikhaṇḍin came to the rescue. At this point Bhīṣma turned away. He considered Śikhaṇḍin to be a woman, and he would not fight with women. Droṇa attacked Śikhaṇḍin and compelled him to withdraw. There ensued a big, confused battle in which the sons of Sātyaki were slain. Sātyaki had attacked Bhūriśravas in an effort to protect them, but Bhūriśravas killed them all. Bhīma rescued Sātyaki. Duryodhana rescued Bhūriśravas. Arjuna slew thousands. It was a big Pāṇḍava victory.

On the *sixth day* Droṇa's charioteer was killed (foul play). There was great slaughter. Bhīma fought eleven of the Sons of Dhṛtarāṣṭra all by himself, scattered them and pursued them on foot wielding his mace. He got behind the Kāurava lines and Dhṛṣṭadyumna went to rescue him. Duryodhana and the other Kāuravas attacked Bhīma and Dhṛṣṭadyumna who were in their midst. At this point Dhṛṣṭadyumna, being surrounded along with Bhīma, used a secret weapon (the Pramohana, "that which bewilders the mind") which he had received from Droṇa as a student, and with it stupefied the Kāuravas. Then Duryodhana arrived with a similar secret weapon (it must have resembled tear, or nerve gas) and stupefied the Pāṇḍavas. But Yudhiṣṭhira came on with a large force to support Bhīma, who promptly revived and joined in. Droṇa killed Dhṛṣṭadyumna's horses (foul play) and shattered his chariot. Dhṛṣṭadyumna took refuge in Abhimanyu's chariot. The Pāṇḍavas wavered. Duryodhana was wounded by Bhīma and rescued by Kṛpa. Bhīṣma scattered the Pāṇḍavas, and the day was declared a victory for the Kāuravas.

On the *seventh day* there were many single combats. Virāṭa was defeated by Droṇa. Virāṭa's son Śaṁga was killed (this was the third of Virāṭa's sons to be slain). But the Kāuravas were getting the worst of it. Later, Yudhiṣṭhira defeated Śrutāyu, killing his horses and charioteer (foul play). Duryodhana's army was demoralized. Cekitāna attacked Kṛpa, killing *his* charioteer and horses (more foul play). Kṛpa retaliated by engaging Cekitāna in single combat on the ground, fighting until both fell, wounded and exhausted. Bhīma took Cekitāna away in his chariot. Śakuni performed a similar service for Kṛpa. Bhīṣma attacked Abhimanyu, but Abhimanyu was rescued by his father Arjuna. The other four Pāṇḍava Princes joined in, but Bhīṣma held his own against all five. At sunset, the warriors of both sides retired to their tents, nursing their wounds.

On the *eighth day* Bhīma killed eight of Dhṛtarāṣṭra's sons. Irāvat, Arjuna's son by his Nāga princess wife, was killed by the rākṣasa warrior Alambuṣa. Arjuna was downcast. Ghaṭotkaca attacked the Kāuravas with great slaughter. Duryodhana advanced and was almost killed by Ghaṭotkaca, being rescued at the last minute by Droṇa. Sixteen sons of Dhṛtarāṣṭra were killed that day.

On the *ninth day* Bhīṣma slew Pāṇḍavas by the thousand. Abhimanyu defeated the rākṣasa warrior Alambuṣa. Sātyaki duelled with Aśvatthāman, Droṇa with Arjuna, and Bhīṣma again attacked the Pāṇḍavas. Krishna suggested that Arjuna kill Bhīṣma, but, again, Arjuna had not the heart to kill his old teacher. Exasperated, Krishna got down from the chariot and proposed to attack Bhīṣma on foot, but Arjuna pulled him back. The day was generally victorious for the Kāuravas.

On the *tenth day* Bhīṣma was killed, or to be more precise, mortally wounded. Arjuna attacked him with Śikhaṇḍin as his charioteer (Bhīṣma had already prophesied that he would be invincible except in the presence of Śikhaṇḍin, whom he considered to be a woman). Śikhaṇḍin shot arrows at Bhīṣma. Arjuna sent a hail of arrows, piercing Bhīṣma's armor at points that Śikhaṇḍin had missed. Bhīṣma died very slowly, supported by a cushion of arrows. He claimed that he had been killed by Arjuna (an honor), though Śikhaṇḍin felt that he, or she, had fulfilled Aṁbā's vow by bringing the great son of King Śaṁtanu to his end. The gods folded their hands in reverent salutation as Bhīṣma was defeated. The battle stopped while both sides paid homage to the old warrior. Bhīṣma asked for water, and Arjuna shot an arrow into the ground. Water sprang forth. "Gaṅgā (the Ganges) has come up to quench her son's thirst," they said. Bhīṣma still counselled peace. Karṇa approached him asking for his blessing. Bhīṣma advised him not to fight. But Karṇa insisted that since he had cast his lot with Duryodhana, he had no choice but to continue. Bhīṣma survived for fifty-eight days (he kept himself alive deliberately so that he could die during the "upper going," or northern phase of the sun, and thus attain nirvāṇa (see footnote to stanza 23, book VIII of the Gītā). He delivered several didactic discourses: he was still living, in fact, after the battle had ended.

The Kāuravas then made a plan to capture Yudhiṣṭhira alive. It was Duryodhana's idea, and Droṇa took it up gladly because he did not want to see Yudhiṣṭhira killed (it will be remembered that Yudhiṣṭhira was the rightful heir to the throne of Hāstinapura, and that Duryodhana was seeking to deprive him of the right). Duryodhana's fundamental purpose was to get Yudhiṣṭhira into another game of dice. The Pāṇḍavas, however, heard of the plan and made their preparations to counter it.

On the *eleventh day* Droṇa attempted to capture Yudhiṣṭhira, but Yudhiṣṭhira fled on a swift horse, holding that it was no disgrace for a warrior to flee before a brāhman. There was single combat between Sahadeva and Śakuni. Śalya was defeated by Nakula; Dhṛstaketu was defeated by Kṛpa. Sātyaki engaged Kṛtavarman; Virāṭa engaged Karṇa. Abhimanyu engaged four prominent Kāuravas at once. Bhīma defeated Śalya. The Kāuravas began to lose courage. Droṇa again attempted to capture Yudhiṣṭhira, but was foiled by Arjuna, who forced Droṇa to retreat. The day was a defeat for the Kāuravas.

On the *twelfth day* the Kāuravas, seeing that they could not capture Yudhiṣṭhira while Arjuna was present in the field, made a plan to draw Arjuna off and kill him. Suśarman, chief of the army of the King of Trigarta, along with his four brothers, attacked Arjuna. He slew them all. Droṇa again tried to capture Yudhiṣṭhira, but Dhṛṣṭadyumna and the other Pāñcāla Princes stood by to protect him. Dhṛṣṭadyumna attacked Droṇa, but Droṇa avoided him to get at Arjuna.

Drupada stood in his way. Droṇa attacked him, and then made for Yudhiṣṭhira. Two Pāñcāla princes, Vṛka and Satyajit, were killed, and Virāṭa's son Śatānīka was killed by Droṇa while Śatānīka was attempting to attack him. Pāñcālya, another Pāñcāla prince, was killed by Droṇa. Then occurred one of the most heroic feats of the entire battle. Arjuna's son, Abhimanyu, broke through the line of the Kāurava forces, and found himself surrounded. In a tremendous display of valor, he fended off the entire Kāurava army, including Duryodhana. The Pāṇḍavas tried to get to Abhimanyu to rescue him, but were prevented. The Kāuravas, throwing good form to the winds, ganged up on Abhimanyu and disarmed him. He continued to fight with a chariot wheel as his only weapon. Finally, Lakṣmaṇa, son of Duḥśāsana, struck him to the ground, killing him. Dhṛtarāṣṭra's son Yuyutsu, who was fighting on the Pāṇḍava side, was so disgusted by this performance that he left the field. Yudhiṣṭhira blamed himself for the death of Abhimanyu. Arjuna was told about his son's death, and vowed vengeance on Jayadratha, King of the Sindhus, who was indirectly responsible (he had helped to trap Abhimanyu)

The battle continued. Droṇa failed in all his attempts to capture Yudhiṣṭhira. The Kāurava forces were stampeded. Bhagadatta, King of Prāgjyotiṣa, was indignant over the rout of the Kāuravas. He attacked Bhīma and destroyed his chariot and horses. Bhīma, on foot, attacked the underside of Bhagadatta's elephant, inflicting wounds and driving the animal mad. All these were unfair tactics, but the rules of war were rapidly breaking down. Bhagadatta was attacked on all sides by the Pāṇḍavas, but Bhagadatta's maddened elephant caused great havoc among them. Arjuna, with Krishna as his charioteer, then made a tremendous attack on Bhagadatta, killing both him and his elephant. Śakuni's brothers, Vṛṣa and Acala, tried to rally the Kāurava forces, but were killed by Arjuna. Śakuni attacked Arjuna, but was forced to flee.

On the *thirteenth day* Arjuna, raining showers of arrows, penetrated the Kāurava ranks, and many Kāuravas fled. Duḥśāsana became infuriated, and rushed against Arjuna with a force of elephants. But Arjuna pierced the elephant host, and Duḥśāsana's force, along with Duḥśāsana himself, fled, seeking Droṇa's protection. Arjuna proceeded against Droṇa's army with the object of getting at Jayadratha. Yudhāmanyu and Uttamāujas followed him to protect him. Arjuna smote the Kāurava army, including an elephant force brought against him by the Aṅgas and Kaliṅgas. Arjuna slew horses, elephants and warriors. Meanwhile, Bhīma attacked a Kāurava warrior named Jalasaṁdha, Son of Dhṛtarāṣṭra, while Yudhiṣṭhira engaged Kṛtavarman and Dhṛṣṭadyumna engaged Droṇa. Seeing the Kāurava forces slaughtered by Sātyaki, Droṇa rushed toward him. At that point, Arjuna who was fighting the army of Jayadratha, blew his conch horn. Yudhiṣṭhira, hearing it, and suspecting that Arjuna was in trouble, sent Sātyaki to the rescue. Then, Bhīma attacked Droṇa with some success, and proceeded through the Kāurava lines, seeking Arjuna. Karṇa rushed at Bhīma, and caused him to retreat. Five of Dhṛtarāṣṭra's sons attacked Bhīma, but he dispatched them all.

On the *fourteenth day* Bhūriśravas, Prince of the Bāhlīkas, advanced against

Sātyaki and brought him to the ground, dragging him by the hair and striking him on the chest with his feet. Seeing Sātyaki's plight, Arjuna, from a distance where he was engaged with Jayadratha, sent a stream of arrows at Bhūriśravas, cutting off his right arm. Bhūriśravas sat upon the ground in Yoga position. Sātyaki then beheaded Bhūriśravas as he sat. Arjuna pressed Jayadratha. There had been a vow made by Jayadratha's father Vṛddhakṣatra that the head of whoever caused his son's head to fall to the ground would burst into a hundred pieces. Krishna informed Arjuna of this vow, and Arjuna, as he beheaded Jayadratha, caused a stream of arrows to convey the head into the lap of his father, who was meditating nearby. When his father roused himself from meditation, *he* let his son's head fall to the ground and his head burst into a hundred pieces. The battle continued into the night by torchlight, and the Pāṇḍavas attacked Droṇa, but Droṇa slew his old enemy Drupada as well as Virāṭa.

On the evening of the *fifteenth day* all knightly ethics were totally discarded. Even Krishna had lost all sense of honor – a rather surprising state considering that he was the avatār of Vishnu or the Supreme Spirit. He suggested naming one of the Pāṇḍava elephants Aśvatthāman, after Droṇa's son and then killing the animal. The idea was carried out. During a lull in the fighting, Droṇa was told that Aśvatthāman was dead, and thought that he had lost his son. He appealed to Yudhiṣṭhira for confirmation knowing that Yudhiṣṭhira never lied. But honor was at such a low ebb that Yudhiṣṭhira did lie, confirming the death of Aśvatthāman. Droṇa, grieving, laid down his arms and was promptly decapitated by Dhṛṣṭadyumna. After Droṇa's death, Karṇa took charge of the Kāurava army.

On the *sixteenth day* Karṇa challenged Yudhiṣṭhira to fight, but during the ensuing combat Yudhiṣṭhira ignominously fled for the second time. A little later Bhīma, recalling Drāupadī's humiliation after the dice game, attacked Duḥśāsana, who had dragged Drāupadī before the assembled Kāuravas, tore him apart and drank his blood as he had promised to do. The warriors on both sides were horrified by Bhīma's act.

On the *seventeenth day* there was a long and terrible duel between Arjuna and Karṇa. At one point a wheel of Karṇa's chariot became stuck in the mud, and he was forced to leap to the ground to try to raise it. He invoked the laws of chivalry, and asked Arjuna not to attack him while he was engaged in this task. He also thought of the *mantra* that he had learned from the brāhman warrior Paraśurāma to use with the Śakti. But, as predicted, he could not remember it. Krishna egged Arjuna on, and Arjuna unethically slew Karṇa. A little later, Yudhiṣṭhira, who had previously fled before Karṇa's attack, reproached Arjuna for not supporting him at the time. This enraged Arjuna, and he would have turned on his brother to kill him, but for the intervention of Krishna (even the Pāṇḍavas were now quarreling among themselves). After the death of Karṇa, Śalya assumed command of the Kāurava forces.

On the *eighteenth and last day* the tide turned definitely in favor of the Pāṇḍavas. Duryodhana was now practically alone. He fled and concealed himself in a nearby lake (he possessed the power of remaining under water). A little later Sahadeva slew Śakuni and Yudhiṣṭhira slew Śalya. After Śalya's death, Aśvatthāman took charge of the Kāurava forces. Bhīma next killed all the remaining Sons of Dhṛtarāṣṭra except the absent Duryodhana. Then he searched for Duryodhana and discovered his hiding place in the lake. He taunted Duryodhana, and forced him to emerge. A tremendous battle with clubs ensued between Bhīma and Duryodhana. Finally, Bhīma, hitting below the belt, broke both Duryodhana's legs with his club, and trampled upon his body. This unfair and brutal act aroused the anger of Yudhiṣṭhira, who struck Bhīma across the face and asked Arjuna to take him away. Balarāma, Krishna's brother, had finally appeared on the field, had witnessed Bhīma's foul blow, and was so disgusted that he attacked Bhīma with a plow (Balarāma's customary weapon). He was stopped by Krishna, and left angrily for their capital city Dvārakā. Duryodhana, still alive, rebuked Krishna, calling him the son of a slave (an allusion to his cowherd foster father).

Then Aśvatthāman took an oath to exterminate the Pāṇḍavas, and egged on by the dying Duryodhana, he, Kṛpa and Kṛtavarman, the last remaining Kāurava nobles decided on a night raid, approaching the Pāṇḍavas in their camp. Kṛpa was against this idea, but he went along. The Pāṇḍava Princes were away at the time, Aśvatthāman first killed his father's slayer, Dhṛṣṭadyumna by stamping on him as he slept. Next he killed Śikhaṇḍin who was also asleep, as well as the warriors Uttamāujas, Prativindhya, Sutasoma, Śatānīka and Śrutakīrti. Using a magic weapon (the brahmāstra), he slew the unborn Parikṣit, son of Abhimanyu, who was still in his mother's womb. However, Parikṣit came alive again, owing to Krishna's magic intervention. Aśvatthāman then killed the five young sons of Drāupadī by her five husbands. Kṛpa and Kṛtavarman took no part in this cowardly slaughter; they were keeping watch at the gates of the camp. Aśvatthāman brought the five heads of the sons of Drāupadī back to Duryodhana, saying that they were the heads of the five Pāṇḍava Princes. But Duryodhana knew better, and he reproached Aśvatthāman for slaying innocent children. Then he died.

The Pāṇḍava Princes, returning to their camp, saw what Aśvatthāman had done, and pursued him furiously. Bhīma fought with Aśvatthāman and overcame him. Aśvatthāman took a jewel from his forehead and presented it to Bhīma in token of defeat. Bhīma gave the jewel to Drāupadī, who later presented it to Yudhiṣṭhira as an ornament for his crown.

The battle was over. Only three of the warriors on the Kāurava side – Kṛpa, Aśvatthāman and Kṛtavarman – survived. The children of the Pāṇḍavas had all been killed except Arjuna's grandchild Parikṣit. The bodies of the slain warriors were gathered up, wrapped in perfumed linen, laid upon a great funeral pyre and burned. Yudhiṣṭhira was proclaimed King of Hāstinapura. Dhṛtarāṣṭra mourned the loss of his hundred sons. He embraced Yudhiṣṭhira as a token of peace. But when Bhīma was announced to the blind king, Krishna put a metal statue in his place, and Dhṛtarāṣṭra crushed it to powder. Gāndhārī, wife of Dhṛtarāṣṭra and mother of his hundred sons, did not forgive, but nevertheless blessed the Pāṇḍavas. Yudhiṣṭhira reigned at Hāstinapura, but he was not happy. Krishna returned to Dvārakā. Yudhiṣṭhira's reign lasted for fifteen years, during which he treated the blind Dhṛtarāṣṭra with respect. As for Dhṛtarāṣṭra himself, he practiced austerities and went to live in the forest, accompanied by Kuntī, Gāndhārī and his minister Saṁjaya. They returned after three years only to be burned to death as their house caught fire. Saṁjaya, however, escaped the fire and went to the Himālaya as a *saṁnyāsin*, or renouncer of all the things of life.

Krishna ruled in Dvārakā for thirty-six years, but his tribe, the Yādavas, gave themselves up to drunken revelry. In one of their drunken orgies Krishna's son, Pradyumna, and also Sātyaki were killed. Balarāma was so disgusted at this that he retired to the forest, assumed a Yoga position and died. Krishna realized that the time had come to end his role as the *avatār* of Vishnu. He was shot by a hunter as the *avatār* escaped. The Pāṇḍavas crowned Parikṣit, son of Abhimanyu and Uttara, and grandson of Arjuna, king. Then they departed for the Himālaya along with Drāupadī. On the way, Drāupadī, Sahadeva and Nakula died. Then Arjuna and Bhīma died. Yudhiṣṭhira alone was left, and he continued to climb. A dog had joined him. The god Indra sent a chariot to take Yudhiṣṭhira to heaven but would not take the dog. Yudhiṣṭhira had become fond of the dog and refused to go without it. Then the dog vanished. It had been the god Dharma (Yudhiṣṭhira's father) in disguise. Yudhiṣṭhira finally found himself on Mount Meru, the Olympos of India, and, much to his disgust, found Duryodhana there. A messenger took Yudhiṣṭhira through a sort of hades, where he found the other Pāṇḍava Princes and Karṇa. He chose to remain with them. Then heaven opened, and Yudhiṣṭhira and the others became godlike.

LIST OF ABBREVIATIONS USED IN THE VOCABULARIES

abl., ablative.
acc., accusative.
act., active.
adj., adjective.
adv., adverb.
*BV cpd., Bahuvrīhi compound. A compound which is always adjectival to a noun or pronoun, either expressed or implicit. The last member is a noun and the first usually an adjective. Its structure can be most simply explained by examples: "He whose B (last member) is A (first member)" or "This of which the B (last member) is A (first member)." Examples can readily be found in English: "redneck," i.e. he whose neck is red; "bluebeard," i.e. he whose beard is blue; "hardhat," i.e. he whose hat is hard. In Sanskrit: mahāratha, he whose chariot is mighty; Dhṛtarāṣṭra (proper name), he by whom the kingdom is held; mahābāho (vocative), O Thou whose arms are mighty; anantarūpa, that of which the form is unending: avyaktādīni, such that their beginnings are unmanifest.
dat., dative.
DV cpd., Dvandva (copulative) compound.
esp., especially.
f., feminine.
fut., future.
gen., genitive.
indic., indicative.
ifc., "in fine compositi," "at the end of a compound," indicating the last member of a compound.
inst., instrumental.
interrog., interrogative.
irreg., irregular.
*KD cpd., Karmadhāraya compound, a compound the members of which have the same case. There are three types: (a) the first member is an adjective, the second a noun. Example in English: "highway," in Sanskrit: "mahādhana," "great wealth." (b) both members are nouns. Example in English: "gentleman-thief," i.e. a thief who is a gentleman; "boy-actress" (in Shakespeare's time), i.e. an actress who is really a boy. Examples in Sanskrit: "rājarṣi," "king-sage;" "devajana," "god people." (c) both members are adjectives. Examples in English: "pale-red," "snow-white." Examples in Sanskrit: "dhūmarohita," "greyish red," "uttarapūrva," "north-east."
lit., literally
loc., locative.
loc. absol., locative absolute.
m., masculine.
mid., middle.
n., neuter.
nom., nominative.
p., past.
pass., passive.
pl., plural.
pr., present.
saṁdhi – not an abbreviation, but a term indicating an alteration in accord with the laws of euphonious combination of words.
sg., singular.
*TP cpd., Tatpuruṣa compound. A compound of two words which would ordinarily have different case endings. Examples in English:

"mountain peak," i.e. the peak of a mountain, etc. In Sanskrit: jīvaloka (jīva, living; loka, world), the world of the living; rājendra (rāja, king; Indra, chief), chief of kings, etc. The members of these compounds are nouns.

voc., vocative.

---

* I am indebted to the Sanskrit scholar J. A. B. van Buitenen of the University of Chicago for these remarkably clear definitions of Sanskrit compounds. They are far preferable to the ones listed in Whitney's Sanskrit Grammar.

EPITHETS (NICKNAMES) USED IN THE BHAGAVAD GĪTĀ

For Krishna:

Hṛṣīkeśa – The Bristling-haired One.
Acyuta – Imperishable One, or One who has not Fallen.
Mādhava – Descendant of Madhu (a Yādava or Mādhava patriarch).
Keśava – The Handsome-haired One.
Govinda – Chief of Herdsmen.
Madhusūdana – Destroyer of the Demon Madhu (properly an epithet of Vishnu).
Janārdana – Agitator of Men, or Mankind-tormenting (an epithet of Vishnu).
Vārṣṇeya – Clansman of the Vṛṣnis.
Keśinisūdana – Slayer of the Demon Keśin.
Arisūdana – Destroyer of the Enemy.
Bhagavān – Blessed One.
Vāsudeva – Son of Vasudeva.
Prabho – Splendid One (voc.).
Mahābāho – Mighty Armed One (a general epithet of warriors).
Yādava – Descendant of Yadu.

And in the Great Manifestation of Book XI:

Puruṣottama – Supreme Spirit, or Best of Men.
Mahātman – whose self is great.
Visṇu – Vishnu (whose avatār Krishna is).
Deveśa (Deva Īśa) – Lord of Gods.
Anantarūpa – whose form is endless, Infinite Form.
Prajāpati – Lord of Creatures.
Aprameya – Immeasurable One.
Apratimaprabhāva – Incomparable Glory.
Īśam Īḍyam – Lord to be Praised.
Deva – God.
Sahasrabāho – Thousand-armed One (voc.).

For Arjuna:

Dhanaṁjaya – Conqueror of Wealth.
Pāṇḍava – Son of Pāṇḍu.
Kapidhvaja – The Monkey-bannered (a descriptive term rather than an epithet).
Pārtha – Son of Pṛthā.
Kāunteya – Son of Kuntī.
Guḍākeśa – Thick-haired One.
Paraṁtapa – Scorcher of the Foe.
Puruṣarṣabha – Bull among Men.
Mahābāho – Mighty Armed One (a general epithet of warriors).
Kurunandana – Son of Kuru, or Joy of Kuru.*
Anagha – Blameless One.
Bhārata – Descendant of Bharata (a general epithet, also applied to King Dhṛtarāṣṭra).
Bharatarṣabha – Bull of the Bharatas.
Dehabhṛtām Vara – Best of the Embodied.
Kuruśreṣtha – Best of Kurus.*
Savyasācin – Ambidextrous Archer.
Kirīṭin – Diademed One.
Kurupravīra – Chief Kuru* Hero.
Bharataśreṣṭha – Best of the Bharatas.
Bharatasattama – Highest of the Bharatas.
Puruṣavyāghra – Tiger among Men.

---

* Reference to the ancient patriarch Kuru testifies to the fact that he was the common ancestor of both the Pāṇḍavas and the Kāuravas (Sons of Kuru).

BOOK I

धृतराष्ट्र उवाच ।
dhṛtarāṣṭra uvāca
Dhṛtarāṣṭra spoke:

dhṛtarāṣṭras (m. nom. sg.), Dhṛtarāṣṭra, the blind Kuru king to whom the Bhagavad Gītā is to be related by Saṁjaya, his minister. The name, a BV cpd., means "He by whom the kingdom is held."
uvāca (3rd sg. perfect act. √*vac*), he said, he spoke.

1

धर्मक्षेत्रे कुरुक्षेत्रे
*dharmakṣetre kurukṣetre**
when in the field of virtue, in the field of Kuru

समवेता युयुत्सवः ।
samavetā yuyutsavaḥ
assembled together, desiring to fight

मामकाः पाण्डवाश्चैव
māmakāḥ pāṇḍavāś cāiva
mine and the Sons of Pāṇḍu

किम् अकुर्वत संजय ॥
kim akurvata saṁjaya
what they did? Saṁjaya?

dharma (m.), duty, law, righteousness, virtue, honor.
kṣetre (n. loc. sg.), in the field, on the field.
kuru (m.), Kuru, the royal dynasty to which Dhṛtarāṣṭra belongs.
kṣetre (n. loc. sg.), in the field, on the field.
samavetās (m. nom. pl. p. pass. participle *sam ava* √*i*), come together, assembled.
yuyutsavas (m. nom. pl. desiderative adj. from √*yudh*), desiring to fight, battle-hungry, desiring to do battle.
māmakās (m. nom. pl.), mine, my.
pāṇḍavās (m. nom. pl.), the Sons of Pāṇḍu.
ca, and.
eva, indeed (used as a rhythmic filler).
kim (interrog.), what?
akurvata (3rd imperf. middle √*kṛ*), they did.
saṁjaya (voc.), Saṁjaya, minister to King Dhṛtarāṣṭra, who relates to him the bulk of the Bhagavad Gītā. The name means "completely victorious."

Dhṛtarāṣṭra spoke:
When in the field of virtue, in the field of Kuru,*
Assembled together, desiring to fight,
What did my army and that of the Sons of Pāṇḍu do, Saṁjaya?

* Kurukṣetra is an actual place, a small plain in the Panjab north of Delhi near Panipat.

I

संजय उवाच ।
saṁjaya uvāca
Saṁjaya spoke:

saṁjdyas (m. nom. sg.), the narrator, minister to King Dhṛtarāṣṭra.
uvāca (3rd sg. perfect act. √*vac*), he said, he spoke.

2

दृष्ट्वा तु पाण्डवानीकं
dṛṣṭvā tu pāṇḍavānīkaṁ
seeing indeed the Pāṇḍava army

व्यूढं दुर्योधनस् तदा ।
vyūḍhaṁ duryodhanas tadā
arrayed, Duryodhana then

आचार्यमुपसंगम्य
ācāryamupasaṁgamya
the Master (Droṇa) approaching,

राजा वचनमब्रवीत् ॥
rājā vacanam abravīt
the King (Duryodhana) word he spoke:

Saṁjaya spoke:

Seeing indeed the army
Of the Sons of Pāṇḍu arrayed,
King Duryodhana, approaching the Master (Droṇa),
Spoke this word:

dṛṣṭvā (gerund √*dṛś*), seeing, having seen.
tu, indeed, truly.
pāṇḍava (adj.), pertaining to the Sons of Pāṇḍu.
anīkam (m. n. acc. sg.), army, fighting force, face, appearance, edge.
(*pāṇḍava-anīkam*, m. n. acc. sg. TP cpd., army of the Sons of Pāṇḍu.)
vyūḍham (m. n. acc. sg.), arrayed, drawn up in battle formation.
duryodhanas (m. nom. sg.), Duryodhana, chief of the Kāurava (Kuru) army, son of Dhṛtarāṣṭra and chief inciter of the battle. The name means "Dirty fighter."
tadā, then, at that time.
ācāryam (m. acc. sg.), teacher, master, to the teacher, to the master (Droṇa).
upasaṁgamya (gerund *upa sam* √*gam*), approaching, going up to.
rājā (m. nom. sg.), the King, royal personage, here referring to Duryodhana.
vacanam (n. acc. sg.), word, speech.
abravīt (3rd sg. imperf. act. √*brū*), he said, he spoke.

3

पश्यैतां पाण्डुपुत्राणाम्
paśyāitāṁ pāṇḍuputrāṇām
behold this of the sons of Pāṇḍu

आचार्य महतीं चमूम् ।
ācārya mahatīṁ camūm
Master, the great army,

व्यूढां द्रुपदपुत्रेण
vyūḍhāṁ drupadaputreṇa
arrayed by the Son of Drupada

तव शिष्येण धीमता ॥
tava śiṣyeṇa dhīmatā
of thee as student wise.

Behold, O Master, this great army
Of the Sons of Pāṇḍu
Arrayed by the Son of Drupada,
Wise by thine instruction.*

paśya (2nd imperative act. √*paś*), behold! perceive! see!
etām (f. acc. sg.), this.
pāṇḍuputrāṇām (m. gen. pl.), of the Sons of Pāṇḍu.
ācārya (voc.), O Master, O Teacher (here applied to the aged warrior Droṇa,* who has instructed many warriors on both sides of the battle).
mahatīm (f. acc. sg.), great, mighty.
camūm (f. acc. sg.), army, division of warriors.
vyūḍhām (f. acc. sg. p. pass. participle *vi* √*vah*), arrayed, arranged in battle formation.
drupada, Drupada,* father of Dhṛṣṭadyumna, who is chief of the Pāṇḍava army. The name means "rapid step."
putreṇa (m. inst. sg.), by the son, i.e., by Dhṛṣṭadyumna, whose name means "bold splendor" or "audacious majesty."
tava (gen. sg.), of thee.
śiṣyeṇa (m. inst. sg.), "by the to be taught," by student, as a student.
dhīmatā (m. inst. sg.), by wise, by intelligent.

* Both Droṇa and Drupada, as befits great heroes in mythology, had odd births. Drupada's father, Pṛṣata, lost his seed at the sight of Menakā, an apsarā (nymph), wife of a Gandharva (aereal being). He tried to trample out the seed. Hence his name "rapid step." Nevertheless, Drupada was born from this seed. Droṇa's father, Bharadvāja, lost his seed under similar circumstances. It fell into a bucket he was carrying. Droṇa means "bucket" – see chapter on the setting of the Bhagavad Gītā.

4

अत्र शूरा महेष्वासा
atra śūrā maheṣvāsā
here (are) heroes, mighty archers

भीमार्जुनसमा युधि ।
bhīmārjunasamā yudhi
Bhīma and Arjuna equal to in battle.

युयुधानो विराटश्च
yuyudhāno virāṭaś ca
Yuyudhāna and Virāṭa

द्रुपदश्च महारथः ॥
drupadaś ca mahārathaḥ
and Drupada, whose chariot is great.

Here are heroes, mighty archers,
Equal in battle to Bhīma and Arjuna,
Yuyudhāna and Virāṭa,
And Drupada, the great warrior;

atra, here, in this case.
śūrās (m. nom. pl.), heroes.
maheṣvāsās (m. nom. pl.), *mahā iṣu āsās* "mighty arrow hurlers," mighty archers.
bhīma, Bhīma, a powerful warrior, brother of Arjuna, son of Kuntī by the wind god Vāyu. The name means "tremendous," or "awful."
arjuna, Arjuna, the warrior hero of the Bhagavad Gītā, son of Kuntī or Pṛthā. The name means "silver white."
samās (m. nom. pl.), the same, equivalent, equal.
(*bhīma-arjuna-samās* m. nom. pl., TP cpd., equal to Bhīma and Arjuna.)
yudhi (m. loc. sg.), in battle, in fighting.
yuyudhānas (m. nom. sg.), Yuyudhāna, son of Satyaka. A Pāṇḍava ally. The name means "anxious to fight."
virāṭas (m. nom. sg.), Virāṭa, a warrior king with whom the Pāṇḍavas once took refuge. A Pāṇḍava ally. The name refers to a district in India.
ca, and.
drupadas (m. nom. sg.), Drupada ("Rapid Step"), a Pāṇḍava warrior (see footnote on p. 53 above).
ca, and.
mahārathas (m. nom. sg.), epithet for Drupada, mighty warrior (as BV cpd.), he whose chariot is great.

5

धृष्टकेतुश्चेकितानः
dhṛṣṭaketuś cekitānaḥ
Dhṛṣṭsaketu, Cekitāna

काशिराजश्च वीर्यवान् ।
kāśirājaś ca vīryavān
and the King of Kasi, valorous,

पुरुजित् कुन्तिभोजश्च
purujit kuntibhojaś ca
Purujit and Kuntibhoja

शैब्यश्च नरपुङ्गवः ॥
śāibyaś ca narapuṅgavaḥ
and Śāibya, man-bull:

Dhṛṣṭaketu, Cekitāna
And the valorous King of the Kāśis
Purujit and Kuntibhoja*
And Śāibya, bull among men;

dhṛṣṭaketus (m. nom. sg.), Dhṛṣṭaketu, King of Cedi, a Pāṇḍava ally. The name means "bold leader."
cekitānas (m. nom. sg.), Cekitāna, a prince, ally of the Pāṇḍavas. The name means "highly intelligent."
kāśirājas (m. nom. sg.), the King of the Kāśis, thought to be a tribe inhabiting the vicinity of modern Benares, an ally of the Pāṇḍavas.
ca, and.
vīryavān (m. nom. sg.), valorous, full of heroism.
purujit (m. nom. sg.), brother of Kuntibhoja, a prince of the Kunti people. The name means "he who conquers widely." A Pāṇḍava ally.
kuntibhojas (m. nom. sg.), Kuntibhoja, a Pāṇḍava ally.
ca, and.
śāibyas (m. nom. sg.), Śāibya, King of the Śibis, a Pāṇḍava ally.
ca, and.
nara (m.), man.
puṅgavas (m. nom. sg.), bull.
(*narapuṅgavas* m. nom. sg., man-bull, bull among men.)

* Kuntibhoja, a Yādava prince, has an interesting relationship with the Pāṇḍava princes. He is, by adoption, their father-in-law, having adopted Pṛthā, daughter of his cousin Śūra, who was also a Yādava prince. Upon adoption, Pṛthā took her foster father's name and became known as Kuntī. Kuntī, formerly Pṛthā, thus belonged to the Yādava clan, and was an aunt of Krishna, whose father, Vasudeva, was her brother (and a son of Śūra). Ultimately she became the mother of the first three Pāṇḍava princes (Yudhiṣṭhira, Bhīma and Arjuna), as well as Karṇa. Throughout the Bhagavad Gītā Arjuna is referred to as Pārtha (Son of Pṛthā), or Kāunteya (Son of Kuntī). – See chapter on "The Setting of the Bhagavad Gītā."

6

युधामन्युश्च विक्रान्त
yudhāmanyuś ca vikrānta
and Yudhāmanyu, mighty,

उत्तमौजश्च वीर्यवान् ।
uttamāujaś ca vīryavān
and Uttamāujas, valorous;

सौभद्रो द्रौपदेयाश्च
sāubhadro drāupadeyāś ca
the Son of Subhadrā and the Sons of Drāupadī

सर्वं एव महारथाः ॥
sarva eva mahārathāḥ
of all of whom the chariots are great.

And mighty Yudhāmanyu
And valorous Uttamāujas;
The Son of Subhadrā and the Sons of Drāupadī
All indeed great warriors.

yudhāmanyus (m. nom. sg.), Yudhāmanyu, a warrior ally of the Pāṇḍavas. The name means "fighting with spirit."
ca, and.
vikrāntas (m. nom. sg. p. pass. participle *vi* √*kram*), striding forth, bold, courageous.
uttamāujas (m. nom. sg.), Uttamāujas, a warrior ally of the Pāṇḍavas. The name means "of highest power" or "of supreme valor."
ca, and.
vīryavān (m. nom. sg.), valorous, full of heroism.
sāubhadras (m. nom. sg.), the son of Subhadrā, i.e. Abhimanyu, the son of Subhadrā (Krishna's sister) by Arjuna, who abducted her with Krishna's consent.
drāupadeyās (m. nom. pl.), the Sons of Drāupadī, who was the collective wife of the five Pāṇḍava princes and the daughter of Drupada. There were five sons of Drāupadī: Prativindhya (by Yudhiṣṭhira), Sutasoma (by Bhīma), Śrutakīrti (by Arjuna), Śatānīka (by Nakula) and Śrutakarman (by Sahadeva).
ca, and.
sarva (*saṁdhi* for *sarve*, nom. pl.), all.
eva, indeed (often used as a rhythmic filler).
mahārathās (m. nom. pl.), great warriors, (as BV cpd.), those whose chariots are great.

7

अस्माकं तु विशिष्टा ये
asmākaṁ tu viśiṣṭā ye
ours indeed distinguished who

तान् निबोध द्विजोत्तम ।
tān nibodha dvijottama
them know! OHighest of the Twice-born

नायका मम सैन्यस्य
nāyakā mama sāinyasya
leaders of my army

संज्ञार्थं तान् ब्रवीमि ते ॥
saṃjñārthaṁ tān bravīmi te
for information I name to thee:

Those of ours who are indeed distinguished,
Know them! O Highest of the Twice-born.
The leaders of my army
I name to thee by proper names:

asmākam (gen. pl.), ours, our.
tu, indeed, truly.
viśiṣṭās (m. nom. pl. p. pass. participle *vi* √*śiṣ*), distinguished, particular, preeminent.
ye (m. nom. pl.), who.
tān (m. acc. pl.), them.
nibodha (2nd sg. imperative act. *ni* √*budh*), know! understand!
dvija (m.), twice-born, member of one of the three highest castes.
uttama (m.), highest chief, most excellent.
(*dvijottama*, m. voc. sg. TP cpd., O Highest of the Twice-born, refers to Droṇa.)
nāyakās (m. nom. pl.), leaders, chiefs, commanders.
mama (gen. sg.), of me, of my, of mine.
sāinyasya (m. n. gen. sg.), of army, of troops.
saṁjñārtham (*sam jñā artham,* n. acc. sg.), for the purpose of knowing, for information, by proper names.
tān (acc. pl.), them.
bravīmi (1st sg. pr. indic. act. √*brū*), I tell, I speak, I name.
te (dat. sg.), to thee.

8

भवान् भीष्मश् च कर्णश् च
bhavān bhīṣmaś ca karṇaś ca
Thy Lordship and Bhīṣma and Karṇa

कृपश्च समितिंजयः ।
kṛpaś ca samitiṁjayaḥ
and Kṛpa, victorious in battle

अश्वत्थामा विकर्णश्च
aśvatthāmā vikarṇaś ca
Aśvatthāmān and Vikarṇa

सौमदत्तिस्तथैव च ॥
sāumadattis tathāiva ca
and the Son of Somadatta also;

Your Lordship and Bhiṣma and Karṇa
And Kṛpa, always victorious in battle,
Aśvatthāmān and Vikarṇa
And the Son of Somadatta also;

bhavān (honorific, m. nom. sg.), Thy Lordship, Your Lordship, thou. Refers to Droṇa.
bhīṣmas (m. nom. sg.), Bhīṣma, aged Kāurava warrior, known as "the grand-sire," great uncle of the Pāṇḍava princes, who is fighting on the other side. He is a reluctant participant in the battle. The name means "awe-inspiring," "terrible" or "awful."
ca, and.
karṇas (m. nom. sg.), Karṇa, a Kāurava warrior, unacknowledged half-brother of Arjuna and the other Pāṇḍava princes. He is the son, by the Sun God Sūrya, of Pṛthā or Kuntī, before her marriage to Pāṇḍu. He has an old family grudge against Arjuna.
ca, and.
Kṛpas (m. nom. sg.), Kṛpa, sometimes known as Kṛpācārya, a Kāurava warrior and teacher of warriors, brother-in-law of Droṇa. The name, in its feminine form *kṛpā*, means "pity" or "compassion," a reference to the fact that Kṛpa was found in a clump of grass as an infant, and "compassionately" adopted by King Śaṁtanu (see chapter "The Setting of the Bhagavad Gītā).
ca, and.
samitiṁjayas (m. nom. sg.), victorious in battle.
aśvatthāmā (m. nom. sg. of Aśvatthāmān), Kāurava warrior, son of Droṇa and Kṛpī (sister of Kṛpa). The name means "having the strength of a horse."
vikarṇas (m. nom. sg.), a son of King Dhṛtarāṣṭra and a Kāurava warrior. (The name means either "without ears" or "having wide ears."
ca, and.
sāumadattis (m. nom. sg.), the Son of Somadatta, and a warrior prince on the Kāurava side.
tathā, thus, also.
eva, indeed (used as a rhythmic filler).
ca, and.

9

अन्ये च बहवः शूरा
anye ca bahavaḥ śūrā
and other many heroes

मदर्थे त्यक्तजीविताः
madarthe tyaktajīvitāḥ
for my sake whose lives are risked

नानाशस्त्रप्रहरणाः
*nānāśastrapraharaṇāḥ**
various weapon assailing

सर्वे युद्धविशारदाः ॥
sarve yuddhaviśāradāḥ
all battle-skilled.

And many other heroes
Whose lives are risked for my sake,
Attacking with various weapons,
All skilled in battle.

anye (m. nom. pl.), others, other.
ca, and.
bahavas (m. nom. pl.), many.
śūrās (m. nom. pl.), heroes.
madarthe (m. loc. sg.), for my sake, lit. "of me in purpose."
tyakta (m. nom. p. pass. participle √*tyaj*), abandoned, relinquished.
jīvitās (m. nom. pl.), lives.
(*tyaktajīvitās*, m. nom. pl. BV cpd., they whose lives are risked.)
nānā, various, different, distinct.
śastra (n.), weapon.
praharaṇās (n. nom. pl. adj. from *pra* √*hṛ*), striking, assailing, throwing, discharging.
(*śastra-praharaṇās*, m. nom. pl. TP cpd., throwing weapons.)
sarve (m. nom. pl.), all.
yuddha (n.), battle, fight.
viśāradās (m. nom. pl.), experienced, proficient, skilled.
(*yuddha-viśāradās*, m. nom. pl. TP cpd., skilled in battle.)

* The compond *śastrapraharaṇās* means literally "weapons to strike and weapons to hurl."

10

अपर्याप्तं तद् अस्माकं
aparyāptaṁ tad asmākaṁ
insufficient this of ours

बलं भीष्माभिरक्षितम् ।
balaṁ bhīṣmābhirakṣitam
(the) force (by) Bhīṣma guarded;

पर्याप्तं त्विदम् एतेषां
paryāptaṁ tv idam eteṣāṁ
sufficient though that of these

बलं भीमाभिरक्षितम् ॥
balaṁ bhīmābhirakṣitam
(the) force (by) Bhīma guarded.

Insufficient is that force of ours
By Bhīṣma guarded;
Sufficient though, this of these,
The force by Bhīma guarded.*

aparyāptam (m. nom. sg. p. pass. participle *a pari* √*āp*), incomplete, insufficient, unlimited, unbounded, unequal.
tad (m. nom. sg.), that, this.
asmākam (gen. pl), of us, ours, to us.
balam (n. nom. sg.), strength, force.
Bhīṣma, the old Kāurava warrior, great uncle of the Pāṇḍava princes and a chief of the Kāurave army.
abhirakṣitam (m. nom. sg. p. pass. participle *abhi* √*rakṣ*), guarded, protected.
(*Bhīṣma-abhirakṣitam*, n. nom. sg. TP cpd., guarded by Bhīṣma.)
paryāptam (n. nom. p. pass. participle *pari* √*āp*), sufficient, abundant, equal.
tu, but though.
idam (n. nom. sg.), this.
eteṣām (m. gen. pl.), of these, to them.
balam (n. nom. sg.), strength, force.
Bhīma, Pāṇḍava warrior, brother of Arjuna.
abhirakṣitam (n. nom. p. pass. participle *abhi* √*rakṣ*), protected, guarded.
(*Bhīma-abhivakṣitam*, n. nom. sg., guarded by Bhīma.)

---

* This stanza has puzzled many translators because (1) Duryodhana's (the speaker's) forces are actually greater than those of the Pāṇḍavas (therefore hardly "insufficient"); (2) tad "that" seems to refer to something nearby while idam "this" seems to refer to something far off; (3) Bhīṣma is generally regarded as a much greater leader of troops than Bhīma; (4) the words sound unnatural coming from Duryodhana who is supposed to be encouraging his forces with a pep talk. The eminent Sanskrit scholar J. A. B. van Buitenen has investigated the matter and published his conclusions in the Journal of the American Oriental Society (Vol. 85, No. 1, Jan.–March 1965). The Vulgate version, from which practically all translations have been made, was, according to van Buitenen, preceded by another version used by Bhāskara the Vedāntin, in the ninth century or thereabouts. In that version, which still survives, the names Bhīṣma and Bhīma are transposed and the stanza reads:

aparyāptam tad asmākaṁ
  balaṁ bhīmābhirakṣitam
paryāptam tv idam eteṣāṁ
  balaṁ bhīsmābhirakṣitam

11

अयनेषु च सर्वेषु
ayaneṣu ca sarveṣu
and in all movements,

यथाभागम् अवस्थिताः ।
yathābhāgam avasthitāḥ
in respective places stationed

भीष्मम् एवाभिरक्षन्तु
bhīṣmam evābhirakṣantu
Bhīṣma indeed protect

भवन्तः सर्व एव हि ॥
bhavantaḥ sarva eva hi
your lordships all, thus indeed.

And on all movements,
Stationed each in his respective place,
Protect ye Bhīṣma,
All of you, indeed!

ayaneṣu (n. loc. pl.), in positions, in progress, in goings, in movements.
ca, and.
sarveṣu (n. loc. pl.), in all.
yathābhāgam (adv.), according to shares, each in his respective place.
avasthitās (m. nom. pl. p. pass. participle *ava* √*sthā*), stationed, placed, following (as of a command).
Bhīṣmam (m. acc. sg.), Bhīṣma, the old Kāurava warrior chief.
eva, indeed (often used as a rhythmic filler).
abhirakṣantu (3rd pl. imperative *abhi* √*rakṣ*), *protect ye*! protect!
bhavantas (honorific nom. pl.), ye, your lordships.
sarva (*saṁdhi* for *sarve*, m. nom. pl.), all.
eva, indeed (used here for emphasis.)
hi, of course, truly, indeed.

---

which in van Buitenen's translation reads:

"That army guarded by Bhīma is not equal to us;
On the other hand, this army, guarded by Bhīṣma is equal to them."

Actually, though Bhīṣma is the leader of the Kāuravas, Bhīma is not the leader of the Pāṇḍavas. Edgerton thinks the name Bhīma is chosen in order to make a word play on the two names.

12

तस्य संजनयन् हर्षं
tasya saṁjanayan harṣaṁ
producing joy, of him (Duryodhana)

कुरुवृद्धः पितामहः।
kuruvṛddhaḥ pitāmahaḥ
the Aged Kuru, the Grandfather,

सिंहनादं विनद्योच्चैः
siṁhanādaṁ vinadyoccāiḥ
roaring a lion's roar on high

शङ्खं दध्मौ प्रतापवान्॥
śaṅkhaṁ dadhmāu pratāpavān
conch horn he blew powerfully

Making him (Duryodhana) happy,
The aged Kuru, the Grandsire,
Roaring a lion's roar on high,
Blew his conch horn powerfully.

tasya (m. gen. sg.), of him, i.e. to him, to Duryodhana.
saṁjanayan (m. nom. sg. pr. act. participle caus. *sam* √*jan*), producing, bringing forth.
harṣam (m. acc. sg.), joy, delight.
kuru (m.), Kuru, member of the Kuru tribe.
vṛddhas (m. nom. sg. p. pass. participle √*vṛdh*), grown larger, aged.
pitāmahas (m. nom. sg.), grandfather, lit. "great father," descriptive of Bhīṣma.
siṁha (m.), lion.
nādam (m. acc. sg.), loud sound, roar.
vinadya (gerund *vi* √*nad*), sounding forth, crying, bellowing.
(*siṁhanādam vinadya,* roaring a lion's roar.)
uccāis (inst. pl. adverb), by high, by loud, loudly, elevated, on high.
śaṅkham (m. n. acc. sg.), conch horn.
dadhmāu (3rd sg. perfect √*dhamā*), he blew.
pratāpavān (m. nom. sg. adj. from *pra* √*tap*), full of dignity, full of power, full of strength, full of energy, searingly.

13

ततः शङ्खाश्च भेर्यश्च
tataḥ śaṅkhāś ca bheryaś ca
and thereupon the conch horns and the kettledrums

पणवानकगोमुखाः ।
paṇavānakagomukhāḥ
the cymbals, drums, bull-mouths (trumpets)

सहसैवाभ्यहन्यन्त
sahasāivābhyahanyanta
all at once they were sounded

स शब्दस् तुमुलो ऽभवत् ॥
sa śabdas tumulo 'bhavat
the uproar tumultuous it was.

And thereupon the conch horns and the kettledrums,
The cymbals, drums and bull-mouths (trumpets)
All at once were sounded,
The uproar was tremendous.

tatas, then, thereupon, from thence.
śaṅkhās (m. nom. pl.), conch horns.
ca, and.
bheryas (f. nom. pl.), kettledrums.
ca, and.
paṇava (m.), cymbal, drum.
ānaka (m.), drum.
gomukhās (m. nom. pl.), trumpets, lit. "bull-mouths" or "bull faces" (the plural refers to the whole compound).
(*paṇavanakagomukhās,* m. nom. pl., DV cpd. the cymbals, drums and trumpets.)
sahasā (n. inst. sg.), suddenly, quickly, all at once.
eva, indeed (used as a rhythmic filler).
abhyahanyanta (3rd. pl. imperf. pass. *abhi* √*han*), they were struck, they sounded.
sas (m. nom. sg.), the, this.
śabdas (m. nom. sg.), sound, syllable, uproar.
tumulas (m. nom. sg.), tumultuous, noisy.
abhavat (3rd sg. imperf. act. √*bhū*), it was, it became.

14

ततः श्वेतैर् हयैर् युक्ते
tataḥ śvetāir hayāir yukte
then with white horses yoked

महति स्यन्दने स्थितौ ।
mahati syandane sthitāu
in the great chariot standing

माधवः पाण्डवश्चैव
mādhavaḥ pāṇḍavaścāiva
the Descendant of Madhu (Krishna) and the Son of Pāṇḍu (Arjuna) thus

दिव्यौ शङ्खौ प्रदध्मतुः ॥
divyāu śaṅkhāu pradadhmatuḥ
divine conch horns they blew forth.

Then, standing in the great chariot
Yoked with white horses,*
The Descendant of Madhu (Krishna) and the Son of Pāṇḍu (Arjuna)
Sounded forth their divine conch horns.

tatas, then, thereupon, from thence.
śvetāis (m. inst. pl.), with white, by white.
hayāis (m. inst. pl.), with horses, by horses.
yukte (m. loc. sg. p. pass. participle √*yuj*), yoked, joined, in yoke.
mahati (m. loc. sg.), in the great, in the mighty.
syandane (m. loc. sg.), in the "fast-running," in the chariot.
sthitāu (m. nom. dual), standing, situated.
Mādhavas (m. nom. sg.), descendant of Madhu, Krishna (the Yādavas, Krishna's tribe, was descended from Madhu, not to be confused with the *asura* Madhu who was killed by Vishnu).
pāṇḍavas (m. nom. sg.), Son of Pāṇḍu, Arjuna. Pāṇḍu was a brother of Dhṛtarāṣṭra and officially the father of the five Pāṇḍava brothers, including Arjuna.
ca, and.
eva, indeed (used as a rhythmic filler).
divyāu (m. n. nom. acc. dual), the two divine, the two heavenly.
śaṅkhāu (m. n. nom. acc. dual), the two conch horns.
pradadhmatus (3rd dual perfect act. *pra* √*dhmā*), they two blew forth.

* Arjuna's chariot is drawn by four horses.

15

पाञ्चजन्यं हृषीकेशो
pāñcajanyaṁ hṛṣīkeśo
Pāñcajanya, the Bristling Haired One (Krishna),

देवदत्तं धनंजयः ।
devadattaṁ dhanaṁjayaḥ
Devadatta, Conqueror of Wealth (Arjuna)

पौण्ड्रं दध्मौ महाशङ्खं
pāuṇḍraṁ dadhmāu mahāśañkhaṁ
Pāuṇḍra he blew, the great conch horn,

भीमकर्मा वृकोदरः ॥
bhīmakarmā vṛkodaraḥ
terrible in action, the Wolf-bellied (Bhīma)

The Bristling Haired One (Krishna) (blew) Pāñcajanya
Conqueror of Wealth (Arjuna) blew Devadatta
While the Wolf-bellied (Bhīma), terrible in action,
Blew the great conch horn Pāuṇḍra.

pāñcajanyam (m. acc. sg.), name of Krishna's conch horn which was taken from the demon Pañcajana after Krishna slew him.
hṛṣīkeśas (m. nom. sg.), "Bristling Haired," "Erect Hair," a very frequent epithet of Krishna.
devadattam (m. acc. sg.), "God Given," name of Arjuna's conch horn.
dhanaṁjayas (m. nom. sg.), "Conqueror of Wealth," very common epithet of Arjuna.
pāuṇḍram (m. acc. sg.), name of Bhīma's conch horn. Possibly named for a king of a people in Eastern India, thought to be a brother of Krishna.
dadhmāu (3rd sg. perfect act. √*dhmā*), he blew.
mahā, great, mighty.
śañkham (m. n. acc. sg.), conch horn.
bhīmakarmā (m. nom. sg. BV cpd.), terrible in action, whose actions are terrible.
vṛka (m.), wolf.
udaras (m. nom. sg.), belly, stomach. (The epithet *vṛkodara* was applied to Bhīma because of his enormous appetite.)
(*vṛka-udara*, m. nom. sg. BV cpd., wolf-bellied one.)

16

अनन्तविजयं राजा
anantavijayaṁ rājā
Anantavijaya the king

कुन्तीपुत्रो युधिष्ठिरः ।
kuntīputro yudhiṣṭhiraḥ
son of Kuntī Yudhiṣṭhira

नकुलः सहदेवश्च
nakulaḥ sahadevaś ca
Nakula and Sahadeva

सुघोषमणिपुष्पकौ ॥
sughoṣamaṇipuṣpakāu
Sughoṣa and Maṇipuṣpaka

The king, son of Kunti, Yudhiṣṭhira,
Blew Anantavijaya;
Nakula and Sahadeva
Blew Sughoṣa and Maṇipuṣpaka

anantavijayam (m. acc. sg.), Anantivijaya, Yudhiṣṭhira's conch horn. The name means "unending victory."
rājā (m. nom. sg.), king.
kuntīputras (m. nom. sg.), son of Kuntī.
yudhiṣṭhiras (m. nom. sg.), Yudhiṣṭhira, son of Kuntī by Dharma, god of justice and law, eldest of the Pāṇḍava princes.
nakulas (m. nom. sg.), Nakula, one of the twins, born to Pāṇḍu's second wife, Mādrī by one of the Āśvins. A Pāṇḍava prince. The name means "color of the mongoose."
sahadevas (m. nom. sg.), Sahadeva, the other twin, son of Mādrī by the other Āśvin. A Pāṇḍava prince. The name means "accompanied by the gods."
ca, and.
sughoṣa, the name of Nakula's conch horn (meaning "making a great noise").
maṇipuṣpakāu (m. acc. dual), Maṇipuṣpaka, the name of Sahadeva's conch horn (meaning "jewel bracelet").
(*sughoṣamaṇipuṣpakāu,* m. acc. dual, DV cpd. sughoṣa and maṇipuṣpaka.)

17

काश्यश्च परमेष्वासः
kāśyaś ca parameṣvāsaḥ
and the King of the Kāśis, supreme archer,

शिखण्डी च महारथः।
śikhaṇḍī ca mahārathaḥ
and Śikhaṇḍin, great warrior;

धृष्टद्युम्नो विराटश्च
dhṛṣṭadyumno virāṭaś ca
Dhṛṣṭadyumna and Virāṭa

सात्यकिश्चापराजितः॥
sātyakiścāparājitaḥ
and Sātyaki, the invincible:

And the King of the Kāśis, supreme archer,
And Śikhandin, that great warrior,
Dhṛṣṭadyumna and Virāṭa
And Sātyaki, the invincible;

kāśyas (m. nom. sg.), the King of the Kāśis, a tribe in a district identified with modern Benares.
ca, and.
parama (m.), supreme, highest.
iṣvāsas (m. nom. sg. *iṣu,* arrow; *āsa,* hurler), archer, bowman.
(*parama-iṣvāsas*, m. nom. sg. KD cpd., best archer.)
śikhaṇḍhī (m. nom. sg. of Śikhaṇḍin), a Pāṇḍava warrior, born as a girl and miraculously changed to a male, son of Drupada, and eventual killer of Bhīṣma who would not fight with a woman.
ca, and.
mahārathas (m. nom. sg.), great warrior, (as a BV cpd.) he whose chariot is great.
dhṛṣṭadyumnas (m. nom. sg.), Pāṇḍava warrior; son of Drupada and brother of Drāupadī.
virāṭas (m. nom. sg.), Virāṭa, warrior king of a particular district in India, with whom the Pāṇḍava princes took refuge during the thirteenth year of their exile.
ca, and.
sātyakis (m. nom. sg.), Yuyudhāna, son of Satyaka and an ally of the Pāṇḍavas. The name means "one whose nature is truth."
ca, and.
aparājitas (m. nom. sg.), unconquered, invincible.

18

द्रुपदो द्रौपदेयाश्च
drupado drāupadeyāś ca
Drupada and the Sons of Drāupadī

सर्वशः पृथिवीपते ।
sarvaśaḥ pṛthivīpate
all together, O Lord of the Earth (Dhṛtarāṣṭra)

सौभद्रश्च महाबाहुः
sāubhadraś ca mahābāhuḥ
and the Son of Subadrā, strong armed

शङ्खान् दध्मुः पृथक् पृथक् ॥
śaṅkhān dadhmuḥ pṛthak pṛthak
conch horns they blew respectively

Drupada and the Sons of Drāupadī
All together, O Lord of the Earth,
And the strong armed Son of Subhadrā
Blew their conch horns, each his own.

drupadas (m. nom. sg.), "Rapid Step," king of the Pāñcālas and father of Dhṛṣṭadyumna, Śikhaṇḍin and Drāupadī, the latter the common wife of the five Pāṇḍu princes.
drāupadeyās (m. nom. pl.), the sons of Drāupadī.
ca, and.
sarvaśas (adv.), altogether, wholly, entirely.
pṛthivīpate (m. voc. sg.), O Lord of the Earth, refers here to Dhṛtarāṣṭra, to whom the scene is being described by Saṁjaya.
sāubhadras (m. nom. sg.), the son of Subhadrā, viz., Abhimanyu, son of Arjuna and Subhadrā, his second wife.
mahā, strong, mighty.
bāhus (m. nom. sg.), arm.
(*mahābāhus,* nom. sg., BV cpd., having mighty arms.)
śaṅkhān (m. acc. pl.), conch horns.
dadhmus (3rd pl. perfect act. √*dhmā*), they blew.
pṛthak pṛthak, one by one, respectively, each in turn.

19

स घोषो धार्तराष्ट्राणां
sa ghoṣo dhārtarāṣṭrāṇāṁ
the noise of the Sons of Dhṛtarāṣṭra,

हृदयानि व्यदारयत् ।
hṛdayāni vyadārayat
the hearts it burst asunder

नभश्च पृथिवीं चैव
nabhaś ca pṛthivīṁ cāiva
and the sky and the earth

तुमुलो व्यनुनादयन् ॥
tumulo vyanunādayan
the tumult causing to resound

The noise burst asunder
The hearts of the Sons of Dhṛtarāṣṭra,
And the tumult caused
The sky and the earth to resound.

sas (m. nom. sg), the, this.
ghoṣas (m. nom. sg. from √*ghuṣ*), noise, cry, tumult, sound.
dhārtarāṣṭrāṇām (m. gen. pl.), of the sons of Dhṛtarāṣṭra.
hṛdayāni (n. acc. pl.), hearts.
vyadārayat (3rd sg. causative imperf. act. *vi* √*dṛ*), it burst, it tore, it rent, it lacerated, it caused to burst.
nabhas (n. acc. sg.), sky, firmament.
ca, and.
pṛthivīm (f. acc. sg.), earth.
ca, and.
eva, indeed (used as a rhythmic filler).
tumulas (m. nom. sg.), tumultuous, tumult.
vyanunādayan (m. nom. sg. pr. causative act. participle *vi anu* √*nad*), causing to make resonant, causing to thunder, causing to howl.

20

page 70

अथ व्यवस्थितान् दृष्ट्वा
atha vyavasthitān dṛṣṭvā
then, drawn up in battle array having seen,

धार्तराष्ट्रान् कपिध्वजः ।
dhārtarāṣṭrān kapidhvajaḥ
the Sons of Dhṛtarāṣṭra, the Monkey Bannered (Arjuna)

प्रवृत्ते शस्त्रसंपाते
pravṛtte śastrasaṁpāte
in the coming forth of the clash of weapons,

धनुर् उद्यम्य पाण्डवः ॥
dhanur udyamya pāṇḍavaḥ
the bow raising, the Son of Pāṇḍu

Then, having seen the Sons of Dhṛtarāṣṭra
Drawn up in battle array,
Raising his bow as the clash of weapons began,
The Monkey-Bannered* Son of Pāṇḍu (Arjuna)

atha, then.
vyavasthitān (m. acc. pl. p. pass. participle *vi ava* √*sthā*), drawn up in battle array, arrayed.
dṛṣṭvā (gerund √*dṛś*), seeing, having seen.
dhārtarāṣṭrān (m. acc. pl.), the sons of Dhṛtarāṣṭra.
kapi (m.), ape, monkey.
dhvajas (m. nom. sg.), banner, flag, standard.
(*kapi-dhvajas*, m. nom. sg. BV cpd., banner of the monkey.)
pravṛtte (m. loc. sg.), in the coming forth, in the resulting, in the occurring.
śastra (m.), weapon.
saṁpāte (m. loc. sg.), in the coming together, collision, encounter, confluence (*sam* √*pat*).
(*śastra-saṁpāte*, m. loc. sg. TP cpd., clash of the weapons.)
(*pravṛtte śastrasaṁpāte*, m. loc. absol., when the clash of weapons began.)
dhanus (m. acc. sg.), bow.
udyamya (gerund *ud* √*yam*), raising up, flourishing, brandishing.
pāṇḍavas (m. nom. sg.), Son of Pāṇḍu (Arjuna).

* Arjuna's standard was a flag with the symbol of a monkey. Incidentally, the monkey was Hanumān, the monkey god, who assisted Rāma in bringing back the kidnapped Sītā, his wife, in the Rāmāyana.

21

हृषीकेशं तदा वाक्यम्
hṛṣīkeśaṁ tadā vākyam
to the Bristling Haired One (Krishna) then word

इदम् आह महीपते ।
idam āha mahīpate
this he said: O Lord of the Earth,

सेनयोर् उभयोर् मध्ये
senayor ubhayor madhye
of the two armies both in the middle

रथं स्थापय मे ऽच्युत ॥
rathaṁ sthāpaya me 'cyuta
the chariot cause to stand of me, Imperishable One

To the Bristling Haired one (Krishna) then
Spoke this word: O Lord of the Earth,
Cause my chariot to stand in the middle
Between the two armies, Imperishable One,

hṛṣī (f.), bristling, erect.
keśam (m. acc. sg.), hair.
(*hṛṣīkeśa*, Bristling Haired a common nickname for Krishna.)
tadā, then.
vākyam (n. acc. sg.), word, speech.
idam (n. acc. sg.), this.
āha (3rd sg. perf. act. √*ah*), he said.
mahī (f. nom. sg.), the earth.
pate (m. voc. sg.), O Lord, O Ruler, O Master.
(*mahīpate*, m. voc. sg. TP cpd., O Lord of the Earth.)
senayos (f. gen. dual), of the two armies.
ubhayos (f. gen. dual), of both.
madhye (n. loc. sg.), in the middle, in the midst of.
ratham (m. acc. sg.), chariot.
sthāpaya (2nd sg. causative imperative act. √*sthā*), cause to stand, cause to be situated.
me (gen. sg.), of me.
acyuta (m. voc. sg.), not fallen, unchanging, imperishable, unshaken, firm, an epithet of Vishnu-Krishna.

22

यावद् एतान् निरीक्षे ऽहं
yāvad etān nirīkṣe 'haṁ
until these I behold, I,

योद्धुकामान् अवस्थितान् ।
yoddhukāmān avasthitān
battle-hungry arrayed.

कैर् मया सह योद्धव्यम्
kāir mayā saha yoddhavyam
with whom? by me together to be fought

अस्मिन् रणसमुद्यमे ॥
asmin raṇasamudyame
in this battle in undertaking.

Until I behold these warriors,
Battle-hungry and arrayed.
With whom must I fight
In undertaking this battle?

yāvad, as many, as much, until.
etān (m. acc. pl.), these.
nirīkṣe (1st sg. mid. *nir* √*īkṣ*), I see, I behold.
aham (nom. sg.), I.
yoddhukāmān (m. acc. pl.), wishing to fight, anxious to fight, hungry for battle.
avasthitān (m. acc. pl.), arrayed, arranged in battle formation.
kāis (m. inst. pl. interrog.), by whom? with whom?
mayā (m. inst. sg.), by me, with me.
saha, together, along with.
yoddhavyam (n. nom. sg. gerundive √*yudh* used impersonally), to be fought.
asmin (m. loc. sg.), in this.
raṇa (m.), battle, conflict; *raṇa* also means joy, pleasure, delight, and in its use here means battle as an object of delight.
samudyame (m. loc. sg. derivative noun from *sam ud* √*yam*), in lifting, in raising, in setting about, in undertaking, in readiness for.
(*raṇa-samudyame,* m. loc. pl. TP cpd., in readiness for battle.)

23

योत्स्यमानान् अवेक्षे ऽहं
yotsyamānān avekṣe 'haṁ
those who are about to give battle I behold, I,

य एते ऽत्र समागताः ।
ya ete 'tra samāgatāḥ
who these here come together

धार्तराष्ट्रस्य दुर्बुद्धेर्
dhārtarāṣṭrasya durbuddher
of the Son of Dhṛtarāṣṭra of evil mind

युद्धे प्रियचिकीर्षवः ॥
yuddhe priyacikīrṣavaḥ
in battle wishing to do service."

I behold those who are about to give battle,
Here come together,
Wishing to do service in warfare
For the evil-minded Son of Dhṛtarāṣṭra (Duryodhana).

yotsyamānān (m. acc. pl. mid. fut. act. participle √*yudh*), those who are about to give battle.
avekṣe (1st sg. pr. indic. mid. *ava* √*īkṣ*), I see, I behold.
aham (nom. sg.), I.
ya, saṁdhi for *ye* (m. nom. pl.), who.
ete (m. nom. pl.), these.
atra, here, in this place, in this respect.
samāgatās (m. nom. pl), come together, assembled.
dhārtarāṣṭrasya (m. gen. sg.), of the Son of Dhṛtarāṣṭra, i.e., Duryodhana.
durbuddhes (m. gen. sg. BV cpd.), of evil mind, of evil intuition, whose mind is evil.
yuddhe (n. loc. sg.), in battle, in warfare.
priya (n.), dear, service, kindness.
cikīrṣavas (m. nom. pl. of *cikīrṣu*, desiderative adjective from √*kṛ*), wishing to do, wishing to perform.
(*priyacikīrṣavas,* m. nom. pl. TP cpd., wishing to do a service, wishing to do a kindness.)

24

एवम् उक्तो हृषीकेशो
evam ukto hṛṣīkeśo
thus addressed, the Bristling Haired One (Krishna)

गुडाकेशेन भारत ।
guḍākeśena bhārata
by the Thick Haired One (Arjuna), O Descendant of Bharata

सेनयोर् उभयोर् मध्ये
senayor ubhayor madhye
of the two armies of both in the middle

स्थापयित्वा रथोत्तमम् ॥
sthāpayitvā rathottamam
having caused to stand the chief chariot

Thus the Bristling Haired One (Krishna) was addressed
By the Thick Haired One (Arjuna), O Descendant of Bharata,*
Having caused the chief chariot
To stand in the middle between the two armies.

evam, thus, in this manner.
uktas (m. nom. sg. p. pass. participle √*vac*), said, addressed, bespoken.
hṛṣī (f.), standing on end, erect, bristling.
keśas (m. nom. sg.), hair, shock of hair.
guḍā (f.), thick, a ball, molasses, thickened juice of the sugar cane.
keśa (m.), hair.
(*guḍākeśena,* m. inst. sg., by the Thick Haired One, by Arjuna.)
bhārata (m. voc. sg.), O Descendant of Bharata (here referring to Dhṛtarāṣṭra whom Saṁjaya is addressing).
senayos (f. gen. dual), of the two armies.
ubhayos (f. gen. dual), of both.
madhye (n. loc. sg.), in the middle.
sthāpayitvā (causative gerund √*sthā*), causing to stand, having caused to stand.
rathottamam (*ratha uttamam,* m. acc. sg.), the chief chariot, the highest chariot.

* Dhṛtarāṣṭra the blind king to whom the scene is being described.

25

भीष्मद्रोणप्रमुखतः
bhīṣmadroṇapramukhataḥ
Bhīṣma and Droṇa in front of

सर्वेषां च महीक्षिताम् ।
sarveṣāṁ ca mahīkṣitām
and of all these rulers of the earth

उवाच पार्थ पश्यैतान्
uvāca pārtha paśyāitān
said the Son of Pṛthā: Behold these

समवेतान् कुरून् इति ॥
samavetān kurūn iti
come together the Kurus, thus.

Before the eyes of Bhīṣma and Droṇa
And all these rulers of the earth,
Said the Son of Pṛthā: Behold these,
The Kurus assembled.

bhīṣma, the elderly Kāurava warrior, great uncle of Arjuna.
droṇa, Kāurava warrior, a Brahman by birth and, like Bhīṣma, a teacher of warfare.
pramukhatas (adv.), lit. "before the face," opposite, in front of, before the eyes of.
(*bhīṣma-droṇa-pramukhatas,* TP cpd., in front of Bhīṣma and Droṇa.)
sarveṣām (m. gen. pl.), of all these.
ca, and.
mahī (f.), earth, world.
kṣitām (m. gen. pl.), of governors, rulers (√*kṣi*).
(*mahīkṣitām,* m. gen. pl., TP cpd., of world-rulers, of earth-rulers.)
uvāca (3rd sg. imperf. act. √*vac*), he said.
pārthas (m. voc. sg.), the Son of Pṛthā, i.e., Arjuna.
paśya (2nd sg. imperative act. √*paś*), behold! look at! see!
etān (m. acc. pl.), these.
samavetān (m. acc. pl. p. pass. participle *sam ava* √*i*), come together, assembled, united.
kurūn (m. acc. pl.), Kurus, the ancient tribe from which both the Pāṇḍavas and the Kāuravas are descended.
iti, thus, indeed (used here, and frequently, at the close of a quotation).

26

तत्रापश्यत् स्थितान् पार्थः
tatrāpaśyat sthitān pārthaḥ
there he saw standing, the Son of Pṛthā (Arjuna)

पितॄन् अथ पितामहान् ।
pitṝn atha pitāmahān
fathers, then grandfathers,

आचार्यान् मातुलान् भ्रातॄन्
ācāryān mātulān bhrātṝn
teachers, maternal uncles, brothers,

पुत्रान् पौत्रान् सखींस् तथा ॥
putrān pāutrān sakhīṅs tathā
sons, grandsons, friends as well

There the Son of Pṛthā (Arjuna) saw standing
Fathers, then grandfathers,
Teachers, maternal uncles, brothers,
Sons, grandsons, friends as well;

tatra, there, thither.
apaśyat (3rd sg. imperfect act. √*paś*), he saw.
sthitān (m. acc. pl. p. pass. participle √*sthā*), standing situated.
pārthas (m. nom. sg.), the Son of Pṛthā, epithet frequently applied to Arjuna.
pitṝn (m. acc. pl.), fathers.
atha, then, and.
pitāmahān (m. acc. pl.), grandfathers.
ācāryān (m. acc. pl.), teachers, masters.
mātulān (m. acc. pl.), maternal uncles.
bhrātṝn (m. acc. pl.), brothers.
putrān (m. acc. pl.), sons.
pāutrān (m. acc. pl.), grandsons.
sakhīn (m. acc. pl.), friends, companions.
tathā, likewise, as well.

27

श्वशुरान् सुहृदश्चैव
śvaśurān suhṛdaścāiva
fathers in law and companions

सेनयोर् उभयोर् अपि ।
senayor ubhayor api
in the two armies, in all two

तान् समीक्ष्य स कौन्तेयः
tān samīkṣya sa kāunteyaḥ
them contemplating, he, the Son of Kuntī,

सर्वान् बन्धून् अवस्थितान् ॥
sarvān bandhūn avasthitān
all relatives arrayed

Fathers in law, companions,
In the two armies, in all two,
Contemplating them, all his kinsmen, arrayed,
He, the Son of Kuntī,

śvaśurān (m. acc. pl.), fathers-in-law.
suhṛdas (m. acc. pl.), companions.
ca, and.
eva, indeed (used as a rhythmic filler).
senayos (f. loc. dual), in the two armies.
ubhayos (f. loc. dual), in both.
api, even, also.
(*ubhayor api*, in all two.)
tān (m. acc. pl.), them.
samīkṣya (gerund *sam* √*īkṣ*), contemplating, regarding, looking at.
sas (m. nom. sg.), he, this.
kāunteyas (m. nom. sg.), the son of Kuntī, epithet often applied to Arjuna.
sarvān (m. acc. pl.), all.
bandhūn (m. acc. pl.), relatives, kinsmen.
avasthitān (m. acc. pl. p. pass. participle), arrayed, arranged in battle order.

28

कृपया परयाविष्टो
kṛpayā parayāviṣṭo
filled with infinite pity

विषीदन्न् इदम् अब्रवीत् ।
viṣīdann idam abravīt
desponding, this he said:

दृष्ट्वेमं स्वजनं कृष्ण
dṛṣṭvemaṁ svajanaṁ kṛṣṇa
"having seen this, my own people Krishna,

युयुत्सुं समुपस्थितम् ॥
yuyutsuṁ samupasthitam
desiring to fight, approaching,

Filled with infinite pity,
Desponding, this he said:
Having seen this, my own people, Krishna,
Desiring to fight, approaching,

kṛpayā (f. inst. sg.), by pity, with pity.
parayā (f. inst. sg.), by infinite, by profound, by deep.
āviṣṭas (m. nom. sg. p. pass. participle *ā* √*viś*), entered, subject to, possessed by, filled with.
viṣīdan (m. n. sg. pr. participle *vi* √*sad*), despairing, despondent.
idam (n. acc. sg.), this.
abravīt (3rd sg. imperf. act. √*brū*), he said, he spoke.
dṛṣṭvā (gerund √*dṛś*), seeing, having seen.
imam (m. acc. sg.), this.
svajanam (m. acc. sg.), own people, own family.
kṛṣṇa (m. voc. sg.), Krishna (the name means black, dark, or dark blue), Arjuna's charioteer, the avatār of Vishnu and the principal spokesman in the Bhagavad Gītā.
yuyutsum (m. acc. sg. desiderative adjective from √*yudh*), desiring to fight, anxious to fight.
samupasthitam (m. acc. sg. p. pass. participle *sam upa* √*sthā*), approaching, coming near, standing near.

29

सीदन्ति मम गात्राणि
sīdanti mama gātrāṇi
"they sink down, my limbs

मुखं च परिशुष्यति।
mukhaṁ ca pariśuṣyati
and (my) mouth dries up

वेपथुश्च शरीरे मे
vepathuś ca śarīre me
and trembling in the body of me

रोमहर्षश्च जायते ॥
romaharṣaś ca jāyate
and bristling of the hair is brought forth.

My limbs sink down
And my mouth dries up
And my body trembles
And my hair stands on end.

sīdanti (3rd pl. pr. indic. act. √*sad*), they sink down, they sit.
mama (gen. sg.), of me, my.
gātrāṇi (n. nom. pl.), limbs, legs, instruments of motion (from √*gā*, go).
mukham (n. nom. sg.), mouth, face.
ca, and.
pariśuṣyati (3rd sg. pr. indic. act. *pari* √*śuṣ*), it dries up, it makes dry.
vepathus (m. nom. sg. from √*vip*), a trembling, a quivering, a quaking.
ca, and.
śarīre (m. loc. sg.), in the body.
me (gen.sg.), of me, my.
roma (n.), hair, body hair.
harṣas (m. nom. sg. derivative noun √*hṛṣ*), standing on end, bristling, standing erect.
(*roma-harṣas*, m. nom. sg. TP cpd., bristling of the hair.)
ca, and.
jāyate (3rd sg. pr. indic. passive √*jan*), it is born, it is brought forth, produced.

30

गाण्डीवं स्रंसते हस्तात्
gāṇḍīvaṁ sraṁsate hastāt
Gāṇḍīva falls from (my) hand

त्वक् चैव परिदह्यते ।
tvak cāiva paridahyate
and (my) skin it burns

न च शक्नोम्य् अवस्थातुं
na ca śaknomy avasthātuṁ
and not I am able to remain as I am,

भ्रमतीव च मे मनः ॥
bhramatīva ca me manaḥ
and it rambles-like of me the mind,

Gāṇḍiva (Arjuna's bow) falls from (my) hand,
And my skin burns,
And I am unable to remain as I am,
And my mind seems to ramble,

gāṇḍīvam (n. nom. sg.), Gāṇḍīva, the name of Arjuna's bow.
sraṁsate (3rd sg. pr. indic. mid. √*sraṁs*), it falls, it drops.
hastāt (m. abl. sg.), from the hand.
tvac (f. nom. sg.), skin.
ca, and.
eva, indeed (used as a rhythmic filler).
paridahyate (3rd sg. pr. indic. passive *pari* √*dah*), it is burned, it burns.
na, not.
ca, and.
śaknomi (1st. sg. pr. indic. act. √*śak*), I am able, I can, I have the power to.
avasthātum (infinitive *ava* √*sthā*), to remain as I am, to stand.
bhramati (3rd sg. pr. indic. act. √*bhram*), it wanders, it rambles.
iva, like, as it were.
me (gen. sg.), of me.
manas (n. nom. sg.), mind, intellect, understanding.

31

निमित्तानि च पश्यामि
nimittāni ca paśyāmi
and omens I perceive

विपरीतानि केशव ।
viparītāni keśava
inauspicious, O Handsome-haired One,

न च श्रेयो ऽनुपश्यामि
na ca śreyo 'nupaśyāmi
and not welfare I foresee

हत्वा स्वजनम् आहवे ॥
hatvā svajanam āhave
having destroyed own people in battle.

And I perceive inauspicious omens,
O Handsome-haired One,
And I foresee misfortune
In destroying my own people in battle.

nimittāni (n. acc. pl.), omens, marks, tokens, signs.
ca, and.
paśyāmi (1st sg. pr. indic. act. √*paś*), I see, I perceive.
viparītāni (n. acc. pl.), inauspicious, perverse.
keśava (m. voc. sg.), O Handsome-haired One.
na, not.
ca, and.
śreyas (n. acc. sg.), welfare, prosperity, good fortune.
anupaśyāmi (1st sg. pr. indic. act. *anu* √*paś*), I foresee, I anticipate.
hatvā (gerund √*han*), slaying, destroying, killing, having destroyed, having killed.
svajanam (m. acc. sg.), own people, own kinsmen.
āhave (m. loc. sg. from *ā* √*hve*), in challenge, in battle, in warfare.

32

न काङ्क्षे विजयं कृष्ण
na kāṅkṣe vijayaṁ kṛṣṇa
not I desire victory, Krishna

न च राज्यं सुखानि च ।
na ca rājyaṁ sukhāni ca
and not kingship and pleasures.

किं नो राज्येन गोविन्द
kiṁ no rājyena govinda
what to us with kingship, Chief of Cowherds (Krishna)?

किं भोगैर् जीवितेन वा ॥
kiṁ bhogāir jīvitena vā
what with enjoyments or with life?

I do not desire victory, Krishna,
Nor kingship nor pleasures.
What to us is kingship, Chief of Cowherds* (Krishna)?
What are enjoyments, even life?

na, not.
kāñkṣe (1st sg. pr. indic. mid. √*kāñkṣ*), I desire, I wish for, I hanker after.
vijayam (m. acc. sg.), conquest, victory.
kṛṣṇa (m. voc. sg.), Krishna.
na, not.
ca, and, or.
rājyam (n. acc. sg.), kingship, kingdom, kingly power.
sukhāni (n. acc. pl.), pleasures, happinesses, joys.
ca, and, or.
kim (interrog.), what?
nas (dat. pl.), to us.
rājyena (n. inst. sg.), with kingship, with kingdom, by kingship.
govinda (m. voc. sg.), "Cow Finder," epithet of Krishna, often translated "Chief of Cowherds," because of a presumed Prakrit derivation, the interpretation of which is moot among scholars. See footnote.
kim (interrog.), what?
bhogāis (m. inst. pl.), with pleasures, with enjoyments.
jīvitena (n. inst. sg.), with life, by life.
vā, or.

* Govinda (lit. "cow finder"). "Chief of Cowherds" presumes an adoption into Sanskrit of the Prakrit "gopendra" (gopa Indra), but this is the translation usually accepted.

33

येषाम् अर्थे काङ्क्षितं नो
yeṣām arthe kāṅkṣitaṁ no
of whom for the sake desired of us

राज्यं भोगाः सुखानि च ।
rājyaṁ bhogāḥ sukhāni ca
kingship, enjoyments and pleasures,

त इमे ऽवस्थिता युद्धे
ta ime 'vasthitā yuddhe
they, these arrayed in battle,

प्राणांस् त्यक्त्वा धनानि च ॥
prāṇāṅs tyaktvā dhanāni ca
vital breaths abandoning and riches,

**Those for whose sake we desire
Kingship, enjoyments and pleasures,
They, these arrayed here in battle,
Abandoning lives and riches,**

yeṣām (m. gen. pl.), of whom.
arthe (m. loc. sg.), for the sake of, in sake.
kāṅkṣitam (n. nom. sg. p. pass. participle √*kāṅkṣ*), desired, wished for, hankered after.
nas (gen. pl.), of us, by us.
rājyam (n. nom. sg.), kingship, sovereignty.
bhogās (m. nom. pl.), pleasures, enjoyments (of eating in particular).
sukhāni (n. nom. pl.), pleasures, comforts.
ca. and.
ta (*saṁdhi* for *te*, m. nom. pl.), they.
ime (m. nom. pl.), these.
avasthitās (m. nom. pl. p. pass. participle *ava* √*sthā*), standing, arrayed, arranged in battle formation.
yuddhe (n. loc. sg.), in battle, in warfare.
prāṇān (m. acc. pl.) vital breaths, lives.
tyaktvā (gerund √*tyaj*), abandoning, sacrificing, relinquishing, having abandoned.
dhanāni (n. acc. pl.), riches, booty.
ca, and.

34

आचार्याः पितरः पुत्रास्
ācāryāḥ pitaraḥ putrās
teachers, fathers, sons,

तथैव च पितामहाः ।
tathāiva ca pitāmahāḥ
and also grandfathers,

मातुलाः श्वशुराः पौत्राः
mātulāḥ śvaśurāḥ pāutrāḥ
maternal uncles, fathers in law, grandsons,

श्यालाः संबन्धिनस् तथा ॥
śyālāḥ saṁbandhinas tathā
brothers in law, kinsmen thus

Teachers, fathers, sons,
And also grandfathers,
Maternal uncles, father's in law, grandsons,
Brothers in law, thus kinsmen.

ācāryās (m. nom. pl.), teachers, masters.
pitaras (m. nom. pl.), fathers.
putrās (m. nom. pl.), sons.
tathā, also, thus.
eva, indeed (used as a rhythmic filler).
ca, and.
pitāmahās (m. nom. pl.), grandfathers.
mātulās (m. nom. pl.), maternal uncles.
śvaśurās (m. nom. pl.), fathers-in-law.
pāutrās (m. nom. pl.), grandsons.
śyālās (m. nom. pl.), brothers-in-law.
saṁbandhinas (m. nom. pl.), kinsmen, relatives.
tathā, thus, also.

35

एतान् न हन्तुम् इच्छामि
etān na hantum icchāmi
them not to slay I desire,

घ्नतो ऽपि मधुसूदन ।
ghnato 'pi madhusūdana
who are also killing, Slayer of Madhu,

अपि त्रैलोक्यराज्यस्य
api trāilokyarājyasya
even for the sovereignty of the three worlds

हेतोः किं नु महीकृते ॥
hetoḥ kiṁ nu mahīkṛte
on account; how then for the earth?

I do not desire to kill
Them who are bent on killing, Slayer of Madhu (Krishna),
Even for the sovereignty of the three worlds,
How then for the earth?

etān (m. acc. pl.), them, these.
na, not.
hantum (infinitive √*han*), to kill, to slay.
icchāmi (1st sg. pr. indic. act. √*iṣ*), I desire, I wish.
ghnatas (m. acc. pl. pr. participle √*han*), those who are killing, those who are about to kill.
api, even, also.
madhusūdana (m. voc. sg.), Slayer of the Demon Madhu, epithet of Vishnu-Krishna. This Madhu is not to be confused with the Yādava patriarch who was Krishna's ancestor.
api, even, also.
trāilokya (n.), the three worlds, viz., the paradise of the gods, the realm of atmospheric beings and the earth.
rājyasya (n. gen. sg.), of the sovereignty, for the sovereignty.
(*trāilokyarājyasya,* n. gen. sg. TP cpd, for the sovereignty of the three worlds.)
hetos (m. abl. sg.), because, on account of, cause.
kim (interrog.), what? how?
nu, now, then, indeed.
mahīkṛte (m. loc. sg.), for the sake of the created world, for the earth.

36

निहत्य धार्तराष्ट्रान् नः
nihatya dhārtarāṣṭrān naḥ
striking down the Sons of Dhṛtarāṣṭra to us

का प्रीतिः स्याज् जनार्दन ।
kā prītiḥ syāj janārdana
what joy should it be, O Agitator of Men?

पापम् एवाश्रयेद् अस्मान्
pāpam evāśrayed asmān
evil thus should cling to us

हत्वैतान् आततायिनः ॥
hatvāitān ātatāyinaḥ
having killed these aggressors.

What joy to us should it be
To strike down the Sons of Dhṛtarāṣṭra, O Agitator of Men* (Krishna)?
Evil thus should cling to us
Having killed these aggressors.

nihatya (gerund *ni* √*han*), striking down, killing.
dhārtarāṣṭrān (m. acc. pl.), the Sons of Dhṛtarāṣṭra.
nas (dat. or gen. pl.), to us.
kā (f. nom. sg. interrog.), what?
prītis (f. nom. sg.), joy, pleasure.
syāt (3rd sg. optative act. √*as*), it should be, might it be.
janārdana (m. voc. sg.), Agitator of Men, frequent epithet of Krishna (from *jana*, man; √*ard*, agitate, torment, move).
pāpam (n. nom. sg.), evil, harm, trouble.
eva, thus, even so.
āśrayet (3rd sg. optative act. *ā* √*śri*), it should cling to, it should lean on, take hold of.
asmān (acc. pl.), us.
hatvā (gerund √*han*), killing, having killed.
etān (m. acc. pl.), these.
ātatāyinas (m. acc. pl.), lit. "having bows drawn" (from *ā* √*tan*), murderers, attackers, aggressors, felons.

* Janārdana, "Agitator of Men" is an epithet of the god Vishnu, of whom Krishna is the earthly *avatār*.

37

तस्मान् नार्हा वयं हन्तुं
tasmān nārhā vayaṁ hantuṁ
therefore not justified we to kill

धार्तराष्ट्रान् स्वबान्धवान् ।
dhārtarāṣṭrān svabāndhavān
the Sons of Dhṛtarāṣṭra, own kinsmen,

स्वजनं हि कथं हत्वा
svajanaṁ hi kathaṁ hatvā
own people surely how, having killed,

सुखिनः स्याम माधव ।।
sukhinaḥ syāma mādhava
happy we should be, Descendant of Madhu?

Therefore we are not justified in killing
The Sons of Dhṛtarāṣṭra, our own kinsmen.
How, having killed our own people,
Should we be happy, Descendant of Madhu (Krishna)?

tasmāt (abl. sg.), from this, therefore.
na, not.
arhās (m. nom. pl. from √*arh*), justified, deserving, entitled to.
vayam (nom. pl.), we.
hantum (infinitive √*han*), to kill, to smite.
dhārtarāṣṭrān (m. acc. pl.), the Sons of Dhṛtarāṣṭra.
svabāndhavān (m. acc. pl.), own kinsmen, own relatives.
svajanam (m. acc. sg.), own people.
hi, surely, indeed.
katham (interrog.), how?
hatvā (gerund √*han*), killing, having killed.
sukhinas (m. nom. pl.), happy, possessing happiness.
syāma (1st pl. optative act. √*as*), we should be, we might be.
mādhava (m. voc. sg.), Descendant of Madhu, progenitor of the Yādavas, Krishna's race; thus an epithet of Krishna.

38

यद्यप्येते न पश्यन्ति
yadyapyete na paśyanti
if even these not they see

लोभोपहतचेतसः ।
lobhopahatacetasaḥ
greed overpowered in thought,

कुलक्षयकृतं दोषं
kulakṣayakṛtaṁ doṣaṁ
the destruction-of-family-caused wrong

मित्रद्रोहे च पातकम् ॥
mitradrohe ca pātakam
and in the friend-treachery crime,

Even if they do not perceive,
Those whose thoughts are overpowered by greed,
The wrong caused by destruction of family,
And the crime of treachery to friend,

yadi, if.
api, even.
ete (m. nom. pl.), these.
na, not.
paśyanti (3rd pl. pr. indic. act. √*paś*), they see, they perceive.
lobha (m.), greed, desire.
upahata (p. pass. participle *upa* √*han*), overpowered.
cetasas (n. nom. pl.), thoughts.
(*upahatacetasas*, n. nom. p. BV cpd., with thoughts overpowered, whose thoughts are overpowered.)
kula (n.), family.
kṣaya (m., noun from √*kṣi*), destroying, destruction.
kṛtam (m. acc. sg. p. pass. participle √*kṛ*), made, caused, done.
(*kula-kṣaya-kṛtam*, m. acc. sg. TP cpd., caused destruction of family.)
doṣam (m. acc. sg.), wrong, evil.
mitra (m.), friend.
drohe (m. loc. sg.), in injury, in treachery, in mischief.
(*mitradrohe*, m. loc. sg., treachery to a friend.)
ca, and.
pātakam (n. acc. sg.), crime, evil, lit. "that which causes to fall" (√*pat*).

39

कथं न ज्ञेयम् अस्माभिः
kathaṁ na jñeyam asmābhiḥ
how not to be known by us

पापाद् अस्मान् निवर्तितुम् ।
pāpād asmān nivartitum
from evil from this to turn back

कुलक्षयकृतं दोषं
kulakṣayakṛtaṁ doṣaṁ
the destruction-of-family-caused evil,

प्रपश्यद्भिर् जनार्दन ॥
prapaśyadbhir janārdana
by discernment, Agitator of Men?

Why should we not know enough
To turn back, through discernment,
From this evil, the wrong caused
By destruction of family, O Agitator of Men?

katham (interrog.), how?
na, not.
jñeyam (gerundive √*jñā*), to be known, to be understood.
asmābhis (m. inst. pl.), by us, with us.
pāpāt (n. abl. sg.), from evil, from wrong.
asmāt (n. abl. sg.),from this.
nivartitum (infinitive *ni* √*vṛt*), to turn back.
kula (n.), family.
kṣaya (m. noun from √*kṣi*), destruction.
kṛtam (m. acc. sg. p. pass. participle √*kṛ*), doing, making, done, made, caused.
(*kula-kṣaya-kṛtam*, m. acc. sg. TP cpd., caused destruction of family.)
doṣam (m. acc. sg.), evil, wrong.
prapaśyadbhis (m. inst. pl. pr. participle *pra* √*paś*), by discerning, by discernment.
janārdana (m. voc. sg.), Agitator of Men, Mover of Men, epithet of Vishnu-Krishna.

40

कुलक्षये प्रणश्यन्ति
kulakṣaye praṇaśyanti
in destruction of family, they vanish

कुलधर्माः सनातनाः ।
kuladharmāḥ sanātanāḥ
the family laws, ancient;

धर्मे नष्टे कुलं कृत्स्नम्
dharme naṣṭe kulaṁ kṛtsnam
when law perishes, the family entire

अधर्मो ऽभिभवत्युत ॥
adharmo 'bhibhavatyuta
lawlessness it overpowers also

In the destruction of family
The ancient family laws vanish;
When the law has perished
Lawlessness overpowers the entire family also.

kula (n.), family.
kṣaye (m. loc. sg., a noun from √*kṣi*), in destruction.
(*kula-kṣaye*, m. loc. sg. TP cpd., destruction of family.)
praṇaśyanti (3rd pl. pr. indic. act. *pra* √*naś*), they are lost, they vanish, they perish.
kula (n.), family.
dharmās (m. nom. pl.), laws, customs, rights, duties.
(*kula-dharmās*, m. nom. pl. TP cpd., laws of family.)
sanātanās (m. nom. pl.), eternal, ancient, primaeval.
dhrame (m. loc. sg.), in duty, in law.
naṣṭe (loc. sg. p. pass. participle √*naś*), in the perishing, in the loss.
(*dharme-naṣṭe,* loc. absol., when law perishes.)
kulam (n. acc. sg.), family.
kṛtsnam (n. acc. sg.), entire.
adharmas (m. nom. sg.), lawlessness, dutilessness.
abhibhavati (3rd sg. pr. indic. act. *abhi* √*bhū*), it overcomes, overpowers, predominates, conquers, surpasses.
uta, and, also, even.

41

अधर्माभिभवात् कृष्ण
adharmābhibhavāt kṛṣṇa
from overpowering by lawlessness, Krishna,

प्रदुष्यन्ति कुलस्त्रियः ।
praduṣyanti kulastriyaḥ
they are corrupted, the family women;

स्त्रीषु दुष्टासु वार्ष्णेय
strīṣu duṣṭāsu vārṣṇeya
in women corrupted, O Clansman of Vṛṣṇi,

जायते वर्णसंकरः ॥
jāyate varṇasaṁkaraḥ
is born the intermixture of caste

Because of the ascendancy of lawlessness, Krishna,
The family women are corrupted;
When women are corrupted, O Clansman of Vṛṣṇi (Krishna).
The intermixture of caste is born.

adharmābhibhavāt (m. abl. sg.), from overpowering by lawlessness, because of the ascendancy of lawlessness (*adharma*, lawlessness; *abhibhavāt*, from over-powering).
kṛṣṇa, (m. voc. sg.), Krishna.
praduṣyanti (3rd pl. pr. indic. act. *pra* √*duṣ*), they become spoiled, they are corrupted.
kula (n.), family.
striyas (f. nom. pl.), women.
(*kula-striyas*, f. nom. pl., women of the family.)
strīṣu (f. loc. pl.), in women.
duṣṭāsu (f. loc. pl. p. pass. participle √*duṣ*), corrupted, spoiled.
(*striṣu duṣṭāsu*, loc. absol., when women are corrupted.)
vārṣṇeya (m. voc. sg.), Clansman of Vṛṣṇi, frequent epithet of Krishna. Vṛṣṇi ("potent," "manly") is a name of the Yādava or Mādhava tribe, or another closely related tribe, to which Krishna belongs.
jāyate (3rd sg. pr. indic. passive √*jan*), it is born, it is produced.
varṇa (m.), caste, color.
saṁkaras (m. nom. sg. from *sam* √*kṝ*), intermixture, pouring together, becoming confused.
(*varṇa-saṁkaras*, m. nom. sg. TP cpd., intermixture of caste.)

42

संकरो नरकायैव
saṁkaro narakāyāiva
intermixture to hell

कुलघ्नानां कुलस्य च ।
kulaghnānāṁ kulasya ca
of the family destroyers and of the family

पतन्ति पितरो ह्येषां
patanti pitaro hyeṣāṁ
they fall, the ancestors indeed of these

लुप्तपिण्डोदकक्रियाः ॥
luptapiṇḍodakakriyāḥ
deprived of offerings of rice and water

Intermixture is to hell
For the family destroyers and for the family, too;
The ancestors of these indeed fall,
Deprived of rites of rice and water.

saṁkaras (m. nom. sg. from *sam* √*kṛ*), intermixture, pouring together.
narakāya (m. dat. sg.), to hell.
eva, indeed (used as a rhythmic filler).
kula (n.) family.
ghnānām (m. g. pl.), destroyers (ghna from √*han*).
(*kulāghānām*, m. g. pl., TP cpd., of family destroyers.)
kulasya (n. gen. sg.), of the family.
ca, and.
patanti (3rd pl. pr. act. indic. √*pat*), they fall.
pitaras (m. nom. pl.), the fathers, the ancestors, the manes.
hi, indeed, truly.
eṣām (m. gen. pl.), of these.
lupta (m. p. pass. participle √*lup*), deprived, robbed, plundered.
piṇḍa (m.), ball, cake, lump, mouthful of rice (offered to ancestors).
udaka (n.), water.
kriyās (f. nom. pl.), rites, offerings.
(*luptapiṇḍodakakriyās*, m. nom. pl., DV cpd. deprived of offerings of balls of rice, and water.)

43

दोषैर् एतैः कुलघ्नानां
doṣāir etāiḥ kulaghnānāṁ
by wrongs these of the family destroyers

वर्णसंकरकारकैः ।
varṇasaṁkarakārakāiḥ
by intermixture of caste producing,

उत्साद्यन्ते जातिधर्माः
utsādyante jātidharmāḥ
they are abolished, caste duties,

कुलधर्माश्च शाश्वताः ॥
kuladharmāś ca śāśvatāḥ
and family laws eternal

By these wrongs of the family destroyers,
Producing intermixture of caste,
Caste duties are abolished,
And eternal family laws also.

doṣāis (m. inst. pl.), by wrongs, by sins, by evils.
etāis (m. inst. pl.), by these.
kulaghnānām (m. gen. pl.), of the family destroyers.
varṇa (m.), caste, color.
saṁkara (m. from *sam* √*kṝ*), intermixture, pouring together.
kārakāis (m. inst. pl. from √*kṛ*), by producing, by making, by creating.
(*varṇasaṁkarakārakāis*, m. inst. pl. TP cpd., by creating intermixture of caste.)
utsādyante (3rd pl. pr. indic. passive causative *ud* √*sad*), they are withdrawn, they leave off, they disappear, they are obliterated, they are abolished.
jāti (f.), birth, caste, race, lineage.
dharmās (m. nom. pl.), duties, laws, rights.
(*jāti-dharmās*, m. nom. pl. TP cpd., laws of caste.)
kuladharmās (m. nom. pl.), family laws, family duties.
ca, and.
śāśvatās (m. nom. pl.), eternal, perpetual, continuing.

44

उत्सन्नकुलधर्माणां
utsannakuladharmāṇāṁ
of obliterated family laws

मनुष्याणां जनार्दन ।
manuṣyāṇāṁ janārdana
of men, O Agitator of Men

नरके ऽनियतं वासो
narake 'niyataṁ vāso
in hell indefinitely dwelling

भवतीत्यनुशुश्रुम ॥
bhavatītyanuśuśruma
it is, thus we have heard repeatedly.

Men whose family laws have been obliterated,
O Agitator of Men (Krishna),
Dwell indefinitely in hell,
Thus we have heard repeatedly.

utsanna (p. pass. participle *ud* √*sad*), obliterated, disappeared, abolished.
kula (n.), family.
dharmāṇām (m. gen. pl.), of laws, of duties.
(*utsannakuladharmāṇām,* m. gen. pl. BV cpd., whose family laws are obliterated.)
manuṣyāṇām (m. gen. pl.), of men, of mankind.
janārdana (m. voc. sg.), Agitator of Men, frequent epithet of Krishna.
narake (m. loc. sg.), in hell.
aniyatam (adv.), uncertainly, indefinitely, irregularly, unrestrictedly, eternally.
vāsas (m. nom. sg. derivative noun √3 *vas*), dwelling.
bhavati (3rd sg. pr. indic. act. √*bhū*), it is, there is.
iti, thus.
anuśuśruma (1st pl. perf. act. *anu* √*śru*), we have heard, we have heard repeatedly.

45

अहो बत महत् पापं
aho bata mahat pāpaṁ
ah! alas! great evil

कर्तुं व्यवसिता वयम् ।
kartuṁ vyavasitā vayam
to do resolved upon we

यद् राज्यसुखलोभेन
yad rājyasukhalobhena
which with greed for royal pleasures

हन्तुं स्वजनम् उद्यताः ॥
hantuṁ svajanam udyatāḥ
to kill own people prepared for.

Aho! Alas! We are resolved
To do a great evil,
Which is to be intent on killing
Our own people, through greed for royal pleasures.

aho, ah!
bata, alas!
mahat (n. acc. sg.), great.
pāpam (m. acc. sg.), evil, wickedness.
kartum (infinitive √*kṛ*), to do, to perpetrate.
vyavasitās (m. nom. pl. p. pass. participle *vi ava* √*so*), determined, resolved, ended, finished.
vayam (nom. sg.), we.
yad (n. acc. sg.), which.
rājya (n.), kingship, royal.
sukha (m. n.), pleasure.
lobhena (m. inst. sg.), with greed, by greed.
(*rājyasukhalobhena,* m. inst. sg. TP cpd., with greed for royal pleasures.)
hantum (infinitive √*han*), to kill, to slay.
svajanam (m. acc. sg.), own people.
udyatās (m. nom. pl. p. pass. participle *ud* √*yam*), eager for, intent on, undertaken, commenced, prepared for.

46

यदि माम् अप्रतीकारम्
yadi mām apratīkāram
if me, unresisting,

अशस्त्रं शस्त्रपाणयः ।
aśastraṁ śastrapāṇayaḥ
unarmed, those whose hands are with weapons

धार्तराष्ट्रा रणे हन्युस्
dhārtarāṣṭrā raṇe hanyus
the Sons of Dhṛtarāṣṭra, in battle they should kill

तन् मे क्षेमतरं भवेत् ॥
tan me kṣemataraṁ bhavet
this to me greater happiness would be.

If the armed Sons of Dhṛtarāṣṭra
Should kill me in battle
While I was unresisting and unarmed,
This would be to me a greater happiness.

yadi, if.
mām (acc. sg.), me.
apratīkāram or *apratikāram* (m. acc. sg. adv. from a *prati* √*kṛ*), unopposing, unresisting, without remedy, without return.
aśastram (n. acc. sg.), unarmed, without weapon.
śastra (m.) weapon
pāṇayaḥ (m. nom. pl.) hand
(*śastrapāṇayas*, m. nom. pl. BV cpd., weapon armed, those armed with weapons, (as BV cpd.) whose hands are with weapons.)
dhārtarāṣṭrās (m. nom. pl.), the Sons of Dhṛtarāṣṭra.
raṇe (m. loc. sg.), in battle, in the joy of battle.
hanyus (3rd pl. optative act. √*han*), they should kill, they may kill, they might kill.
tad (n. nom. sg.), that, this.
me (gen. sg.), to me, of me.
kṣemataram (comparative), greater ease, greater tranquility, greater happiness.
bhavet (3rd sg. optative act. √*bhū*), it would be.

47

एवम् उक्त्वा ऽर्जुन संख्ये
evam uktvā 'rjuna saṁkhye
thus having spoken, Arjuna, in the battle

रथोपस्थ उपाविशत्।
rathopastha upāviśat
upon the chariot seat sat down,

विसृज्य सशरं चापं
visṛjya saśaraṁ cāpaṁ
throwing down both arrow and bow,

शोकसंविग्नमानसः ॥
śokasaṁvignamānasaḥ
with a heart overcome by sorrow.

Thus having spoken, in the battle,
Arjuna sat down upon the seat of the chariot,
Throwing down both arrow and bow,
With a heart overcome by sorrow.

evam, thus, so.
uktvā (gerund √*vac*), speaking, having spoken.
arjunas (m. nom. sg.), Arjuna.
saṁkhye (n. loc. sg.), in the battle, in the challenge, in the conflict.
ratha (m.), chariot, car.
upastha (m.), seat, stool.
(*rathopastha*, *saṁdhi* for *rathopasthe*, m. loc. sg., on the chariot seat.)
upāviśat (3rd sg. imperf. act. *upa ā* √*viś*), he sat down, he settled upon.
visṛjya (gerund *vi* √*sṛj*), throwing down, casting aside.
saśaram (n. acc. sg.), together with arrow.
cāpam (m./n. acc. sg.), bow.
śoka (m.), sorrow, grief.
saṁvigna (p. pass. participle *sam* √*vij*), starting back, recoiling, overcome.
mānasas (m. nom. sg.), mind, heart, spirit.
(*śokasaṁvignamānasas*, m. nom. sg., with a heart overcome by sorrow, as BV cpd., whose heart was overcome by sorrow.)

End of Book I

The Despondency of Arjuna

BOOK II

संजय उवाच ।
saṁjaya uvāca
Saṁjaya spoke:

saṁjayas (m. nom. sg.), *Saṁjaya,* the minister of the blind King Dhṛtarāṣṭra, who is narrating the story.
uvāca (3rd sg. perf. act. √*vac*), he said, he spoke.

1

तं तथा कृपयाविष्टम्
taṁ tathā kṛpayāviṣṭam
to him thus overcome by pity,

अश्रुपूर्णाकुलेक्षणम् ।
aśrupūrṇākulekṣaṇam
whose eyes were filled with tears and downcast,

विषीदन्तम् इदं वाक्यम्
viṣīdantam idaṁ vākyam
despairing, this word

उवाच मधुसूदनः ॥
uvāca madhusūdanaḥ
said the Slayer of Madhu

Saṁjaya spoke:

To him thus overcome by pity, despairing,
Whose eyes were filled with tears and downcast,
The Slayer of Madhu (Krishna)
Spoke this word:

tam (m. acc. sg.), him, to him.
tathā, thus, in this way, also, as well.
kṛpayā (f. inst. sg.), by pity, by sorrow.
aviṣṭam (m. acc. sg. p. pass. participle *a* √*viś*), taken possession of, fallen into, overcome by.
aśru (n.), tear.
pūrṇa (p. pass. participle √*pṛ*), filled with, full of.
ākula (adj.), downcast, disturbed.
īkṣaṇam (n. acc. sg. from √*īkṣ*), eye.
(*aśrupūrṇākulekṣaṇam,* n. acc. sg. BV cpd., whose eyes were filled with tears and downcast.)
viṣīdantam (n. acc. sg. pr. participle *vi* √*sad*), despairing, desponding, dejected.
idam (n. acc. sg.), this.
vākyam (n. acc. sg.), word, speech.
uvāca (3rd sg. perf. act. √*vac*), he said, he spoke.
Madhusūdanas (m. nom. sg.), Slayer of Madhu, epithet of Krishna referring to Vishnu-Krishna's slaying of the demon Madhu.

II

श्रीभगवान् उवाच।
śrībhagavān uvāca
the Blessed Lord spoke:

śrībhagavān (m. nom. sg.), the Blessed Lord, the Blessed One.
uvāca (3rd sg. perf. act. √*vac*), he said, he spoke.

2

कुतस्त्वा कश्मलम् इदं
kutastvā kaśmalam idaṁ
whence of thee timidity this,

विषमे समुपस्थितम्।
viṣame samupasthitam
in danger come,

अनार्यजुष्टम् अस्वर्ग्यम्
anāryajuṣṭam asvargyam
not befitting an Aryan, not leading to heaven,

अकीर्तिकरम् अर्जुन॥
akīrtikaram arjuna
disgrace causing, Arjuna?

The Blessed Lord spoke:
Whence this timidity of thine,
Come to thee in time of danger,
Not acceptable in an Aryan, not leading to heaven,
Causing disgrace, Arjuna?

kutas (interrog.), whence? from where? from whom? wherefore? how?
tvā (acc. sg.), thee, to thee.
kaśmalam (n. acc. sg.), timidity, impurity, faintheartedness.
idam (n. acc. sg.), this.
viṣame (m. n. loc. sg.), in distress, in misfortune, in difficulty, in danger.
samupasthitam (n. acc. sg. participle *sam upa* √*sthā*), approaching, come near to.
anārya (adj.), not honorable, unaryan.
juṣṭam (n. acc. sg.), acceptable, agreeable, welcome.
(*anāryajuṣṭam,* n. acc. sg., not suitable to an Aryan, not acceptable in an Aryan.)
asvargyam (n. acc. sg.), not leading to heaven (*svarga,* heaven).
akīrti (f.), disgrace, infamy.
karam (n. acc. sg.), making, causing.
(akīrti-karam, n. acc. sg. TP cpd., causing disgrace.)
arjuna (m. voc. sg.), Arjuna.

3

क्लैब्यं मा स्म गमः पार्थ
klāibyaṁ mā sma gamaḥ pārtha
cowardice never indeed thou shouldst entertain, Son of Pṛthā

नैतत् त्वय्युपपद्यते ।
nāitat tvayyupapadyate
not this in thee it is suitable,

क्षुद्रं हृदयदौर्बल्यं
kṣudraṁ hṛdayadāurbalyaṁ
base faintheartedness

त्यक्त्वोत्तिष्ठ परंतप ॥
tyaktvottiṣṭha paraṁtapa
abandoning, stand up! Scorcher of the Foe.

Do not become a coward, Son of Pṛthā,
This, in thee, is not suitable.
Abandoning base faint heartedness,
Stand up! Scorcher of the Foe.

klāibyam (n. acc. sg.), cowardice.
mā (prohibitive), not, never.
sma, indeed, in truth.
gamas (2nd sg. aorist subjunctive √*gam*), thou shouldst undergo, thou shouldst partake of, thou shouldst entertain.
(*klāibyam mā gamas,* do not become a coward.)
pārtha (m. voc. sg.), Son of Pṛthā, frequent epithet of Arjuna, referring to his mother Pṛthā or Kuntī.
na, not.
etad (n. nom. sg.), this.
tvayi (loc. sg.), in thee.
upapadyate (3rd sg. pr. indic. mid. *upa* √*pad*), it is suitable, it is possible, it is according to rule.
kṣudram (n. acc. sg.), base, low, despicable.
hṛdaya (n.), heart.
dāurbalyam (n. acc. sg.), lack of strength, weakness, impotence.
(*hṛdayadāurbalyam,* n. acc. sg., faintheartedness.)
tyaktvā (gerund √*tyaj*), abandoning, having abandoned.
uttiṣṭha (2nd sg. imperative act. *ud* √*sthā*), stand up! arise!
paraṁtapa (m. voc. sg.), Scorcher of the Foe.

अर्जुन उवाच
arjuna uvāca
Arjuna spoke:

arjunas (m. nom. sg.), Arjuna.
uvāca (3rd sg. perfect act. √*vac*), he said, he spoke.

4

कथं भीष्मम् अहं संख्ये
kathaṁ bhīṣmam ahaṁ saṁkhye
how Bhīṣma I in battle

द्रोणं च मधुसूदन ।
droṇaṁ ca madhusūdana
and Droṇa, O Slayer of Madhu

इषुभिः प्रतियोत्स्यामि
iṣubhiḥ pratiyotsyāmi
with arrows I shall fight against

पूजार्हावरिसूदन ॥
pūjārhāvarisūdana
the two reverence-worthy, O Slayer of the Foe (Krishna)?

Arjuna spoke:

How can I kill in battle
Bhiṣma and Droṇa, O Slayer of Madhu?
How can I fight with arrows against
These two venerable men, O Slayer of the Foe (Krishna)?

katham (interrog.), how? in what way?
bhīṣmam (m. acc. sg.), Bhīṣma, the old Kāurava warrior, great uncle of Arjuna.
aham (nom. sg.), I.
saṁkhye (n. loc. sg.), in battle, in conflict.
droṇam (m. acc. sg.), Droṇa, a brāhman and Arjuna's teacher, fighting on the Kāurava side.
ca, and.
madhusūdana, (m. voc. sg.), Slayer of Madhu, epithet of Krishna.
iṣubhis (m. inst. pl.), by arrows, with arrows.
pratiyotsyāmi (1st sg. fut. *prati* √*yudh*), I shall fight against, I shall attack.
pūjā (f.), reverence, honor, veneration.
arhāu (m. acc. dual), worthy, deserving.
(*pūjārhāu,* m. acc. dual, two reverence-worthy, two venerable.)
ari (m.), enemy, foe.
sūdana (m. nom. acc. sg.), slayer, slaying.
(*arisūdana,* m. voc. sg. TP cpd., Slayer of the Enemy, epithet of Krishna.)

5*

गुरून् अहत्वा हि महानुभावान्
gurūn ahatvā hi mahānubhāvān
the gurus instead of slaying, indeed, the noble,

श्रेयो भोक्तुं भैक्ष्यमपीह लोके ।
śreyo bhoktuṁ bhāikṣyamapīha loke
preferable to eat the food of mendicancy here on earth

हत्वार्थकामांस् तु गुरूनिहैव
hatvārthakāmāṅs tu gurūn ihāiva
having slain, with desire for gain indeed, the gurus here on earth,

भुञ्जीय भोगान् रुधिरप्रदिग्धान् ॥
bhuñjīya bhogān rudhirapradigdhān
I should enjoy enjoyments smeared with blood

Indeed, instead of slaying these noble gurus
It would be preferable to eat the food of beggars here on earth;
Having slain the gurus, with desire for worldly gain,
I should enjoy here on earth enjoyments smeared with blood.

gurūn (m. acc. pl.), elders, gurus, teachers.
ahatvā (gerund *a* √*han*), not slaying, instead of slaying.
hi, indeed, in truth.
mahānubhāvān (m. acc. pl.), of great might, mighty, high-minded, noble, generous.
śreyas (comparative), better, preferable.
bhoktum (infinitive √*bhuj*), to eat, to enjoy.
bhāikṣyam (n. acc. sg.), living on alms, begging, mendicancy.
api, even, also.
iha, here, here in the world, here below.
loke (m. loc. sg.), on earth.
hatvā (gerund √*han*), having slain, slaying.
artha (m.), gains, property, booty, object.
kāmān (m. acc. pl.), desires, greed.
(*arthakāmān*, m. acc. pl. BV cpd., desirous of gain.)
tu, indeed, but.
gurūn (m. acc. pl.), elders, gurus, teachers.
iha, here on earth, here in the world.
eva, indeed (used as a rhythmic filler).
bhuñjīya (1st sg. opt. mid. √*bhuj*), I should enjoy, I should eat.
bhogān (m. acc. pl.), enjoyments, pleasures.
rudhira (adj.), red, bloody.
pradigdhān (m. acc. pl. from *pra* √*dih*), smeared, covered.
(*rudhirapradigdhān*, m. acc. pl. TP cpd. from *pra* √*dih*, smeared with blood.)

* This and the next three stanzas are in *triṣṭubh* metre, otherwise known as the kṣatriya metre, eleven syllables to the line. This differs from the *śloka* metre (eight syllables per line) used in most of the poem.

6

न चैतद् विद्मः कतरन् नो गरीयो
*na cāitad vidmaḥ kataran no garīyo**
not and this we know, which for us (is) preferable

यद् वा जयेम यदि वा नो जयेयुः ।
yad vā jayema yadi vā no jayeyuḥ
whether we should conquer, or if us they should conquer

यान् एव हत्वा न जिजीविषामस्
yān eva hatvā na jijīviṣāmas
whom having killed, not we desire to live,

ते ऽवस्थिताः प्रमुखे धार्तराष्ट्राः
te 'vasthitāḥ pramukhe dhārtarāṣṭrāḥ
they standing before us, the Sons of Dhṛtarāṣṭra

And this we do not know: which for us is preferable,
Whether we should conquer them or they should conquer us,
Those whom, having killed, we should not desire to live
Those standing before us, the Sons of Dhṛtarāṣṭra.

na, not.
ca, and.
etad (n. acc. sg.), this.
vidmas (1st pl. pr. indic. act. √*vid*), we know.
katarat (n. acc. dual), which of two?
nas (dat. pl.), of us, to us, for us.
garīyas (comparative), heavier, more precious, more important, preferable.
yad vā, whether, if, if either.
jayema (1st pl. opt. act. √*ji*), we should conquer, we should prevail.
yadi, if.
vā, or.
nas (acc. pl.), us.
jayeyus (3rd pl. opt. act. √*ji*), they should conquer, they should be victorious over.
yān (m. acc. pl.), whom.
eva, indeed (used as a rhythmic filler).
hatvā (gerund √*han*), killing, having killed.
na, not.
jijīviṣāmas (1st pl. desiderative act. √*jīv*), we desire to live.
te (m. nom. pl.), they.
avasthitās (m. nom. pl. p. pass. participle *ava* √*sthā*), standing, arrayed in battle order, arrayed.
pramukhe (n. loc. sg.), face to face, before us.
Dhārtarāṣṭrās (m. nom. pl.), the Sons of Dhṛtarāṣṭra.

* The first two lines of this stanza contain an extra syllable apiece – not uncommon in ***triṣṭubh*** metre.

7

कार्पण्यदोषोपहतस्वभावः
kārpaṇyadoṣopahatasvabhāvaḥ
pity-weakness-overcome own being

पृच्छामि त्वां धर्मसंमूढचेताः ।
pṛcchāmi tvāṁ dharmasaṁmūḍhacetāḥ
I ask thee, duty uncertain in thought,

यच्छ्रेयः स्यान् निश्चितं ब्रूहि तन् मे
yacchreyaḥ syān niścitaṁ brūhi tan me
which preferably should it be for certain?
Tell that to me,

शिष्यस् ते ऽहं शाधि मां त्वां प्रपन्नम् ॥
śiṣyas te 'haṁ śādhi māṁ tvāṁ prapannam
pupil of thee, I, correct me, thy suppliant.

With my own being overcome by pity-weakness,
I, whose mind is confused as to my duty, ask thee
Which should be preferable, for certain?
Tell that to me, thy pupil. Correct me, thy suppliant.

kārpaṇya (n.), poorness of spirit, pity.
doṣa (m.), wrong, weakness, sin.
upahata (p. pass. participle *upa* √*han*), damaged, afflicted, overcome, discour-aged.
svabhavas (nom. sg.), own being.
(*kārpaṇyadoṣopahatasvabhāvas,* nom. sg. BV cpd., whose own being was overcome by the weakness of pity.)
pṛcchāmi (1st sg. pr. indic. act. √*prach*), I ask, I pray.
tvām (acc. sg.), thee, to thee.
dharma (m.), duty, right, law.
saṁmūḍha (p. pass. participle *sam* √*muh*), uncertain, confused, bewildered, crazed.
cetās (n. nom. sg.), thoughts, heart, mind.
(*dharmasaṁmūḍhacetās,* n. nom. sg. BV cpd., whose mind is confused as to duty.)
yad (n. nom. sg.), which, what.
śreyas (comparative), better, preferable.
syāt (3rd sg. optative √*as*), it should be.
niścitam (adv.), for certain, without doubt, surely.
brūhi (2nd sg. imperative act. √*brū*), say! tell!
tad (n. acc. sg.), this, that.
me (dat. sg.), to me.
śiṣyas (m. nom. sg.), pupil, student.
te (gen. sg.), of thee.
aham (nom. sg.), I.
śādhi (2nd sg. imperative act. √*śādh*), correct! order!
mām (acc. sg.), me.
tvām (acc. sg.), thee, of thee.
prapannam (acc. sg. p. pass. participle *pra* √*pad*), fallen before the feet, suppliant.

8

न हि प्रपश्यामि ममापनुद्याद्
na hi prapaśyāmi mamāpanudyād
not indeed I perceive of me it should dispel

यच्छोकम् उच्छोषणम् इन्द्रियाणाम् ।
yacchokam ucchoṣaṇam indriyāṇām
what, the sorrow, drying up of the senses,

अवाप्य भूमावसपत्नमृद्धं
avāpya bhūmāvasapatnaṁ ṛddhaṁ
(even) having obtained on earth unrivaled prosperous

राज्यं सुराणाम् अपि चाधिपत्यम् ॥
rājyaṁ surāṇām api cādhipatyam
royal power, or of the gods even, the sovereignty."

Indeed, I do not see what should dispel
This sorrow of mine which dries up the senses,
Though I should obtain on earth unrivaled and
Prosperous royal power, or even the sovereignty of the gods.

na, not.
hi, indeed, truly.
prapaśyāmi (1st sg. pr. indic. act. *pra* √*paś*), I see, I perceive.
mama (gen. sg.), of me.
apanudyāt (3rd sg. optative act. *apa* √*nud*), it should remove, it should take away, it should dispel.
yad (n. acc. sg.), what, which.
śokam (m. acc. sg.), sorrow.
ucchoṣaṇam (m. acc. sg. from *ud* √*śuṣ*), drying up.
indriyāṇām (m. gen. pl.), of the powers, of the senses.
avāpya (gerund *ava* √*āp*), obtaining, attaining, having obtained, having attained.
bhūmāu (f. loc. sg.), on earth, in the world.
asapatnam (n. acc. sg.), not with a rival, unrivaled.
ṛddham (n. acc. sg.), prosperous.
rājyam (n. acc. sg.), royal power, dominion, kingship.
surāṇām (m. gen. pl.), of the gods.
api ca, or even, and even.
ādhipatyam (m. acc. sg.), sovereignty, rulership.

संजय उवाच ।
saṁjaya uvāca
Saṁjaya spoke:

saṁjayas (nom. sg.), Saṁjaya, the narrator, minister to the blind king Dhṛtarāṣṭra, to whom the battle of Kurukṣetra is being described.
uvāca (3rd sg. perfect act. √*vac*), he said, he spoke.

9

एवम् उक्त्वा हृषीकेशं
evam uktvā hṛṣīkeśaṁ*
thus having addressed the Bristling Haired One,

गुडाकेशः परंतप ।
guḍākeśaḥ† *paraṁtapa*
The Thick Haired One, O Scorcher of the Foe,

न योत्स्य इति गोविन्दम्
na yotsya iti govindam
"not I shall fight," thus to the Chief of Cowherds

उक्त्वा तूष्णीं बभूव ह ॥
uktvā tūṣṇīṁ babhūva ha
having spoken, silent he became in truth.

evam, thus.
uktvā (gerund √*vac*), saying, having said, having addressed.
hṛṣīkeśam (m. acc. sg.), the Bristling Haired One, frequent epithet of Krishna.
guḍākeśas (m. nom. sg.), the Thick Haired One, epithet of Arjuna.
paraṁtapa (m. voc. sg.), O Scorcher of the Foe, epithet of warriors (here applied to King Dhṛtarāṣṭra).
na, not.
yotsye (1st sg. pr. future mid. √*yudh*), I will fight, I shall fight. (Saṁdhi changes final vowel from e to a before a vowel.)
iti, thus, often used to close a quotation.
govindam (m. acc. sg.), the Chief Cowherd, to the Chief of Cowherds, lit. "Cow Finder," epithet of Krishna.
uktvā (gerund √*vac*), speaking, having spoken.
tūṣṇīm (adv.), silently.
babhūva (3rd sg. perf. act. √*bhū*), he was, he became.
ha (asseverative particle), indeed, in truth.

Saṁjaya spoke:
Thus having addressed the Bristling Haired One (Krishna)
The Thick Haired One (Arjuna), O Scorcher of the Foe,
Said "I shall not fight" thus to the Chief of Cowherds (Krishna),
And having spoken, he became silent.

* *Śloka* metre resumes.

† *guḍākeśa* has been translated by some native translators as *guḍāka īśa*, "Conqueror of Sleep." It is generally believed that *guḍāka*, "sleep," is an artificial word, invented to explain *guḍākeśa*, and not the other way around.

10

तम् उवाच हृषीकेशः
tam uvāca hṛṣīkeśaḥ
to him spoke the Bristling Haired One

प्रहसन्न् इव भारत।
prahasann iva bhārata
beginning to laugh, so to speak, O Descendant of Bharata,

सेनयोर् उभयोर् मध्ये
senayor ubhayor madhye
of armies of both in the middle,

विषीदन्तम् इदं वचः ॥
viṣīdantam idaṁ vacaḥ
dejected, this word:

To him, the dejected one, the Bristling Haired One (Krishna)
Beginning to laugh, so to speak, O Descendant of Bharata,
In the middle, between the two armies,
Spoke this word:

tam (m. acc. sg.), him, to him.
uvāca (3rd sg. perf. acc. √*vac*), he spoke, he said.
hṛṣīkeśas (m. nom. sg.), the Bristling Haired One, Krishna.
prahasant (m. nom. sg. pr. participle *pra* √*has*), smiling, laughing, beginning to laugh.
iva, like, so to speak.
bhārata (m. voc. sg.), O Descendant of Bharata, epithet here of Dhṛtarāṣṭra, the king to whom the scene is being described.
senayos (f. gen. dual), of the two armies.
ubhayos (f. gen. dual), of both.
madhye (m. loc. sg.), in the middle.
viṣīdantam (m. acc. sg. pr. participle *vi* √*sad*), dejected, despondent, sunk down.
idam (n. acc. sg.), this.
vacas (n. acc. sg.), word, speech.

II

श्रीभगवान् उवाच ।
śrībhagavān uvāca
The Blessed Lord spoke:

śrībhagavān (m. nom. sg.), the Blessed Lord, the Blessed One.
uvāca (3rd sg. perf. act. √*vac*), he spoke, he said.

11

अशोच्यान् अन्वशोचस् त्वं
aśocyān anvaśocas tvaṁ
the not to be mourned, thou hast mourned, thou,

प्रज्ञावादांश्च भाषसे ।
prajñāvādāṅś ca bhāṣase
and (yet) wisdom words thou speakest;

गतासून् अगतासूंश्च
gatāsūn agatāsūṅś ca
the dead and the not dead

नानुशोचन्ति पण्डिताः ॥
nānuśocanti paṇḍitāḥ
not they mourn, the paṇḍits

The Blessed Lord spoke:

Thou hast mourned the not-to-be-mourned
And yet thou speakest words as if with wisdom;
For the dead and for the not dead
The paṇḍits do not mourn.

aśocyān (m. acc. pl. gerundive *a* √*śuc*), not to be lamented, not to be mourned.
anvaśocas (*anu a śocas,* 2nd sg. imperfect act. *anu* √*śuc*), thou hast lamented, thou hast mourned.
tvam (nom. sg.), thou.
prajñā (f.), wisdom.
vādān (m. acc. pl.), words.
(*prajñāvādān,* m. acc. pl., wisdom words, i.e. words that appear to be wisdom though they are not.) TP cpd.
ca, and.
bhāṣase (2nd sg. mid. √*bhāṣ*), thou speakest, thou sayest.
gatāsūn (m. acc. pl.), the gone, the dead (from *gata*, gone, *asu*, breath). BV cpd.
agatāsūn (m. acc. pl.), the not gone, the not dead. BV cpd.
ca, and.
na, not.
anuśocanti (3rd pl. pr. indic. act. *anu* √*śuc*), they mourn, they lament.
paṇḍitās (m. nom. pl.), the paṇḍits, the wise men.

12

न त्वेवाहं जातु नासं
na tvevāhaṁ jātu nāsaṁ
not truly I ever not I was

न त्वं नेमे जनाधिपाः ।
na tvaṁ neme janādhipāḥ
nor thou nor these lords of men

न चैव न भविष्यामः
na cāiva na bhaviṣyāmaḥ
and not either *not* we shall be

सर्वे वयम् अतः परम् ॥
sarve vayam ataḥ param
all we from this time onward.

Truly there was never a time when I was not,
Nor thou, nor these lords of men;
And neither will there be a time when we shall cease to be;
All of us exist from this time onward.

na, not.
tu, truly, indeed.
eva, indeed (used as a rhythmic filler).
aham (nom. sg.), I.
jātu, ever.
na, not.
āsam (1st sg. imperf. act. √*as*), I was, I existed.
na, not, nor.
tvam (nom. sg.), thou.
na, not, nor.
ime (m. nom. pl.), these.
janādhipās (m. nom. pl.), lords of men, rulers of men. TP cpd.
na, not, nor.
ca, and, or.
eva, either, indeed (often used as a rhythmic filler).
na, not.
bhaviṣyāmas (3rd pl. fut. act. √*bhū*), we shall be, we shall exist.
sarve (m. nom. pl.), all.
vayam (nom. pl.), we.
atas, from here.
param (adj. acc. sg.), beyond, after.
(*ataḥ param,* henceforth, further on, from this time onward.)

13

देहिनो ऽस्मिन् यथा देहे
dehino 'smin yathā dehe
of the embodied, as in this body,

कौमारं यौवनं जरा ।
kāumāraṁ yāuvanaṁ jarā
childhood, youth and age,

तथा देहान्तरप्राप्तिर्
tathā dehāntaraprāptir
so also acquisition of another body.

धीरस् तत्र न मुह्यति ॥
dhīras tatra na muhyati
the wise one in this not he is deluded.

Just as in the body childhood, adulthood and senescence
Happen to the embodied one,*
So also it (the embodied one) acquires another body.
The wise one, in this, is not deluded.

dehinas (m. gen. sg.), of the embodied,* i.e. the *ātman* or soul.
asmin (m. loc. sg.), in this.
yathā, in which way, as.
dehe (m./n. loc. sg.), in the body.
kāumāram (n. nom. sg.), childhood.
yāuvanam (m. nom. sg.), youth.
jarā (f. nom. sg.), age, old age.
tathā, in this way, so, so also.
deha (m./n.), body.
antara, other, another.
prāptis (f. nom. sg. from *pra* √*āp*), acquisition, attainment, obtaining, advent, reaching, arrival at.
(*deha-antara-prāptis*, TP cpd., obtaining another body.)
dhīras (m. nom. sg.),, wise one, wise man.
tatra, there, in that, in this, in this matter.
na, not.
muhyati (3rd sg. pr. indic. act. √*muh*), he is deluded, he is confused.

* The embodied, i.e. that which is in, but not of, the body, viz. the ātman, or self.

14

मात्रास्पर्शास् तु कौन्तेय
mātrāsparśās tu kāunteya
material sensations, truly, O Son of Kuntī,

शीतोष्णसुखदुःखदाः ।
śītoṣṇasukhaduḥkhadāḥ
cold heat pleasure pain causing,

आगमापायिनो ऽनित्यास्
āgamāpāyino 'nityās
coming and going, impermanent,

तांस् तितिक्षस्व भारत ॥
tāṅs titikṣasva bhārata
them thou must endeavor to endure, Descendant of Bharata.

Material sensations, truly, Son of Kuntī
Causing cold, heat, pleasure or pain,
Come and go and are impermanent.
Do manage to endure them, Descendant of Bharata (Arjuna).

mātrā (f.), material, measure, quantity.
sparśās (m. nom. pl. derivative noun from √*spṛś*), touchings, sensations.
(*mātrā-sparśās,* m. nom. pl. KD cpd., material sensations.)
tu, indeed, truly, but.
kāunteya (voc.), O Son of Kuntī, epithet of Arjuna, referring to his mother Pṛthā or Kuntī.
śīta (n.), cold.
uṣṇa (n.), heat.
sukha (n.), pleasure, happiness.
duḥkha (n.), pain, misfortune.
dās (m. nom. pl. suffix), causing, bringing about.
āgama (from *ā* √*gam*), coming.
apāyinas (m. nom. pl. from *apa* √*i*), going.
anityās (m. nom. sg.), impermanent, transient, not eternal.
tān (m. acc. pl.), them.
titikṣasva (2nd sg. imperative mid. desiderative √*tij*), thou must endeavor to endure, do manage to endure!
bhārata (m. voc. sg.), Descendant of Bharata, epithet of Arjuna.

15

यं हि न व्यथयन्त्येते
yaṁ hi na vyathayantyete
whom indeed not they afflict these

पुरुषं पुरुषर्षभ ।
puruṣaṁ puruṣarṣabha
the man, O Man-Bull,

समदुःखसुखं धीरं
samaduḥkhasukhaṁ dhīraṁ
constant in pain and pleasure, the wise one,

सो ऽमृतत्वाय कल्पते ॥
so 'mṛtatvāya kalpate
he for immortality is ready.

Indeed, the man whom these (i.e. the sensations) do not afflict,
O Bull among Men,
The wise one, to whom happiness and unhappiness are the same,
Is ready for immortality.

yam (m. acc. sg.), whom.
hi, indeed, truly.
na, not.
vyathayanti (3rd pl. causative act. √*vyath*), they cause to tremble, they afflict.
ete (m. nom. pl.), these.
puruṣam (m. acc. sg.), man, spirit.
puruṣarṣabha (m. voc. sg.) (*purṣa ṛṣabha*), O Man-Bull, O Bull among Men, O Leader among Men. BV cpd.
sama, the same, equal, constant.
duḥkha (n.), pain, misfortune.
sukham (n. nom. acc. sg.), pleasure, happiness.
(*samaduḥkhasukham,* m. acc. sg. BV cpd., to whom pain and pleasure are alike.)
dhīram (m. acc. sg.), wise, wise one, wise man.
sas (m. nom. sg.), he, this.
amṛtatvāya (n. dat. sg.), to immortality, for immortality.
kalpate (3rd sg. pr. indic. mid. √*klp*), he is ready, he is prepared, he is fit, he is adapted.

16

नासतो विद्यते भावो
nāsato vidyate bhāvo
not of the non-existent, there is found coming to be,

नाभावो विद्यते सतः ।
nābhāvo vidyate sataḥ
in the *not* non-existent, there is found the real;

उभयोर् अपि दृष्टो ऽन्तस्
ubhayor api dṛṣṭo 'ntas
of both surely perceived the certainty

त्वनयोस्तत्त्वदर्शिभिः ।।
tvanayor tattvadarśibhiḥ
of these two by the truth perceivers.

It is found that there is no coming to be of the non-existent;
It is found that the *not* non-existent constitutes the real.
The certainty of both these propositions is indeed surely seen.
By the perceivers of truth.

na, not.
asatas (n. gen. sg. pr. participle *a* √*as*), of the nonexistent, of the not real.
vidyate (3rd sg. pr. indic. pass. √2 *vid*), it is found.
bhāvas (m. nom. sg.), being, coming to be, becoming.
na, not.
abhāvas (m. nom. sg.), not being, not existing, not becoming.
vidyate (3rd sg. pr. indic. pass. √2 *vid*), it is found.
satas (n. gen. sg. pr. participle √*as*), of the real, of the true, of the existent.
ubhayos (m. gen. dual), of both.
api, indeed, surely, also, even.
dṛṣṭas (n. nom. sg. p. pass. participle √*dṛś*), seen, perceived, discerned.
antas (m. nom. sg.), certainty, conclusion, end.
tu, indeed, but.
anayos (m. gen. dual), of these two.
tattva (n.), truth, reality, "thatness."
darśibhis (m. inst. pl. from √*dṛś* TP cpd.), by the seers, by the perceivers, by the discerners, by the knowers.

17

अविनाशि तु तद् विद्धि
avināśi tu tad viddhi
indestructible indeed that, know!

येन सर्वम् इदं ततम् ।
yena sarvam idaṁ tatam
by which all this universe pervaded

विनाशम् अव्ययस्यास्य
vināśam avyayasyāsya
destruction of the imperishable, of this,

न कश्चित् कर्तुम् अर्हति ॥
na kaścit kartum arhati
not anyone to accomplish is capable.

Know that that by which all this universe
Is pervaded is indeed indestructible;
No one is able to accomplish
The destruction of this imperishable.*

avināśi (n. acc. sg. from *a vi* √*naś*), indestructible, not to be lost.
tu, indeed, but.
tad (n. acc. sg.), this, that.
viddhi (2nd sg. imperative act. √*vid*), know! learn!
yena (n. inst. sg.), by which.
sarvam idam (n. acc. sg.), all this, used in the meaning of "all this visible universe."
tatam (n. acc. sg. p. pass. participle √*tan*), extended, diffused, pervaded.
vināśam (m. acc. sg. from *vi* √*naś*), destruction, loss.
avyayasya (n. gen. sg.), of the imperishable, of the eternal.
asya (n. gen. sg.), of it, of this.
na, not.
kaścid, anyone, anyone whoever.
kartum (infinitive √*kṛ*), to do, to make, to accomplish.
arhati (3rd sg. pr. indic. acc. √*arh*), he is worthy, he is able, he is capable.

* I.e. the *ātman* (self) or *Brahman.*

18

अन्तवन्त इमे देहा
antavanta ime dehā
having an end these bodies

नित्यस्योक्ताः शरीरिणः ।
nityasyoktāḥ śarīriṇaḥ
of the eternal, said, of the embodied,

अनाशिनो ऽप्रमेयस्य
anāśino 'prameyasya
of the indestructible, of the immeasurable.

तस्माद् युध्यस्व भारत ॥
tasmād yudhyasva bhārata
therefore fight, Descendant of Bharata!

These bodies inhabited by the eternal,
The indestructible, the immeasurable embodied one,*
Are said to come to an end.
Therefore fight, Descendant of Bharata (Arjuna)!

antavantas (m. nom. pl.), having an end, impermanent.
ime (m. nom. pl.), these.
dehās (m. nom. pl.), bodies.
nityasya (m. gen. sg.), of the eternal, of the undying.
uktās (m. nom. pl. p. pass. participle √*vac*), said, declared.
śarīriṇas (m. gen. sg.), of the embodied, of the soul, of the *ātman*.
anāśinas (m. gen. sg. derivative noun *a* √*naś*), of the indestructible, of the not lost.
aprameyasya (m. gen. sg. derivative noun from *a pra* √*mā*), of the not to be measured, of the immeasurable.
tasmāt (m. abl. sg.), from that, therefore.
yudhyasva (2nd sg. imperative mid. √*yudh*), fight! join in battle!
bhārata (m. voc. sg.), Descendant of Bharata, epithet of Arjuna.

* I.e. the *ātman* or *Brahman*.

19

य एनं वेत्ति हन्तारं
ya enaṁ vetti hantāraṁ
who this he thinks the slayer

यश्चैनं मन्यते हतम् ।
yaścāinaṁ manyate hatam
and who this he thinks slain

उभौ तौ न विजानीतो
ubhāu tāu na vijānīto
both they two not they understand

नायं हन्ति न हन्यते ॥
nāyaṁ hanti na hanyate
not this it slays, not it is slain.

He who imagines this (the embodied one) the slayer
And he who imagines this (the embodied one) the slain,
Neither of them understands;
This (the embodied one) does not slay, nor is it slain.

yas (m. nom. sg.), who.
enam (m. acc. sg.), this.
vetti (3rd sg. pr. indic. act. √*vid*), he thinks, he knows, he imagines.
hantāram (m. acc. sg. derivative noun from √*han*), slayer, killer.
yas (m. nom. sg.), who, which.
ca, and.
enam (m. acc. sg.), this.
manyate (3rd sg. pr. indic. mid. √*man*), he thinks, he imagines.
hatam (m. acc. sg. p. pass. participle √*han*), slain, killed.
ubhāu (m. nom. dual), both.
tāu (m. nom. dual), they two.
na, not.
vijānītas (3rd dual pr. indic. mid. *vi* √*jñā*), they two know, they two understand.
na, not.
ayam (m. nom. sg.), this.
hanti (3rd sg. pr. indic. act. √*han*), he slays, he kills.
na, not.
hanyate (3rd sg. pr. indic. pass. √*han*), he is slain, he is killed.

20

न जायते म्रियते वा कदाचिन्
na jāyate mriyate vā kadācin
not it is born, dies neither at any time

नायं भूत्वा भविता वा न भूयः।
nāyaṁ bhūtvā bhavitā vā na bhūyaḥ
nor this, having been, will come to be or not again;

अजो नित्यः शाश्वतो ऽयं पुराणो
ajo nityaḥ śāśvato 'yaṁ purāṇo
unborn, eternal, perpetual this, primaeval,

न हन्यते हन्यमाने शरीरे ॥
*na hanyate hanyamāne śarīre**
not it is slain in being slain in the body

Neither is this (the embodied one) born nor does it die at any time,
Nor, having been, will it again come not to be.
Birthless, eternal, perpetual, primaeval,
It is not slain when the body is slain.

na, not.
jāyate (3rd sg. pr. pass. √*jan*), he is born.
mriyate (3rd sg. pr. pass. √*mṛ*), he dies, he is dead.
vā-vā, either-or.
kadācit, at any time, at any time whatever.
na, not.
ayam (m. nom. sg.), this.
bhūtvā (gerund √*bhū*), being, having been.
bhavitā (3rd sg. periphrastic fut. √*bhū*), he, it will be, he, it will become.
na, not.
bhūyas (m. nom. sg.), again.
ajas (m. nom. sg. √*jan*), unborn, birthless.
nityas (m. nom. sg.), eternal, indestructible.
śāśvatas (m. nom. sg.), perpetual, continuing.
ayam (m. nom. sg.), this.
purāṇas (m. nom. sg.), primaeval, from former time, primordial.
na, not.
hanyate (3rd sg. pr. indic. pass. √*han*), it is slain, it is killed, he is slain.
hanyamāne (m. loc. sg. pr. mid. participle √*han*), in being slain, in being killed.
śarīre (m. loc. sg.), in the body.

* *Triṣṭubh* metre.

21

वेदाविनाशिनं नित्यं
vedāvināśinaṁ nityaṁ
he knows, the indestructible, the eternal,

य एनम् अजम् अव्ययम् ।
ya enam ajam avyayam
who this, the unborn the imperishable,

कथं स पुरुषः पार्थ
kathaṁ sa puruṣaḥ pārtha
in what way this man, Son of Pṛthā,

कं घातयति हन्ति कम् ॥
*kaṁ ghātayati hanti kam**
whom he causes to slay? he slays whom?

He who knows this, the indestructible, the eternal,
The birthless, the imperishable,
In what way, this man, Son of Pṛthā (Arjuna),
Whom does he cause to slay? He slays whom?

veda (3rd sg. perf. act. √*vid*, with present meaning), he knows.
avināśinam (n. acc. sg. from *a vi* √*naś*), indestructible, not subject to loss.
nityam (n. acc. sg.), eternal.
yas (m. nom. sg.), who.
enam (m. acc. sg.), this.
ajam (n. nom. acc. sg.), unborn, birthless.
avyayam (n. acc. sg.), imperishable.
katham (interrog.), how? in what way?
sas (m. nom. sg.), this, the, he.
puruṣas (m. nom. sg.), man.
pārtha (m. voc. sg.), O Son of Pṛthā, epithet of Arjuna referring to his mother Pṛthā.
kam (m. acc. sg. interrog.), whom? which?
ghātayati (3rd sg. causative act. √*han*), he causes to slay.
hanti (3rd sg. pr. indic. act. √*han*), he slays.
kam (m. acc. sg. interrog.), whom?

* *Śloka* metre resumes.

22

वासांसि जीर्णानि यथा विहाय
vāsāṁsi jīrṇāni yathā vihāya
garments worn out as casting away,

नवानि गृह्णाति नरो ऽपराणि ।
navāni gṛhṇāti naro 'parāṇi
new he takes, a man, others

तथा शरीराणि विहाय जीर्णान्य्
tathā śarīrāṇi vihāya jīrṇāny
so bodies casting away, worn out,

अन्यानि संयाति नवानि देही ॥
*anyāni saṁyāti navāni dehī**
others it encounters, new, the embodied one.

vāsāṁsi (n. acc. pl.), garments, clothes.
jīrṇāni (n. acc. pl.), worn out, old.
yathā, in which way, as.
vihāya (gerund *vi* √*hā*), abandoning, casting away.
navāni (n. acc. pl.), new.
gṛhṇāti (3rd sg. pr. indic. act. √*grabh*), he seizes, he grasps, he takes.
naras (m. nom. sg.), man.
aparāṇi (n. acc. pl.), others.
tathā, in this way, so.
śarīrāṇi (n. acc. pl.), bodies.
vihāya (gerund *vi* √*hā*), abandoning, casting away.
jīrṇāni (n. acc. pl.), worn out, old.
anyāni (n. acc. pl.), others.
saṁyāti (3rd sg. pr. indic. act. *sam* √*yā*), he meets with, he encounters.
navāni (n. acc. pl.), new.
dehī (m. nom. sg.), the embodied, the soul, the *ātman*, the self.

As, after casting away worn out garments,
A man later takes new ones,
So, after casting away worn out bodies,
The embodied one encounters other, new ones.

* *Triṣṭubh* metre.

23

नैनं छिन्दन्ति शस्त्राणि
nāinaṁ chindanti śastrāṇi
not this they pierce, weapons,

नैनं दहति पावकः ।
nāinaṁ dahati pāvakaḥ
not this it burns, fire,

न चैनं क्लेदयन्त्यापो
na cāinaṁ kledayantyāpo
and not this they cause to wet, the waters

न शोषयति मारुतः ॥
*na śoṣayati mārutaḥ**
nor it causes to wither, the wind.

na, not.
enam (m. acc. sg.), this.
chindanti (3rd pl. pr. indic. act. √*chid*), they cut, they pierce, they chop.
śastrāṇi (n. nom. pl.), weapons.
na, not.
enam (m. acc. sg.), this.
dahati (3rd sg. pr. indic. act. √*dah*), it burns.
pāvakas (m. nom. sg.), fire, flame.
na, not.
ca, and.
enam (m. acc. sg.), this.
kledayanti (3rd pl. pr. indic. causative act. √*klid*), they cause to become wet, they wet, they moisten.
āpas (f. nom. pl.), waters, the waters.
na, not, nor.
śoṣayati (3rd sg. pr. indic. causative act. √*śuṣ*), it causes to dry, it causes to wither.
mārutas (m. nom. sg.), wind, the wind.

Weapons do not pierce this (the embodied one),
Fire does not burn this,
And the waters do not wet this,
Nor does the wind cause it to wither.

* *Śloka* metre resumes.

24

अच्छेद्यो ऽयम् अदाह्यो ऽयम्
acchedyo 'yam adāhyo 'yam
not to be pierced, this, not to be burned, this,

अक्लेद्यो ऽशोष्य एव च ।
akledyo 'śoṣya eva ca
not to be wetted and not to be withered,

नित्यः सर्वगतः स्थाणुर्
nityaḥ sarvagataḥ sthāṇur
eternal, all pervading, fixed,

अचलो ऽयं सनातनः ॥
acalo 'yaṁ sanātanaḥ
unmoving, this, primaeval

Not to be pierced, this, not to be burned, this,
Not to be wetted and not to be withered;
This is eternal, all pervading, fixed;
This is unmoving and primaeval.

acchedyas (m. nom. sg. gerundive *a* √*chid*), not to be pierced.
ayam (m. nom. sg.), this.
adāhyas (m. nom. sg. gerundive *a* √*dah*), not to be burned.
ayam (m. nom. sg.), this.
akledyas (m. nom. sg. gerundive *a* √*klid*), not to be wetted.
aśoṣyas (m. nom. sg. gerundive √*śuṣ*), not to be dried.
eva, indeed (used as a rhythmic filler).
ca, and.
nityas (m. nom. sg.), eternal, imperishable.
sarvagatas (m. nom. sg.), "all going," all pervading.
sthāṇus (m. nom. sg.), fixed, standing firmly, immovable.
acalas (m. nom. sg.), unmoving, immovable.
ayam (m. nom. sg.), this.
sanātanas (m. nom. sg.), primaeval, ancient, primordial, eternal.

25

अव्यक्तो ऽयम् अचिन्त्यो ऽयम्
avyakto 'yam acintyo 'yam
unmanifest this, unthinkable this,

अविकार्यो ऽयम् उच्यते ।
avikāryo 'yam ucyate
unchanging this, it is said.

तस्माद् एवं विदित्वैनं
tasmād evaṁ viditvāinaṁ
therefore thus having known this,

नानुशोचितुम् अर्हसि ॥
nānuśocitum arhasi
not to mourn thou shouldst.

Unmanifest, this, unthinkable, this,
Unchanging, this, it is said.
Therefore thus having understood this,*
Thou shouldst not mourn.

avyaktas (m. nom. sg. p. pass. participle *a vi* √*añj*), unmanifest, undisplayed.
ayam (m. nom. sg.), this.
acintyas (m. nom. sg. gerund *a* √*cint*), unthinkable, unimaginable.
ayam (m. nom. sg.), this.
avikāryas (m. nom. sg. gerund *a vi* √*kṛ*), unchanging, invariable.
ayam (m. nom. sg.), this.
ucyate (3rd sg. pr. indic. pass. √*vac*), it is said, it is spoken.
tasmāt (m./n. abl. sg.), from this, therefore.
evam, thus.
viditvā (gerund √*vid*), knowing, having known.
enam (m. acc. sg.), this.
na, not.
anuśocitum (infinitive *anu* √*śuc*), to mourn, to lament.
arhasi (2nd sg. pr. indic. act. √*arh*), thou shouldst, thou art obliged, thou art able, thou art worthy.

* I.e. the foregoing propositions.

26

अथ चैनं नित्यजातं
atha cāinaṁ nityajātaṁ
and moreover (if) this, being eternally born,

नित्यं वा मन्यसे मृतम् ।
nityaṁ vā manyase mṛtam
or eternally, thou thinkest, dead,

तथापि त्वं महाबाहो
tathāpi tvaṁ mahābāho
then even thou, Mighty Armed One,

नैनं शोचितुमर्हसि ॥
nāinaṁ śocitumarhasi
not this to mourn thou shouldst.

And moreover even if thou thinkest this
To be eternally born or eternally dead,
Even then, thou, O Mighty Armed One (Arjuna),
Shouldst not mourn for this.

atha ca, and moreover, and further, and if.
enam (m. acc. sg.), this.
nitya (adj.), eternal, imperishable, eternally.
jātam (m. acc. sg.), born.
(*nityajātam*, KD cpd., eternally born.)
nityam (adv.), eternally.
vā, or.
manyase (2nd sg. pr. indic. mid. √*man*), thou thinkest, thou believest, thou imaginest.
mṛtam (m. acc. p. pass. participle √*mṛ*), dead, dying.
tathāpi (tathā api), then even.
tvam (nom. sg.), thou.
mahābāho (m. voc. sg.), O Mighty Armed One, frequent eipthet of Arjuna, also applied to other warriors.
na, not.
enam, this.
śocitum (infinitive √*śuc*), to mourn, to lament, to be sorrowful.
arhasi (2nd sg. pr. indic. act. √*arh*), thou shouldst, thou art obliged, thou art able, thou art worthy.

27

जातस्य हि ध्रुवो मृत्युर्
jātasya hi dhruvo mṛtyur
of the born indeed certain death

ध्रुवं जन्म मृतस्य च ।
dhruvaṁ janma mṛtasya ca
and certain birth of the dead

तस्मादपरिहार्येऽर्थे
tasmādaparihārye 'rthe
therefore, inevitable in purpose,

न त्वं शोचितुमर्हसि ॥
na tvaṁ śocitumarhasi
not thou, to mourn thou shouldst.

For the born, death is certain;
For the dead there is certainly birth.
Therefore, for this, inevitable in consequence,
Thou shouldst not mourn.

jātsaya (m. gen. sg.), of the born.
hi, indeed, truly.
dhruvas (n. nom. sg.), certain, safe, fixed.
mṛtyus (m. nom. sg.), death.
dhruvam (n. nom. sg.), certain, undoubted.
janma (n. nom. sg.), birth.
mṛtasya (m. gen. sg.), of the dead.
ca, and.
tasmāt (abl. sg.), from this, for this, therefore.
aparihārye (m. loc. sg. gerundive *a pari* √*hṛ*), in unavoidable, in inevitable.
arthe (m. loc. sg.), in purpose, in aim, in consequence.
na, not.
tvam (nom. sg.), thou.
śocitum (infinitive √*śuc*), to mourn, to lament.
arhasi (2nd sg. pr. indic. act. √*arh*), thou shouldst, thou art obliged, thou art able.

28

अव्यक्तादीनि भूतानि
avyaktādīni bhūtāni
unmanifest beginnings, beings,

व्यक्तमध्यानि भारत ।
vyaktamadhyāni bhārata
manifest middles, Descendant of Bharata,

अव्यक्तनिधनान्येव
avyaktanidhanānyeva
unmanifest ends again,

तत्र का परिदेवना ॥
tatra kā paridevanā
over this, what complaint?

Beings are such that their beginnings are unmanifest,
That their middles are manifest,
That their ends are unmanifest again.
What complaint can there be over this?

avyakta (p. pass. participle *a vi* √*añj*), unmanifest.
ādīni (n. nom. pl.), beginnings, commencements.
(*avyaktādīni*, n. nom. pl. BV cpd., such that their beginnings are unmanifest.)
bhūtāni (n. nom. pl.), beings, creatures.
vyakta (p. pass. participle *vi* √*añj*), manifest.
madhyāni (n. nom. pl.), middles.
(*vyaktamadhyāni*, n. nom. pl. BV cpd., such that their middles are manifest.)
bhārata (m. voc. sg.), Descendant of Bharata, epithet of Arjuna.
avyakta (p. pass. participle *a vi* √*añj*), unmanifest.
nidhanāni (n. nom. pl.), ends, deaths.
(*avyaktanidhanāni*, n. nom. acc. pl. BV cpd., such that their ends are unmanifest.)
eva, again, indeed (often used as a rhythmic filler).
tatra, there, over this, about this.
kā (f. nom. sg. interrog.), what?
paridevanā (f. nom. sg.), complaint, lamentation.

29

आश्चर्यवत् पश्यति कश्चिदेनम्
āścaryavat paśyati kaścidenam
wondrously he perceives someone, this,

आश्चर्यवद् वदति तथैव चान्यः ।
āścaryavad vadati tathāiva cānyaḥ
and wondrously he declares indeed another,

आश्चर्यवच्चैनम् अन्यः शृणोति
āścaryavaccāinam anyaḥ śṛṇoti
and wondrously this another he hears,

श्रुत्वाप्येनं वेद न चैव कश्चित् ॥
*śrutvāpyenaṁ veda na cāiva kaścit**
and having heard this, this knows not thus anyone.

Marvellously, someone perceives this;
Marvellously, another declares this;
Marvellously, still another hears of this;
But even having heard of this, no one knows it.†

āścaryavat (adv.), wondrously, full of marvels.
paśyati (3rd sg. pr. indic. act. √*paś*), he perceives, he sees.
kaścid, someone, anyone.
enam (m. acc. sg.), this.
āścaryavat (adv.), wondrously, marvellously.
vadati (3rd sg. pr. indic. act. √*vad*), he says, he tells, he declares.
tathā, thus, indeed.
eva, indeed (used as a rhythmic filler).
ca, and.
anyas (m. nom. sg.), another, other.
āścaryavat (adv.), wondrously, marvellously.
ca, and.
enam (m. acc. sg.), this.
anyas (m. nom. sg.), another, other.
śṛṇoti (3rd sg. pr. indic. act. √*śru*), he hears.
śrutvā (gerund √*śru*), hearing, having heard.
api, even also.
enam (m. acc. sg.), this.
veda (3rd sg. perf. act. √*vid*, with present meaning), he knows.
na, not.
ca, and.
eva, indeed (used as a rhythmic filler).
kaścid, anyone, anything.

* ***Triṣṭubh*** metre with second line one syllable too long.

† This stanza explains the mystical nature of ***Brahman*** and the ***ātman***.

30

देही नित्यं अवध्यो ऽयं
*dehī nityaṁ avadhyo 'yaṁ**
embodied (one) eternally inviolable, this,

देहे सर्वस्य भारत ।
dehe sarvasya bhārata
in the body of all, Descendant of Bharata,

तस्मात् सर्वाणि भूतानि
tasmāt sarvāṇi bhūtāni
therefore all beings

न त्वं शोचितुमर्हसि ॥
na tvaṁ śocitumarhasi
not thou to mourn shouldst.

dehī (m. nom. sg.), the embodied, the soul, the *ātman*.
nityam (adv.), eternally.
avadhyas (m. nom. sg. gerundive *a* √*vadh*), inviolable, not to be harmed.
ayam (m. nom. sg.), this.
dehe (m./n. loc. sg.), in the body.
sarvasya (m. gen. sg.), of all, of anyone, of everyone.
bhārata (m. voc. sg.), Descendant of Bharata, epithet of Arjuna, sometimes applied to other worthies of the tribe.
tasmāt (abl. sg.), from this, therefore.
sarvāṇi (n. acc. pl.), all.
bhūtāni (n. acc. pl.), beings, creatures.
na, not.
tvam (m. nom. sg.), thou.
śocitum (infinitive √*śuc*), to mourn, to lament.
arhasi (2nd sg. pr. indic. act. √*arh*), thou shouldst, thou art able, thou art obliged.

This, the embodied one, is eternally inviolable
In the body of all, Descendant of Bharata.
Therefore thou shouldst not mourn
For any being.

* *Śloka* metre resumes.

31

स्वधर्मम् अपि चावेक्ष्य
svadharmam api cāvekṣya
and own (caste) duty just perceiving,

न विकम्पितुम् अर्हसि ।
na vikampitum arhasi
not to tremble thou shouldst

धर्म्याद् धि युद्धाच्छ्रेयो ऽन्यत्
dharmyād dhi yuddhācchreyo 'nyat
than righteous indeed battle, greater other

क्षत्रियस्य न विद्यते ॥
kṣatriyasya na vidyate
for the kṣatriya not it is found.

And, perceiving just thine own caste duty,
Thou shouldst not tremble.
Indeed, anything superior to righteous battle,
For the kṣatriya (man of the warrior caste), does not exist.

svadharmam (m. acc. sg.), own duty, here "own caste duty" as a *kṣatriya,* or warrior.
api ca, even though, although, just.
avekṣya (gerund *ava* √*īkṣ*), looking at, perceiving, beholding.
na, not.
vikampitum (infinitive *vi* √*kamp*), to tremble, to waver.
arhasi (2nd sg. pr. indic. act. √*arh*), thou shouldst, thou art obliged, thou art able.
dharmyāt (n. abl. sg.), than righteous, than lawful.
dhi = *hi,* indeed, truly.
yuddhāt (n. abl. sg.), than battle, from fighting.
śreyas (comparative), better, preferable.
anyat (n. n. s.), other.
kṣatriyasya (m. gen. sg.), of the *kṣatriya,* of the warrior, of the member of the warrior caste.
na, not.
vidyate (3rd sg. pr. indic. pass. √2 *vid*), it is found.

32

यदृच्छया चोपपन्नं
yadṛcchayā copapannaṁ
and by good fortune gained

स्वर्गद्वारम् अपावृतम् ।
svargadvāram apāvṛtam
the gate of heaven open,

सुखिनः क्षत्रियाः पार्थ
sukhinaḥ kṣatriyāḥ pārtha
happy kṣatriyas, Son of Pṛthā,

लभन्ते युद्धम् ईदृशम् ॥
labhante yuddham īdṛśam
when they encounter battle such

yadṛcchayā (f. inst. sg.), by a lucky chance, by good fortune, by accident.
ca, and.
upapannam (n. acc. sg. p. pass. participle *upa* √*pad*), gained, happened, fallen to one's lot.
svarga (m.), heaven.
dvāram (n. acc. sg. TP cpd.), door, gate.
apāvṛtam (acc. sg. p. pass. participle *apa ā* √*vṛ*), open, unconcealed.
sukhinas (m. nom. pl.), happy, lucky.
kṣatriyās (m. nom. pl.), the *kṣatriyas*, the warriors, members of the warrior caste.
pārtha (m. voc. sg.), Son of Pṛthā, epithet of Arjuna.
labhante (3rd pl. pr. indic. mid. √*labh*), they encounter, they attain, they find.
yuddham (n. acc. sg.), battle, fighting.
īdṛśam (n. acc. sg.), such, of such a kind.

And if by good fortune they gain
The open gate of heaven
Happy are the kṣatriyas, Son of Pṛthā,
When they encounter such a fight.

33

अथ चेत् त्वम् इमं धर्म्यं
atha cet tvam imaṁ dharmyaṁ
now if thou this proper

संग्रामं न करिष्यसि ।
saṁgrāmaṁ na kariṣyasi
engagement not thou shalt undertake

ततः स्वधर्मं कीर्तिं च
tataḥ svadharmaṁ kīrtiṁca
thereupon, own duty and glory

हित्वा पापम् अवाप्स्यसि ॥
hitvā pāpam avāpsyasi
having avoided, evil thou shalt incur.

atha, now, then.
ced, if.
tvam (nom. sg.), thou.
imam (m. acc. sg.), this.
dharmyam (m. acc. sg.), proper, lawful, dutiful.
saṁgrāmam (m. acc. sg.), assembly, army, combat, fight, engagement.
na, not.
kariṣyasi (2nd sg. fut. act. √*kṛ*), thou shalt undertake, thou shalt do, make, etc.
tatas, then, thereupon.
svadharmam (m. acc. sg.), own duty.
kīrtim (f. acc. sg.), glory, fame.
ca, and.
hitvā (gerund √*hā*), having avoided, having left.
pāpam (n. acc. sg.), evil, sin.
avāpsyasi (2nd sg. fut. act. *ava* √*āp*), thou shalt attain, thou shalt incur.

Now, if thou wilt not undertake
This proper engagement,
Thereupon, having avoided thine own duty and glory,
Thou shalt incur evil.

34

अकीर्तिं चापि भूतानि
akīrtiṁ cāpi bhūtāni
and disgrace also people

कथयिष्यन्ति ते ऽव्ययाम् ।
kathayiṣyanti te 'vyayām
they will relate of thee, forever,

संभावितस्य चाकीर्तिर्
saṁbhāvitasya cākīrtir
and for the honored, disgrace

मरणाद् अतिरिच्यते ॥
maraṇād atiricyate
than dying it is worse.

And also people will relate
Thine undying infamy;
And, for the honored,
Disgrace is worse than dying.

akīrtim (f. acc. sg.), disgrace, absence of glory, infamy.
ca, and.
api, also.
bhūtāni (n. nom. sg.), beings, people.
kathayiṣyanti (3rd pl. fut. act. √*kath*), they will relate, they will tell how it was.
te (gen. sg.), of thee.
avyayām (f. acc. sg.), eternal, undying.
saṁbhāvitasya (m. gen. sg. p. pass. causative participle *sam* √*bhū*), of the honored, of the famous, of the esteemed.
ca, and.
akīrtis (f. nom. sg.), disgrace, infamy.
maraṇāt (n. abl. sg.), than dying, from dying.
atiricyate (3rd sg. pr. indic. mid. *ati* √*ric*), it exceeds, it surpasses.

35

भयाद् रणाद् उपरतं
bhayād raṇād uparataṁ
through fear, from delight in battle abstaining,

मंस्यन्ते त्वां महारथाः
maṅsyante tvāṁ mahārathāḥ
they will think thee, the great warriors,

येषां च त्वं वहुमतो
yeṣāṁ ca tvaṁ bahumato
and among whom thou, much thought of

भूत्वा यास्यसि लाघवम् ॥
bhūtvā yāsyasi lāghavam
having been, thou shalt come to lightness.

The great warriors will think
That thou abstainest from joy in battle through fear,
And among those by whom thou hast been held in high esteem
Thou shalt come to be held lightly.

bhayāt (n. abl. sg.), from fear, through fear.
raṇāt (m. abl. sg.), from delight in battle, from battle.
uparatam (m. acc. sg. p. pass. participle *upa* √*ram*), withdrawn from, abstaining, ceased, stopped.
maṅsyante (3rd pl. fut. mid. √*man*), they will think, they will believe.
tvām (acc. sg.), thee.
mahārathās (m. nom. pl.), the great warriors, (as BV cpd.) "those whose chariots are great."
yeṣām (m. gen. pl.), of whom, among whom.
ca, and.
tvam (nom. sg.), thou.
bahu (m.), much, many.
matas (m. nom. sg. pass. participle √*man*), thought, believed, esteemed.
bhūtvā (gerund √*bhū*), having been.
yāsyasi (2nd sg. fut. act. √*yā*), thou shalt go, thou shalt come.
lāghavam (m. acc. sg.), lightness, insignificance.

36

अवाच्यवादांश्च बहून्
avācyavādāṅśca bahūn
and not to be spoken words, many

वदिष्यन्ति तवाहिताः ।
vadiṣyanti tavāhitāḥ
they will speak of thee, the hostile ones,

निन्दन्तस् तव सामर्थ्यं
nindantas tava sāmarthyaṁ
deriding of thee the capacity.

ततो दुःखतरं तु किम् ॥
tato duḥkhataraṁ tu kim
than that greater hardship, indeed, what?

And the hostile ones will speak of thee
Many words that should not be spoken,
Deriding thy capacity.
What greater hardship than that?

avācya (gerundive *a* √*vac*), not to be spoken.
vādān (m. acc. pl.), words, speeches.
ca, and.
bahūn (m. acc. pl.), many, much.
vadiṣyanti (3rd pl. fut. act. √*vad*), they will speak, they will say.
tava (gen. sg.), of thee.
ahitās (m. nom. pl.), noxious, hostile, enemies.
nindantas (m. nom. pl. pr. act. participle √*nind*), deriding, ridiculing.
tava (gen. sg.), of thee, thy.
sāmarthyam (n. acc. sg.), fitness, power, strength, adequacy, capacity.
tatas, from thence, from that.
duḥkhataram (n. acc. sg. comparative), greater hardship, greater pain, greater misery.
tu, indeed, but.
kim (interrog.), what?

37

हतो वा प्राप्स्यसि स्वर्गं
hato vā prāpsyasi svargaṁ
slain either, thou shalt attain heaven,

जित्वा वा भोक्ष्यसे महीम् ।
jitvā vā bhokṣyase mahīm
having conquered, or, thou shalt enjoy the earth;

तस्माद् उत्तिष्ठ कौन्तेय
tasmād uttiṣṭha kāunteya
therefore stand up, Son of Kuntī,

युद्धाय कृतनिश्चयः ॥
yuddhāya kṛtaniścayaḥ
to battle resolved.

Either, having been slain, thou shalt attain heaven,
Or, having conquered, thou shalt enjoy the earth.
Therefore stand up, Son of Kunti,
Resolved to battle.

hatas (m. nom. sg. p. pass. participle √*han*), slain, killed.
vā-vā, either-or.
prāpsyasi (2nd sg. fut. act. *pra* √*āp*), thou shalt attain, thou shalt reach.
svargam (m. acc. sg.), heaven.
jitvā (gerund √*ji*), having conquered.
bhokṣyase (2nd sg. fut. mid. √*bhuj*), thou shalt enjoy, thou shalt eat.
mahīm (f. acc. sg.), the earth.
tasmāt (abl. sg.), from this, therefore.
uttiṣṭha (2nd sg. imperative act. *ud* √*sthā*), stand up! arise!
kāunteya (m. voc. sg.), Son of Kuntī, epithet of Arjuna.
yuddhāya (m. dat. sg.), to battle, to fighting.
kṛtaniścayas (m. n. s.), resolved (*kṛta*, made; *niścaya,* conviction).

38

सुखदुःखे समे कृत्वा
sukhaduḥkhe same kṛtvā
pleasure and pain alike having made,

लाभालाभौ जयाजयौ ।
lābhālābhāu jayājayāu
gain and loss, victory and defeat,

ततो युद्धाय युज्यस्व
tato yuddhāya yujyasva
then to battle yoke thyself!

नैवं पापम् अवाप्स्यसि ॥
nāivaṁ pāpam avāpsyasi
not thus evil thou shalt incur.

Holding pleasure and pain to be alike,
Likewise gain and loss, victory and defeat,
Then yoke thyself to battle!
Thus thou shalt not incur evil.

sukha (n.), pleasure, happiness.
duḥkhe (n. nom. acc. dual), pain, misery.
(*sukhaduḥkhe,* n. acc. dual DV cpd., pleasure and pain.)
same (n. acc. dual), in similar state, alike, the same.
kṛtvā (gerund √*kṛ*), having made, having done.
lābhālābhāu (m. acc. dual), gain and loss (*lābha alābha*). DV cpd.
jayājayāu (m. acc. dual), victory and defeat (*jaya ajaya*). DV cpd.
tatas, then, from there.
yuddhāya (n. dat. sg.), to battle, to fighting.
yujyasva (2nd sg. imperative mid. √*yuj*), join! engage! yoke thyself!
na, not.
evam, thus.
pāpam (n. acc. sg.), evil, sin.
avāpsyasi (2nd sg. fut. act. *ava* √*āp*), thou shalt incur, thou shalt attain, thou shalt obtain.

39

एषा ते ऽभिहिता सांख्ये
eṣā te 'bhihitā sāṁkhye
this to thee declared in the Sāṁkhya.

बुद्धिर् योगे त्विमां शृणु ।
buddhir yoge tvimāṁ śṛṇu
insight in yoga, however, this hear!

बुद्ध्या युक्तो यया पार्थ
buddhyā yukto yayā pārtha
by insight yoked by which, Son of Pṛthā,

कर्मबन्धं प्रहास्यसि ॥
karmabandhaṁ prahāsyasi
karma-bondage thou shalt avoid.

This (insight) is intuitive determination as declared in the theory of Sāṁkhya;*
Now hear it as applied in arduous practice;
Yoked with this determination, Son of Pṛthā
Thou shalt rid thyself of the bondage of karma.

eṣā (f. nom. sg.), this.
te (dat. sg.), to thee.
abhihitā (f. nom. sg. p. pass. participle *abhi* √*dhā*), named, called, declared, spoken.
Sāṁkhye (m. loc. sg.), in the *Sāṁkhya* philosophy, among the followers of the *Sāṃkhya*.
buddhis (f. nom. sg.), insight, enlightenment, intelligence, mental determination.
yoge (m. loc. sg.), in Yoga, in arduous practice.
tu, but, however, indeed.
imām (f. acc. sg.), this.
śṛṇu (2nd sg. imperative act. √*śru*), hear! learn!
buddhyā (f. inst. sg.), by insight, with insight.
yuktas (m. nom. sg. p. pass. participle √*yuj*), joined, disciplined, yoked.
yayā (f. inst. sg.), by which.
Pārtha (m. voc. sg.), Son of Pṛthā, epithet of Arjuna referring to his mother Pṛthā or Kuntī.
karma (n. sg., here untranslated), the sum of one's past actions by which one is bound in a future life.
bandham (m. acc. sg.), bondage.
(*karma-bandham*, m. acc. sg. TP cpd., bondage of karma.)
prahāsyasi (2nd sg. fut. act. *pra* √*hā*), thou shalt leave, thou shalt abandon, thou shalt avoid.

* *Sāṁkhya*, one of the six traditional systems of Hindu philosophy, and one of the oldest. The others are *Mīmāṁsā*, *Yoga*, *Vedānta*, *Vāiśeṣika*, and *Nyāya*. The *Sāṁkhya* system is attributed to the sage Kapila (circa 500 B.C.) and is known as the "reason method" of salvation, while *Yoga*, or at least *karma-Yoga* (the *Yoga* of action) is the "action method." The two often overlap in the Bhagavad Gītā, and are not always distinct. *Sāṁkhya* is the older of the two. From it comes the concept of the *guṇas*. It postulates a cosmology in which results are implied in causes, and in which the universe remains constant, nothing new ever being added to or subtracted from it. Nothing is ever created. Everything is a manifestation or mutation of what has always existed. Thus death is merely a transitory state leading to other states. In this, *Sāṁkhya* has a parallel in the modern scientific theory of the conservation of matter and energy. *Sāṁkhya* does not recognize gods or sacrifices. It is said to have influenced Buddhism.

40

नेहाभिक्रमनाशो ऽस्ति
nehābhikramanāśo 'sti
not in this an effort lost it is.

प्रत्यवायो न विद्यते ।
pratyavāyo na vidyate
reverse not it is found.

स्वल्पम् अप्य् अस्य धर्मस्य
svalpam apy asya dharmasya
a little even of it, of this discipline,

त्रायते महतो भयात् ॥
trāyate mahato bhayāt
protects from great danger.

Here (in the Yoga doctrine of practice) no effort is lost,
Nor is any loss of progress found.
Even a little of this discipline
Protects one from great danger.

na, not.
iha, here, here in the world.
abhikrama (m.), undertaking, effort.
nāśas (m. nom. sg. derivative noun from √*naś*), loss, disappearance, destruction.
(*abhikrama-nāsa*, m. nom. sg. TP cpd., destruction of effort.)
asti (3rd sg. pr. indic. √*as*), it is, there is.
pratyavāyas (m. nom. sg. from *prati ava* √*i*), decrease, diminution, reverse, contrary course, opposite action.
na, not.
vidyate (3rd sg. pr. indic. pass. √2 *vid*), it is found.
svalpam (m. acc. sg.), little, very small.
api, even, also.
asya (gen. sg.), of it, of this.
dharmasya (m. gen. sg.), of discipline, of law, of virtue.
trāyate (3rd sg. pr. indic. mid. √*trāi*), it protects, it rescues.
mahatas (n. abl. sg.), from great.
bhayāt (n. abl. sg.), from danger, from fear.

It is known as "the way of knowledge," and it proposes knowledge as the principal means of salvation. Still other means of salvation mentioned in the Gītā are meditation and love of God.

41

व्यवसायात्मिका बुद्धिर्
vyavasāyātmikā buddhir
resolute-natured insight

एकेह कुरुनन्दन ।
ekeha kurunandana
one in this matter, Descendant of Kuru (Arjuna),

बहुशाखा ह्यनन्ताश्च
bahuśākhā hyanantāś ca
having many branches, indeed endless,

बुद्धयो ऽव्यवसायिनाम् ॥
buddhayo 'vyavasāyinām
the insights of the irresolute.

Resolute-natured insight
Is one in this matter, Descendant of Kuru (Arjuna),
The insights of the irresolute
Have many branches and are, indeed, endless.

vyavasāya (m. noun from *vi ava* √*so*), determination, resolve, purpose, intention.
ātmikā (f. nom. sg. ifc.), of the nature of, "selved."
buddhis (f. nom. sg.), insight, enlightenment, intelligence.
ekā (f. nom. sg.), one.
iha, here, in this place, in this world, in this matter.
kurunandana (m. voc. sg.), Descendant of Kuru, epithet of Arjuna, referring to the ancestor of the Kuru people, progenitor of both Pāṇḍu and Dhṛtarāṣṭra, thus the ancestor of most of the warriors on both sides in the Battle of Kurukṣetra.
bahu, many, much.
śākhās (f. nom. pl.), branches.
hi, indeed, truly.
anantās (f. nom. pl.), endless, infinite, having no end.
ca, and.
buddhayas (f. nom. pl.), insights, intelligences, enlightenments.
avyavasāyinām (m. gen. pl. from *a vi ava* √*so*), of the irresolute, of the wavering.

42

याम् इमां पुष्पितां वाचं
yām imāṁ puṣpitāṁ vācaṁ
which, this flowery word

प्रवदन्त्यविपश्चितः ।
pravadantyavipaścitaḥ
they proclaim, the ignorant ones,

वेदवादरताः पार्थ
vedavādaratāḥ pārtha
delighting in the word of the Veda, Son of Pṛthā (Arjuna),

नान्यद् अस्तीति वादिनः ॥
nānyad astīti vādinaḥ
"not anything else there is" thus saying,

This flowery discourse which
The ignorant ones proclaim, Son of Pṛthā,
Delighting in the letter of the Veda
And saying "there is nothing else,"

yām (f. acc. sg.), which.
imām (f. acc. sg.), this.
puṣpitām (f. acc. sg.), flowery.
vācam (f. acc. sg.), word, speech, language, discourse.
pravadanti (3rd pl. pr. indic. act. *pra* √*vad*), they proclaim, they declare.
avipaścitas (m. nom. pl.), the ignorant ones.
veda (m.), the Veda.
vāda (m.), word, quotation, doctrine.
ratās (m. nom. pl. p. pass. participle √*ram*), delighted, delighting.
(*veda-vāda-ratās*, m. nom. pl. TP cpd., delighting in the letter of the Veda.)
pārtha (m. voc. sg.), Son of Pṛthā, epithet of Arjuna.
na, not.
anyat (n. nom. sg.), anything, other, else.
asti (3rd sg. pr. indic. √*as*), there is, it is.
iti, thus (used to close a quotation).
vādinas (m. nom. pl.), saying, declaring, holding doctrinally.

43

कामात्मानः स्वर्गपरा
kāmātmānaḥ svargaparā
Being of desirious natures, intent on heaven

जन्मकर्मफलप्रदाम् ।
janmakarmaphalapradām
offering rebirth as the fruit of action,

क्रियाविशेषबहुलां
kriyāviśeṣabahulāṁ
abounding in many specific rites,

भोगैश्वर्यगतिं प्रति ॥
bhogāiśvaryagatiṁ prati
enjoyment and power goal with regard to

Being of desirous natures,* intent on heaven,
Offering rebirth as the fruit of action,
Addicted to many specific rites,
Aimed at the goal of enjoyment and power;

kāmātmānas (m. nom. pl. BV cpd.), men of desirous natures, those whose selves are desirous.
svarga (m.), heaven.
parās (m. nom. pl. ifc.), intent on, having as highest object.
janma (n.), birth.
karma (n.), action.
phala (n.), fruit.
pradām (f. acc. sg.), offering, giving.
(*janmakarmaphalapradām,* (f. acc. sg. TP cpd., offering rebirth as the fruit of action.)
kriyā (f.), rite, making, performing, doing, esp. a religious or ritual act.
viśeṣa (*vi śiṣ*), differentiation, specification, various, varieties of.
bahulām (f. acc. sg.), much, many.
(*kriyāviśeṣabahulām,* f. acc. sg. TP cpd., abounding in various species of rites, addicted to many various rites.)
bhoga (m.), enjoyment, pleasure, especially in eating.
āiśvarya (n.), power, lordliness.
gatim (f. acc. sg.), goal, path, aim.
(*bhogāiśvaryagatim,* f. acc. sg. TP cpd., the goal of enjoyment and power.)
prati, (adv.), opposite, in the vicinity of, in regard to.

* I.e. the "ignorant ones" of the preceding stanza.

44

भोगैश्वर्यप्रसक्तानां
bhogāiśvaryaprasaktānāṁ
of the enjoyment-and-power-attached (pl.)

तयापहृतचेतसाम् ।
tayāpahṛtacetasām
of the by-this (i.e. this discourse)-stolen-away-thoughts,

व्यवसायात्मिका बुद्धिः
vyavasāyātmikā buddhiḥ
resolute-natured insight

समाधौ न विधीयते ॥
samādhāu na vidhīyate
in meditation not it is granted.

To those (the ignorant ones) attached to enjoyment and power,
Whose thought is stolen away by this discourse,
Resolute-natured insight
In meditation is not granted.

bhoga (m., from √*bhuj*), enjoyment, pleasure.
āiśvarya (n.), power, lordship.
prasaktānām (m. gen. pl.), of the attached.
(*bhogāiśvaryaprasaktānām,* gen. pl. BV cpd., of those attached to pleasure and power.)
tayā (f. inst. sg.), by this.
apahṛta (n. p. pass. participle *apa* √*hṛ*), stolen away.
cetasām (n. gen. pl.), of thoughts, of minds.
(*tayāpahṛtacetasām,* m. gen. pl. BV cpd., of those whose thoughts are stolen away by this.)
vyavasāya (from *vi ava* √*so*), resolution.
ātmikā (f. nom. sg. ifc.), having the nature of, "selved," "natured."
buddhis (f. nom. sg.), insight, enlightenment, intelligence.
samādhāu (m. loc. sg.), in meditation.
na, not.
vidhīyate (3rd sg. p. indic. passive *vi* √*dhā*), it is granted, it is given.

45

त्रैगुण्यविषया वेदा
trāiguṇyaviṣayā vedā
three guṇas territories in the Vedas

निस्त्रैगुण्यो भवार्जुन ।
nistrāiguṇyo bhavārjuna
without the three guṇas be! Arjuna

निर्द्वन्द्वो नित्यसत्त्वस्थो
nirdvandvo nityasattvastho
indifferent toward the pairs of opposites, eternally fixed in truth,

निर्योगक्षेम आत्मवान् ॥
niryogakṣema ātmavān
free from (thoughts of) acquisition and comfort, possessed of the self.

The Vedas are such that their scope is confined to the three guṇas;
Be free from those three guṇas, Arjuna,
Indifferent toward the pairs of opposites, eternally fixed in truth,
Free from thoughts of acquisition and comfort, possessed of the self.

trāiguṇya (n.), three guṇas, the triad of guṇas.
viṣayās (m. nom. pl.), territories, spheres of action, belonging to, category.
(*trāiguṇa-viṣagās,* m. nom. pl. TP cpd., belonging to the three guṇas.)
vedās (m. nom. pl.), the Vedas.
nistrāiguṇyas (m. nom. sg.), without the three guṇas, without the triad of guṇas.
bhava (2nd sg. imperative act. √*bhū*), be! exist! become!
arjuna (m. voc. sg.), Arjuna.
nirdvandvas (m. nom. sg.), without the pairs of opposites (heat, cold; pain, pleasure, etc.), indifferent to the pairs of opposites, indifferent to the polarities.
nitya, (adv.), eternal, eternally.
sattva (n.), truth, reality, goodness.
-sthas (suffix, m. nom. sg.), fixed, standing, staying, abiding.
niryogakṣemas (m. nom. sg.), without thoughts of acquisition and conservation.
ātmavān (m. nom. sg.), possessed of the self, full of the self.

46

यावानर्थ उदपाने
yāvān artha udapāne
as much value in a well

सर्वतः संप्लुतोदके ।
sarvataḥ saṁplutodake
when on every side, water overflowing,

तावान्सर्वेषु वेदेषु
tāvān sarveṣu vedeṣu
so much in all the Vedas

ब्राह्मणस्य विजानतः ॥
brāhmaṇasya vijānataḥ
for the brāhman, knowing.

**As much value as there is in a well
When water is flooding on every side,
So much is the value in all the Vedas
For a brāhman who knows.**

yāvān (m. nom. sg.), as much, so much.
arthas (m. nom. sg.), use, object, aim, value.
udapāne (m. loc. sg.), in a well.
sarvatas, (adv.), on all sides, everywhere.
saṁpluta (p. pass. participle *sam* √*plu*), overflowing.
udake (n. loc. sg.), in water, with water.
(*saṁpluta-udake,* n. loc. sg. KD cpd., overflowing with water.)
tāvān (m. nom. sg.), so much.
sarveṣu (m. loc. pl.), in all.
vedeṣu (m. loc. pl.), in the Vedas.
brāhmaṇasya (m. gen. sg.), of the brāhman, for the brāhman.
vijānatas (m. gen. sg. pr. participle *vi* √*jñā*), knowing, wise.

47

कर्मण्येवाधिकारस्ते
karmaṇyevādhikāraste
in action alone the jurisdiction of thee,

मा फलेषु कदाचन ।
mā phaleṣu kadācana
never in fruits at any time,

मा कर्मफलहेतुर् भूर्
mā karmaphalahetur bhūr
never action-fruit motive should arise,

मा ते सङ्गो ऽस्त्व् अकर्मणि ॥
mā te sañgo 'stv akarmaṇi.
never of thee attachment let there be in inaction.

Thy jurisdiction is in action alone;
Never in its fruits at any time.
Never should the fruits of action be thy motive;*
Never let there be attachment in thee to inaction.

karmaṇi (n. loc. sg.), in action, in deeds.
eva, alone, indeed (often used as a rhythmic filler).
adhikāras (m. nom. sg.), jurisdiction, authority, prerogative, office, claim, privilege.
te (gen. sg.), of thee, thy.
mā (prohibitive), not, never.
phaleṣu (n. loc. pl.), in fruits, in results.
kadācana, (adv.), at any time, at any time whatsoever.
mā (prohibitive), not, never.
karmaphala (n.), fruit of action, result of action.
hetus (m. nom. sg.), motive, cause.
(*karma-phala-hetus*, m. nom. sg. TP cpd., motive in fruit-of-action.)
bhūs (3rd sg. aorist subjunctive √*bhū*), it should be, it should arise.
mā (prohibitive), not, never.
te (gen. sg.), of thee, thy.
sañgas (m. nom. sg.), attachment.
astu (3rd sg. imperative act. √*as*), let there be!
akarmaṇi (n. loc. sg.), in inaction, in non-action.

* Acting without regard or desire for the fruits of action is one of the most constant teachings of the Bhagavad Gītā. It refers to "disinterested action," which is not to be confused with irresponsible or careless action. According to the law of *karma* an individual is responsible for his actions throughout eternity, or until he achieves *nirvāṇa*. The "fruits" (usually translated in the plural, though the singular *phalam* is used in the Sanskrit) mean the results of action, and they are of three kinds: those of obligatory action, those of action prompted by desire, and those that arise from delusion (see XVIII 23, 24, 25). The first of these is really action without desire for the fruits, i.e. action which is a duty. The second and third are related to desire, and the elimination of desire for the fruits of action is basic to the Gītā's teaching. The last line, about "inaction" is an injunction against sloth – one of the evils associated with the *guṇa* of *tamas*, or darkness. Action prompted by delusion (see above) is also associated with *tamas*. Thus, action prompted by greed, desire for wealth, desire for power, or desire for fame is not advised.

48

योगस्थः कुरु कर्माणि
yogasthaḥ kuru karmāṇi
in Yoga fixed, perform actions,

सङ्गं त्यक्त्वा धनंजय ।
saṅgaṁ tyaktvā dhanaṁjaya
attachment having abandoned, Conqueror of Wealth,

सिद्ध्यसिद्ध्योः समो भूत्वा
siddhyasiddhyoḥ samo bhūtvā
to success or failure indifferent having become

समत्वं योग उच्यते ॥
samatvaṁ yoga ucyate
indifference (is) Yoga, it is said.

Fixed in Yoga, perform actions,
Having abandoned attachment, Conqueror of Wealth (Arjuna).
Having become indifferent to success or failure.
It is said that indifference is Yoga.

yoga (m.), Yoga, discipline, steadfastness.
-sthas (m. nom. sg. suffix), fixed, abiding in.
kuru (2nd sg. imperative act. √*kṛ*), do! make! perform!
karmāṇi (n. acc. pl.), actions, deeds.
saṅgam (m. acc. sg.), attachment, adherence, clinging.
tyaktvā (gerund √*tyaj*), abandoning, having abandoned.
dhanaṁjaya (m. voc. sg.), Conqueror of Wealth, frequent epithet of Arjuna.
siddhi (f.), success, attainment, fulfillment.
asiddhi (f.), non-success, failure.
(*siddhyasiddhyos,* f. loc. dual, in success and failure, in success or failure.)
samas (m. nom. sg.), the same, equal, indifferent (as between two alternatives).
bhūtvā (gerund √*bhū*), being, becoming, having become.
samatvam (n. nom. sg.), equanimity, indifference, equableness.
yogas (m. nom. sg.), Yoga.
ucyate (3rd sg. pr. indic. passive √*vac*), it is said, it is declared.

49

दूरेण ह्यवरं कर्म
dūreṇa hyavaraṁ karma
by far, indeed, inferior, action

बुद्धियोगाद् धनंजय ।
buddhiyogād dhanaṁjaya,
to intelligence-discipline, Conqueror of Wealth.

बुद्धौ शरणम् अन्विच्छ
buddhāu śaraṇam anviccha
in insight refuge seek;

कृपणाः फलहेतवः ॥
kṛpaṇāḥ phalahetavaḥ
despicable (are) those who are motivated by fruit.

dūreṇa (n. inst. sg.), by far, by distance, by a long way.
hi, indeed.
avaram (n. nom. sg.), inferior, below, low, unimportant.
karma (n. nom. sg.), action, doing, making.
buddhiyogāt (m. abl. sg.), from the Yoga of intelligence, to the Yoga of intelligence, to mental determination, intuitive determination. TP cpd.
dhanaṁjaya, (m. voc. sg.), Conqueror of Wealth, frequent epithet of Arjuna.
buddhāu (f. loc. sg.), in insight, in enlightenment, in intelligence, in mental determination.
śaraṇam (n. acc. sg.), refuge.
anviccha (2nd imperative act. *anu* √*iṣ*), seek! wish for! desire!
kṛpaṇās (m. nom. pl.), despicable, pitiable.
phalahetavas (m. nom. pl. BV cpd.), those whose motives are based on fruit, those who are motivated by the fruit.

Action is inferior by far
To the Yoga of intuitive determination, Conqueror of Wealth (Arjuna).
Seek refuge in intuitive determination!
Despicable are those whose motives are based on the fruit of action.

50

बुद्धियुक्तो जहातीह
buddhiyukto jahātīha
He who is disciplined in intuitive determination casts off here in the world

उभे सुकृतदुष्कृते ।
ubhe sukṛtaduṣkṛte
both good and evil deeds;

तस्माद् योगाय युज्यस्व
tasmād yogāya yujyasva
therefore to Yoga yoke thyself!

योगः कर्मसु कौशलम् ॥
yogaḥ karmasu kāuśalam
Yoga in actions (is) skill.

buddhiyuktas (m. nom. sg. p. pass. participle √*yuj*), the yoked intelligence, the disciplined in intelligence, the disciplined in mental determination, (as BV cpd.) he who is disciplined in intuitive determination.
jahāti (3rd sg. pr. indic. act. √*hā*), he leaves, he casts off.
iha, here, here in the world.
ubhe (n. acc. dual), both.
sukṛta (m.), good deed.
duṣkṛte (n. acc. dual), evil deeds.
(*sukṛtaduṣkṛte,* n. acc. dual, good and evil deeds.)
tasmāt (abl. sg.), from this, therefore.
yogāya (m. dat. sg.), to Yoga.
yujyasva (2nd sg. imperative mid. √*yuj*), yoke! yoke thyself! join thyself!
yogas (m. nom. sg.), Yoga, discipline.
karmasu (n. loc. pl.), in actions, in deeds.
kāuśalam (n. nom. acc. sg.), skill, health, ease.

He whose intuitive determination is disciplined
Casts off, here in the world, both good and evil actions;
Therefore yoke thyself to Yoga!
Yoga is skill in actions.

51

कर्मजं बुद्धियुक्ता हि
karmajaṁ buddhiyuktā hi
born of action, the intelligence-disciplined (pl.) indeed,

फलं त्यक्त्वा मनीषिणः ।
phalaṁ tyaktvā manīṣiṇaḥ
fruit having abandoned, the wise,

जन्मबन्धविनिर्मुक्ताः
janmabandhavinirmuktāḥ
rebirth bondage freed from,

पदं गच्छन्त्य् अनामयम् ॥
padam gacchanty anāmayam
(to the) place they go, free from pain.

Those who are disciplined in intuitive determination,
The wise ones, who have abandoned the fruit born of action,
And are freed from the bondage of rebirth,
Go to the place that is free from pain.

karmajam (*karma* √*ja*, n. acc. sg.), born of action, produced by action.
buddhi (f.), intelligence, enlightenment, intuitive determination.
yuktās (m. nom. pl. p. pass. participle √*yuj*), yoked, joined, disciplined.
hi, indeed.
phalam (n. acc. sg.), fruit, result.
tyaktvā (gerund √*tyaj*), abandoning, having abandoned, having cast aside.
manīṣiṇas (m. nom. pl.), wise, wise ones.
janma (n.), birth, rebirth.
bandha (m.), bondage.
vinirmuktās (m. nom. pl. participle *vi nir* √*muc*), released, freed from.
(*janmabandhavinirmuktās*, m. nom. pl., freed from the bondage of rebirth.)
padam (n. acc. sg.), place, way, abode.
gacchanti (3rd pl. pr. indic. act. √*gam*), they go.
anāmayam (n. acc. sg.), free from disease, free from pain, healthy, salubrious.

52

यदा ते मोहकलिलं
yadā te mohakalilaṁ
when of thee the delusion-thicket

बुद्धिर् व्यतितरिष्यति ।
buddhir vyatitariṣyati
the intelligence shall cross beyond

तदा गन्तासि निर्वेदं
tadā gantāsi nirvedaṁ
then thou shalt become disgusted

श्रोतव्यस्य श्रुतस्य च ॥
śrotavyasya śrutasya ca
with the to-be-heard and with the heard.

When thine intelligence shall cross beyond
The thicket of delusion, then thou shalt become disgusted
With that which is to be heard
And with that which has been heard (in the Veda).

yadā, when.
te (gen. sg.), of thee, thy.
moha (m.), delusion.
kalilam (m. acc. sg.), thicket, heap, confusion.
buddhis (f. nom. sg.), intelligence, enlightenment, mental determination.
vyatitariṣyati (3rd sg. fut. act. *vi ati* √*tṛ*), it shall cross over, it shall pass beyond.
tadā, then.
gantāsi (2nd sg. periphrastic fut. act. √*gam*), thou shalt go.
nirvedam (m. acc. sg.), disgust, disgusted.
śrotavyasya (m. gen. sg. gerundive √*śru*), of the to-be-heard, with that which is to be heard.
śrutasya (m. gen. sg. p. pass. participle √*śru*), of the heard, of that which has been heard.
ca, and.

53

श्रुतिविप्रतिपन्ना ते
śrutivipratipannā te
disregarding ritual-centered revelation (i.e. of the Veda), of thee

यदा स्थास्यति निश्चला ।
yadā sthāsyati niścalā
when it shall stand unmoving

समाधावचलाबुद्धिस्
samādhāvacalābuddhis
in deep meditation, immovable, (thine) intelligence,

तदा योगम् अवाप्स्यसि ॥
tadā yogam avāpsyasi
then Yoga thou shalt attain.

When thine intelligence shall stand
Fixed in deep meditation, unmoving,
Disregarding Vedic doctrine,
Then thou shalt attain Yoga.

śruti (f.), heard, what is heard.
vipratipannā (f. nom. sg. p. pass. participle *vi prati* √*pad*), perplexed, false, mistaken, contrary.
(*śrutivipratipannā,* f. nom. sg., contrary to ritual-centered revelation, disregarding Vedic doctrine.) TP cpd.
te (gen. sg.), of thee, by thee, thine.
yadā, when.
sthāsyati (3rd sg. fut. act. √*sthā*), it shall stand.
niścalā (f. nom. sg.), unmoving, motionless, fixed.
samādhāu (m. loc. sg.), in meditation, in deep meditation.
acalā (f. nom. sg.), immovable, unmoving.
buddhis (f. nom. sg.), intelligence, mental determination.
tadā, then.
yogam (m. acc. sg.), Yoga.
avāpsyasi (2nd sg. fut. act. *ava* √*āp*), thou shalt attain, thou shalt obtain, thou shalt reach.

अर्जुन उवाच ।
arjuna uvāca
Arjuna spoke:

arjunas (m. nom. sg.), Arjuna.
uvāca (3rd sg. per. act. √*vac*), he said, he spoke.

54

स्थितप्रज्ञस्य का भाषा
sthitaprajñasya kā bhāṣā
of him who is steady of insight, what description?

समाधिस्थस्य केशव ।
samādhisthasya keśava
of him who is steadfast in deep meditation, Handsome Haired One (Krishna)?

स्थितधीः किं प्रभाषेत
sthitadhīḥ kiṁ prabhāṣeta
he who is steady in thought, how he should speak?

किम् आसीत व्रजेत किम् ॥
kim āsīta vrajeta kim
how should he sit, he should move how?

Arjuna spoke:

How does one describe him who is steady of insight?
Him who is steadfast in deep meditation, Handsome Haired One (Krishna)?
How should he who is steady in thought speak?
How should he sit? How should he move?

sthitaprajñasya (m. gen. sg. BV cpd.), of him who is steady of insight.
kā (f. nom. sg. interrog.), what?
bhāṣā (f. nom. sg.), description, definition, identification, language, speech.
samādhisthasya (m. gen. sg. BV cpd.), of him who is steadfast in deep meditation.
keśava (m. voc. sg.), Handsome Haired One, frequent epithet of Krishna.
sthitadhīs (f. nom. sg. BV cpd.), he who is steady in thought, man of stable thoughts.
kim (interrog.), what? how?
prabhāṣeta (3rd sg. opt. act. *pra* √*bhāṣ*), he might speak, he should speak.
kim (interrog.), what? how?
āsīta (3rd sg. opt. mid. √*ās*), he might sit, he should sit.
vrajeta (3rd sg. opt. mid. √*vraj*), he might go, he should travel, he should move, he should proceed.
kim (interrog.), what? how?

श्रीभगवान् उवाच ।
śrībhagavān uvāca
the Blessed Lord spoke:

śrībhagavān (m. nom. sg.), the Blessed Lord, the blessed one.
uvāca (3rd sg. perf. act. √*vac*), he said, he spoke.

55

प्रजहाति यदा कामान्
prajahāti yadā kāmān
he leaves behind, when, desires

सर्वान् पार्थ मनोगतान् ।
sarvān pārtha manogatān
all, Son of Pṛthā, emerging from the mind,

आत्मन्येवात्मना तुष्टः
ātmanyevātmanā tuṣṭaḥ
in the self by the self contented,

स्थितप्रज्ञस्तदोच्यते ॥
sthitaprajñastadocyate
one whose insight is steady then he is said to be.

prajahāti (3rd sg. pr. indic. act. *pra* √*hā*), he leaves behind, he relinquishes, he abandons, he renounces.
yadā, when.
kāmān (m. acc. pl.), desires, addictions, cravings.
sarvān (m. acc. pl.), all.
pārtha (m. voc. sg.), Son of Pṛthā, frequent epithet of Arjuna.
manogatān (m. acc. pl.), "mind gone," emerging from the mind, originating in the mind. TP cpd.
ātmani (m. loc. sg.), in the self.
eva, indeed (used as a rhythmic filler).
ātmanā (m. inst. sg.), by the self.
tuṣṭas (m. nom. sg. p. pass. participle √*tuṣ*), satisfied, contented.
sthitaprajñas (m. nom. sg.), steady of insight, wise, prudent, (as BV cpd.) one whose insight is steady.
tadā, then.
ucyate (3rd sg. pr. indic. passive √*vac*), it is said, he is said to be.

The Blessed Lord spoke:

When he leaves behind all desires
Emerging from the mind, Son of Pṛthā,
And is contented in the self by the self,
Then he is said to be one whose insight is steady.

56

दुःखेष्वनुद्विग्नमनाः
duḥkheṣvanudvignamanāḥ
in misfortunes not agitated the mind

सुखेषु विगतस्पृहः ।
sukheṣu vigataspṛhaḥ
in pleasures freed from desire

वीतरागभयक्रोधः
vītarāgabhayakrodhaḥ
departed passion, fear, anger,

स्थितधीर् मुनिर् उच्यते ॥
sthitadhīr munir ucyate
steady in thought, a sage he is said to be.

He whose mind is not agitated in misfortune,
Whose desire for pleasures has disappeared,
Whose passion, fear and anger have departed,
Whose meditation is steady, is said to be a sage.

duḥkheṣu (n. loc. pl.), in misfortunes, in miseries, in unhappinesses.
anudvigna (p. pass. participle *an ud* √*vij*), free from anxiety, not agitated, free from perplexity.
manās (m. nom. sg. ifc.), mind, minded.
(*anudvignamanās,* m. nom. sg. BV cpd., whose mind is not agitated.)
sukheṣu (n. loc. pl.), in pleasures, in happinesses, in joys.
vigataspṛhas (m. nom. sg.), "gone away desire," (as BV cpd.) whose desire has disappeared, freed from desire, freed from greed.
vīta (p. pass. participle *vi* √*i*), departed, gone.
rāga (m.), passion.
bhaya (n.), fear, danger.
krodhas (m. nom. sg.), anger.
(*vītarāgabhayakrodhas,* m. nom. sg. BV cpd., whose passion, fear and anger have departed.)
sthitadhīs (f. nom. sg.), steady of thought, steady in meditation, (as BV cpd.) whose meditation is steady.
munis (m. nom. sg.), sage, wise man.
ucyate (3rd sg. pr. indic. pass. √*vac*), he is called, he is said to be, it is said.

57

यः सर्वत्रानभिस्नेहस्
yaḥ sarvatrānabhisnehas
who on all sides non-desirous,

तत्तत् प्राप्य शुभाशुभम् ।
tattat prāpya śubhāśubham
this or that encountering, pleasant or unpleasant,

नाभिनन्दति न द्वेष्टि
nābhinandati na dveṣṭi
not he rejoices, not he dislikes

तस्य प्रज्ञा प्रतिष्ठिता ।।
tasya prajñā pratiṣṭhitā
of him the wisdom standing firm.

He who is non-desirous on all sides,
Encountering this or that, pleasant or unpleasant,
Neither rejoicing nor disliking;
His wisdom stands firm.

yas (m. nom. sg.), who.
sarvatra, on all sides, everywhere, in all things.
anabhisnehas (m. nom. sg. from *an abhi* √*snih*), without affection, unimpassioned, nondesirous.
tat tad (n. nom. sg.), this or that.
prāpya (gerund *pra* √*āp*), encountering, obtaining, attaining, incurring.
śubhāśubham (n. acc. sg. *śubha aśubha*), pleasant and unpleasant, pleasant or unpleasant. DV cpd.
na, not.
abhinandati (3rd sg. pr. indic. act. *abhi* √*nand*), he rejoices, he salutes, he approves.
na, not.
dveṣṭi (3rd sg. pr. indic. act. √*dviṣ*), he dislikes, he hates.
tasya (gen. sg.), of this, of it, of him.
prajñā (f. nom. sg.), wisdom, understanding, knowledge, discrimination, judgement.
pratiṣṭhitā (f. nom. sg. p. pass. participle), standing firm, established.

58

यदा संहरते चायं
yadā saṁharate cāyaṁ
and when he withdraws, this one,

कूर्मो ऽङ्गानीव सर्वशः ।
kūrmo 'ṅgānīva sarvaśaḥ
the tortoise-limbs-like completely,

इन्द्रियाणीन्द्रियार्थेभ्यस्
indriyāṇīndriyārthebhyas
the senses from the objects of the sense,

तस्य प्रज्ञा प्रतिष्ठिता ॥
tasya prajñā pratiṣṭhitā
of him the wisdom standing firm.

And when he withdraws completely
The senses from the objects of the senses,
As a tortoise its limbs into its shell,
His wisdom stands firm.

yadā, when.
saṁharate (3rd. sg. pr. indic. mid. *sam* √*hṛ*), he withdraws, he draws together.
ca, and.
ayam (m. nom. sg.), this, this one.
kūrmas (m. nom. sg.), tortoise, turtle.
aṅgāni (n. acc. pl.), limbs, legs and arms.
iva, like, similarly.
sarvaśas, completely, wholly, altogether.
indriyāṇi (n. acc. pl.), senses, powers.
indriyārthebhyas (m. abl. pl.), from the objects of sense, from the objects of the senses. TP cpd.
tasya (m. gen. sg.), of this, of it, of him.
prajñā (f. nom. sg.), wisdom, understanding, judgement, discrimination.
pratiṣṭhitā (f. nom. sg. p. pass. participle *prati* √*sthā*), standing firm, established.

59

विषया विनिवर्तन्ते
viṣayā vinivartante
the objects turn away

निराहारस्य देहिनः ।
nirāhārasya dehinaḥ
from the fasting of the embodied one,

रसवर्जं रसो ऽप्यस्य
rasavarjaṁ raso 'pyasya
flavor excepted; flavor also from him,

परं दृष्ट्वा निवर्तते ॥
paraṁ dṛṣṭvā nivartate
the supreme having seen, it turns away.

The objects turn away
From the fasting embodied one,
Except flavor;* flavor also turns away
From him who has seen the Supreme.†

viṣayās (m. nom. pl.), objects, dominions, spheres of influence.
vinivartante (3rd pl. pr. indic. mid. *vi ni* √*vṛt*), they turn away.
nirāhārasya (m. gen. sg. from *nir āhāra*, food), from the fasting, from the without-food.
dehinas (m. gen. sg.), of the embodied one, of the *ātman*, of the self.
rasa (m.), flavor, taste.
varjam (adv.), excluding, with the exception of. TP cpd.
rasas (m. nom. sg.), flavor, taste.
api, also, even.
asya (m. gen. sg.), of him.
param (m. acc. sg.), the highest, the supreme.
dṛṣṭvā (gerund √*dṛś*), seeing, having seen.
nivartate (3rd sg. pr. indic. mid. *ni* √*vṛt*), it turns away.

---

* Flavor being the object of hunger, most basic of desires.
† The *ātman*.

60

यततो ह्यपि कौन्तेय
yatato hyapi kāunteya
of the striving, indeed even, Son of Kuntī,

पुरुषस्य विपश्चितः।
puruṣasya vipaścitaḥ
of the man of wisdom,

इन्द्रियाणि प्रमाथीनि
indriyāṇi pramāthīni
the senses tormenting

हरन्ति प्रसभं मनः॥
haranti prasabhaṁ manaḥ
they carry away forcibly the mind.

The tormenting senses
Carry away forcibly
The mind, Son of Kuntī,
Even of the striving man of wisdom.

yatatas (m. gen. sg. pr. act. participle √*yat*), of the striving, of the eager, of the one who strives.
hi, indeed, truly.
api, even, also.
kāunteya (m. voc. sg.), Son of Kuntī, frequent epithet of Arjuna.
puruṣasya (m. gen. sg.), of the man.
vipaścitas (m. gen. sg. from √*vip*), of wisdom, of learning.
indriyāṇi (n. nom. pl.), the senses, the powers.
pramāthīni (n. nom. pl.), tearing, rending, harassing, destroying, tormenting.
haranti (3rd pl. pr. indic. act. √*hṛ*), they carry away, they seize, they take.
prasabham (adv.), forcibly, violently.
manas (n. acc. sg.), mind, thoughts.

61

तानि सर्वाणि संयम्य
tāni sarvāṇi saṁyamya
these (i.e. the senses) all restraining

युक्त आसीत मत्परः ।
yukta āsīta matparaḥ
disciplined, he should sit, me intent on;

वशे हि यस्येन्द्रियाणि
vaśe hi yasyendriyāṇi
in control surely of whom the senses,

तस्य प्रज्ञा प्रतिष्ठिता ॥
tasya prajñā pratiṣṭhitā
of him the wisdom standing firm.

**Restraining all these senses,
Disciplined, he should sit, intent on Me;
He of whom the senses are controlled,
His wisdom stands firm.**

tāni (n. acc. pl.), these.
sarvāṇi (n. acc. pl.), all.
saṁyamya (gerund *sam* √*yam*), restraining, holding back.
yuktas (m. nom. sg. p. pass. participle √*yuj*), disciplined, yoked, joined (usually refers to being steadfast in Yoga).
āsīta (3rd sg. opt. mid. √*ās*), he should sit.
matparas (m. nom. sg.), me intent on, with me as highest object.
vaśe (m. loc. sg.), in control, in wish, in desire, in dominion.
hi, surely, indeed, truly.
yasya (m. gen. sg.), of whom.
indriyāṇi (n. nom. pl.), the senses, the powers.
tasya (m. gen. sg.), of this, of him.
prajñā (f. nom. sg.), wisdom, understanding, discrimination.
pratiṣṭhitā (f. nom. sg. p. pass. participle *prati* √*sthā*), standing firm, stabilized, steadfast, established.

62

ध्यायतो विषयान् पुंसः
dhyāyato viṣayān puṁsaḥ
contemplating objects, for a man

सङ्गस् तेषूपजायते ।
saṅgas teṣūpajāyate
attachment to them it is born

सङ्गात् संजायते कामः
saṅgāt saṁjāyate kāmaḥ
from attachment is born desire

कामात् क्रोधो ऽभिजायते ॥
kāmāt krodho 'bhijāyate
from desire anger is born

For a man dwelling on the objects of the senses,
An attachment to them is born;
From attachment, desire is born;
From desire, anger is born;

dhyāyatas (m. gen. sg. pr. act participle √*dhyā*), of dwelling on, of contemplating.
viṣayān (m. acc. pl.), objects, departments, spheres of action, provinces, fields.
puṁsas (m. gen. sg.), of a man, for a man.
saṅgas (m. nom. sg.), attachment, clinging.
teṣu (m. loc. pl.), in them, to them.
*upajāyate** (3rd sg. pr. indic. passive *upa* √*jan*), it is born, it is produced.
saṅgāt (m. abl. sg.), from attachment, from clinging.
*saṁjāyate** (3rd pl. pr. indic. passive *sam* √*jan*), it is born, it is produced.
kāmas (m. nom. sg.), desire, craving, greed.
kāmāt (m. abl. sg.), from desire, from craving.
krodhas (m. nom. sg.), anger, wrath, fury.
*abhijāyate** (3rd sg. pr. indic. passive *abhi* √*jan*), it is born, it is produced.

* The use of three different prefixes to *jāyate* (it is born), viz., *upa, sam, abhi,* testifies to the fact that in Sanskrit, such prefixes are sometimes used merely for elegance (in this case avoidance of repetition), and do not necessarily convey any difference in meaning.

63

क्रोधाद् भवति संमोहः
krodhād bhavati saṁmohaḥ
from anger arises delusion,

संमोहात् स्मृतिविभ्रमः ।
saṁmohāt smṛtivibhramaḥ
from delusion, memory wandering,

स्मृतिभ्रंशाद् बुद्धिनाशो
smṛtibhraṁśād buddhināśo
from memory wandering, intelligence destruction,

बुद्धिनाशात् प्रणश्यति ॥
buddhināśāt praṇaśyati
from intelligence-destruction one is lost.

From anger arises delusion;
From delusion, wandering of the memory;
From memory-wandering, destruction of the intelligence;
From destruction of the intelligence one is lost.

krodhāt (m. abl. sg.), from anger, from wrath.
bhavati (3rd sg. √*bhū*), it arises, it comes to be, it is.
saṁmohas (m. nom. sg. from *sam* √*muh*), delusion, confusion.
saṁmohāt (m. abl. sg.), from delusion, from confusion.
smṛti (f.), memory, wisdom remembered.
vibhramas (m. nom. sg. from *vi* √*bhram*), wandering away. TP cpd.
smṛti (f.), memory, wisdom remembered.
bhraṁśāt (m. abl. sg.), from wandering.
(*smṛtibhraṁśāt,* abl. sg., from memory wandering away.) TP cpd.
buddhi (f.), intelligence.
nāśas (m. nom. sg.), destruction, loss. TP cpd.
buddhi (f.), intelligence.
nāśāt (m. abl. sg.), from destruction.
(*buddhināśāt*, m. abl. sg. TP cpd., from destruction of the intelligence, from loss of the intelligence.)
praṇaśyati (3rd sg. pr. indic. act. *pra* √*naś*), he is lost, he is destroyed, one is lost, one is destroyed.

64

रागद्वेषवियुक्तस्तु
rāgadveṣaviyuktas tu
desire and hate eliminated, however,

विषयान् इन्द्रियैश्चरन् ।
viṣayān indriyāiścaran
(even though) objects by the senses engaging,

आत्मवश्यैर् विधेयात्मा
ātmavaśyāir vidheyātmā
by self-restraint, the self-controlled,

प्रसादम् अधिगच्छति ॥
prasādam adhigacchati
tranquility he attains.

With the elimination of desire and hatred,
Even though engaging the objects of the senses,
He who is susceptible of control by the self,
By self-restraint, attains tranquility.

rāga (m.), passion, desire.
dveṣa (m.), hatred, loathing.
viyuktas (m. nom. sg. p. pass. participle *vi* √*yuj*), unjoined, eliminated.
tu, but, however.
viṣayān (m. acc. pl.), objects, spheres of action, provinces, fields.
indriyāīs (n. inst. pl.), by the senses, with the senses.
caran (m. nom. sg. pr. participle act. √*car*), moving, engaging.
ātmavaśyāis (m. inst. pl.), controlled by self-restraints, by self-controls, with self-restraints.
vidheya (gerundive *vi* √*dhā*), to be enjoined, to be governed, to be subdued, to be controlled.
ātmā (m. nom. sg.), self.
(*vidheyātmā*, m. nom. sg. BV cpd., he whose self is controllable.)
prasādam (m. acc. sg.), tranquility, peace.
adhigacchati (3rd sg. pr. indic. act. *adhi* √*gam*), he goes to, he attains, he reaches.

65

प्रसादे सर्वदुःखानां
prasāde sarvaduḥkhānāṁ
in tranquility, of all sorrows

हानिर् अस्योपजायते ।
hānir asyopajāyate
cessation for him it is born.

प्रसन्नचेतसो ह्याशु
prasannacetaso hyāśu
of the tranquil minded, indeed, at once

बुद्धिः पर्यवतिष्ठते ॥
buddhiḥ paryavatiṣṭhate
the intelligence it becomes steady.

In tranquility the cessation of all sorrows
Is born for him.
Indeed, for the tranquil-minded
The intelligence at once becomes steady.

prasāde (m. loc. sg.), in tranquility, in peace.
sarva, all.
duḥkhānām (n. gen. pl.), of sorrows, of misfortunes.
hānis (f. nom. sg. from √*hā,* leave), cessation, withdrawal.
asya (m. gen. sg.), of him, of it, for him.
upajāyate (3rd sg. pr. indic. passive *upa* √*jan*), it is born, it is produced.
prasanna (p. pass. participle *pra* √*sad*), clear, bright, tranquil, placid.
cetasas (m. gen. sg.), of mind, minded, of thought.
(*prasannacetasas,* m. gen. sg. BV cpd., of him whose mind is tranquil.)
hi, indeed, truly.
āśu (adv.), quickly, at once, immediately.
buddhis (f. nom. sg.), intelligence, enlightenment, discrimination.
paryavatiṣṭhate (3rd sg. pr. indic. mid. *pari ava* √*sthā*), it becomes steady, it steadies, it stands.

66

नास्ति बुद्धिर् अयुक्तस्य
nāsti buddhir ayuktasya
not there is intelligence of the uncontrolled,

न चायुक्तस्य भावना ।
na cāyuktasya bhāvanā
and not of the uncontrolled, concentration,

न चाभावयतः शान्तिर्
na cābhāvayataḥ śāntir
and not of the non-concentrating, peace.

अशान्तस्य कुतः सुखम् ॥
aśāntasya kutaḥ sukham
of the unpeaceful, whence happiness?

There is no intuitive determination in him who is uncontrolled,
And there is likewise no concentration in him who is uncontrolled,
And in him who does not concentrate, there is no peace.
Whence can come happiness to him who is not peaceful?

na, not.
asti (3rd sg. pr. indic. $\sqrt{as}$), it is, there is.
buddhis (f. nom. sg.), intelligence, discrimination, intuitive determination.
ayuktasya (m. gen. sg.) of the uncontrolled, of the undisciplined one, of him who is undisciplined.
na, not.
ca, and.
ayuktasya (m. gen. sg.), of the uncontrolled, of the undisciplined, of the unsteadfast in Yoga.
bhāvanā (f. nom. sg.), meditation, perception, concentration.
na, not.
ca, and.
abhāvayatas (m. gen. sg.), of the non-meditating, of the non-perceiving, of the non-concentrating.
śāntis (f. nom. sg.), peace, tranquility.
aśāntasya (m. gen. sg.), of the unpeaceful, of the unpeaceful one.
kutas (interrog.), whence? from where?
sukham (n. acc. sg.), happiness, joy, good fortune.

67

इद्रियाणां हि चरतां
indriyāṇāṁ hi caratāṁ
of the senses, indeed, wandering,

यन् मनो ऽनुविधीयते ।
yan mano 'nuvidhīyate
when the mind is guided by,

तदस्य हरति प्रज्ञां
tadasya harati prajñāṁ
then of him it carries away the understanding

वायुर् नावम् इवाम्भसि ॥
vāyur nāvam ivāmbhasi
wind-a-ship-like on the water.

indriyāṇām (n. gen. pl.), of the senses, of the powers.
hi, indeed, truly.
caratām (m. gen. pl. pr. participle √*car*), of wandering, of roving.
yad (n. nom. sg.), which, what, when.
manas (n. nom. sg.), mind, thought.
anuvidhīyate (3rd sg. pr. passive *anu vi* √*dhā*), it is guided, it is led, it is ordered, it is regulated.
tad (n. nom. sg.), this, that, then.
asya (gen. sg.), of it, of him.
harati (3rd sg. act. √*hṛ*), it carries away, it steals.
prajñām (f. acc. sg.), wisdom, understanding, discrimination.
vāyus (m. nom. sg.), wind.
nāvam (f. acc. sg.), ship, boat.
iva, like.
ambhasi (n. loc. sg.), on the water.

When the mind is guided
By the wandering senses,
Then it carries away one's understanding
As does the wind a ship on the water.

68

तस्माद् यस्य महाबाहो
tasmād yasya mahābāho
therefore of whom, Mighty Armed One,

निगृहीतानि सर्वशः ।
nigṛhītāni sarvaśaḥ
withdrawn on all sides

इन्द्रियाणीन्द्रियार्थेभ्यस्
indriyāṇīndriyārthebhyas
the senses from the objects of the senses

तस्य प्रज्ञा प्रतिष्ठिता ॥
tasya prajñā pratiṣṭhitā
of him the wisdom standing firm.

Therefore, O Mighty Armed One,
The wisdom of him whose senses
Are withdrawn from the objects of the senses;
That wisdom stands firm.

tasmāt (m. abl. sg.), from this, therefore.
yasya (m. gen. sg.), of whom, of which.
mahābāho (m. voc. sg.), O Mighty Armed One, frequent epithet of Arjuna, also applied to other warriors.
nigṛhītāni (n. nom. pl. p. pass. participle *ni* √*grah*), withdrawn, held back, suppressed.
sarvaśas (adv.), on all sides, in all respects.
indriyāṇi (n. nom. pl.), senses, powers.
indriyārthebhyas (m. abl. pl.), from the objects of the senses.
tasya (m. gen. sg.), of it, of him, of this.
prajñā (f. nom. sg.), wisdom, understanding.
pratiṣṭhitā (f. nom. sg. p. pass. participle *prati* √*sthā*), standing firm, established.

69

या निशा सर्वभूतानां
yā niśā sarvabhūtānāṁ
what (is) the night of all beings

तस्यां जागर्ति संयमी ।
tasyāṁ jāgarti saṁyamī
in this he is wakeful, the man of restraint;

यस्यां जाग्रति भूतानि
yasyāṁ jāgrati bhūtāni
in what they are wakeful, beings,

सा निशा पश्यतो मुनेः ॥
sā niśā paśyato muneḥ
that (is) the night of the seeing sage.

yā (f. nom. sg.), what, which.
niśā (f. nom. sg.), night.
sarvabhūtānām (n. gen. pl.), of all beings.
tasyām (f. loc. sg.), in it, in this.
jāgarti (3rd sg. pr. indic. act. √*jāgṛ*), he is wakeful, he is watchful.
saṁyamī (m. nom. sg.), the restrained one, the man of restraint.
yasyām (f. loc. sg.), in what, in that which.
jāgrati (3rd pl. pr. indic. act. √*jāgṛ*), they are wakeful, they are watchful.
bhūtāni (n. nom. pl.), beings, existences.
sā (f. nom. sg.), this, that.
niśā (f. nom. sg.), night.
paśyatas (m. gen. sg. pr. participle √*paś*), of the seeing, of the perceiving.
munes (m. gen. sg.), of the sage, of the wise man.

The man of restraint is wakeful
In that which is the night of all beings;
The time in which all beings are wakeful
Is the night of the sage who sees.*

* Meaning that the "sage who sees" perceives the light of the *ātman*, which is dark as night to others, while the others see the light of the senses which is dark as night to the sage.

70

आपूर्यमाणम् अचलप्रतिष्ठं
*āpūryamāṇam acalapratiṣṭhaṁ**
becoming filled (yet) unmoved, standing still,

समुद्रम् आपः प्रविशन्ति यद्वत् ।
samudram āpaḥ praviśanti yadvat
the ocean, the waters they enter in which way,

तद्वत् कामा यं प्रविशन्ति सर्वे
tadvat kāmā yaṁ praviśanti sarve
in this way desires whom they enter all

स शान्तिम् आप्नोति न कामकामी ॥
sa śāntim āpnoti na kāmakāmī
he peace attains; not the desirer of desires.

Like the ocean, which becomes filled yet remains unmoved and standing still
As the waters enter it,
He whom all desires enter and who remains unmoved
Attains peace; not so the desirer of objects of desire.

āpūryamāṇam (m. acc. sg. pr. mid. participle from *ā* √*pṝ*) becoming filled, becoming full.
acala (m.), unmoved, unmoving.
pratiṣṭham (n. acc. sg. from *prati* √*sthā*), standing still, stable.
(*acalapratiṣṭham*, n. acc. sg. BV cpd., which is unmoved and standing still.)
samudram (n. acc. sg.), ocean, sea.
āpas (f. nom. pl.), water, the waters.
praviśanti (3rd pl. pr. indic. act. *pra* √*viś*), they enter, they sit upon, they dissolve in.
yadvat, in which way, as.
tadvat, in this way, so.
kāmās (m. nom. pl.), desires, appetites.
yam (m. acc. sg.), whom.
praviśanti (3rd pl. act. pr. indic. *pra* √*viś*), they enter, they encounter, they dissolve in.
sarve (m. nom. pl.), all.
sas (m. nom. sg.), he.
śāntim (f. acc. sg.), peace, tranquility.
āpnoti (3rd sg. act. √*āp*), he attains, he obtains, he reaches.
na, not.
kāmakāmī (m. nom. sg.), desirer of desires, desirer of the objects of desire. TP cpd.

* *Triṣṭubh* metre.

71

विहाय कामान् यः सर्वान्
*vihāya kāmān yaḥ sarvān**
abandoning desires who all,

पुमांश्चरति निःस्पृहः।
pumāṅścarati niḥspṛhaḥ
the man acts free from lust.

निर्ममो निरहंकारः
nirmamo nirahaṁkāraḥ
indifferent to possessions, free from egotism,

स शान्तिम् अधिगच्छति ॥
sa śāntim adhigacchati
he peace attains.

The man who abandons all desires
Acts free from lust.
Indifferent to possessions, free from egotism,
He attains peace.

vihāya (gerund *vi* √*hā*), abandoning, casting away.
kāmān (m.acc. pl.), desires, cravings.
yas (m. nom. sg.), who.
sarvān (m. acc. pl.), all.
pumān (m. nom. sg.), the man, a man, man.
carati (3rd sg. pr. indic. act. √*car*), he moves, he lives, he acts.
niḥspṛhas (m. nom. sg.), free from desire, free from lust.
nirmamas (m. nom. sg.), indifferent to "mine," indifferent to possessions.
nirahaṁkāras (m. nom. sg.), free from "I making," free from egotism.
sas (m. nom. sg.), he, this.
śāntim (f. acc. sg.), peace.
adhigacchati (3rd sg. pr. indic. act. *adhi* √*gam*), he goes to, he attains.

* *Śloka* metre resumes.

72

एषा ब्राह्मी स्थितिः पार्थ
eṣā brāhmī sthitiḥ pārtha
this the brāhmanic position, Son of Pṛthā.

नैनां प्राप्य विमुह्यति ।
nāināṁ prāpya vimuhyati
not, this having attained, he is deluded.

स्थित्वा ऽस्याम् अन्तकाले ऽपि
sthitvā 'syām antakāle 'pi
fixed in it, at time of death even

ब्रह्मनिर्वाणम् ऋच्छति ॥
brahmanirvāṇam ṛcchati
brahmanirvāṇa he reaches.

This is the Brahmanic state, Son of Pṛthā (Arjuna).
Having attained this, he is not deluded;
Fixed in it, even at the hour of death,
He reaches the nirvāṇa of Brahman.

eṣā (f. nom. sg.), this.
brāhmī (adj., f. nom. sg.), holy, divine, pertaining to Brahman.
brāhmī sthitis (f. nom. sg.), the state of Brahman, Brahmanic state, state concerning Brahman, Brahmanic position.
pārtha, Son of Pṛthā, frequent epithet of Arjuna.
na, not.
enām (f. acc. sg.), this.
prāpya (gerund *pra* √*āp*), attaining, having attained.
vimuhyati (3rd sg. pr. indic. act. *vi* √*muh*), he is deluded, he is confused.
sthitvā (gerund √*sthā*), fixed, standing firm.
asyām (f. loc. sg.), in it, in this.
antakāle (m. loc. sg.), in time of end, at time of death.
api, even, also.
brahmanirvāṇam (n. acc. sg.), Brahmanirvāṇa, the nirvāṇa (ceasing to exist) in Brahman (the word nirvāṇa—from *nir* √*vā*, blow—means "blown out" in the sense that a candle is blown out).
ṛcchati (3rd sg. pr. indic. act. √*ṛ*), he reaches, he attains.

End of Book II

The Yoga of Knowledge

BOOK III

अर्जुन उवाच ।
arjuna uvāca
Arjuna spoke:

arjunas (m. nom. sg.), Arjuna.
uvāca (3rd sg. perf. act. √*vac*), he said, he spoke.

1

ज्यायसी चेत् कर्मणस् ते
jyāyasī cet karmaṇas te
better if than action of thee

मता बुद्धिर्जनार्दन ।
matā buddhirjanārdana
thought, intelligence, Agitator of Men,

तत्किं कर्मणि घोरे मां
tatkiṁ karmaṇi ghore māṁ
then why to action terrible me

नियोजयसि केशव ॥
niyojayasi keśava
thou urgest, Handsome Haired One?

jyāyasī (f. nom. sg. comparative), better, superior, larger, stronger.
ced, if.
karmaṇas (n. abl. sg.), than action, than deeds.
te (gen. sg.), of thee, thy.
matā (f. nom. sg.), thought, idea, conviction.
buddhis (f. nom. sg.), intelligence, enlightenment, mental determination.
janārdana, (m. voc. sg.), Mover of Men, Agitator of Men, epithet of Krishna.
tad (n. nom. sg.), then.
kim (n. nom. sg. interrog.), what? why?
karmaṇi (n. loc. sg.), in action, to action.
ghore (n. loc. sg.), terrible, frightful, awful, venerable, sublime.
mām (acc. sg.), me, to me.
niyojayasi (2nd sg. pr. indic. causative act. *ni* √*yuj*), thou causest to yoke, thou urgest.
keśava (m. voc. sg.), O Handsome Haired One, epithet of Krishna.

Arjuna spoke:

If it is thy conviction that intuitive determination
Is better than action, O Agitator of Men,
Then why dost thou urge me to terrible action,
O Handsome Haired One?

2

व्यामिश्रेणेव वाक्येन
vyāmiśreṇeva vākyena
by equivocal-like speech

बुद्धिं मोहयसीव मे ।
buddhiṁ mohayasīva me
the intelligence thou confusest-like, of me;

तद् एकं वद निश्चित्य
tad ekaṁ vada niścitya
this one tell! surely

येन श्रेयो ऽहम् आप्नुयाम् ॥
yena śreyo 'ham āpnuyām
by which the highest good I should attain.

With speech that seems equivocal
Thou confusest mine intelligence.
This one thing tell me surely:
That by which I should attain the highest good.

vyāmiśreṇa (n. inst. sg. from *vi ā* √*miś*), by mixed, by manifold, by troubled, by distracted, by equivocal.
iva like, so to speak.
vākyena (n. inst. sg.), by words, with words, with speech.
buddhim (f. acc. sg.), intelligence, discrimination.
mohayasi (2nd sg. causative act. √*muh*), thou deludest, thou confusest.
iva, like, as it were.
me (gen. sg.), of me, my.
tad (n. acc. sg.), that, this.
ekam (n. acc. sg.), one.
vada (2nd sg. imperative act. √*vad*), tell! say!
niścitya (gerund *nis* √*ci*), surely, without doubt.
yena (inst. sg.), by which, with which.
śreyas (n. nom. sg. compar.), the higher good, the supreme good.
aham (nom. sg.), I.
āpnuyām (1st sg. opt. act. √*āp*), I should attain, I should reach.

III

श्रीभगवान् उवाच ।
śrībhagavān uvāca
the Blessed Lord spoke:

śrībhagavān (m. nom. sg.), the Blessed Lord, the Blessed One.
uvāca (3rd sg. perfect act. √*vac*), he said, he spoke.

3

लोके ऽस्मिन् द्विविधा निष्ठा
loke 'smin dvividhā niṣṭhā
in world in this, two-fold basis (of devotion)

पुरा प्रोक्ता मया ऽनघ ।
purā proktā mayā 'nagha
anciently taught by me, Blameless One (Arjuna),

ज्ञानयोगेन सांख्यानां
jñānayogena sāṁkhyānāṁ
by knowledge Yoga of the Sāṁkhyas;

कर्मयोगेन योगिनाम् ॥
karmayogena yoginām
by action Yoga of the Yogins.

loke (m. loc. sg.), in the world.
asmin (m. loc. sg.), in this.
dvividhā (f. nom. sg.), of two kinds, two-fold.
nisṭhā (f. nom. sg. from *ni* √*sthā*), basis, steadfastness, attachment.
purā (adv.), anciently, previously, in older times.
proktā (f. nom. sg. p. pass. participle *pra* √*vac*), declared, proclaimed, taught.
mayā (inst. sg.), by me.
anagha (m. voc. sg.), Blameless One, epithet of Arjuna.
jñānayogena (m. inst. sg.), by knowledge-Yoga, by the Yoga of knowledge. TP cpd.
*sāṁkhyānām** (m. gen. pl.), of the Sāṁkyas, of the followers of the Sāṁkhya doctrine.
karmayogena (m. inst. sg.), by action Yoga, by the Yoga of action. TP cpd.
yoginām (m. gen. pl.), of the Yogins, of the followers of Yoga.

The Blessed Lord spoke:

In this world there is a two-fold basis (of devotion)
Taught anciently by me, Blameless One (Arjuna),
That of the knowledge-Yoga of the followers of the Sāṁkhya*
And that of the action-Yoga of the Yogins.

* See footnote on p. 136.

4

न कर्मणाम् अनारम्भान्
na karmaṇām anārambhān
not of actions from non-commencement

नैष्कर्म्यं पुरुषो ऽश्नुते ।
nāiṣkarmyaṁ puruṣo 'śnute
the state beyond karma a man he attains

न च संन्यसनादेव
na ca saṁnyasanādeva
and not from renunciation alone

सिद्धिं समधिगच्छति ॥
siddhiṁ samadhigacchati
perfection he approaches.

Not by abstention from actions
Does a man attain the state beyond karma,
And not by renunciation alone
Does he approach perfection.

na, not.
karmaṇām (n. gen. pl.), of actions, of deeds, from actions.
anārambhāt (m. abl. sg. from *an ā √rambh*), from non-commencement, from non-undertaking, from abstention.
nāiṣkarmyam (n. acc. sg.), freedom from action, inactivity, state beyond karma.
puruṣas (m. nom. sg.), man, spirit.
aśnute (3rd sg. pr. indic. mid. *√aś*), he attains.
na, not.
ca, and.
saṁnyasanāt (n. abl. sg.), from renunciation, from relinquishment.
eva, indeed, alone (often used as a rhythmic filler).
siddhim (f. acc. sg.), perfection, fulfillment, success.
samadhigacchati (3rd sg. pr. indic. act. *sam adhi √gam*), he approaches, he comes near, he surpasses.

5

न हि कश्चित् क्षणमपि
na hi kaścit kṣaṇamapi
not indeed anyone in the twinkling of an eye even

जातु तिष्ठत्यकर्मकृत् ।
jātu tiṣṭhatyakarmakṛt
ever he exists not doing action;

कार्यते ह्यवशः कर्म
kāryate hyavaśaḥ karma
he is forced to perform, indeed without will, action,

सर्वः प्रकृतिजैर् गुणैः ॥
sarvaḥ prakṛtijāir guṇāiḥ
everyone by the nature-born guṇas

Indeed, no one, even in the twinkling of an eye,
Ever exists without performing action;
Everyone is forced to perform action, even that action which is against his will,
By the guṇas, which originate in material nature.

na, not.
hi, indeed, truly.
kaścid, anyone, anyone whatsoever.
kṣaṇam (n. nom. sg.), an instant, a moment, the twinkling of an eye.
api, even, also.
jātu, ever, at any time.
tiṣṭhati (3rd sg. pr. indic. act. √*sthā*), he stands, he exists, he remains.
akarmakṛt (m. nom. sg.), not action doing, not performing action.
kāryate (3rd sg. pr. indic. pass. causative √*kṛ*), he is caused to perform, he is forced to perform.
hi, indeed, truly.
avaśas (m. nom. sg.), without will, against will.
karma (n. acc. sg.), action.
sarvas (m. nom. sg.), all, everyone.
prakṛtijāis (m. inst. pl.), by original sources born, by material nature born.
guṇāis (m. inst. pl.), by the guṇas.

6

कर्मेन्द्रियाणि संयम्य
karmendriyāṇi saṁyamya
action powers restraining,

य आस्ते मनसा स्मरन् ।
ya āste manasā smaran
who he sits by the mind remembering

इन्द्रियार्थान् विमूढात्मा
indriyārthān vimūḍhātmā
the objects of the senses, deluded self,

मिथ्याचारः स उच्यते ॥
mithyācāraḥ sa ucyate
a hypocrite, he, it is said.

He who sits, restraining his powers of action,
While in his mind brooding over
The objects of the senses, with a deluded self,
Is said to be a hypocrite.

karmendriyāṇi (n. acc. pl. TP cpd. *karma indriyāṇi*), action-powers, powers of action.
saṁyamya (gerund *sam* √*yam*), restraining, subduing, controlling.
yas (m. nom. sg.), who, which.
āste (3rd sg. pr. indic. mid. √*ās*), he sits.
manasā (n. inst. sg.), by the mind, with the mind.
smaran (m. nom. sg. pr. participle √*smṛ*), remembering, thinking of.
indriyārthān (*indriya arthān*, m. acc. pl. TP cpd.), sense-objects, objects of the senses, objects of the powers.
vimūḍha (p. pass. participle *vi* √*muh*), deluded, confused.
ātmā (m. nom. sg.), self.
mithyācāras (m. nom. sg.), of false behavior, hypocrisy, a hypocrite.
sas (m. nom. sg.), he, this.
ucyate (3rd sg. pr. indic. passive √*vac*), it is said, he is called, he is said to be.

7

यस् त्विन्द्रियाणि मनसा
yas tvindriyāṇi manasā
who but the senses by the mind

नियम्यारभते ऽर्जुन ।
niyamyārabhate 'rjuna
controlling he undertakes, Arjuna,

कर्मेन्द्रियैः कर्मयोगम्
karmendriyāiḥ karmayogam
by the action-organs, action yoga,

असक्तः स विशिष्यते ॥
asaktaḥ sa viśiṣyate
unattached, he is distinguished.

**But he who undertakes the control
Of the senses by the mind, Arjuna,
And, without attachment, engages the
  organs of action
In the Yoga of action, is superior.**

yas (m. nom. sg.), who.

tu, but.

indriyāṇi (n. acc. pl.), senses, powers.

manasā (n. inst. sg.), by the mind, with the mind.

niyamya (gerund *ni √yam*), controlling, subduing.

ārabhate (3rd sg. pr. indic. mid. *ā √rambh*), he undertakes, he commences, he begins, he engages.

arjuna (m. voc. sg.), Arjuna.

karmendriyāis (*karma indriyāis,* m. inst. pl. TP cpd.), by the organs of action, by the powers of action.

karmayogam (m. acc. sg. TP cpd.), action-Yoga, the Yoga of action.

asaktas (m. nom. sg. p. pass. participle *a √sañj*), unattached, not hanging onto.

sas (m. nom. sg.), he, this.

viśiṣyate (3rd sg. pr. pass. *vi √śiṣ*), he is distinguished, he is superior.

8

नियतं कुरु कर्म त्वं
niyatam̐ kuru karma tvam̐
enjoined perform action thou,

कर्म ज्यायो ह्यकर्मणः ।
karma jyāyo hyakarmaṇaḥ
action better indeed than non-action

शरीरयात्रापि च ते
śarīrayātrāpi ca te
and body conduct even of thee

न प्रसिद्ध्येद् अकर्मणः ॥
na prasiddhyed akarmaṇaḥ
not it could be accomplished without action.

Perform enjoined action, thou!
Action is indeed better than non-action,
And even the mere maintenance of thy body
Could not be accomplished without action.

niyatam (m. acc. sg. p. pass. participle *ni* √*yam*), enjoined, subdued.
kuru (2nd sg. imperative act. √*kṛ*), peform! do!
karma (n. acc. sg.), action, deeds.
tvam (nom. sg.), thou
karma (n. nom. sg.), action.
jyāyas (comparative), better, superior.
hi, indeed, truly.
akarmaṇas (n. abl. sg.), from inaction, than non-action.
śarīra (n.), body.
yā trā (f. nom. sg.), conduct, maintenance.
api, even, also.
ca, and.
te (gen. sg.), of thee, thy.
na, not.
prasiddhyet (3rd sg. opt. act. *pra* √*sidh*), it should be accomplished, it might be accomplished, it should succeed, it should be attained.
akarmaṇas (n. abl. sg.), without action, from non-action, from inaction.

9

यज्ञार्थात् कर्मणो ऽन्यत्र
yajñārthāt karmaṇo 'nyatra
from sacrifice-purpose from action aside,

लोको ऽयं कर्मबन्धनः ।
loko 'yaṁ karmabandhanaḥ
world this action-bound

तदर्थं कर्म कौन्तेय
tadarthaṁ karma kāunteya
(for) that purpose, action, Son of Kuntī,

मुक्तसङ्गः समाचर ॥
muktasañgaḥ samācara
free from attachment, perform!

Aside from action for the purpose of sacrifice,
This world is bound by action.
Perform action for this purpose of sacrifice, Son of Kuntī,
Free from attachment.

yajña (m.), sacrifice.
arthāt (m. abl. sg.), from object, from purpose, from aim.
(*yajñārthāt*, m. abl. sg. TP cpd., for the purpose of sacrifice.)
karmaṇas (n. abl. sg.), from action.
anyatra, adv., aside from, elsewhere, otherwise.
lokas (m. nom. sg.), world.
ayam (m. nom. sg.), this.
karmabandhanas (m. nom. sg. BV cpd.) such that it is bound by action.
tad (n. acc. sg.), that, this.
artham (m. acc. sg.), purpose, aim, object.
karma (n. acc. sg.), action, deeds.
kāunteya (m. voc. sg.), Son of Kuntī, epithet of Arjuna referring to his mother.
mukta (p. pass. participle √*muc*), freed, released.
sañgas (m. nom. sg. √*sañj*), attachment, clinging.
(*muktasañgas,* m. nom. sg. BV cpd., being free from attachment.)
samācara (2nd sg. imperative act. *sam ā* √*car*), perform! accomplish!

10

सहयज्ञाः प्रजाः सृष्ट्वा
sahayajñāḥ prajāḥ sṛṣṭvā
together with sacrifices mankind having created,

पुरोवाच प्रजापतिः ।
purovāca prajāpatiḥ
anciently said Prajapati (the Lord of Creatures)

अनेन प्रसविष्यध्वम्
anena prasaviṣyadhvam
"by this may ye bring forth;

एष वो ऽस्त्विष्टकामधुक्
eṣa vo 'stviṣṭakāmadhuk
this of you may it be the milch cow of desires.

Having created mankind along with sacrifices,
Prajāpati (the Lord of Creatures) anciently said,
"By this (i.e. sacrifice), may you bring forth;
May this be the milch cow of your desires.

sahayajñās (f. acc. pl.), together with sacrifices, along with sacrifices.
prajās (f. acc. pl.), progeny, mankind.
sṛṣṭvā (gerund √*sṛj*), having created, having sent forth, having let go.
purā (adv.), anciently, previously, in olden times.
uvāca (3rd sg. perf. act. √*vac*), he said, he spoke.
prajāpatis (m. nom. sg.), Lord of Creatures, Brahmā, also applied to other figures.
anena (m. inst. sg.), by this.
prasaviṣyadhvam (2nd pl. imperative future act. *pra* √*su*), may you bring forth! bring ye forth!
eṣas (m. nom. sg.), this.
vas (gen. pl.), of you, your.
astu (3rd sg. imperative act. √*as*), may it be!
iṣṭakāmadhuk (f. nom. sg.), Granting Desires, name of the Cow of Plenty.

11

देवान् भावयतानेन
devān bhāvayatānena
"the gods may you cherish by this

ते देवा भावयन्तु वः ।
te devā bhāvayantu vaḥ
they the gods may they cherish you;

परस्परं भावयन्तः
parasparaṁ bhāvayantaḥ
(by) each other cherishing

श्रेयः परम् अवाप्स्यथ ॥
śreyaḥ param avāpsyatha
welfare the highest will you attain

"By this (i.e. sacrifice) may you cherish* the gods;
May the gods cherish you!
By cherishing each other
You shall attain the highest welfare.

devān (m. acc. pl.), the gods.
bhāvayata (2nd pl. causative opt. act. √*bhū*), may you cherish, may you foster, lit. "may you cause to be," may you produce, may you increase the well-being of.
anena (m. inst. sg.), by this (i.e. sacrifice).
te (m. nom. pl.), they.
devās (m. nom. pl.), the gods.
bhāvayantu (3rd pl. causative imperative act. √*bhū*), may they cherish, may they foster, may they increase the well-being of, may they produce, lit. "may they cause to be."
vas (acc. pl.), you, ye.
parasparam, each other, one another.
bhāvayantas (m. nom. pl. pr. particple √*bhū*), cherishing, fostering, lit. "causing to be."
śreyas (n. acc. sg.), welfare, bliss, happiness.
param (n. acc. sg.), highest, supreme.
avāpsyatha (2nd pl. future mid. *ava* √*āp*), you shall attain, you shall achieve, you shall reach.

* *bhāvayate,* "may you cherish," sometimes translated "may you foster," "prosper ye" or "may you nourish," is actually a causative form of the root, √*bhū*, "be," "exist." Thus its literal meaning is "may you cause (the gods) to be." The metaphysical inference is interesting. Man causes the gods to be, and in return the gods cause man to be. This is by no means the only place in religious literature where a mutual creation is hinted at – man creating god and god creating man. The idea also reminds one of William James' statement in "Essays on Faith and Morals": "I confess that I do not see why the very existence of an invisible world may not depend in part on the personal response which any one of us may make to the religious appeal. God himself, in short, may draw vital strength and increase of very being from our fidelity."

12

इष्टान् भोगान् हि वो देवा
iṣṭān bhogān hi vo devā
"desired enjoyments indeed to you the gods

दास्यन्ते यज्ञभाविताः।
dāsyante yajñabhāvitāḥ
they will give, sacrifice-produced;

तैर् दत्तान् अप्रदायैभ्यो
tāir dattān apradāyāibhyo
by these gifts not offering to them

यो भुङ्क्ते स्तेन एव सः॥
yo bhuṅkte stena eva saḥ
who he enjoys, a thief, he."

"The gods, brought into being by sacrifice,
Will indeed give you desired enjoyments;
He who enjoys while not offering these gifts to them,
A thief is he."

iṣṭān (m. acc. pl. p. pass. participle √*iṣ*), desired, wished for, sought for, asked for.
bhogān (m. acc. pl.), enjoyments, pleasures.
hi, indeed, truly.
vas (dat. pl.), to you.
devās (m. nom. pl.), the gods.
dāsyante (3rd pl. future mid. √*dā*), they will give.
yajñabhāvitās (*yajña* + m. nom. pl. p. pass. participle √*bhū*), sacrifice-produced, (as TP cpd.) brought into being by sacrifice.
tāis (m. inst. pl.), by these.
dattān (m. acc. pl.), gifts.
apradāya (gerund *a pra* √*dā*), not giving, not offering.
ebhyas (m. dat. pl.), to them.
yas (m. nom. sg.), who.
bhuṅkte (3rd sg. pr. indic. mid. √*bhuj*), he enjoys, he eats, he possesses.
stenas (m. nom. sg.), thief.
eva, indeed, only (often used as a rhythmic filler).
sas (m. nom. sg.), he, this.

13

यज्ञशिष्टाशिनः सन्तो
yajñaśiṣṭāśinaḥ santo
the sacrifice remainder eating, the good,

मुच्यन्ते सर्वकिल्बिषैः ।
mucyante sarvakilbiṣāiḥ
they are released from all evils,

भुञ्जते ते त्वघं पापा
bhuñjate te tvaghaṁ pāpā
they eat they indeed, evils the wicked

ये पचन्त्यात्मकारणात् ॥
ye pacantyātmakāraṇāt
who they cook for own sake.

The good, who eat the remainder of the sacrifice,
Are released from all evils,
But the wicked, who cook only for their own sake,
Eat their own impurity.

yajñaśiṣṭa (n.), the "sacrifice remainder" which is eaten by the faithful after the gods and priests have consumed their share.
āśinas (m. nom. pl. from √*aś*), eating, enjoying.
(*yajñaśiṣṭāśinas*, m. nom. pl. TP cpd., those who eat the remainder of the sacrifice.)
santas (m. nom. pl.), good, existing, true.
mucyante (3rd pl. pr. indic. passive √*muc*), they are released, they are liberated.
sarvakilbiṣāis (n. inst. pl.), by sins, from wrongs, from evils. KD cpd. from all evils.
bhuñjate (3rd pl. pr. indic. mid. √*bhuj*), they enjoy, they eat.
te (m. nom. pl.), they.
tu, indeed, but.
agham (n. acc. sg.), impurity, pain, suffering.
pāpās (m. nom. pl.), the wicked, the evil ones.
ye (m. nom. pl.), who.
pacanti (3rd pl. pr. indic. act. √*pac*), they cook, they digest.
ātma (n.), self, own.
kāraṇāt (n. abl. sg.), from reason, from cause, for the sake of.
(*ātmakāraṇāt*, n. abl. sg. TP cpd., for their own sake.)

14

अन्नाद् भवन्ति भूतानि
annād bhavanti bhūtāni
from food they exist, beings;

पर्जन्याद् अन्नसंभवः ।
parjanyād annasaṁbhavaḥ
from the rain god, food the origin;

यज्ञाद् भवति पर्जन्यो
yajñād bhavati parjanyo
from sacrifice exists the rain god;

यज्ञः कर्मसमुद्भवः ॥
yajñaḥ karmasamudbhavaḥ
sacrifice action origin

Beings exist from food,
Food is brought into being by the rain god,
The rain god is cherished through sacrifice,
Sacrifice is brought into being by action.*

annāt (n. abl. sg.), from food.
bhavanti (3rd pl. pr. indic. act. √*bhu*), they exist, they are, they come to be.
bhūtāni (n. nom. sg.), beings, living beings, existences.
parjanyāt (m. abl. sg.), from the rain cloud, from the rain god.
anna (n.), food.
saṁbhavas (m. nom. sg.), origin, source.
(*annasaṁbhavas*, m. nom. sg. BV cpd., of which food is the source.)
yajñāt (m. abl. sg.), from sacrifice.
bhavati (3rd sg. pr. indic. act. √*bhū*), it, he, exists, it, he, comes to be.
parjanyas (m. nom. sg.), the rain cloud, the rain god.
yajñas (m. nom. sg.), sacrifice, worship.
*karma** (n.), action, doing, deeds.
samudbhavas (m. nom. sg. from *sam ud* √*bhū*), origin, source, cause of being.
(*karmasamudbhavas*, m. nom. sg. BV cpd., brought into being by action, whose origin is in action.)

* Throughout the Bhagavad Gītā, the word *karma* (action) is used in several senses. Sometimes, as here, it refers to religious action, the ritual action of the priest performing the sacrifice. Elsewhere it refers to the warlike action proper to the warrior caste to which Arjuna belongs. At still other places it has the meaning of the sum of past actions that is carried into a future life.

15

कर्म ब्रह्मोद्भवं विद्धि
karma brahmodbhavaṁ viddhi
action Brahman origin, know!

ब्रह्माक्षरसमुद्भवम् ।
brahmākṣarasamudbhavam
Brahman the imperishable arising from

तस्मात् सर्वगतं ब्रह्म
tasmāt sarvagataṁ brahma
therefore all-pervading Brahman

नित्यं यज्ञे प्रतिष्ठितम् ॥
nityaṁ yajñe pratiṣṭhitam
eternally in sacrifice established.

Know that (ritual) action originates in Brahman (the Vedas)
Brahman arises from the Imperishable;
Therefore all-pervading Brahman
Is eternally established in sacrifice.*

karma (n. acc. sg.), action, deeds.
brahma (n.), Brahman, the all-pervading spirit of the universe. Here meaning the Vedas.
udbhavam (m. acc. sg. from *ud* √*bhū*), origin, originating, coming to be.
brahmodbhavam (m. acc. sg. TP cpd.), originating in Brahman.
viddhi (2nd sg. imperative act. √*vid*), know! learn!
brahma (n.), Brahman, the Vedas.
akṣara (adj.), imperishable, eternal, indestructible.
samudbhavam (m. acc. sg.), origin, originating, coming to be, arising from.
(*brahmākṣarasamudbhavam*, m. acc. sg. BV cpd., of which imperishable Brahman is the source).
tasmāt (n. abl. sg.), from this, therefore.
sarvagatam (n. nom. sg.), all-pervading, omnipresent.
brahma (n. nom. sg.), Brahman, the Vedas.
nityam (adv.), eternally.
yajñe (m. loc. sg.), in sacrifice.
pratiṣṭhitam (n. nom. sg. p. pass. participle *prati* √*sthā*), established, standing, remaining.

* Edgerton has pointed out that this stanza does not constitute the logical syllogism that it seems on first reading to be. "Sacrifice" is not the starting point of the series, but an intermediate term.

16

एवं प्रवर्तितं चक्रं
evaṁ pravartitaṁ cakraṁ
thus set in motion the wheel

नानुवर्तयतीह यः ।
nānuvartayatīha yaḥ
not he causes to turn (the wheel) here in the world, who,

अघायुरिन्द्रियारामो
aghāyurindriyārāmo
malicious, sense-delighted,

मोघं पार्थ स जीवति ॥
moghaṁ pārtha sa jīvati
vain, Son of Pṛthā, he lives.

evam, thus, so.
pravartitam (n. acc. sg. causative p. pass. participle *pra* √*vṛt*), set in motion, turning.
cakram (n. acc. sg.), wheel.
na, not.
anuvartayati (3rd sg. causative act. *anu* √*vṛt*), he causes to turn.
iha, here on earth, here in the world.
yas (m. nom. sg.), who.
aghāyus (m. nom. sg.), intending to injure malicious.
indriyārāmas (m. nom. sg.), sense-delighted, (as BV cpd.), one whose senses are delighted (*indriya*, senses; *ārāma*, delight).
mogham (adv.), vainly, uselessly, fruitlessly, vain, useless.
pārtha (m. voc. sg.), Son of Pṛthā, epithet of Arjuna referring to his mother, Pṛthā or Kuntī.
sas (m. nom. sg.), he, this one.
jīvati (3rd sg. pr. indic. act. √*jīv*), he lives.

He who does not cause to turn here on earth
The wheel* thus set in motion,
Lives, Son of Pṛthā (Arjuna),
Malicious, sense-delighted, and in vain.

* I.e. The circular sequence: sacrifice, the rain god, food, beings, sacrifice, the rain god, etc. etc.

17

यस्त्वात्मरतिरेव स्याद्
yastvātmaratireva syād
who only gratified in the self he should be

आत्मतृप्तश्च मानवः ।
ātmatṛptaśca mānavaḥ
and satisfied in the self, the man

आत्मन्येव च संतुष्टस्
ātmanyeva ca saṁtuṣṭas
and in the self content

तस्य कार्यं न विद्यते ॥
tasya kāryaṁ na vidyate
of him the to-be-done, not it is found.

He whose delight is only in the self,
And whose satisfaction is in the self,
And who is content only in the self;
For him the need to act does not exist.

yas (m. nom. sg.), who, which, what.
tu, indeed.
ātma (m.), self.
ratis (f. nom. sg.), pleasure, gratified, pleased, content.
(*ātmaratis*, f. nom. sg. BV cpd., whose delight is in the self.)
eva, indeed, only (often used as a rhythmic filler).
syāt (3rd sg. opt. act. √*as*), he should be, he may be.
ātma (m.), self.
tṛptas (m. nom. sg. p. pass. participle √*tṛp*), pleased, satisfied.
(*ātmatṛptas*, n. nom. sg. BV cpd., who is content in the self.)
ca, and.
mānavas (m. nom. sg.), man, a man, a descendant of Manu, the primal ancestor.
ātmani (m. loc. sg.), in the self.
eva, indeed, only (often used as a rhythmic filler).
ca, and.
saṁtuṣṭas (m. nom. sg.), content, satisfied, pleased.
tasya (m. gen. sg.), of him.
kāryam (n. nom. sg. gerundive √*kṛ*), to-be-done, to be accomplished, task, duty.
na, not.
vidyate (3rd sg. pr. indic. passive √2 *vid*), it is found.

18

नैव तस्य कृतेनार्थो
nāiva tasya kṛtenārtho
not indeed of him with action a purpose

नाकृतेनेह कश्चन ।
nākṛteneha kaścana
nor with non-action in this case any whatever,

न चास्य सर्वभूतेषु
na cāsya sarvabhūteṣu
and not of him in all beings

कश्चिद् अर्थव्यपाश्रयः ॥
kaścid arthavyapāśrayaḥ
any whatever purpose need

He has no purpose at all in action,
Nor any whatever in non-action,
And he has no need of any purpose whatever
In regard to any being.

na, not.
eva, indeed (often used as a rhythmic filler).
tasya (m. gen. sg.), of him, of this.
kṛtena (n. inst. sg. p. pass. participle √*kṛ*), with action, with deeds.
arthas (m. nom. sg.), purpose, aim, acquisition.
na, not.
akṛtena (inst. sg. p. pass. participle *a* √*kṛ*), with non-action, with inaction, by in-action.
iha, here, in this case.
kaścana, anyone whoever, anything whatever.
na, not.
ca, and.
asya (m. gen. sg.), of him, of it.
sarvabhūteṣu (m. loc. pl.), in all beings, in all existences.
kaścid, any whatever.
artha (m.), purpose, aim, acquisition.
vyapāśrayas (m. nom. sg. from *vi apa ā* √*śri*), need, needing, depending on, clinging to.
artha-vyapāśrayas (m. nom. sg. TP cpd.) need of purpose.

19

तस्माद् असक्तः सततं
tasmād asaktaḥ satataṁ
therefore unattached constantly

कार्यं कर्म समाचर।
kāryaṁ karma samācara
to be done action perform!

असक्तो ह्याचरन्कर्म
asakto hyācarankarma
unattached indeed performing action,

परम् आप्नोति पूरुषः ॥
param āpnoti pūruṣaḥ
the Supreme he attains, man.

tasmāt (m. abl. sg.), from this, therefore.
asaktas (m. nom. sg. p. pass. participle *a* √*sañj*), unattached, not clinging.
satatam (adv.), constantly, perpetually, always.
kāryam (n. acc. sg. gerundive √*kṛ*), to be done, to be accomplished, duty, task.
karma (n. acc. sg.), action, deeds.
samācara (2nd sg. imperative act. *sam ā* √*car*), perform! practice! conduct! act!
asaktas (m. nom. sg. p. pass. participle *a* √*sañj*), unattached, not clinging.
hi, indeed, truly.
ācaran (m. nom. sg. pr. participle act. *ā* √*car*), performing, acting, practicing.
karma (n. acc. sg.), actions, deeds.
param (m. acc. sg.), the highest, the supreme.
āpnoti (3rd sg. pr. indic. act. √*āp*), he attains, he obtains, he reaches.
pūruṣas (m. nom. sg.), man, spirit.

Therefore, constantly unattached,
Perform that action which is thy duty.
Indeed, by performing action while unattached,
Man attains the Supreme.*

* The "therefore" is not a consequence of the preceding stanzas, which describe the person who has attained complete concentration on the *ātman*. This stanza is the advice to Arjuna to perform action while unattached, in order to attain the state described in III 17 and 18.

20

कर्मणैव हि संसिद्धिम्
karmaṇāiva hi saṁsiddhim
by action only indeed perfection

आस्थिता जनकादयः ।
āsthitā janakādayaḥ
attained Janaka* commencing with,

लोकसंग्रहमेवापि
lokasaṁgrahamevāpi
the world holding together even,

संपश्यन् कर्तुमर्हसि ॥
saṁpaśyan kartum arhasi
beholding, to act thou shouldst.

With action alone, indeed,
Perfection was attained by kings like Janaka;*
Beholding the mere holding together of the world,
Thou shouldst act.

karmaṇā (n. inst. sg.), by action, by deeds.
eva, indeed, only (often used as a rhythmic filler).
hi, indeed, truly.
saṁsiddhim (f. acc. sg.), perfection, fulfillment, success.
āsthitā (m. nom. pl. p. pass. participle *ā* √*sthā*), attained, obtained.
*janaka,** name of an ancient philosopher-king.
ādayas (m. nom. pl.), commencing with, beginning with, (as BV cpd.) "they whose first was," the Sanskrit equivalent of "and so forth," "etcetera," "and others."
(*janakādayas,* m. nom. pl. BV cpd., those (kings) whose first was Janaka.)
loka (m.), world.
saṁgraham (m. acc. sg.), holding together, maintenance.
loka-saṁgraham (m. acc. sg. TP cpd.), maintenance of the world.
eva, indeed (used as a rhythmic filler).
api, even, also.
saṁpaśyan (m. nom. sg. pr. participle act. *sam* √*paś*), beholding, seeing, observing.
kartum (infinitive √*kṛ*), to act, to do.
arhasi (2nd sg. pr. indic. act. √*arh*), thou shouldst, thou art obliged, thou art able.

* Janaka, a famous philosopher king who, with his priest and adviser, Yājñavalkya, opposed the brāhman priesthood, claiming that he himself, though a member of the warrior caste, could perform sacrifices without brāhman help. Eventually he became a brāhman and a *rājarṣi,* or royal seer. He was the father of Sītā, the heroine of the Rāmāyaṇa. He is thought to have influenced the Buddha, who was also a member of the *kṣatriya* caste. The reference is to Janaka, as a *kṣatriya* (warrior or doer) attaining perfection through deeds rather than austerities.

21

यद्यद् आचरति श्रेष्ठस्
yadyad ācarati śreṣṭhas
whatever he does the best

तत्तद् एवेतरो जनः ।
tattad evetaro janaḥ
this and that, thus the rest, man;

स यत् प्रमाणं कुरुते
sa yat pramāṇaṁ kurute
he what standard sets

लोकस्तदनुवर्तते ॥
lokastadanuvartate
the world that it follows.

Whatever the greatest man does,
Thus do the rest;
Whatever standard he sets,
The world follows that.

yad yad, whatever.
ācarati (3rd sg. pr. indic. act. *ā* √*car*), he does, he behaves, he practices.
śreṣṭhas (m. nom. sg. superl.), best, most splendid, most excellent.
tattad (*tad tad*), this and that.
eva, indeed (used as a rhythmic filler).
itaras (m. nom. sg.), the other, another, the rest.
janas (m. nom. sg.), man.
sas (m. nom. sg.), he, the, this.
yad (n. acc. sg.), what, which.
pramāṇam (n. acc. sg. from *pra* √*mā*), measure, scale, standard.
kurute (3rd sg. pr. indic. mid. √*kṛ*), he makes, he sets.
lokas (m. nom. sg.), world, aggregate of people.
tad (n. acc. sg.), that, this.
anuvartate (3rd sg. pr. indic. mid. *anu* √*vṛt*), it follows.

22

न मे पार्थास्ति कर्तव्यं
na me pārthāsti kartavyaṁ
not of me, Son of Pṛthā, there is to-be-done

त्रिषु लोकेषु किंचन ।
triṣu lokeṣu kiṁcana
in the three worlds anything whatever

नानवाप्तमवाप्तव्यं
nānavāptamavāptavyaṁ
nor not attained to be attained,

वर्त एव च कर्मणि ॥
varta eva ca karmaṇi
I engage nevertheless in action.

For me, Son of Pṛthā, there is nothing whatever
To be done in the three worlds,
Nor is there anything not attained to be attained.
Nevertheless I engage in action.

na, not.
me (gen. sg.), of me, my.
pārtha (m. voc. sg.), Son of Pṛthā, epithet of Arjuna.
asti (3rd sg. pr. indic. √*as*), there is, it is.
kartavyam (n. nom. sg. gerundive √*kṛ*), to be done, to be accomplished.
triṣu (m. loc. pl.), in the three.
lokeṣu (m. loc. pl.), in the worlds.
kiṁcana, anything whatever, anyone whoever.
na, not, nor.
anavāptam (m. acc. sg. p. pass. participle *an ava* √*āp*), unattained, not attained, not reached.
avāptavyam (m. acc. sg. gerundive *ava* √*āp*), to be attained, to be reached.
varta (*saṃdhi* for *varte,* 1st sg. pr. indic. mid. √*vṛt*), I work, I move, I engage.
eva ca, nevertheless, notwithstanding.
karmaṇi (n. loc. sg.), in action, in deeds.

23

यदि ह्यहं न वर्तेयं
yadi hyahaṁ na varteyaṁ
if indeed I not should engage

जातु कर्मण्यतन्द्रितः ।
jātu karmaṇyatandritaḥ
at all in action, unwearied,

मम वर्त्मानुवर्तन्ते
mama vartmānuvartante
of me the path they follow

मनुष्याः पार्थ सर्वशः ॥
manuṣyāḥ pārtha sarvaśaḥ
mankind, Son of Pṛthā, everywhere.

yadi, if.
hi, indeed, truly.
aham (nom. sg.), I.
na, not.
varteyam (1st sg. opt. act. √*vṛt*), I should engage, I should be occupied with.
jātu, ever, at all.
karmaṇi (n. loc. sg.), in action, in deeds.
atandritas (m. nom. sg.), free from lassitude, unwearied.
mama (gen. sg.), of me, my.
vartma (n. acc. sg.), path, turning, way.
anuvartante (3rd pl. pr. indic. mid. *anu* √*vṛt*), they follow.
manuṣyās (m. nom. pl.), men, mankind.
pārtha (m. voc. sg.), Son of Pṛthā, epithet of Arjuna.
sarvaśas (adv.), wholly, completely, universally, altogether, everywhere.

Indeed, if I, unwearied, should not engage
In action at all,
Mankind would follow
My path everywhere, Son of Pṛthā (Arjuna).

24

उत्सीदेयुर् इमे लोका
utsīdeyur ime lokā
they would perish, these worlds,

न कुर्यां कर्म चेदहम् ।
na kuryāṁ karma cedaham
not I should perform action, if I,

संकरस्य च कर्ता स्याम्
saṁkarasya ca kartā syām
and of confusion maker I should be,

उपहन्याम् इमाः प्रजाः ॥
upahanyām imāḥ prajāḥ
I should destroy these creatures.

If I should not perform action,
These worlds would perish
And a maker of confusion I should be;
I should destroy these creatures.

utsīdeyus (3rd pl. opt. act. *ud* √*sad*), they would sink down, they should perish.
ime (m. nom pl.), these.
lokās (m. nom. pl.), worlds.
na, not.
kuryām (1st sg. opt. act. √*kṛ*), I should perform, I should do.
karma (n. acc. sg.), action, deeds.
ced, if.
aham (nom. sg.), I.
saṁkarasya (m. gen. sg.), of confusion, "of together-pouring," or scattering to-gether.
ca, and.
kartā (m. nom. sg.), maker, doer, performer, creator.
syām (1st sg. opt. √*as*), I should be.
upahanyām (1st sg. opt. act. *upa* √*han*), I should destroy, I should smite.
imās (f. acc. pl.), these.
prajās (f. acc. pl.), creatures, beings, progeny, offspring, descendants, people.

25

सक्ता: कर्मण्यविद्वांसो
saktāḥ karmaṇyavidvāṁso
attached in action, the unwise

यथा कुर्वन्ति भारत ।
yathā kurvanti bhārata
as they act, Descendant of Bharata (Arjuna);

कुर्याद् विद्वांस् तथासक्तश्
kuryād vidvāṅs tathāsaktaś
he should act, the wise, so, unattached,

चिकीर्षुर् लोकसंग्रहम् ॥
cikīrṣur lokasaṁgraham
intending to do the holding together of the world.

While those who are unwise act, Descendant of Bharata (Arjuna),
Attached in action,
So the wise one should act unattached,
Intending to maintain the holding together of the world.

saktās (m. nom. pl. p. pass. participle √*sañj*), attached, clinging.
karmaṇi (n. loc. pl.), in action, in deeds.
avidvāṁas (m. nom. pl. perf. act. particple *a* √*vid*), the unwise, the unwise ones.
yathā, in which way, as.
kurvanti (3rd pl. pr. indic. act. √*kṛ*), they act, they do.
bhārata (m. voc. sg.), Descendant of Bharata, epithet of Arjuna, and others. Bharata was the patriarch of the dominant tribes about whom the Mahābhārata was sung, and later written.
kuryāt (3rd sg. opt. act. √*kr*), he should act, he should perform, he should do.
vidvān (m. nom. sg. participle √*vid*), the wise, the wise one.
tathā, thus, in this way, so.
asaktas (m. nom. sg. p. pass. participle *a* √*sañj*), unattached, not clinging.
cikīrṣus (3rd sg. desiderative √*kṛ*), desiring to do, desiring to make, intending to do.
loka (m.), world.
saṁgraham (m. acc. sg.), holding together, maintenance.
(*loka-saṁgraham*, m. acc. sg. TP cpd., maintenance of the world.)

26

न बुद्धिभेदं जनयेद्
na buddhibhedaṁ janayed
not intelligence-fragmentation one should produce

अज्ञानां कर्मसङ्गिनां
ajñānāṁ karmasaṅgināṁ
of the ignorant, of the action attached;

जोषयेत् सर्वकर्माणि ।
joṣayet sarvakarmāṇi
one should cause (them) to enjoy all actions,

विद्वान् युक्तः समाचरन् ॥
vidvān yuktaḥ samācaran
the wise, disciplined performing.

One should not produce fragmentation of the mind
Among the ignorant who are attached to action;
The wise one should cause them to enjoy all actions,
While himself performing actions in a disciplined manner.

na, not.
buddhi (f.), intelligence.
bhedam (m. acc. sg. from √*bhid*), breaking, rending, tearing, bursting, rupture, fragmentation, splitting.
(*buddhibhedam*, m. acc. sg. TP cpd., fragmentation of the mind.)
janayet (3rd sg. opt. act. caus. √*jan*), he should give birth to, he should cause to arise, one should produce.
ajñānām (m. gen. pl.), of the ignorant, among the ignorant ones.
karmasaṅginām (m. gen. pl.), of the action-attached, (as TP cpd.) of those who cling to action.
joṣayet (3rd sg. opt. causative act. √*juṣ*), he should cause to enjoy, he should cause to delight.
sarvakarmāṇi (n. acc. pl.), all actions.
vidvān (m. nom. sg.), the wise, the wise one.
yuktas (m. nom. sg. p. pass. participle √*yuj*), joined, yoked, disciplined, stead-fast in Yoga.
samācaran (m. nom. sg. pr. participle act. *sam ā* √*car*), performing, practicing, observing.

27

प्रकृतेः क्रियमाणानि
prakrteḥ kriyamāṇāni
of material nature performed

गुणैः कर्माणि सर्वशः ।
guṇāiḥ karmāṇi sarvaśaḥ
by the guṇas, actions in all cases

अहंकारविमूढात्मा
ahaṁkāravimūḍhātmā
the egotism-confused self

कर्ताहम् इति मन्यते ॥
kartāham iti manyate
"doer I" thus he thinks.

Actions in all cases are performed
By the guṇas of material nature;
He whose self is confused by egotism,
"I am the doer," thus he imagines.

prakṛtes (f. gen. sg.), of material nature, of nature.
kriyamāṇāni (n. nom. pl. pr. mid. participle √*kṛ*), being performed, performed.
guṇāis (m. inst. pl.), by the guṇas.
karmāṇi (n. nom. pl.), actions.
sarvaśas, adv., everywhere, in all cases, altogether, entirely.
ahaṁkāra (m.), lit. "I making," egotism.
vimūḍha (m. p. pass. participle *vi* √*muh*), deluded, confused.
ātmā (m. nom. sg.), self.
(*ahaṁkāravimuḍhātmā,* m. nom. sg. BV cpd., he whose self is confused by egotism.)
kartā (m. nom. sg.), doer, creator.
aham (nom. sg.), I.
iti, thus (used to close quotations).
manyate (3rd sg. mid. √*man*), he thinks, he believes, he imagines.

28

तत्त्ववित् तु महाबाहो
tattvavit tu mahābāho
The truth-knowing, but, Mighty Armed One,

गुणकर्मविभागयोः ।
guṇakarmavibhāgayoḥ
guṇa and action of the two roles

गुणा गुणेषु वर्तन्त
guṇā guṇeṣu vartanta
"the guṇas in the guṇas they are working,"

इति मत्वा न सज्जते ॥
iti matvā na sajjate
thus having thought, not he is attached.

But he who knows the truth, O Mighty Armed One,
The fact of the two roles of guṇa and action,
"The guṇas work among the guṇas,"
Thus having thought, he is not attached.

tattvavid (m. nom. sg.), truth-knowing, "thatness knowing."
tu, but.
mahābāho (m. voc. sg.), O Mighty Armed, O Long Armed, epithet of Arjuna and other warriors.
guṇa (m.), guṇa.
karma (n.), action.
vibhāgayos (m. gen. dual), in the two roles, in the two spheres, in the two shares.
(*guṇakarmavibhāgayos,* m. loc. gen. TP cpd., of the two roles of guṇa and action.)
guṇās (m. nom. pl.), guṇas, the guṇas.
guṇeṣu (m. loc. pl.), in the guṇas.
vartanta (*saṁdhi* for *vartante*, 3rd pl. pr. indic. √*vṛt*), they work, they act.
iti, thus.
matvā (gerund √*man*), thinking, having thought.
na, not.
sajjate (3rd sg. pr. indic. mid. √*sañj*), he is attached.

29

प्रकृतेर् गुणसंमूढाः
prakṛter guṇasaṁmūḍhāḥ
of material nature, the guṇa-deluded

सज्जन्ते गुणकर्मसु ।
sajjante guṇakarmasu
they are attached in guṇa actions

तान् अकृत्स्नविदो मन्दान्
tān akṛtsnavido mandān
them incomplete-knowing, foolish;

कृत्स्नविन् न विचालयेत् ॥
kṛtsnavin na vicālayet
the complete knower not he should disturb.

prakṛtes (f. gen. sg.), of material nature, of nature.
guṇa (m.), guṇa.
saṁmūḍhās (m. nom. pl.), the deluded, those who are deluded.
(*guṇa-saṁmūḍhās*, m. nom. pl. TP cpd., those who are deluded by the guṇas.)
sajjante (3rd pl. pr. indic. mid. $\sqrt{}$*sañj*), they are attached.
guṇakarmasu (n. loc. pl.), in guṇa actions.
tān (m. acc. pl.), them.
akṛtsnavidas (m. acc. pl.), incomplete knowing, not knowing the whole, not knowing the entirety.
mandān (m. acc. pl.), foolish, fools, dullards.
kṛtsnavid (m. nom. sg.), the complete knower, the knower of the whole.
na, not.
vicālayet (3rd sg. causative act. opt. *vi* $\sqrt{}$*cal*), he should cause to waver.

Those deluded by the guṇas of material nature
Are attached to the actions of the guṇas.
Them, foolish men of incomplete knowledge,
The complete knower should not disturb.

30

मयि सर्वाणि कर्माणि
mayi sarvāṇi karmāṇi
on Me all actions

संन्यस्याध्यात्मचेतसा ।
saṁnyasyādhyātmacetasā
relinquishing, meditating on the Supreme Spirit

निराशीर् निर्ममो भूत्वा
nirāśīr nirmamo bhūtvā
free from desire, indifferent to "mine" having become,

युध्यस्व विगतज्वरः ॥
yudhyasva vigatajvaraḥ
fight! gone away fever.

Deferring all actions to Me,*
Meditating on the Supreme Spirit,
Having become free from desire, indifferent to possessions,
Fight! thy fever departed.

mayi (loc. sg.), in me, to me, on me.
sarvāṇi (n. acc. pl.), all.
karmāṇi (n. acc. pl.), actions, deeds.
saṁnyasya (gerund *sam ni* √*as*), relinquishing, entrusting, renouncing.
adhyātmacetasā (n. inst. sg.), by meditating on the Supreme Spirit (*adhyātma*), by thinking on the Supreme Self.
nirāśīs (m. nom. sg.), not wishing for, not asking for, free from asking, free from desire.
nirmamas (m. nom. sg.), indifferent to "mine," free from desire for possessions.
bhūtvā (gerund √*bhū*), becoming, being, having become, having been.
yudhyasva (2nd imperative mid. √*yudh*), fight! engage in battle!
vigata (p. pass. participle *vi* √*gam*), gone away, departed, disappeared.
jvaras (m. nom. sg.), fever, grief.
vigata-jvaras (m. nom. sg. BV cpd.), one whose fever is departed.

* I.e. allowing God to initiate all actions.

31

ये मे मतम् इदं नित्यम्
ye me matam idaṁ nityam
who of me doctrine this constantly

अनुतिष्ठन्ति मानवाः ।
anutiṣṭhanti mānavāḥ
they practice, men,

श्रद्धावन्तो ऽनसूयन्तो
śraddhāvanto 'nasūyanto
believing, not sneering,

मुच्यन्ते ते ऽपि कर्मभिः ॥
mucyante te 'pi karmabhiḥ
they are released, they also by actions.

Men who constantly practice
This doctrine of Mine,
Believing, not sneering,
Are also released from the bondage of actions.

ye (m. nom. pl.), who, which.
me (gen. sg.), of me, my.
matam (n. acc. sg.), thought, doctrine.
idam (n. acc. sg.), this.
nityam (adv.), constantly, eternally, perpetually.
anutiṣṭhanti (3rd pl. pr. indic. act. *anu* √*sthā*), they practice, they follow, they carry out.
mānavās (m. nom. pl.), men, mankind, descendants of Manu, progenitor of the human race.
śraddhāvantas (m. nom. pl.), believing, full of faith.
anasūyantas (m. nom. pl. pr. participle *an* √*asūya*), not sneering, not spiteful, not envious, not caviling, not grumbling, not speaking ill of, not showing jealousy.
mucyante (3rd pl. pr. pass. √*muc*), they are released, they are liberated.
te, (m. nom. pl.), they.
api, even, also.
karmabhis (n. inst. pl.), by actions, from actions.

32

ये त्वेतद् अभ्यसूयन्तो
ye tvetad abhyasūyanto
who, but, this sneering at,

नानुतिष्ठन्ति मे मतम् ।
nānutiṣṭhanti me matam
not they practice of me the doctrine,

सर्वज्ञानविमूढांस् तान्
sarvajñānavimūḍhāṅs tān
all wisdom confusing; them

विद्धि नष्टान् अचेतसः ।।
viddhi naṣṭān acetasaḥ
know to be lost and mindless.

But those who, sneering at this,
Do not practice My doctrine,
Confusing all wisdom,
Know them to be lost and mindless.

ye (m. nom. pl.), who.
tu, but.
etad, (n. acc. sg.), this.
abhyasūyantas (m. nom. pl. pr. participle *abhi* √*asūya*), sneering, showing ill will, caviling.
na, not.
anutiṣṭhanti (3rd pl. pr. indic. act. *anu* √*sthā*), they practice, they follow, they carry out.
me (gen. sg.), of me, my.
matam (n. acc. sg.), thought, doctrine.
sarva, all.
jñāna (n.), knowledge, wisdom.
vimūḍhān (m. acc. pl. p. pass. participle *vi* √*muh*), confusing, deluding.
(*sarva-jñāna-vimūḍhān*, m. acc. pl. TP cpd., confusing all knowledge.)
tān (m. acc. pl.), them.
viddhi (2nd sg. imperative act. √*vid*), know! learn!
naṣṭān (m. acc. pl. p. pass. participle √*naś*), lost, destroyed.
acetasas (m. acc. pl.), them whose minds are not, them who are mindless, the stupid ones.

33

सदृशं चेष्टते स्वस्याः
sadṛśaṁ ceṣṭate svasyāḥ
according to one acts from own

प्रकृतेर् ज्ञानवान् अपि ।
prakṛter jñānavān api
material nature, the wise man even.

प्रकृतिं यान्ति भूतानि
prakṛtiṁ yānti bhūtāni
material nature they follow, beings;

निग्रहः किं करिष्यति ॥
nigrahaḥ kiṁ kariṣyati
restraint what it will accomplish?

One acts according to one's own material nature.
Even the wise man does so.
Beings follow (their own) material nature;
What will restraint accomplish?

sadṛśam (adv.), according to.
ceṣṭate (3rd sg. pr. indic. mid. √*ceṣṭ*), he, she, one acts, one strives, one moves, one struggles.
svasyās (f. gen. sg.), from own, through own.
prakṛtes (f. gen. sg.), from material nature.
jñānavān (m. nom. sg.), full of wisdom, wise, wise man.
api, even, also.
prakṛtim (f. acc. sg.), material nature.
yānti (3rd pl. pr. indic. act. √*yā*), they go, they follow.
bhūtāni (n. nom. pl.), beings, existences.
nigrahas (m. nom. sg.), restraint, control, subduing.
kim (interrog.), what?
kariṣyati (3rd sg. future act. √*kṛ*), it will make, it will do, it will accomplish.

34

इन्द्रियस्येन्द्रियस्यार्थे
indriyasyendriyasyārthe
in of a sense of a sense-object

रागद्वेषौ व्यवस्थितौ ।
rāgadveṣāu vyavasthitāu
passion and hatred seated.

तयोर् न वशम् आगच्छेत्
tayor na vaśam āgacchet
of these two not the power one should come under;

तौ ह्यस्य परिपन्थिनौ ॥
tāu hyasya paripanthināu
they two indeed, of one, two antagonists.

In a sense in relation to an object of that sense,
Passion and hatred are seated.
One should not come under the power of these two;
They are indeed one's two antagonists.

indriyasya (n. gen. sg.), of a sense, of a power.
indriyasya (n. gen. sg.), of a sense, of a power.
artha (m.), object, purpose.
(*indriyasyendriyasyārthe,* m. loc. sg., of a sense in relation to an object of that sense.)
rāga (m.), passion, desire.
dveṣa (m.), hatred, aversion.
(*rāgadveṣāu,* m. nom. dual DV cpd., passion and hatred.)
vyavasthitāu (m. nom. dual p. pass. participle *vi ava* √*sthā*), seated, abiding in.
tayos (m. gen. dual), of these two.
na, not.
vaśam (m. acc. sg.), power, will, authority, control.
āgacchet (3rd sg. opt. act. *ā* √*gam*), one should come, one should come near, one should fall into, one should come under.
tāu (m. nom. dual), they two, them two.
hi, indeed, truly.
asya (m. gen. sg.), of him, of it, of one.
paripanthināu (m. nom. dual), two enemies, two hindrances, two things that stand in the way, two adversaries, two antagonists.

35

श्रेयान् स्वधर्मो विगुणः
śreyān svadharmo viguṇaḥ
better own duty deficient

परधर्मात् स्वनुष्ठितात् ।
paradharmāt svanuṣṭhitāt
than duty of another (caste), well performed.

स्वधर्मे निधनं श्रेयः
svadharme nidhanaṁ śreyaḥ
in own duty death better,

परधर्मो भयावहः ॥
paradharmo bhayāvahaḥ
duty of another (caste), danger inviting.

Better one's own duty deficient
Than the duty of another caste well performed.
Better death in one's own duty;
The duty of another caste invites danger.

śreyān (m. nom. sg. comparative), better, superior, preferable.
svadharmas (m. nom. sg.), own duty (here meaning duty of one's own caste).
viguṇas (m. nom. sg.), deficient, imperfect, ineffective, unsuccessful.
paradharmāt (m. abl. sg.), from duty of another, than duty of another (here meaning of another caste).
sv, su well, good.
anuṣṭhitāt (abl. p. pass. participle *anu* √*sthā*), than done, than practiced, than performed.
svadharme (m. loc. sg.), in own duty, in own caste duty.
nidhanam (n. nom. sg.), settling down, end, death.
śreyas (n. nom. sg. compar.), better, superior, preferable.
paradharmas (m. nom. sg.), duty of another, opposite duty.
bhaya (n.), danger, fear.
āvahas (from *ā* √*vah*), inviting, bringing.
(*bhaya-āvahaḥ*, m. nom. sg. TP cpd., bringing fear.)

III

अर्जुन उवाच।
arjuna uvāca
Arjuna spoke:

arjunas (m. nom. sg.), Arjuna.
uvāca (3rd sg. perf. act. √*vac*), he said, he spoke.

36

अथ केन प्रयुक्तो ऽयं
atha kena prayukto 'yaṁ
then, by what impelled this

पापं चरति पूरुषः।
pāpaṁ carati pūruṣaḥ
evil he commits a man

अनिच्छन्नपि वार्ष्णेय
anicchannapi vārṣṇeya
unwillingly even, Clansman of Vṛṣṇi

बलाद् इव नियोजितः॥
balād iva niyojitaḥ
from force, as if, urged

Arjuna spoke:

Then, by what impelled
Does a man commit this evil?
Unwillingly even, Clansman of Vṛṣṇi (Krishna),
As if urged by force?

atha, then, in this case.
kena (inst. sg. interrog.), by what?
prayuktas (m. nom. sg. p. pass. participle *pra* √*yuj*), impelled, ordered, set in motion, caused.
ayam (m. nom. sg.), this.
pāpam (n. acc. sg.), evil, misfortune, harm.
carati (3rd sg. pr. indic. act. √*car*), he moves, he acts, he commits.
pūruṣas (m. nom. sg.), man, spirit.
anicchan (m. nom. sg. pr. participle *an* √*iṣ*), not wishing, unwilling, not desiring.
api, even, also.
vārṣṇeya (m. voc. sg.), Clansman of Vṛṣṇi, epithet of Krishna, refers to the race of the Yādavas or Mādhavas. Vṛṣṇi was the name of a Yādava dynasty to which Krishna traced his lineage (this refers to the earthly Krishna, not the *avatār* of Vishnu which entered Krishna's body).
balāt (n. abl. sg.), from force, from strength.
iva, like, as if.
niyojitas (m. nom. sg. p. pass. participle causative *ni* √*yuj*), attached to, enjoined, commanded, urged.

श्रीभगवान् उवाच ।
śrībhagavān uvāca
the Blessed Lord spoke:

śrībhagavān (m. nom. sg.), the Blessed Lord, the Blessed One.
uvāca (3rd sg. perf. act. √*vac*), he said, he spoke.

37

काम एष क्रोध एष
kāma eṣa krodha eṣa
desire this anger this

रजोगुणसमुद्भवः ।
rajoguṇasamudbhavaḥ
rajas guṇa the source

महाशनो महापाप्मा
mahāśano mahāpāpmā
mighty eating, greatly injurious

विद्ध्येनम् इह वैरिणम् ॥
viddhyenam iha vāiriṇam
know this, in this case, the enemy.

The Blessed Lord spoke:

This force is desire, this force is anger
Of which the rajas guṇa is the source.
Voracious and greatly injurious;
Know this to be, in this matter, the enemy.

kāmas (m. nom. sg.), desire, love, greed.
eṣas (m. nom. sg.), this.
krodhas (m. nom. sg.), anger, wrath, fury.
eṣas (m. nom. sg.), this (refers to the "force" of stanza 36).
rajas (n.), the guṇa or rajas, of desire and power.
guṇa (m.), guṇa.
samudbhavas (m. nom. sg. from *sam ud* √*bhū*), source, cause, origin.
(*rajo-guṇa-samudbhavas*, m. nom. sg. TP cpd., born of the guna of rajas.)
mahā, great, mighty.
aśana (n. nom. acc. sg. pr. participle √*aś*), eating, consuming.
(*mahāśanas*, m. nom. sg. voracious.)
mahā, great, mighty.
pāpmā (m. nom. sg.), misfortune, evil, crime, sin, hurtful, injurious.
(*mahāpāpmās*, m. nom. sg. BV cpd., it of which the evil is great.)
viddhi (2nd sg. imperative act. √*vid*), know! learn!
enam (m. acc. sg.), this.
iha, here, in this case, in this matter.
vāiriṇam (m. acc. sg.), enemy, foe, hostile.

38

धूमेनाव्रियते वह्निर्
dhūmenāvriyate vahnir
by smoke he is covered, the bearer (Agni, god of fire),

यथा ऽदर्शो मलेन च ।
yathā 'darśo malena ca
and as similarly a mirror by dust,

यथोल्बेनावृतो गर्भस्
yatholbenāvṛto garbhas
as membrane-covered, the embryo,

तथा तेनेदम् आवृतम् ॥
tathā tenedam āvṛtam
thus by this that covered.

As fire is obscured by smoke,
And similarly a mirror by dust,
As the embryo is enveloped by the membrane,
So the intelligence is obscured by passion.

dhūmena (m. inst. sg.), by smoke, with smoke.
āvriyate (3rd sg. pr. indic. pass. *ā* √*vṛ*), he is covered, he is enveloped.
vahnis (m. nom. sg.), bearer (applied to draught animals, charioteers; here to Agni, the god of fire, who bears oblations to the gods).
yathā, in which way, similarly as.
ādarśas (m. nom. sg. from *ā* √*dṛś*), mirror.
malena (n. inst. sg.), by dust, with dust.
ca, and.
yathā, in which way, similarly as.
ulbena (n. inst. sg.), by membrane, by envelope.
āvṛtas (m. nom. sg. p. pass. participle *ā* √*vṛ*), covered, enveloped.
garbhas (m. nom. sg.), embryo, womb, foetus.
tathā, thus, so.
tena (n. inst. sg.), by this.
idam (n. nom. sg.), that, this.
āvṛtam (n. nom. sg. p. pass. participle *ā* √*vṛ*), covered, enveloped.

39

आवृतं ज्ञानम् एतेन
āvṛtaṁ jñānam etena
covered knowledge by this

ज्ञानिनो नित्यवैरिणा ।
jñānino nityavāiriṇā
of the knowers by the eternal enemy

कामरूपेण कौन्तेय
kāmarūpeṇa kāunteya
by the form of desire, Son of Kuntī,

दुष्पूरेणानलेन च ॥
duṣpūreṇānalena ca
and by hard-to-fill fire.

By this eternal enemy,
Having the form of desire,
And of insatiable fire,
The knowledge even of the wise ones
is obscured.

āvṛtam (n. nom. sg. p. pass. participle *ā* √*vṛ*), covered, enveloped, obscured.
jñānam (n. nom. sg.), knowledge, wisdom.
etena (m. inst. sg.), by this, with that.
jñāninas (m. nom. pl.), the knowing, the wise ones.
nitya (adj.), eternal, imperishable.
vāiriṇā (m. inst. sg.), by the enemy, by the adversary.
kāma (m.), desire, lust.
rūpeṇa (n. inst. sg.), by the form, with the shape.
(*kāma-rūpeṇa*, m. instr. sg. TC cpd., with the form of desire.)
kāunteya (m. voc. sg.), Son of Kuntī, epithet of Arjuna referring to his mother.
duṣpūreṇa (m. inst. sg.), by hard to fill, by insatiable.
analena (m. inst. sg.), by fire, with fire.
ca, and.

40

इन्द्रियाणि मनो बुद्धिर्
indriyāṇi mano buddhir
the senses, the mind, the intelligence

अस्याधिष्ठानमुच्यते ।
asyādhiṣṭhānam ucyate
of it the abode, it is said;

एतैर् विमोहयत्येष
etāir vimohayatyeṣa
with these, it confuses, this,

ज्ञानम् आवृत्य देहिनम् ॥
jñānam āvṛtya dehinam
knowledge-obscuring, the embodied one.

indriyāṇi (n. nom. pl.), senses, powers.
manas (n. nom. sg.), mind, thought.
buddhis (f. nom. sg.), intelligence, intuitive knowledge.
asya (m. gen. sg.), of it, of this.
adhiṣṭhānam (n. nom. sg.), abode, resting place.
ucyate (3rd sg. pr. indic. passive √*vac*), it is said.
etāis (m. inst. pl.), by these, with these.
vimohayati (3rd sg. pr. indic. causative act. *vi* √*muh*), it causes to confuse, it confuses, it deludes.
eṣas (m. nom. sg.), this.
jñānam (n. acc. sg.), knowledge, wisdom.
āvṛtya (gerund *ā* √*vṛ*), obscuring, covering, enveloping.
dehinam (m. acc. sg.), the embodied one, the embodied soul, the *ātman*.

The senses, the mind and the intelligence
Are said to be its (i.e. the eternal enemy's) abode;
With these, it confuses the embodied one,
Obscuring this knowledge.

41

तस्मात् त्वम् इन्द्रियाण्यादौ
tasmāt tvam indriyāṇyādāu
therefore thou, the senses first

नियम्य भरतर्षभ ।
niyamya bharatarṣabha
restraining, Bull of the Bharatas,

पाप्मानं प्रजहि ह्येनं
pāpmānaṁ prajahi hyenaṁ
evil demon kill indeed this

ज्ञानविज्ञाननाशनम् ॥
jñānavijñānanāśanam
knowledge and discrimination destroying.

Therefore thou, restraining the senses
First, Bull of the Bharatas,
Kill this evil demon
Which destroys knowledge and discrimination.

tasmāt (m. abl. sg.), from this, therefore.
tvam (nom. sg.), thou.
indriyāṇi (n. acc. pl.), the senses.
ādāu (m. loc. sg.), in first, at first, in the beginning.
niyamya (gerund *ni* √*yam*), restraining, controlling, subduing.
bharatarṣabha (m. voc. sg.), Bull of the Bharatas, epithet of Arjuna.
pāpmānam (m. acc. sg.), devil, evil being.
prajahi (2nd sg. imperative act. *pra* √*han*), kill! destroy!
hi, indeed, truly.
enam (n. acc. sg.), this.
jñāna (n.), knowledge.
vijñāna (n.), discrimination, understanding.
nāśanam (m. acc. sg. from √*naś*), destroying, losing.
(*jñānavijñānanāśanam*, m. acc. sg. TP cpd., knowledge and discrimination-destroying.)

42

इन्द्रियाणि पराण्याहुर्
indriyāṇi parāṇyāhur
the senses high, they say,

इन्द्रियेभ्यः परं मनः ।
indriyebhyaḥ paraṁ manaḥ
than the senses higher, the mind,

मनसस् तु परा बुद्धिर्
manasas tu parā buddhir
than the mind, moreover, higher, the intelligence,

यो बुद्धेः परतस् तु सः ॥
yo buddheḥ paratas tu saḥ
which than the intelligence much higher indeed, this (i.e. the ātman or self, see foll. stanza)

They say that the senses are high (i.e. powerful, important).
The mind is higher than the senses;
Moreover, the intelligence is higher than the mind;
That which is much higher than the intelligence is this.*

indriyāṇi (n. nom. pl.), senses.
parāṇi (n. nom. pl.), high, elevated, important.
āhus (3rd pl. perfect √*ah*, with present meaning), they say, they assert.
indriyebhyas (n. abl. pl.), from the senses, than the senses.
param (n. nom. sg.), higher, superior.
manas (n. acc. sg.), mind.
manasas (n. abl. sg.), from the mind, than the mind.
tu, but, moreover, indeed.
parā (f. nom. sg.), higher.
buddhis (f. nom. sg.), intelligence.
yas (m. nom. sg.), who, which, what.
buddhes (f. abl. sg.), from the intelligence, than the intelligence.
paratas (adv.), higher, highest.
tu, but, indeed.
sas (m. nom. sg.), this.

* I.e. the Yoga of action, without desire for the fruits of action, see following stanza, also stanzas 40 and 41.

43

एवं बुद्धेः परं बुद्ध्वा
evaṁ buddheḥ paraṁ buddhvā
thus than the intelligence higher having learned,

संस्तभ्यात्मानम् आत्मना ।
saṁstabhyātmānam ātmanā
together sustaining the self by the self

जहि शत्रुं महाबाहो
jahi śatruṁ mahābāho
kill the enemy, O Mighty Armed One,

कामरूपं दुरासदम् ॥
kāmarūpaṁ durāsadam
having the form of desire, difficult to approach.

Thus having learned that which is higher than the intelligence,
Sustaining the self by the self,
Kill the enemy, O Mighty Armed One,
Which has the form of desire and is difficult to approach.

evam, thus, even so.
buddhes (f. abl. sg.), from the intelligence, than the intelligence.
param (n. nom. sg.), higher.
buddhvā (gerund √*budh*), having learned.
saṁstabhya (gerund *sam* √*stabh*), together sustaining, upholding.
ātmānam (m. acc. sg.), self.
ātmanā (m. inst. sg.), by the self.
jahi (2nd sg. imperative act. √*han*), kill! destroy!
śatrum (m. acc. sg.), enemy, adversary.
mahābāho (m. voc. sg.), O Mighty Armed One, epithet of Arjuna and other warriors.
kāmarūpam (n. acc. sg.), desire-form, having the form of desire, (as BV cpd.) which has the form of desire.
durāsadam (n. acc. sg.), difficult to approach, encountered wtih difficulty.

End of Book III

The Yoga of Action

BOOK IV

श्रीभगवान् उवाच ।
śrībhagavān uvāca
the Blessed Lord spoke:

śrībhagavān (m. nom. sg.), the Blessed Lord, the Blessed One.
uvāca (3rd sg. perfect act. √*vac*), he said, he spoke.

1

इमं विवस्वते योगं
imaṁ vivasvate yogaṁ
this, to Vivasvat, Yoga

प्रोक्तवान् अहम् अव्ययम् ।
proktavān aham avyayam
having declared, I, imperishable,

विवस्वान् मनवे प्राह
vivasvān manave prāha
Vivasvat to Manu communicated,

मनुर् इक्ष्वाकवे ऽब्रवीत् ॥
manur ikṣvākave 'bravīt
Manu to Ikṣvāku imparted.

The Blessed Lord spoke:

I, having proclaimed this imperishable Yoga
To Vivasvat;*
Vivasvat communicated it to Manu;†
Manu imparted it to Ikṣvāku.‡

imam (m. acc. sg.), this.
vivasvate (m. dat. sg.), to Vivasvat, "Shining Forth," the Sun God, father of Manu Vāivasvata who was the seventh of the fourteen Manus, the Noah of Hindu mythology and the progenitor of the human race.
yogam (m. acc. sg.), Yoga.
proktavān (m. nom. sg. perf. act. participle *pra* √*vac*), declaring, having declared.
aham (nom. sg.), I.
avyayam (m. acc. sg.), imperishable, eternal.
vivasvān (m. nom. sg.), Vivasvat.
manave (m. dat. sg.), to Manu, i.e. Manu Vāivasvata, see above.
prāha (3rd sg. perf. act. *pra* √*ah*), he told, he communicated.
manus (m. nom. sg.), Manu, Manu Vāivasvata.
ikṣvākave (m. dat. sg.), to Ikṣvāku. Ikṣvāku was a son of Manu Vāivasvata, and founder of a dynasty of kings.
abravīt (3rd sg. imperf. act. √*brū*), he told, he imparted, he related.

---

* Vivasvat, the Sun god.
† Manu, Manu Vāivasvata, son of the Sun god.
‡ Ikṣvāku, son of Manu Vāivasvata. All are early legendary figures. See chapter on "The Setting of the Bhagavad Gītā."

2

एवं परम्पराप्राप्तम्
evaṁ paramparāprāptam
thus, succession-received,

इमं राजर्षयो विदुः ।
imaṁ rājarṣayo viduḥ
this the royal seers they knew;

स कालेनेह महता
sa kāleneha mahatā
this with time here on earth long,

योगो नष्टः परंतप ॥
yogo naṣṭaḥ paraṁtapa
Yoga lost, Scorcher of the Foe.

Thus received by succession,
The royal seers knew this;
After a long time here on earth,
This Yoga was lost, Scorcher of the Foe.

evam, thus, so.
paramparā (f. nom. sg.), succession, one to another.
prāptam (acc. sg. p. pass. participle *pra* √*āp*), received, obtained, attained.
imam (m. acc. sg.), this.
rājarṣayas (m. nom. pl. *rāja ṛsayas*), royal *ṛsis,* royal seers.
vidus (3rd sg. perfect act. √*vid*), they knew.
sas (m. nom. sg.), it, this.
kālena (m. inst. sg.), by time, in time, with time.
iha, here, here on earth.
mahatā (m. inst. sg.), long, great, extended.
yogas (m. nom. sg.), Yoga.
naṣṭas (m. nom. sg. p. pass. participle √*naś*), lost, destroyed.
paraṁtapa (m. voc. sg.), Scorcher of the Foe, epithet of Arjuna and other warriors.

3

स एवायं मया ते ऽद्य
sa evāyaṁ mayā te 'dya
it this by me to thee today

योगः प्रोक्तः पुरातनः।
yogaḥ proktaḥ purātanaḥ
Yoga, declared, ancient

भक्तो ऽसि मे सखा चेति
bhakto 'si me sakhā ceti
devoted thou art of me, comrade, and thus.

रहस्यं ह्येतद् उत्तमम्॥
rahasyaṁ hyetad uttamam
secret indeed this supreme.

This ancient Yoga is today
Declared by Me to thee,
Since thou art My devotee and comrade.
This secret is supreme indeed.

sas (m. nom. sg.), it, this.
eva, indeed (often used as a rhythmic filler).
ayam (m. nom. sg.), this.
mayā (inst. sg.), by me.
te (dat. sg.), to thee.
adya, today, now, nowadays.
yogas (m. nom. sg.), Yoga.
proktas (m. nom. sg. p. pass. participle *pra* √*vac*), declared, proclaimed, described, imparted.
purātanas (m. nom. sg.), ancient, primaeval, of olden times.
bhaktas (m. nom. sg. p. pass. participle √*bhaj*), devoted, worshipped, shared, devotee.
asi (2nd sg. pr. indic. √*as*), thou art.
me (gen. sg.), of me.
sakhā (m. nom. sg.), comrade, friend.
ca, and.
iti, thus, so.
rahasyam (n. nom. sg.), private, secret, esoteric teaching.
hi, indeed, truly.
etad (n. nom. sg.), this.
uttamam (n. nom. sg.), supreme.

IV

अर्जुन उवाच।
arjuna uvaca
Arjuna spoke:

arjunas (m. nom. sg.), Arjuna.
uvāca (3rd sg. perf. act. √*vac*), he said, he spoke.

4

अपरं भवतो जन्म
aparaṁ bhavato janma
later of your lordship the birth

परं जन्म विवस्वतः।
paraṁ janma vivasvataḥ
earlier the birth of Vivasvat;

कथम् एतद् विजानीयां
katham etad vijānīyāṁ
how this I should understand

त्वम् आदौ प्रोक्तवान् इति॥
tvam ādāu proktavān iti
thou in the beginning declaring thus?

aparam (n. nom. sg.), later, not earlier, not previous.
bhavatas (formal address, m. gen. sg.), of you, of your lordship.
janma (n. nom. sg.), birth.
param (n. nom. sg.), earlier, prior, previous.
janma (n. nom. sg.), birth.
vivasvatas (m. gen. sg.), of Vivasvat, of the Sun God.
katham (interrog.), how?
etad (n. acc. sg.), this.
vijānīyām (1st sg. opt. act. *vi* √*jñā*), I should understand, I should comprehend.
tvam (nom. sg.), thou.
ādāu (loc. sg.), in the beginning.
proktavān (m. nom. sg. perf. act. participle *pra* √*vac*), declaring, having declared.
iti, thus, so.

Arjuna spoke:

Your Lordship's birth was later,
The birth of Vivasvat earlier;
How should I understand this,
That thou didst declare it in the beginning?

IV

श्रीभगवान् उवाच ।
śrībhagavān uvāca
the Blessed Lord spoke:

śrībhagavān (m. nom. sg.), the Blessed Lord, the Blessed One.
uvāca (3rd sg. perf. act. √*vac*), he said, he spoke.

5

बहूनि मे व्यतीतानि
bahūni me vyatītāni
many of me passed away

जन्मानि तव चार्जुन ।
janmāni tava cārjuna
births, and of thee Arjuna

तान्यहं वेद सर्वाणि
tānyahaṁ veda sarvāṇi
them I know all

न त्वं वेत्थ परंतप ॥
na tvaṁ vettha paraṁtapa
not thou knowest, Scorcher of the Foe.

bahūni (n. nom. pl.), many.
me (gen. sg.), of me, my.
vyatītāni (n. nom. pl. p. pass. participle *vi ati* √*i*), passed away, gone away, passings away.
janmāni (n. nom. pl.), births.
tava (gen. sg.), of thee, thy.
ca, and.
arjuna (m. voc. sg.), Arjuna.
tāni (n. acc. pl.), them.
aham (nom. sg.), I.
veda (1st sg. perfect act. √*vid*, with present meaning), I know.
sarvāṇi (n. acc. pl.), all.
na, not.
tvam (nom. sg.), thou.
vettha (2nd sg. perfect act. √*vid*, with present meaning), thou knowest.
paraṁtapa (m. voc. sg.), Scorcher of the Foe, epithet of Arjuna and other warriors.

The Blessed Lord spoke:

Many of my births have passed away,
And also the births of thee, Arjuna.
I know them all;
Thou dost not know them, Scorcher of the Foe (Arjuna).

6

अजो ऽपि सन्न् अव्ययात्मा
ajo 'pi sann avyayātmā
birthless although being, imperishable self,

भूतानाम् ईश्वरो ऽपि सन् ।
bhūtānām īśvaro 'pi san
of beings, the lord although being,

प्रकृतिं स्वाम् अधिष्ठाय
prakṛtiṁ svām adhiṣṭhāya
material nature own controlling

संभवाम्यात्ममायया ॥
saṁbhavāmyātmamāyayā
I come into being by own supernatural power.

ajas (m. nom. sg.), unborn, birthless.
api, even, although.
san (m. nom. sg. pr. participle √*as*), being.
avyaya (m.), imperishable.
ātmā (m. nom. sg.), shelf.
(*avyaya-atmā*, m. nom. sg. KD cpd., imperishable self).
bhūtānām (m. gen. pl.), of beings.
īśvaras (m. nom. sg.), lord.
api, even, although.
san (m. nom. sg. pr. participle √*as*), being.
prakṛtim (f. acc. sg.), material nature.
svām (f. acc. sg.), own.
adhiṣṭhāya (gerund *adhi* √*sthā*), controlling, governing, standing over.
saṁbhavāmi (1st sg. pr. indic. act. *sam* √*bhū*), I come into being, I originate myself.
ātma (m.), self, own.
māyayā (f. inst. sg.), by magic, by supernatural power, by power of illusion.
(*ātmamāyayā*, f. inst. sg. TP cpd., by own supernatural power.)

Although I am birthless* and my self imperishable,
Although I am the Lord of All Beings,
Yet, by controlling my own material nature,
I come into being by my own supernatural power.

* There appears to be a contradiction here between "birthless" and "many of my births" of the preceding stanza, but Krishna's "births" refer to his "giving forth" of himself – see following stanza.

7

यदा यदा हि धर्मस्य
yadā yadā hi dharmasya
whenever indeed of righteousness

ग्लानिर् भवति भारत ।
glānir bhavati bhārata
decrease exists, Descendant of Bharata,

अभ्युत्थानम् अधर्मस्य
abhyutthānam adharmasya
rising up of unrighteousness

तदा ऽत्मानं सृजाम्यहम् ॥
tadā 'tmānaṁ sṛjāmyaham
then myself give forth I.

Whenever a decrease of righteousness
Exists, Descendant of Bharata,
And there is a rising up of unrighteous-ness,
Then I give forth myself,

yadā yadā, whenever.
hi, indeed, truly.
dharmasya (m. gen. sg.), of righteousness, of duty, of law.
glānis (f. nom. sg.), exhaustion, decrease.
bhavati (3rd sg. pr. indic. act. √*bhū*), it is, it exists, it comes to be.
bhārata (m. voc. sg.), Descendant of Bharata, epithet of Arjuna.
abhyutthānam (n. acc. sg. verbal noun from *abhi ud* √*sthā*), rising up, emerging, standing up.
adharmasya (m. gen. sg.), of unrighteousness, of undutifulness, of unlawfulness.
tadā, then.
ātmānam (m. acc. sg.), self, myself.
sṛjāmi (1st sg. pr. indic. act. √*sṛj*), I give forth, I let go, I create.
aham (nom. sg.), I.

8

परित्राणाय साधूनां
paritrāṇāya sādhūnāṁ
to protecting of the good

विनाशाय च दुष्कृताम् ।
vināśāya ca duṣkṛtām
and to the destruction of evil doers

धर्मसंस्थापनार्थाय
dharmasaṁsthāpanārthāya
for the sake of establishing righteousness,

संभवामि युगे युगे ॥
saṁbhavāmi yuge yuge
I come into being from age to age.

For the protection of the good
And the destruction of evil doers;
For the sake of establishing righteousness,
I come into being from age to age.*

paritrāṇāya (n. dat. sg. from *pari* √*trā*), to refuge, to protecting, to preservation, to deliverance.
sādhūnām (m. gen. pl.), of the righteous, of the good, of the virtuous ones.
vināśāya (m. dat. sg. from *vi* √*naś*), to the destruction, to the loss, to the perishing.
ca, and.
duṣkṛtām (m. gen. pl.), of evil doers, of doers of wicked deeds.
dharma (m.), righteousness, duty, law.
saṁsthāpana (pr. causative noun from *sam* √*sthā*), the establishing.
arthāya (m. dat. sg.), for the purpose of, with the aim of, for the sake of.
(*dharmasaṁsthāpanārthāya,* m. dat. sg. TP cpd., for the sake of the establishing of righteousness.)
saṁbhavāmi (1st sg. pr. indic. act. *sam* √*bhū*), I come into being, I originate myself.
yuge yuge (n. loc. sg.), from age to age, in age after age. The conception of the Hindu *yuga* is explained at length in a footnote to stanza 17 of Book VIII.

* This conception of the "coming into being" from age to age to protect the good and punish the evil is not confined to Hunduism. Buddhism has a Buddha who arrives at different times for that purpose. Messianic Judaism, and thus Christianity, have parallels, though they require only one visitation of the Messiah, or *avatār* of God.

9

जन्म कर्म च मे दिव्यम्
janma karma ca me divyam
birth and action of me divine

एवं यो वेत्ति तत्त्वतः ।
evaṁ yo vetti tattvataḥ
thus who knows in truth

त्यक्त्वा देहं पुनर्जन्म
tyaktvā dehaṁ punarjanma
having left the body, (to) rebirth

नैति माम् एति सो ऽर्जुन ॥
nāiti mām eti so 'rjuna
not he goes; to me goes he, Arjuna.

He who knows in truth
My divine birth and action,
Having left the body, does not go
To rebirth; he goes to Me, Arjuna.

janma (n. acc. sg.), birth.
karma (n. acc. sg.), action, deeds.
ca, and.
me (gen. sg.), of me, my.
divyam (n. acc. sg.), divine, heavenly, god-like.
evam, thus.
yas (m. nom. sg.), who.
vetti (3rd sg. pr. indic. act. √*vid*), he knows.
tattvatas (adv.), "by thatness," by the truth about, in truth, truly.
tyaktvā (gerund √*tyaj*), leaving, renouncing, abandoning, having left, having abandoned.
deham (n. acc. sg.), body, material body.
punarjanma (n. acc. sg.), "again birth," rebirth.
na, not.
eti (3rd sg. pr. indic. act. √*i*), he goes, he comes.
mām (m. acc. sg.), me, to me.
eti (3rd sg. pr. indic. act. √*i*), he goes, he comes.
sas (m. nom. sg.), he, the, this.
arjuna (m. voc. sg.), Arjuna.

10

वीतरागभयक्रोधा
vītarāgabhayakrodhā
gone passion fear and anger

मन्मया माम् उपाश्रिताः ।
manmayā mām upāśritāḥ
absorbed in me, me resorting to,

बहवो ज्ञानतपसा
bahavo jñānatapasā
many, by knowledge austerity

पूता मद्भावम् आगताः ।।
pūtā madbhāvam āgatāḥ
purified, my state of being (have) attained.

Thinking solely of Me, resorting to Me,
Many, whose greed, fear and anger have departed,
Purified by the austerity of knowledge,
Have attained My state of being.

vitā (p. pass. participle *vi* √*i*), gone away, disappeared.
rāga (m.), passion, greed.
bhaya (n.), fear, danger.
krodhās (m. nom. pl.), anger.
(*vītarāgabhayakrodhās,* m. nom. pl. disappeared greed, fear and anger; free of passion, fear and anger; (as BV cpd.) whose greed, fear and anger have departed.)
manmayā (m. nom. pl.), absorbed in me, thinking solely of me.
mām (acc. sg.), me.
upāśritās (m. nom. pl. p. pass. participle *upa ā* √*śri*), resorting to, clinging to.
bahavas (m. nom. pl.), many.
jñānatapasā (n. inst. sg. TP cpd.), by knowledge-austerity, by the austerity of wisdom.
pūtās (m. nom. pl. p. pass. participle √*pū*), purified, cleansed.
madbhāvam (m. acc. sg.), "of me being," my state of being.
āgatās (m. nom. pl. p. pass. participle *ā* √*gam*), come to, attained, reached.

11

ये यथा मां प्रपद्यन्ते
ye yathā māṁ prapadyante
who, in whatever way Me they take refuge in

तांस् तथैव भजाम्यहम् ।
tāṁs tathāiva bhajāmyaham
them thus reward I;

मम वर्त्मानुवर्तन्ते
mama vartmānuvartante
my path they follow

मनुष्याः पार्थ सर्वशः ॥
manuṣyāḥ pārtha sarvaśaḥ
men, Son of Pṛthā, everywhere.

ye (m. nom. pl.), who.
yathā, in which way, as.
mām (acc. sg.), me.
prapadyante (3rd pl. pr. indic. mid. *pra* √*pad*), they take refuge in, they resort to.
tām (m. acc. pl.), them.
tathā, thus, in this way, so.
eva, indeed (used as a rhythmic filler).
bhajāmi (1st sg. pr. indic. act. √*bhaj*), I share with, I love, I reward.
aham (nom. sg.), I.
mama (gen. sg.), of me, my.
vartma (n. acc. sg.), path, road, turning.
anuvartante (3rd pl. pr. indic. mid. *anu* √*vṛt*), they follow.
manuṣyāś (m. nom. pl.), men, human beings.
pārtha (m. voc. sg.), Son of Pṛthā, epithet of Arjuna.
sarvaśas (adv.), everywhere, on all sides.

They who, in whatever way,
Take refuge in Me, them I reward.
Men everywhere, Son of Pṛthā,
Follow My path.

12

काङ्क्षन्तः कर्मणां सिद्धिं
kāṅkṣantaḥ karmaṇāṁ siddhiṁ
desiring of (ritual) acts the success

यजन्त इह देवताः ।
yajanta iha devatāḥ
they sacrifice here in the world to the (Vedic) godheads

क्षिप्रं हि मानुषे लोके
kṣipraṁ hi mānuṣe loke
quickly indeed in the human world

सिद्धिर् भवति कर्मजा ॥
siddhir bhavati karmajā
the success comes to be (of ritual) acts born.

Desiring the success of ritual acts,
Men sacrifice here on earth to the Vedic godheads.
Quickly indeed in the world of men
The success born of ritual acts comes to be.

kāṅkṣantas (m. nom. pl. pr. participle √*kāṅkṣ*), desiring, wishing for, hankering after.
karmaṇām (n. gen. pl.), of acts, of ritual acts.
siddhim (f. acc. sg.), success, accomplishment, fulfillment.
yajanta (*saṁdhi* for *yajante*, 3rd pl. pr. indic. mid. √*yaj*), they sacrifice, they worship.
iha, here, here in the world, here on earth.
devatās (f. acc. pl.), to the godheads, to the Vedic godheads.
kṣipram (adv.), quickly, instantly.
hi, indeed, truly.
mānuṣe (m. loc. sg.), in human, belonging to mankind.
loke (m. loc. sg.), in the world.
(*mānuṣe loke*, m. loc. sg., in the world of men, in the human world.)
siddhis (f. nom. sg.), success, accomplishment, fulfillment.
bhavati (3rd sg. pr. indic. act. √*bhū*), it is, it comes to be.
karmajā (f. nom. sg.), born of action, born of ritual acts.

13

चातुर्वर्ण्यं मया सृष्टं
cāturvarṇyaṁ mayā sṛṣṭaṁ
the four caste system by me created

गुणकर्मविभागशः ।
guṇakarmavibhāgaśaḥ
guṇa action-distribution according to;

तस्य कर्तारम् अपि मां
tasya kartāram api māṁ
of it the creator although me

विद्ध्यकर्तारम् अव्ययम् ॥
viddhyakartāram avyayam
know (me to be) non-doer eternal.

The system of four castes was created by Me,
According to the distribution of the guṇas and their acts.
Although I am the creator of this (the system),
Know Me to be the eternal non-doer.

cāturvarṇyam (n. nom. sg.), four-caste system, system of four castes.
mayā (inst. sg.), by me.
sṛṣṭam (n. nom. sg. p. pass. participle √*sṛj*), created, brought forth, let go.
guṇa (m.), guṇa.
karma (n.), action.
vibhāga (m. from *vi* √*bhaj*), distribution, sharing.
-*śas* (adverbial suffix), according to.
(*guṇakarmavibhāgaśas*, adverbial TP cpd., according to the distribution of the guṇas and their acts.)
tasya (m. gen. sg.), of it, of this.
kartāram (m. acc. sg.), creator, maker.
api, even, also, although.
mām (acc. sg.), me.
viddhi (2nd sg. imperative act. √*vid*), know! learn!
akartāram (m. acc. sg.), non-doer, one who does not act.
avyayam (m. acc. sg.), eternal, imperishable.

14

न मां कर्माणि लिम्पन्ति
na māṁ karmāṇi limpanti
not me actions they befoul

न मे कर्मफले स्पृहा।
na me karmaphale spṛhā
not of me in action-fruit desire

इति मां योऽभिजानाति
iti māṁ yo 'bhijānāti
thus me who comprehends

कर्मभिर न स बध्यते ॥
karmabhir na sa badhyate
by actions not he is bound.

na, not.
mām (acc. sg.), me.
karmāṇi (n. nom. pl.), actions.
limpanti (3rd pl. pr. indic. act. √*lip*), they smear, they defile, they befoul.
na, not.
me (gen. sg.), of me, my.
karmaphale (n. loc. sg.), in action fruit, in the fruit of action.
spṛhā (f. nom. sg.), desire, covetousness.
iti, thus, so.
mām (acc. sg.), me.
yas (m. nom. sg.), who.
abhijānāti (3rd sg. pr. indic. act. *abhi* √*jñā*), he comprehends, he understands.
karmabhis (n. inst. pl.), by actions, by deeds.
na, not.
sas (m. nom. sg.), he.
badhyate (3rd sg. pr. indic. passive √*bandh*), he is bound, he is fettered.

Actions do not befoul me;
I have no desire for the fruit of action;
Thus he who comprehends me
Is not bound by actions.

15

एवं ज्ञात्वा कृतं कर्म
evaṁ jñātvā kṛtaṁ karma
thus having known performed action

पूर्वैर् अपि मुमुक्षुभिः ।
pūrvāir api mumukṣubhiḥ
by the ancients, also, by the seekers for release.

कुरु कर्मैव तस्मात् त्वं
kuru karmāiva tasmāt tvaṁ
perform action therefore thou

पूर्वैः पूर्वतरं कृतम् ॥
pūrvaiḥ pūrvataraṁ kṛtam
(as was) by the ancients earlier done.

They having known this, action was performed
Also by the ancients, seeking release.
Therefore perform action
As it was earlier performed by the ancients.

evam, thus.
jñātvā (gerund √*jñā*), knowing, having known.
kṛtam (n. acc. sg. p. pass. participle √*kṛ*), performed, done, made.
karma (n. acc. sg.), action.
pūrvāis (m. inst. pl.), by the ancients, by the prior ones.
api, even, also.
mumukṣubhis (inst. pl. desiderative noun from √*muc*), by the desirers of release, by the seekers of liberation.
kuru (2nd sg. imperative act. √*kṛ*), do! perform! make!
karma (n. acc. sg.), action, deeds.
eva, indeed (used as a rhythmic filler).
tasmāt (m. abl. sg.), from this, therefore.
tvam (nom. sg.), thou.
pūrvāis (inst. pl.), by the ancients, by the prior ones.
pūrvataram (comparative), earlier, in olden times.
kṛtam (n. acc. p. pass. participle √*kṛ*), done, performed, made.

16

किं कर्म किम् अकर्मेति
kiṁ karma kim akarmeti
"what, action? what, non-action?" thus

कवयो ऽप्य् अत्र मोहिताः ।
kavayo 'py atra mohitāḥ
the poets even in this matter confused.

तत् ते कर्म प्रवक्ष्यामि
tat te karma pravakṣyāmi
this to thee action I shall explain

यज् ज्ञात्वा मोक्ष्यसे ऽशुभात् ।।
yaj jñātvā mokṣyase 'śubhāt
which having known thou shalt be released from evil.

"What is action? What is non-action?" thus,
Even the poets* are confused in this matter.
This action I shall explain to thee,
Having known which, thou shalt be released from evil.

kim (interrog.), what?
karma (n. nom. sg.), action.
kim (interrog.), what?
akarma (n. nom. sg.), non-action, inaction.
iti, thus (often used to close a quotation).
kavayas (m. nom. pl.), poets, sages.
api, even, also.
atra, in this matter, in this respect, here.
mohitās (m. nom. pl. p. pass. participle √*muh*), confused, deluded.
tad (n. acc. sg.), this, that.
te (dat.), to thee.
karma (n. acc. sg.), action.
pravakṣyāmi (1st sg. future act. *pra* √*vac*), I shall speak, I shall explain, I shall declare.
yad (n. acc. sg.), which.
jñātvā (gerund √*jñā*), knowing, having known.
mokṣyase (2nd sg. future passive √*muc*), thou shalt be released, thou shalt be liberated.
aśubhāt (m. abl. sg.), from evil, from sin, from viciousness, from the disagreeable.

* *kavayas*, poets. One must remember that much of Sanskrit religious literature was conceived in poetic form. Thus "poets" here (often translated "sages") were religious teachers who wrote, or rather *sang*, in verse.

17

कर्मणो ह्यपि बोद्धव्यं
karmaṇo hyapi boddhavyaṁ
of action indeed also to be known,

बोद्धव्यं च विकर्मणः ।
boddhavyaṁ ca vikarmaṇaḥ
and to be known of wrong action

अकर्मणश्च बोद्धव्यं
akarmaṇaśca boddhavyaṁ
and of non-action to be known

गहना कर्मणो गतिः ॥
gahanā karmaṇo gatiḥ
profound, of action the way.

One must know the nature of action
And also the nature of wrong action,
As well as the nature of inaction.
The way of action is profound.

karmaṇas (n. gen. sg.), of action.
hi, indeed, truly.
api, even, also.
boddhavyam (n. nom. sg. gerundive √*budh*), to be known, to be enlightened, to be taught.
ca, and.
vikarmaṇas (n. gen. sg.), of wrong action, of unsuitable action.
akarmaṇas (n. gen. sg.), of non-action, of inaction.
ca, and.
boddhavyam (n. nom. sg. gerundive √*budh*), to be known, to be enlightened, to be learned.
gahanā (f. nom. sg.), difficult to understand, hard to comprehend, deep, dense, thick, profound.
karmaṇas (n. gen. sg.), of action.
gatis (f. nom. sg.), way, path, road, going.

18

कर्मण्यकर्म यः पश्येद्
karmaṇyakarma yaḥ paśyed
in action non-action who should perceive,

अकर्मणि च कर्म यः ।
akarmaṇi ca karma yaḥ
and in non-action, action, who,

स बुद्धिमान् मनुष्येषु
sa buddhimān manuṣyeṣu
he wise among men;

स युक्तः कृत्स्नकर्मकृत् ।।
sa yuktaḥ kṛtsnakarmakṛt
he disciplined all action performing.

He who perceives non-action in action,
And action in non-action,
Is wise among men;
He performs all action in a disciplined manner.

karmaṇi (n. loc. sg.), in action, in deeds.
akarma (n. acc. sg.), non-action, inaction.
yas (m. nom. sg.), who.
paśyet (3rd sg. optative act. √*paś*), he should see, he should perceive.
akarmaṇi (n. loc. sg.), in non-action, in inaction.
ca, and.
karma (n. acc. sg.), action.
yas (m. nom. sg.), who.
sas (m. nom. sg.), he, the, this.
buddhimān (m. nom. sg.), full of wisdom, wise, intelligent.
manuṣyeṣu (m. loc. pl.), in men, among men.
sas (m. nom. sg.), he, the, this.
yuktas (m. nom. sg. p. pass. participle √*yuj*), yoked, disciplined, steadfast in Yoga.
kṛtsna (adj.), whole, entire, all.
karma (n.), action.
-kṛt (n. nom. sg. suffix), performing, doing, making.

19

यस्य सर्वे समारम्भाः
yasya sarve samārambhāḥ
of whom all enterprises

कामसंकल्पवर्जिताः ।
kāmasaṁkalpavarjitāḥ
desire and purpose excluded,

ज्ञानाग्निदग्धकर्माणं
jñānāgnidagdhakarmāṇaṁ
who has consumed his karma in the fire of knowledge,

तम् आहुः पण्डितं बुधाः ॥
tam āhuḥ paṇḍitaṁ budhāḥ
him they call paṇḍit, the wise ones.

He who has excluded desire and purpose
From all his enterprises,
And has consumed his karma in the fire of knowledge,
Him the wise men call a paṇḍit.

yasya (m. gen. sg.), of whom.
sarve (m. nom. pl.), all.
samārambhās (m. nom. pl. from *sam ā* √*rabh*√*rambh*), enterprises, undertakings.
kāma (m.), desire, love.
saṁkalpa (m.), purpose, aim.
varjitās (m. nom. pl. p. pass. participle √*vṛj*), twisted off, withheld, excluded.
(*kāma-saṁkalpa-varjitās*, m. nom. pl. BV cpd., ones who have excluded desirous intentions.)
jñāna (n.), knowledge, wisdom.
agni (m.), fire, the god of fire.
dagdha (p. pass. participle √*dah*), burned, consumed.
karmāṇam (m. acc. sg.), action, deeds, karma.
(*jñānāgnidagdhakarmāṇam*, m. acc. sg. BV cpd., he who has consumed his karma in the fire of knowledge.)
tam (m. acc. sg.), him, this.
āhus (3rd pl. perfect acc. √*ah*, used in present sense), they call, they designate, they say.
paṇḍitam (m. acc. sg.), paṇḍit, pundit, wise man.
budhās (m. nom. pl.), the intelligent, the wise ones.

20

त्यक्त्वा कर्मफलासङ्गं
tyaktvā karmaphalāsaṅgaṁ
having abandoned action-fruit attachment,

नित्यतृप्तो निराश्रयः ।
nityatṛpto nirāśrayaḥ
always satisfied, not dependent,

कर्मण्य् अभिप्रवृत्तो ऽपि
karmaṇy abhipravṛtto 'pi
in action proceeding even

नैव किंचित् करोति सः ॥
nāiva kiṁcit karoti saḥ
not anything does he.

He who has abandoned all attachment to the fruits of action,
Always satisfied, not dependent,
Even when proceeding in action,
Does, in effect, nothing at all.

tyaktvā (gerund √*tyaj*), abandoning, having abandoned.
karma (n.), action.
phala (n.), fruit, result.
āsaṅgam (m. acc. sg.), attachment, clinging.
(*karmaphalāsaṅgam*, m. acc. sg. TP cpd., attachment to the fruit of action.)
nitya, always, eternally.
tṛptas (m. nom. sg. p. pass. participle √*tṛp*), satisfied, content.
nirāśrayas (m. nom. sg. *nis ā* √*śri*), not dependent, not resorting to, whose dependence is lacking.
karmaṇi (n. loc. sg.), in action.
abhipravṛttas (m. nom. sg. p. pass. participle *abhi pra* √*vṛt*), turning ahead, proceeding, engaging.
api, even, also.
na, not.
eva, indeed (used as a rhythmic filler).
kiṁcid, anything whatever.
karoti (3rd sg. pr. indic. act. √*kṛ*), he does, he performs, he makes.
sas (m. nom. sg.), he, this one.

21

निराशीर् यतचित्तात्मा
nirāśīr yatacittātmā
without wish, restrained thought and self,

त्यक्तसर्वपरिग्रहः ।
tyaktasarvaparigrahaḥ
abandoned all acquisition,

शारीरं केवलं कर्म
śārīraṁ kevalaṁ karma
(with) the body alone action

कुर्वन् नाप्नोति किल्बिषम् ॥
kurvan nāpnoti kilbiṣam
performing, not he incurs guilt.

Performing action with the body alone,
Without wish, restrained in thought and self,
With all motives of acquisition abandoned,
He incurs no evil.

nirāśīs (m. nom. sg.), hopeless, free from desires, indifferent, without wishes.
yata (m. p. pass. participle √*yam*), restrained, controlled.
citta (n.), thought, mind.
ātmā (m. nom. sg.), self.
(*yata-citta-ātmā*, m. nom. sg. BV cpd., having a self with a controlled mind.)
tyakta (p. pass. participle √*tyaj*), abandoned, left, renounced.
sarva, all.
parigrahas (m. nom. sg. from *pari* √*grah*), getting, attaining, grasping, acquisition, possessions, property.
śārīram (n. acc. sg.), bodily, with the body.
kevalam (n. acc. sg.), alone, exclusively, only, merely.
karma (n. acc. sg.), action.
kurvan (m. nom. sg. pr. act. participle √*kṛ*), performing, doing, making.
na, not.
āpnoti (3rd sg. pr. indic. act. √*āp*), he attains, he obtains, he reaches, he incurs.
kilbiṣam (n. acc. sg.), guilt, fault, evil.

22

यदृच्छालाभसंतुष्टो
yadṛcchālābhasaṁtuṣṭo
chance gain content,

द्वन्द्वातीतो विमत्सरः।
dvandvātīto vimatsaraḥ
the dualities transcending, free from envy,

समः सिद्धाव् असिद्धौ च
samaḥ siddhāv asiddhāu ca
constant in success and in failure,

कृत्वा ऽपि न निबध्यते ॥
kṛtvā 'pi na nibadhyate
having acted even, not he is bound.

Content with gain by chance,
Transcending the dualities (i.e. pleasure, pain, etc.), free from envy,
Constant in mind whether in success or in failure,
Even though he has acted, he is not bound.

yadṛcchā (f. nom. sg.), chance, accidental, spontaneous.
lābha (m.), obtaining, gain.
saṁtuṣṭas (m. nom. sg. p. pass. participle *sam* √*tuṣ*), content, satisfied.
(*lābha-samtuṣṭas*, m. nom. sg. BV cpd., one who has contentment.)
dvandva (n.), pairs, dualities, polarity of opposites.
atītas (m. nom. sg. p. pass. participle *ati* √*i*), going beyond, transcending.
(*dvandva-atītas*, m. nom. sg. BV cpd., gone beyond opposites.)
vimatsaras (m. nom. sg.), whose envy is gone, free from envy, free from greed, free from malice.
samas (m. nom. sg.), constant, the same, indifferent.
siddhāu (f. loc. sg.), in success, in accomplishment.
asiddhāu (f. loc. sg.), in failure, in nonsuccess.
ca, and.
kṛtvā (gerund √*kṛ*), making, having made, having done, having acted.
api, even, also.
na, not.
nibadhyate (3rd sg. pr. indic. passive *ni* √*badh*), he is bound down, he is bound.

23

गतसङ्गस्य मुक्तस्य
gatasaṅgasya muktasya
of the free from attachment, of the released,

ज्ञानावस्थितचेतसः ।
jñānāvasthitacetasaḥ
of him whose thought is established in knowledge,

यज्ञायाचरतः कर्म
yajñāyācarataḥ karma
for sacrifice undertaking, action

समग्रं प्रविलीयते ॥
samagraṁ pravilīyate
wholly it melts away.

Of one who is free from attachment, of one who is released,
Whose thought is established in knowledge,
Action undertaken only as a sacrifice
Wholly melts away.

gata (m. p. pass. participle √*gam*), gone.
saṅgasya (m. gen. sg.), of attachment, of clinging.
(*gatasaṅgasya,* m. gen. sg., of the free from attachment, (as BV cpd.) of one from whom attachment is gone.)
muktasya (m. gen. sg. p. pass. participle √*muc*), of the released, of the liberated one.
jñāna (n.), knowledge.
avasthita (p. pass. participle *ava* √*sthā*), established, supported.
cetasas (n. gen. sg.), of thought, of mind.
(*jñānāvasthitacetasas,* m gen. sg. BV cpd., of him whose thought is established in knowledge.)
yajñāya (m. dat. sg.), to sacrifice, for sacrifice.
ācaratas (m. nom. sg. pr. participle act. *ā* √*car*), undertaking, moving towards.
karma (n. nom. sg.), action, ritual action.
samagram (adv.), wholly, together, in the aggregate.
pravilīyate (3rd sg. pr. indic. pass. *pra vi* √*lī*), is is melted away, it becomes dissolved, it vanishes.

24

ब्रह्मार्पणं ब्रह्म हविर्
brahmārpaṇaṁ brahma havir
Brahman the offering, Brahman the oblation,

ब्रह्माग्नौ ब्रह्मणा हुतम् ।
brahmāgnāu brahmaṇā hutam
in the fire of Brahman by Brahman poured out

ब्रह्मैव तेन गन्तव्यं
brahmāiva tena gantavyaṁ
Brahman by him to be attained

ब्रह्मकर्मसमाधिना ॥
brahmakarmasamādhinā
by him who contemplates the action of Brahman.

brahma (n. nom. sg.), Brahman.
arpaṇam (n. nom. sg.), offering, placing upon, entrusting.
brahma (n. nom. sg.), Brahman.
havis (n. nom., sg.), oblation, pouring out.
brahma (n.), Brahman.
agnāu (m. loc. sg.), in the fire.
(*brahma-agnau*, m. loc. sg. TP cpd., in the fire of Brahman.)
brahmaṇā (n. inst. sg.), by Brahman.
hutam (m. acc. sg. p. pass. participle √*hu*), poured out into the sacrificial fire.
brahma (n. nom. sg.), Brahman.
eva, indeed (used as a rhythmic filler).
tena (m. inst. sg.), by it, by him.
gantavyam (gerundive √*gam*), to be attained, to be gone, to be approached, to be accomplished.
brahmakarma (n.), Brahman action, action of Brahman.
samādhinā (m. inst. sg. from *sam ā* √*dhā*), by contemplating, by absorption, in contemplation.
(*brahmakarmasamādhinā,* m. inst. sg. BV cpd., by one who contemplates the action of Brahman.)

Brahman is the offering, Brahman is the oblation,
Poured out by Brahman into the fire of Brahman,
Brahman is to be attained by him
Who contemplates the action of Brahman.*

* "The entire act consists of *Brahman* because it is of *Brahman*'s nature: the sacrifice is *Brahman*, the utensils are *Brahman*, the fire in which the sacrifice is offered is *Brahman*, the sacrificer himself is *Brahman*. He who contemplates this insight, contemplates the act-as-*Brahman*. Such a one is capable of knowing the proper form of the *ātman* – which is *Brahman* – through his acts, because his acts are of *Brahman*'s nature. In other words, the acts performed by an aspirant have the form of knowledge because they imply the realization that they consist of *Brahman* and are therefore a means of contemplating the *ātman*..." Rāmānuja, tr. van Buitenen.

25

दैवम् एवापरे यज्ञं
dāivam evāpare yajñaṁ
to a god some, sacrifice,

योगिनः पर्युपासते ।
yoginaḥ paryupāsate
yogins they practice

ब्रह्माग्नाव् अपरे यज्ञं
brahmāgnāv apare yajnaṁ
in the fire of Brahman, others, sacrifice,

यज्ञेनैवोपजुह्वति ।।
yajñenāivopajuhvati
by sacrifice (itself) they offer.

Some yogins practice
Sacrifice to a god;
Others offer sacrifice,
By sacrifice itself, in the fire of Brahman;

dāivam (m. acc. sg.), to a god, relating to a god.
eva, indeed (used as a rhythmic filler).
apare (m. nom. pl.), some, others.
yajñam (m. acc. sg.), sacrifice, religious offering.
yoginas (m. nom. pl.), yogins.
paryupāsate (3rd pl. pr. indic. mid. *pari upa* √*ās*), they practice.
brahmāgnāu (m. loc. sg.), in Brahman fire, in the fire of Brahman.
apare (m. nom. pl.), some, others.
yajñam (m. acc. sg.), sacrifice, religious offering.
yajñena (m. inst. sg.), by sacrifice.
eva, indeed (used as a rhythmic filler).
upajuhvati (3rd pl. pr. indic. act. *upa* √*hu*), they offer, they sacrifice, they present oblations.

26

श्रोत्रादीनीन्द्रियाण्य् अन्ये
śrotrādīnīndriyāṇy anye
hearing like senses others

संयमाग्निषु जुह्वति ।
saṁyamāgniṣu juhvati
in the restraint fires they offer

शब्दादीन् विषयान् अन्य
śabdādīn viṣayān anya
sound commencing with, objects of the senses others

इन्द्रियाग्निषु जुह्वति ॥
indriyāgniṣu juhvati
in the sense fires they offer.

Others offer senses like hearing
In the fires of restraint;
Still others offer sound and other objects of the senses
In the fires of the senses;

śrotra (n.), hearing.
ādīni (n. acc. pl.), commencing with, and so forth, lit. "whose first was."
indriyāṇi (n. acc. sg.), senses, powers.
anye (m. nom. pl.), others.
saṁyamāgniṣu (*saṁyama agniṣu*, m. loc. pl.), in restraint fires, in the fires of restraint, in the fires of control.
juhvati (3rd pl. pr. indic. act. √*hu*), they offer, they sacrifice, they honor.
śabda (m.), sound.
ādīn (m. acc. pl.), commencing with, and so forth, "whose first was."
viṣayān (m acc. pl.), objects of the senses, provinces of the senses.
anya (*saṁdhi* for *anye*, m. nom. pl.), others.
indriyāgniṣu (m. loc. pl.), in sense fires, in the fires of the senses.
juhvati (3rd pl. pr. indic. act. √*hu*), they offer, they sacrifice.

27

सर्वाणीन्द्रियकर्माणि
sarvāṇīndriyakarmāṇi
all sense actions

प्राणकर्माणि चापरे ।
prāṇakarmāṇi cāpare
and vital breath action others

आत्मसंयमयोगाग्नौ
ātmasaṁyamayogāgnāu
in the self-restraint-of-Yoga fire

जुह्वति ज्ञानदीपिते ॥
juhvati jñānadīpite
they offer, in knowledge kindled.

Others offer all actions of the senses,
And actions of the vital breath,
In the fire of the Yoga of self restraint
Which is kindled by knowledge.

sarvāṇi (n. acc. pl.), all.
indriyakarmāṇi (n. acc. pl.), sense actions, actions of the senses.
prāṇa (m.), vital breath.
karmāṇi (n. acc. pl.), actions.
ca, and.
apare (m. nom. pl.), some, others.
ātmasaṁyama, self restraint, self control.
yogāgnāu (m. loc. sg.), in Yoga fire.
(*ātmasaṁyamayogāgnāu,* m. loc. sg. TP cpd., in the fire of the Yoga of self restraint.)
juhvati (3rd pl. pr. indic. act. √*hu*), they offer, they sacrifice.
jñāna (n.), knowledge.
dīpite (m. loc. sg. caus. p. pass. participle √*dīp*), in kindled.
(*jñānadīpite,* m. loc. sg. TP cpd., kindled by knowledge.)

28

द्रव्ययज्ञास् तपोयज्ञा
dravyayajñās tapoyajñā
material possession sacrifices, austerity sacrifices,

योगयज्ञास् तथापरे ।
yogayajñās tathāpare
Yoga sacrifices, thus some;

स्वाध्यायज्ञानयज्ञाश्च
svādhyāyajñānayajñāśca
whose sacrifices consist of Vedic recitation and the knowledge sacrifice,

यतयः संशितव्रताः ॥
yatayaḥ saṁśitavratāḥ
ascetics (with) sharpened vows.

Those whose sacrifices are made with material possessions,
Likewise those whose sacrifices take the form of Yoga,
And those whose sacrifices consist in Vedic recitation and the knowledge-sacrifice
Are to be deemed ascetics with sharpened vows.

dravya (n.), substance, thing, object, material possession.
yajñās (m. nom. pl.), sacrifices, offerings.
(*dravyayajñās,* m. nom. pl. BV cpd., those whose sacrifices are made with material things.)
tapas (n.), austerity, self-denial.
yajñās (m. nom. pl.), sacrifices, offerings.
(*tapoyajñās,* m. nom. pl. BV cpd., those whose sacrifices are made in the form of austerity.)
yoga (m.), Yoga.
yajñās (m. nom. pl.), sacrifices, offerings.
(*yogayajñās,* m. nom. pl. BV cpd., those whose sacrifices take the form of Yoga.)
tathā, thus, also, likewise.
apare (m. nom. pl.), some, others.
svādhyāya (m.), Veda study, reciting the Veda to oneself.
jñāna (n.), knowledge, wisdom.
yajñās (m. nom. pl.), sacrifices, offerings.
(*svādhyāyajñānayajñās,* m. nom. pl. BV cpd., those whose sacrifices consist of Veda study and the knowledge sacrifice.)
ca, and.
yatayas (m. nom. pl.), ascetics, men of austerity.
saṁśita (p. pass. participle *sam* $\sqrt{}$*śi*), sharpened, whetted.
vratās (m. nom. pl.), vows, ordinances, rules, commands.

29

अपाने जुह्वति प्राणं
apāne juhvati prāṇaṁ
in exhalation they offer inhalation,

प्राणे ऽपानं तथापरे ।
prāṇe 'pānaṁ tathāpare
in inhalation, exhalation thus others

प्राणापानगती रुद्ध्वा
prāṇāpānagatī ruddhvā
the path of inhalation and exhalation restraining,

प्राणायामपरायणाः ॥
prāṇāyāmaparāyaṇāḥ
control of the breath intent upon.

Some offer inhalation into exhalation,
And others exhalation into inhalation,
Restraining the path of inhalation and exhalation,
Intent on control of the vital breath.*

apāne (m. loc. sg.), in exhalation, in the abdominal breath (the Hindus believed in two breaths: the vital breath (prāṇa), and the abdominal breath (apāna), supposed to have been breathed through the anus, though the two terms were also used for inhalation and exhalation respectively, which is their meaning here).
juhvati (3rd pl. pr. indic. act. √*hu*), they offer, they sacrifice.
prāṇam (m. acc. sg.), inhalation, vital breath.
prāṇe (m. loc. sg.), in inhalation, in the vital breath.
apānam (m. acc. sg.), exhalation, the abdominal breath.
tathā, thus, also.
apare (m. nom. pl.), some, others.
prāṇāpānagatī (f. acc. dual), the paths of inhalation and exhalation.
ruddhvā (gerund √2 *rudh*), restraining.
prāṇa (m.), vital breath, inhalation.
āyāma (m. from *ā* √*yam*), control, stopping.
parāyaṇās (m. nom. pl. ifc.), intent upon.
(*prāṇāyāma-parūyaṇās,* m. nom. pl., TP cpd, intent on breath control.)

* These are Yoga breathing excercises, as yet understood by few in the West, but familiar to all Yogins.

30

अपरे नियताहाराः
apare niyatāhārāḥ
others who have been restrained in foods

प्राणान् प्राणेषु जुह्वति ।
prāṇān prāṇeṣu juhvati
inhalations into inhalations they offer,

सर्वे ऽप्येते एते यज्ञविदो
sarve 'pyete yajñavido
all even these sacrifice knowing

यज्ञक्षपितकल्मषाः ॥
yajñakṣapitakalmaṣāḥ
whose evils have been destroyed through sacrifice.

Others who have restricted their foods
Offer inhalations into inhalations;
All these are the sacrifice-knowing,
Whose evils have been destroyed through sacrifice.

apare (m. nom. pl.), some, others.
niyatāhārās (m. nom. pl. BV cpd.), who have been restrained in food.
prāṇān (m. acc. pl.), inhalations, vital breaths.
prāṇeṣu (m. loc. pl.), in inhalations, in vital breaths.
juhvati (3rd pl. pr. indic. act. √*hu*), they sacrifice, they offer.
sarve (m. nom. pl.), all.
api, even, also.
ete (m. nom. pl.), these.
yajñavidas (m. nom. pl.), the sacrifice-knowing, those with knowledge of sacrifice.
yajñakṣapita (*yajña* + p. pass. causative participle √4*kṣi*), sacrifice-destroyed, destroyed by sacrifice.
kalmaṣās (m. nom. pl.), evils, wrongs.
(*yajñakṣapitakalmaṣās*, m. nom. pl. BV cpd., whose evils have been destroyed through sacrifice.)

31

यज्ञशिष्टामृतभुजो
yajñaśiṣṭāmṛtabhujo
the sacrifice-remnant-nectar-enjoying

यान्ति ब्रह्म सनातनम् ।
yānti brahma sanātanam
they go to Brahman, primaeval;

नायं लोको ऽस्त्य् अयज्ञस्य
nāyaṁ loko 'sty ayajñasya
not this world it is for the non-sacrificing,

कुतो ऽन्यः कुरुसत्तम ॥
kuto 'nyaḥ kurusattama
how the other, Best of Kurus?

The enjoyers of the nectar of the sacrificial remnants
Go to primaeval Brahman.
Not even this world is for the non-sacrificing;
How then the other, Best of Kurus?

yajñaśiṣṭa (n.), sacrifice remainder, remainder of the offering, remainder consumed after the gods have taken their portion of the sacrifice.
amṛta (n.), nectar, immortality.
bhujas (f. nom. pl.), enjoying, eating.
(*yajñaśiṣṭa-amṛta-bhujas*, f. nom. pl., BV, sacrifice-remnant-nectar-enjoying ones.
yānti (3rd sg. pr. indic. act. √*yā*), they go, they come.
brahma (n. acc. sg.), to Brahman, Brahman.
sanātanam (n. acc. sg.), primaeval, aged, ancient.
na, not.
ayam (m. nom. sg.), this.
lokas (m. nom. sg.), world.
asti (3rd sg. pr. indic. √*as*), it is.
ayajñasya (m. gen. abl. sg.), of the non-sacrificing, for the non-sacrificing one.
kutas (interrog.), how?
anyas (m. nom. sg.), other.
kurusattama (m. voc. sg.), Best of Kurus, Highest of Kurus, epithet of Arjuna.

32

एवं बहुविधा यज्ञा
evaṁ bahuvidhā yajñā
thus of many kinds, sacrifices,

वितता ब्रह्मणो मुखे ।
vitatā brahmaṇo mukhe
arranged of Brahman in the mouth,

कर्मजान् विद्धि तान् सर्वान्
karmajān viddhi tān sarvān
action born, know them all (to be).

एवं ज्ञात्वा विमोक्ष्यसे ॥
evaṁ jñātvā vimokṣyase
thus knowing, thou shalt be released.

Thus sacrifices are of many kinds,
Arranged in the mouth of Brahman.
Know them all to be born of action.
Thus knowing, thou shalt be released.

evam, thus, accordingly.
bahuvidhās (m. nom. pl.), of many kinds, of many sorts.
yajñās (m. nom. pl.), sacrifices, offerings.
vitatās (m. nom. pl. sg. p. pass. participle *vi* √*tan*), stretched, arranged, spread.
brahmaṇas (n. gen. sg.), of Brahman.
mukhe (n. loc. sg.), in the mouth, in the face.
karmajān (m. acc. pl.), action born, born of action, arising from action.
viddhi (2nd sg. imperative act. √*vid*), know! learn!
tān (m. acc. pl.), them.
sarvān (m. acc. pl.), all.
evam, thus, this.
jñātvā (gerund √*jñā*), knowing, having known.
vimokṣyase (2nd sg. fut. pass. *vi* √*muc*), thou shalt be released, thou shalt be liberated.

33

श्रेयान् द्रव्यमयाद् यज्ञाज्
śreyān dravyamayād yajñāj
better than material-possession sacrifice

ज्ञानयज्ञः परंतप ।
jñānayajñaḥ paraṁtapa
(is) knowledge sacrifice, Scorcher of the Foe.

सर्वं कर्माखिलं पार्थ
sarvaṁ karmākhilaṁ pārtha
all action without a gap, Son of Pṛthā

ज्ञाने परिसमाप्यते ॥
jñāne parisamāpyate
in knowledge is fully comprehended.

Better than the sacrifice of material possessions
Is the knowledge sacrifice, Scorcher of the Foe (Arjuna),
All action, without exception, Son of Pṛthā (Arjuna),
Is fully comprehended in knowledge.

śreyān (m. nom. sg. comparative), better, preferable.
dravyamayāt (n. abl. sg.), than consisting of material possessions, than property, than material, than substance.
yajñāt (m. abl. sg.), than sacrifice, than offering.
jñāna (n.), knowledge, wisdom.
yajñas (m. nom. sg.), sacrifice, offering.
(*jñāna-yajñas*, m. nom. sg. TP cpd., sacrifice of knowledge.)
paraṁtapa (m. voc. sg.), Scorcher of the Foe, epithet of Arjuna and other warriors.
sarvam (n. nom. sg.), all.
karma (n. nom. sg.), action.
akhilam (adv.), without a gap, completely, without exception.
pārtha (m. voc. sg.), Son of Pṛthā, epithet of Arjuna.
jñāne (n. loc. sg.), in knowledge, in wisdom.
parisamāpyate (3rd sg. pr. indic. passive *pari sam* √*āp*), it is fully comprehended, it is contained in, it is finished.

34

तद् विद्धि प्रणिपातेन
tad viddhi praṇipātena
this know! by humble submission,

परिप्रश्नेन सेवया।
paripraśnena sevayā
by enquiry, by service,

उपदेक्ष्यन्ति ते ज्ञानं
upadekṣyanti te jñānaṁ
they will teach to thee knowledge,

ज्ञानिनस् तत्त्वदर्शिनः ॥
jñāninas tattvadarśinaḥ
the knowing, the perceivers of truth.

This know! Through humble submission,
Through enquiry, through service (on thine own part),
The knowing ones, the perceivers of truth,
Will be led to teach thee knowledge,

tad, (n. acc. sg.) this, that.
viddhi (2nd sg. imperative act. √*vid*), know! learn!
praṇipātena (m. inst. sg. from *pra ni* √*pat*), by bowing respectfully to, by humble submission, by prostrating oneself.
paripraśnena (m. inst. sg. from *pari* √*prach*), by interrogation, by enquiry.
sevayā (f. inst. sg.), by service, by waiting on, by attendance.
upadeksyanti (3rd pl. fut. act. *upa* √*diś*), they will point out, they will instruct, they will teach.
te (dat. sg.), thee, to thee.
jñānam (n. acc. sg.), knowledge, wisdom.
jñāninas (m. nom. pl.), the knowing, the wise ones.
tattva (n.), "thatness," truth.
darśinas (m. nom. pl. from √*dṛś*), perceivers, seers, understanders.
(*tattva-darśinas*, m. nom. pl. TP cpd., seers of truth.)

35

यज् ज्ञात्वा न पुनर् मोहम्
yaj jñātvā na punar moham
which, having known, not again delusion

एवं यास्यसि पाण्डव ।
evaṁ yāsyasi pāṇḍava
thus thou shalt fall into, Son of Pāṇḍu

येन भूतान्य् अशेषेण
yena bhūtāny aśeṣeṇa
by which beings without remainder

द्रक्ष्यस्य् आत्मन्य् अथो मयि ॥
drakṣyasy ātmany atho mayi
thou shalt see in thyself, then in me.

**Knowing which, thou shalt not again
Fall into delusion, Son of Pāṇḍu
  (Arjuna);
And by which knowledge thou shalt
  see all beings
In thyself, and then in Me.**

yad (n. acc. sg.), which, what.
jñātvā (gerund √*jñā*), knowing, having known.
na, not.
punar, again.
moham (m. acc. sg.), delusion, confusion.
evam, thus, so.
yāsyasi (2nd sg. fut. act. √*yā*), thou shalt go to, thou shalt come to, thou shalt fall into.
pāṇḍava (m. voc. sg.), Son of Pāṇḍu, epithet of Arjuna.
yena (m. inst. sg.), by which, with which.
bhūtāni (n. acc. sg.), beings, creatures.
aśeṣeṇa (m. inst. sg.), without remainder, all.
drakṣyasi (2nd sg. fut. act. √*dṛś*), thou shalt see, thou shalt perceive, thou shalt behold.
ātmani (m. loc. sg.), in the self, in thyself.
atho, then.
mayi (loc. sg.), in me.

36

अपि चेद् असि पापेभ्यः
api ced asi pāpebhyaḥ
even if thou art of evil-doers

सर्वेभ्यः पापकृत्तमः ।
sarvebhyaḥ pāpakṛttamaḥ
of all the most evil doing,

सर्वं ज्ञानप्लवेनैव
sarvaṁ jñānaplavenāiva
all by knowledge boat

वृजिनं संतरिष्यसि ॥
vṛjinaṁ saṁtariṣyasi
wickedness thou shalt transcend.

Even if thou wert the most evil
Of all evildoers,
Thou wouldst cross over all wickedness
By the boat of knowledge.

api, even, also.
ced, if.
asi (2nd sg. pr. indic. √*as*), thou art.
pāpebhyas (m. abl. pl.), of evil-doers, of sinners.
sarvebhyas (m. abl. pl.), of all.
pāpakṛttamas (m. nom. sg. superl.), the greatest evil-doer, the greatest sinner, the most evil-doing.
sarvam (n. acc. sg.), all.
jñāna (n.), knowledge.
plavena (m. n. inst. sg.), by the boat.
(*jñāplavena,* m. inst. sg. TP cpd., by the boat of knowledge.)
eva, indeed (used as a rhythmic filler).
vṛjinam (n. acc. sg.), wickedness, sinfulness.
saṁtariṣyasi (2nd sg. fut. act. *sam* √*tṛ*), thou shalt cross over, thou shalt transcend.

37

यथैधांसि समिद्धो ऽग्निर्
yathāidhāṁsi samiddho 'gnir
as firewood the kindled fire

भस्मसात्कुरुते ऽर्जुन ।
bhasmasāt kurute 'rjuna
to ashes it reduces, Arjuna,

ज्ञानाग्निः सर्वकर्माणि
jñānāgniḥ sarvakarmāṇi
the fire of knowledge all actions

भस्मसात् कुरुते तथा ॥
bhasmasāt kurute tathā
to ashes it reduces so.

As the kindled fire
Reduces firewood to ashes, Arjuna,
So the fire of knowledge
Reduces all actions to ashes.

yathā, in which way, as.
edhāṁsi (n. nom. pl.), firewood, kindling.
samiddhas (m. nom. sg. p. pass. participle *sam* √*indh*), set on fire, kindled.
agnis (m. nom. sg.), fire.
bhasmasāt kurute (*bhasmasāt* adv. + 3rd sg. pr. indic. mid. √*kṛ*), it reduces to ashes.
arjuna (m. voc. sg.), Arjuna.
jñāna (n.), knowledge, wisdom.
agnis (m. nom. sg.), fire.
(*jñānāgnis,* m. nom. sg. KD cpd., the fire of knowledge.)
sarva, all.
karmāṇi (n. acc. pl.), actions.
bhasmasāt (adv.), to ashes.
kurute (3rd sg. pr. indic. mid. √*kṛ*), it reduces.
tathā, thus, in this way, so.

38

न हि ज्ञानेन सदृशं
na hi jñānena sadṛśaṁ
not indeed to knowledge similar

पवित्रम् इह विद्यते ।
pavitram iha vidyate
purifier here in the world it is found;

तत् स्वयं योगसंसिद्धः
tat svayaṁ yogasaṁsiddhaḥ
that himself the perfected in Yoga

कालेनात्मनि विन्दति ॥
kālenātmani vindati
with time in the self he finds.

No purifier equal to knowledge
Is found here in the world;
He who is himself perfected in Yoga
In time finds that knowledge in the self.

na, not.
hi, indeed.
jñānena (n. inst. sg.), by knowledge, to knowledge.
sadṛśam (n. nom. sg.), similar, equal.
pavitram (n. nom. sg.), purifier, cleanser.
iha, here, here in the world.
vidyate (3rd sg. pr. indic. passive √2 *vid*), it is found.
tad, (n. acc. sg.), that.
svayam (adv.), himself, own, self.
yoga (m.), Yoga.
saṁsiddhas (m. nom. sg. p. pass. participle *sam* √*sidh*), perfected, accomplished, successful.
(*yoga-saṁsiddhas*, m. nom. sg. TP cpd., perfected in yoga.)
kālena (m. inst. sg.), by time, with time, in time.
ātmani (m. loc. sg.), in the self.
vindati (3rd sg. pr. indic. acc. √2 *vid*), he finds, one finds.

39

श्रद्धावाँल् लभते ज्ञानं
śraddhāvāṁl labhate jñānaṁ
possessing faith he attains knowledge

तत्परः संयतेन्द्रियः ।
tatparaḥ saṁyatendriyaḥ
devoted to that, restraining sense,

ज्ञानं लब्ध्वा परां शान्तिम्
jñānaṁ labdhvā parāṁ śāntim
knowledge having attained, to supreme peace

अचिरेणाधिगच्छति ॥
acireṇādhigacchati
not slowly he goes.

He who possesses faith attains knowledge;
Devoted to that (knowledge), restraining his senses,
Having attained knowledge, he goes speedily
To supreme peace.

śraddhāvān (m. nom. sg.), full of faith, possessing faith.
labhate (3rd sg. pr. indic. mid. √*labh*), he attains, he obtains, he meets with.
jñānam (n. acc. sg.), knowledge, wisdom.
tad (m. acc. sg.), that.
paras (m. nom. sg.), devoted to, holding as highest object.
saṁyata (p. pass. participle *sam* √*yam*), restraining, controlling, subduing.
indriyas (m. nom. sg.), sense, power.
(*saṁyata-indriyas*, m. nom. sg., BV cpd., one with restrained senses.)
jñānam (n. nom. acc. sg.), knowledge, wisdom.
labdhvā (gerund √*abh*), attaining, obtaining, having attained.
parām (f. acc. sg.), supreme, highest.
śāntim (f. acc. sg.), peace, tranquility.
acireṇa (adv.), by not slowly, by not for long, speedily, soon.
adhigacchati (3rd sg. pr. indic. act. *adhi* √*gam*), he attains, he goes, he meets with.

40

अज्ञश्चाश्रद्दधानश्च
ajñaścāśraddadhānaśca
and ignorant and not faith giving

संशयात्मा विनश्यति ।
saṁśayātmā vinaśyati
he whose self is doubtful is destroyed;

नायं लोको ऽस्ति न परो
nāyaṁ loko 'sti na paro
not this world it is, nor beyond,

न सुखं संशयात्मनः ॥
na sukhaṁ saṁśayātmanaḥ
not happiness for the doubting self.

The self of him who is ignorant, and does not give faith,
Of him whose self doubts, is destroyed.
Neither this world nor that beyond,
Nor happiness, is for him whose self doubts.

ajñas (m. nom. sg.), ignorant, unknowing.
ca, and.
aśraddadhānas (m. nom. sg.), not giving faith, without giving faith, not placing faith.
ca, and.
saṁśaya (m. from *sam* √*śi*), doubting, hesitating, lacking in resolution.
ātmā (m. nom. sg.), self.
(*saṁśayātmā,* nom. sg. BV cpd., he whose self doubts.)
vinaśyati (3rd sg. pr. indic. act. *vi* √*naś*), he is lost, he is destroyed.
na, not.
ayam (m. nom. sg.), this.
lokas (m. nom. sg.), world.
asti (3rd sg. pr. indic. √*as*), it is, there is.
na, not.
paras, beyond, distant, remote, former, later.
na, not, nor.
sukham (n. nom. sg.), happiness, bliss, agreeableness, comfort, pleasure, delight, joy.
saṁśaya (m. from *sam* √*śi*), doubting, hesitating.
ātmanas (m. gen. sg.), of the self, for the self.
(*saṁśayātmanas*, m. gen. sg. BV cpd., of the self of him who doubts, for him whose self is doubtful.)

41

योगसंन्यस्तकर्माणं
yogasaṁnyastakarmāṇaṁ
him whose actions are renounced in Yoga,

ज्ञानसंछिन्नसंशयम् ।
jñānasaṁchinnasaṁśayam
whose doubt is cut away by knowledge,

आत्मवन्तं न कर्माणि
ātmavantaṁ na karmāṇi
self-possessed, not actions

निबध्नन्ति धनंजय ॥
nibadhnanti dhanaṁjaya
they bind, Conqueror of Wealth.

Action does not bind him
Who has renounced action through Yoga,
Whose doubt is cut away by knowledge
And who is possessed of the self, Conqueror of Wealth.

yoga (m.), Yoga.
saṁnyasta (p. pass. participle *sam ni* √2 *as*), renounced, abandoned, give up, thrown down.
karmāṇam (n. acc. sg.), action.
(*yogasaṁnyastakarmāṇam*, n. acc. sg. BV cpd., him who has renounced action in Yoga.)
jñāna (n.), knowledge.
saṁchinna (p. pass. participle *sam* √*chid*), cut away, severed.
saṁśayam (m. acc. sg.), doubt, irresolution, hesitation.
(*jñānasaṁchinnasaṁśayam*, m. acc. sg. BV cpd., whose doubt is cut away by knowledge.)
ātmavantam (m. acc. sg.), self possessed, composed, prudent, having a self.
na, not.
karmāṇi (n. nom. pl.), actions.
nibadhnanti (3rd pl. pr. indic. act. *ni* √*badh* √*bandh*), they bind, they bind down, they fetter.
dhanaṁjaya (m. voc. sg.), Conqueror of Wealth, epithet of Arjuna.

42

तस्माद् अज्ञानसंभूतं
tasmād ajñānasaṁbhūtaṁ
therefore ignorance proceeding from

हृत्स्थं ज्ञानासिना ऽत्मनः ।
hṛtsthaṁ jñānāsinā 'tmanaḥ
abiding in the heart, with thine own knowledge-sword from thyself

छित्त्वैनं संशयं योगम्
chittvāinaṁ saṁśayaṁ yogam
having cut away this doubt, to Yoga

आतिष्ठोत्तिष्ठ भारत ॥
ātiṣṭhottiṣṭha bhārata
resort! stand up! Descendant of Bharata.

Therefore, having cut away with thine own sword of knowledge,
This doubt that proceeds from ignorance and abides in thy heart,
Resort to Yoga!
Stand up, Descendant of Bharata! (Arjuna).

tasmāt (m. abl. sg.), from this, therefore.
ajñāna (n.), ignorance, non-knowledge.
saṁbhūtam (m. acc. sg.), proceeding from, produced by, originating in.
hṛtstham (m. acc. sg.), abiding in the heart, situated in the heart.
jñāna (n.), knowledge.
asinā (m. inst. sg.), by the sword, by the knife, with the knife.
(*jñāna-asinā*, m. inst. sg., TP cpd., with the sword of knowledge.)
ātmanas (m. gen. sg.), of the self, of thyself, own.
chittvā (gerund √*chid*), cutting away, severing, having cut away, having severed.
enam (m. acc. sg.), this.
saṁśayam (m. acc. sg.), doubt, hesitation, irresolution.
yogam (m. acc. sg.), Yoga, to Yoga.
ātiṣṭha (2nd sg. imperative act. *ā* √*sthā*), resort! go towards! perform!
uttiṣṭha (2nd sg. imperative act. *ud* √*sthā*), stand up! arise!
bhārata (m. voc. sg.), Descendant of Bharata, epithet of Arjuna.

End of Book IV

The Yoga of Renunciation of
Action in Knowledge

BOOK V

अर्जुन उवाच ।
arjuna uvāca
Arjuna spoke:

arjunas (m. nom. sg.), Arjuna.
uvāca (3rd sg. perf. act. √*vac*), he said, he spoke.

1

संन्यासं कर्मणां कृष्ण
saṁnyāsaṁ karmaṇāṁ kṛṣṇa
renunciation of actions, Krishna,

पुनर् योगं च शंससि ।
punar yogaṁ ca śaṁsasi
and again Yoga thou praisest.

यच्छ्रेय एतयोर् एकं
yacchreya etayor ekaṁ
which better of these two, the one?

तन् मे ब्रूहि सुनिश्चितम् ॥
tan me brūhi suniścitam
this to me tell definitely.

Arjuna spoke:

Thou praisest renunciation of actions,
And again thou praisest Yoga, Krishna.
Which one is the better of these two?
Tell this to me definitely.

saṁnyāsam (m. acc. sg. from *sam ni* √2 *as*), renunciation, throwing down, abandonment.
karmaṇām (n. gen. pl.), of actions, of deeds.
kṛṣṇa (m. voc. sg.), Krishna.
punar, again.
yogam (m. acc. sg.), Yoga.
ca, and.
śaṁsasi (2nd sg. pr. indic. act. √*śaṁs*), thou praisest, thou recitest, thou approvest, thou declarest.
yad (n. nom. sg.), which, what.
śreyas, better, preferable.
etayos (m. gen. dual), of these two.
ekam (acc. sg.), one, the one.
tad (n. acc. sg.), this, that.
me (dat. sg.), to me.
brūhi (2nd sg. imperative act. √*brū*), tell! say!
suniścitam (adv. from p. pass. participle *su nis* √*ci*), definitely, firmly resolved, in a settled way.

V

श्रीभगवान् उवाच।
śrībhagavān uvāca
the Blessed Lord spoke:

śrībhagavān (m. nom. sg.), the Blessed Lord, the Blessed One.
uvāca (3rd sg. perfect act. √*vac*), he said, he spoke.

2
संन्यासः कर्मयोगश्च
saṁnyāsaḥ karmayogaśca
renunciation and the Yoga of action

निःश्रेयसकराव् उभौ।
niḥśreyasakarāv ubhāu
ultimate bliss effecting, both;

तयोस् तु कर्मसंन्यासात्
tayos tu karmasaṁnyāsāt
of the two, however, than renunciation of action,

कर्मयोगो विशिष्यते॥
karmayogo viśiṣyate
the Yoga of action is better.

saṁnyāsas (m. nom. sg.), renunciation, abandonment, throwing down.
karmayogas (m. nom. sg. TP cpd.,), the Yoga of action.
ca, and.
niḥśreyasa (n.), ultimate bliss, incomparable bliss, highest happiness.
karāu (m. nom. du.), leading to, making for, inviting, intending to accomplish, effecting.
(*niḥśreyasa-kārau*, m. nom. dual, leading to bliss.)
ubhāu (m. nom. dual), both.
tayos (m. gen. dual), of the two, of these two.
tu, but, however.
karmasaṁnyāsāt (m. abl. sg. TP cpd.), from renunciation of action, than renunciation of action.
karmayogas (m. nom. sg. TP cpd.), action-Yoga, the Yoga of action.
viśiṣyate (3rd sg. pr. indic. passive √*śiṣ*), it is distinguished, it is better, it is superior, it excels.

The Blessed Lord spoke:

Both renunciation and the Yoga of action
Lead to incomparable bliss;
Of the two, however, the Yoga of action
Is superior to the renunciation of action.*

* Rāmānuja: "Both the Yoga of action and the Yoga of knowledge are...equally autonomous means of attaining beatitude. But the Yoga of action is better than the Yoga of knowledge." The reason is that the ātman can be secured through the Yoga of action. The aim of both is the same, but the Yoga of knowledge cannot be attained without the prior acquisition of the Yoga of action.

3

ज्ञेयः स नित्यसंन्यासी
jñeyaḥ sa nityasaṁnyāsī
to be known, he the eternal renouncer,

यो न द्वेष्टि न काङ्क्षति ।
yo na dveṣṭi na kāñkṣati
who not he hates not he desires,

निर्द्वन्द्वो हि महाबाहो
nirdvandvo hi mahābāho
indifferent to the opposites, in truth, O Mighty Armed One,

सुखं बन्धात् प्रमुच्यते ॥
sukhaṁ bandhāt pramucyate
easily from bondage he is liberated.

jñeyas (m. nom. sg. gerundive √*jñā*), to be known.
sas (m. nom. sg.), he, the.
nitya, eternal perpetual.
saṁnyāsī (m. nom. sg.), renouncer, one who throws down.
yas (m. nom. sg.), who.
na, not.
dveṣṭi (3rd sg. pr. indic. act. √*dviṣ*), he hates.
na, not, nor.
kāñkṣati (3rd sg. pr. indic. act. *kāñkṣ*), he desires, he covets.
nirdvandvas (m. nom. sg.), indifferent to pairs of opposites (heat, cold, pleasure pain, etc.).
hi, indeed, truly.
mahābāho (m. voc. sg.), O Mighty Armed One, epithet of Arjuna and other warriors.
sukham (adv.), easily, pleasantly.
bandhāt (m. abl. sg.), from bondage.
pramucyate (3rd sg. pr. indic. passive *pra* √*muc*), he is liberated, he is released.

He who neither hates nor desires
Is to be known as the eternal renouncer,
Who is indifferent to the pairs of opposites, O Mighty Armed One.
He is easily liberated from bondage.

4

सांख्ययोगौ पृथग्बालाः
sāṁkhyayogāu pṛthagbālāḥ
sāṁkhya and yoga distinct, the childish

प्रवदन्ति न पण्डिताः ।
pravadanti na paṇḍitāḥ
declare; not the paṇḍits;

एकम् अप्य् आस्थितः सम्यग्
ekam apy āsthitaḥ saṁyag
one even practiced correctly

उभयोर् विन्दते फलम् ॥
ubhayor vindate phalam
of both one finds the fruit.

"Sāṁkhya and Yoga are distinct,"
The childish declare; not the paṇḍits.
Even with one of them, practiced correctly,
One finds the fruit of both.

sāṁkhya, Sāṁkhya, one of the oldest of Hindu philosophies, non-theistic, concerned with theory (see discussion in footnote to II 39).
yogāu (m. nom. dual DV cpd.), Yoga.
pṛthak (adv.), distinct, separate, single, one by one.
bālās (m. nom. pl.), childish, foolish.
pravadanti (3rd sg. pr. indic. act. *pra* √*vad*), they declare, they maintain.
na, not.
paṇḍitās (m. nom. pl.), paṇḍits, wise men.
ekam (n. nom. sg.), one.
api, even.
āsthitas (m. nom. sg. p. pass. participle *ā* √*sthā*), practiced, followed, undertaken, performed.
saṁyañc (adv.), correctly, (adj.) true, right.
ubhayos (m. gen. dual), of both.
vindate (3rd sg. pr. indic. mid. √2 *vid*), he finds, one finds.
phalam (n. acc. sg.), fruit.

5

यत् सांख्यैः प्राप्यते स्थानं
yat sāṁkhyāiḥ prāpyate sthānaṁ
which by the Sāṁkhyas is attained, the place,

तद् योगैर् अपि गम्यते ।
tad yogāir api gamyate
that by Yogas also it is attained.

एकं सांख्यं च योगं च
ekaṁ sāṁkhyaṁ ca yogaṁ ca
one Sāṁkhya and Yoga

यः पश्यति स पश्यति ॥
yaḥ paśyati sa paśyati
who perceives, he perceives.

The place that is attained by the followers of Sāṁkhya
Is also attained by the followers of Yoga.
Sāṁkhya and Yoga are one.
He who perceives this, truly perceives.

yad (n. nom. sg.), which, what.
sāṁkhyāis (m. inst. pl.), by the Sāṁkhyas, by the followers of the Sāṁkhya doctrine.
prāpyate (3rd sg. pr. passive *pra* √*āp*), it is attained, it is obtained, it is reached.
sthānam (n. acc. sg.), place, standing, position.
tad (n. nom. sg.), this, that.
yogāis (m. inst. pl.), by Yogas, by the followers of Yoga.
api, also, even.
gamyate (3rd sg. pr. passive √*gam*), it is attained, it is gone to, it is reached.
ekam (m. acc. sg.), one.
sāṁkhyam (m. acc. sg.), Sāṁkhya.
ca, and.
yogam (m. acc. sg.), Yoga.
ca, and.
yas (m. nom. sg.), who.
paśyati (3rd sg. pr. indic. act. √*paś*), he perceives, he sees.
sas (m. nom. sg.), he.
paśyati (3rd sg. pr. indic. act. √*paś*), he perceives, he sees.

6

संन्यासस् तु महाबाहो
saṁnyāsas tu mahābāho
renunciation indeed, O Mighty Armed One,

दुःखम् आप्तुम् अयोगतः ।
duḥkham āptum ayogataḥ
difficult to attain without yoga

योगयुक्तो मुनिर् ब्रह्म
yogayukto munir brahma
the Yoga-disciplined sage Brahman

नचिरेणाधिगच्छति ॥
nacireṇādhigacchati
in no long time he attains.

Renunciation indeed, O Mighty Armed One,
Is difficult to attain without Yoga;
The sage who is disciplined in Yoga
Quickly attains Brahman.

saṁnyāsas (m. nom. sg.), renunciation, throwing down.
tu, indeed, but.
mahābāho (m. voc. sg.), O Mighty Armed One, epithet of Arjuna and other warriors.
duḥkham (n. nom. sg.), difficult, painful.
āptum (infinitive √*āp*), to attain, to obtain, to encounter.
ayogatas (m. abl. sg.), without Yoga.
yogayuktas (m. nom. sg.), Yoga yoked, Yoga disciplined, (as TP cpd.) disciplined in Yoga.
munis (m. nom. sg.), sage, wise man.
brahma (n. acc. sg.), Brahman.
nacireṇa (adv.), in no long time, quickly.
adhigacchati (3rd sg. pr. indic. act. *adhi* √*gam*), he attains, he reaches.

7

योगयुक्तो विशुद्धात्मा
yogayukto viśuddhātmā
he who is yoked to Yoga, whose self is purified,

विजितात्मा जितेन्द्रियः ।
vijitātmā jitendriyaḥ
whose self is subdued, whose senses are conquered,

सर्वभूतात्मभूतात्मा
sarvabhūtātmabhūtātmā
whose self has become the self of all beings,

कुर्वन्न् अपि न लिप्यते ॥
kurvann api na lipyate
acting even, he is not befouled.

He who is yoked to Yoga, whose self is purified,
Whose self is subdued, whose senses are conquered,
Whose self has become the self of all beings,
Is not befouled even when acting.

yogayuktas (m. nom. sg. TP cpd.), he who is disciplined in Yoga, he who is yoked to Yoga.
viśuddha (p. pass. participle *vi* √*śudh*), purified, cleansed.
ātmā (m. nom. sg.), self.
(*viśuddhātmā,* m. nom. sg. BV cpd., whose self is purified, whose self is cleansed.)
vijita (p. pass. participle *vi* √*ji*), conquered, subdued, controlled.
ātmā (m. nom. sg.), self.
(*vijitātmā,* m. nom. sg. BV cpd., whose self is subdued, whose self is conquered.)
jita (p. pass. participle √*ji*), conquered, subdued, controlled.
indriyas (n. with m. nom. sg. ending), sense.
(*jitendriyas,* m. nom. sg. BV cpd., whose senses are conquered.)
sarva, all.
bhūta (m.), being.
ātma (m.), self.
bhūta (m.), being, becoming.
ātmā (m. nom. sg.), self.
(*sarvabhūtātmabhūtātmā,* m. nom. sg. BV cpd., whose self has become the self of all beings.)
kurvan (pr. participle act. √*kṛ*), acting, doing.
api, even, also.
na, not.
lipyate (3rd sg. pr. indic. passive √*lip*), he is smeared, he is befouled, he is defiled.

8

नैव किञ्चित् करोमीति
nāiva kiñcit karomīti
"not anything I do," thus,

युक्तो मन्यते तत्त्ववित् ।
yukto manyate tattvavit
steadfast, he thinks, the knower of truth,

पश्यञ्शृण्वन् स्पृशञ्जिघ्रन्
paśyañśṛṇvan spṛśañjighrann
seeing, hearing, touching, smelling,

अश्नन् गच्छन् स्वपञ्श्वसन् ।।
aśnan gacchan svapañśvasan
eating, walking, sleeping, breathing,

"I do not do anything," thus,
Steadfast in Yoga, the knower of truth should think,
Whether seeing, hearing, touching, smelling,
Eating, walking, sleeping, breathing,

na, not.
eva, indeed (used as a rhythmic filler).
kiñcid or *kiṁcid,* anything, anything whatever, even a little.
karomi (1st sg. pr. indic. act. √*kṛ*), I do, I make, I act.
iti, thus (often used to close a quotation).
yuktas (m. nom. sg. p. pass. participle √*yuj*), disciplined, steadfast, yoked in Yoga, fixed in Yoga.
manyate (3rd sg. pr. indic. mid. √*man*), he thinks.
tattvavid (m. nom. sg.), the knower of "thatness," the knower of truth.
paśyan (m. nom. sg. pr. act. participle √*paś*), seeing, perceiving, observing.
śṛṇvan (m. nom. sg. pr. act. participle √*śru*), hearing.
spṛśan (m. nom. sg. pr. act. participle √*spṛś*), touching.
jighran (m. nom. sg. pr. act. participle √*ghrā*), smelling, scenting.
aśnan (m. nom. sg. pr. act. participle √*aś*), eating.
gacchan (m. nom. sg. pr. act. participle √*gam*), going, walking.
svapan (m. nom. sg. pr. act. participle √*svap*), sleeping.
śvasan (m. nom. sg. pr. act. participle √*śvas*), breathing, blowing.

9

प्रलपन् विसृजन् गृह्णन्न्
pralapan visrjan gṛhṇann
talking, excreting, grasping,

उन्मिषन् निमिषन्न् अपि ।
unmiṣan nimiṣann api
opening the eyes, shutting the eyes also.

इन्द्रियाणीन्द्रियार्थेषु
indriyāṇīndriyārtheṣu
"the senses in the objects of the senses

वर्तन्त इति धारयन् ॥
vartanta iti dhārayan
abide," thus believing.

Talking, excreting, grasping,
Opening the eyes and shutting the eyes,
"The senses abide in the objects of the senses,"
Thus believing.

pralapan (m. nom. sg. pr. act. participle *pra* √*lap*), talking, chattering, addressing.
visrjan (m. nom. sg. pr. act. participle *vi* √*sṛj*), defecating, eliminating, letting go, discharging, sending forth, evacuating the bowels.
gṛhṇan (m. nom. sg. pr. act. participle √*grah*), grasping, laying hold of.
unmiṣan (m. nom. sg. pr. act. participle *ud* √*miṣ*), opening the eyes.
nimiṣan (m. nom. sg. pr. act. participle *ni* √*miṣ*), shutting the eyes.
api, also, even.
indriyāṇi (n. nom. pl.), senses, powers.
indriyārtheṣu (n. loc. pl.), in the sense objects, in the objects of the senses.
vartanta (*saṁdhi* for *vartante*, 3rd pl. mid. pr. indic. √*vṛt*), they abide, they dwell, they work, they turn.
iti, thus (often used to close a quotation).
dhārayan (m. nom. sg. pr. causative act. participle √*dhṛ*), resolving, maintaining, believing, being convinced.

10

ब्रह्मण्य् आधाय कर्माणि
brahmaṇy ādhāya karmāṇi
on Brahman placing actions,

सङ्गं त्यक्त्वा करोति यः ।
saṅgaṁ tyaktvā karoti yaḥ
attachment having abandoned, he acts, who

लिप्यते न स पापेन
lipyate na sa pāpena
defiled not he by evil

पद्मपत्त्रम् इवाम्भसा ॥
padmapattram ivāmbhasā
lotus-leaf-like by water.

Placing his actions on Brahman,
Having abandoned attachment,
He who acts is not befouled by evil
Any more than a lotus leaf by water.

brahmaṇi (n. loc. sg.), in Brahman, on Brahman.
ādhāya (gerund *ā* √*dhā*), placing, putting.
karmāṇi (n. acc. pl.), actions, deeds.
saṅgam (m. acc. sg.), attachment, clinging.
tyaktvā (gerund √*tyaj*), abandoning, having abandoned.
karoti (3rd sg. pr. indic. act. √*kṛ*), he acts.
yas (m. nom. sg.), who.
lipyate (3rd sg. pr. passive √*lip*), he is smeared, he is befouled, he is defiled.
na, not.
sas (m. nom. sg.), he, this.
pāpena (n. inst. sg.), by evil, by wrong.
padma (m.), lotus.
pattram (n. nom. sg.), leaf.
(*padma-pattra*, KD cpd., n. nom. sg., lotus leaf.)
iva, like.
ambhasā (n. inst. sg.), by water.

11

कायेन मनसा बुद्ध्या
kāyena manasā buddhyā
with the body, with the mind, with the intelligence,

केवलैर् इन्द्रियैर् अपि ।
kevalāir indriyāir api
merely with the senses even

योगिनः कर्म कुर्वन्ति
yoginaḥ karma kurvanti
the yogins action perform

सङ्गं त्यक्त्वा ऽत्मशुद्धये ॥
saṅgaṁ tyaktvā 'tmaśuddhaye
attachment having abandoned, toward self purification.

With the body, with the mind, with the intelligence,
Even merely with the senses,
The yogins perform action toward self purification,
Having abandoned attachment.

kāyena (m. inst. sg.), by the body, with the body.
manasā (n. inst. sg.), by the mind, with the mind.
buddhyā (f. inst. sg.), by the intelligence, with the intelligence.
kevalāis (m. inst. pl.), merely, solely, alone, wholly.
indriyāis (m. inst. pl.), by the senses, with the senses.
api, even, also.
yoginas (m. nom. pl.), yogins.
karma (n. acc. sg.), action.
kurvanti (3rd pl. pr. indic. act. $\sqrt{}$*kṛ*), they perform, they do, they make.
saṅgam (m. acc. sg.), attachment, clinging.
tyaktvā (gerund $\sqrt{}$*tyaj*), abandoning, having abandoned.
ātma (m.), self, own.
śuddhaye (f. dat. sg.), to purification, toward purification.
(*ātma-śuddhaye*, f. dat. sg. TP cp., for self purification.)

12

युक्तः कर्मफलं त्यक्त्वा
yuktaḥ karmaphalaṁ tyaktvā
he who is disciplined, action fruit having abandoned,

शान्तिमाप्नोति नैष्ठिकीम् ।
śāntimāpnoti nāiṣṭhikīm
peace he attains complete;

अयुक्तः कामकारेण
ayuktaḥ kāmakāreṇa
he who is undisciplined, by desire-action,

फले सक्तो निबध्यते ॥
phale sakto nibadhyate
in fruit attached, he is bound.

He who is disciplined in Yoga, having abandoned the fruit of action,
Attains steady peace;
The undisciplined one, attached to fruit,
Is bound by actions prompted by desire.

yuktas (m. nom. sg. p. pass. participle √*yuj*), disciplined, steadfast, fixed in Yoga.
karmaphalam (n. acc. sg.), action fruit, fruit of action.
tyaktvā (gerund √*tyaj*), abandoning, having abandoned.
śāntim (f. acc. sg.), peace, tranquility.
āpnoti (3rd sg. pr. indic. act. √*āp*), he attains, he obtains, he reaches.
nāiṣṭhikīm (f. acc. sg.), final, complete, last, decided, highest, definitive, steady.
ayuktas (m. nom. sg.), undisciplined, unfixed in Yoga, unsteadfast.
kāmakāreṇa (m. inst. sg.), by desire-action, by action resulting from desire.
phale (n. loc. sg.), in fruit.
saktas (m. nom. sg. p. pass. participle √*sañj*), attached, clinging.
nibadhyate (3rd sg. pr. indic. passive *ni* √*bandh*), he is bound, he is bound down, he is fettered.

13

सर्वकर्माणि मनसा
sarvakarmāṇi manasā
all actions with the mind

संन्यस्यास्ते सुखं वशी ।
saṁnyasyāste sukhaṁ vaśī
renouncing it sits happily, ruler

नवद्वारे पुरे देही
navadvāre pure dehī
in the nine-gated city, the embodied one,

नैव कुर्वन् न कारयन् ॥
nāiva kurvan na kārayan
not at all acting, not causing to act.

Renouncing all actions with the mind,
The embodied one sits happily, as the ruler
Within the city whose gates are nine,*
Not acting at all, nor causing action.

sarva, all.
karmāṇi (n. acc. pl.), actions, deeds.
manasā (n. inst. sg.), with the mind, by the mind.
saṁnyasya (gerund *sam ni* √2 *as*), renouncing, throwing down.
āste (3rd sg. pr. indic. mid. √*ās*), he sits, it sits.
sukham (adv.), happily, pleasantly.
vaśī (m. nom. sg.), having mastery, ruler, lord.
nava, nine.
dvāre (m. loc. sg.), in the gate, inside the gate, within the gate.
(*navadvāre,* m. loc. sg. BV cpd., whose gates are nine.)
pure (m. loc. sg.), in the city.
dehī (m. nom. sg.), the embodied one, the embodied soul, the ātman.
na, not.
eva, at all, indeed (often used as a rhythmic filler).
kurvan (m. nom. sg. pr. act. participle √*kṛ*), acting, doing, making.
na, not, nor.
kārayan (m. nom. sg. pr. causative act. participle √*kṛ*), causing to act, causing action, causing deeds.

* "the city whose gates are nine." The "city" is the body. The "nine gates" are the two eyes, the two ears, the two nostrils, the mouth and the organs of excretion and generation.

14

न कर्तृत्वं न कर्माणि
na kartṛtvaṁ na karmāṇi
not agency not actions

लोकस्य सृजति प्रभुः ।
lokasya sṛjati prabhuḥ
of people He creates, the Lord,

न कर्मफलसंयोगं
na karmaphalasaṁyogaṁ
nor action-fruit union.

स्वभावस् तु प्रवर्तते ॥
svabhāvas tu pravartate
inherent nature, on the other hand, proceeds.

The Lord does not create
Either the agency (the means of action) or the actions of people,
Or the union of action with its fruit.
Nature, on the other hand, proceeds (in all this).

na, not.
kartṛtvam (n. acc. sg.), agency, means of action, state of performing action.
na, not, nor.
karmāṇi (n. acc. pl.), actions.
lokasya (m. gen. sg.), of the world, of people.
sṛjati (3rd sg. pr. indic. act. √*sṛj*), he creates, he brings forth, it creates, it lets flow.
prabhus (m. nom. sg.), the Lord, the Mighty One, the ātman or self.
na, not, nor.
karma (n.), action.
phala (n.), fruit.
saṁyogam (m. acc. sg.), yoking together, union.
(*karmaphalasaṁyogam,* m. acc. sg. TP cpd., the union of action with its fruit.)
svabhāvas (m. nom. sg.), nature, spontaneousness (in the sense of nature's spontaneousness).
tu, but, on the other hand.
pravartate (3rd sg. pr. indic. mid. *pra* √*vṛt*), it proceeds, it turns, it works.

15

नादत्ते कस्यचित् पापं
nādatte kasyacit pāpaṁ
not it receives of anyone the evil

न चैव सुकृतं विभुः ।
na cāiva sukṛtaṁ vibhuḥ
and not either the good doing, the Omnipresent,

अज्ञानेनावृतं ज्ञानं
ajñānenāvṛtaṁ jñānaṁ
by ignorance (is) enveloped knowledge

तेन मुह्यन्ति जन्तवः ॥
tena muhyanti jantavaḥ
by it (i.e. ignorance) they are deluded the people.

The Omnipresent does not receive
Either the evil or the good deeds of anyone.
Knowledge is enveloped by ignorance.
By it (ignorance) people are deluded.

na, not.
ādatte (3rd sg. pr. indic. mid. *ā* √*dā*), it takes, it receives, it accepts.
kasyacid (m. gen. sg.), of anyone, of anyone whatever.
pāpam (n. acc. sg.), evil, sin, wrong.
na, not.
ca, and.
eva, either, indeed (often used as a rhythmic filler).
sukṛtam (n. acc. sg.), good doing, goodness, virtue.
vibhus (m. nom. sg.), the Omnipresent, the All Pervading, the Eternal, the ātman.
ajñānena (n. inst. sg.), by ignorance.
āvṛtam (n. nom. sg. p. pass. participle *ā* √*vṛ*), enveloped, concealed, surrounded.
jñānam (n. nom. sg.), knowledge, wisdom.
tena (n. inst. sg.), by it, by this.
muhyanti (3rd pl. pr. indic. act. √*muh*), they are deluded, they are crazed, they are confused.
jantavas (m. nom. pl.), people, offspring, living beings, men.

16

ज्ञानेन तु तद् अज्ञानं
jñānena tu tad ajñānaṁ
by knowledge, however, this ignorance

येषां नाशितम् आत्मनः ।
yesāṁ nāśitam ātmanaḥ
of whom (pl.) destroyed of the self

तेषाम् आदित्यवज् ज्ञानं
teṣām ādityavaj jñānaṁ
of them like the sun knowledge

प्रकाशयति तत् परम् ॥
prakāśayati tat param
it illumines that Supreme.

But of those in whom this ignorance in the self
Is destroyed by knowledge,
That knowledge of theirs
Causes the Supreme to shine like the sun.

jñānena (n. inst. sg.), by knowledge, with knowledge.
tu, but, however.
tad (n. nom. sg.), this, that.
ajñānam (n. nom. sg.), ignorance.
yeṣām (m. gen. pl.), of whom.
nāśitam (n. nom. sg. causative p. pass. participle √*naś*), lost, destroyed.
ātmanas (m. gen. sg.), of the self.
teṣām (m. gen. pl.), of them.
ādityavat, like the sun.
jñānam (n. nom. sg.), knowledge.
prakāśayati (3rd sg. causative act. *pra* √*kāś*), it illumines, it causes to appear, it causes to shine.
tad (n. nom. sg.), this, that.
param (n. nom. sg.), Supreme Highest.

17

तद्बुद्धयस् तदात्मानस्
tadbuddhayas tadātmānas
they whose minds are absorbed in that, whose selves are fixed on that,

तन्निष्ठास् तत्परायणाः ।
tanniṣṭhās tatparāyaṇāḥ
whose basis is that, who hold that as highest object,

गच्छन्त्यपुनरावृत्तिं
gacchantyapunarāvṛttiṁ
they go to rebirthlessness,

ज्ञाननिर्धूतकल्मषाः ॥
jñānanirdhūtakalmaṣāḥ
their evils shaken off by knowledge.

They whose minds are absorbed in that (i.e. the Supreme),
Whose selves are fixed on that,
Whose basis is that, who hold that as highest object,
Whose evils have been shaken off by knowledge, go to the end of rebirth.

tadbuddhyas (m. nom. pl. BV cpd.), they whose minds are absorbed in that.
tadātmānas (m. nom. pl. BV cpd.), they whose selves are fixed on that.
tanniṣṭhās (m. nom. pl. BV cpd. from *tad niṣṭhā*), they whose basis is that, they whose foundation is that.
tatparāyaṇās (m. nom. pl. BV cpd.), they who hold that as highest object.
gacchanti (3rd pl. pr. indic. act. *gam*), they go.
apunar, not again.
āvṛttim (f. acc. sg. from *ā* √*vṛt*), return, rebirth.
(*apunarāvṛttim,* f. acc. sg., to rebirthlessness, to the end of rebirth.)
jñāna (n.), knowledge, wisdom.
nirdhūta (p. pass. participle, *nir* √*dhū*), shaken, shaken off.
kalmaṣās (m. nom. pl.), evils, wrongs.
(*jñānanirdhūtakalmaṣās,* m. nom. pl. BV cpd., they whose evils have been shaken off by knowledge.)

18

विद्याविनयसंपन्ने
vidyāvinayasaṁpanne
on a wisdom and cultivation endowed

ब्राह्मणे गवि हस्तिनि ।
brāhmaṇe gavi hastini
Brahman, on a cow, on an elephant

शुनि चैव श्वपाके च
śuni cāiva śvapāke ca
and on a dog and on a dog-cooker*

पण्डिताः समदर्शिनः ॥
paṇḍitāḥ samadarśinaḥ
the Paṇḍits the same seeing.

In a brāhman endowed with wisdom and cultivation,
In a cow, in an elephant,
And even in a dog or in a dog-cooker*
The paṇḍits see the same (ātman).

vidyā (f. sg.), wisdom, knowledge.
vinaya (m. from *vi* √*nī*), training, educated, cultivated, cultivation.
saṁpanne (m. loc. sg. p. pass. participle *sam* √*pad*), accomplished, endowed.
(*vidyā-vinaya-saṁpanne*, m. loc. sg. TP cpd., endowed with education and wisdom.)
brāhmaṇe (m. loc. sg.), on a Brāhman, on a member of the priestly caste.
gavi (f. loc. sg.), on a cow.
hastini (m. loc. sg.), on an elephant.
śuni (m. loc. sg.), on a dog.
ca, and.
eva, indeed (used as a rhythmic filler).
śvapāke (m. loc. sg.), on a dog-cooker, on an outcaste.
ca, and.
paṇḍitās (m. nom pl.), paṇḍits, wise men.
sama, (adv.), same, equally, impartially.
darśinas (m. nom. pl.), looking, seeing, observing, finding.

* Dog-cooker, a type of outcaste, offspring of a *śūdra* father and a *brāhman* mother, or offspring of a *cāṇḍāla* (son of a *śūdra* father and a *brāhman* mother), or of a prostitute, or of parents of various foreign mountain tribes, or of parents of a mixed *kṣatriya* and *śūdra* lineage, or of mixed *kṣatriya* and *vāiśya* lineage. Such people served as public executioners and in other menial or unpleasant occupations.

19

इहैव तैर् जितः सर्गो
ihāiva tāir jitaḥ sargo
here on earth by those conquered birth,

येषां साम्ये स्थितं मनः ।
yeṣāṁ sāmye sthitaṁ manaḥ
of whom in impartiality established the mind;

निर्दोषं हि समं ब्रह्म
nirdoṣaṁ hi samaṁ brahma
guiltless, indeed impartial, Brahman

तस्माद् ब्रह्मणि ते स्थिताः ॥
tasmād brahmaṇi te sthitāḥ
therefore in Brahman they established.

Even here on earth, rebirth is conquered
By those whose mind is established in impartiality.*
Brahman is guiltless and impartial;*
Therefore they are established in Brahman.

iha, here, here on earth.
eva, indeed (used as a rhythmic filler).
tāis (m. inst. pl.), by those, by them.
jitas (m. nom. sg. p. pass. participle √*ji*), conquered, subdued, controlled.
sargas (m. nom. sg.), birth, coming forth.
yeṣām (m. gen. pl.), of whom.
sāmye (n. loc. sg.), in equality, in sameness, in equability, in impartiality, in disinterestedness.
sthitam (n. nom. sg.), established, situated, abiding in, remaining.
manas (n. nom. sg.), mind, thought.
nirdoṣam (n. nom. sg.), guiltless, without evil.
hi, indeed, truly.
samam (n. nom. sg.), impartial, equable, equal, same, dispassionate, disinterested.
brahma (n. nom. sg.), Brahman.
tasmāt (m. abl. sg.), from this, therefore.
brahmaṇi (n. loc. sg.), in Brahman.
te, they.
sthitās (m. nom. pl.), established, abiding in, situated.

---

* The word "impartial" refers to those who "see the same," i.e. see that all ātmans are identical with their own (see introductory chapter on Cosmology).

20

न प्रहृष्येत् प्रियं प्राप्य
na prahṛṣyet priyaṁ prāpya
not one should rejoice, the cherished attaining,

नोद्विजेत् प्राप्य चाप्रियम् ।
nodvijet prāpya cāpriyam
and not one should shudder, attaining the uncherished.

स्थिरबुद्धिर् असंमूढो
sthirabuddhir asaṁmūḍho
(with) firm intelligence, undeluded,

ब्रह्मविद् ब्रह्मणि स्थितः ॥
brahmavid brahmaṇi sthitaḥ
Brahman knowing, in Brahman (one is) established.

na, not.
prahṛṣyet (3rd sg. optative act. *pra* √*hṛṣ*), one should rejoice, one should be excited.
priyam (m. acc. sg.), the cherished, the dear, the preferred.
prāpya (gerund *pra* √*āp*), attaining, reaching.
na, not.
udvijet (3rd sg. opt. act. *ud* √*vij*), one should shudder, one should tremble.
prāpya (gerund *pra* √*āp*), attaining, reaching.
ca, and.
apriyam (m. acc. sg.), uncherished, undesired, non-dear.
sthira (f.), firm, solid, unshakable.
buddhis (f. nom. sg.), intelligence.
(*sthira-buddhis*, f. nom. sg. KD cpd., firm intelligence.)
asaṁmūḍhas (m. nom. sg. p. pass. participle *a sam* √*muh*), undeluded, unconfused.
brahmavid (m. nom. sg.), Brahman knowing, a knower of Brahman.
brahmaṇi (n. loc. sg.), in Brahman.
sthitas (m. nom. sg.), established, abiding, situated.

One should not rejoice upon attaining the cherished,
Nor should one shudder upon encountering the uncherished;
With firm intelligence, undeluded,
Brahman-knowing, one is established in Brahman.

21

बाह्यस्पर्शेष्वसक्तात्मा
bāhyasparśeṣvasaktātmā
whose self is unattached to external contacts,

विन्दत्यात्मनि यत् सुखम् ।
vindatyātmani yat sukham
he finds in the self, who happiness,

स ब्रह्मयोगयुक्तात्मा
sa brahmayogayuktātmā
he whose self is united with Brahman by Yoga,

सुखम् अक्षयम् अश्नुते ॥
sukham akṣayam aśnute
happiness imperishable he reaches.

He whose self is unattached to external sensations,
Who finds happiness in the self,
Whose self is united with Brahman through Yoga,
Reaches imperishable happiness.

bāhya, outside, situated without.
sparśeṣu (m. loc. pl. from √*spṛś*), in touchings, in contacts.
asakta (p. pass. participle *a* √*sañj*), unattached, not clinging.
ātmā (m. nom. sg.), self, soul.
(*bāhyasparśeṣvasaktātmā,* m. nom. sg. BV cpd., he whose self is unattached to external sensations.)
vindati (3rd sg. pr. indic. act. √2 *vid*), he finds.
ātmani (m. loc. sg.), in the self.
yad (n. acc. sg.), what, which, who.
sukham (n. acc. sg.), happiness, bliss.
sas (m. nom. sg.), he, this.
brahma (n.), Brahman.
yoga (m.), Yoga.
yukta (p. p ss. participle √*yuj*), joined, united, yoked.
ātmā (m. nom. sg.), self.
(*brahmayogayuktātmā,* m. nom. sg. BV cpd., whose self is united in Yoga with Brahman.)
sukham (n. acc. sg.), happiness, bliss.
akṣayam (n. acc. sg.), imperishable, indestructible.
aśnute (3rd sg. pr. indic. mid. √*aś*), he reaches, he attains.

22

ये हि संस्पर्शजा भोगा
ye hi saṁsparśajā bhogā
which indeed contact-born pleasures

दुःखयोनय एव ते ।
duḥkhayonaya eva te
wombs (i.e. sources) of pain, they

आद्यन्तवन्तः कौन्तेय
ādyantavantaḥ kāunteya
having a beginning and an end, Son of Kuntī,

न तेषु रमते बुधः ॥
na teṣu ramate budhaḥ
not in them he is content, the wise man.

Pleasures born of contact, indeed,
Are wombs (i.e. sources) of pain.
Since they have a beginning and an end (i.e. are not eternal), Son of Kuntī,
The wise man is not content in them.

ye (m. nom. pl.), who, which.
hi, indeed, truly.
saṁsparśajās (m. nom. pl.), born of touching, born of contact.
bhogās (m. nom. pl.), pleasures, gratifications.
duḥkha (n.), pain, misery, unhappiness.
yonayas (m. nom. pl.), wombs, sources.
(*duḥkha-yonayas*, m. n. pl. TP cpd., sources of pain.)
eva, indeed (used as a rhythmic filler).
te (m. nom. sg.), they.
ādi, beginning, commencement.
anta, end.
-vantas (m. nom. pl. suffix), having, rich in, tending toward.
(*ādyantavantas*, m. nom. pl., having a beginning and an end.)
kāunteya (m. voc. sg.), Sun of Kuntī, epithet of Arjuna.
na, not.
teṣu (m. loc. pl.), in them.
ramate (3rd sg. mid. √*ram*), he is content, he is delighted, he rejoices.
budhas (m. nom. sg.), wise man, man of intelligence.

23

शक्नोतीहैव यः सोढुं
śaknotīhāiva yaḥ soḍhuṁ
he is able here on earth, who, to endure,

प्राक् शरीरविमोक्षणात् ।
prāk śarīravimokṣaṇāt
before liberation from the body

कामक्रोधोद्भवं वेगं
kāmakrodhodbhavaṁ vegaṁ
desire-and-anger-origination agitation

स युक्तः स सुखी नरः ॥
sa yuktaḥ sa sukhī naraḥ
he disciplined, he happy man.

He who is able to endure here on earth,
Before liberation from the body,
The agitation that arises from desire and anger,
Is disciplined; he is a happy man.

śaknoti (3rd sg. pr. indic. act. √*śak*), he is able, he can.
iha, here, here on earth.
eva, indeed (used as a rhythmic filler).
yas (m. nom. sg.), who.
soḍhum (infinitive √*sah*), to bear, to endure, to tolerate.
prāk (*prāñc,* n. nom. sg.), before, previously, former.
śarīra, body, bodily frame.
vimokṣaṇāt (m. abl. sg. verbal noun from *vi* √*muc*), from liberation, from release.
(*śarīravimokṣaṇāt,* m. abl. sg., liberation from the body.)
kāma (m.), desire, love, greed.
krodha (m.), anger, wrath.
udbhavam (m. acc. sg.), origination.
vegam (m. acc. sg.), agitation, impetus, shock, momentum, onset, orgasm.
sas (m. nom. sg.), he, this.
yuktas (m. nom. sg. p. pass. participle √*yuj*), disciplined, fixed in Yoga, steadfast in Yoga.
sas (m. nom. sg.), he, this.
sukhī (m. nom. sg.), happy, fortunate.
naras (m. nom. sg.), man.

24

यो ऽन्तःसुखो ऽन्तरारामस्
yo 'ntaḥsukho 'ntarārāmas
who (having) happiness within, delight within,

तथान्तर्ज्योतिर् एव यः ।
tathāntarjyotir eva yaḥ
as a consequence inner radiance, thus who

स योगी ब्रह्मनिर्वाणं
sa yogī brahmanirvāṇaṁ
this yogin Brahmanirvāṇa,

ब्रह्मभूतो ऽधिगच्छति ॥
brahmabhūto, 'dhigacchati
absorbed in Brahman, he attains.

He who has happiness within, delight within,
And, as a consequence, inner radiance;
This yogin attains to Brahmanirvāṇa,*
Absorbed in Brahman.

yas (m. nom. sg.), who.
antaḥsukhas (m. nom. sg.), "withinhappiness," having happiness within, (as BV cpd.) he who has happiness within.
antarārāmas (m. nom. sg.), interior delight, delight within, content within, interior contentment, (as BV cpd.) he who has delight within.
tathā, thus, in this way, as a consequence.
antarjyotis (n. nom. sg.), inner radiance, interior brightness, radiance within, (as BV cpd.) he who has radiance within.
eva, indeed (used as a rhythmic filler).
yas (m. nom. sg.), who.
sas (m. nom. sg.), he, this.
yogī (m. nom. sg.), yogin.
brahmanirvāṇam (n. acc. sg.), Brahmanirvāṇa, the nirvāṇa of Brahman, the extinction of the self in Brahman.
brahmabhūtas (m. nom. sg.), absorbed in Brahman, indentical in being with Brahman.
adhigacchati (3rd sg. pr. indic. act. *adhi* √*gam*), he attains, he goes, he ascends to.

* *nirvāṇa*, from *nir* √*vā*, "blow out" as a candle is blown out, refers to the final extinction of the "self," following the round of rebirths, which the Hindus (Buddhists of the Theravāda School too) regard as the ultimately desirable state of nonbeing. It is related to the Hindu belief that to be born at all is a tragedy.

25

लभन्ते ब्रह्मनिर्वाणम्
labhante brahmanirvāṇam
they attain Brahmanirvāṇa

ऋषयः क्षीणकल्मषाः ।
ṛṣayaḥ kṣīṇakalmaṣāḥ
the seers (of) destroyed evils,

छिन्नद्वैधा यतात्मानः
chinnadvāidhā yatātmānaḥ
whose doubts have been cut away, whose selves are restrained,

सर्वभूतहिते रताः ॥
sarvabhūtahite ratāḥ
who delight in the welfare of all beings

The seers, whose evils have been destroyed,
Whose doubts have been cut away, whose selves are restrained,
Who delight in the welfare of all beings,
Attain Brahmanirvāṇa.

labhante (3rd pl. pr. indic. mid. √*labh*), they attain, they acquire, they obtain.
brahmanirvāṇam (n. acc. sg.), the *nirvāṇa* of Brahman, the extinction of the self in Brahman.
ṛṣayas (m. nom. pl.), the *ṛṣis*, the seers.
kṣīṇa (m. p. pass. participle √*ksi*), destroyed, passed away, made an end of.
kalmaṣās (m. nom. pl.), sins, evils, wrongs.
(*kṣīṇa-kalmaṣās*, m. nom. pl. BV cpd., whose evils are diminished.)
chinna (p. pass. participle √*chid*), cut away, severed.
dvāidhās (m. nom. pl.), twofold states, dualities, disputes, doubts, uncertainties.
(*chinna-dvaidhās*, m. nom. pl. BV cpd., whose doubts are dispelled.)
yata (p. pass. participle √*yam*), restrained, controlled.
ātmānas (m. nom. pl.), selves, souls.
(*yata-ātmānas*, m. nom. pl. BV cpd., whose selves are restrained.)
sarva, all.
bhūta (m.), being, creature.
hite (m. loc. sg. p. pass. participle √*dhā*), in welfare, in friendship, in favorableness, in benefit, in advantage.
(*sarvabhūtahite*, m. loc. sg., in the welfare of all beings.)
ratās (m. nom. pl. p. pass. participle √*ram*), delighted, content, rejoicing.

26

कामक्रोधवियुक्तानां
kāmakrodhaviyuktānāṁ
of the desire-and-anger-separated-from

यतीनां यतचेतसाम् ।
yatīnāṁ yatacetasām
of the ascetics, of the restrained in thought,

अभितो ब्रह्मनिर्वाणं
abhito brahmanirvāṇaṁ
close Brahmanirvāṇa

वर्तते विदितात्मनाम् ॥
vartate viditātmanām
it lies, of the knowing selves.

To those who have cast aside desire and anger,
To the ascetics, to those whose thought is controlled,
To the knowers of the self,
The nirvāṇa of Brahman lies close.

kāma (m.), desire, love, greed.
krodha (m.), anger, wrath.
viyuktānām (m. gen. pl. p. pass. participle *vi* √*yuj*), of the separated from, of the unyoked, of the disjoined.
(*kāmakrodhaviyuktānām,* m. gen. pl. TP cpd., of those who are separated from desire and anger.)
yatīnām (m. gen. pl.), of the ascetics.
yatacetasām (m. gen. pl.), of the restrained in thought, (as BV cpd.) of those whose thoughts are controlled.
abhitas (adv.), close, near.
brahmanirvāṇam (n. nom. sg.), the *nirvāṇa* of Brahman, the extinction of the self in Brahman.
vartate (3rd sg. pr. indic. mid. √*vṛt*), it lies, it exists, it works, it turns.
vidita (p. pass. participle √*vid*), known, learned, knowing, knower.
ātmanām (m. gen. pl.), of the selves, of the souls.
(*viditātmanām*, m. gen. pl. BV cpd., of the knowers of the self, of those to whom the self is known.)

27

स्पर्शान् कृत्वा बहिर् बाह्यांश्
sparśān kṛtvā bahir bāhyāṁś
contacts having made outside (to be) expelled,

चक्षुश्चैवान्तरे भ्रुवोः ।
cakṣuścāivāntare bhruvoḥ
and the gaze in between the two brows,

प्राणापानौ समौ कृत्वा
prāṇāpānāu samāu kṛtvā
inhalation and exhalation equal making,

नासाभ्यन्तरचारिणौ ॥
nāsābhyantaracāriṇāu
the nose within moving,

Expelling outside contacts
And putting the gaze between the two eye-brows,*
Making inhalation and exhalation equal,
Moving within the nose,

sparśān (m. acc. pl. from √*spṛś*), touchings, contacts.
kṛtvā (gerund √*kṛ*), making, doing, performing, having made, having performed.
bahis (adv.), outside, exterior.
bāhyān (m. acc. pl.), expelled, external, foreign, excluded.
cakṣus (m. nom. sg.), seeing, gaze, eye.
ca, and.
eva, indeed (used as a rhythmic filler).
antare (m. loc. sg.), in between, inside.
bhruvos (f. gen. dual), of the two eyebrows, of the two brows.
prāṇa (m.), vital breath, inhalation.
apāna (m.), abdominal breath, exhalation.
(*prāṇāpānāu,* m. acc. dual, the vital breath and the abdominal breath, inhalation and exhalation.)
samāu (m. acc. dual), equal, the same, similar.
kṛtvā (gerund √*kṛ*), making, having made.
nāsā (f.), nose.
abhyantara, within, interiorly.
cāriṇāu (dual from √*car*), moving.
(*nāsābhyantaracāriṇāu,* m. acc. dual, moving within the nose.)

* These are elementary Yoga exercises, well-known to all yogins. It might be remarked that, according to modern physiology and psychology, eye movement is apt to accompany thought, even such unconscious thought as occurs in dreams. "Putting the gaze between the two eyebrows," in other words rolling the eyeballs to their highest attainable point and drawing them toward the nose, keeping them there steadily, is a method of inhibiting thought. The other directions are for Yoga breathing exercises.

28

यतेन्द्रियमनोबुद्धिर्
yatendriyamanobuddhir
with controlled sense, mind and intelligence,

मुनिर् मोक्षपरायणः ।
munir mokṣaparāyaṇaḥ
the sage, (with) release as highest aim,

विगतेच्छाभयक्रोधो
vigatecchābhayakrodho
gone desire, fear and anger,

यः सदा मुक्त एव सः ॥
yaḥ sadā mukta eva saḥ
who, forever released, he.

The sage whose highest aim is release,
Whose senses, mind and intelligence are controlled,
From whom desire, fear and anger have departed,
Is forever liberated.

yata (p. pass. participle √*yam*), controlled, subdued.
indriya (n.), sense, sensation.
manas (n.), mind.
buddhis (f. nom. sg.), intelligence, mental determination, intuition.
(*yatendriyamanobuddhis,* f. nom. sg. BV cpd., whose senses, mind and intelligence are controlled.)
munis (m. nom. sg.), sage, wise man.
mokṣaparāyaṇas (m. nom. sg. BV cpd.), who has release as highest aim, whose highest course is release.
vigata (p. pass. participle *vi* √*gam*), gone away, disappeared.
icchā (f.), desire.
bhaya (n.), fear.
krodhas (m. nom. sg.), anger, wrath.
(*vigatecchābhayakrodhas,* m. nom. sg. BV cpd., from whom desire, fear and anger have disappeared.)
yas (m. nom. sg.), who.
sadā, always, perpetually, forever.
muktas (m. nom. sg. p. pass. participle √*muc*), released, liberated.
eva, indeed (used as a rhythmic filler).
sas (m. nom. sg.), he, this one.

29

भोक्तारं यज्ञतपसां
bhoktāraṁ yajñatapasāṁ
the enjoyer of the sacrificial austerities

सर्वलोकमहेश्वरम् ।
sarvalokamaheśvaram
(of) all the world the Mighty Lord,

सुहृदं सर्वभूतानां
suhṛdaṁ sarvabhūtānāṁ
friend of all creatures,

ज्ञात्वा मां शान्तिमृच्छति ॥
jñātvā māṁ śāntimṛcchati
having known me, peace he attains.

Having known Me, the enjoyer of sacrificial austerities,
The Mighty Lord of all the world,
The friend of all creatures,
He (the sage) attains peace.

bhoktāram (m. acc. sg.), enjoyer, eater.
yajña (m.), sacrifice, offering, sacrificial.
tapasām (n. gen. pl.), of the austerities, of the heatings.
(*yajñatapasām,* n. gen. pl., of the sacrificial austerities.)
sarva, all.
loka (m.), world.
maheśvaram (m. acc. sg.), Mighty Lord.
(*sarva-loka-maheśvaram,* m. acc. sg. TP cpd., mighty Lord of all the world.)
suhṛdam (m. acc. sg.), friend, companion.
sarvabhūtānām (m. gen. pl.), of all beings, of all creatures.
jñātvā (gerund √*jñā*), knowing, having known.
mām (acc. sg.), me.
śāntim (f. acc. sg.), peace, tranquility.
ṛcchati (3rd sg. pr. indic. act. √*ṛ*), he reaches, he attains, he ascends to, he obtains.

End of Book V

The Yoga of Renunciation

BOOK VI

श्रीभगवान् उवाच ।
śrībhagavān uvāca
the Blessed Lord spoke:

śrībhagavān (n. nom. sg.), the Blessed Lord, the Blessed One.
uvāca (3rd sg. perfect act. √*vac*), he said, he spoke.

1

अनाश्रितः कर्मफलं
anāśritaḥ karmaphalaṁ
not depending (on) action fruit

कार्यं कर्म करोति यः ।
kāryaṁ karma karoti yaḥ
the to-be-done (ritual) action he does, who

स संन्यासी च योगी च
sa saṁnyāsī ca yogī ca
he a renouncer and a yogin

न निरग्निर् न चाक्रियः ॥
na niragnir na cākriyaḥ
not (he who is) without a (consecrated) fire, and without sacred rites.

The Blessed Lord spoke:

He who performs that ritual action which is his duty,
While renouncing the fruit of action,
Is a renouncer and a yogin;
Not he who is without a consecrated fire, and who fails to perform sacred rites.

anāśritas (m. nom. sg. p. pass. participle *an ā* √*śri*), not resorting to, not depending on.
karmaphalam (n. acc. sg.), action fruit, the fruit of action.
kāryam (m. acc. sg. gerundive √*kṛ*), to be done, prescribed duty.
karma (n. acc. sg.), action, ritual action.
karoti (3rd sg. pr. indic. act. √*kṛ*), he does, he performs.
yas (m. nom. sg.), who.
sas (m. nom. sg.), he, this.
saṃnyāsī (m. nom. sg.), renouncer, thrower down.
ca, and.
yogī (m. nom. sg.), yogin.
ca, and.
na, not.
niragnis (m. nom. sg.), without fire, without consecrated fire, (as BV cpd.) he who is without a consecrated fire.
na, not, nor.
ca, and.
akriyas (m. nom. sg.), without sacred rites, without ritual action, (as BV cpd.) he who is without sacred rites.

2

यं संन्यासम् इति प्राहुर्
yaṁ saṁnyāsam iti prāhur
which renunciation thus they call

योगं तं विद्धि पाण्डव ।
yogaṁ taṁ viddhi pāṇḍava
Yoga it know, Son of Pāṇḍu

न ह्य् असंन्यस्तसंकल्पो
na hy asaṁnyastasaṁkalpo
not indeed without renounced purpose

योगी भवति कश्चन ॥
yogī bhavati kaścana
a yogin he becomes, anyone.

That which they call renunciation,
That know to be Yoga, Son of Pāṇḍu.
Not without renounced purpose
Does anyone become a yogin.

yam (m. acc. sg.), which.
saṁnyāsam (m. acc. sg.), renunciation, throwing down, casting aside.
iti, thus.
prāhus (3rd pl. perfect act. *pra* √*ah* with present meaning), they call, they say.
yogam (m. acc. sg.), Yoga.
tam (m. acc. sg.), it, this.
viddhi (2nd sg. imperative act. √*vid*), know! learn!
pāṇḍava (m. voc. sg.), Son of Pāṇḍu, epithet of Arjuna.
na, not.
hi, indeed, truly.
asaṁnyasta (m.), not renounced, without renounced.
saṁkalpas (m. nom. sg.), volition, desire, purpose.
(*asaṁnyasta-saṁkalpus*, m. nom. sg., without renounced purpose.)
yogī (m. nom. sg.), yogin.
bhavati (3rd sg. pr. indic. act. √*bhū*), he is, he becomes.
kaścana, anyone, anyone whatever.

3

आरुरुक्षोर् मुनेर् योगं
ārurukṣor muner yogaṁ
of the desirous of ascending, of the sage, to Yoga

कर्म कारणम् उच्यते ।
karma kāraṇam ucyate
action the means it is said;

योगारूढस्य तस्यैव
yogārūḍhasya tasyāiva
of the Yoga-ascended, of him,

शमः कारणम् उच्यते ॥
śamaḥ kāraṇam ucyate
tranquility the means it is said.

For the sage desirous of ascending to Yoga,
Action is said to be the means;
For him who has already ascended to Yoga,
Tranquility is said to be the means.*

ārurukṣos (m. gen. sg. desiderative noun from *ā* √*ruh*), of the desirous of ascending, of the desirous of climbing.
munes (m. gen. sg.), of the sage, of the wise man.
yogam (m. acc. sg.), to yoga, yoga.
karma (n. nom. sg.), action, deeds.
kāraṇam (n. acc. sg.), method, cause, means.
ucyate (3rd sg. pr. indic. passive √*vac*), it is said, it is called.
yogārūḍhasya (m. gen. sg. p. pass. participle *yoga ā* √*ruh*), of the Yoga ascended, (as TP cpd.) of him who has ascended to Yoga.
tasya (m. gen. sg.), of him, of this.
eva, indeed (used as a rhythmic filler).
śamas (m. nom. sg.), calmness, tranquility, quiet.
kāraṇam (n. acc. sg.), method, means.
ucyate (3rd sg. pr. indic. passive √*vac*), it is said, it is called.

* By *karmayoga* (the Yoga of Action) one is able to succeed in Yoga because in *karmayoga* one does not risk being negligent about it. When a man aspires to the contemplation, i.e. to release, *karmayoga* will cause him to succeed; only when the contemplation of the *ātman* has already been secured, will *jñānayoga* (the Yoga of Knowledge), i.e. inactivity, cause him to succeed; or, in other words, a man must perform acts until he has attained release. Now, when has a man attained Yoga? When the yogin is no longer able to interest himself in the objects of *prakṛti* (material nature) differing from the *ātman*, or in corresponding acts, because naturally he does not experience anything but the *ātman*; for then all desires have gone. When a man wishes to attain Yoga, then he can only do so by practicing *karmayoga*, for at that stage one is still unable *not* to experience the objects and therefore *karmayoga* is one's only resource, because *karmayoga* means practicing one's interest in objects. However, one should save oneself by disengaging one's mind from its interest in objects and not perish by neglecting to do so. – Rāmānuja.

4

यदा हि नेन्द्रियार्थेषु
yadā hi nendriyārtheṣu
when indeed not in the objects of the senses

न कर्मस्व् अनुसज्जते ।
na karmasv anusajjate
nor in actions he is attached

सर्वसंकल्पसंन्यासी
sarvasaṁkalpasaṁnyāsī
all purpose renouncing

योगारूढस् तदोच्यते ॥
yogārūḍhas tadocyate
Yoga-ascended then he is said to be.

When he is attached neither to the objects of the senses
Nor to actions,
And has renounced all purpose,
He is then said to be ascended to Yoga.*

yadā, when.
hi, indeed, truly.
na, not.
indriyārtheṣu (n. loc. pl.), in the objects of the senses.
na, not, nor.
karmasu (n. loc. pl.), in actions, in deeds.
anusajjate (3rd sg. pr. indic. mid. *anu* √*saj* √*sañj*), he is attached, he clings, he hangs onto.
sarvasaṁkalpa (m.), all purpose, all resolve, all determination.
saṁnyāsī (m. nom. sg.), renouncing, throwing down, casting aside.
(*sarvasaṁkalpasṁnyāsī,* m. nom. sg. TP cpd., renouncing all purpose, renouncing all determination.)
yoga (m.), Yoga.
ārūḍhas (m. nom. sg. p. pass. participle *ā* √*ruh*), ascended, climbed.
(*yogārūḍhas*, m. nom. sg. TP cpd., ascended to Yoga, mounted to Yoga.)
tadā, then.
ucyate (3rd. sg. pr. indic. passive √*vac*), it is said, he is said to be.

* See footnote previous stanza.

5

उद्धरेद् आत्मना ऽत्मानं
uddhared ātmanā 'tmānaṁ
one should uplift by the self the self;

नात्मानम् अवसादयेत् ।
nātmānam avasādayet
not the self one should degrade.

आत्मैव ह्यात्मनो बन्धुर्
ātmāiva hyātmano bandhur
the self indeed of the self a friend

आत्मैव रिपुर् आत्मनः ॥
ātmāiva ripur ātmanaḥ
the self alone enemy of the self.

One should uplift the self by the self;
One should not degrade the self;
Thus the self alone can be a friend to the self,
And the self alone can be an enemy of the self.*

uddharet (3rd sg. optative act. *ud* √*dhṛ*), one should uplift, he should rise up, one should lift up.
ātmanā (m. inst. sg.), by the self.
ātmānam (m. acc. sg.), the self.
na, not.
ātmānam (m. acc. sg.), the self.
avasādayet (3rd sg. causative act. optative *ava* √*sad*), one should degrade, one should cause to sink, one should render downhearted.
ātmā (m. nom. sg.), self.
eva, alone, indeed (often used as a rhythmic filler).
hi, indeed, truly, alone.
ātmanas (m. gen. sg.), of the self.
bandhus (m. nom. sg.), friend, companion, relative.
ātmā (m. nom. sg.), self.
eva, alone, indeed (often used as a rhythmic filler).
ripus (m. nom. sg.), enemy.
ātmanas (m. gen. sg.), of the self.

* In the case of one who is saving himself by disengaging his mind from its interest in the objects of sense, the mind (*manas*) will be his friend; in the case of one who wishes not to perish by neglecting to so disengage his mind, mind (*manas*) will be his enemy and bring about the opposite of beatitude – freely adapted from Rāmānuja, who thus equates *manas* (mind) with *ātman* (self) in interpreting this stanza.

6

बन्धुर् आत्मा ऽत्मनस् तस्य
bandhur ātmā 'tmanas tasya
a friend the self of the self of him

येनात्मैवात्मना जितः ।
yenātmāivātmanā jitaḥ
by whom the self by the self conquered

अनात्मनस् तु शत्रुत्वे
anātmanas tu śatrutve
he whose self is not, indeed, in enmity

वर्तेतात्मैव शत्रुवत् ॥
vartetātmāiva śatruvat
it would exist, the self, like an enemy

For him who has conquered his self by the self,
The self is a friend;
But for him whose self is not conquered,
The self remains hostile, like an enemy.*

bandhus (m. nom. sg.), friend, companion, relative.
ātmā (m. nom. sg.), self.
ātmanas (m. gen. sg.), of the self.
tasya (m. gen. sg.), of him, of this.
yena (m. inst. sg.), by whom.
ātmā (m. nom. sg.), self.
eva, indeed (used as a rhythmic filler).
ātmanā (m. inst. sg.), by the self.
jitas (m. nom. sg. p. pass. participle √*ji*), conquered, subdued, controlled.
anātmanas (m. gen. sg.), of the not-self, of the unconquered self, (as BV cpd.) for him whose self is not.
tu, indeed, but, however.
śatrutve (m. loc. sg.), in enmity, in rivalry, in hostility.
varteta (3rd sg. optative mid. √*vṛt*), it should exist, it might exist.
ātmā (m. nom. sg.), self.
eva, indeed (used as a rhythmic filler).
śatruvat (n. nom. sg.), like an enemy, in the manner of an enemy.

* See previous footnote.

7

जितात्मनः प्रशान्तस्य
jitātmanaḥ praśāntasya
of the conquered self, of the peaceful

परमात्मा समाहितः ।
paramātmā samāhitaḥ
the highest self (is) steadfast,

शीतोष्णसुखदुःखेषु
śītoṣṇasukhaduḥkheṣu
in cold, heat, pleasure, pain,

तथा मानापमानयोः ॥
tathā mānāpamānayoḥ
thus (also) in honor and dishonor.

The highest self* of him who has conquered himself,
Of the peaceful man, is steadfast
In cold, heat, pleasure and pain;
Thus also in honor and dishonor.

jita (p. pass. participle √*ji*), conquered, subdued.
ātmanas (m. gen. sg.), of the self.
(*jitāmanas,* m. gen. sg. BV cpd., of him who has conquered himself.)
praśāntasya (m. gen. sg. p. pass. participle *pra* √*śam*), of the peaceful, of him who is peaceful.
paramātmā (m. nom. sg.), highest self, Supreme Self.
samāhitas (m. nom. sg. p. pass. participle *sam ā* √*dhā*), steadfast, combined, united, composed, collected, devoted.
śīta (n.), cold.
uṣṇa (n.), heat.
sukha (n.), pleasure, happiness.
duḥkha (n.), pain, misery.
(*śītoṣṇasukhaduḥkheṣu,* n. loc. pl. DV cpd., in cold, heat, pleasure and pain.)
tathā, thus, in this way.
māna (m.), honor, pride, fame.
apamāna (m.), dishonor, ill fame.
(*mānāpamānayos,* m. loc. DV cpd. dual, in honor and dishonor.)

* Highest self, the self which has been exalted by Yoga practice.

8

ज्ञानविज्ञानतृप्तात्मा
jñānavijñānatṛptātmā
the knowledge-discrimination-satisfied self

कूटस्थो विजितेन्द्रियः ।
kūṭastho vijitendriyaḥ
unchanging, (with) conquered sense,

युक्त इत्युच्यते योगी
yukta ityucyate yogī
disciplined, thus he is said to be, the yogin

समलोष्टाश्मकाञ्चनः ॥
samaloṣṭāśmakāñcanaḥ
to whom a clod, a stone and gold are the same,

The yogin whose self is satisfied with knowledge and discrimination,*
Who is unchanging, with conquered senses,
To whom a clod, a stone and gold are the same,
Is said to be disciplined.

jñāna (n.), knowledge.
vijñāna (n.), discrimination, perception, understanding.
tṛpta (p. pass. participle √*tṛp*), satisfied, content.
ātmā (m. nom. sg.), self.
(*jñānavijñānatṛptātmā,* m. nom. sg. BV cpd., he whose self is satisfied with knowledge and discrimination.)
kūṭasthas (m. nom. sg.), unchanging, standing at the top, immovable.
vijita (p. pass. participle *vi* √*ji*), conquered, subdued.
indriyas (m. nom. sg.), sense, power.
(*vijita-indriyah,* m. n. sg. BV cpd., one whose senses are subdued.)
yuktas (m. nom. sg. p. pass. participle √*yuj*), disciplined, fixed in Yoga, steadfast.
iti, thus.
ucyate (3rd sg. pr. indic. passive √*vac*), he is called, he is said to be.
yogī (m. nom. sg.), yogin.
sama, the same, similar, equal.
loṣṭa (m.), clod, lump of clay.
aśma (m.), stone.
kāñcanas (m. nom. sg.), gold.
(*samaloṣṭāśmakāñcanas,* m. nom. sg. BV cpd., to whom a clod, a stone and gold are the same.)

* Discrimination, i.e. knowledge of the *ātman* as well as of the *ātman* as a different entity from *prakṛti* (material nature).

9

सुहृन्मित्रार्युदासीन-
suhṛnmitrāryudāsīna-
friend-companion-enemy sitting apart,

मध्यस्थद्वेष्यबन्धुषु ।
madhyasthadveṣyabandhuṣu
standing in the middle among enemies and kinsmen

साधुष्व् अपि च पापेषु
sādhuṣv api ca pāpeṣu
among the righteous and also among the evil

समबुद्धिर् विशिष्यते ॥
samabuddhir viśiṣyate
impartial minded, he is to be distinguished.

He who is indifferent toward friend, companion and enemy,
Who is neutral among enemies and kinsmen,
And who is of impartial insight among the righteous and also among the evil,
Is to be distinguished among men.*

suhṛd (m.), friend, companion.
mitra (m.), associate, companion.
ari (m.), enemy.
udāsīna (m. pr. participle *ud* √*ās*), sitting apart, free from affection or hatred, impartial, disinterested, dispassionate, in-different.
madhyastha (m.), standing in the middle, neutral.
dveṣya (m.), enemy, foe.
bandhu (m.), kinsman, friend. companion.
(*suhṛnmitrāryudāsīnamadhyasthadveṣyabandhuṣu,* m. loc. pl., impartial toward friend, companion and enemy, and neutral among enemies and kinsmen.)
sādhuṣu (m. loc. pl.), among the good, among the righteous.
api, also, even.
ca, and.
pāpeṣu (m. loc. pl.), among the sinful, among the evil ones.
samabuddhis (f. nom. sg.), impartial minded, (as BV cpd.) he who is of impartial insight.
viśiṣyate (3rd sg. pr. indic. mid. *vi śiṣ*), he is to be distinguished, he is preeminent.

* A consequence of contemplation of the *ātman* exclusively.

10

योगी युञ्जीत सततम्
yogī yuñjīta satatam
the yogin should concentrate constantly

आत्मानं रहसि स्थितः ।
ātmānaṁ rahasi sthitaḥ
on the self, in solitude remaining,

एकाकी यतचित्तात्मा
ekākī yatacittātmā
alone controlled thought and self

निराशीर् अपरिग्रहः ॥
nirāśīr aparigrahaḥ
having no desires, destitute of possessions.

The yogin should concentrate constantly
On the self, remaining in solitude,
Alone, with controlled thought and self,
Having no desires and destitute of possessions.

yogī (m. nom. sg.), yogin.
yuñjīta (3rd sg. optative mid. √*yuj*), he should concentrate, he should yoke himself, he should discipline himself.
satatam (adv.), constantly.
ātmānam (m. acc. sg.), the self, to the self, on the self.
rahasi (n. loc. sg.), in solitude, alone.
sthitas (m. nom. sg. p. pass. participle √*sthā*), remaining, situated.
ekākī (m. nom. sg.), alone, solitary.
yata (p. pass. participle √*yam*), controlled, subdued.
citta (n.), thought, mind.
ātmā (m. nom. sg.), self.
(*yata-citta-ātmā*, m. nom. sg. KD cpd., with controlled thought and self.)
nirāśīs (m. nom. sg.), without desires, without asking, without wish.
aparigrahas (m. nom. sg.), destitute, nonaccepting, without possessions or a wife.

11

शुचौ देशे प्रतिष्ठाप्य
śucāu deśe pratiṣṭhāpya
in a clean place establishing

स्थिरम् आसनम् आत्मनः ।
sthiram āsanam ātmanaḥ
a firm seat for himself

नात्युच्छ्रितं नातिनीचं
nātyucchritaṁ nātinīcaṁ
not too high, not too low,

चैलाजिनकुशोत्तरम् ॥
cāilājinakuśottaram
a cloth, an antelope skin and kuśa grass cover.

Establishing a firm seat for himself
In a clean place,
Not too high, not too low,
Covered with a cloth, an antelope skin and kuśa grass,*

śucāu (f. loc. sg.), in clean, in white, in undefiled, in radiant, in virtuous, in holy, in pure.
deśe (m. loc. sg.), in a place, in a region, in a spot.
pratiṣṭhāpya (causative gerund *prati* √*sthā*), establishing, causing to fix, locating.
sthiram (m. acc. sg.), firm, steady.
āsanam (n. acc. sg.), seat.
ātmanas (m. gen. sg.), of himself, for himself.
na, not.
atyucchritam (m. acc. sg. p. pass. participle *ati ud* √*śri*), raised too high, too much elevated.
na, not.
atinīcam (n. acc. sg. from *ati ni* √2 *añc*), too low, too short, too mean, too base.
cāila (m.), cloth.
ajina (n.), skin of an antelope.
kuśa (m.), kuśa grass, a kind of fragrant grass.
uttaram (n. acc. sg.), covering, ultimate layer, bottom.
(*cāilājinakuśottaram*, n. acc. sg. BV cpd., whose covering is cloth, antelope hide and kuśa grass.)

* N.B. The kuśa grass is on the bottom, the antelope skin on top of it, and the cloth topmost. This was the proper seat for the meditating yogin.

12

तत्रैकाग्रं मनः कृत्वा
tatrāikāgraṁ manaḥ kṛtvā
there, directed to a single object the mind having made

यतचित्तेन्द्रियक्रियः ।
yatacittendriyakriyaḥ
controlling thought and sense-activity,

उपविश्यासने युञ्ज्याद्
upaviśyāsane yuñjād
seating himself on the seat, he should practice

योगमात्मविशुद्धये ॥
yogamātmaviśuddhaye
yoga to self purification.

There, having directed his mind to a single object,*
He who controls thought and the activity of the senses,
Seating himself on the seat, should yoke himself
To Yoga for the purpose of self-purification.

tatra, there.
ekāgram (n. acc. sg.), directed to a single point, concentrated on a single object.
manas (n. acc. sg.), mind, thought.
kṛtvā (gerund √*kṛ*), making, having made, having performed.
yata (p. pass. participle √*yam*), controlled, restrained.
citta (n.), thought.
indriyakriyas (m. nom. sg.), sense activity, activity of the senses.
(*yatacittendriyakriyas*, m. nom. sg. BV cpd., he who controls the activity of thought and the senses.)
upaviśya (gerund, *upa* √*viś*), seating himself, sitting.
āsane (n. loc. sg.), on the seat.
yuñjāt (3rd sg. optative act. √*yuj*), he should practice, he should concentrate, he should yoke himself, he should fix himself.
yogam (m. acc. sg.), Yoga, to Yoga.
ātma (m.), self.
viśuddhaye (f. dat. sg.), to purification, toward purification, for the purpose of purification.
(*ātma-viśuddhaye*, f. dat. sg. TP cpd., for purfication of self.)

* Directing the mind (concentrating it) on a single point or object is one of the preliminary techniques of Yoga. Its purpose is control of the mind, which tends to wander. It is very difficult for the average person to keep the mind concentrated on a single object for any length of time.

13

समं कायशिरोग्रीवं
samaṁ kāyaśirogrīvaṁ
erect the body, head and neck

धारयन्न् अचलं स्थिरः ।
dhārayann acalaṁ sthiraḥ
holding, motionless, steady

संप्रेक्ष्य नासिकाग्रं स्वं
saṁprekṣya nāsikāgraṁ svaṁ
looking at the tip of the nose own

दिशश्चानवलोकयन् ॥
diśaścānavalokayan
and (any) direction not looking towards.

Holding the body, head and neck erect,
Motionless and steady,
Gazing at the tip of his own nose
And not looking in any direction,*

samam (m. acc. sg.), balanced, equal, erect.
kāya (m.), body.
śiras (n.), head.
grīvam (m. acc. sg.), neck.
(*kāyaśirogrīvam,* m. acc. sg., body, head and neck.)
dhārayan (m. nom. sg. pr. causative participle √*dhṛ*), holding, placing.
acalam (m. acc. sg.), motionless, unmoving.
sthiras (m. nom. sg.), steady, immovable.
saṁprekṣya (gerund *sam pra* √*īkṣ*), looking at, concentrating the eyes on.
nāsikā (f.), nose, nostril.
agram (n. acc. sg.), foremost point, tip.
svam (m. acc. sg.), own, of oneself.
diśas (f. acc. pl.), regions, quarters, directions.
ca, and.
anavalokayan (m. nom. sg. pr. indic. causative act. participle *an ava* √*lok*), not looking toward, not looking.

* This and the following stanza concern yoga techniques aimed at controlling the mind. The sitting position is, of course, the lotus position with legs intertwined and feet emerging behind the opposite knee.

14

प्रशान्तात्मा विगतभीर्
praśāntātmā vigatabhīr
(with) quieted self, banishing fear,

ब्रह्मचारिव्रते स्थितः ।
brahmacārivrate sthitaḥ
in brahmacārin vow (of continence) established,

मनः संयम्य मच्चित्तो
manaḥ saṁyamya maccitto
the mind controlling, thoughts fixed on me,

युक्त आसीत मत्परः ॥
yukta āsīta matparaḥ
concentrated he should sit, devoted to me.

With quieted self, banishing fear,
Established in the brahmacārin vow of continence,
Controlling the mind, with thoughts fixed on Me,
He should sit, concentrated, devoted to Me.

praśānta (m. p. pass. participle *pra* √*śam*), quieted, made peaceful.
ātmā (m. nom. sg.), self.
vigata (p. pass. participle *vi* √*gam*), gone away, disappeared, banished, banishing.
bhīs (f. nom. sg.), fear, apprehension, fright, dread.
(*vigata-bhīs*, f. nom. sg. KD cpd., banishing fear.)
brahmacārivrate (n. loc. sg.), in brahmacārin vow, in pledge of chastity, in vow of continence.
sthitas (m. nom. sg.), established, standing.
manas (n. acc. sg.), mind, thought.
saṁyamya (gerund *sam* √*yam*), controlling, subduing.
maccittas (m. nom. sg.), thinking of me, thoughts fixed on me.
yuktas (m. nom. sg. p. pass. participle √*yuj*), concentrated, disciplined, steadfast, yoked.
āsīta (3rd sg. optative mod. √*ās*), he should sit.
matparas (m. nom. sg.), devoted to me, holding me as highest object.

15

युञ्जन्न् एवं सदा ऽत्मानं
yuñjann evaṁ sadā 'tmānaṁ
disciplining thus always himself,

योगी नियतमानसः ।
yogī niyatamānasaḥ
the yogin of subdued mind

शान्तिं निर्वाणपरमां
śāntiṁ nirvāṇaparamāṁ
to peace, to nirvāṇa supreme

मत्संस्थाम् अधिगच्छति ॥
matsaṁsthām adhigacchati
to union with me, he goes.

yuñjan (m. nom. sg. pr. act. participle √*yuj*), disciplining, concentrating.
evam, thus.
sadā (adv.), always, perpetually.
ātmānam (m. acc. sg.), himself.
yogī (m. nom. sg.), yogin.
niyatamānasas (m. gen. sg.), of subdued mind, (as BV cpd.) whose mind is subdued.
śāntim (f. acc. sg.), peace, tranquility.
nirvāṇa, nirvāṇa, extinction of the self in Brahman.
paramām (f. acc. sg.), highest, supreme.
(*nirvāna-paramām*, f. acc. sg. KD cpd., nirvāna supreme.)
matsaṁsthām (f. acc. sg.), "me together standing," union with me.
adhigacchati (3rd sg. pr. indic. act. *adhi* √*gam*), he attains, he goes.

Thus, continually disciplining himself,
The yogin whose mind is subdued
Goes to nirvāṇa, to supreme peace,
To union with Me.

16

नात्यश्नतस् तु योगो ऽस्ति
nātyaśnatas tu yogo 'sti
not of eating too much, indeed, Yoga it is

न चैकान्तम् अनश्नतः ।
na cāikāntam anaśnataḥ
and not absolutely of not eating

न चातिस्वप्नशीलस्य
na cātisvapnaśīlasya
and not of the too-much-sleeping habit

जाग्रतो नैव चार्जुन ॥
jāgrato nāiva cārjuna
and of keeping awake not either, Arjuna.

Yoga is not eating too much,
Nor is it absolutely not eating.
And not the habit of sleeping too much,
And not keeping awake either,* Arjuna.

na, not.
atyaśnatas (m. gen. sg. pr. act. participle *ati* √*aś*), of eating too much.
tu, indeed, but.
yogas (m. nom. sg.), Yoga.
asti (3rd sg. pr. indic. √*as*), it is, there is.
na, not.
ca, and.
ekāntam (adv.), absolutely, of necessity, solely, only, exclusively.
anaśnatas (m. gen. sg. pr. participle *an* √*aś*), of one who does not eat, of one who refrains from food.
na, not.
ca, and.
atisvapna (m.), too much sleeping, oversleeping.
śīlasya (m. gen. sg.), of habit, of custom, of usage.
(*atisvapnaśīlasya,* m. gen. sg. BV cpd., of him who has the habit of sleeping too much.)
jāgratas (m. gen. sg. pr. participle √*jagṛ*), of keeping awake, of being watchful, of awakening.
na, not.
eva, indeed (used as a rhythmic filler).
ca, and.
arjuna (m. voc. sg.), Arjuna.

* This statement, not dissimilar to the "middle way" of the Buddha, is among several references in the Bhagavad Gītā to extreme practices on the part of some ascetics. The following stanza continues the idea.

17

युक्ताहारविहारस्य
yuktāhāravihārasya
of the moderate in food and diversion,

युक्तचेष्टस्य कर्मसु ।
yuktaceṣṭasya karmasu
of the disciplined in performance of actions,

युक्तस्वप्नावबोधस्य
yuktasvapnāvabodhasya
of the moderate in sleep and waking

योगो भवति दुःखहा ॥
yogo bhavati duḥkhahā
yoga it is sorrow destroying.

For him who is moderate in food and diversion,
Whose actions are disciplined,
Who is moderate in sleep and waking,
Yoga destroys all sorrow.

yukta (p. pass. participle √*yuj*), disciplined, moderate, yoked.
āhāra (m.), food.
vihārasya (m. gen. sg.), of sport, of play, of diversion.
(*yukta-āhāra-vihārasya*, m. g. sg. BV cpd., one moderate in food and diversion.)
yukta (p. pass. participle √*yuj*), disciplined, moderate.
ceṣṭasya (m. gen. sg.), of actions.
(*yuktaceṣṭasya*, m. gen. sg. BV cpd., whose actions are disciplined.)
karmasu (n. loc. pl.), in actions.
yukta (p. pass. participle √*yuj*), disciplined, moderate.
svapna (m.), sleep.
avabodhasya (m. gen. sg.), of waking, of being awake.
(*yuktasvapnāvabodhasya*, m. gen. sg. BV cpd., who is moderate in sleeping and staying awake.)
yogas (m. nom. sg.), Yoga.
bhavati (3rd sg. pr. indic. act. √*bhū*), it is, it becomes.
duḥkhahā (m. nom. sg. from *duḥkha* √*han*), sorrow destroying.

18

यदा विनियतं चित्तम्
yadā viniyataṁ cittam
when (with) controlled thought

आत्मन्य् एवावतिष्ठते ।
ātmany evāvatiṣṭhate
in the self alone he is absorbed,

निःस्पृहः सर्वकामेभ्यो
niḥspṛhaḥ sarvakāmebhyo
free from longing, from all desires,

युक्त इत्य् उच्यते तदा ॥
yukta ity ucyate tadā
"disciplined" thus, he is said to be, then.

yadā, when.
viniyatam (n. nom. sg. p. pass. participle *vi ni* √*yam*), controlled, subdued.
cittam (n. nom. sg.), thought.
ātmani (m. loc. sg.), in the self.
eva, indeed (used as a rhythmic filler).
avatiṣṭhate (3rd sg. pr. indic. mid. *ava* √*sthā*), he is absorbed, he abides in, he remains.
niḥspṛhas (m. nom. sg.), free from desire, free from longing.
sarva, all.
kāmebhyas (m. abl. sg.), from desires, from lust.
yuktas (m. nom. sg.), disciplined, steadfast.
iti, thus.
ucyate (3rd sg. pr. indic. passive √*vac*), he is said to be, he is called.
tadā, then.

When he is absorbed in the self alone,
With controlled thought,
Free from longing, from all desires,
Then he is said to be disciplined.

19

यथा दीपो निवातस्थो
yathā dīpo nivātastho
as a lamp in a windless place

नेङ्गते सोपमा स्मृता ।
neṅgate sopamā smṛtā
not it flickers, the simile is recorded

योगिनो यतचित्तस्य
yogino yatacittasya
of the yogin, of controlled thought,

युञ्जतो योगम् आत्मनः ॥
yuñjato yogam ātmanaḥ
of performing the Yoga of the self.

As a lamp in a windless place
Does not flicker, so the simile is recorded
Of the yogin of controlled thought,
Performing the Yoga of the self.

yathā, as, in which way.
dīpas (m. nom. sg.), lamp, lantern.
nivāta (m.), without wind, windless.
-sthas (m. nom. sg. suffix), situated, being situated in, standing in.
na, not.
iṅgate (3rd sg. pr. indic. md. √*iṅg*), it flickers, it stirs.
sas (m. nom. sg.), simile.
smṛtā (f. nom. sg. p. pass. participle √*smṛ*), recorded, remembered, thought.
yoginas (m. gen. sg.), of the yogin.
yatacittasya (m. gen. sg. BV cpd.), of him of controlled thought, of one of subdued thought.
yuñjatas (m. gen. sg. pr. act. participle √*yuj*), of concentrated, of steadfast, of performing.
yogam (m. acc. sg.), Yoga.
ātmanas (m. gen. sg.), of the shelf.

20

यत्रोपरमते चित्तं
yatroparamate cittaṁ
where it is at rest, thought

निरुद्धं योगसेवया ।
niruddhaṁ yogasevayā
restrained by Yoga practice

यत्र चैवात्मना ऽत्मानं
yatra cāivātmanā 'tmānaṁ
and where by the self the self

पश्यन्न् आत्मनि तुष्यति ॥
paśyann ātmani tuṣyati
beholding in the self he is content,

Where thought comes to rest,
Restrained by the practice of Yoga,
And where beholding the self, by the self,
He is content in the self,

yatra, where.
uparamate (3rd sg. pr. indic. mid. *upa* √*ram*), it is at rest, it pauses, it stops, it is inactive, it ceases.
cittam (n. nom. sg.), thought, reflection.
niruddham (n. nom. sg. p. pass. participle *ni* √*rudh*), restrained, held back.
yoga (m.), Yoga.
sevayā (f. inst. sg.), by practice, by service.
(*yoga-sevayā*, f. inst. sg., TP cpd., by practice of yoga.)
yatra, where.
ca, and.
eva, indeed (used as a rhythmic filler).
ātmanā (m. inst. sg.), by the self.
ātmānam (m. acc. sg.), the self.
paśyan (m. nom. sg. pr. participle act. √*paś*), beholding, seeing.
ātmani (m. loc. sg.), in the self.
tuṣyati (3rd sg. pr. indic. act. √*tuṣ*), he is content, he is satisfied.

21

सुखम् आत्यन्तिकं यत् तद्
sukham ātyantikaṁ yat tad
happiness infinite which that

बुद्धिग्राह्यम् अतीन्द्रियम् ।
buddhigrāhyam atīndriyam
(by) intelligence grasped, transcending the senses

वेत्ति यत्र न चैवायं
vetti yatra na cāivāyaṁ
he knows where, and not this (one),

स्थितश्चलति तत्त्वतः ॥
sthitaścalati tattvataḥ
established, he deviates from the truth;

He knows the location of that infinite happiness
Which is grasped by the intelligence and transcends the senses,
And, established there,
Does not deviate from the truth;

sukham (n. acc. sg.), happiness, joy, pleasure.
ātyantikam (n. acc. sg.), endless, infinite, perpetual.
yad (n. acc. sg.), which.
tad (n. acc. sg.), this, that.
buddhigrāhyam (n. acc. sg.), grasped by the intelligence.
atīndriyam (n. acc. sg.), transcending the senses, beyond the realm of the senses.
vetti (3rd sg. pr. indic. act. √*vid*), he knows.
yatra, where.
na, not.
ca, and.
eva, indeed (used as a rhythmic filler).
ayam (m. nom. sg.), this, he, this one.
sthitas (m. nom. sg.), established, standing, abiding.
calati (3rd sg. pr. indic. act. √*cal*), he moves, he deviates.
tattvatas (n. abl. sg.), from "thatness," from the truth.

22

यं लब्ध्वा चापरं लाभं
yaṁ labdhvā cāparaṁ lābhaṁ
and which having attained, other gain

मन्यते नाधिकं ततः ।
manyate nādhikaṁ tataḥ
he thinks not greater from there,

यस्मिन् स्थितो न दुःखेन
yasmin sthito na duḥkhena
in which established not by sorrow,

गुरुणापि विचाल्यते ॥
guruṇāpi vicālyate
profound even, he is shaken;

And which, having attained,
No greater gain can he imagine;
In which established,
He is not moved even by profound sorrow;

yam (m. acc. sg.), which, who.
labdhvā (gerund √*abh*), attaining, having attained, obtaining, having obtained.
ca, and.
aparam (m. acc. sg.), other.
lābham (m. acc. sg.), gain, attainment, obtainment.
manyate (3rd sg. pr. indic. mid. √*man*), he thinks, he imagines.
na, not.
adhikam (m. acc. sg.), greater, additional, subsequent, superior.
tatas (m. abl. sg.), from there, from this point.
yasmin (m. loc. sg.), in which, in whom.
sthitas (m. nom. sg.), established, situated, abiding in.
na, not.
duḥkhena (n. inst. sg.), by sorrow, by misfortune.
guruṇā (n. inst. sg.), by heavy, by profound.
api, even, also.
vicālyate (3rd sg. pr. indic. causative passive *vi* √*cal*), he is shaken, he is moved.

23

तं विद्याद् दुःखसंयोग-
taṁ vidyād duḥkhasaṁyoga-
this, let it be known, union-with-pain-

वियोगं योगसंज्ञितम् ।
viyogaṁ yogasaṁjñitam
dissolution, Yoga called

स निश्चयेन योक्तव्यो
sa niścayena yoktavyo
this, with determination to be practiced,

योगो ऽनिर्विण्णचेतसा ॥
yogo 'nirviṇṇacetasā
Yoga with undismayed mind.

This, the dissolution of union with pain,
Let it be known, is called Yoga;
This Yoga to be practiced with determination
And with undismayed mind.

tam (m. acc. sg.), it, him, this.
vidyāt (3rd sg. active optative √*vid*), may it be known, let it be known.
duḥkha (n. nom. acc. sg.), pain.
saṁyoga (m.), union, coming together.
viyogam (m. acc. sg.), dissolution, sundering, moving apart.
(*duḥkha-samyoga-viyogam*, m. acc. sg. TP cpd., dissolution of union with pain.)
yoga (m.), Yoga.
saṁjñitam (m. acc. sg. p. pass. participle from noun *saṁjñā*), known as, called, recognized as.
(*yoga-saṁjñitam*, m. acc. sg. TP cpd., known as yoga.)
sas (m. nom. sg.), this, he.
niścayena (m. inst. sg. from *niś* √*ci*), by determination, with determination, with absence of doubt.
yoktavyas (m. nom. sg. gerundive √*yuj*), to be practiced, to be concentrated on.
yogas (m. nom. sg.), Yoga.
anirviṇṇa (p. pass. participle *a nir* √*vid*), not downcast, undismayed.
cetasā (n. inst. sg.), with mind, with thought.
(*anirviṇṇacetasā*, m. inst. sg. KD cpd., with undismayed mind, with thoughts which are not downcast.)

24

संकल्पप्रभवान् कामांस्
saṁkalpaprabhavān kāmāṅs
whose origins lie in one's intention, desires

त्यक्त्वा सर्वान् अशेषतः ।
tyaktvā sarvān aśeṣataḥ
having abandoned all without remainder,

मनसैवेन्द्रियग्रामं
manasāivendriyagrāmaṁ
by the mind the multitude of senses,

विनियम्य समन्ततः ॥
viniyamya samantataḥ
restraining completely,

Abandoning those desires whose origins lie in one's intention,
All of them, without exception,
And completely restraining
The multitude of senses with the mind,

saṁkalpa (m), purpose, aim, intention.
prabhavān (m. acc. pl.), produced, born, come into being, origins.
(*saṁkalpaprabhavān,* m. acc. pl. BV cpd., whose origins lie in one's intention.)
kāmān (m. acc. pl.), desires, cravings, lusts.
tyaktvā (gerund √*tyaj*), abandoning, having abandoned, having forsaken, having renounced.
sarvān (m. acc. pl.), all.
aśeṣatas (adv.), without remainder, entirely, wholly.
manasā (n. inst. sg.), by mind, by thought.
eva, indeed (used as a rhythmic filler).
indriyagrāmam (m. acc. sg.), the multitude of senses, the aggregate of senses.
viniyamya (gerund *vi ni* √*yam*), restraining, subduing, controlling.
samantatas (adv.), wholly, completely.

25

शनैः शनैर् उपरमेद्
śanāiḥ śanāir uparamed
by little by little he should cease from action

बुद्ध्या धृतिगृहीतया ।
buddhyā dhṛtigṛhītayā
with the intelligence firmly grasped.

आत्मसंस्थं मनः कृत्वा
ātmasaṁsthaṁ manaḥ kṛtvā
the self fixed, the mind having made,

न किंचिद् अपि चिन्तयेत् ॥
na kiṁcid api cintayet
not anything even he should think of.

Little by little, he should come to rest,
With the intelligence firmly grasped.
His mind having been fixed in the self,
He should not think of anything.

śanāiḥ śanāis (adv.), little by little, gradually.
uparamet (3rd sg. optative act. *upa* √*ram*), he should cease from action, he should renounce action, he should be quiet.
budhyā (f. inst. sg.), by the intelligence, with the intelligence.
dhṛti (f.), firmness, firm, firmly.
gṛhītayā (f. inst. sg. p. pass. participle √*grah*), grasped, controlled, gripped.
(*dhṛti-gṛhītayā*, f. instr. sg. KD cpd., firmly grasped.)
ātma- (m.), self, own.
saṁstham (m. acc. sg.), "together standing," fixed, situated together with.
manas (n. acc. sg.), mind, thought.
kṛtvā (gerund √*kṛ*), making, having made.
na, not.
kiṁcid, anything, anything whatever.
api, even, also.
cintayet (3rd sg. causative optative act. √*cint*), he should think of, he should reflect on, he should consider.

26

यतो यतो निश्चरति
yato yato niścarati
wheresoever it wanders away,

मनश्चञ्चलम् अस्थिरम् ।
manaścañcalam asthiram
the mind, moving to and fro, unsteady,

ततस्ततो नियम्यैतद्
tatastato niyamyāitad
from thence holding back this (i.e. the mind)

आत्मन्य् एव वशं नयेत् ॥
ātmany eva vaśaṁ nayet
in the self to control he should lead.

Whenever the unsteady mind,
Moving to and fro, wanders away,
From there he should hold it back
To control in the self.

yatas yatas, whensoever, whencesoever, wheresoever.
niścarati (3rd sg. pr. indic. act. *niś* √*car*), it moves away, it wanders away.
manas (n. nom. sg.), mind, thought.
cañcalam (n. nom. sg. intensive verbal noun from √*cal*), moving to and fro, dancing here and there, wandering.
asthiram (n. nom. sg.), unsteady, unfixed.
tatas tatas, from thence, from there.
niyamya (gerund *ni* √*yam*), holding back, subduing, controlling.
etad (n. acc. sg.), this.
ātmani (m. loc. sg.), in the self.
eva, indeed (used as a rhythmic filler).
vaśam (m. acc. sg.), control, dominance, to the will, to the control.
nayet (3rd sg. optative act. √*nī*), he should lead, he should direct.

27

प्रशान्तमनसं ह्येनं
praśāntamanasaṁ hyenaṁ
composed in mind indeed, him

योगिनं सुखम् उत्तमम् ।
yoginaṁ sukham uttamam
the yogin; happiness supreme

उपैति शान्तरजसं
upāiti śāntarajasaṁ
he approaches, pacified passion

ब्रह्मभूतम् अकल्मषम् ॥
brahmabhūtam akalmaṣam
one with Brahman become, without evil.

The yogin whose mind is composed,
Whose passions are calmed,
Who is free of evil and has become one with Brahman,
Approaches the highest happiness.

praśānta (n. p. pass. participle *pra* √*śam*), composed, peaceful.
manasam (m. acc. sg.), mind.
(*praśāntamanasam,* m. acc. sg. BV cpd., whose mind is tranquil.)
hi, indeed, truly.
enam (m. acc. sg.), him, this.
yoginam (m. acc. sg.), yogin.
sukham (n. nom. sg.), happiness, joy, bliss.
uttamam (n. nom. sg.), highest, supreme.
upāiti (3rd sg. pr. indic. act. *upa* √*i*), he approaches, he attains, he goes to.
śānta (m.), calmed, pacified, appeased.
rajasam (m. acc. sg.), passion, emotion.
(*śāntarajasam* (m. acc. sg. BV cpd., whose passions are calmed.)
brahmabhūtam (m. acc. sg.), one with Brahman, united with Brahman, become one with Brahman.
akalmaṣam (m. acc. sg.), without wrong, free of evil.

28

युञ्जन् एवं सदा ऽत्मानं
yuñjann evaṁ sadā 'tmānaṁ
practicing Yoga thus constantly himself

योगी विगतकल्मषः ।
yogī vigatakalmaṣaḥ
the yogin, freed from evil,

सुखेन ब्रह्मसंस्पर्शम्
sukhena brahmasaṁsparśam
easily Brahman contact

अत्यन्तं सुखम् अश्नुते ॥
atyantaṁ sukham aśnute
beyond end happiness he attains.

yuñjan (m. nom. sg. pr. participle act. √*yuj*), practicing Yoga, yoking, performing Yoga.
evam, thus.
sadā, always, constantly, perpetually.
ātmānam (m. acc. sg.), himself.
yogī (m. nom. sg.), yogin.
vigatakalmaṣas (m. nom. sg.), "gone away evil," freed from sin, freed from evil, vanished evil, (as BV cpd.) whose evil has vanished.
sukhena (n. inst. sg.), by happiness, easily, readily.
brahmasaṁsparśam (n. acc. sg.), contact with Brahman, touching Brahman, encountering Brahman.
atyantam (n. acc. sg.), beyond end, endless, boundless.
sukham (n. acc. sg.), happiness, joy, bliss.
aśnute (3rd sg. pr. indic. mid. √*aś*), he attains, he reaches.

**Thus constantly disciplining himself,
The yogin, freed from evil,
Easily encountering Brahman,
Attains happiness beyond end.**

29

सर्वभूतस्थम् आत्मानं
sarvabhūtastham ātmānaṁ
present in all beings, the self,

सर्वभूतानि चात्मनि ।
sarvabhūtāni cātmani
and a'l beings in the self,

ईक्षते योगयुक्तात्मा
īkṣate yogayuktātmā
he sees, the yoga-disciplined self

सर्वत्र समदर्शनः ॥
sarvatra samadarśanaḥ
at all times seeing the same.*

sarvabhūtastham (n. acc. sg.), existing in all beings, present in all beings.
ātmānam (m. acc. sg.), self.
sarvabhūtāni (n. acc. pl.), all beings, all creatures.
ca, and.
ātmani (m. loc. sg.), in the self.
īkṣate (3rd sg. pr. indic. mid. √*īkṣ*), he sees, he observes.
yogayukta (m.), disciplined in Yoga, steadfast in Yoga, yoked to Yoga.
ātmā (m. nom. sg.), self.
(*yogayuktātmā*, m. nom. sg. BV cpd., whose self is disciplined by Yoga.)
sarvatra, at all times, everywhere, in all cases.
samadarśanas (m. nom. sg.), seeing the same,* seeing equally.

With the self present in all beings,
And all beings present in the self,
The self of him who is disciplined by Yoga
Sees the same* (self) at all times.

* *Samadarśana* has a special meaning which the words "seeing the same" scarcely convey. The *ātmans*, or selves, of all creatures are conceived to be the same once they have been separated from the material nature with which they are temporarily conjoined in life. "A person who has brought his *ātman* into Yoga, will see similarity in all *ātmans* when separated from *prakṛti* (material nature); he will see that all beings are in his own *ātman*; in other words he will see that his own *ātman* has the same form as the *ātmans* of all other beings and contrariwise, so that he has seen all that is *ātman* when he has seen one *ātman*." – Rāmānuja.

30

यो मां पश्यति सर्वत्र
yo māṁ paśyati sarvatra
who me he sees everywhere

सर्वं च मयि पश्यति
sarvaṁ ca mayi paśyati
and all in me he sees,

तस्याहं न प्रणश्यामि
tasyāhaṁ na praṇaśyāmi
of him I not I am lost

स च मे न प्रणश्यति ॥
sa ca me na praṇaśyati
and he of me not he is lost.

yas (m. nom. sg.), who.
mām (m. acc. sg.), me.
paśyati (3rd sg. pr. indic. act. √*paś*), he sees, he observes, he perceives.
sarvatra, everywhere, at all times, in everything.
sarvam (m. acc. sg.), all.
ca, and.
mayi (m. loc. sg.), in me.
paśyati (3rd sg. pr. indic. act. √*paś*), he sees.
tasya (m. gen. sg.), of him, to him.
aham (nom. sg.), I.
na, not.
praṇaśyāmi (1st sg. pr. indic. act. *pra* √*naś*), I am lost.
sas (m. nom. sg.), he.
ca, and.
me (gen. sg.), of me, to me.
na, not.
praṇaśyati (3rd sg. pr. indic. act. *pra* √*naś*), he is lost, he is destroyed.

He who sees Me everywhere,
And sees all things in Me;*
I am not lost to him,
And he is not lost to Me.

* Krishna (the Supreme Spirit) is here equating himself with the *ātman.*

31

सर्वभूतस्थितं यो मां
sarvabhūtasthitaṁ yo māṁ
(as) all-beings-abiding who me

भजत्य् एकत्वम् आस्थितः ।
bhajaty ekatvam āsthitaḥ
he honors, oneness established in,

सर्वथा वर्तमानो ऽपि
sarvathā vartamāno 'pi
in whatever way (otherwise) acting even

स योगी मयि वर्तते ॥
sa yogī mayi vartate
he, the yogin, in me he dwells.

sarvabhūtasthitam (m. acc. sg. TP cpd.), abiding in all beings, situated in all beings.
yas (m. nom. sg.), who.
mām (acc. sg.), me.
bhajati (3rd sg. pr. indic. act. √*bhaj*), he honors, he worships, he resorts to.
ekatvam (n. nom. sg.), oneness.
āsthitas (n. nom. sg. p. pass. participle *ā* √*sthā*), established in, abiding in, resorting to, having regard for, practiced in.
sarvathā, in whatever way.
vartamānas (m. nom. sg. pr. middle participle √*vṛt*), turning, moving, existing, acting.
api, even, also.
sas (m. nom. sg.), he, this.
yogī (m. nom. sg.), yogin.
mayi (loc. sg.), in me.
vartate (3rd sg. pr. indic. mid. √*vṛt*), he lives, he dwells, he abides, he turns.

The yogin who, established in oneness,*
Honors Me as abiding in all beings,
In whatever way he otherwise acts,
Dwells in Me.

* I.e. who recognizes that all *ātmans* are one, and all pervaded by the Supreme Spirit.

32

आत्मौपम्येन सर्वत्र
ātmāupamyena sarvatra
himself by comparison in all cases

समं पश्यति यो ऽर्जुन ।
samaṁ paśyati yo 'rjuna
the same he sees, who, Arjuna,

सुखं वा यदि वा दुःखं
*sukhaṁ vā yadi vā duḥkhaṁ**
pleasure whether or pain,

स योगी परमो मतः ॥
sa yogī paramo mataḥ
he a yogin supreme thought to be.

ātmā (m.), self, himself, oneself.
āupamyena (n. inst. sg.), by comparison, by resemblance, by analogy.
sarvatra (adv.), in all cases, everywhere.
samam (m. acc. sg.), the same, similarly.
paśyati (3rd sg. pr. indic. act. √*paś*), he sees, he considers.
yas (m. nom. sg.), who.
arjuna (m. voc. sg.), Arjuna.
*sukham** (n. acc. sg.), pleasure, happiness.
vā yadi vā, whether, or if.
*duḥkham** (n. acc. sg.), pain, misery.
sas (m. nom. sg.), he, this.
yogī (m. nom. sg.), yogin.
paramas (m. nom. sg.), highest, supreme.
matas (m. nom. sg. p. pass. participle √*man*), thought, thought to be.

He who sees by comparison with himself,
The same in all cases, Arjuna,
Whether as to pleasure or as to pain,†
Is thought to be a supreme yogin.

* It is perhaps amusing to note the etymology of the words "*sukha*" (pleasure, comfort, bliss) and "*duḥkha*" (misery, unhappiness, pain). The ancient Aryans who brought the Sanskrit language to India were a nomadic, horse- and cattle-breeding people who travelled in horse- or ox-drawn vehicles. "*Su*" and "*dus*" are prefixes indicating good or bad. The word "*kha,*" in later Sanskrit meaning "sky," "ether," or "space," was originally the word for "hole," particularly an axle hole of one of the Aryan's vehicles. Thus "*sukha*" (a BV cpd.) meant, originally, "having a good axle hole," while "*duḥkha*" meant "having a poor axle hole," leading to discomfort.

† I.e. that pleasure and pain in others is the same as pleasure and pain in himself, since the selves of all beings are equal to his own self, or identical with it.

अर्जुन उवाच ।
arjuna uvāca
Arjuna spoke:

arjunas (m. nom. sg.), Arjuna.
uvāca (3rd sg. perfect act. √*vac*), he said, he spoke.

33

यो ऽयं योगस् त्वया प्रोक्तः
yo 'yaṁ yogas tvayā proktaḥ
which this yoga by thee declared

साम्येन मधुसूदन ।
sāmyena madhusūdana
with evenness of mind, Slayer of Madhu,

एतस्याहं न पश्यामि
etasyāhaṁ na paśyāmi
of this I, not I perceive,

चञ्चलत्वात् स्थितिं स्थिराम् ।।
cañcalatvāt sthitiṁ sthirām
because of instability the foundation permanent.

Arjuna spoke:

This Yoga which is declared by Thee
As evenness of mind, Slayer of Madhu,
Of this, I do not perceive
The permanent foundation, because of (the mind's) instability.

yas (m. nom. sg.), which, who.
ayam (m. nom. sg.), this.
yogas (m. nom. sg.), Yoga.
tvayā (inst. sg.), by thee.
proktas (m. nom. sg. p. pass. participle *pra* √*vac*), declared, propounded, explained.
sāmyena (n. inst. sg.), with eveness of mind, with equilibrium, with impartiality.
madhusūdana, (m. voc. sg.), Slayer of Madhu, epithet of Krishna, referring to an *asura,* or demon, killed by Vishnu (Krishna), not to be confused with Madhu, the *Yādava*, who was Krishna's ancestor.
etasya (m. gen. sg.), of this.
aham (nom. sg.), I.
na, not.
paśyāmi (1st sg. pr. indic. act. √*paś*), I see, I perceive.
cañcalatvāt (m. abl. sg.), from instability, from unsteadiness, from capriciousness, because of instability.
sthitim (f. acc. sg.), foundation, standing, maintenance, permanence, continued existence.
sthirām (f. acc. sg.), permanent, immovable, fixed, steady, changeless.

34

चञ्चलं हि मनः कृष्ण
cañcalaṁ hi manaḥ kṛṣṇa
unstable indeed the mind, Krishna,

प्रमाथि बलवद् दृढम् ।
pramāthi balavad dṛḍham
troubling, powerful, intense,

तस्याहं निग्रहं मन्ये
tasyāhaṁ nigrahaṁ manye
of it I restraining, I think,

वायोर् इव सुदुष्करम् ॥
vāyor iva suduṣkaram
of-the-wind-like difficult to achieve.

The mind, indeed, is unstable, Krishna,
Troubling, powerful and intense;
The restraining of it, I think
Is, like the restraining of the wind, difficult to achieve.

cañcalam (n. nom. sg.), unstable, unsteady, wandering.
hi, indeed, truly.
manas (n. nom. acc. sg.), mind.
kṛṣṇa (m. voc. sg.), Krishna.
pramāthi (n. nom. sg.), troubling, harassing, destroying.
balavat (n. nom. sg.), powerful, strong.
dṛḍham (n. nom. sg.), intense, hard, fixed, massive, unyielding.
tasya (n. gen. sg.), of it, of this.
aham (nom. sg.), I.
nigraham (m. acc. sg. noun from *ni* √*grah*), keeping back, restraining, suppression, subjugation.
manye (1st sg. pr. indic. mid. √*man*), I think, I believe.
vāyos (m. gen. sg.), of the wind.
iva, like.
suduṣkaram (n. acc. sg.), difficult to do, hard to achieve, hard to bring about.

श्रीभगवान् उवाच ।
śrībhagavān uvāca
the Blessed Lord spoke:

śrībhagavān (m. nom. sg.), the Blessed Lord, the Blessed One.
uvāca (3rd sg. perfect act. √*vac*), he said, he spoke.

35

असंशयं महाबाहो
asaṁśayaṁ mahābāho
without doubt, O Mighty Armed One,

मनो दुर्निग्रहं चलम् ।
mano durnigrahaṁ calam
the mind difficult to restrain, unsteady;

अभ्यासेन तु कौन्तेय
abhyāsena tu kāunteya
by practice, but, Son of Kuntī,

वैराग्येण च गृह्यते ॥
vāirāgyeṇa ca gṛhyate
and by indifference it is restrained.

asaṁśayam (adv.), without doubt, doubtless.
mahābāho (m. voc. sg.), O Mighty Armed One, epithet of Arjuna and other warriors.
manas (n. nom. sg.), mind.
durnigraham (n. nom. sg. from *dur ni* √*grah*), difficult to restrain, hard to control, hard to subdue.
calam (n. nom. sg.), moving, unsteady, unstable, restless.
abhyāsena (m. inst. sg.), by practice, by performance.
tu, but.
kāunteya (m. voc. sg.), Son of Kuntī, epithet of Arjuna.
vāirāgyeṇa (n. inst. sg.), by indifference, by disgust, by aversion to worldly objects.
ca, and.
gṛhyate (3rd sg. pr. indic. passive √*grah*), it is restrained, it is gripped, it is subdued, it is controlled.

The Blessed Lord spoke:
Without doubt, O Mighty Armed One (Arjuna),
The mind is unsteady and difficult to restrain;
But by practice, Son of Kuntī,
And by indifference to worldly objects, it is restrained.

36

असंयतात्मना योगो
asaṁyatātmanā yogo
by him whose self is uncontrolled, Yoga

दुष्प्राप इति मे मतिः ।
duṣprāpa iti me matiḥ
difficult to attain, thus of me the thought;

वश्यात्मना तु यतता
vaśyātmanā tu yatatā
by him whose self is controlled, but, by striving,

शक्यो ऽवाप्तुम् उपायतः ॥
śakyo 'vāptum upāyataḥ
possible to attain through a (proper) course.

Yoga is difficult to attain
By him whose self is uncontrolled, thus is my thought;
But by him whose self is controlled, by striving,
It is possible to attain through proper means.

asaṁyata (p. pass. participle *a sam* √*yam*), uncontrolled, unsubdued.
ātmanā (m. inst. sg.), by the self.
(*asaṁyatātmanā,* m. inst. sg. BV cpd., by him whose self is uncontrolled.)
yogas (m. nom. sg.), Yoga.
duṣprāpas (m. nom. sg. from *duṣ pra* √*āp*), difficult to attain, hard to reach.
iti, thus.
me (gen. sg.), of me, my.
matis (f. nom. sg.), thought, opinion.
vaśya (m.), controlled, subject to the will.
ātmanā (m. inst. sg.), by the self.
(*vaśyātmanā,* m. inst. sg. BV cpd., by him whose self is controlled.)
tu, but, however.
yatatā (m. inst. sg. pr. act. participle √*yat*), by striving, with effort.
śakyas (m. nom. sg. gerund √*śak*), possible, able.
avāptum (infinitive *ava* √*āp*), to attain, to reach, to obtain.
upāya (m.), means, course.
-tas (adverbial suffix), through, by.

VI

अर्जुन उवाच ।
arjuna uvāca
Arjuna spoke:

arjunas (m. nom. sg.), Arjuna.
uvāca (3rd sg. perf. act. √*vac*), he said, he spoke.

37

अयतिः श्रद्धयोपेतो
ayatiḥ śraddhayopeto
the uncontrolled one who has arrived at faith,

योगाच्चलितमानसः ।
yogāccalitamānasaḥ
whose mind has fallen away from Yoga

अप्राप्य योगसंसिद्धिं
aprāpya yogasaṁsiddhiṁ
not attaining Yoga-perfection

कां गतिं कृष्ण गच्छति ॥
kāṁ gatiṁ kṛṣṇa gacchati
what road, Krishna, he goes?

ayatis (m. nom. sg.), the uncontrolled one, the unsubdued one.
śraddhayā (f. inst. sg.), by faith, with faith.
upetas (m. nom. sg. p. pass. participle *upa* √*i*), arrived at.
yogāt (m. abl. sg.), from Yoga.
calita (p. pass. participle √*cal*), moved, gone astray, deviated, fallen away.
mānasas (m. nom. sg.), mind, spirit.
(*calitamānasas*, m. nom. sg. BV cpd., whose mind has fallen away.)
aprāpya (gerund *a pra* √*āp*), not attaining, not reaching, without attaining.
yogasaṁsiddhim (f. acc. sg.), Yoga-perfection, perfection in Yoga.
kām (f. acc. sg. interrog.), what?
gatim (f. acc. sg.), road, goal, path.
kṛṣṇa (m. voc. sg.), Krishna.
gacchati (3rd sg. pr. indic. act. √*gam*), he goes, he walks, he moves.

Arjuna spoke:

The uncontrolled one who has arrived at faith,
Whose mind has fallen away from Yoga,
Who does not attain perfection in Yoga,
What road, Krishna, does he go?

38

कच्चिन् नोभयविभ्राष्टश्
kaccin nobhayavibhraṣṭaś
is it that not (from) both (worlds) fallen,

छिन्नाभ्रम् इव नश्यति ।
chinnābhram iva naśyati
disappearing-cloud-like, he is lost,

अप्रतिष्ठो महाबाहो
apratiṣṭho mahābāho
having no solid ground, O Mighty Armed One (Krishna),

विमूढो ब्रह्मणः पथि ॥
vimūḍho brahmaṇaḥ pathi
confused of Brahman on the path?

Is he not lost like a disappearing cloud,
Having fallen from both worlds,*
Having no solid ground, O Mighty Armed One,†
Confused on the path of Brahman?

kaccid, is it that?
na, not.
ubhaya (m.), both.
vibhraṣṭas (m. nom. sg. p. pass. participle *vi* √*bhraṅś*), fallen, failed, deserted.
ubhaya-vibhraṣṭas, (m. nom. sg. TP cpd., failed in both.)
chinna (p. pass. participle √*chid*), cut off, split, pierced, effaced, blotted out, disappeared.
abhram (n. nom. sg.), cloud, thunder cloud.
(*chinna-abhram,* m. nom. sg. KD cpd., blotted-out cloud.)
iva, like.
naśyati (3rd sg. pr. indic. act. √*naś*), he is lost, he is destroyed.
aprastiṣhas (m. nom. sg.), having no solid ground, fluctuating, unsafe.
mahābāho (m. voc. sg.), O Mighty Armed One, epithet here applied to Krishna.
vimūḍhas (m. nom. sg. p. pass participle *vi* √*muh*), confused, deluded.
brahmaṇas (n. gen. sg.), of Brahman.
pathi (m. loc. sg.), on the path, on the road.

* "Both worlds," viz. the here and the hereafter, earth and heaven.

† This is one of two instances in the Bhagavad Gītā where Krishna is addressed as "Mighty Armed," usually Arjuna's nickname. The other instance is in XI 23. The nickname is used throughout the Mahābhārata as a designation for eminent warriors.

39

एतन् मे संशयं कृष्ण
etan me saṁśayaṁ kṛṣṇa
this of me doubt, Krishna

छेत्तुम् अर्हस्य् अशेषतः।
chettum arhasy aśeṣataḥ
to efface thou art able without remainder;

त्वदन्यः संशयस्यास्य
tvadanyaḥ saṁśayasyāsya
other than thee, of (this) doubt, of it,

छेत्ता न ह्य् उपपद्यते ॥
chettā na hy upapadyate
an effacer not indeed he comes forth.

Thou art able, Krishna,
To efface the totality of this doubt of mine;
Other than thee, no effacer of this doubt,
Comes forth to help me.

etad (n. acc. sg.), this.
me (gen. sg.), of me, my.
saṁśayam (m. acc. sg.), doubt, uncertainty, irresolution.
kṛṣṇa (m. voc. sg.), Krisha.
chettum (infinitive √*chid*), to cut away, to efface.
arhasi (2nd sg. pr. indic. act. √*arh*), thou art able, thou art capable, please to.
aśeṣatas (adv.), without remainder, wholly, totally.
tvadanyas (m. nom. sg.), other than thee.
saṁśayasya (m. gen. sg.), of doubt, of uncertainty.
asya (m. gen. sg.), of it, of this.
chettā (m. nom. sg.), cutter-away, effacer.
na, not.
hi, indeed, truly.
upapadyate (3rd sg. pr. indic. mid. *upa* √*pad*), he arrives, he comes forth, he exists.

श्रीभगवान् उवाच
śrībhagavān uvāca
the Blessed Lord spoke:

śrībhagavān (m. nom. sg.), the Blessed Lord, the Blessed One.
uvāca (3rd sg. perfect act. √*vac*), he said, he spoke.

40

पार्थ नैवेह नामुत्र
pārtha nāiveha nāmutra
Son of Pṛthā, neither here on earth, nor there above

विनाशस् तस्य विद्यते।
vināśas tasya vidyate
destruction of him it is found

न हि कल्याणकृत् कश्चिद्
na hi kalyāṇakṛt kaścid
not indeed good-doing anyone

दुर्गतिं तात गच्छति ॥
durgatiṁ tāta gacchati
to misfortune, my son, he goes.

The Blessed Lord spoke:

Son of Pṛthā, neither here on earth nor in heaven above
Is there found to be destruction of him;*
No one who does good
Goes to misfortune, My Son.

pārtha (m. voc. sg.), Son of Pṛthā, epithet of Arjuna.
na, not, neither.
eva, indeed (used as a rhythmic filler).
iha, here, here on earth.
na, not, nor.
amutra (adv.), there above, there in heaven.
vināśas (m. nom. sg. verbal noun from *vi* √*naś*), destruction, loss.
tasya (m. gen. sg.), of him, of this.
vidyate (3rd sg. pr. indic. passive √2 *vid*), it is found, it is to be found.
na, not.
hi, indeed, truly.
kalyāṇakṛt (m. nom. sg. from *kalyāṇa* + √*kṛ*), virtuous, doing good.
kaścid anyone, anyone whatever.
durgatim (f. acc. sg.), misfortune, "hard road," to misfortune, to the unfortunate goal.
tāta (m. voc. sg.), my son, father (term of affection between seniors and juniors).
gacchati (3rd sg. pr. indic. act. √*gam*), he goes, he walks.

* I.e. the uncontrolled man who has arrived at faith but has fallen from Yoga.

41

प्राप्य पुण्यकृतां लोकान्
prāpya puṇyakṛtāṁ lokān
attaining of the meritorious doing, the worlds

उषित्वा शाश्वतीः समाः ।
uṣitvā śāśvatīḥ samāḥ
having dwelt for endless years

शुचीनां श्रीमतां गेहे
śucīnāṁ śrīmatāṁ gehe
of the radiant and of the illustrious in the dwelling

योगभ्रष्टो ऽभिजायते ॥
yogabhraṣṭo 'bhijāyate
he who has fallen from Yoga, he is born again.

prāpya (gerund *pra* √*āp*), attaining, reaching.
puṇyakṛtām (m. gen. pl.), of the meritorious acting, of the auspicious making, of the virtuous acting, of the good doing.
lokān (m. acc. pl.), worlds.
uṣitvā (gerund √3 *vas*), dwelling, having dwelt.
śāśvatīs (f. acc. pl.), constant, perpetual, endless.
samās (f. acc. pl.), years.
śucīnām (m. gen. pl.), of the radiant, of the happy.
śrīmatām (m. gen. pl.), of the illustrious, of the famous.
gehe (n. loc. sg.) in the dwelling, in the house.
yogabhraṣṭas (m. nom. sg. p. pass. participle *yoga* √*bhraṅś*), BV cpd., fallen from Yoga, gone from Yoga, lost to Yoga.
abhijāyate (3rd sg. pr. indic. passive *abhi* √*jan*), he is born, he is reborn, he is born again.

Attaining the worlds of the meritorious,
Having dwelt for endless years
In the dwelling of the radiant and the illustrious,
He who has fallen from Yoga is born again.

42

अथवा योगिनाम् एव
athavā yogināṁ eva
or else of yogins

कुले भवति धीमताम् ।
kule bhavati dhīmatām
in the family he comes to be, of wise,

एतद् धि दुर्लभतरं
etad dhi durlabhataraṁ
this indeed more difficult to attain

लोके जन्म यद् ईदृशम् ॥
loke janma yad īdṛśam
in the world birth which such.

Or he may be born in the family
Of wise yogins,
Such a birth as this being more difficult
To attain in the world.

athavā, or else, otherwise.
yoginām (m. gen. pl.), of yogins.
eva, indeed (used as a rhythmic filler).
kule (n. loc. sg.), in the family.
bhavati (3rd sg. pr. indic. act. √*bhū*), he comes to be, he exists.
dhīmatām (m. gen. pl.), of the wise, of the learned ones.
etad (n. nom. sg.), this.
hi, indeed, truly.
durlabhataram (n. nom. sg. comparative), more difficult to attain, harder to obtain.
loke (m. loc. sg.), in the world.
janma (n. nom. sg.), birth.
yad (n. nom. sg.), which.
īdṛśam (n. nom. sg.), such, of such a kind.

43

तत्र तं बुद्धिसंयोगं
tatra taṁ buddhisaṁyogaṁ
there it, intelligence-accretion,

लभते पौर्वदेहिकम् ।
labhate pāurvadehikam
he receives, derived from a former body,

यतते च ततो भूयः
yatate ca tato bhūyaḥ
and he strives from thence once more

संसिद्धौ कुरुनन्दन ॥
saṁsiddhāu kurunandana
toward perfection, Son of Kuru.

tatra, there.
tam (m. acc. sg.), it, him, this.
buddhisaṁyogam (m. acc. sg. TP cpd.), intelligence-accretion, accretion of knowledge, accretion of experience, joining together of knowledge.
labhate (3rd sg. pr. indic. mid. √*labh*), he receives, he obtains.
pāurvadehikam (m. acc. sg.), from a former body, from a previous birth, derived from a former incarnation.
yatate (3rd sg. pr. indic. mid. √*yat*), he strives, he makes effort.
ca, and.
tatas, from there, from thence.
bhūyas (adv.), again, once more.
saṁsiddhāu (f. loc. sg.), toward perfection, toward success.
kurunandana (m. voc. sg.), Descendant of Kuru, Joy of Kuru, epithet of Arjuna.

There he regains the accretion of knowledge
Derived from a former body,
And he strives onward once more
Toward perfection, Descendant of Kuru.

44

पूर्वाभ्यासेन तेनैव
pūrvābhyāsena tenāiva
by prior practice, by it,

ह्रियते ह्य् अवशो ऽपि सः ।
hriyate hy avaśo 'pi saḥ
he is carried on, indeed against will even, he,

जिज्ञासुर् अपि योगस्य
jijñāsur api yogasya
the wishing to know even, of Yoga

शब्दब्रह्मातिवर्तते ॥
śabdabrahmātivartate
word Brahman (i.e. Vedic recitation) he transcends.

pūrva-abhyāsena (m. inst. sg. KD cpd.), by prior practice, by prior performance.
tena (m. inst. sg.), by it, by this.
eva, indeed (used as a rhythmic filler).
hriyate (3rd sg. pr. indic. passive √*hṛ*), he is carried on, he is conveyed, he is brought.
hi, indeed, truly.
avaśas (m. nom. sg.), without will, without wish, against will.
api, also, even.
sas (m. nom. sg.), he, this.
jijñāsus (m. nom. sg. from desiderative √*jñā*), desirous of knowing, examining, anxious to know, wishing to know.
api, even, also.
yogasya (m. gen. sg.), of Yoga.
śabda (m.), sound, word.
brahma (n. acc. sg.), Brahman.
(*śabda-brahma*, n. acc. sg. KD cpd., word-brahman.)
ativartate (3rd sg. pr. indic. mid. *ati* √*vṛt*), he goes beyond, he transcends.

He is carried on, even against his will,
By prior practice;
He who even wishes to know of Yoga
Transcends word Brahman (i.e. Vedic recitation).

45

प्रयत्नाद् यतमानस् तु
prayatnād yatamānas tu
from presevering effort (and) controlled mind indeed

योगी संशुद्धकिल्बिषः ।
yogī saṁśuddhakilbiṣaḥ
the yogin, completely cleansed of guilt,

अनेकजन्मसंसिद्धस्
anekajanmasaṁsiddhas
not-one-birth-perfected,

ततो याति परां गतिं ॥
tato yāti parāṁ gatiṁ
then he goes to the Supreme Goal.

Through persevering effort and controlled mind,
The yogin, completely cleansed of evil,
And perfected through many births,
Then goes to the Supreme Goal.

prayatnāt (m. abl. sg.), from persevering effort, from exertion.
yatamānas (m. nom. sg. pr. mid. participle), controlled, restrained.
tu, indeed, but.
yogī (m. nom. sg.), yogin.
saṁśuddha (p. pass. participle *sam* √*śudh*), completely cleansed, completely purified.
kilbiṣas (m. nom. sg.), guilt, sin, evil.
(*saṁśuddhakilbiṣas,* m. nom. sg. BV cpd., who is completely cleansed of evil.)
aneka (n.), not one, i.e. many.
janma (n.), birth.
saṁsiddhas (m. nom. sg. p. pass. participle *sam* √*sidh*), perfected, successful.
(*anekajanmasaṁsiddhas*, m. nom. sg. TP cpd., perfected through many births, successful through many incarnations.)
tatas (m. abl. sg.), then, from there.
yāti (3rd sg. pr. indic. act. √*yā*), he goes.
parām (f. acc. sg.), to the highest, to the supreme, the supreme.
gatim (f. acc. sg.), goal, path.

46

तपस्विभ्यो ऽधिको योगी
tapasvibhyo 'dhiko yogī
to the ascetics superior the yogin;

ज्ञानिभ्यो ऽपि मतो ऽधिकः ।
jñānibhyo 'pi mato 'dhikaḥ
to the learned also thought to be superior;

कर्मिभ्यश् चाधिको योगी
karmibhyaś cādhiko yogī
and to the active (in ritual) superior the yogin

तस्माद् योगी भवार्जुन ॥
tasmād yogī bhavārjuna
therefore a yogin be! Arjuna.

tapasvibhyas (m. abl. pl.), to the ascetics.
adhikas (m. nom. sg.), superior, going beyond.
yogī (m. nom. sg.), yogin.
jñānibhyas (m. abl. pl.), to the knowing, to the learned.
api, also, even.
matas (m. nom. sg. p. pass. participle √*man*), thought, thought to be, believed to be.
adhikas (m. nom. sg.), superior, going beyond.
karmibhyas (m. abl. pl.), to the active, to those active in ritual.
ca, and.
adhikas (m. nom. sg.), superior, going beyond.
yogī (m. nom. sg.), yogin.
tasmāt (m. abl. sg.), from this, therefore.
yogī (m. nom. sg.), yogin.
bhava (2nd sg. imperative act. √*bhū*), be!
arjuna (m. voc. sg.), Arjuna.

The yogin is superior to the ascetics;
He is also thought to be superior to the learned;
And the yogin is superior to those who are active in ritual.
Therefore, be a yogin, Arjuna.

47

योगिनाम् अपि सर्वेषां
yogināṁ api sarveṣāṁ
of the yogins even, of all these,

मद्गतेनान्तरात्मना ।
madgatenāntarātmanā
to me by going with inner self,

श्रद्धावान् भजते यो मां
śraddhāvān bhajate yo māṁ
full of faith he honors, who, me

स मे युक्ततमो मतः ॥
sa me yuktatamo mataḥ
he to me the most devoted thought to be.

yoginām (m. gen. pl.), of the yogins.
api, even, also.
sarveṣām (m. gen. pl.), of all these.
madgatena (m. inst. sg.), gone to me, by going to me.
antarātmanā (m. inst. sg.), by the inner self, with the inner self.
śraddhāvān (m. nom. sg.), full of faith, rich in faith.
bhajate (3rd sg. pr. indic. mid. √*bhaj*), he honors, he worships, he loves.
yas (m. nom. sg.), who.
mām (acc. sg.), me.
sas (m. nom. sg.), he, this.
me (dat. sg.), to me.
yuktatamas (m. nom. sg. superlative of *yukta*, p. pass. part. of √*yuj*), most devoted, most attached, most steadfast.
matas (m. nom. sg. p. pass. participle √*man*), thought, believed, thought to be, believed to be.

Of all these yogins,
He who has gone to Me with his inner self,*
Who honors Me, full of faith,
Is thought to be the most devoted to Me.

End of Book VI

The Yoga of Meditation

* I.e. whose mind is perpetually fixed on God, or the Supreme Spirit, through *bhakti*, or love.

BOOK VII

श्रीभगवान् उवाच ।
śrībhagavān uvāca
the Blessed Lord spoke:

śrībhagavān (m. nom. sg.), the Blessed Lord, the Blessed One.
uvāca (3rd sg. perfect act. √*vac*), he said, he spoke.

1

मय्य् आसक्तमनाः पार्थ
mayy āsaktamanāḥ pārtha
in me whose mind is absorbed, Son of Pṛthā,

योगं युञ्जन् मदाश्रयः ।
yogaṁ yuñjan madāśrayaḥ
Yoga practicing, dependent on me,

असंशयं समग्रं मां
asaṁśayaṁ samagraṁ māṁ
without doubt, entirely me;

यथा ज्ञास्यसि तच्छृणु ॥
yathā jñāsyasi tac chṛṇu
how thou shalt know, that hear!

The Blessed Lord Spoke:

With mind absorbed in Me, Son of Pṛthā,
Practicing Yoga, dependent on Me,
How thou shalt know Me entirely,
Without doubt; hear that!

mayi (loc. sg.), in me.
āsakta (p. pass. participle *ā* √*sañj*), absorbed in, intent on, attached to.
manās (n. nom. sg.), mind, thought, devotion.
(*āsaktamanās*, m. nom. sg. BV cpd., one whose mind is attached, one whose mind is absorbed.)
pārtha (m. voc. sg.), Son of Pṛthā, epithet of Arjuna.
yogam (m. acc. sg.), Yoga.
yuñjan (m. nom. sg. pr. participle √*yuj*), practicing, performing.
madāśrayas (m. nom. sg.), dependent on me, taking refuge in me.
asaṁśayam (adv.), without doubt, without irresolution, without qualification.
samagram (adv.), wholly, entirely.
mām (acc. sg.), me.
yathā, how, in which way.
jñāsyasi (2nd sg. future act. √*jñā*), thou shalt know.
tad (n. acc. sg.), that, this.
śṛṇu (2nd sg. imperative √*śru*), hear!

2

ज्ञानं ते ऽहं सविज्ञानम्
jñānaṁ te 'haṁ savijñānam
knowledge to thee I, along with discrimination,

इदं वक्ष्याम्य् अशेषतः ।
idaṁ vakṣyāmy aśeṣataḥ
this I shall explain without remainder

यज् ज्ञात्वा नेह भूयो ऽन्यज्
yaj jñātvā neha bhūyo 'nyaj
which, having been known, not here in the world further (anything) other

ज्ञातव्यम् अवशिष्यते ॥
jñātavyam avaśiṣyate
to be known it remains.

To thee I shall explain in full this knowledge,
Along with discrimination,
Which, having been understood, nothing further
Remains to be known here in the world.

jñānam (n. acc. sg.), knowledge, wisdom.
te (dat. sg.), to thee.
aham (nom. sg.), I.
savijñānam (n. acc. sg.), with discrimination, with understanding, along with discrimination.
idam (n. acc. sg.), this.
vakṣyāmi (1st sg. future act. √*vac*), I shall say, I shall tell, I shall explain.
aśeṣatas (adv.), without remainder, in full.
yad (n. acc. sg.), which.
jñātvā (gerund √*jñā*), knowing, having known, having understood (here in a passive sense, as "having been understood").
na, not.
iha, here, here on earth.
bhūyas, (adv.), again, further.
anyat (n. nom. sg.), other.
jñātavyam (n. nom. sg. gerundive √*jñā*), to be known.
avaśiṣyate (3rd sg. pr. indic. passive *ava* √*śiṣ*), it remains, it is left.

VII

3

मनुष्याणां सहस्रेषु
manuṣyāṇāṁ sahasreṣu
of mankind in thousands

कश्चिद् यतति सिद्धये ।
kaścid yatati siddhaye
(scarcely) anyone strives for perfection;

यतताम् अपि सिद्धानां
yatatām api siddhānāṁ
of the striving even, of the perfected,

कश्चिन् मां वेत्ति तत्त्वतः ॥
kaścin māṁ vetti tattvataḥ
(scarcely) anyone me he knows in reality.

Of mankind in thousands,
Scarcely anyone strives for perfection;
Of the striving even, of the perfected,
Scarcely anyone knows Me in truth.

manuṣyāṇām (m. gen. pl.), of men, of mankind.
sahasreṣu (m. loc. pl.), in thousands.
kaścid, anyone, anyone whatever (here, scarcely anyone).
yatati (3rd sg. pr. indic. act. √*yat*), he strives, he stretches.
siddhaye (f. dat. sg.), to perfection, toward perfection.
yatatām (gen. pl. pr. act. participle √*yat*), of the striving.
api, even, also.
siddhānām (m. gen. pl.), of the perfected.
kaścid, anyone (here, scarcely anyone).
mām (acc. sg.), me.
vetti (3rd sg. pr. indic. act. √*vid*), he knows.
tattvatas (adv.), truly, in reality.

4

भूमिर् आपो ऽनलो वायुः
bhūmir āpo 'nalo vāyuḥ
earth, water, fire, wind,

खं मनो बुद्धिर् एव च ।
khaṁ mano buddhir eva ca
ether, mind, intelligence and

अहंकार इतीयं मे
ahaṁkāra itīyaṁ me
self consciousness thus this of me

भिन्ना प्रकृतिर् अष्टधा ॥
bhinnā prakṛtir aṣṭadhā
divided nature eightfold.

Earth, water, fire, wind,
Ether, mind, intelligence
And self-consciousness,* thus this,
My material nature, is divided, eight-fold.

bhūmis (f. nom. sg.), earth.
āpas (f. nom. pl.), water, the waters.
analas (m. nom. sg.), fire.
vāyus (m. nom. sg.), wind.
kham (n. nom. sg.), ether, sky, space.
manas (n. nom. sg.), mind, thought.
buddhis (f. nom. sg.), intelligence.
eva, indeed (used as a rhythmic filler).
ca, and.
ahaṁkāras (m. nom. sg.), "I making," consciousness of the self (sometimes, "egotism").
iti, thus, so.
iyam (f. nom. sg.), this.
me (gen. sg.), of me, my.
bhinnā (f. nom. sg. p. pass. participle √*bhid*), divided, split.
prakṛtis (f. nom. sg.), nature, material nature.
aṣṭadhā (adv.), eightfold.

* These are *Sāṁkhya* categories.

5

अपरेयम् इतस् त्व् अन्यां
apareyam itas tv anyāṁ
inferior this; but other

प्रकृतिं विद्धि मे पराम् ।
prakṛtiṁ viddhi me parām
nature know of me the highest,

जीवभूतां महाबाहो
jīvabhūtāṁ mahābāho
the spiritual beings, O Mighty Armed One

ययेदं धार्यते जगत् ॥
yayedaṁ dhāryate jagat
by which this it is sustained the universe.

aparā (f. nom. sg.), lower, inferior.
iyam (f. nom. sg.), this.
itas, this, here.
tu, indeed.
anyām (f. acc. sg.), other.
prakṛtim (f. acc. sg.), nature.
viddhi (2nd sg. imperative act. √*vid*), know! learn!
me (gen. sg.), of me, my.
parām (f. acc. sg.), highest, supreme.
jīvabhūtām (f. acc. sg.), consisting of the *jīvas,* consisting of souls, consisting of spiritual beings.
mahābāho (m. voc. sg.), O Mighty Armed One, epithet of Arjuna and other warriors.
yayā (f. inst. sg.), by which.
idam (n. nom. sg.), this.
dhāryate (3rd sg. pr. indic. causative passive √*dhṛ*), it is sustained, it is supported.
jagat (n. nom. sg.), world, universe.

Such is my inferior nature, but elsewhere
Know My highest nature –
That which consists of spiritual beings,* O Mighty Armed One,
By which this universe is sustained.

* God has two *prakṛtis,* a lower and a higher one. The lower one is the *prakṛti* of this world consisting of endless various objects, means and occasions of material experience and divided into eight categories" (see stanza 4)..."God's higher *prakrti,* however, is not of the same order of this non-spiritual *prakṛti* which solely consists of the objects experienced by the spiritual beings, but is constituted by the spiritual beings themselves, the jīvas." – Rāmānuja.

6

एतद्योनीनि भूतानि
etadyonīni bhūtāni
this (my highest nature) the wombs (of) beings,

सर्वाणीत्य् उपधारय ।
sarvāṇīty upadhāraya
all, thus understand!

अहं कृत्स्नस्य जगत:
ahaṁ kṛtsnasya jagataḥ
I of the entire universe

प्रभव: प्रलयस् तथा ॥
prabhavaḥ pralayas tathā
the origin and the dissolution also.

All creatures have their wombs in this,
My highest nature.
Understand this!
I am the origin and also the dissolution
Of the entire universe.

etad (n. nom. sg.), this.
yonīni (n. nom. pl.), wombs, origins.
bhūtāni (n. nom. pl.), beings, creatures.
sarvāṇi (n. nom. pl.), all.
(*etadyonīni bhūtāni sarvāṇi,* all creatures have their wombs in this.)
iti, thus.
upadhāraya (2nd sg. pr. indic. causative act. imperative *upa* √*dhṛ*), understand! comprehend!
aham (nom. sg.), I.
kṛtsnasya (n. gen. sg.), of the entire, of the whole.
jagatas (n. gen. sg.), of the universe, of the world.
prabhavas (m. nom. sg.), origin, coming to be.
pralayas (m. nom. sg.), dissolution, ceasing to exist.
tathā, thus, also.

7

मत्तः परतरं नान्यत्
mattaḥ parataraṁ nānyat
than me higher not other

किंचिद् अस्ति धनंजय ।
kiṁcid asti dhanaṁjaya
anything there is, Conqueror of Wealth.

मयि सर्वम् इदं प्रोतं
mayi sarvam idaṁ protaṁ
on me all this universe strung

सूत्रे मणिगणा इव ॥
sūtre maṇigaṇā iva
on-a-thread-pearls-like.

mattas (abl. sg.), from me, than me.
parataram (n. nom. sg. comparative), higher, superior.
na, not.
anyat (n. nom. sg.), other.
kiṁcid, anything, anything whatever.
asti (3rd sg. pr. indic. √*as*), there is, it is.
dhanaṁjaya (m. voc. sg.), Conqueror of Wealth, epithet of Arjuna.
mayi (loc. sg.), on me, in me.
sarvam (n. nom. sg.), all.
idam (n. nom. sg.), this.
protam (n. nom. sg. participle *pra* √*ve*), strung, woven.
sūtre (n. loc. sg.), on a thread.
maṇigaṇās (m. nom. pl.), pearls, clusters of pearls, clusters of jewels.
iva, like.

Nothing higher than Me exists,
O Conqueror of Wealth.
On Me all this universe is strung
Like pearls on a thread.

8

रसो ऽहम् अप्सु कौन्तेय
raso 'ham apsu kāunteya,
the liquidity I in the waters, Son of Kuntī,

प्रभास्मि शशिसूर्ययोः ।
prabhāsmi śaśisūryayoḥ
the radiance I am in that which contains the rabbit,* and the sun,

प्रणवः सर्ववेदेषु
praṇavaḥ sarvavedeṣu
the sacred syllable (Oṁ) in all the Vedas

शब्दः खे पौरुषं नृषु ॥
śabdaḥ khe pāuruṣaṁ nṛṣu
the sound in the air, the manhood in men.

I am the liquidity in the waters, Son of Kuntī,
I am the radiance in the moon and sun,
The sacred syllable (Oṁ) in all the Vedas,
The sound in the air, the manhood in men.

rasas (m. nom. sg.), flavor, liquidity, taste.
aham (nom. sg.), I.
apsu (f. loc. pl.), in the waters, in water.
kāunteya (m. voc. sg.), Son of Kuntī, epithet of Arjuna.
prabhā (f. nom. sg.), radiance, light, splendor.
asmi (1st sg. pr. indic. $\sqrt{}$*as*), I am.
śaśi (m.), that which contains the rabbit (*śaśa*), i.e. the moon.
sūrya (m.), the sun.
(*śaśisūryayos*, m. gen. dual, of the moon and sun.)
praṇavas (m. nom. sg.), the sacred syllable "Oṁ."
sarvavedeṣu (m. loc. pl.), in all the Vedas.
śabdas (m. nom. sg.), sound.
khe (n. loc. sg.), in the air, in the ether.
pāuruṣam (n. nom. sg.), manhood, potency, virility.
nṛṣu (m. loc. pl.), in men.

* "That which contains the rabbit" (*śaśin*), along with *śaśāṅka* (rabbit marked) one of the most common of all Sanskrit terms for the moon, said to arise because the Hindus saw a "rabbit in the moon."

9

पुण्यो गन्धः पृथिव्यां च
puṇyo gandhaḥ pṛthivyāṁ ca
and the pure fragrance in the earth,

तेजश्चास्मि विभावसौ ।
tejaścāsmi vibhāvasāu
and the brilliance I am in the sun,

जीवनं सर्वभूतेषु
jīvanaṁ sarvabhūteṣu
the life in all beings

तपश्चास्मि तपस्विषु ॥
tapaścāsmi tapasviṣu
and the austerity I am in ascetics.

**And the pure fragrance in the earth,
And I am the brilliance in the sun;
The life in all beings,
And the austerity in ascetics.**

puṇyas (m. nom. sg.), pure, pleasant, auspicious, sacred.
gandhas (m. nom. sg.), fragrance, smell.
pṛthivyām (f. loc. sg.), in the earth, of the earth.
ca, and.
tejas (n. nom. sg.), splendor, brilliance, radiance.
ca, and.
asmi (1st sg. pr. indic. √*as*), I am.
vibhāvasāu (m. loc. sg.), in the sun, in flame.
jīvanam (n. nom. sg.), life.
sarvabhūteṣu (m. loc. pl.), in all beings.
tapas (n. nom. sg.), austerity, heat, self-denial.
ca, and.
asmi (1st sg. pr. indic. √*as*), I am.
tapasviṣu (m. loc. pl.), in ascetics, in holy men.

10

बीजं मां सर्वभूतानां
bījaṁ māṁ sarvabhūtānāṁ
the seed, me, of all creatures

विद्धि पार्थ सनातनम्
viddhi pārtha sanātanam
know, Son of Pṛthā, primaeval

बुद्धिर् बुद्धिमताम् अस्मि
buddhir buddhimatām asmi
the intelligence of the intelligent I am

तेजस् तेजस्विनाम् अहम् ॥
tejas tejasvinām-aham
the splendor of the splendid, I.

bījam (n. nom. sg.), seed, germ, primary cause.
mām (acc. sg.), me.
sarvabhūtānām (m. gen. pl.), of all beings, of all creatures.
viddhi (2nd sg. imperative act. √*vid*), know! learn!
pārtha (m. voc. sg.), Son of Pṛthā, epithet of Arjuna.
sanātanam (n. nom. sg.), ancient, primaeval.
buddhis (f. nom. sg.), intelligence.
buddhimatām (m. gen. pl.), of the intelligent, of those who are intelligent.
asmi (1st sg. pr. indic. √*as*), I am.
tejas (n. nom. sg.), splendor, brilliance, radiance.
tejasvinām (m. gen. pl.), of the splendid, of the brilliant, of the radiant.
aham, I.

Know Me to be the primaeval seed
Of all creatures, Son of Pṛthā (Arjuna);
I am the intelligence of the intelligent;
The splendor of the splendid, I.

11

बलं बलवतां चाहं
balaṁ balavatāṁ cāhaṁ
and the might of the mighty, I,

कामरागविवर्जितम् ।
kāmarāgavivarjitam
desire and passion freed from,

धर्माविरुद्धो भूतेषु
dharmāviruddho bhūteṣu
according to law in beings

कामो ऽस्मि भरतर्षभ ।।
kāmo 'smi bharatarṣabha
love I am, Bull of the Bharatas.

And the might of the mighty I am,
Which is freed from lust and passion,
And I am that love in beings
Which is according to law, Bull of the Bharatas (Arjuna).

balam (n. nom. sg.), strength, force, might.
balavatām (m. gen. pl.), of the strong, of the mighty.
ca, and.
aham (nom. sg.), I.
kāma (m.), desire, love.
rāgavivarjitam (n. nom. sg. p. pass. participle *raga vi* √*vṛj*), freed from passion, diverted from passion, with passion set aside.
(*kāma-rāga-vivarjitam*, n. nom. sg. TP cpd., freed from passion and desire.)
dharma (m.), law, justice, rule, duty.
aviruddhas (m. nom. sg. p. pass. participle *a vi* √*rudh*), according to, consistent with, not encountering resistance from, not opposed to.
(*dharma-aviruddhas*, m. nom. sg. TP cpd., not opposed to law.)
bhūteṣu (m. loc. pl.), in beings, in creatures.
kāmas (m. nom. sg.), desire, love.
asmi (1st sg. pr. indic. √*as*), I am.
bharatarṣabha (m. voc. sg.), Bull of the Bharatas, epithet of Arjuna.

12

ये चैव सात्त्विका भावा
ye cāiva sāttvikā bhāvā
and which (are) sattvic states of being

राजसास् तामसाश्च ये ।
rājasās tāmasāśca ye
rajasic and tamasic which

मत्त एवेति तान् विद्धि
matta eveti tān viddhi
from Me indeed them know!

न त्व् ग्रहं तेषु ते मयि ॥
na tv ahaṁ teṣu te mayi
not, but, I in them; they in me.

And those states of being which are sattvic,
And those which are rajasic and tamasic,
Know that they proceed from Me.
But I am not in them; they are in Me.*

ye (m. nom. pl.), which, who.
ca, and.
eva, indeed (used as a rhythmic filler).
sāttvikās (m. nom. pl.), sattvic, derived from the sattva guṇa (the guṇa of goodness).
bhāvās (m. nom. pl.), states of being, comings into existence, modes of behavior.
rājasās (m. nom. pl.), rajasic, derived from the rajas guṇa (guṇa of passion and power).
tāmasās (m. nom. pl.), tamasic, derived from the tamas guṇa (guṇa of darkness and sloth).
ca, and.
ye (m. nom. pl.), which, who.
mattas (abl. sg.), from me.
eva, indeed (used as a rhythmic filler).
iti, thus.
tān (m. acc. pl.), them.
viddhi (2nd sg. imperative act. √*vid*), know! learn!
na, not.
tu, but.
aham (nom. sg.), I.
teṣu (m. loc. pl.), in them.
te (m. nom. pl.), they.
mayi (m. loc. sg.), in me.

* All these entities with their peculiar individuality and characteristics have originated from God, are *śeṣas* (remainders) of God and depend on God inasmuch as they constitute his body, and God himself is modified by all these entities of which He is the *ātman.* These entities which are of the nature of *sattva, rajas* and *tamas* and which exist in this world in the form of body, senses, material objects and their causes, depend on God whose body they constitute. God himself, however, does not depend on them. – Rāmānuja.

13

त्रिभिर् गुणमयैर् भावैर्
tribhir guṇamayāir bhāvāir
by the three guṇa-made states of being,

एभिः सर्वम् इदं जगत् ।
ebhiḥ sarvam idaṁ jagat
by these, all this universe

मोहितं नाभिजानाति
mohitaṁ nābhijānāti
deluded, not it recognizes

माम् एभ्यः परम् अव्ययम् ॥
mām ebhyaḥ param avyayam
me, than these higher (and) eternal.

tribhis (m. inst. pl.), by three, by the three.
guṇamayāis (m. inst. pl.), by guṇa made, by guṇa produced, by guṇa formed. *
bhāvāis (m. inst. pl.), by states of being, by modes of behavior.
ebhis (m. inst. pl.), by these.
sarvam (n. nom. sg.), all.
idam (n. nom. sg.), this.
jagat (n. nom. sg.), world, universe.
mohitam (n. nom. sg. causative participle √*muh*), deluded, confused.
na, not.
abhijānāti (3rd sg. pr. indic. act. *abhi* √*jñā*), it recognizes, it perceives, it becomes aware of.
mām (acc. sg.), me.
ebhyas (m. abl. pl.), than these, from these.
param (m. acc. sg.), higher, highest.
avyayam (m. acc. sg.), eternal, imperishable.

By these three guṇa-made states of being,
All this universe is deluded.
It does not recognize Me,
Who am higher than these, and eternal.

---

* The three guṇas – *sattva*, or illumination and truth, *rajas*, or passion and desire, and *tamas* or darkness, sloth and dullness – were originally thought, by the Sāṁkhya philosophers who first identified and named them, to be substances. Later they became attributes of the psyche. *Sattva* has been equated with essence, *rajas* with energy and *tamas* with mass. According to still another interpretation, *sattva* is intelligence, *rajas* is movement and *tamas* is obstruction. The word *guṇa* means "strand," "thread" or "rope," and *prakṛti*, or material nature is conceived as a cord woven from the three *guṇas*. They chain down the soul to thought and matter. They can exist in different proportions in a single being, determining his mental outlook and his actions. A man whose nature is dominated by *sattva* will be clear thinking, radiant and truthful. A man whose nature is dominated by *rajas* will be passionate, quick to anger and greedy. A man whose nature is dominated by *tamas* will be stupid, lazy and stubborn. But most men will be found to have elements of *guṇas* different from their dominating ones, i.e. to be motivated by a combination of *guṇas*. The aim of the upward reaching *ātman*, or self, is to transcend the *guṇas*, break free of their bondage, and attain liberation and union with *Brahman*. The *guṇas*, moreover, are constituents of that *māyā*, or power of illusion, possessed by Qualified (*Saguṇa*) *Brahman*. Through the *guṇas*, this *Saguṇa Brahman* creates and maintains the world (or the cosmic illusion) by its powers of projection and concealment. All the universe and all the things in it are the creations of *Saguṇa Brahman*, and all are subject to the influences of the *guṇas*. Only the sages are able to lift the veil of *māyā* and perceive the reality that is *Brahman* behind it. And only those who persevere in meditation, right action and the aquisition of knowledge through many lives are permitted to voyage beyond *māyā* and the *guṇas*, finally to reach *Brahmanirvāṇa* or the *nirvāṇa* of *Brahman*.

14

दैवी ह्य् एषा गुणमयी
dāivī hy eṣā guṇamayī
divine indeed this guṇa-made

मम माया दुरत्यया।
mama māyā duratyayā
of me illusion, difficult to penetrate,

माम् एव ये प्रपद्यन्ते
mām eva ye prapadyante
me only who they resort to

मायाम् एतां तरन्ति ते ॥
māyām etāṁ taranti te
illusion this they transcend, they.

Divine indeed is this My guṇa-made illusion,
And difficult to penetrate;
Only those who resort to Me
Transcend this illusion.

dāivī (f. nom. sg.), divine, heavenly.
hi, indeed, truly.
eṣā (f. nom. sg.), this.
guṇamayī (f. nom. sg.), guṇa-made, guṇa-produced.
mama (gen. sg.), of me, my.
māyā (f. nom. sg.), illusion, magic, power.
duratyayā (f. nom. sg. from *dur ati* √*i*), difficult to penetrate, hard to go beyond, difficult to master.
mām (acc. sg.), me.
eva, indeed (used as a rhythmic filler).
ye (m. nom. pl.), who.
prapadyante (3rd pl. pr. indic. mid. *pra* √*pad*), they resort to, they take refuge with, they attain.
māyām (f. acc. sg.), illusion, magic power.
etām (f. acc. sg.), this.
taranti (3rd pl. pr. indic. act. √*tṛ*), they transcend, they penetrate, they pass beyond.
te (m. nom. pl.), they.

15

न मां दुष्कृतिनो मूढाः
na māṁ duṣkṛtino mūḍhāḥ
not me evil-doers deluded

प्रपद्यन्ते नराधमाः ।
prapadyante narādhamāḥ
they resort to, men lowest

माययापहृतज्ञाना
māyayāpahṛtajñānā
by illusion bereft of knowledge

आसुरं भावम् आश्रिताः ॥
āsuraṁ bhāvam āśritāḥ
demon existence attached.

Evil doers, lowest of men,
Bereft of knowledge by illusion,
Do not resort to Me,
Attached as they are to a demonic existence.

na, not.
mām (acc. sg.), me.
duṣkṛtinas (m. nom. pl.), evil doers, wrong doers.
mūḍhās (m. nom. pl. p. pass. participle √*muh*), deluded, confused.
prapadyante (3rd pl. pr. indic. mid. *pra* √*pad*), they resort to, they take refuge with, they attain.
narā (m. nom. pl.), men.
adhamās (m. nom. pl.), lowest, vilest, worst.
māyayā (f. inst. sg.), by illusion, by magic power.
apahṛta (p. pass. participle *apa* √*hṛ*), taken away, bereft, carried off, removed.
jñānās (m. nom. pl.), knowledge, wisdom (plural because of *narās*, men).
(*apahṛtajñānās,* m. nom. pl. BV cpd., whose knowledge has been carried away.)
āsuram (m. acc. sg.), demon, demonic.
bhāvam (m. acc. sg.), existence, being.
āśritās (m. nom. pl. p. pass. participle *ā* √*śri*), attached, resorting to, having recourse to.

16

चतुर्विधा भजन्ते मां
caturvidhā bhajante māṁ
four kinds they honor me

जनाः सुकृतिनो ऽर्जुन ।
janāḥ sukṛtino 'rjuna
(among) men good-doing, Arjuna,

आर्तो जिज्ञासुर् अर्थार्थी
ārto, jijñāsur arthārthī
those bereft who seek to regain spiritual power, those who desire knowledge, the desirous of wealth,*

ज्ञानी च भरतर्षभ ॥
jñānī ca bharatarṣabha
and the man of wisdom, Bull of the Bharatas.

caturvidhās (m. nom. pl.), of four kinds, fourfold.
bhajante (3rd pl. pr. indic. mid. √*bhaj*), they worship, they honor.
mām (acc. sg.), me.
janās (m. nom. pl.), men.
sukṛtinas (m. nom. pl.), benevolent, good-doing.
arjuna (m. voc. sg.), Arjuna.
ārtas (m. nom. sg. p. pass. participle *a* √*ṛ*), bereft, afflicted, suffering.
jijñāsus (m. nom. sg. from desiderative √*jñā*), he who is desirous of knowing, desirous of knowledge.
arthārthī (m. nom. sg.), he who is desirous of wealth, he who desires the Highest Truth.
jñānī (m. nom. sg.), man of wisdom, learned man, wise man.
ca, and.
bharatarṣabha (m. voc. sg.), Bull of the Bharatas, epithet of Arjuna.

Among benevolent men, four kinds worship Me, Arjuna:
The bereft who desire to regain spiritual power,
The desirous of knowledge, the desirous of attaining the Highest Truth
And the Man of wisdom, Bull of the Bharatas.

* The common translation "desirous of wealth," which is favored by many native translators, is obviously so much at odds with the other teachings of the Bhagavad Gītā, that it cannot be entertained by the thoughtful reader. Śrī Krishna Prem has suggested that "*artha*" here refers to the *paramārtha*, or highest spiritual knowledge. Rāmānuja says that the expression *arthārthī* (which is the nom. sg. of *arthārthin*) refers to "those who aspire to acquire knowledge of the *ātman* as distinct from *prakṛti*," or material nature. The meaning of the last three catagories of "benevolent men" is further explained in the next book (VIII) from stanza 8 onward.

17

तेषां ज्ञानी नित्ययुक्त
teṣāṁ jñānī nityayukta
of them, the man of wisdom, eternally steadfast,

एकभक्तिर् विशिष्यते ।
ekabhaktir viśiṣyate
devoted to one alone, he is pre-eminent

प्रियो हि ज्ञानिनो ऽत्यर्थम्
priyo hi jñānino 'tyartham
fond indeed of the man of wisdom exceedingly

अहं स च मम प्रियः ॥
ahaṁ sa ca mama priyaḥ
I, and he of Me fond.

Of them the man of wisdom, eternally steadfast,
Devoted to One alone, is pre-eminent.
I am indeed exceedingly fond of the man of wisdom,
And he is fond of Me.

teṣām (m. gen. pl.), of them.
jñānī (m. nom. sg.), man of wisdom, wise man, learned man.
nitya (adv.), eternally, imperishably.
yuktas (m. nom. sg.), steadfast, disciplined, joined to Yoga.
ekabhaktis (f. nom. sg.), "one devoted," devoted to one alone, worshipping a single god or absolute (as BV cpd.), whose devotion is to one.
viśiṣyate (3rd. sg. pr. indic. passive *vi* √*śiṣ*), he is distinct, he is distinguished, he is pre-eminent.
priyas (m. nom. sg.), fond, dear.
hi, indeed, truly.
jñāninas (m. gen. sg.), of the man of wisdom, of the wise man.
atyartham (adv.), exceedingly, extraordinarily.
aham (nom. sg.), I.
sas (m. nom. sg.), he.
ca, and.
mama (gen. sg.), of me.
priyas (m. nom. sg.), fond, dear.

18

उदाराः सर्व एवैते
udārāḥ sarva evāite
noble all indeed these;

ज्ञानी त्व् आत्मैव मे मतम् ।
jñānī tv ātmāiva me matam
the man of wisdom, but, the self thus of me thought to be;

आस्थितः स हि युक्तात्मा
āsthitaḥ sa hi yuktātmā
abiding in, he indeed, the steadfast self,

माम् एवानुत्तमां गतिम् ॥
mām evānuttamāṁ gatim
me, the Supreme Goal.

udārās (m. nom. pl.), noble, exalted.
sarve (m. nom. pl.), all.
eva, indeed (often used as a rhythmic filler).
ete (m. nom. pl.), these.
jñānī (m. nom. sg.), man of wisdom, wise man.
tu, but.
ātmā (m. nom. sg.), self.
eva, indeed (used as a rhythmic filler).
me (gen. sg.), of me, my.
matam (n. nom. sg.), thought, thought to be.
āsthitas (m. nom. sg.), abiding in, situated in.
sas (m. nom. sg.), he, this.
hi, indeed, truly.
yuktātmā (m. nom. sg. BV cpd.), whose self is steadfast.
mām (acc. sg.), me.
eva, indeed (used as a rhythmic filler).
anuttamām (f. acc. sg.), supreme, unsurpassed.
gatim (f. acc. sg.), goal, path, way.

All these are indeed noble;
But the man of wisdom is thought to be my very self.
He, indeed, whose self is steadfast,
Abides in Me, the Supreme Goal.

19

बहूनां जन्मनाम् अन्ते
bahūnāṁ janmanām ante
of many births at the end

ज्ञानवान् मां प्रपद्यते ।
jñānavān māṁ prapadyate
the man of wisdom me he resorts to

वासुदेवः सर्वम् इति
vāsudevaḥ sarvam iti
"Vāsudeva (Krishna) (is) all," thus

स महात्मा सुदुर्लभः ॥
sa mahātmā sudurlabhaḥ
this great soul hard to find.

bahūnām (n. gen. pl.), of many, of much.
janmanām (n. gen. pl.), of births.
ante (m. loc. sg.), at the end, in the end.
jñānavān (m. nom. sg.), wise man, man of wisdom.
mām (acc. sg.), me.
prapadyate (3rd sg. pr. indic. mid. *pra* √*pad*), he resorts to, he takes refuge in, he attains.
vāsudevas (m. nom. sg.), Son of Vasudeva, i.e. Krishna.
sarvam (n. nom. sg.), all.
iti, thus.
sas (m. nom. sg.), this, he.
mahātmā (m. nom. sg.), great soul, great self, (as BV cpd.) one whose self is great.
sudurlabhas (m. nom. sg. from *su dur* √*labh*), hard to find, difficult to obtain.

At the end of many births,
The man of wisdom resorts to Me,
Thinking "Vāsudeva* (Krishna) is all."
Such a great self is hard to find.

* Vāsudeva, literally "the son of Vasudeva," or Krishna, whose father was a son of Śūra, descendant of Yadu. At the birth of Vasudeva, the father, the gods sounded the heavenly drums, knowing that an *avatār* of Vishnu (i.e. Krishna) was to be born into his family. Krishna was a brother of Kuntī, mother of the three principal Paṇḍu princes (see chapter "The Setting of the Bhagavad Gītā"). Here Krishna is identified with Brahman.

20

कामैस् तैस्तैर् हृतज्ञानाः
kāmāis tāistāir hṛtajñānāḥ
by desires, be these and those, bereft of knowledge

प्रपद्यन्ते ऽन्यदेवताः ।
prapadyante 'nyadevatāḥ
they resort to other gods

तंतं नियमम् आस्थाय
taṁtaṁ niyamam āsthāya
this or that religious obligation having recourse to

प्रकृत्या नियताः स्वया ॥
prakṛtyā niyatāḥ svayā
by nature constrained by own.

Men whose knowledge has been carried away
By these and those desires, resort to other gods,
Having recourse to this and that religious obligation,
Constrained by their own material natures.

kāmāis (m. inst. pl.), by desires, by lusts.
tāis tāis (m. inst. pl.), by these and those.
hṛta (p. pass. participle √*hṛ*), bereft, stolen away, taken away.
jñānās (m. nom. pl.), knowledge, wisdom.
(*hṛtajñānās,* m. nom. pl. BV cpd., whose knowledge has been carried away.)
prapadyante (3rd pl. pr. indic. mid. *pra* √*pad*), they resort to, they take refuge with, they worship.
anya-, other.
devatās (m. nom. pl.), gods, godheads.
taṁ tam (m. acc. sg.), this or that.
niyamam (m. acc. sg.), religious obligation, discipline, worship.
āsthāya (gerund *ā* √*sthā*), having recourse to, following, practicing.
prakṛtyā (f. inst. sg.), by material nature.
niyatās (m. nom. pl.), constrained, held down, controlled, subdued.
svayā (f. inst. sg.), by own.

21

यो यो यां यां तनुं भक्तः
yo yo yāṁ yāṁ tanuṁ bhaktaḥ
whoever whatever form worshipped

श्रद्धयार्चितुम् इच्छति ।
śraddhayārcitum icchati
with belief to honor he desires,

तस्य तस्याचलां श्रद्धां
tasya tasyācalāṁ śraddhāṁ
on him on him immovable faith

ताम् एव विदधाम्य् अहम् ॥
tām eva vidadhāmy aham
it I bestow, I.

Whoever desires to honor with belief
Whatever worshipped form,
On him I bestow
Immovable faith.

yas yas (m. nom. sg.), whoever.
yām yām (f. acc. sg.), whatever.
tanum or *tanūm* (f. acc. sg.), form, body.
bhaktas (m. nom. sg. p. pass. participle √*bhaj*), worshipped, honored.
śraddhayā (f. inst. sg.), with faith, with belief.
arcitum (infinitive √*arc*), to worship, to praise, to honor.
icchati (3rd sg. pr. indic. act. √*iṣ*), he desires, he wishes.
tasya tasya (m. gen. sg.), on him, on whoever he is.
acalām (f. acc. sg.), immovable, unmoving, steady, steadfast.
śraddhām (f. acc. sg.), faith.
tām (f. acc. sg.), it, this.
eva, indeed (used as a rhythmic filler).
vidadhāmi (1st sg. pr. indic. act. *vi* √*dhā*), I bestow, I grant, I establish.
aham (nom. sg.), I.

22

स तया श्रद्धया युक्तस्
sa tayā śraddhayā yuktas
he with this faith endowed

तस्याराधनम् ईहते ।
tasyārādhanam īhate
of this (source) propitiation he desires,

लभते च ततः कामान्
labhate ca tataḥ kāmān
and he receives from thence (his) desires

मयैव विहितान् हि तान् ॥
mayāiva vihitān hi tān
by me decreed, indeed, them.

He, who, endowed with this faith,
Desires to propitiate this (God),
Receives from thence his desires
Because those desires are decreed by Me.*

sas (m. nom. sg.), he, this.
tayā (f. inst. sg.), by this, with this.
śraddhayā (f. inst. sg.), by faith, with faith.
yuktas (m. nom. sg. p. pass. participle √*yuj*), joined, endowed, yoked to.
tasya (m. gen. sg.), of him, of it, of this.
ārādhanam (n. acc. sg. from *ā* √*rādh*), propitiation.
īhate (3rd sg. pr. indic. mid. √*īh*), he is eager for, he desires to obtain.
labhate (3rd sg. pr. indic. mid. √*labh*), he receives, he obtains.
ca, and.
tatas, from thence, from there.
kāmān (m. acc. pl.), desires, wishes.
mayā (inst. sg.), by me.
eva, indeed (used as a rhythmic filler).
vihitān (m. acc. pl. p. pass. participle *vi* √*dhā*), determined, ordained, decreed.
hi, indeed, truly.
tān (m. acc. pl.), them.

* All religions are subsumed here, and the speaking God explains that all worship, of whatever kind, goes to Him, and that all boons, begged from whatever gods, are granted by Him alone. The stanza is an instance of the strong monotheistic element in the Gītā, also of its religious tolerance.

23

अन्तवत् तु फलं तेषां
antavat tu phalaṁ teṣāṁ
temporary, but, the fruit for them

तद् भवत्य् अल्पमेधसाम् ।
tad bhavaty alpamedhasām
this it becomes, of the small in understanding,

देवान् देवयजो यान्ति
devān devayajo yānti
to the gods, the god-worshipping they go

मद्भक्ता यान्ति माम् अपि ॥
madbhaktā yānti mām api
the *me*-worshipping, they go to me surely.

But temporary this fruit becomes
For those of small understanding.
To the gods the god-worshipping go;
My worshippers go surely to Me.

antavat (n. nom. sg.), having an end, temporary, fleeting.
tu, but, indeed.
phalam (n. nom. sg.), fruit, result.
teṣām (gen. pl.), of them, for them.
tad (n. nom. sg.), this, that.
bhavati (3rd sg. pr. indic. √*bhū*), it is, it becomes.
alpamedhasām (m. gen. pl.), of the small in understanding, of those of little intelligence.
devān (m. acc. pl.), the gods, to the gods.
devayajas (m. nom. pl. from *deva* √*yaj*), the god worshipping, those who worship the gods.
yānti (3rd pl. pr. indic. act. √*yā*), they go, they attain.
madbhaktās (m. nom. pl.), "those worshipping me," those who worship me.
yānti (3rd pl. pr. indic. act. √*yā*), they go, they attain.
mām (acc. sg.), me, to me.
api, surely, indeed, even.

24

अव्यक्तं व्यक्तिम् आपन्नं
avyaktaṁ vyaktim āpannaṁ
(though) unmanifest, manifestation fallen into

मन्यन्ते माम अबुद्धयः।
manyante mām abuddhayaḥ
they think me, the unintelligent,

परं भावम् अजानन्तो
paraṁ bhāvam ajānanto
higher being not knowing

ममाव्ययम् अनुत्तमम् ॥
mamāvyayam anuttamam
of me imperishable, unsurpassed.

avyaktam (m. acc. sg. p. pass. participle *a vi* √*añj*), unmanifest, invisible, unapparent.
vyaktim (f. acc. sg.), manifestation, visibility.
āpannam (m. acc. sg. p. pass. participle *ā* √*pad*), fallen into, changed into, entered into.
manyante (3rd pl. pr. indic. mid. √*man*), they think, they imagine.
mām (acc. sg.), me.
abuddhayas (m. nom. pl.), the unintelligent, the stupid ones.
param (m. acc. sg.), higher, highest.
bhāvam (m. acc. sg.), being, existence.
ajānantas (m. nom. sg. pl. pr. participle *a* √*jñā*), not knowing, not being aware of.
mama (gen. sg.), of me, my.
avyayam (m. acc. sg.), imperishable, eternal.
anuttamam (m. acc. sg.), unsurpassed, incomparable.

Though I am unmanifest, the unintelligent
Think of Me as fallen into manifestation,
Not knowing My higher being
Which is imperishable and unsurpassed.*

* This stanza discusses idolatry, the worship of the God "fallen into manifestation," i.e. as a statue, or image, or as a human being, or even an animal or inanimate object.

25

नाहं प्रकाशः सर्वस्य
nāhaṁ prakāśaḥ sarvasya
not I manifest to all,

योगमायासमावृतः।
yogamāyāsamāvṛtaḥ
Yoga magic enveloped,

मूढो ऽयं नाभिजानाति
mūḍho 'yaṁ nābhijānāti
deluded, this not it recognizes,

लोको माम् अजम् अव्ययम् ॥
loko mām ajam avyayam
the world, me, unborn, imperishable.

I am not manifest to all,
Being enveloped in Yoga magic;
This deluded world does not recognize Me,
The Birthless and Imperishable.

na, not.
aham (nom. sg.), I.
prakāśas (m. nom. sg.), manifest, apparent, visible, shining.
sarvasya (m. gen. sg.), of all, to all.
yoga (m.), Yoga.
māyā (f.), power of illusion, magic.
samāvṛtas (m. nom. sg. p. pass. participle *sam a* √*vṛ*), enveloped, covered.
(*yoga-māyā-samāvṛtas*, m. nom. sg. TP cpd., covered by the illusion of my yoga.)
mūḍhas (m. nom. sg. p. pass. participle √*muh*), deluded, confused.
ayam (m. nom. sg.), this.
na, not.
abhijānāti (3rd sg. pr. indic. act. *abhi* √*jñā*), it recognizes, it perceives.
lokas (m. nom. sg.), world.
mām (acc. sg.), me.
ajam (m. acc. sg.), unborn, birthless.
avyayam (m. acc. sg. gerund *a vi* √*i*), imperishable, eternal, not passing away.

26

वेदाहं समतीतानि
vedāhaṁ samatītāni
I know, I, the departed

वर्तमानानि चार्जुन।
vartamānāni cārjuna
and the living, Arjuna

भविष्याणि च भूतानि
bhaviṣyāṇi ca bhūtāni
and the yet-to-be beings

मां तु वेद न कश्चन॥
māṁ tu veda na kaścana
me, but, he knows not anyone.

I know the departed beings
And the living, Arjuna,
And those who are yet to be;
But Me no one knows.

veda (1st sg. perfect act. √*vid* with present meaning), I know.
aham (nom. sg.), I.
samatītāni (n. acc. pl. participle *sam ati* √*i*), the departed, the passed beyond, the crossed over, the dead.
vartamānāni (n. acc. pl. pr. participle √*vṛt*), turning, moving, living, existing.
ca, and.
arjuna (m. voc. sg.), Arjuna.
bhaviṣyāṇi (n. acc. pl.), yet to be, about to become, future.
ca, and.
bhūtāni (n. acc. pl.), beings, creatures.
mām (acc. sg.), me.
tu, but, indeed.
veda (3rd sg. perfect. act. √*vid* with present meaning), he knows.
na, not.
kaścana, anyone, anyone whatever.

27

इच्छाद्वेषसमुत्थेन
icchādveṣasamutthena
by desire and hatred rising up

द्वन्द्वमोहेन भारत ।
dvandvamohena bhārata
by duality delusion, Descendant of Bharata,

सर्वभूतानि संमोहं
sarvabhūtāni saṁmohaṁ
all beings delusion

सर्गे यान्ति परंतप ॥
sarge yānti paraṁtapa
at birth they fall into, Scorcher of the Foe.

icchā (f.), desire.
dveṣa (m.), hatred, loathing, aversion, antipathy.
samutthena (m. inst. sg. from *sam ud* √*sthā*), by the rising up, by the coming forth.
(*icchā-dveṣa-samutthena*, m. instr. sg. TP cpd., by the arising of desire and hatred.)
dvandvamohena (m. inst. sg.), by the delusion of the dualities (desire-hatred, heat-cold, etc.).
bhārata (m. voc. sg.), Descendant of Bharata, epithet of Arjuna.
sarva-, all.
bhūtāni (n. nom. pl.), beings, creatures.
saṁmoham (n. acc. sg.), delusion, confusion.
sarge (m. loc. sg.), at creation, at birth.
yānti (3rd pl. pr. indic. act. √*yā*), they go, they go to, they fall into.
paraṁtapa (m. voc. sg.), Scorcher of the Foe, epithet of Arjuna.

Because of the coming forth of desire and hatred,
Because of the deluding (power) of the opposites, Descendant of Bharata,
All beings fall into delusion
At birth, Scorcher of the Foe.

28

येषां त्व् अन्तगतं पापं
yeṣāṁ tv antagataṁ pāpaṁ
of whom, but, come-to-an-end evil,

जनानां पुण्यकर्मणाम् ।
janānāṁ puṇyakarmaṇām
of men whose actions are pure,

ते द्वन्द्वमोहनिर्मुक्ता
te dvandvamohanirmuktā
they, duality delusion liberated from,

भजन्ते मां दृढव्रताः ॥
bhajante māṁ dṛḍhavratāḥ
they worship me (with) firm vows.

But those in whom evil has come to an end,
Those men whose actions are pure;
They, liberated from the deluding power of the opposites,
Worship Me with firm vows.

yeṣām (m. gen. pl.), of whom.
tu, but.
antagatam (m. acc. sg. p. pass. participle *anta* √*gam*), gone to an end, come to an end, "end gone."
pāpam (m. acc. sg.), evil, sin, wrong.
janānām (m. gen. pl.), of men.
puṇyakarmaṇām (n. gen. pl.), of those of pure actions, of those of righteous acts, of those of good deeds, (as BV cpd.) of those whose actions are pure.
te (m. nom. pl.), they.
dvandva (n.), duality, polarity.
moha (m.), delusion, confusion.
nirmuktās (m. nom. pl. p. pass. participle *nir* √*muc*), liberated from, freed from.
(*dvandva-moha-nirmuktās,* m. nom. pl. TP cpd., liberated from duality and delusion.)
bhajante (3rd pl. pr. indic. mid. √*bhaj*), they worship, they honor.
mām (acc. sg.), me.
dṛḍha (m.), firm, solid, stable.
vratās (m. nom. pl.), vows, commands, ordinances.
(*dṛḍhavratās,* m. nom. pl. BV cpd., whose vows are firm.)

29

जरामरणमोक्षाय
jarāmaraṇamokṣāya
toward old age and dying release from

माम् आश्रित्य यतन्ति ये ।
mām āśritya yatanti ye
me depending on, they strive, who

ते ब्रह्म तद् विदुः कृत्स्नम्
te brahma tad viduḥ kṛtsnam
they Brahman this they know entirely

अध्यात्मं कर्म चाखिलम् ॥
adhyātmaṁ karma cākhilam
the Supreme Self and action without gap.

Those who strive toward release from
Old age and death, depending on Me,
Know this Brahman thoroughly
As well as the Adhyātman and all action.

jarā (f.), old age.
maraṇa (n.), dying.
mokṣāya (m. dat. sg.), toward release, to liberation.
(*jarāmaraṇamokṣāya,* m. dat. sg. TP cpd., toward release from old age and dying.)
mām (acc. sg.), me.
āśritya (gerund *ā* √*śri*), depending on, taking refuge in, resorting to.
yatanti (3rd pl. pr. indic. act. √*yat*), they strive, they stretch.
ye (m. nom. pl.), who.
te (m. nom. pl.), they.
brahma (n. acc. sg.), Brahman.
tad (n. acc. sg.), this, that.
vidus (3rd pl. perfect act. √*vid* with present meaning), they know.
kṛtsnam (adv.), entirely, wholly.
adhyātmam (m. acc. sg.), the Supreme Self, the Adhyātman.
karma (n. acc. sg.), action, deeds.
ca, and.
akhilam (adv.), without a gap, completely.

30

साधिभूताधिदैवं मां
sādhibhūtādhidāivaṁ māṁ
along with the adhibhūta,* and the adhidāiva,* me

साधियज्ञं च ये विदुः ।
sādhiyajñaṁ ca ye viduḥ
and along with the chief sacrifice, who they know

प्रयाणकालेऽपि च मां
prayāṇakāle 'pi ca māṁ
and at departure time even me

ते विदुर् युक्तचेतसः ।।
te vidur yuktacetasaḥ
they know, with steadfast thought.

They who know Me as the Adhibhūta* and the Adhidāiva,*
As well as the Chief of Sacrifice,
And know Me even at the hour of death,
They truly know Me with steadfast thought.

sa- (prefix), with, along with.
adhibhūta (m.), Supreme Being.
adhidāivam (m. acc. sg.), Supreme God.
mām (acc. sg.), me.
sa- (prefix), with, along with.
adhiyajñam (m. acc. sg.), Chief Sacrifice, Lord of Sacrifice, Basis of Sacrifice.
ca, and.
ye (m. nom. pl.), who.
vidus (3rd pl. perfect act. √*vid* with present meaning), they know.
prayāṇakāle (m. loc. sg.), at the time of departure, at the time of death, at the hour of death.
api, even, also.
ca, and.
mām (acc. sg.), me.
te (m. nom. pl.), they.
vidus (3rd pl. perfect act. √*vid* with present meaning), they know.
yuktacetasas (m. nom. pl. BV cpd.), those whose thought is steadfast, having steadfast thought.

End of Book VII

The Yoga of Knowledge and Discrimination

* *adhibhūta* (supreme being) and *adhidāiva* (supreme god) are sometimes translated as "the penetrating influence of the Supreme Spirit" and "the divine agent operating on material objects" respectively. The two terms are further explained in the following chapter.

BOOK VIII

अर्जुन उवाच ।
arjuna uvāca
Arjuna spoke:

arjunas (m. nom. sg.), Arjuna.
uvāca (3rd sg. perfect act. √*vac*), he said, he spoke.

1

किं तद् ब्रह्म किम् अध्यात्मं
kiṁ tad brahma kim adhyātmaṁ
what this Brahman, what the adhyātma?

किं कर्म पुरुषोत्तम ।
kiṁ karma puruṣottama
what action? highest among spirits.

अधिभूतं च किं प्रोक्तम्
adhibhūtaṁ ca kiṁ proktam
and adhibūta what declared to be?

अधिदैवं किम् उच्यते ॥
adhidāivaṁ kim ucyate
and adhidāiva what it is said to be?

kim (interrog. n. nom. sg.), what?
tat (n. nom. sg.), this, that.
brahma (n. nom. sg.), Brahman.
kim (interrog. n. nom. sg.), what?
adhyātmam (n. nom. sg.), Supreme Self, aggregate of elements of the individual self.
kim (interrog. n. nom. sg.), what?
karma (n. nom. sg.), action.
puruṣottama (m. voc. sg.), Highest among Men, Highest among Spirits, here applied to Krishna.
adhibhūtam (n. nom. sg.), Supreme Being, aggregate of physical elements.
ca, and.
kim (interrog. n. nom. sg.), what?
proktam (n. nom. sg. participle *pra* √*vac*), declared, declared to be, said to be.
adhidāivam (n. nom. sg.), Supreme God.
kim (ingerrog. n. nom. sg.), what?
ucyate (3rd sg. pr. passive √*vac*), it is said, it is said to be.

Arjuna spoke:

What is this Brahman? what is the Adhyātma?
What is action, O Highest among Spirits?
And the Adhibhūta, what is it declared to be?
And the Adhidāiva, what is it said to be?

2

अधियज्ञः कथं को ऽत्र
adhiyajñaḥ kathaṁ ko 'tra
the Adhiyajña in what manner, what? here

देहे ऽस्मिन् मधुसूदन ।
dehe 'smin madhusūdana
in the body, in this, O Slayer of Madhu

प्रयाणकाले च कथं
prayāṇakāle ca kathaṁ
and at time of death; how?

ज्ञेयो ऽसि नियतात्मभिः ॥
jñeyo 'si niyatātmabhiḥ
to be known thou art by the controlled selves

In what manner, and what, is the Adhiyajña
Here in this body, O Slayer of Madhu?
And how at the hour of death
Art Thou to be known by those whose selves are controlled?

adhiyajñas (m. nom. sg.), Chief Sacrifice, Lord of Sacrifice, Basis of Sacrifice.
katham (interrog.), how? in what manner?
kas (m. nom. sg. interrog.), who, what?
atra, here, in this case, in this instance.
dehe (n. loc. sg.), in the body.
asmin (n. loc. sg.), in this.
madhusūdana (m. voc. sg.), Slayer of Madhu, epithet of Krishna-Vishnu referring to his killing of the demon Madhu.
prayāṇakāle (m. loc. sg.), at the time of death, at the hour of death, at the time of departure.
ca, and.
katham (interrog.), how? in what way?
jñeyas (m. nom. sg. gerundive √*jñā*), to be known.
asi (2nd sg. pr. indic. √*as*), thou art.
niyata (m. p. pass. participle *ni* √*yam*), controlled, subdued.
ātmabhis (m. inst. pl.), by selves.
(*niyatātmabhis,* m. inst. pl. BV cpd., by those whose selves are controlled.)

VIII

श्रीभगवान् उवाच ।
śrībhagavān uvāca
the Blessed Lord spoke:

śrībhagavān (m. nom. sg.), the Blessed Lord, the Blessed One.
uvāca (3rd sg. perfect act. √*vac*), he said, he spoke.

3

अक्षरं ब्रह्म परमं
akṣaraṁ brahma paramaṁ
imperishable Brahman supreme;

स्वभावो ऽध्यात्मम् उच्यते ।
svabhāvo 'dhyātmam ucyate
inherent nature the adhyātman it is said,

भूतभावोद्भवकरो
bhūtabhāvodbhavakaro
which originates the being of creatures;

विसर्गः कर्मसंज्ञितः ॥
visargaḥ karmasaṁjñitaḥ
creative power, action known as.

The Blessed Lord spoke:

Brahman is the Supreme Imperishable;
The Adhyātma is said to be the inherent nature of the individual,
Which originates the being of creatures;
Action is known as the creative power (of the individual, which causes him to be reborn in this or that condition of being).*

akṣaram (n. nom. sg.), imperishable, eternal.
brahma (n. nom. sg.), Brahman.
paramam (n. nom. sg.), supreme, highest.
svabhāvas (m. nom. sg.), own nature, inherent nature.
adhyātmam (n. nom. sg.), Supreme Self, aggregation of elements of the individual personality.
ucyate (3rd sg. pr. indic. passive √*vac*), it is said, it is called.
bhūtabhāva (m.), state of being.
udbhava (m.), origin, existence, production.
karas (m. nom. sg.), making, causing, doing.
(*bhūtabhāvodbhavakaras,* m. nom. sg. TP cpd., which originates the being of creatures.)
visargas (m. nom. sg.), creative power, sending forth, discharging.
karma (n. nom. sg.), action.
saṁjñitas (n. nom. sg. from *samjñā*), known as, understood to be, called.

* But Rāmānuja says: "*Karman* (action) is the procreative act connected with a woman which causes a human being, etc., to originate. An aspirant to *kāivālya* (complete detachment of the *ātman* from material nature) should know that all this, and all that is connected with it, is to be feared and avoided." The point is debatable. *Karma* has many meanings.

4

अधिभूतं क्षरो भावः
adhibhūtaṁ kṣaro bhāvaḥ
the adhibhūta perishable existence

पुरुषश्चाधिदैवतम् ।
puruṣaścādhidāivatam
and the Spirit (is the) Supreme Divine Agent

अधियज्ञो ऽहम् एवात्र
adhiyajño 'ham evātra
the adhiyajña I here

देहे देहभृतां वर ॥
dehe dehabhṛtāṁ vara
in the body, O Best of the Embodied.

adhibhūtam (n. nom. sg.), aggregate of physical elements.
kṣaras (m. nom. sg. noun from √*kṣar*), perishable, destructible.
bhāvas (m. nom. sg.), existence, being.
puruṣa (m. nom. sg.), spirit, man, soul.
ca, and.
adhidāivatam (n. nom. sg.), Supreme, Divine agent.
adhiyajñas (m. nom. sg.), Chief of Sacrifice, Basis of Sacrifice, Lord of Sacrifice.
aham (nom. sg.), I.
eva, indeed (used as a rhythmic filler).
atra, here, in this case.
dehe (n. loc. sg.), in the body.
dehabhṛtām vara (m. voc. sg.), O Chosen of the Embodied, O Best of the Embodied, applied to Arjuna.

The Adhibhūta is the perishable nature of being (or the sphere of the Supreme Spirit in acting on the individual, i.e. nature)*
The Adhidāivata is the Supreme Divine Agent itself (the puruṣa)
The Adhiyajña (Basis, or Lord of Sacrifice) is Myself,
Here in this body, O Best of the Embodied.

* All the terms here are technical and sometimes puzzling. Edgerton regards the language of these stanzas as grandiloquent. But native commentators take it very seriously, and some of their definiions are included here.

Rāmānuja identifies the *Adhyātman* with *svabhāva* (inherent disposition) or *prakṛti* (material nature) – "that which is not the self, but is conjoined with the self." The *Adhibhūta*, according to him, is "the transitoriness of the elements, ether, etc., of which elements sound, touch, etc., are developments." The *Adhidāivata* "connotes the *puruṣa*; it means 'being beyond the pantheon of Indra, Prajāpati, etc.' The *Adhiyajña* is God – He who is to be propitiated by sacrifice."

5

अन्तकाले च माम् एव
antakāle ca mām eva
and at the end-time me

स्मरन् मुक्त्वा कलेवरम् ।
smaran muktvā kalevaram
remembering, having relinquished the body,

यः प्रयाति स मद्भावं
yaḥ prayāti sa madbhāvaṁ
who dies, he to my state of being

याति नास्त्य् अत्र संशयः ॥
yāti nāsty atra saṁśayaḥ
he goes, not there is in this case doubt.

And at the hour of death, remembering Me,
Having relinquished the body,
He who dies goes to My state of being.
In this matter there is no doubt.

antakāle (m. loc. sg.), at the time of departure, at the hour of death, lit. "at end time."
ca, and.
mām (acc. sg.), me.
eva, indeed (used as a rhythmic filler).
smaran (pr. act. participle √*smṛ*), remembering, thinking on, thinking of.
muktvā (gerund √*muc*), relinquishing, having relinquished, having been liberated from.
kalevaram (m. acc. sg.), body, cadaver.
yas (m. nom. sg.), who, which.
prayāti (3rd sg. pr. indic. act. *pra* √*yā*), he departs, he dies.
sas (m. nom. sg.), he, this.
madbhāvam (m. acc. sg.), my state of being, to my state of being, to my being.
yāti (3rd sg. pr. indic. act. √*yā*), he goes, he attains.
na, not.
asti (3rd sg. pr. indic. √*as*), it is, he is, there is.
atra, here, in this case, in this instance.
saṁśayas (m. nom. sg.), doubt, question, irresolution.

6

यं यं वापि स्मरन् भावं
yaṁ yaṁ vāpi smaran bhāvaṁ
whatever, moreover, remembering, state of being

त्यजत्य् अन्ते कलेवरम् ।
tyajaty ante kalevaram
(when) he gives up at the end the body,

तं तं एवैति कौन्तेय
taṁ ṭaṁ evāiti kāunteya
to respectively that he goes, O Son of Kuntī (Arjuna)

सदा तद्भावभावितः ॥
sadā tadbhāvabhāvitaḥ
always that state of being caused to become.

Moreover whatever state of being he remembers
When he gives up the body at the end,
He goes respectively to that state of being, Son of Kuntī,
Always transformed into that state of being.

yam yam (m. acc. sg.), whatever.
vā api, moreover, or also.
smaran (m. nom. sg. pr. act. participle √*smṛ*), remembering, thinking of.
bhāvam (m. acc. sg.), state of being, being.
tyajati (3rd sg. pr. indic. act. √*tyaj*), he abandons, he gives up.
ante (m. loc. sg.), in the end, at the end.
kalevaram (m. acc. sg.), body, physical body.
tam tam (repetition indicates distribution, m. acc. sg.), to that, respectively that.
eva, indeed (used as a rhythmic filler).
eti (3rd sg. pr. indic. act. √*i*), he goes, he attains.
kāunteya (m. voc. sg.), O Son of Kuntī, epithet of Arjuna.
sadā, always, invariably.
tad (n. nom. sg.), that, this.
bhāva (m.), state of being, being.
bhāvitas (m. nom. sg. causative participle √*bhū*), transformed into, caused to become.
(*bhāva-bhāvitas*, m. nom. sg. TP cpd., transformed into that state of being.)

7

तस्मात् सर्वेषु कालेषु
tasmāt sarveṣu kāleṣu
therefore at all times

माम् अनुस्मर युद्य च ।
mām anusmara yudhya ca
me remember, and fight

मय्य् अर्पितमनोबुद्धिर्
mayy arpitamanobuddhir
on me fixed mind and intelligence

माम् एवैष्यस्य् असंशयम् ॥
mām evāiṣyasy asaṁśayam
to me thus thou shalt come, without doubt.

tasmāt (abl. sg.), from this, therefore.
sarveṣu (m. loc. pl.), in all, at all.
kāleṣu (m. loc. pl.), in times, at times.
mām (acc. sg.), me.
anusmara (2nd sg. imperative act. *anu* √*smṛ*), remember! think of!
yudhya (2nd sg. imperative act. √*yudh*), fight!
ca, and.
mayi (m. loc. sg.), on me, in me.
arpita (m.), fixed, placed, entrusted.
manobuddhis (f. nom. sg.), mind and intelligence.
(*arpitamanobuddhis,* m. nom. sg. BV cpd., having mind and intelligence fixed.)
mām (acc. sg.), me, to me.
eva, indeed (used as a rhythmic filler).
eṣyasi (2nd sg. future act. √*i*), thou shalt come, thou shalt attain.
asaṁśayam (adv.), without doubt, surely.

Therefore, at all times
Meditate on Me, and fight,
Thy mind and intelligence fixed on Me.
In this way, thou shalt surely come to Me.

8

अभ्यासयोगयुक्तेन
abhyāsayogayuktena
by the practice of Yoga disciplined,

चेतसा नान्यगामिना ।
cetasā nānyagāminā
by thought, by no other going toward,

परमं पुरुषं दिव्यं
paramaṁ puruṣaṁ divyaṁ
to the Supreme Spirit divine

याति पार्थानुचिन्तयन् ॥
yāti pārthānucintayan
one goes, Son of Pṛthā, meditating (on him).

With a mind disciplined by the practice of Yoga,
Which does not turn to anything else,
To the divine Supreme Spirit
One goes, Son of Pṛthā, meditating on Him.*

abhyāsa (m. from *abhi* √2 *as*), practice, performance.
yoga (m.), Yoga.
yuktena (m. inst. sg.), by one who is disciplined.
(*abhyāsayogayuktena,* m. inst. sg. TP cpd., disciplined by the practice of Yoga.)
cetasā (n. inst. sg.), by thought, by mind.
na, not.
anya, other.
gāminā (m. inst. sg.), by going toward, by going.
(*nānyagāminā,* m. inst. sg. TP cpd., which does not turn to anything else.)
paramam (m. acc. sg.), to the Supreme, the Highest.
puruṣam (m. acc. sg.), Spirit, Soul, Person.
(*paramam puruṣam,* m. acc. sg., the Supreme Spirit, to the Supreme Spirit.)
divyam (m. acc. sg.), divine, heavenly.
yāti (3rd sg. pr. indic. act. √*yā*), he, she, it, one goes.
pārtha (m. voc. sg.), Son of Pṛthā, epithet of Arjuna.
anucintayan (m. nom. sg. pr. act. causative participle *anu* √*cint*), meditating, thinking of.

* According to Rāmānuja's commentary, stanzas 8, 9 and 10 refer to the *āiśvaryārthin* (He who aims at superhuman power), who sees God in terms of God's power, and who "remains fixed on God as the result of daily practice of Yoga." He is the "desirous of knowledge" of VII 16, where he is referred to as the *jijñāsu.*

9

कविं पुराणम् अनुशासितारम्
*kaviṁ purāṇam anuśāsitāram**
the poet, the ancient, the ruler

अणोर् अणीयांसम् अनुस्मरेद् यः ।
aṇor aṇīyāṁsam anusmared yaḥ
than the atom subtler, he should meditate on, who

सर्वस्य धातारम् अचिन्त्यरूपम्
sarvasya dhātāram acintyarūpam
of all supporter, the unthinkable form,

आदित्यवर्णं तमसः परस्तात् ॥
ādityavarṇaṁ tamasaḥ parastāt
the color of the sun, from darkness beyond,

He who meditates on the ancient seer,
The ruler, smaller than the atom,
Who is the supporter of all, whose form is unthinkable,
And who is the color of the sun, beyond darkness†

kavim (m. acc. sg.), the poet, the seer. (N.B. Much Sanskrit religious thought was expressed in poetry, hence the poet was its chronicler or expositor.)
purāṇam (m. acc. sg.), ancient, former, previous.
anuśāsitāram (m. acc. sg. noun from *anu* √*śās*), ruler, governor, censor, punisher, controller, chastiser.
aṇos (m. abl. sg.), from the atom, than the atom.
aṇīyāṁsam (m. acc. sg. comparative), more minute, smaller, subtler.
anusmaret (3rd sg. optative act. *anu* √*smṛ*), he should meditate on, he should call to mind.
yas (m. nom. sg.), who.
sarvasya (m. gen. sg.), of all.
dhātāram (m. acc. sg.), the supporter, the one who places or puts.
acintya (n.), unthinkable, unimaginable.
rūpam (n. acc. sg.), form, shape, entity.
(*acintyarūpam*, n. acc. sg. BV cpd., whose form is unthinkable.)
āditya (m.), the sun.
varṇam (m. acc. sg.), color, caste.
(*ādityavarṇam*, m. acc. sg. BV cpd., whose color is that of the sun.)
tamasas (n. abl. sg.), than darkness.
parastāt (n. abl. sg.), beyond, further.

* *Triṣṭubh* metre.

† "He will attain the *āiśvarya* (power) which God himself possesses, when he has concentrated his *prāṇa* (vital breath) between the brows and then, in virtue of his daily practiced worship, with his mind unwavering because all *saṁskāras* (preparatory reformations of the mind) have been passed, represents God to himself as the omniscient, primaeval Lord of the universe, the creator of all, subtler than the *jīva* (monad of the life principle), whose proper form is of another order than everything else and who is possessed of a divine form peculiar to none but Him." – Rāmānuja.

10

प्रयाणकाले मनसाचलेन
*prayāṇakāle manasācalena**
at departure time with mind unmoving

भक्त्या युक्तो योगबलेन चैव ।
bhaktyā yukto yogabalena cāiva
with devotion yoked and with Yoga power

भ्रुवोर् मध्ये प्राणम् आवेश्य सम्यक्
bhruvor madhye prāṇam āveśya samyak
of the two eyebrows in the middle, the vital breath entering correctly,

स तं परं पुरुषम् उपैति दिव्यम् ॥
sa taṁ paraṁ puruṣam upāiti divyam
he this Supreme Spirit approaches, divine.

At the hour of death, with unmoving mind,
With devotion yoked and with Yoga power,
Having made the vital breath enter correctly between the two eyebrows,†
He approaches this divine Supreme Spirit.

prayāṇakāle (m. loc. sg.), at departure, at the time of death.
manasā (n. inst. sg.), by mind, with mind.
acalena (n. inst. sg.), by unmoving, motionless.
bhaktyā (f. inst. sg.), with devotion, with worship, with love.
yuktas (m. nom. sg. p. pass. participle √*yuj*), united, held, joined, yoked.
yogabalena (m. inst. sg.), with Yoga power, with the strength of Yoga.
ca, and.
eva, indeed (used as a rhythmic filler).
bhruvos (f. gen. dual), of the two eyebrows.
madhye (m. loc. sg.), in the middle.
prāṇam (m. acc. sg.), the vital breath.
āveśya (causative gerund *ā* √*viś*), having caused to enter.
samyak (adv.), directly, united, in one direction, correctly, properly.
sas (m. nom. sg.), he, this.
tam (m. acc. sg.), him, this.
param (m. acc. sg.), Highest, Supreme.
puruṣam (m. acc. sg.), Spirit, Soul.
upāiti (3rd sg. pr. indic. act. *upa* √*i*), he approaches, he goes to.
divyam (m. acc. sg.), divine, heavenly.

* *Triṣṭubh* metre continues. The last line is one syllable too long.

† As in several such Yoga techniques, the anatomical elements are vague to the non-yogin.

11

यद् अक्षरं वेदविदो वदन्ति
*yad akṣaraṁ vedavido vadanti**
which the imperishable the Veda-knowing they call,

विशन्ति यद् यतयो वीतरागाः ।
viśanti yad yatayo vītarāgāḥ
they enter which the ascetics, the free from passion,

यद् इच्छन्तो ब्रह्मचर्यं चरन्ति
yad icchanto brahmacaryaṁ caranti
which desiring, a life of chastity they follow,

तत् ते पदं संग्रहेण प्रवक्ष्ये ।।
tat te padaṁ saṁgraheṇa pravakṣye
that to thee path in brief I shall declare.

That which the Veda-knowing call the Imperishable,
Which the ascetics, free from passion, enter,
Desiring which they follow a life of chastity,
That path I shall explain to thee briefly.

yad (n. nom. sg.), which.
akṣaram (n. acc. sg.), imperishable, eternal.
vedavidas (m. nom. pl.), the Veda-knowing, those versed in the Vedas.
vadanti (3rd pl. pr. indic. act. √*vad*), they say, they call, they say to be.
viśanti (3rd pl. pr. indic. act. √*viś*), they enter, they go into, they pervade.
yad (n. nom. sg.), which.
yatayas (m. nom. pl.), the ascetics, the strivers, the performers of austerities.
vītarāgās (m. nom. pl.), free from passion, free from lust, free from desire.
yad (n. nom. sg.), which.
icchantas (m. nom. pl. pr. act. participle √*iṣ*), desiring, wishing for.
brahmacaryam (n. acc. sg.), life of chastity, life of a Brahmacārin.
caranti (3rd pl. pr. indic. act. √*car*), they move, they follow.
tad (n. acc. sg.), this, that.
te (dat. sg.), to thee.
padam (n. acc. sg.), path, step.
saṁgraheṇa (m. inst. sg. or adv.), briefly, in brief.
pravakṣye (1st sg. future *pra* √*vac*), I shall declare, I shall speak of, I shall explain.

* *Triṣṭubh* metre continues.

12

सर्वद्वाराणि संयम्य
*sarvadvārāṇi saṁyamya**
all the gates (of the body) controlling,

मनो हृदि निरुध्य च।
mano hṛdi nirudhya ca
and the mind in the heart shutting up,

मूर्ध्न्य् आधायात्मनः प्राणम्
mūrdhny ādhāyātmanaḥ prāṇam
in the head having placed own vital breath,

आस्थितो योगधारणाम् ॥
āsthito yogadhāraṇām
established in Yoga concentration,

sarvā-, all.
dvārāṇi (n. acc. pl.), gates, doors, gates of the body.
saṁyamya (gerund *sam* √*yam*), controlling.
manas (n. acc. sg.), mind.
hṛdi (n. loc. sg.), in the heart.
nirudhya (gerund *ni* √*rudh*), shutting up, confining, suppressing.
ca, and.
mūrdhni (n. loc. sg.), in the head.
ādhāya (gerund *ā* √*dhā*), placing, having placed.
ātmanas (m. gen. sg.), of the self, own.
prāṇam (m. acc. sg.), vital breath, inhalation.
āsthitas (m. nom. sg.), established, seated, situated in.
yogadhāraṇām (f. acc. sg.), Yoga concentration, Yoga fixation.

Controlling all the gates of the body,†
And shutting up the mind in the heart,
Having placed the vital breath in the head,
Established in Yoga concentration,

* *Śloka* metre resumes.

† Gates of the body, nine in number, viz. the two eyes, two nostrils, two ears, mouth, organ of generation, organ of excretion.

13

ओम् इत्य् एकाक्षरं ब्रह्म
om ity ekākṣaraṁ brahma
"Om" thus, the single-syllabled Brahman

व्याहरन् माम् अनुस्मरन् ।
vyāharan mām anusmaran
uttering, me meditating on,

यः प्रयाति त्यजन् देहं
yaḥ prayāti tyajan dehaṁ
who he goes forth, renouncing the body,

स याति परमां गतिम् ॥
sa yāti paramāṁ gatim
he goes to the highest goal.

"Om," thus uttering the single-syllable Brahman,
Meditating on Me,
He who goes forth, renouncing the body,
Goes to the Supreme Goal.*

om, the sacred syllable, said to embrace all the secrets of the universe.
iti, thus.
ekākṣaram (n. acc. sg.), one syllabled, single syllabled.
brahma (n. acc. sg.), Brahman.
vyāharan (pr. act. participle *vi ā* √*hṛ*), uttering, pronouncing, speaking.
mām (acc. sg.), me.
anusmaran (m. nom. sg. pr. act. participle *anu* √*smṛ*), meditating on, thinking about, remembering.
yas (m. nom. sg.), who.
prayāti (3rd sg. pr. indic. act. *pra* √*yā*), he goes forth, he dies.
tyajan (m. nom. sg. pr. participle act. √*tyaj*), renouncing, abandoning.
deham (m./n. acc. sg.), body.
sas (m. nom. sg.), he, this one.
yāti (3rd sg. pr. indic. act. √*yā*), he goes, he attains.
paramām (f. acc. sg.), to the highest, to the supreme.
gatim (f. acc. sg.), goal, path.

* According to Rāmānuja's commentary, stanzas 12 and 13 refer to the *kāivalyārthin* (seeker of complete detachment) who seeks the complete severance of the *ātman* from the body, and worships God as the *akṣara*, or indestructible, eternal essence (*Brahman*). He is mentioned in VII 16, as the *arthārthin*, or seeker of knowledge of the *ātman* as different from *prakṛti*, or material nature. This is the "Highest Truth" of VII 16.

14

अनन्यचेताः सततं
ananyacetāḥ satataṁ
whose mind does not go elsewhere, ever,

यो मां स्मरति नित्यशः ।
yo māṁ smarati nityaśaḥ
who me he thinks of constantly,

तस्याहं सुलभः पार्थ
tasyāhaṁ sulabhaḥ pārtha
for him I easy to reach, Son of Pṛthā,

नित्ययुक्तस्य योगिनः ॥
nityayuktasya yoginaḥ
for the constantly yoked yogin.

ananyacetās (m. nom. sg. BV cpd.), whose mind does not go elsewhere.
satatam (adv.), perpetually, ever.
yas (m. nom. sg.), who.
mām (acc. sg.), me.
smarati (3rd sg. pr. indic. act. √*smṛ*), he thinks of, he remembers.
nityaśas (adv.), constantly, always.
tasya (m. gen. sg.), of him, for him.
aham (nom. sg.), I.
sulabhas (m. nom. sg.), easy to reach, easy to attain.
pārtha (m. voc. sg.), Son of Pṛthā, epithet of Arjuna.
nityayuktasya (m. gen. sg.), of the constantly disciplined, of the eternally yoked in Yoga, (as BV cpd.) of him who is constantly yoked.
yoginas (m. gen. sg.), of the yogin, for the yogin.

He who thinks of Me constantly,
Whose mind does not go elsewhere, ever,
For him, the yogin who is constantly yoked,
I am easy to reach, Son of Pṛthā.*

* According to Rāmānuja's commentary, this and stanzas 15 and 16 are devoted to the *jñānin* of VII 16, the "man of wisdom," who is never without direct concentration on God, "his mind focussed on God alone because God is incomparably dear to him, and because he cannot sustain his *ātman* without representing God (to himself).... And God himself, unable to endure separation from his worshipper, will choose him." According to the same source, the *āiśvaryārthin* (stanza 8 *et seq.*) is reborn. But the *kāivalyārthin* (stanzas 12 and 13) and the *jñānin*, described in this and the following stanzas, are not reborn, but go to union with Brahman, or God.

15

माम् उपेत्य पुनर्जन्म
mām upetya punarjanma
me approaching, rebirth

दुःखालयम् अशाश्वतम् ।
duḥkhālayam aśāśvatam
misfortune home, impermanent,

नाप्नुवन्ति महात्मानः
nāpnuvanti mahātmānaḥ
not they incur, the great selves,

संसिद्धिं परमां गताः ॥
saṁsiddhiṁ paramāṁ gatāḥ
to perfection the highest gone.

Approaching Me, those whose selves are great,
Who have gone to supreme perfection,
Do not incur rebirth,
That impermanent home of misfortune.

mām (acc. sg.), me, to me.
upetya (gerund *upa* √*i*), approaching, coming near to.
punarjanma (n. acc. sg.), "again birth," rebirth.
duḥkha (n.), misfortune, misery, unhappiness.
ālayam (m. acc. sg.), home, abode.
(*duḥkha-ālayam*, m. acc. sg. TP cpd., home of misery.)
aśāśvatam (m. acc. sg.), impermanent, inconstant.
na, not.
āpnuvanti (3rd pl. pr. indic. act. *āp*), they incur, they attain, they reach.
mahātmānas (m. nom. pl.), great selves, great souls, (as pl. BV cpd.) those whose selves are great.
saṁsiddhim (f. acc. sg.), perfection, to perfection, to accomplishment, to success.
paramām (f. acc. sg.), highest, supreme.
gatās (m. nom. pl. p. pass. participle √*gam*), gone.

16

श्रा ब्रह्मभुवनाल् लोका:
ā brahmabhuvanāl lokāḥ
up to Brahman's realm of being, the worlds

पुनरावर्तिनो ऽर्जुन।
punarāvartino 'rjuna
subject to again return, Arjuna,

माम् उपेत्य तु कौन्तेय
mām upetya tu kāunteya
me approaching, but, Son of Kuntī,

पुनर्जन्म न विद्यते ॥
punarjanma na vidyate
rebirth not it is found.

Up to Brahman's realm of being,
The worlds are subject to successive rebirths, Arjuna;
But, in approaching Me, Son of Kuntī,
Rebirth is not found.

ā, to, up to.
brahmabhuvanāt (n. abl. sg.), to Brahman's world, to Brahman's realm of being.
lokās (m. nom. pl.), worlds, peoples.
punarāvartinas (m. nom. pl.), return to successive births, rebirths.
arjuna (m. voc. sg.), Arjuna.
mām (acc. sg.), me.
upetya (gerund *upa* $\sqrt{i}$), approaching, coming near to.
tu, but.
kāunteya (m. voc. sg.), Son of Kuntī, epithet of Arjuna.
punarjanma (n. nom. sg.), "again birth," rebirth.
na, not.
vidyate (3rd sg. pr. indic. passive $\sqrt{2}$ *vid*), it is found.

17

सहस्रयुगपर्यन्तम्
sahasrayugaparyantam
a thousand yugas* extending as far as,

अहर् यद् ब्रह्मणो विदुः ।
ahar yad brahmaṇo viduḥ
the day which of Brahmā, they know

रात्रिं युगसहस्रान्तां
rātriṁ yugasahasrāntāṁ
the night a thousand yugas ending

ते ऽहोरात्रविदो जनाः ।।
te 'horātravido janāḥ
they the day and night knowing men.

They who know that the day of Brahmā
Extends as far as a thousand yugas,*
And that the night of Brahmā ends only in a thousand yugas;
They are the day- and night-knowing men.

sahasra (n.), a thousand.
yuga (n), age, yuga.*
paryantam (m. acc. sg.), extending as far as, border, limit, end, extremity.
(*sahasra-yuga-paryantam*, m. acc. sg. TP cpd., extending as far as a thousand yugas.)
ahar (n. acc. sg.), day.
yad (n. acc. sg.), which.
brahmaṇas (n. gen. sg.), of Brahmā.
vidus (3rd pl. perfect act. √*vid* with present meaning), they know.
rātrim (f. acc. sg.), night.
yuga (n.), age, yuga.*
sahasra (n.), a thousand.
antām (f. acc. sg.), end, ending.
(*yuga-sahasra-antām*, f. acc. sg. TP cpd., ending in a thousand yugas.)
te (m. nom. pl.), they.
ahorātravidas (m. nom. pl.), day and night knowing, those who know day and night.
janās (m. nom. pl.), men.

---

* *yuga*, an "age" of the world, which is a division of a *mahāyuga*, or period of 4,320,000 years. There are four *yugas*: the *kṛtayuga*, or golden age, which lasts for 1,728,000 years and is named for the side of the die marked with four dots. The *tretā yuga*, which lasts for 1,296,000 years, which is less virtuous and is named for the side of the die with three dots; the *dvāpara yuga*, which lasts for 864,000 years, represents a growing predominance of evil over good and is named for the side of the die marked with two dots; and the *kali yuga*, or dark age, which lasts for 432,000 years, is a period of predominant evil and is named for the side of the die marked with a single dot. It takes a thousand *mahāyugas*, or 4,320,000,000 years, to make a *kalpa*, or one day of Brahmā, an equal number to make one night of Brahmā. We are, as this volume goes to press, in the 5,079th year of a *kali yuga* that began on February 18, 3102 B.C.

18

अव्यक्ताद् व्यक्तयः सर्वाः
avyaktād vyaktayaḥ sarvāḥ
from the unmanifest the manifestations all

प्रभवन्त्य् अहरागमे ।
prabhavanty aharāgame
they come forth at the arrival of the day (of Brahmā);

रात्र्यागमे प्रलीयन्ते
rātryāgame pralīyante
at the arrival of (Brahmā's) night, they are dissolved,

तत्रैवाव्यक्तसंज्ञके ।।
tatrāivāvyaktasaṁjñake
there the unmanifest known as.

From the unmanifest, all manifestations
Come forth at the arrival of (Brahmā's) day;
At the arrival of (Brahmā's) night, they are dissolved,
At that point to be known as the unmanifest again.

avyaktāt (m. abl. sg.), from the unmanifest, from the invisible.
vyaktayas (f. nom. pl.), manifestations, appearances.
sarvās (f. nom. pl.), all.
prabhavanti (3rd pl. pr. indic. act. *pra* √*bhū*), they come forth, they originate.
aharāgame (m. loc. sg.), at the arrival of day.
rātryāgame (m. loc. sg.), at the arrival of night.
pralīyante (3rd pl. pr. indic. pass. *pra* √*lī*), they are dissolved, they are reabsorbed, they disappear.
tatra, there, in that case.
eva, indeed (used as a rhythmic filler).
avyakta (m.), unmanifest.
saṁjñake (m. loc. sg.), known as, in known as, when known as, to be known as.
(*avyaktasaṁjñake,* m. loc. sg. BV cpd., whose name is the unmanifest.)

19

भूतग्रामः स एवायं
bhūtagrāmaḥ sa evāyaṁ
the multitude of existences it this

भूत्वा भूत्वा प्रलीयते ।
bhūtvā bhūtvā pralīyate
having come to be again and again, is dissolved

रात्र्यागमे ऽवशः पार्थ
rātryāgame 'vaśaḥ pārtha
at the arrival of night without will, Son of Pṛthā,

प्रभवत्य् अहरागमे ॥
prabhavaty aharāgame
it comes into existence at the arrival of day.

This multitude of existences,
Having come to be again and again, is dissolved
Willy-nilly at the arrival of night, Son of Pṛthā;
It comes into existence again at the arrival of day.*

bhūtagrāmas (m. nom. sg.), aggregate of beings, multitude of existences.
sas (m. nom. sg.), it, this, he.
eva, indeed (used as a rhythmic filler).
ayam (m. nom. sg.), this.
bhuṭvā bhūtvā (gerund √*bhū*), coming into existence again and again, having come into being again and again.
pralīyate (3rd sg. pr. pass. *pra* √*lī*), it is dissolved, it is reabsorbed, it disappears.
rātryāgame (m. loc. sg.), at the arrival of night.
avaśas (m. nom. sg.), without will, inevitably, willy-nilly.
pārtha (m. voc. sg.), Son of Pṛthā, epithet of Arjuna.
prabhavati (3rd sg. pr. indic. act. *pra* √*bhū*), it comes into existence, it arises.
aharāgame (m. loc. sg.), at the arrival of day.

* This and the previous stanza describe the periodic creation of all beings and their subsequent dissolution. The "night of Brahmā" which lasts for a *kalpa* (4,320,000,000 years, see footnote to VIII 17), and during this time all life is in latent, "unmanifest" form. At the arrival of the "day of Brahmā," all beings, animal, vegetable and mineral, are created again, to go through their much smaller lives and reincarnations, all of which end at the recurrence of the "night of Brahmā," when they pass into the unmanifest again. The day of Brahmā is equal in length to the night of Brahmā.

20

परस् तस्मात् तु भावो ऽन्यो
paras tasmāt tu bhāvo 'nyo
higher than this, but, state of being other

ऽव्यक्तो ऽव्यक्तात् सनातनः ।
'vyakto 'vyaktāt sanātanaḥ
unmanifest, than the unmanifest primaeval,

यः स सर्वेषु भूतेषु
yaḥ sa sarveṣu bhūteṣu
which it in all beings

नश्यत्सु न विनश्यति ॥
naśyatsu na vinaśyati
in the perishings not it perishes.

But higher than this state of being
Is another unmanifest state of being
Higher than the primaeval unmanifest,
Which, when all beings perish, does not perish.

paras (m. nom. sg.), higher.
tasmāt (abl. sg.), from this, than this.
tu, but, indeed.
bhāvas (m. nom. sg.), state of being, existence.
anyas (m. nom. sg.), other.
avyaktas (m. nom. sg. p. pass. participle *a vi* √*añj*), unmanifest, invisible.
avyaktāt (m. abl. sg.), from the unmanifest, than the unmanifest.
sanātanas (m. nom. sg.), ancient, primaeval.
yas (m. nom. sg.), which, who.
sas (m. nom. sg.), it, this.
sarveṣu (m. loc. pl.), in all.
bhūteṣu (m. loc. pl.), in existences, in beings.
naśyatsu (m. loc. pl.), in the perishings, in the losses.
(*sarveṣu bhūteṣu naśyatsu,* loc. absol., when all beings perish.)
na, not.
vinaśyati (3rd sg. pr. indic. act. *vi* √*naś*), it perishes, it is lost, it dies.

21

अव्यक्तो ऽक्षर इत्य् उक्तस्
avyakto 'kṣara ity uktas
the unmanifest (is) the imperishable, thus said.

तम् आहुः परमां गतिम् ।
tam āhuḥ paramāṁ gatim
it they call the supreme goal,

यं प्राप्य न निवर्तन्ते
yaṁ prāpya na nivartante
which attaining, not they return.

तद् धाम परमं मम ॥
tad dhāma paramaṁ mama
that the dwelling place supreme of me.

avyaktas (m. nom. sg. p. pass. participle *a vi* √*añj*), unmanifest, invisible.
akṣaras (m. nom. sg.), imperishable, indestructible, eternal.
iti, thus, so.
uktas (m. nom. sg. p. pass. participle √*vac*), said, declared.
tam (m. acc. sg.), it, this.
āhus (3rd pl. perfect act. √*ah* with present meaning), they say, they declare.
paramām (f. acc. sg.), highest, supreme.
gatim (f. acc. sg.), goal, path, way.
yam (m. acc. sg.), which.
prāpya (gerund *pra* √*āp*), attaining, reaching.
na, not.
nivartante (3rd pl. pr. indic. mid. *ni* √*vṛt*), they return, they turn back.
tad (n. acc. sg.), that, this.
dhāma (n. nom. sg.), dwelling place, domain, abode.
paramam (n. nom. sg.), supreme, highest.
mama (gen. sg.), of me, my.

This unmanifest is the Imperishable, thus it is said.
They call it the Supreme Goal,
Which attaining, they do not return.
This is My supreme dwelling place.

22

पुरुषः स परः पार्थ
puruṣaḥ sa paraḥ pārtha
spirit this supreme, Son of Pṛthā,

भक्त्या लभ्यस् त्व् अनन्यया ।
bhaktyā labhyas tv ananyayā
by devotion attainable, indeed, not by other,

यस्यान्तःस्थानि भूतानि
yasyāntaḥsthāni bhūtāni
of which within-standing (all) beings

येन सर्वम् इदं ततम् ॥
yena sarvam idaṁ tatam
by which all this (universe) pervaded.

This is the Supreme Spirit, Son of Pṛthā,
Attainable by devotion not directed elsewhere,
Within which all beings stand,
By which all this universe is pervaded.

puruṣas (m. nom. sg.), spirit, man.
sas (m. nom. sg.), this, he.
paras (m. nom. sg.), highest, supreme.
pārtha (m. voc. sg.), Son of Pṛthā, epithet of Arjuna referring to his mother Kuntī or Pṛthā.
bhaktyā (f. inst. sg.), by devotion, by worship.
labhyas (m. nom. sg. gerundive √*labh*), to be attained, attainable.
tu, but, indeed.
ananyayā (f. inst. sg.), not by it directed elsewhere.
yasya (m. gen. sg.), of which.
antaḥsthāni (n. nom. pl.), standing within, existing within.
bhūtāni (n. nom. pl.), beings, all beings.
yena (m. inst. sg.), by which.
sarvam idam (n. nom. sg.), all this, all this universe.
tatam (n. nom. p. pass. participle √*tan*), stretched, pervaded.

23

यत्र काले त्व् अनावृत्तिम्
yatra kāle tv anāvṛttim
where in time, but, non-return

आवृत्तिं चैव योगिनः ।
āvṛttiṁ cāiva yoginaḥ
and return the yogins

प्रयाता यान्ति तं कालं
prayātā yānti taṁ kālaṁ
departing they go, (of) this time

वक्ष्यामि भरतर्षभ ॥
vakṣyāmi bharatarṣabha
I shall speak, Bull of the Bharatas.

yatra where, whither.
kāle (m. loc. sg.), in time.
tu, but, indeed.
anāvṛttim (f. acc. sg.), non-return, not turning back.
āvṛttim (f. acc. sg.), return, turning back.
ca, and.
eva, indeed (used as a rhythmic filler).
yoginas (m. nom. pl.), yogins.
prayātās (m. nom. pl. pr. participle *pra* √*yā*), departing, dying.
yānti (3rd pl. act. √*yā*), they go.
tam (m. acc. sg.), this, him.
kālam (m. acc. sg.), time.
vakṣyāmi (1st sg. future act. √*vac*), I shall speak.
bharatarṣabha (m. voc. sg.), Bull of the Bharatas, epithet of Arjuna.

But at what time the yogins
Achieve non-return or return,
As they go, departing in death,
Of this time I shall speak, Bull of the Bharatas.

24

अग्निर् ज्योतिर् अहः शुक्लः
agnir jyotir ahaḥ śuklaḥ
fire, brightness, day, the bright lunar fortnight,

षण्मासा उत्तरायणम् ।
ṣaṇmāsā uttarāyaṇam
the six months of the upper going† (northern phase of the sun),

तत्र प्रयाता गच्छन्ति
tatra prayātā gacchanti
there departing, they go

ब्रह्म ब्रह्मविदो जनाः ॥
brahma brahmavido janāḥ
to Brahman, the Brahman-knowing men.

agnis (m. nom. sg.), fire, god of fire.
jyotis (n. nom. sg.), brightness, bright.
ahar (n. nom. sg.), day.
śuklas (n. nom. sg.), the bright lunar fortnight.
ṣaṇmāsās (m. nom. pl.), six months.
uttarāyaṇam (n. nom. sg.), upper going of the sun, i.e. the northern phase of the sun.
tatra, there, thither.
prayātās (m. nom. pl. pr. participle *pra* √*yā*), departing, dying.
gacchanti (3rd pl. pr. indic. act. √*gam*), they go, they attain.
brahma (n. acc. sg.), to Brahman, Brahman.
brahmavidas (m. nom. pl.), Brahman knowing.
janās (m. nom. pl.), men.

Fire, brightness, day, the bright lunar fortnight,
The six months of the northern course of the sun:
Then departing, the men who know Brahman
Go forth to Brahman.*

* This and the following stanzas present a formula to be found in the Chāndogya Upanishad, V 9, 1 to 5, and in the Bṛhadāraṇyaka Upanishad, VI 2, 15 and 16. There is also a shorter reference in Chandyoga IV 15, 5, which does not mention the "dark" path. In the Bṛhadāraṇyaka Upanishad, the distinction between those who follow the path of light and those who follow the path of darkness lies not only in the time of death but also between those who meditate on the "five fires" (viz. Heaven, the Rain god, the World, Man and Woman) and those who merely perform rituals, the latter going the path of darkness and rebirth.

† "upper going" means northern because the north of India is higher than the south.

25

धूमो रात्रिस् तथा कृष्णः
dhūmo rātris tathā kṛṣṇaḥ
smoke, night, and so the dark lunar fortnight,

षण्मासा दक्षिणायनम् ।
ṣaṇmāsā dakṣiṇāyanam
the six months of the right hand going (southern phase of the sun),*

तत्र चान्द्रमसं ज्योतिर्
tatra cāndramasaṁ jyotir
there lunar brightness

योगी प्राप्य निवर्तते ॥
yogī prāpya nivartate
the yogin attaining, he is born again.

dhūmas (m. nom. sg.), smoke.
rātris (f. nom. sg.), night.
tathā, thus, so.
kṛṣṇas (m. nom. sg.), the dark lunar fortnight (also the name Krishna, but that is not meant here).
ṣaṇmāsās (m./n. nom. pl.), six months.
dakṣiṇāyanam (n. nom. sg.), "the right hand going," the southern phase of the sun.
tatra, there, thither.
cāndramasam (n. acc. sg.), lunar.
jyotis (n. acc. sg.), brightness, light.
yogī (m. nom. sg.), yogin.
prāpya (gerund *pra* √*āp*), attaining, reaching.
nivartate (3rd sg. mid. *ni* √*vṛt*), he returns, he turns back, he is born again.

Smoke, night, and the dark lunar fortnight,
The six months of the southern course of the sun;
There attaining the lunar light,
The yogin is born again.

* When identifying directions, the Hindu faces east where the sun rises. Thus "right hand" means south.

26

शुक्लकृष्णे गती ह्येते
śuklakṛṣṇe gatī hyete
light and dark two paths indeed these

जगतः शाश्वते मते
jagataḥ śāśvate mate
for the universe eternal thought to be

एकया यात्य् अनावृत्तिम्
ekayā yāty anāvṛttim
by one he goes to non-return

अन्ययावर्तते पुनः ।।
anyayāvartate punaḥ
by the other he returns again.

śuklakṛṣṇe (f. nom. dual), light and dark.
gatī (f. nom. dual), two paths, two goals.
hi, indeed, truly.
ete (f. nom. dual), these two.
jagatas (n. gen. sg.), of the universe, for the world.
śāśvate (f. nom. dual), eternal, perpetual.
mate (f. nom. dual), thought, thought to be.
ekayā (f. inst. sg.), by one.
yāti (3rd sg. act. √*yā*), he goes, one goes, he attains.
anāvṛttim (f. acc. sg.), to non-return, non-return.
anyayā (f. inst. sg.), by the other.
āvartate (3rd sg. mid. *ā* √*vṛt*), he returns, he turns back.
punar (adv.), again, once more.

These are the two paths, light and dark,
Thought to be eternal for the universe.
By one he goes to non-return;
By the other he returns again.*

* The choice of whether to return or not is apparently up to the yogin. The literature abounds with yogins who have delayed their deaths so as to reach the half-year that will eventuate in either return or non-return. (Cf. the case of Bhīṣma, who delayed his death at the Battle of Kurukṣetra – see chapter "The Setting of the Bhagavad Gītā.)"

The existence of the "two paths" (light and dark) must seem rather arbitrary to the Western reader. Rāmānuja refers them to the *jñānin* and *kāivalyārthin* of VII 16 on the one hand, and the *āiśvaryārthin* of the same stanza on the other. But this does not explain the element of free will which allows the yogin to fix the time of his death and choose between the two paths.

27

नैते सृती पार्थ जानन्
nāite sṛtī pārtha jānan
not these two paths, Son of Pṛthā, knowing,

योगी मुह्यति कश्चन ।
yogī muhyati kaścana
the yogin he is confused at all

तस्मात् सर्वेषु कालेषु
tasmāt sarveṣu kāleṣu
therefore at all times

योगयुक्तो भवार्जुन ॥
yogayukto bhavārjuna
steadfast in Yoga be, Arjuna.

na, not.
ete (f. nom. dual), these two.
sṛtī (f. nom. dual), two paths, two roads, two wanderings.
pārtha (m. voc. sg.), Son of Pṛthā, epithet of Arjuna.
jānan (m. nom. sg. pr. act. participle √*jñā*), knowing.
yogī (m. nom. sg.), yogin.
muhyati (3rd sg. pr. indic. act. √*muh*), he is deluded, he is confused.
kaścana, at all, in any way.
tasmāt (m. abl. sg.), from this, therefore.
sarveṣu (m. loc. pl.), at all, in all.
kāleṣu (m. loc. pl.), at times, in times.
yoga-yuktas (m. nom. sg. TP cpd. p. pass participle √*yuj*), steadfast, united to Yoga, disciplined, yoked.
bhava (3rd sg. imperative act. √*bhū*), be!
arjuna (m. voc. sg.), Arjuna.

Knowing these two paths, Son of Pṛthā,
The yogin is not confused at all.
Therefore, at all times,
Be steadfast in Yoga, Arjuna.

28

वेदेषु यज्ञेषु तपःसु चैव
*vedeṣu yajñeṣu tapaḥsu cāiva**
in the Vedas, in sacrifices and in austerities,

दानेषु यत् पुण्यफलं प्रदिष्टम् ।
dāneṣu yat puṇyaphalaṁ pradiṣṭam
in gifts, which pure fruit ordained

अत्येति तत् सर्वम् इदं विदित्वा
atyeti tat sarvam idaṁ viditvā
he goes beyond that, all this having known

योगी परं स्थानम् उपैति चाद्यम् ॥
yogī paraṁ sthānam upāiti cādyam
and the yogin to the supreme state he goes, primal.

The yogin, having known all this, goes beyond
The pure fruit of action which is ordained in the Vedas,
In sacrifices, in austerities and in gifts,
And goes to the Supreme Primal State.

vedesu (m. loc. pl.), in the Vedas.
yajñeṣu (m. loc. pl.), in sacrifices.
tapaḥsu (m. loc. pl.), in austerities.
ca, and.
eva, indeed (used as a rhythmic filler).
dāneṣu (n. loc. pl.), in gifts, in charities.
yad (n. acc. sg.), which.
puṇya (n.), pure, sacred.
phalam (n. acc. sg.), fruit.
(*punya-phalam*, n. acc. sg. KD cpd., pure fruit.)
pradiṣṭam (n. acc. sg. p. pass. participle *pra* √*diś*), ordained, commanded, prescribed.
atyeti (3rd sg. pr. indic. act. *ati* √*i*), he goes beyond, he transcends.
tad (n. acc. sg.), this, that.
sarvam idam (n. acc. sg.), all this.
viditvā (gerund √*vid*), knowing, having known.
yogī (m. nom. sg.), yogin.
param (n. acc. sg.), to the highest, the supreme.
sthānam (n. acc. sg.), state, place, abode, station.
upāiti (3rd sg. act. *upa* √*i*), he goes, he attains.
ca, and.
ca, and.
ādyam (n. acc. sg.), primal, ancient, original, being at the beginning.

End of Book VIII

The Yoga of Imperishable Brahman

* *Triṣṭubh* metre.

BOOK IX

श्रीभगवान् उवाच ।
śrībhagavān uvāca
the Blessed Lord spoke:

śrībhagavān (m. nom. sg.), the Blessed Lord, the Blessed One.
uvāca (3rd sg. perfect act. √*vac*), he said, he spoke.

1

इदं तु ते गुह्यतमं
*idaṁ tu te guhyatamaṁ**
this, but, to thee the most secret

प्रवक्ष्याम्य् अनसूयवे ।
pravakṣyāmy anasūyave
I shall declare, to the not disbelieving,

ज्ञानं विज्ञानसहितं
jñānaṁ vijñānasahitaṁ
knowledge and discrimination combined,

यज् ज्ञात्वा मोक्ष्यसे ऽशुभात् ॥
yaj jñātvā mokṣyase 'śubhāt
which having known, thou shalt be released from evil.

idam (n. acc. sg.), this.
tu, but, indeed.
te (dat. sg.), to thee.
guhyatamam (superl.), most secret.
pravakṣyāmi (1st sg. future act. *pra* √*vac*), I shall declare, I shall explain.
anasūyave (m. dat. sg.), to the not sneering, to the not disbelieving.
jñānam (n. acc. sg.), knowledge.
vijñāna (n.), discrimination, understanding, realization.
sahitam (n. acc. sg.), combined, together with, placed together.
yad (n. acc. sg.), which.
jñātvā (gerund √*jñā*), knowing, having known.
mokṣyase (2nd sg. future pass. √*muc*), thou shalt be released, thou shalt be freed, thou shalt be liberated.
aśubhāt (m. abl. sg.), from evil, from impurity.

The Blessed Lord spoke:
But this most secret thing
I shall declare to thee, who dost not disbelieve:
Knowledge and discrimination combined,
Which, having learned, thou shalt be released from evil.

* *Śloka* metre resumes.

2

राजविद्या राजगुह्यं
rājavidyā rājaguhyaṁ
royal knowledge, royal secret,

पवित्रम् इदम् उत्तमम् ।
pavitram idam uttamam
purifier this supreme,

प्रत्यक्षावगमं धर्म्यं
pratyakṣāvagamaṁ dharmyaṁ
as if before the eyes, intelligible, righteous,

सुसुखं कर्तुम् अव्ययम् ॥
susukhaṁ kartum avyayam
easy to practice, imperishable.

A royal knowledge, a royal secret,
A supreme purifier, this,
Plainly intelligible, righteous,
Easy to practice, imperishable.

rājavidyā (f. nom. sg.), royal knowledge, royal wisdom.
rājaguhyam (n. nom. sg.), royal secret.
pavitram (n. nom. sg.), purifier, cleanser.
idam (n. nom. sg.), this.
uttamam (n. nom. sg.), highest, supreme.
pratyakṣa, before the eyes.
avagamam (n. nom. sg.), intelligible, understanding.
(*pratyakṣāvagamam,* n. nom. sg. BV cpd., which is intelligible before the eyes, which can be plainly understood, whose understanding is before the eyes.)
dharmyam (n. nom. sg.), righteous, lawful.
susukham (n. nom. sg.), easy, pleasant.
kartum (infinitive √*kṛ*), to do, to practice.
avyayam (n. nom. sg.), imperishable, eternal.

3

अश्रद्दधानाः पुरुषा
aśraddadhānāḥ puruṣā
who do not give faith men,

धर्मस्यास्य परंतप।
dharmasyāsya paraṁtapa
of this law, of it, Scorcher of the Foe,

अप्राप्य मां निवर्तन्ते
aprāpya māṁ nivartante
not attaining to me, they are born again

मृत्युसंसारवर्त्मनि ॥
mṛtyusaṁsāravartmani
in the death transmigration path.

Men who hold no faith
In this worship, Scorcher of the Foe,
Not attaining to Me, are born again
In the path of death and transmigration.

aśraddadhānās (m. nom. pl. pr. participle *a śradda* √*dhā*), non-faith-holding, without faith, without giving faith.
puruṣās (m. nom. pl.), men, spirits.
dharmasya (m. gen. sg.), of law, of this law, of this rule, of this worship.
asya (m. gen. sg.), of it.
paraṁtapa (m. voc. sg.), Scorcher of the Foe, epithet of Arjuna.
aprāpya (gerund *a pra* √*āp*), not attaining, not reaching.
mām (acc. sg.), me, to me.
nivartante (3rd pl. pr. indic. mid. *ni* √*vṛt*), they are born again, they are reborn.
mṛtyu (m.), death.
saṁsāra (m.), transmigration, succession of rebirths.
vartmani (n. loc. sg.), in the path.
(*mṛtyu-samsāra-vartmani*, n. loc. sg., TP cpd., in the path of death and transmigration.)

4

मया ततम् इदं सर्वं
mayā tatam idaṁ sarvaṁ
by me pervaded this whole

जगद् अव्यक्तमूर्तिना ।
jagad avyaktamūrtinā
universe by unmanifest aspect

मत्स्थानि सर्वभूतानि
matsthāni sarvabhūtāni
me abiding all beings

न चाहं तेष्व् अवस्थितः ॥
na cāhaṁ teṣv avasthitaḥ
and not I in them abiding.

**This whole universe is pervaded
By Me in my unmanifest aspect.
All beings abide in Me;
I do not abide in them.**

mayā (inst. sg.), by me.
tatam (n. nom. sg. p. pass. participle √*tan*), pervaded, stretched.
idam (n. nom. sg.), this.
sarvam (n. nom. sg.), whole, all, entire.
jagat (n. nom. sg.), universe, world.
avyakta (p. pass. participle *a vi* √*añj*), unmanifest.
mūrtinā (f. inst. sg.), by aspect, by image.
(*avyaktamūrtinā*, f. inst. sg., by unmanifest aspect; as BV cpd., by me whose aspect is unmanifest.)
matsthāni (n. nom. pl.), in me abiding, in me situated.
sarvabhūtāni (n. acc. pl.), all beings, all creatures.
na, not.
ca, and.
aham (nom. sg.), I.
teṣu (n. loc. pl.), in them.
avasthitas (m. nom. sg.), resting, abiding, standing.

5

न च मत्स्थानि भूतानि
na ca matsthāni bhūtāni
and (yet) not from me abiding beings.

पश्य मे योगम् ऐश्वरम् ।
paśya me yogam āiśvaram
behold of me the power majestic!

भूतभृन् न च भूतस्थो
bhūtabhṛn na ca bhūtastho
beings sustaining and not beings dwelling in;

ममात्मा भूतभावनः ॥
mamātmā bhūtabhāvanaḥ
myself beings causing to be.

na, not.
ca, and.
matsthāni (n. acc. pl.), abiding in me.
bhūtāni (n. acc. pl.), beings, creatures.
paśya (2nd sg. pr. imperative act. √*paś*), behold! see!
me (gen. sg.), of me, my.
yogam (m. acc. sg.), Yoga, power.
āiśvaram (m. acc. sg.), majestic, lordly.
bhūtabhṛt (m. nom. sg.), beings, sustaining, sustaining beings, supporting beings, bearing beings.
na, not.
ca, and.
bhūtasthas (m. nom. sg.), beings dwelling in, abiding in beings, existing in beings.
mama (gen. sg.), of me, my.
ātmā (m. nom. sg.), self.
bhūtabhāvanas (m. nom. sg.), causing beings to be, causing beings to come into existence.

And yet beings do not abide in Me.*†
Behold My majestic power!
Sustaining beings and not dwelling in beings
Is Myself, causing beings to be.

---

* The explanation of the apparent paradox follows: "God is the source of all phenomena, but is not touched by them" – Radhakrishnan.

† "God pervades beings by virtue of his will... God supports all beings, but no being is of use to him." – freely excerpted from Rāmānuja.

6

यथाकाशस्थितो नित्यं
yathākāśasthito nityaṁ
as (in) space dwelling eternally

वायुः सर्वत्रगो महान् ।
vāyuḥ sarvatrago mahān
the wind everywhere going, mighty,

तथा सर्वाणि भूतानि
tathā sarvāṇi bhūtāni
so all beings

मत्स्थानीत्य् उपधारय ॥
matsthānīty upadhāraya
in me abiding, thus consider!

yathā, as, in which way.
ākāśa- (m./n.), space, ether.
sthitas (m. nom. sg.), situated, dwelling in.
nityam (adv.), eternally, perpetually.
vāyus (m. nom. sg.), wind.
sarvatragas (m. nom. sg.), "everywhere going," omnipresent.
mahān (m. nom. sg.), mighty, strong.
tathā, so, in this way.
sarvāṇi (n. nom. pl.), all.
bhūtāni (n. nom. pl.), beings, creatures.
matsthāni (n. nom. pl.), in me existing, in me abiding.
iti, thus, this.
upadhāraya (2nd sg. pr. imperative causative act. *upa* √*dhṛ*), consider! reflect!

As the mighty wind, going everywhere,
Dwells eternally in space,
So all beings
Dwell in Me. Consider this!

7

सर्वभूतानि कौन्तेय
sarvabhūtāni kāunteya
all beings, Son of Kuntī

प्रकृतिं यान्ति मामिकाम् ।
prakṛtiṁ yānti māmikām
(into) material nature, they go, my own,

कल्पक्षये पुनस् तानि
kalpakṣaye punas tāni
at the end of a kalpa;* again them

कल्पादौ विसृजाम्य् अहम् ॥
kalpādāu visṛjāmy aham
at the beginning of a kalpa I send forth, I.

All beings, Son of Kuntī,
Go into My own material nature
At the end of a kalpa;*
At the beginning of a kalpa, I send them forth;

sarvabhūtāni (n. nom. pl.), all beings.
kāunteya (m. voc. sg.), Son of Kuntī, epithet of Arjuna referring to his mother, Kuntī or Pṛthā.
prakṛtim (f. acc. sg.), to material nature, material nature.
yānti (3rd pl. act. √*yā*), they go.
māmikām (f. acc. sg.), my, mine, my own.
kalpakṣaye (m. loc. sg.), at the end of a kalpa, at the destruction of a kalpa, at the burning of a kalpa.
punar, again.
tāni (n. acc. pl.), they, them.
kalpādāu (m. loc. sg.), at the beginning of a kalpa, at the originating of a kalpa.
visṛjāmi (1st sg. pr. indic. act. *vi* √*sṛj*), I send forth, I create, I let go.
aham (nom. sg.), I.

* Day of Brahman, see Book VIII 17, note (i.e. 4,320,000,000 years).

8

प्रकृतिं स्वाम् अवष्टभ्य
prakṛtiṁ svām avaṣṭabhya
material nature own resting on,

विसृजामि पुनः पुनः ।
visṛjāmi punaḥ punaḥ
I send forth again and again

भूतग्रामम् इमं कृत्स्नम्
bhūtagrāmam imaṁ kṛtsnam
multitude of beings this entire,

अवशं प्रकृतेर् वशात् ॥
avaśaṁ prakṛter vaśāt
without will, of material nature, from the will.

prakṛtim (f. acc. sg.), material nature.
svām (f. acc. sg.), own.
avaṣṭabhya (gerund *ava* √*stabh*), resting on, supported by, propped up by.
visṛjāmi (1st sg. pr. indic. act. *vi* √*sṛj*), I send forth, I create.
punaḥ punaḥ, again and again.
bhūtagrāmam (m. acc. sg.), the multitude of beings, the aggregate of beings.
imam (m. acc. sg.), this.
kṛtsnam (m. acc. sg.), entire, whole.
avaśam (m. acc. sg.), powerless, without will, willy-nilly.
prakṛtes (f. gen. sg.), of material nature.
vaśāt (m. abl. sg.), from the will, from the power, by the power.

Resting on My own material nature,
I send forth again and again
This entire multitude of beings,
Which is powerless, by the power of My material nature.*

* God creates these beings anew (at the beginning of a new *kalpa*), reposing upon his own *prakṛti* (material nature), which is capable of development into various shapes. God creates the fourfold creation of gods, men, animals and immovables every now and then because of his bewildering *prakṛti* which consists of *guṇas*. He develops this *prakṛti* into eight forms (cf. VII 4 and following stanza). – Rāmānuja.

9

न च मां तानि कर्माणि
na ca māṁ tāni karmāṇi
and not me these actions

निबध्नन्ति धनंजय ।
nibadhnanti dhanaṁjaya
they bind, conqueror of wealth.

उदासीनवद् आसीनम्
udāsīnavad āsīnam
indifferently sitting

असक्तं तेषु कर्मसु ॥
asaktaṁ teṣu karmasu
unattached in these actions.

And these actions do not bind Me,
Conqueror of Wealth;
I sit indifferently,
Unattached by these actions.

na, not.
ca, and.
mām (acc. sg.), me
tāni (n. nom. pl.), these.
karmāṇi (n. nom. pl.), actions, deeds.
nibadhnanti (3rd pl. pr. indic. act. *ni* √*badh*), they bind, they fetter, they bind down.
dhanaṁjaya (m. voc. sg.), Conqueror of Wealth, epithet of Arjuna.
udāsīnavat (adv.), "like one sitting apart," indifferently, impartially.
āsīnam (m. acc. sg. from √*ās*), sitting, seated.
asaktam (m. acc. sg. p. pass. participle *a* √*sañj*), unattached, not clinging.
teṣu (n. loc. pl.), in these.
karmasu (n. loc. pl.), in actions, in deeds, to actions.

10

मयाध्यक्षेण प्रकृतिः
mayādhyakṣeṇa prakṛtiḥ
with me as overseer, material nature

सूयते सचराचरम् ।
sūyate sacarācaram
it produces both animate and inanimate (things)

हेतुनानेन कौन्तेय
hetunānena kāunteya
from this cause, Son of Kuntī,

जगद् विपरिवर्तते ॥
jagad viparivartate
the universe, it revolves.

With Me as overseer, material nature
Produces all things animate and inanimate.
From this cause, Son of Kuntī,
The universe revolves.

mayā (inst. sg.), by me, with me.
adhyakṣeṇa (m. inst. sg.), as overseer, as inspector, as eye witness.
prakṛtis (f. nom. sg.), material nature.
sūyate (3rd sg. pr. indic. mid. √*sū*), it produces, it impels, it creates.
sacarācaram (m. acc. sg. DV cpd.), both the animate(*cara*) and inanimate (*acara*), both the moving and the unmoving.
hetunā (m. inst. sg.), by cause, from cause, by reason, from reason.
anena (m. inst. sg.), by this, from this, with this.
kāunteya (m. voc. sg.), Son of Kuntī, epithet of Arjuna.
jagat (n. nom. acc.), world, universe.
viparivartate (3rd sg. pr. indic. mid. *vi pari* √*vṛt*), it revolves, it exists.

11

अवजानन्ति मां मूढा
avajānanti māṁ mūḍhā
they despise me, the deluded,

मानुषीं तनुम् आश्रितम् ।
mānuṣīṁ tanum āśritam
human form assuming

परं भावम् अजानन्तो
paraṁ bhāvam ajānanto
higher being not knowing

मम भूतमहेश्वरम् ॥
mama bhūtamaheśvaram
of me, the Great Lord of Beings.

The deluded despise Me
When I assume human form,
Not knowing My higher being
As the Great Lord of Beings.

avajānanti (3rd pl. pr. indic. act. *ava* √*jñā*), they despise, they disesteem, they treat with contempt.
mām (acc. sg.), me.
mūḍhas (m. nom. pl. p. pass. participle √*muh*), the deluded, the confused ones, fools.
mānusīm (f. acc. sg.), human.
tanum (f. acc. sg.), body, form.
āśritam (m. acc. sg. p. pass. participle *ā* √*śri*), having recourse to, dwelling in, employing, using, assuming.
param (m. acc. sg.), higher.
bhāvam (m. acc. sg.), being, existence.
ajānantas (m. nom. pl. pr. participle act. *a* √*jñā*), not knowing, ignorant of.
mama (gen. sg.), of me, my.
bhūta (m.), being, creature.
maheśvaram (m. acc. sg.), mighty lord, great lord.
(*maheśvaram*, m. acc. sg. TP cpd., Great Lord of Beings.)

12

मोघाशा मोघकर्माणो
moghāśā moghakarmāṇo
those of vain hopes, vain actions,

मोघज्ञाना विचेतसः ।
moghajñānā vicetasaḥ
vain knowledges, without thought,

राक्षसीम् आसुरीं चैव
rākṣasīm āsurīṁ cāiva
fiendish and demonic thus

प्रकृतिं मोहिनीं श्रिताः ॥
prakṛtiṁ mohinīṁ śritāḥ*
nature delusive abiding.

Those of vain hopes, vain actions,
Vain knowledge, devoid of thought,
Abide in a fiendish and demonic nature,*
Which is deluding.

moghāśās (*mogha āśās,* m. nom. pl. BV cpd.), those of vain hopes, those whose hopes are vain.
moghakarmāṇas (m. nom. pl. BV cpd.), those whose actions are vain, those of vain actions.
moghajñānās (m. nom. pl. BV cpd.), those whose knowledges are vain, those of vain knowledges.
vicetasas (m. nom. pl.), without thought, without sense, (as BV cpd.) those whose thoughts are lacking.
rākṣasīm (f. acc. pl.), fiendish, evil.
āsurīm (f. acc. pl.), demonic, pertaining to devils.
ca, and.
eva, indeed (used as a rhythmic filler).
prakṛtim (f. acc. sg.), nature, character.
mohinīm (f. acc. sg.), delusive, confused.
śritās (m. nom. pl. p. pass. participle √*śri*), abiding, resorting to, resting on, clinging to.

* *prakṛtim* (nature) is not used here in the usual sense of "material nature," but is part of a simple attribute.

13

महात्मानस् तु मां पार्थ
mahātmānas tu māṁ pārtha
those whose selves are great, but, me, Son of Pṛthā,

दैवीं प्रकृतिम् आश्रिताः ।
dāivīṁ prakṛtim āśritāḥ
celestial nature abiding in,

भजन्त्य् अनन्यमनसो
bhajanty ananyamanaso
they worship not other-mindedly,

ज्ञात्वा भूतादिम् अव्ययम् ॥
jñātvā bhūtādim avyayam
knowing (me as) the beginning of beings, the Imperishable.

But those whose selves are great, Son of Pṛthā,
Abiding in celestial nature,
Worship Me single-mindedly,
Knowing Me as the origin of beings and as the Imperishable.

mahātmānas (m. nom. pl.), great selves, great souls, mighty souls, (as BV cpd.) those whose selves are great.
tu, but.
mām (acc. sg.), me.
pārtha (m. voc. sg.), Son of Pṛthā, epithet of Arjuna.
dāivīm (f. acc. sg.), celestial, heavenly, divine.
prakṛtim (f. acc. sg.), nature, character.
āśritās (m. nom. pl. p. pass. participle *ā* √*śri*), abiding in, resorting to, clinging to, resting on.
bhajanti (3rd pl. pr. indic. act. √*bhaj*), they worship, they honor, they share with.
ananyamanasas (m. nom. pl. BV cpd.), those whose minds are not elsewhere.
jñātvā (gerund √*jñā*), knowing, having known.
bhūtādim (m. acc. sg.), the origin of beings, the beginning of beings.
avyayam (m. acc. sg.), imperishable, eternal.

14

सततं कीर्तयन्तो मां
satataṁ kīrtayanto māṁ
perpetually glorifying me

यतन्तश्च दृढव्रताः ।
yatantaśca dṛḍhavratāḥ
and striving with firm vows

नमस्यन्तश्च मां भक्त्या
namasyantaśca māṁ bhaktyā
and honoring me with devotion

नित्ययुक्ता उपासते ॥
nityayuktā upāsate
ever steadfast they worship.

Perpetually glorifying Me
And striving, with firm vows,
And honoring Me with devotion,
Ever steadfast, they worship.

satatam (adv.), perpetually, continually.
kīrtayantas (m. nom. pl. pr. causative participle √*kīrt*), glorifying, making mention of, praising, celebrating.
mām (acc. sg.), me.
yatantas (m. nom. pl. pr. act. participle √*yat*), striving, stretching.
ca, and.
dṛḍha (p. pass. participle √*dṛh*), firm, solid, sincere.
vrata (n.), vow.
(*dṛḍhavratās*, m. nom. pl. BV cpd., those vows are firm.)
namasyantas (m. nom. pl. pr. act. participle √*nam*), paying homage to, honoring.
ca, and.
mām (acc. sg.), me.
bhaktyā (f. inst. sg.), with devotion, with piety, with love.
nitya (adv.), always, ever, eternally.
yuktās (m. nom. pl. p. pass. participle √*yuj*), steadfast, united in Yoga, yoked.
upāsate (3rd pl. pr. indic. mid. *upa* √*ās*), they worship, they honor.

15

ज्ञानयज्ञेन चाप्य् अन्ये
jñānayajñena cāpy anye
and by the knowledge-sacrifice also others,

यजन्तो माम् उपासते ।
yajanto mām upāsate
sacrificing, me they worship

एकत्वेन पृथक्त्वेन
ekatvena pṛthaktvena
as the one, as the manifold,

बहुधा विश्वतोमुखम् ॥
bahudhā viśvatomukham
variously manifested, facing in all directions.

jñānayajñena (m. inst. sg.), by the knowledge sacrifice, by the sacrifice of knowledge.
ca, and.
api, also, even.
anye (m. nom. pl.), others.
yajantas (m. nom. pl. pr. act. participle √*yaj*), sacrificing, worshipping.
mām (acc. sg.), me.
upāsate (3rd pl. pr. indic. mid. *upa* √*ās*), they worship, they honor.
ekatvena (n. inst. sg.), by oneness, as the one.
pṛthaktvena (n. inst. sg.), by manifoldness, as the manifold.
bahudhā (adv.), variously manifested, variously placed.
viśvatomukham (adv.), facing in all directions, omniscient.

**And by the knowledge sacrifice,
Others, sacrificing, worship Me,
As the one and as the manifold,
Variously manifested, facing in all directions (i.e. omniscient).**

IX

16

अहं क्रतुर् अहं यज्ञः
ahaṁ kratur ahaṁ yajñaḥ
I the ritual, I the sacrifice,

स्वधाहम् अहम् औषधम् ।
svadhāham aham āuṣadham
the offering I, I the medicinal herb,

मन्त्रो ऽहम् अहम् एवाज्यम्
mantro 'ham aham evājyam
the sacred text I, I also the clarified butter,

अहम् अग्निर् अहं हुतम् ॥
aham agnir ahaṁ hutam
I the fire, I the pouring out:

I am the ritual, I am the sacrifice,
The offering am I, I am the medicinal herb,
The sacred text am I, I am also the clarified butter,
I am the fire and I am the pouring out (of the oblation);

aham (nom. sg.), I.
kratus (m. nom. sg.), ritual, intention, plan, ceremony.
aham, I.
yajñas (m. nom. sg.), sacrifice.
svadhā (n. nom. sg.), offering.
aham, I.
aham, I.
āuṣadham (n. nom. sg.), medicine, medicinal herb, remedy.
mantras (m. nom. sg.), sacred text, formula.
aham I.
aham, I.
eva, indeed (used as a rhythmic filler).
ājyam (n. nom. sg.), clarified butter, ghee.
aham, I.
agnis (m. nom. sg.), fire.
aham, I.
hutam (n. nom. sg.), the oblation, the pouring out.

17

पिताहम् अस्य जगतो
pitāham asya jagato
the father I of it, of the universe

माता धाता पितामहः ।
mātā dhātā pitāmahaḥ
the mother, the establisher, the grandfather,

वेद्यं पवित्रम् ओंकार
vedyaṁ pavitram oṁkāra
the to-be-known, the purifier, the sacred syllable "Oṁ,"

ऋक् साम यजुर् एव च ।।
ṛk sāma yajur eva ca
the Ṛg, the Sāma and the Yajur (Vedas).

I am the father of the universe,
The mother, the establisher, the grandfather,
The object of knowledge, the purifier, the sacred syllable "Oṁ,"
The Ṛg, Sāma and Yajur Vedas,*

pitā (m. nom. sg.), father.
aham (nom. sg.), I.
asya (gen. sg.), of it, of this.
jagatas (n. gen. sg.), of the world, of the universe.
mātā (f. nom. sg.), mother.
dhātā (m. nom. sg.), the establisher, the arranger.
pitāmahas (m. nom. sg.), grandfather.
vedyam (n. nom. sg. gerundive √*vid*), the to-be-known, the object of knowledge.
pavitram (n. nom. sg.), the purifier, the cleanser.
oṁkāras (m. nom. sg.), the syllable "Oṁ."
ṛk, Ṛg Veda.
sāma, Sāma Veda.
yajur, Yajur Veda.
eva, indeed (used as a rhythmic filler).
ca, and.

* The Ṛg, Sāma and Yajur Vedas are the three principal Vedas, or compilations of ancient Vedic lore, the first being devoted to verses of praise, the second to the traditions of chant applied largely to the same verses, and the third to ritual formulas.

18

गतिर् भर्ता प्रभुः साक्षी
gatir bhartā prabhuḥ sākṣī
the goal, the supporter, the Great Lord, the eye witness,

निवासः शरणं सुहृत् ।
nivāsaḥ śaraṇaṁ suhṛt
the abode, the refuge, the friend,

प्रभवः प्रलयः स्थानं
prabhavaḥ pralayaḥ sthānaṁ
the origin, the dissolution, the staying

निधानं बीजम् अव्ययम् ॥
nidhānaṁ bījam avyayam
the treasure house, the seed imperishable.

The goal, the supporter, the Great Lord, the eye witness,
The abode, the refuge, the friend,
The origin, the dissolution and the staying,
The treasure house and the imperishable seed.

gatis (f. nom. sg.), goal, path.
bhartā (m. nom. sg.), supporter, bearer, sustainer.
prabhus (m. nom. sg.), great lord.
sākṣī (m. nom. sg.), eye-witness, observer.
nivāsas (m. nom. sg.), abode, home.
śaraṇam (n. nom. sg.), refuge, shelter.
suhṛd (m. nom. sg.), friend, companion, (as BV cpd.) he whose heart is good.
prabhavas (m. nom. sg.), origin, bringing forth, birth.
pralayas (m. nom. sg.), dissolution, dying.
sthānam (n. nom. sg.), maintenance, basis, support.
nidhānam (n. nom. sg.), treasure house.
bījam (n. nom. sg.), seed.
avyayam (n. nom. sg.), imperishable, eternal.

19

तपाम्य् अहम् अहं वर्षं
tapāmy aham ahaṁ varṣaṁ
I radiate heat, I, I the rain,

निगृह्णाम्य् उत्सृजामि च ।
nigṛhṇāmy utsṛjāmi ca
I withhold, and I send forth;

अमृतं चैव मृत्युश्च
amṛtaṁ cāiva mṛtyuśca
and immortality thus and death,

सद असच् चाहम् अर्जुन ॥
sad asac cāham arjuna
being and non-being, I, Arjuna.

I radiate heat, I withhold and
Send forth the rain;
And both immortality and death,
Being and non-being, I am, Arjuna.

tapāmi (1st sg. pr. indic. act. √*tap*), I radiate heat, I heat up.
aham (nom. sg.), I.
aham, I.
varṣam (m. acc. sg.), rain.
nigṛhṇāmi (1st sg. pr. indic. act. *ni* √*grah*), I withhold, I hold back.
utsṛjāmi (1st sg. pr. indic. act. *ud* √*sṛj*), I send forth, I let go.
ca, and.
amṛtam (n. nom. sg.), immortality, nectar.
ca, and.
eva, indeed (used as a rhythmic filler).
mṛtyus (m. nom. sg.), death.
ca, and.
sat (n. nom. sg. pr. participle √*as*), being, truth.
asat (n. nom. sg.), non-being, untruth.
ca, and.
aham, I.
arjuna (m. voc. sg.), Arjuna.

20

त्रैविद्या मां सोमपाः पूतपापा
*trāividyā māṁ somapāḥ pūtapāpā**
The three-Veda knowers, me, the soma drinkers, the cleansed of evils,

यज्ञैर् इष्ट्वा स्वर्गतिं प्रार्थयन्ते ।
yajñāir iṣṭvā svargatiṁ prārthayante
with sacrifices worshipping, heaven goal they seek;

ते पुण्यम् आसाद्य सुरेन्द्रलोकम्
te puṇyam āsādya surendralokam
they, the pure, attaining the god-Indra-world,

अश्नन्ति दिव्यान् दिवि देवभोगान् ॥
aśnanti divyān divi devabhogān
they enjoy divine, in the sky, godly pleasures.

Those who know the three Vedas, the soma drinkers, those whose evils are cleansed,
Worship Me with sacrifices and seek to go to heaven.
They, attaining the pure world of the Indra† of the gods,
Enjoy in the sky the gods' celestial pleasures.

trāividyās (m. nom. pl.), knowers of the three Vedas.
mām (acc. sg.), me.
somapās (m. nom. pl.), soma drinkers.
pūta (m.), purified, cleansed.
pāpās (m. nom. pl.), evils, sins.
(*pūtapāpās*, m. nom. sg. BV cpd., whose evils are cleansed.)
yajñāis (m. inst. pl.), with sacrifices, by sacrifices.
iṣṭvā (gerund √*yaj*), worshipping, offering.
svargatim (f. acc. sg.), heaven goal, goal of heaven, path of heaven.
prārthayante (3rd pl. pr. indic. mid. *pra* √*arth*), they seek, they ask for, they desire.
te (m. nom. pl.), they.
puṇyam (m. acc. sg.), pure, meritorious, holy.
āsādya (gerund *ā* √*sad*), attaining, going toward, approaching, encountering.
surendra (m.), the lord of the gods, the Indra (chief) of the gods.
lokam (m. acc. sg.), world.
(*surendra-loka*, m. acc. sg. TP cpd., world of Indra.)
aśnanti (3rd pl. pr. indic. act. √*aś*), they eat, they enjoy.
divyān (m. acc. pl.), divine, heavenly.
divi (n. loc. sg.), in the sky, in heaven.
devabhogān (m. acc. pl.), god pleasures, divine enjoyments.

* *Triṣṭubh* metre.

† This is the only mention in the Gītā of the chief of the Vedic gods, Indra, though the surviving mutation of his name in the word "*indriya*" meaning "sense" or "power" is common, and he is mentioned in X 22, by another name. The use of the name here is in its common meaning, "chief" – thus the Indra or "chief" of the gods.

21

ते तं भुक्त्वा स्वर्गलोकं विशालं
*te taṁ bhuktvā svargalokaṁ viśālaṁ**
they, it having enjoyed, the world of heaven, wide,

क्षीणे पुण्ये मर्त्यलोकं विशन्ति ।
kṣīṇe puṇye martyalokaṁ viśanti
with exhausted merit, the world of mortals they enter.

एवं त्रयीधर्मम् अनुप्रपन्ना
evaṁ trayīdharmam anuprapannā
thus the law of the three Vedas conforming to,

गतागतं कामकामा लभन्ते ॥
gatāgataṁ kāmakāmā labhante
going and coming, desiring objects of desire, they obtain (them).

Having enjoyed the wide world of heaven,
They enter the world of mortals when their merit is exhausted.
Thus conforming to the law of the three Vedas,
Desiring objects of desire, they obtain what comes and goes.

te (m. nom. pl.), they.
tam (m. acc. sg.), it, this.
bhuktvā (gerund √*bhuj*), enjoying, having enjoyed.
svarga (m.), heaven.
lokam (m. acc. sg.), world.
(*svargalokam*, m. acc. sg. TP cpd., the world of heaven.)
viśālam (m. acc. sg.), wide, spacious, extensive.
kṣīṇe (m. loc. sg. p. pass. participle √*kṣi*), in exhausted, in destroyed.
puṇye (m. loc. sg.), in merit, in goodness, in virtue, in purity.
martyalokam (m. acc. sg.), mortal world, world of mortals.
viśanti (3rd pl. pr. indic. act. √*viś*), they enter.
evam, thus, in this manner.
trayīdharmam (m. acc. sg.), "three law," law of the three Vedas.
anuprapannās (m. nom. pl. p. pass. participle *anu pra* √*pad*), conforming to, following, carrying out.
gatāgatam (m. acc. sg.), going and coming, what comes and goes.
kāmakāmās (m. nom. pl.), desiring objects of desire.
labhante (3rd pl. pr. indic. mid. √*labh*), they obtain, they get.

* *Triṣṭubh* metre continues.

22

अनन्याश् चिन्तयन्तो मां
*ananyāś cintayanto māṁ**
without other (thoughts), directing thoughts to me,

ये जनाः पर्युपासते ।
ye janāḥ paryupāsate
which men, they worship,

तेषां नित्याभियुक्तानां
teṣāṁ nityābhiyuktānāṁ
of them of those who are constantly steadfast,

योगक्षेमं वहाम्य् अहम् ॥
yogakṣemaṁ vahāmy aham
acquisition and possession I bring, I.

Those men who worship, directing their thoughts to Me,
Whose minds do not go elsewhere;
To them, who are constantly steadfast,
I bring acquisition and possession of their goal.

ananyās (m. nom. pl.), not directed to another.
cintayantas (m. nom. pl. pr. participle √*cint*), directing thoughts to, meditating on.
mām (acc. sg.), me.
ye (m. nom. pl.), which, who.
janās (m. nom. pl.), men.
paryupāsate (3rd pl. pr. indic. mid. *pari upa* √*ās*), they worship, they honor.
teṣām (gen. pl.), of them, to them.
nitya (adv.), constantly, eternally.
abhiyuktānām (m. gen. pl.), of the steadfast ones, of those united to Yoga.
(*nityābhiyuktānām*, m. gen. pl. BV cpd., of those who are eternally steadfast.)
yogakṣemam (m. acc. sg.), to acquisition and possession, to the acquiring and protection of property.
vahāmi (1st sg. pr. indic. act. √*vah*), I lead, I carry, I bring.
aham (nom. sg.), I.

* *Śloka* metre resumes.

23

ये ऽप्य् अन्यदेवताभक्ता
ye 'py anyadevatābhaktā
who even other gods worshipping

यजन्ते श्रद्धयान्विताः ।
yajante śraddhayānvitāḥ
they sacrifice by faith accompanied

ते ऽपि माम् एव कौन्तेय
te 'pi mām eva kāunteya
they also to me, Son of Kuntī,

यजन्त्य् अविधिपूर्वकम् ॥
yajanty avidhipūrvakam
(though) they sacrifice not according to rule.

Even those who worship other gods,
Sacrificing with faith,
Also sacrifice to Me, Son of Kuntī,
Though they do not sacrifice according to rule.

ye (m. nom. pl.), who.
api, even, also.
anya-, other.
devatās (f.), gods, godheads.
bhaktās (m. nom. pl. p. pass. participle √*bhaj*), worshipping, sharing with.
(*anya-devatā-bhaktās*, m. nom. pl. TP cpd., worshipping other gods.)
yajante (3rd pl. pr. indic. mid. √*yaj*), they sacrifice, they worship.
śraddhayā (f. inst. sg.), with faith, by faith.
anvitās (m. nom. pl.), along with, accompanied by.
te (m. nom. pl.), they.
api, also, even.
mām (acc. sg.), me, to me.
eva, indeed (used as a rhythmic filler).
kāunteya (m. voc. sg.), Son of Kuntī, epithet of Arjuna.
yajanti (3rd pl. pr. indic. act. √*yaj*), they sacrifice, they worship.
avidhipūrvakam (adv.), not according to rule, in the absence of fixed rules.

24

अहं हि सर्वयज्ञानां
ahaṁ hi sarvayajñānāṁ
I indeed of all sacrifices

भोक्ता च प्रभुर् एव च ।
bhoktā ca prabhur eva ca
the enjoyer and the lord.

न तु माम् अभिजानन्ति
na tu mām abhijānanti
not, but, me they recognize

तत्त्वेनातश् च्यवन्ति ते ॥
tattvenātaś cyavanti te
in truth, hence they fall, they.

For I am the enjoyer and the Lord
Of all sacrifices.
But they do not recognize Me in truth;
Hence they fall.

aham (nom. sg.), I.
hi, indeed, truly.
sarvayajñānām (m. gen. pl.), of all sacrifices.
bhoktā (m. nom. sg.), enjoyer.
ca, and.
prabhus (m. nom. sg.), lord.
eva, indeed (used as a rhythmic filler).
ca, and.
na, not.
tu, but, indeed.
mām (acc. sg.), me.
abhijānanti (3rd pl. pr. indic. act. *abhi* √*jñā*), they recognize, they know.
tattvena (n. inst. sg.), by truth, in truth, in "thatness."
atas, hence, from this.
cyavanti (3rd pl. pr. indic. act. √*cyu*), they fall, they deviate, they vanish.
te (m. nom. pl.), they.

25

यान्ति देवव्रता देवान्
yānti devavratā devān
they go, those who are devoted to the gods, to the gods,

पितॄन् यान्ति पितृव्रताः ।
pitṝn yānti pitṛvratāḥ
to the ancestors go those who are devoted to the ancestors;

भूतानि यान्ति भूतेज्या
bhūtāni yānti bhūtejyā
to the spirits go those who sacrifice to the spirits;

यान्ति मद्याजिनो ऽपि माम् ॥
yānti madyājino 'pi mām
they go, those who sacrifice to me, surely to me.

yānti (3rd pl. act. √*yā*), they go, they attain.
devavratās (m. nom. pl.), the god-devoted, those devoted to the gods.
devān (m. acc. pl.), to the gods, the gods.
pitṝn (m. acc. pl.), to the ancestors, the ancestors.
yānti (3rd pl. pr. indic. act. √*yā*), they go, they attain.
pitṛvratās (m. nom. pl.), the ancestor-devoted, those who are devoted to the ancestors.
bhūtāni (n. acc. pl.), beings, spirits, to the spirits.
yānti (3rd pl. pr. indic. act. √*yā*), they go, they attain.
bhūtejyās (m. nom. pl.), the spirit-sacrificing, those devoted to the spirits.
yānti (3rd pl. pr. indic. act. √*yā*), they go, they attain.
madyājinas (m. nom. pl.), the me-sacrificing, those who are devoted to me.
api, even, also, surely.
mām (acc. sg.), me, to me.

Those who are devoted to the gods go to the gods;
To the ancestors go those who are devoted to the ancestors;
To the spirits go those who are devoted to the spirits;
Those who sacrifice to Me go surely to Me.

26

पत्त्रं पुष्पं फलं तोयं
pattraṁ puṣpaṁ phalaṁ toyaṁ
a leaf, a flower, a fruit, water,

यो मे भक्त्या प्रयच्छति ।
yo me bhaktyā prayacchati
who to me with devotion, he offers,

तद् अहं भक्त्युपहृतम्
tad ahaṁ bhaktyupahṛtam
that I devotion offered

अश्नामि प्रयतात्मनः ॥
aśnāmi prayatātmanaḥ
I eat* from him whose self is pure.

He who offers to Me with devotion
A leaf, a flower, a fruit or water,
That offering of devotion
I accept from him whose self is pure.

pattram (n. acc. sg.), leaf.
puṣpam (n. acc. sg.), flower.
phalam (n. acc. sg.), fruit.
toyam (n. acc. sg.), water.
yas (m. nom. sg.), who.
me (m. dat. sg.), to me.
bhaktyā (f. inst. sg.), with devotion, with love.
prayacchati (3rd sg. pr. indic. act. *pra* √*yam*), he offers, he presents, he goes toward.
tad (n. acc. sg.), this, that.
aham, I.
bhakti (f.), devotion, love.
upahṛtam (n. acc. sg. p. pass. participle *upa* √*hṛ*), offered, presented.
(*bhakti-upahṛtam*, n. acc. sg. TP cpd., offering of devotion.)
aśnāmi (1st sg. pr. indic. act. √*aś*), I eat, I partake, I accept.
prayata (m. p. pass. participle *pra* √*yam*), pure, controlled, dutiful.
ātmanas (m. abl. sg.), of the self, from the self.
(*prayatātmanas*, m. abl. sg. BV cpd., from him whose self is pure.)

* "I eat." The ancient belief was that the gods actually "ate" part of the sacrificial offering.

27

यत् करोषि यद् अश्नासि
yat karoṣi yad aśnāsi
what thou doest, what thou eatest,

यज् जुहोषि ददासि यत् ।
yaj juhoṣi dadāsi yat
what thou offerest, thou givest what,

यत् तपस्यसि कौन्तेय
yat tapasyasi kāunteya
what thou performest in austerities, Son of Kuntī,

तत् कुरुष्व मदर्पणम् ॥
tat kuruṣva madarpaṇam
that do (as) an offering to me.

Whatever thou doest, whatever thou eatest,
Whatever thou offerest, whatever thou givest,
Whatever austerities thou performest, Son of Kunti;
That do as an offering to Me.

yad (n. acc. sg.), what, which.
karoṣi (2nd sg. pr. indic. act. √*kṛ*), thou doest, thou makest.
yad (n. acc. sg.), what.
aśnāsi (2nd sg. pr. indic. act. √*aś*), thou eatest.
yad (n. acc. sg.), what, which.
juhoṣi (2nd sg. pr. indic. act. √*hu*), thou offerest (in sacrifice).
dadāsi (2nd sg. pr. indic. act. √*dā*), thou givest.
yad (n. acc. sg.), what, which.
yad (n. acc. sg.), what, which.
tapasyasi (2nd sg. pr. indic. act. √*tapasya*), thou performest (in the way of austerities), thou strivest.
kāunteya (m. voc. sg.), Son of Kuntī, epithet of Arjuna.
tad (n. acc. sg.), this, that.
kuruṣva (2nd sg. mid. imperative √*kṛ*), do! make!
madarpaṇam (n. acc. sg.), as an offering to me.

28

शुभाशुभफलैर् एवं
śubhāśubhaphalāir evaṁ
from good and evil fruits certainly,

मोक्ष्यसे कर्मबन्धनैः ।
mokṣyase karmabandhanāiḥ
thou shalt be liberated from the bonds of action;

संन्यासयोगयुक्तात्मा
saṁnyāsayogayuktātmā
thou whose self is disciplined in the Yoga of renunciation,

विमुक्तो माम् उपैष्यते ॥
vimukto mām upāiṣyate
liberated, me thou shalt come to.

Thou shalt certainly be liberated
From good and evil fruits, from the bonds of action;
Liberated, with thyself disciplined by the Yoga of renunciation,
Thou shalt come to Me.

śubhāśubha (n.), good and evil, auspicious and unfortunate.
phalāis (n. inst. pl.), by the fruits, from the fruits.
(*śubhāśubhaphalāis,* n. inst. pl., from good and evil fruits, by good and evil fruits.)
evam, thus, certainly.
mokṣyase (2nd sg. future pass. √*muc*), thou shalt be liberated, thou shalt be freed.
karmabandhanāis (n. inst. pl.), from the bonds of action, by the fetters of action.
saṁnyāsa (m.), renunciation, relinquishment.
yoga (m.), Yoga.
yukta (p. pass. participle √*yuj*), disciplined, joined in Yoga, steadfast, yoked.
ātmā (m. nom. sg.), self, thyself.
(*saṁnyāsayogayuktātmā,* m. nom. sg. BV cpd., whose self is disciplined in the Yoga of renunciation.)
vimuktas (m. nom. sg. p. pass. participle *vi* √*muc*), liberated, freed.
mām (acc. sg.), me.
upāiṣyate (3rd future 2nd sg. *upa* √*i*), thou shalt come, thou shalt attain, thou shalt go.

29

समो ऽहं सर्वभूतेषु
samo 'haṁ sarvabhūteṣu
the same I am in all beings;*

न मे द्वेष्यो ऽस्ति न प्रियः ।
na me dveṣyo 'sti na priyaḥ
not of me disliked there is, nor dear;

ये भजन्ति तु मां भक्त्या
ye bhajanti tu māṁ bhaktyā
who they worship, but, Me with devotion

मयि ते तेषु चाप्य् अहम् ॥
mayi te teṣu cāpy aham
in me they, and in them also I.

I am the same (self) in all beings;
There is none disliked or dear to Me.
But they who worship Me with devotion
They are in Me, and I also am in them.

samas (m. nom. sg.), the same, impartial, disinterested.
aham (nom. sg.), I.
sarvabhūteṣu (n. loc. pl.), in all beings, to all beings.
na, not.
me (m. gen. sg.), of me.
dveṣyas (m. nom. sg.), disliked, hated.
asti (3rd sg. pr. indic. √*as*), there is, it is.
na, not, nor.
priyas (m. nom. sg.), dear, favored.
ye (m. nom. pl.), who.
bhajanti (3rd pl. pr. indic. act. √*bhaj*), they worship, they honor.
tu, but, indeed.
mām (acc. sg.), me.
bhaktyā (f. inst. sg.), with devotion, with love.
mayi (m. loc. sg.), in me.
te (m. nom. pl.), they.
teṣu (m. loc. pl.), in them.
ca, and.
api, also, even.
aham (nom. sg.), I.

* "Being a refuge for all, God is the same toward all *ātmans* (selves) of gods, men, animals and immovables, which, according to their class, configuration, nature and knowledge, exist in an infinite plurality of forms." – Rāmānuja. The meaning is that God exists in all *ātmans* (selves) and is therefore a part, equal in quantity, of all beings, thus "the same" in all beings.

30

अपि चेत् सुदुराचारो
api cet sudurācāro
even if the evil doer

भजते माम् अनन्यभाक् ।
bhajate mām ananyabhāk
he worships me (with) not-another devoted,

साधुर् एव स मन्तव्यः
sādhur eva sa mantavyaḥ
righteous he to be thought.

सम्यग् व्यवसितो हि सः ॥
samyag vyavasito hi saḥ
rightly resolved indeed he.

If even the evil doer
Worships Me with undivided devotion,
He is to be thought of as righteous.
He is indeed rightly resolved.

api, even, also.
ced, if.
sudurācāras (m. nom. sg. from *su dur ā* √*car*), evil doing, evil doer.
bhajate (3rd sg. pr. indic. mid. √*bhaj*), he worships, he honors.
mām (acc. sg.), me.
ananyabhāk (m. nom. sg.), devoted to no one else.
sādhus (m. nom. sg.), righteous, good.
eva, indeed (used as a rhythmic filler).
sas (m. nom. sg.), he, this.
mantavyas (m. nom. sg. gerundive √*man*), to be thought, to be considered.
samyañc (adv.), rightly.
vyavasitas (m. nom. sg. p. pass. participle *vi ava* √*so*), resolved, determined, settled, undertaken.
hi, indeed, truly.
sas (m. nom. sg.), he, this.

31

क्षिप्रं भवति धर्मात्मा
kṣipraṁ bhavati dharmātmā
quickly he becomes one whose self is virtuous,

शश्वच्छान्तिं निगच्छति ।
śaśvacchāntiṁ nigacchati
everlasting peace he goes to

कौन्तेय प्रतिजानीहि
kāunteya pratijānīhi
Son of Kuntī, be aware!

न मे भक्तः प्रणश्यति ॥
na me bhaktaḥ praṇaśyati
not of me a devotee he is lost.

Quickly he becomes one whose self is virtuous;
He goes to everlasting peace.
Son of Kuntī, be aware!
No devotee of Mine is ever lost.

kṣipram (adv.), quickly, immediately.
bhavati (3rd sg. pr. indic. act. √*bhū*), he is, he becomes.
dharma (m.), virtuous, dutiful, righteous, law, rule.
ātmā (m. nom. sg.), self.
(*dharmātmā*, m. nom. sg. BV cpd., one whose self is virtuous.)
śaśvat, everlasting, perpetual, eternal.
śāntim (f. acc. sg.), peace, tranquility.
nigacchati (3rd sg. pr. indic. act. *ni* √*gam*), he goes to, he enters, he acquires.
kāunteya (m. voc. sg.), Son of Kuntī, epithet of Arjuna.
pratijānīhi (2nd sg. imperative act. *prati* √*jñā*), be aware! become aware! understand!
na, not.
me (m. gen. sg.), of me, my.
bhaktas (m. nom. sg. p. pass. participle √*bhaj*), worshipping, worshipper.
praṇaśyati (3rd sg. pr. indic. act. *pra* √*naś*), he is lost, he is destroyed.

32

मां हि पार्थ व्यपाश्रित्य
mām hi pārtha vyapāśritya
me indeed, Son of Pṛthā, taking refuge in

ये ऽपि स्युः पापयोनयः ।
ye 'pi syuḥ pāpayonayaḥ
who, even be they (from) evil wombs

स्त्रियो वैश्यास् तथा शूद्रास्
striyo vāiśyās tathā śūdrās
women, vaiśyas, even śūdras

ते ऽपि यान्ति परां गतिम् ॥
te 'pi yānti parām gatim
they also go to the highest goal.

They who take refuge in me, Son of Pṛthā,
Even if they are born of those whose wombs are evil (i.e. those of low origin),
Women, Vaiśyas,* even Śūdras,†
Also go to the highest goal.

mām (acc. sg.), me.
hi, indeed, truly.
pārtha, (m. voc. sg.), Son of Pṛthā, epithet of Arjuna.
vyapāśritya (gerund *vi apa ā* √*śri*), taking refuge in, having recourse to.
ye (m. nom. pl.), who.
api, even, also.
syus (3rd pl. optative act. √*as*), be they, should they be, they should be.
pāpa (m.), evil, wicked, sinful.
yonayas (m. nom. pl.), wombs, origins.
(*pāpayonayas,* m. nom. pl. BV cpd., those whose wombs are evil.)
striyas (f. nom. pl.), women.
vāiśyās (m. nom. pl.), Vāiśyas, members of the third caste.
tathā, even, thus, also.
śūdrās (m. nom. pl.), Sūdras, members of the fourth caste.
te (m. nom. pl.), they.
api, also, even.
yānti (3rd sg. pr. indic. act. √*yā*), they go, they attain.
parām (f. acc. sg.), highest, to the highest.
gatim (f. acc. sg.), goal, path, to the goal.

* *vāiśyās* – members of the merchant or peasant caste, third in order of rank.

† *śūdrās* – members of the servant caste, fourth in order of rank and lowest of the four original castes.

33

किं पुनर् ब्राह्मणाः पुण्या
kiṁ punar brāhmaṇāḥ puṇyā
how much more the brāhmans pure,

भक्ता राजर्षयस् तथा ।
bhaktā rājarṣayas tathā
devoted royal seers too

अनित्यम् असुखं लोकम्
anityam asukhaṁ lokam
impermanent unhappy world

इमं प्राप्य भजस्व माम् ॥
imaṁ prāpya bhajasva mām
this attaining, devote thyself to me.

How much more easily then, the pure Brāhmans
And the devoted royal seers!
Having attained this impermanent and unhappy world,
Devote thyself to Me.

kim (interrog.), what? how?
punar, again, more.
brāhmaṇās (m. nom. pl.), the Brahmans.
puṇyās (m. nom. pl.), pure, holy.
bhaktās (m. nom. pl.), devoted.
rājarṣayas (m. nom. pl.), royal seers.
tathā, also, too, thus.
anityam (m. acc. sg.), impermanent, perishable.
asukham (m. acc. sg.), unhappy, unpleasant.
lokam (m. acc. sg.), world.
imam (m. acc. sg.), this.
prāpya (gerund *pra* √*āp*), attaining, reaching.
bhajasva (2nd sg. imperative mid. √*bhaj*), devote thyself! honor! worship!
mām (acc. sg.), me, to me.

34

मन्मना भव मद्भक्तो
manmanā bhava madbhakto
by thought be to me devoted,

मद्याजी मां नमस्कुरु ।
madyājī māṁ namaskuru
to me sacrificing to me reverence make!

माम् एवैष्यसि युक्त्वैवम्
mām evāiṣyasi yuktvāivam
to me thou shalt come, made steadfast thus,

आत्मानं मत्परायणः ॥
ātmānaṁ matparāyaṇaḥ
thyself (with) me as supreme aim.

manmanās (m. nom. sg.), me-minded, (as BV cpd.) one whose mind is fixed on me, with me in mind, thinking of me.
bhava (2nd sg. imperative act. √*bhū*), be!
madbhaktas (m. nom. sg.), me worshipping, of me devoted.
madyājī (m. nom. sg.), to me sacrificing, me worshipping.
mām (acc. sg.), me, to me.
namaskuru (2nd sg. imperative, *namas* √*kṛ*), make reverence! make obeisance!
mām (acc. sg.), me, to me.
eva, indeed (used as a rhythmic filler).
eṣyasi (2nd sg. future √*i*), thou shalt come, thou shalt go.
yuktvā (gerund √*yuj*), made steadfast, steadfast, united in Yoga, disciplined, yoked.
evam, thus.
ātmānam (m. acc. sg.), thyself, self.
matparāyaṇas (m. nom. sg.), with me as supreme aim, with me as supreme object.

With mind fixed on Me, be devoted to Me;
Sacrificing to Me, make reverence to Me.
Thus steadfast, with Me as supreme aim,
Thou thyself shalt come to Me.

End of Book IX

The Yoga of Royal Knowledge and of Royal Mystery

BOOK X

श्रीभगवान् उवाच ।
śrībhagavān uvāca
the Blessed Lord spoke:

śrībhagavān (m. nom. sg.), the Blessed Lord, the Blessed one.
uvāca (3rd sg. perfect act. √*vac*), he said, he spoke.

1

भूय एव महाबाहो
bhūya eva mahābāho
again, Mighty Armed One,

शृणु मे परमं वचः ।
śṛṇu me paramaṁ vacaḥ
hear of me the supreme word

यत् ते ऽहं प्रीयमाणाय
yat te 'haṁ prīyamāṇāya
which to thee, I, to the beloved one,

वक्ष्यामि हितकाम्यया ॥
vakṣyāmi hitakāmyayā
I shall speak with desire for (thy) welfare.

bhūyas, again, once more.
eva, indeed (used as a rhythmic filler).
mahābāho (m. voc. sg.), O Mighty Armed One, epithet of Arjuna and other warriors.
śṛṇu (2nd sg. imperative act. √*śru*), hear!
me (gen. sg.), of me, from me.
paramam (n. acc. sg.), supreme, highest.
vacas (n. acc. sg.), word, advice.
yad (n. acc. sg.), which.
te (dat. sg.), to thee.
aham (nom. sg.), I.
prīyamāṇāya (m. dat. sg. pr. mid. participle √*prī*), to the delighting one, to the one who is beloved.
vakṣyāmi (1st sg. future act. √*vac*), I shall speak, I shall tell.
hitakāmyayā (f. inst. sg.), with desire for welfare.

The Blessed Lord spoke:

Again O Mighty Armed One (Arjuna),
Hear My supreme word
Which I shall speak to thee, who art beloved,
With desire for thy welfare.

X

2

न मे विदुः सुरगणाः
na me viduḥ suragaṇāḥ
not of me they know, the multitudes of gods,

प्रभवं न महर्षयः ।
prabhavaṁ na maharṣayaḥ
the origin, nor the great seers.

अहम् आदिर् हि देवानां
aham ādir hi devānāṁ
I the source, in truth, of the gods,

महर्षीणां च सर्वशः ॥
maharṣīṇāṁ ca sarvaśaḥ
and of the great seers universally.

na, not.
me (gen. sg.), of me.
vidus (3rd pl. perfect act. √*vid* with present meaning), they know.
suragaṇās (m. nom. pl.), the multitudes of gods, the aggregate of gods.
prabhavam (m. acc. sg.), origin, coming to be.
na, not, nor.
maharṣayas (m. nom. pl.), the great seers.
aham (nom. sg.), I.
ādis (m. nom. sg.), source, beginning.
hi, indeed, truly.
devānām (m. gen. pl.), of the gods.
maharṣīṇām (m. gen. pl.), of the great seers.
ca, and.
sarvaśas (adv.), in every way, in all cases, universally.

Neither the multitude of gods
Nor the great seers know My origin.
In truth I am the source of the gods
And of the great seers universally.

3

यो माम् अजम् अनादिं च
yo mām ajam anādiṁ ca
who me, the birthless and the beginningless

वेत्ति लोकमहेश्वरम् ।
vetti lokamaheśvaram
he knows, the World's Mighty Lord,

असंमूढः स मर्त्येषु
asaṁmūḍhaḥ sa martyeṣu
undeluded he among mortals

सर्वपापैः प्रमुच्यते ॥
sarvapāpāiḥ pramucyate
from all evils he is released.

He who knows Me, the Birthless and the Beginningless,
The Mighty Lord of the World,
He among mortals is undeluded;
From all evils he is released.

yas (m. nom. sg.), who.
mām (acc. sg.), me.
ajam (m. acc. sg.), unborn, birthless.
anādim (m. acc. sg.), beginningless, without beginning.
ca, and.
vetti (3rd sg. pr. indic. act. √*vid*), he knows.
lokamaheśvaram (m. acc. sg.), world's mighty lord, great lord of the world.
asaṁmūḍhas (m. nom. sg. p. pass. participle *a sam* √*muh*), undeluded, unconfused.
sas (m. nom. sg.), he, this.
martyeṣu (m. loc. pl.), in mortals, among mortals.
sarvapāpāis (m. inst. pl.), by all evils, from all evils, from all sins.
pramucyate (3rd sg. pr. indic. passive *pra* √*muc*), he is released, he is liberated, he is freed.

4

बुद्धिर् ज्ञानम् असंमोहः
buddhir jñānam asaṁmohaḥ
intelligence, knowledge, non-delusion,

क्षमा सत्यं दमः शमः ।
kṣamā satyaṁ damaḥ śamaḥ
patience, veracity, self restraint, tranquility,

सुखं दुःखं भवो ऽभवो
sukhaṁ duḥkhaṁ bhavo 'bhavo
pleasure, pain, becoming, passing away,

भयं चाभयम् एव च ॥
bhayaṁ cābhayam eva ca
and fear and fearlessness

Intelligence, knowledge, freedom from delusion,
Patience, veracity, self restraint, tranquility,
Pleasure, pain, becoming, passing away,
And fear and fearlessness,

buddhis (f. nom. sg.), intelligence.
jñānam (n. nom. sg.), knowledge, wisdom.
asaṁmohas (m. nom. sg.), non-delusion, non-confusion.
kṣamā (f. nom. sg.), patience, forbearance, tameness.
satyam (n. nom. sg.), truth, veracity, sincerity.
damas (m. nom. sg.), self restraint, control, domination of the self.
śamas (m. nom. sg.), tranquility, calmness, equanimity.
sukham (n. nom. sg.), pleasure, comfort, happiness.
duḥkham (n. nom. sg.), pain, discomfort, misery.
bhavas (m. nom. sg.), being, becoming, arising.
abhavas (m. nom. sg.), non-being, passing away.
bhayam (n. nom. acc. sg.), fear, terror.
ca, and.
abhayam (n. nom. sg.), fearlessness, absence of fear.
eva, indeed (used as a rhythmic filler).
ca, and.

5

अहिंसा समता तुष्टिस्
ahiṁsā samatā tuṣṭis
non-violence, impartiality, contentment,

तपो दानं यशो ऽयशः ।
tapo dānaṁ yaśo 'yaśaḥ
austerity, charity, fame, disrepute,

भवन्ति भावा भूतानां
bhavanti bhāvā bhūtānāṁ
they arise conditions of beings

मत्त एव पृथग्विधाः ॥
matta eva pṛthagvidhāḥ
from me alone manifold.

Non-violence, impartiality, contentment,
Austerity, charity, fame, disrepute,
The manifold conditions of beings,
Arise from Me alone.

ahiṁsā (f. nom. sg.), non-violence, harmlessness.
samatā (f. nom. sg.), impartiality, equableness.
tuṣṭis (f. nom. sg.), contentment, satisfaction.
tapas (m. nom. sg.), austerity, heat.
dānam (n. nom. sg.), charity, benevolence, gift.
yaśas (n. nom. sg., here m.), fame, celebrity, good name.
ayaśas (n. nom. sg., here m.), disrepute, bad reputation.
bhavanti (3rd pl. pr. indic. act. √*bhū*), they are, they arise, they come to be.
bhāvās (m. nom. pl.), conditions, states of being.
bhūtānām (m. gen. pl.), of beings, of creatures.
mattas (abl. sg.), from me.
eva, alone, indeed (often used as a rhythmic filler).
pṛthagvidhās (f. nom. pl.), manifold, existing in many forms, placed many times, of many varieties.

6

महर्षयः सप्त पूर्वे
maharṣayaḥ sapta pūrve
the great seers seven in the past

चत्वारो मनवस् तथा
catvāro manavas tathā
the four Manus also,

मद्भावा मानसा जाता
madbhāvā mānasā jātā
from me the origins, mentally brought forth,

येषां लोक इमाः प्रजाः ।।
yeṣāṁ loka imāḥ prajāḥ
from whom the world these creatures

The seven great seers of old*
And also the four Manus†
From whom have sprung these creatures of the world,
Originated from Me, born of My mind.

maharṣayas (m. nom. pl), great seers, mighty seers.
sapta, seven.
pūrve (m. loc. sg.), in the past, in previous times.
catvāras (m. nom. sg.), four.
manavas (m. nom. pl.), Manus, ancestors of the human race.
tathā, thus, also.
madbhāvās (m. nom. pl.), from me origins, originating from me.
mānasās (m. nom. pl.), mentally, deriving from mind.
jātās (m. nom. pl.), born, brought forth.
yeṣām (m. gen. pl.), of whom.
lokas (m. nom. sg.), world.
imās (f. nom. pl.), these.
prajās (f. nom. pl.), creatures, beings.

* Seven legendary seers (*ṛṣis*) – Kaśyapa, Atri, Vasiṣṭha, Viśvāmitra, Gotama, Jamadagni and Bharadvāja – sometimes identified with the seven stars of the Lesser Bear constellation, sometimes with other heavenly bodies. For Kaśyapa see chapter "The Setting of the Bhagavad Gītā."

† Manus seem to come in various quantities. Fourteen are commonly listed. All are purely legendary figures. One, Manu Vāivasvata, is supposed to have been the great Hindu lawgiver, author of the post-Vedic *Mānava dharmaśāstra,* and progenitor of the human race.

7

एतां विभूतिं योगं च
etāṁ vibhūtiṁ yogaṁ ca
this manifested lordship and power

मम यो वेत्ति तत्त्वतः ।
mama yo vetti tattvataḥ
of me who knows in truth

सो ऽविकम्पेन योगेन
so 'vikampena yogena
he by unwavering Yoga

युज्यते नात्र संशयः ॥
yujyate nātra saṁśayaḥ
is united (with me), not here doubt.

He who knows in truth
This, My manifested lordship and power,
Is united with Me by unwavering Yoga,
Of this there is no doubt.

etām (f. acc. sg.), this.
vibhūtim (f. acc. sg.), manifested might, manifested power.
yogam (m. acc. sg.), Yoga, power.
ca, and.
mama (gen. sg.), of me, my.
yas (m. nom. sg.), who.
vetti (3rd sg. pr. indic. act. √*vid*), he knows.
tattvatas (n. abl. sg.), in truth, from "thatness."
sas (m. nom. sg.), he, this.
avikampena (m. inst. sg. from *a vi* √*kamp*), by unwavering, by untrembling.
yogena (m. inst. sg.), by Yoga.
yujyate (3rd sg. pr. indic. passive √*yuj*), he is joined, he is united, he is yoked.
na, not.
atra, here, in this case.
saṁśayas (m. nom. sg.), doubt, irresolution, questioning.

8

अहं सर्वस्य प्रभवो
ahaṁ sarvasya prabhavo
I of all the origin

मत्तः सर्वं प्रवर्तते ।
mattaḥ sarvaṁ pravartate
from me all proceeds

इति मत्वा भजन्ते मां
iti matvā bhajante māṁ
thus thinking they worship me

बुधा भावसमन्विताः ॥
budhā bhāvasamanvitāḥ
the intelligent, endowed with the faculty of meditation.

I am the origin of all;
From Me all proceeds.
Thinking thus, the intelligent ones,
Endowed with the faculty of meditation, worship Me.

aham (nom. sg.), I.
sarvasya (m. gen. sg.), of all.
prabhavas (m. nom. sg.), origin, bringing to be.
mattas (m. abl. sg.), from me.
sarvam (m. acc. sg.), all.
pravartate (3rd sg. pr. indic. mid. *pra* √*vṛt*), it proceeds, it rolls onward, it happens, it begins.
iti, thus, so.
matvā (gerund √*man*), thinking, having thought, having considered.
bhajante (3rd pl. pr. indic. mid. √*bhaj*), they worship, they honor.
mām (acc. sg.), me.
budhās (m. nom. pl.), intelligent, learned, wise men.
bhāva (m.), state of being, disposition, contemplation, meditation, state of mind.
(*bhāva-samanvitās*, m. nom. pl. TP cpd., endowed with state of being.)
samanvitās (m. nom. pl.), endowed with, accompanied by.

9

मच्चित्ता मद्गतप्राणा
maccittā madgataprāṇā
those who think of me, who concentrate the vital breath on me,

बोधयन्तः परस्परम् ।
bodhayantaḥ parasparam
awakening each other,

कथयन्तश्च मां नित्यं
kathayantaśca māṁ nityaṁ
and speaking of me constantly,

तुष्यन्ति च रमान्ति च ॥
tuṣyanti ca ramanti ca
they are content and they rejoice.

Those who think of Me, who concentrate the vital breath on Me,
Enlightening each other,
And speaking of Me constantly,
They are content and they rejoice.

maccittās (m. nom. pl. BV cpd.), those who think of me.
madgataprāṇās (m. nom. pl. BV cpd.), those who have concentrated the vital breath on me.
bodhayantas (m. nom. pl. pr. act. causative participle √*budh*), enlightening, causing to enlighten, awakening.
parasparam, each other, one another.
kathayantas (m. nom. pl. pr. act. participle √*kath*), speaking of, relating about, explaining.
ca, and.
mām (acc. sg.), me.
nityam (adv.), constantly, eternally.
tuṣyanti (3rd pl. pr. indic. act. √*tuṣ*), they are content.
ca, and.
ramanti (3rd pl. pr. indic. act. √*ram*), they rejoice, they are delighted, they are pleased.
ca, and.

10

तेषां सततयुक्तानां
teṣāṁ satatayuktānāṁ
of them, of those who are constantly steadfast,

भजतां प्रीतिपूर्वकम् ।
bhajatāṁ prītipūrvakam
of the worshipping with affection,

ददामि बुद्धियोगं तं
dadāmi buddhiyogaṁ taṁ
I give intelligence-Yoga, it,

येन माम् उपयान्ति ते ॥
yena mām upayānti te
by which me they come to, they.

To them, those who are constantly steadfast,
Those who worship with affection,
I give the Yoga of discrimination
By which they come to Me.

teṣām (m. gen. pl.), of them, to them.
satata (adv.), constantly, perpetually.
yuktānām (m. gen. pl.), of the steadfast, of the disciplined.
(*satatayuktānām,* m. gen. pl. KD cpd., of those who are constantly steadfast.)
bhajatām (m. gen. pl. pr. act. participle √*bhaj*), of the worshippers, of the worshipping, of those who worship.
prītipūrvakam (adv.), with the accompaniment of kindness, with affection, affectionately.
dadāmi (1st sg. pr. indic. act. √*dā*), I give, I bestow.
buddhiyogam (m. acc. sg. TP cpd.), intelligence Yoga, the Yoga of intelligence, discipline of mind, Yoga of discrimination, power of discrimination.
tam (m. acc. sg.), it, this.
yena (m. inst. sg.), by which.
mām (acc.), me, to me.
upayānti (3rd pl. pr. indic. act. *upa* √*yā*), they come, they go.
te (m. nom. pl.), they.

11

तेषाम् एवानुकम्पार्थम्
teṣām evānukampārtham
of them (with) compassion aim,

अहम् अज्ञानजं तमः ।
aham ajñānajaṁ tamaḥ
I ignorance-born darkness

नाशयाम्य् आत्मभावस्थो
nāśayāmy ātmabhāvastho
I cause to be destroyed, in their own beings dwelling,

ज्ञानदीपेन भास्वता ॥
jñānadīpena bhāsvatā
with knowledge lamp, shining.

Out of compassion for them,
I, who dwell within their own beings,*
Destroy the darkness born of ignorance
With the shining lamp of knowledge.

teṣām (m. gen. pl.), of them.
eva, indeed (used as a rhythmic filler).
anukampā (f. from *anu* √*kamp*), sympathy, compassion, lit. "trembling alongside."
artham (m. acc. sg. ifc.), aim, goal, purpose.
(*anukampā-artha*, m. acc. sg., out of compassion.)
aham (nom. sg.), I.
ajñānajam (n. acc. sg.), ignorance-born, produced by ignorance.
tamas (n. acc. sg.), darkness, murk, guṇa of tamas.
nāśayāmi (1st causative pr. indic. √*naś*), I cause to be destroyed, I cause to be lost.
ātmabhāvasthas (m. nom. sg.), situated in own being, dwelling in own being.
jñānadīpena (m. inst. sg.), by the lamp of knowledge, with the lantern of knowledge.
bhāsvatā (m. inst. sg.), shining, luminous, bright.

* This phrase has been variously translated. Edgerton makes it "while remaining in my own true state," and some others follow him. I prefer the present translation.

अर्जुन उवाच ।
arjuna uvāca
Arjuna spoke:

arjunas (m. nom. sg.), Arjuna.
uvāca (3rd sg. perfect act. √*vac*), he said, he spoke.

12

मरं ब्रह्मपरं धाम
paraṁ brahma paraṁ dhāma
the Supreme Brahman, the supreme abode,

पवित्रं परमं भवान् ।
pavitraṁ paramaṁ bhavān
Purifier Supreme Thou (honorific),

पुरुषं शाश्वतं दिव्यम्
puruṣaṁ śāśvataṁ divyam
spirit eternal divine

आदिदेवम् अजं विभुम् ।।
ādidevam ajaṁ vibhum
the Primal God, birthless, all-pervading,

param (n. acc. sg.), highest, supreme.
brahma (n. acc. sg.), Brahman.
param (n. acc. sg.), highest, supreme.
dhāma (n. acc. sg.), dwelling, place, abode, domain.
pavitram (n. acc. sg.), purifier, cleanser.
paramam (n. acc. sg.), highest, supreme.
bhavān (m. acc. sg., honorific), thou, thy Lordship.
puruṣam (m. acc. sg.), spirit, being, person, man.
śāśvatam (m. acc. sg.), eternal, perpetual.
divyam (m. acc. sg.), divine, godly, heavenly.
ādidevam (m. acc. sg.), primal god, god existing from the beginning.
ajam (m. acc. sg.), birthless, unborn.
vibhum (m. acc. sg.), all-pervading, omnipresent.

Arjuna spoke:

Thou art the Supreme Brahman, the Supreme Abode,
The Supreme Purifier,
The eternal Divine Spirit,
The Primal God, birthless and all-pervading,

13

आहुस् त्वाम् ऋषयः सर्वे
āhus tvām ṛṣayaḥ sarve
they call Thee, the seers all

देवर्षिर् नारदस् तथा ।
devarṣir nāradas tathā
the divine seer Nārada, also

असितो देवलो व्यासः
asito devalo vyāsaḥ
Asita Devala and Vyāsa,

स्वयं चैव ब्रवीषि मे ॥
svayaṁ cāiva bravīṣi me
and Thyself Thou tellest me.

Thus they call Thee, the seers all,
The divine seer Nārada,*
Also Asita Devala† and Vyāsa,‡
And Thou Thyself (now) tellest me.

āhus (3rd pl. perfect act √*ah* with present meaning), they say, they tell, they call.
tvām (m. acc. sg.), thee.
ṛṣayas (m. nom. pl.), seers, wise men.
sarve (m. nom. pl.), all.
devarṣis (m. nom. sg.), divine seer.
nāradas (m. nom. sg.), Nārada, said to have been the composer of some hymns in the Ṛg Veda.
tathā, also, thus.
asitas devalas (m. nom. sg.), Asita Devala, legendary sage.
vyāsas (m. nom. sg.), Vyāsa, legendary compiler of the Vedas and natural grandfather of the Pāṇḍava Princes.
svayam (adv.), thyself, own, oneself.
ca, and.
eva, indeed (used as a rhythmic filler).
bravīṣi (2nd sg. pr. indic. act. √*brū*), thou sayest, thou tellest.
me (dat. sg.), to me, me.

* Nārada, a legendary seer to whom some of the verses of the Ṛg Veda are ascribed.

† Asita Devala, legendary composer of some other hymns of the Ṛg Veda.

‡ Vyāsa, legendary compiler of the Vedas and the Mahābhārata. The name means "arranger," "compiler," or "divider."

14

सर्वम् एतद् ऋतं मन्ये
sarvam etad ṛtaṁ manye
all this true I believe

यन् मां वदसि केशव ।
yan māṁ vadasi keśava
which to me thou speakest, Handsome Haired One (Krishna)

न हि ते भगवन् व्यक्तिं
na hi te bhagavan vyaktiṁ
not indeed of thee, O Blessed One, the manifestation

विदुर् देवा न दानवाः ॥
vidur devā na dānavāḥ
they know, the gods nor the demons.

sarvam (n. acc. sg.), all.
etad (n. acc. sg.), this.
ṛtam (n. acc. sg.), true, right.
manye (1st sg. pr. indic. mid. √*man*), I think, I believe.
yad (n. acc. sg.), which, what.
mām (acc. sg.), me, to me.
vadasi (2nd sg. pr. indic. act. √*vad*), thou sayest, thou tellest.
keśava (m. voc. sg.), O Handsome Haired One.
na, not.
hi, indeed, truly.
te (gen. sg.), of thee, thy.
bhagavan (m. voc. sg.), O Blessed One.
vyaktim (f. acc. sg.), manifestation, becoming visible.
vidus (3rd pl. perfect √*vid* with present meaning), they know.
devās (m. nom. pl.), the gods.
na, not, nor.
dānavās (m. nom. pl.), demons, evil spirits.

All this which Thou speakest to me, Handsome Haired One,
I believe to be true;
Indeed, neither the gods nor the demons, O Blessed One,
Know Thy manifestation.

15

स्वयम् एवात्मना ऽत्मानं
svayam evātmanā 'tmānaṁ
thyself alone through thyself thyself

वेत्थ त्वं पुरुषोत्तम ।
vettha tvaṁ puruṣottama
thou knowest, thou, Highest of Spirits,

भूतभावन भूतेश
bhūtabhāvana bhūteśa
causing welfare in beings, Lord of Beings,

देवदेव जगत्पते ॥
devadeva jagatpate
God of gods, O Lord of the Universe.

Thou knowest Thyself through Thyself alone,
Highest of Spirits,
Source of Welfare in Beings, Lord of Beings,
God of gods, O Lord of the Universe.

svayam, thyself, oneself, own.
eva, alone, indeed (often used as a rhythmic filler).
ātmanā (m. inst. sg.), by thyself, through thyself.
ātmānam (m.acc. sg.), thyself, self.
vettha (2nd sg. pr. indic. act. √*vid*), thou knowest.
tvam (m. nom. sg.), thou.
puruṣottama (m. voc. sg.), highest of spirits, highest of men, Supreme Spirit.
bhūtabhāvana (m. voc. sg.), causing welfare in beings, bringing welfare to be in beings.
bhūteśa (*bhūta īśa,* m. voc. sg.), Lord of Beings.
devadeva (m. voc. sg.), God of Gods.
jagatpate (m. voc. sg.), Lord of the Universe.

16

वक्तुम् अर्हस्य् अशेषेण
vaktum arhasy aśeṣeṇa
to describe please do without remainder

दिव्या ह्य् आत्मविभूतयः ।
divyā hy ātmavibhūtayaḥ
the divine indeed self-manifestations

याभिर् विभूतिभिर् लोकान्
yābhir vibhūtibhir lokān
by which manifestations the worlds

इमांस् त्वं व्याप्य तिष्ठसि ॥
imāṅs tvaṁ vyāpya tiṣṭhasi
these Thou, pervading, abidest in.

vaktum (infinitive √*vac*), to speak, to tell, to describe.
arhasi (2nd sg. pr. indic. act. √*arh*), thou art able, thou canst, please do!
aśeṣeṇa (m. inst. sg.), without remainder, completely.
divyās (m. nom. pl.), divine.
hi, indeed, truly.
ātmavibhūtayas (f. nom. pl.), self manifestations, self powers.
yābhis (f. inst. pl.), by which, with which.
vibhūtibhis (f. inst. pl.), manifestations, powers, appearances.
lokān (m. acc. pl.), worlds.
imān (m. acc. pl.), these.
tvam (m. nom. sg.), thou.
vyāpya (gerund *vi* √*āp*), pervading, permeating.
tiṣṭhasi (2nd sg. pr. indic. act. √*sthā*), thou abidest in, thou are situated in.

Be pleased to describe with completeness
The divine self-manifestations
By which Thou pervadest
These worlds, and abidest in them.

17

कथं विद्याम् अहं योगिंस्
kathaṁ vidyām ahaṁ yogiṅs
how may I know, I, O Yogin

त्वां सदा परिचिन्तयन् ।
tvāṁ sadā paricintayan
on thee constantly meditating?

केषुकेषु च भावेषु
keṣukeṣu ca bhāveṣu
and in what particular aspects of being

चिन्त्यो ऽसि भगवन् मया ॥
cintyo 'si bhagavan mayā
to be thought thou art, O Blessed One, by me?

How may I know Thee, O Yogin,
Constantly meditating on Thee?
And in what various aspects of being
Art Thou to be thought of by me, O Blessed One?

katham (interrog.), how? in what way?
vidyām (1st sg. optative act. √*vid*), I shall know, may I know.
aham (m. nom. sg.), I.
yogin (m. voc. sg.), O Yogin.
tvām (m. acc. sg.), thee.
sadā, always, constantly.
paricintayan (m. nom. sg. pr. causative participle act. *pari* √*cint*), meditating on, reflecting on, thinking about.
keṣu keṣu (m. loc. pl. interrog., repetition indicates distribution), in what various?
ca, and.
bhāveṣu (m. loc. pl.), in states of being, in aspects of being.
cintyas (m. nom. sg. gerundive √*cint*), to be thought, to be imagined.
asi (2nd sg. pr. indic. √*as*), thou art.
bhagavan (m. voc. sg.), O Blessed One, O Illustrious One.
mayā (m. inst. sg.), by me.

18

विस्तरेणात्मनो योगं
vistareṇātmano yogaṁ
in detail of thyself the power

विभूतिं च जनार्दन ।
vibhūtiṁ ca janārdana
and manifestation, O Agitator of Men,

भूयः कथय तृप्तिर् हि
bhūyaḥ kathaya tṛptir hi
further explain, satiation indeed

शृण्वतो नास्ति मे ऽमृतम् ॥
śṛṇvato nāsti me 'mṛtam
of hearing not there is, to me (of this) nectar.

vistareṇa (m. inst. sg.), in detail, by detail.
ātmanas (m. gen. sg.), of thyself, of self.
yogam (m. acc. sg.), power, Yoga.
vibhūtim (f. acc. sg.), manifestation.
ca, and.
janārdana (m. voc. sg.), O Agitator of Men, O Mover of Men, epithet of Vishnu-Krishna.
bhūyas, again, further.
kathaya (2nd sg. act. imperative √*kath*), tell! relate! explain!
tṛptis (f. nom. sg.), satiation.
hi, indeed, truly.
śṛṇvatas (n. gen. sg. participle *śru*), of hearing.
na, not.
asti (3rd sg. pr. indic. √*as*), there is, it is.
me (gen. sg.), of me, to me.
amṛtam (m. acc. sg.), nectar, immortality.

Explain to me further in detail
Thy power and manifestation, O Agitator of Men,
There is for me no satiation
In hearing Thy nectar-like words.

श्रीभगवान् उवाच ।
śrībhagavān uvāca
the Blessed Lord spoke:

śrībhagavān (m. nom. sg.), the Blessed Lord, the Blessed One.
uvāca (3rd sg. perfect act. √*vac*), he said, he spoke.

19

हन्त ते कथयिष्यामि
hanta te kathayiṣyāmi
listen! to thee I shall explain

दिव्या ह्य् आत्मविभूतयः ।
divyā hy ātmavibhūtayaḥ
the divine indeed self-manifestations

प्राधान्यतः कुरुश्रेष्ठ
prādhānyataḥ kuruśreṣṭha
(those that are) prominent, Best of Kurus,

नास्त्य् अन्तो विस्तरस्य मे ॥
nāsty anto vistarasya me
(for) not there is an end of the extent of me.

hanta (exhortative particle), listen! look! let us get on!
te (dat. sg.), to thee.
kathayiṣyāmi (1st sg. future act. √*kath*), I shall say, I shall tell, I shall explain.
divyās (f. acc. pl.), divine.
hi, indeed, truly.
ātmavibhūtayas (f. acc. pl.), self manifestations, own manifestations.
prādhānyatas (adv.), chief, mainly, most prominent.
kuruśreṣṭha (m. voc. sg.), Best of Kurus, epithet of Arjuna.
na, not.
asti (3rd sg. pr. indic. √*as*), there is, it is.
antas (m. nom. sg.), end.
vistarasya (m. gen. sg.), of the extent, of the spreading, of the expansion.
me (gen. sg.), of me, my.

The Blessed Lord spoke:

**Listen! I shall explain to thee
The divine self-manifestations;
Those only that are prominent,
For there is no end to My extent.**

20

अहम् आत्मा गुडाकेश
aham ātmā guḍākeśa
I the self, Thick Haired One,

सर्वभूताशयस्थितः ।
sarvabhūtāśayasthitaḥ
all-being-heart-abiding,

अहम् आदिश्च मध्यं च
aham ādiśca madhyaṁ ca
and I the beginning and the middle

भूतानाम् अन्त एव च ॥
bhūtānām anta eva ca
of beings and the end as well.

I am the ātman, Thick Haired One,
Abiding in the heart of all beings;
And I am the beginning and the middle
Of beings, and the end as well.

aham (m. nom. sg.), I.
ātmā (m. nom. sg.), self.
guḍākeśa (m. voc. sg.), O Thick Haired One, epithet of Arjuna.
sarva (m.), all.
bhūta (m.), being, creature.
āśaya (m.), resting place, heart, mind.
sthitas (m. nom. sg.), abiding in, situated in.
(*sarvabhūtāśayasthitas,* m. nom. sg. TP cpd., abiding in the heart of all beings.)
aham (nom. sg.), I.
ādis (m. nom. sg.), beginning, start, commencement.
ca, and.
madhyam (n. nom. sg.), middle.
ca, and.
bhūtānām (m. gen. pl.), of beings, of creatures.
antas (m. nom. sg.), end.
eva, indeed (often used as a rhythmic filler).
ca, and.
(*eva ca,* as well, also, too.)

21

आदित्यानाम् अहं विष्णुर्
ādityānām ahaṁ viṣṇur
of the Ādityas I Vishnu

ज्योतिषां रविर् अंशुमान् ।
jyotiṣāṁ ravir aṁśumān
of lights, the sun, radiant

मरीचिर् मरुताम् अस्मि
marīci marutām asmi
Marīci of the Maruts I am

नक्षत्राणाम् अहं शशी ॥
nakṣatrāṇām ahaṁ śaśī
of the stars I that which contains the rabbit.

Of the Ādityas,* I am Vishnu;
Of lights, the radiant sun;
I am Marīci† of the Maruts;‡
Among the nightly ones I am the moon;

ādityānām (m. gen. pl.), of the Ādityas.
aham (nom. sg.), I.
viṣṇus (m. nom. sg.), Vishnu.
jyotiṣām (n. gen. pl.), of luminaries, of lights, of stars.
ravis (m. nom. sg.), the sun.
aṁśumān (n. nom. sg.), radiant, shining.
marīcis (m. nom. sg.), Marīci, chief of the storm gods.
marutām (m. gen. pl.), of the Maruts, of the storm gods.
asmi (1st sg. pr. indic. √*as*), I am.
nakṣatrāṇām (n. gen. pl.), of the nightly ones, of the lunar zodiac.
aham (nom. sg.), I.
śaśī (m. nom. sg.), that which contains the rabbit, the moon.

* The Ādityas, originally seven, later twelve in number, were a group of supreme gods.

† Marīci was the chief of the Maruts or storm gods.

‡ Maruts were the storm gods who helped Indra slay the cosmic dragon, in order to bring water to the world.

22

वेदानां सामवेदो ऽस्मि
vedānāṁ sāmavedo 'smi
of the Vedas the Sama Veda I am,

देवानाम् अस्मि वासवः ।
devānām asmi vāsavaḥ
of the gods I am vāsava,

इन्द्रियाणाम् मनश्चास्मि
indriyāṇām manaścāsmi
and of the senses the mind I am,

भूतानाम् अस्मि चेतना ॥
bhūtānām asmi cetanā
of beings I am the consciousness.

vedānām (m. gen. pl.), of the Vedas.
sāmavedas (m. nom. sg.), the Sāma Veda.
asmi (1st sg. pr. indic. √*as*), I am.
devānām (m. gen. pl.), of the gods.
asmi (1st sg. pr. indic. √*as*), I am.
vāsavas (m. nom. sg.), Vāsava, one of the names of Indra, Vedic chief of the gods.
indriyāṇām (m. gen. pl.), of the senses.
manas (n. nom. sg.), mind, thought.
ca, and.
asmi (1st sg. pr. indic. √*as*), I am.
bhūtānām (m. gen. pl.), of beings, of creatures.
asmi (1st sg. pr. indic. √*as*), I am.
cetanā (f. nom. sg.), consciousness, mind, intelligence, thought.

Of the Vedas, I am the Sāma Veda,*
Of the gods, I am Vāsava,†
And of the senses, the mind am I,
I am the consciousness of beings.

* The Veda concerned with chants.
† One of the names of Indra, the chief Vedic god, mentioned by his usual name only in IX 20.

23

रुद्राणां शंकरश्चास्मि
rudrāṇāṁ śaṁkaraścāsmi
and of the Rudras Śaṁkara* I am,

वित्तेशो यक्षरक्षसाम् ।
vitteśo yakṣarakṣasām
Vittesa of the Yakṣas and Rakṣas,

वसूनां पावकश्चास्मि
vasūnāṁ pāvakaścāsmi
and of the Vasus Pavaka I am,

मेरुः शिखरिणाम् अहम् ॥
meruḥ śikhariṇām aham
Meru of mountains, I.

And of the Rudras,* I am Śaṁkara,†
Vitteśa‡ of the Yakṣas and Rakṣas,§
And Pāvaka|| of the Vasus¶ I am,
The Meru of mountains, I.**

rudrāṇām (m. gen. pl.), of the Rudras, of the gods of destruction and renewal.
śaṁkaras (m. nom. sg.), Shiva, chief god of renewal and destruction.
ca, and.
asmi (1st sg. pr. indic. √*as*), I am.
vitteśas (m. nom. sg.), Vitteśa, or Kubera, lord of wealth.
yakṣarakṣasām (m. gen. pl.), of the Yakṣas and Rakṣas.
vasūnām (m. gen. pl.), of the Vasus (a class of gods).
pāvakas (m. nom. sg.), Agni, the flame, God of Fire, the Purifier.
ca, and.
asmi (1st sg. pr. indic. √*as*), I am.
merus (m. nom. sg.), fabulous mountain, Hindu Olympos.
śikhariṇām (m. gen. pl.), of mountains, of mountain peaks.
aham (nom. sg.), I.

---

* Rudras, or "roarers," storm gods and gods of destruction and renewal.

† Śaṁkara, Shiva, god of fertility and destruction.

‡ Vitteśa, otherwise known as Kubera, lord of wealth.

§ Yakṣas and Rakṣas, spirits of vague character, sometimes hostile and sometimes benevolent.

|| Pāvaka, one of the names of Agni, the Vedic god of fire. The word means "purifier."

¶ Vasus, a group of eight "bright" gods.

** Mt. Meru was the Olympos of Hindu mythology.

24

पुरोधसां च मुख्यं मां
purodhasāṁ ca mukhyaṁ māṁ
and of the household priests, the chief, Me

विद्धि पार्थ बृहस्पतिम् ।
viddhi pārtha bṛhaspatim
know to be, Son of Pṛthā, Lord of Sacrifice,

सेनानीनाम् अहं स्कन्दः
senānīnām ahaṁ skandaḥ
of the commanders of armies, I am Skanda,

सरसाम् अस्मि सागरः ॥
sarasām asmi sāgaraḥ
of bodies of water I am the ocean.

purodhasām (m. gen. pl.), of household priests.
ca, and.
mukhyam (m. acc. sg.), the head, the chief.
mām (acc. sg.), me.
viddhi (2nd sg. imperative act. √*vid*), know! know to be!
pārtha (m. voc. sg.), Son of Pṛthā, epithet of Arjuna.
bṛhaspatim (m. acc. sg.), Bṛhaspati, priest of the gods.
senānīnām (m. gen. pl.), of the commanders of armies.
aham (nom. sg.), I.
skandas (m. nom. sg.), Skanda, god of war.
sarasām (n. gen. pl.), of bodies of water.
asmi (1st sg. pr. indic. √*as*), I am.
sāgaras (m. nom. sg.), the ocean.

And the chief of household priests,
Bṛhaspati, know Me to be, Son of Pṛthā,
Of the commanders of armies I am Skanda,*
Of bodies of water, I am the ocean.

* Skanda, the god of war, otherwise known as Kārttikeya.

25

महर्षीणां भृगुर् अहं
maharṣīṇāṁ bhṛgur ahaṁ
of the great seers Bhṛgu, I,

गिराम् अस्म्य् एकम् अक्षरम् ।
girām asmy ekam akṣaram
of utterances I am the one syllable (Oṁ),

यज्ञानां जपयज्ञो ऽस्मि
yajñānāṁ japayajño 'smi
of sacrifices the muttered prayer I am,

स्थावराणां हिमालयः ॥
sthāvarāṇāṁ himālayaḥ
of immovables the Himālaya.

maharṣīṇām (m. gen. pl.), of the great seers.
bhṛgus (m. nom. sg.), Bhṛgu, an illustrious mythical seer.
aham (nom. sg.), I.
girām (f. gen. pl.), of utterances.
asmi (1st sg. pr. indic. √*as*), I am.
ekam akṣaram (n. nom. sg.), the one syllable, the mystic syllable "Om."
yajñānām (m. gen. pl.), of sacrifices.
japayajñas (m. nom. sg.), the muttered prayer.
asmi (1st sg. pr. indic. √*as*), I am.
sthāvarāṇām (m. gen. pl.), of immovables, of unshakables.
himālayas (m. nom. sg.), "abode of snow," the Himālaya.

Of the great seers, I am Bhṛgu,*
Of utterances, I am the single syllable "Oṁ,"
Of sacrifices, I am the muttered prayer,
Of immovables, the Himālaya.

* Bhṛgu, ancient seer, so illustrious that he mediated quarrels among the gods.

26

अश्वत्थः सर्ववृक्षाणां
aśvatthaḥ sarvavṛkṣāṇāṁ
the sacred fig tree among all trees,

देवर्षीणां च नारद ।
devarṣīṇāṁ ca nārada
and of the divine seers, Nārada,

गन्धर्वाणां चित्ररथः
gandharvāṇāṁ citrarathaḥ,
and of the Gandharvas Citraratha

सिद्धानां कपिलो मुनिः ॥
siddhānāṁ kapilo muniḥ
of the perfected Kapila the sage.

aśvatthas (m. nom. sg.), the aśvattha, or sacred fig tree.
sarvavṛkṣāṇām (m. gen. pl.), of all trees, among all trees.
devarṣīṇām (m. gen. pl.), of divine seers.
ca, and.
nāradas (m. nom. sg.), Nārada, an ancient seer.
gandharvāṇām (m. gen. pl.), of the Gandharvas, of the heavenly musicians.
citrarathas (m. nom. sg.), Citraratha, chief of the Gandharvas. The name is a BV cpd. "He whose chariot is bright."
siddhānām (m. gen. pl.), of the perfected, of the successful.
kapilas (m. nom. sg.), Kapila, founder of Sāṁkhya, a school of philosophy.
munis (m. nom. sg.), sage, wise man.

Among all trees, I am the sacred fig tree,
And of the divine seers, Nārada,*
And of the Gandharvas,† Citraratha,‡
Of the perfected, Kapila§ the sage.

* Nārada, ancient seer to whom some verses of the Ṛg Veda are ascribed.
† Gandharvas, the musicians of paradise.
‡ Citraratha, heavenly chief of the Gandharvas.
§ Kapila, a sage, founder of the Sāṁkhya school of philosophy, one of the oldest of the Hindu systems.

27

उच्चैःश्रवसम् अश्वानां
uccāiḥśravasam aśvānāṁ
Uccāiḥśravas of horses

विद्धि माम् अमृतोद्भवम् ।
viddhi mām amṛtodbhavam
know me (to be) born of nectar

ऐरावतं गजेन्द्राणां
āirāvataṁ gajendrāṇāṁ
Āirāvata of princely elephants

नराणां च नराधिपम् ॥
narāṇāṁ ca narādhipam
and of men the Great Lord of men.

Uccaiḥśravas* of horses,
Born of nectar, know Me to be;
Āirāvata† of princely elephants,
And of men, the Great Lord.

uccāiḥśravasam (m. acc. sg.), Uccāiḥśravas, name of Indra's horse.
aśvānām (m. gen. pl.), of horses.
viddhi (2nd sg. imperative act. √*vid*), know! learn! know to be!
mām (acc. sg.), me.
amṛtodbhavam (m. acc. sg.), born of nectar, produced from nectar, originating in nectar.
āirāvatam (m. acc. sg.), Āirāvata, Indra's elephant.
gajendrāṇām (m. gen. pl.), of princely elephants.
narāṇām (m. gen. pl.), men.
ca, and.
narādhipam (m. acc. sg.), lord of men, great lord, king, protector of men.

* Uccāiḥśravas, the name of Indra's horse, or of the horse of the Sun god, born of nectar that was churned from the ocean. The name means "high sounding."

† Āirāvata, Indra's elephant. The name means "produced from the Irāvatī River."

28

आयुधानाम् अहं वज्रं
āyudhānām ahaṁ vajraṁ
of weapons I the thunderbolt,

धेनूनाम् अस्मि कामधुक् ।
dhenūnām asmi kāmadhuk
of cows I am the cow of wishes,

प्रजनश्चास्मि कन्दर्पः
prajanaścāsmi kandarpaḥ
and I am procreating Kandarpa,

सर्पाणाम् अस्मि वासुकिः ॥
sarpāṇām asmi vāsukiḥ
of serpents I am Vasuki.

āyudhānām (n. gen. pl.), of weapons.
aham (nom. sg.), I.
vajram (n. nom. sg.), thunderbolt.
dhenūnām (f. gen. pl.), of cows.
asmi (1st sg. pr. indic. √*as*), I am.
kāmadhuk (f. nom. sg.), Cow of Wishes, legendary cow of plenty.
prajanas (m. nom. sg.), begetting, generation, procreating.
ca, and.
asmi (1st sg. pr. indic. √*as*), I am.
kandarpas (m. nom. sg.), Kāma, god of desire, god of love.
sarpāṇām (m. gen. pl.), of serpents, of snakes.
asmi (1st sg. pr. indic. √*as*), I am.
vāsukis (m. nom. sg.), Vāsuki, king of serpents.

Of weapons, I am the thunderbolt,
Of cows, I am the cow of wishes,*
And I am procreating Kandarpa;†
Of serpents, I am Vāsuki.‡

* Kāmadhuk, a mythical cow, able to provide its master with anything desired.

† Kandarpa, god of love or desire, otherwise known as Kāma.

‡ Vāsuki, a serpent king.

29

अनन्तश्चास्मि नागानां
anantaścāsmi nāgānāṁ
and Ananta I am of snakes,

वरुणो यादसाम् अहम् ।
varuṇo yādasām aham
Varuṇa of the water creatures, I,

पितॄणाम् अर्यमा चास्मि
pitṝṇām aryamā cāsmi
and of the ancestors Aryaman I am,

यमः संयमताम् अहम् ॥
yamaḥ saṁyamatām aham
Yama of the subduers I.

anantas (m. nom. sg.), Ananta, "endless," "eternal," a mythical snake.
ca, and.
asmi (1st sg. pr. indic. √*as*), I am.
nāgānām (m. gen. pl.), of snakes.
varuṇas (m. nom. sg.), Varuṇa, the Supporter, one of the chief Vedic gods, later "King of the waters."
yādasām (n. gen. pl.), of water creatures, of sea monsters.
aham (nom. sg.), I.
pitṝṇām (m. gen. pl.), of the ancestors.
aryamā (m. nom. sg.), Aryaman, chief of the ancestors.
ca, and.
asmi (1st sg. pr. indic. √*as*), I am.
yamas (m. nom. sg.), Yama, god of death.
saṁyamatām (m. gen. pl. pr. participle act. *sam* √*yam*), of the subduers.
aham (nom. sg.), I.

Ananta* I am, of snakes,
Varuṇa† of the water creatures, I,
And of the ancestors I am Aryaman,‡
Yama§ of the subduers, I,

---

* Ananta, a mythical snake whose coils encircle the earth and who symbolizes eternity. The word means "unending."

† Varuṇa, originally a Vedic god, the sustainer of the universe. Here, in the later religion, a water god, the "water king."

‡ Aryaman, chief of the ancestors.

§ Yama, god of death.

30

प्रह्लादश्चास्मि दैत्यानां
prahlādaścāsmi dāityānāṁ
and Prāhlada I am of the Daityas,

कालः कलयताम् अहम् ।
kālaḥ kalayatām aham
Time of the calculators, I,

मृगाणां च मृगेन्द्रो ऽहं
mṛgāṇāṁ ca mṛgendro 'haṁ
and of the beasts the beast king, I,

वैनतेयश्च पक्षिणाम् ॥
vāinateyaśca pakṣiṇām
and Vāinateya of the birds.

prahlādas (m. nom. sg.), Pralādha, a prince of the Dāityas.
ca, and.
asmi (1st sg. pr. indic. √*as*), I am.
dāityānām (m. gen. pl.), of the Dāityas.
kālas (m. nom. sg.), time personified.
kalayatām (m. gen. pl. pr. participle act. √*kal*), of the calculators, of the reckoners.
aham (nom. sg.), I.
mṛgāṇām (m. gen. pl.), of beasts, of animals.
ca, and.
mṛgendras (m. nom. sg.), King of Beasts, the lion.
aham (nom. sg.), I.
vāinateyas (m. nom. sg.), Garuḍa, son of Vinatā, the bird vehicle of Vishnu.
pakṣiṇām (m. gen. pl.), of birds.

And Prahlāda,* I am of the Dāityas,†
Time, of the calculators, I,
And of the beasts, I am the lion,‡
And Vāinateya,§ of the birds.

* Prahlāda, a Dāitya (enemy of the gods) prince who defected from the Dāityas, became pious and worshipped Vishnu.

† Dāityas, demons at war with the gods.

‡ The word "mṛgendra" (*mṛga indra*) means literally "king of beasts."

§ Vāinateya (son of Vinatā), otherwise known as Garuḍa, a fabulous bird, and vehicle of Vishnu.

31

पवनः पवताम् अस्मि
pavanaḥ pavatām asmi
the wind of purifiers I am,

रामः शस्त्रभृताम् अहम् ।
rāmaḥ śastrabhṛtām aham
Rāma of the weapon bearing, I.

झषानां मकरश्चास्मि
jhaṣānāṁ makaraścāsmi
of the sea monsters I am Makara,

स्रोतसाम् अस्मि जाह्नवी ॥
srotasām asmi jāhnavī
of rivers, I am the Daughter of Jahnu (the Ganges).

Of purifiers, I am the wind,
Rāma* of the weapon-bearing, I,
Makara† of the sea monsters I am,
Of rivers, I am the Daughter of Jahnu (the Ganges).‡

pavanas (m. nom. sg.), the wind.
pavatām (m. gen. pl. pr. participle act. √*pu*), of purifiers, of cleansers.
asmi (1st sg. pr. indic. √*as*), I am.
rāmas (m. nom. sg.), Rāma, warrior hero of the Rāmāyaṇa.
śastrabhṛtām (m. gen. pl.), of the weapon bearing, of warriors.
aham (nom. sg.), I.
jhaṣānām (m. gen. pl.), of sea monsters.
makaras (m. nom. sg.), Makara, a sea monster or crocodile, avatār of Varuṇa.
ca, and.
asmi (1st sg. pr. indic. √*as*), I am.
srotasām (m. gen. pl.), of rivers.
asmi (1st sg pr. indic. √*as*), I am.
jāhnavī (f. nom. sg.), the Daughter of Jahnu, the Ganges.

* Rāma, warrior and hero of the epic, the Rāmāyaṇa, or possibly Paraśurāma, see chapter "Setting of the Bhagavad Gītā."

† Makara, a sea monster sometimes equated with a crocodile, shark or dolphin, the Capricorn of the Hindu zodiac, and vehicle of Varuna.

‡ So called because when Vishnu permitted the Ganges to flow, the sage Jahnu drank it up. Later he allowed it to flow from his ear.

32

सर्गाणाम् आदिर् अन्तश्च
sargāṇām ādir antaśca
of creations the beginning and the end

मध्यं चैवाहम् अर्जुन ।
madhyaṁ cāivāham arjuna
and the middle I, Arjuna,

अध्यात्मविद्या विद्यानां
adhyātmavidyā vidyānāṁ
the Supreme Self knowledge, of knowledges,

वादः प्रवदताम् अहम् ॥
vādaḥ pravadatām aham
the discourse of them that speak, I.

Of creations the beginning and the end,
And also the middle I am, Arjuna;
Of knowledges, the knowledge of the Supreme Self.
I am the discourse of those who speak.

sargāṇām (m. gen. pl.), of creations, of bringings forth.
ādis (m. nom. sg.), beginning.
antas (m. nom. sg.), end.
ca, and.
madhyam (n. nom. sg.), middle.
ca, and.
eva, also, indeed (often used as a rhythmic filler).
aham (nom. sg.), I.
arjuna (m. voc. sg.), Arjuna.
adhyātmavidyā (f. nom. sg.), Supreme-Self knowledge, knowledge of the Supreme Self.
vidyānām (f. gen. pl.), of knowledges.
vādas (m. nom. sg.), discourse.
pravadatām (m. gen. pl.), of those who speak.
aham (nom. sg.), I.

33

अक्षराणाम् अकारो ऽस्मि
akṣarāṇām akāro 'smi
of letters the letter A I am,

द्वन्द्वः सामासिकस्य च ।
dvandvaḥ sāmāsikasya ca
and the *dvandva* of compound (words),

अहम् एवाक्षयः कालो
aham evākṣayaḥ kālo
I alone infinite time,

धाताहं विश्वतोमुखः ॥
dhātāhaṁ viśvatomukhaḥ
the establisher, I, facing in all directions.

akṣarāṇām (m. gen. pl.), of letters of the alphabet, lit. "indestructibles" or "irreducibles."
akāras (m. nom. sg.), letter A.
asmi (1st sg. pr. indic. √*as*), I am.
dvaṁdvas or *dvandvas* (m. nom. sg.), simple copulative compound (consisting of two or more words).
sāmāsikasya (m. gen. sg.), of the system of compounds.
ca, and.
aham (nom. sg.), I.
eva, alone, indeed (often used as a rhythmic filler).
akṣayas (m. nom. sg.), infinite, imperishable, indestructible.
kālas (m. nom. sg.), time.
dhātā (m. nom. sg.), establisher, arranger.
aham (nom. sg.), I.
viśvatomukhas (m. nom. sg.), facing in all directions, omniscient.

Of letters I am the letter A
And the dvandva* of compound words;
I alone am infinite Time,
The Establisher, I, facing in all directions (i.e. omniscient).

* *dvandva* is the simple copulative compound, where two or more words are joined together.

34

मृत्युः सर्वहरश्चाहम्
mṛtyuḥ sarvaharaścāham
and death all-destroying, I,

उद्भवश्च भविष्यताम् ।
udbhavaśca bhaviṣyatām
and the origin of those things that are to be,

कीर्तिः श्रीर् वाक् च नारीणां
kīrtiḥ śrīr vāk ca nārīṇām
fame, prosperity, and speech of feminine things,

स्मृतिर् मेधा धृतिः क्षमा ॥
smṛtir medhā dhṛtiḥ kṣamā
(also) memory, wisdom, courage, patience.

mṛtyus (m. nom. sg.), death.
sarvaharas (m. nom. sg.), all-destroying, all seizing.
ca, and.
aham (nom. sg.), I.
udbhavas (m. nom. sg.), origin.
ca, and.
bhaviṣyatām (m. gen. pl.), of those things that are to be, of those events that are to happen.
kīrtis (f. nom. sg.), fame, good name.
śrīs (f. nom. sg.), prosperity, wealth.
vāk (f. nom. sg.), speech.
ca, and.
nārīṇām (f. gen. pl.), of feminine things, of womanly words.
smṛtis (f. nom. sg.), memory, reflection.
medhā (f. nom. sg.), wisdom, mental vigor, intelligence.
dhṛtis (f. nom. sg.), courage, firmness, constancy.
kṣamā (f. nom. sg.), patience, endurance, submissiveness.

And I am all-destroying death,
And the origin of those things that are to be.
Among the feminine,* I am fame, prosperity and speech,
And also memory, wisdom, courage and patience.

* All these listed nouns are of feminine gender.

35

बृहत्साम तथा साम्नां
bṛhatsāma tathā sāmnāṁ
the Bṛhatsaman also of chants,

गायत्री छन्दसाम् अहम् ।
gāyatrī chandasām aham
the gāyatrī of metres, I,

मासानां मार्गशीर्षो ऽहम्
māsānāṁ mārgaśīrṣo 'ham
of months, mārgaśīrṣa, I,

ऋतूनां कुसुमाकरः ॥
ṛtūnāṁ kusumākaraḥ
of seasons, the abounding with flowers (Spring).

bṛhatsāma (n. nom. sg.), the Bṛhatsaman, a type of Vedic melody.
tathā, also, thus.
sāmnām (n. gen. pl.), of chants.
gāyatrī (f. nom. sg.), the gāyatrī metre, used in the Vedas, obsolete in later Sanskrit.
chandasām (n. gen. pl.), of metres.
aham (nom. sg.), I.
māsānām (m. gen. pl.), of months.
mārgaśīrṣas (m. nom. sg.), month of mārgaśīrṣa, roughly November–December.
aham (nom. sg.), I.
ṛtūnām (m. gen. pl.), of seasons.
kusumākaras (m. nom. sg.), abounding with flowers, Spring.

Of chants I am the Bṛhatsāman*
The gāyatrī† of metres I am,
Of months, the mārgaśīrṣa,‡ I,
Of seasons, the Abounding with Flowers (Spring).

---

* *bṛhatsāman*, a type of chant to Indra in the Sāma Veda.

† *gāyatrī*, a Ṛg Vedic metre consisting of three lines of eight syllables each, thought suitable for brāhmans. It exists only in the Vedic literature.

‡ *mārgaśīrṣa*, the month when the moon enters the constellation of *mṛga śiras* ("deer head," fifth lunar mansion), roughly November–December. It is interesting that Krishna's months and seasons are the Spring and Autumn. The hot Indian summer and the damp Indian winter are avoided.

36

द्यूतं छलयताम् अस्मि
dyūtaṁ chalayatām asmi
the gambling of the dishonest I am,

तेजस् तेजस्विनाम् अहम् ।
tejas tejasvinām aham
the splendor of the splendid, I,

जयो ऽस्मि व्यवसायो ऽस्मि
jayo 'smi vyavasāyo 'smi
victory I am, effort I am,

सत्त्वं सत्त्ववताम् अहम् ॥
sattvaṁ sattvavatām aham
the goodness of the good, I.

dyūtam (n. nom. sg.), gambling.
chalayatām (m. gen. pl.), of the dishonest, of cheats.
asmi (1st sg. pr. indic. √*as*), I am.
tejas (n. nom. sg.), splendor, brilliance.
tejasvinām (m. gen. pl.), of the splendid, of the brilliant ones.
aham (nom. sg.), I.
jayas (m. nom. sg.), victory.
asmi (1st sg. pr. indic. √*as*), I am.
vyavasāyas (m. nom. sg.), effort, resolve, exertion.
asmi (1st sg. pr. indic. √*as*), I am.
sattvam (n. nom. sg.), goodness, virtue, truth, reality.
sattvavatām (m. n. gen. pl.), of the good, of the virtuous, of those who are full of truth.
aham (nom. sg.), I.

I am the gambling of the dishonest,
The splendor of the splendid, I,
I am victory, I am effort,
I am the goodness of the good.*

* This line may also be translated: I am the truth of truth-tellers. (*Sattva* means either "good," "true" or "real.")

37

वृष्णीनां वासुदेवो ऽस्मि
vṛṣṇīnāṁ vāsudevo 'smi
of the Vṛṣṇis, Vāsudeva I am,

पाण्डवानां धनंजयः ।
pāṇḍavānāṁ dhanaṁjayaḥ
of the sons of Pāṇḍu, Conqueror of Wealth (Arjuna),

मुनीनाम् अप्य् अहं व्यासः
munīnām apy ahaṁ vyāsaḥ
of the sages, moreover, I, Vyāsa,

कवीनाम् उशना कविः ॥
kavīnām uśanā kaviḥ
of poets, Uśanas the poet.

vṛṣṇīnām (m. gen. pl.), of the Vṛṣṇis, a clan from which Krishna sprang.
vāsudevas (m. nom. sg.), the Son of Vasudeva, Krishna himself.
asmi (1st sg. pr. indic. √*as*), I am.
pāṇḍavānām (m. gen. pl.), of the Sons of Pāṇḍu.
dhanaṁjayas (m. nom. sg.), Conqueror of Wealth, epithet of Arjuna.
munīnām (m. gen. pl.), of sages.
api, moreover, also.
aham (nom. sg.), I.
vyāsas (m. nom. sg.), Vyāsa, "the divider or arranger," legendary compiler of the Vedas.
kavīnām (m. gen. pl.), of poets.
uśanā (m. nom. sg.), Uśanas or Uśanā, an ancient seer.
kavis (m. nom. sg.), poet.

Of the Vṛsnis,* Vāsudeva† I am,
Of the sons of Pāṇḍu, Conqueror of Wealth (Arjuna),
Of the sages, moreover, I am Vyāsa,‡
Of poets, the poet Uśanas.§

* Vṛṣṇis, a clan from which Krishna himself is descended.

† Vāsudeva, patronymic of Krishna himself: "Son of Vasudeva."

‡ Vyāsa, legendary sage supposed to have compiled the Vedas. His identity is chronologically confused. He is supposed to have compiled the *Mahābhārata*, of which the Bhagaved Gītā is a part, and he appears in that Epic as the natural grandfather of the Pāṇḍava princes. (See chapter, "The Setting of the Bhagavad Gītā.")

§ Uśanas or Uśanā, an ancient seer and poet.

38

दण्डो दमयताम् अस्मि
daṇḍo damayatām asmi
the power of rulers I am,

नीतिर् अस्मि जिगीषताम् ।
nītir asmi jigīṣatām
the guidance I am of the desirous of victory,

मौनं चैवास्मि गुह्यानां
māunaṁ cāivāsmi guhyānāṁ,
and the silence also I am of secrets

ज्ञानं ज्ञानवताम् अहम् ॥
jñānaṁ jñānavatām aham
the knowledge of the knowing, I.

I am the power of rulers,
The guidance I am of those desirous of victory,
And I am also the silence of secrets,
The knowledge of the wise, I.

daṇḍas (m. nom. sg.), power (lit. "stick," exactly like the modern word "clout").
damayatām (m. gen. pl. pr. participle act. √*dam*), of rulers, of kings.
asmi (1st sg. pr. indic. √*as*), I am.
nītis (f. nom. sg.), guidance, advice.
asmi (1st sg. pr. indic. √*as*), I am.
jigīṣatām (m. gen. pl. desiderative pr. participle act. √*ji*), of the desirous of victory, of those desiring victory.
māunam (n. nom. sg.), silence, taciturnity.
ca, and.
eva, also, indeed (often used as a rhythmic filler).
asmi (1st sg. pr. indic. √*as*), I am.
guhyānām (n. gen. pl.), of secrets.
jñānam (n. nom. sg.), knowledge.
jñānavatām (m. gen. pl.), of the knowing, of the rich in knowledge.
aham (nom. sg.), I.

39

यच् चापि सर्वभूतानां
yac cāpi sarvabhūtānāṁ
and which also of all creatures

बीजं तद् अहम् अर्जुन ।
bījaṁ tad aham arjuna
the seed, that I, Arjuna

न तद् अस्ति विना यत् स्यान्
na tad asti vinā yat syān
not that there is without which it could
  exist

मया भूतं चराचरम् ॥
mayā bhūtaṁ carācaram
by me existing, moving or not moving.

And also that which is the seed of all
  creatures,
That am I, Arjuna;
There is nothing that could exist
  without
Existing through Me, whether moving
  or not moving.

yad (n. nom. sg.), which.
ca, and.
api, also, even.
sarvabhūtānām (m. gen. pl.), of all beings,
  of all creatures.
bījam (n. nom. sg.), seed.
tad (n. nom. sg.), that.
aham (nom. sg.), I.
arjuna (m. voc. sg.), Arjuna.
na, not.
tad (n. nom. sg.), that.
asti (3rd sg. pr. indic. √*as*), there is, it is.
vinā, without.
yad (n. nom. sg.), which.
syāt (3rd sg. optative act. √*as*), it should be,
  it could exist.
mayā (m. inst. sg.), by me, through me.
bhūtam (n. nom. sg.), being, existing.
carācaram (n. nom. sg.), moving or not
  moving, animate or inanimate.

40

नान्तो ऽस्ति मम दिव्यानां
nānto 'sti mama divyānāṁ
not end there is of me, of the divine

विभूतीनां परंतप ।
vibhūtīnāṁ paraṁtapa
manifestations, Scorcher of the Foe,

एष तूद्देशतः प्रोक्तो
eṣa tūddeśataḥ prokto
this indeed by example declared

विभूतेर् विस्तरो मया ।।
vibhūter vistaro mayā
of manifestation extent by me.

na, not.
antas (m. nom. sg.), end.
asti (3rd sg. pr. indic. √*as*), there is, it is.
mama (gen. sg.), of me, of my.
divyānām (n. gen. pl.), of divine, of heavenly.
vibhūtīnām (n. gen. pl.), of manifestations.
paraṁtapa (m. voc. sg.), Scorcher of the Foe, epithet of Arjuna.
eṣas (m. nom. sg.), this.
tu, indeed, but.
uddeśatas (adv.), by way of explanation, for example.
proktas (m. nom. sg. p. pass. participle *pra* √*vac*), declared, explained.
vibhūtes (n. gen. sg.), of manifestation.
vistaras (m. nom. sg.), extent, expansion, spreading.
mayā (inst. sg.), by me.

There is no end to My divine
Manifestations, Scorcher of the Foe,
This* has been declared by Me
As an example of the extent of my manifestations.

* I.e. the preceding declarations.

41

यद् यद् विभूतिमत् सत्त्वं
yad yad vibhūtimat sattvaṁ
whatever powerful being

श्रीमद् ऊर्जितम् एव वा ।
śrīmad ūrjitam eva vā
glorious or vigorous, indeed,

तत् तद् एवावगच्छ त्वं
tat tad evāvagaccha tvaṁ
in every case understand thou

मम तेजों ऽशसंभवम् ।।
mama tejo'ṁśasaṁbhavam
of me splendor fraction origin.

Whatever manifested being exists,
Glorious and vigorous, indeed,
Understand that in every case
He originates from a fraction of My splendor.

yad yad (n. nom. sg.), whatever.
vibhūtimat (n. nom. sg.), powerful, splendid, glorious.
sattvam (n. nom. sg.), being, existence, truth.
śrīmat (n. nom. sg.), glorious, pleasant, splendid, prosperous.
ūrjitam (n. nom. sg.), vigorous, powerful.
eva, indeed (used as a rhythmic filler).
vā, indeed.
tat tad (n. acc. sg.), that that, this and that, in every case.
eva, indeed (used as a rhythmic filler).
avagaccha (2nd sg. imperative act. *ava* √*gam*), understand! comprehend!
tvam (nom. sg.), thou.
mama (gen. sg.), of me, my.
tejas (n. acc. sg.), splendor, brilliance, power.
aṁśa (m.), fraction, portion, share.
saṁbhavam (m. acc. sg.), origin, coming to be.
(*tejas-aṁsa-saṁbhavam,* m. acc. sg. TP cpd., origion of a fraction of splendor.)

42

अथवा बहुनैतेन
athavā bahunāitena
but with extensive this

किं ज्ञातेन तवार्जुन ।
kiṁ jñātena tavārjuna
what with knowledge to thee, Arjuna?

विष्टभ्याहम् इदं कृत्स्नम्
viṣṭabhyāham idaṁ kṛtsnam
supporting I this entire,

एकांशेन स्थितो जगत् ॥
ekāṁśena sthito jagat
by a single fraction constantly, world.

But what is this extensive
Knowledge to thee, Arjuna?
I support this entire universe constantly
With a single fraction of Myself.

athavā, however, but, or rather.
bahunā (m. inst. sg.), with extensive, with abundant, with much.
etena (m. inst. sg.), with this.
kim (interrog.), what?
jñātena (m. inst. sg. p. pass. participle √*jñā*), with knowledge, by knowledge, "by the known."
tava (gen. sg.), of thee, to thee.
arjuna (m. voc. sg.), Arjuna.
viṣṭabhya (gerund *vi* √*stabh*), supporting, propping up.
aham (nom. sg.), I.
idam (n. acc. sg.), this.
kṛtsnam (n. acc. sg.), entire, whole.
eka, one, single.
aṁśena (m. inst. sg.), by a fraction.
(*ekāṁśena,* m. inst. sg., by a single fraction.)
sthitas (m. nom. sg. perf. √*sthā*), standing, can be rendered adverbially as constantly, continually, remaining.
jagat (n. acc. sg.), universe, world.

End of Book X

The Yoga of Manifestation

BOOK XI

अर्जुन उवाच।
arjuna uvāca
Arjuna spoke:

arjunas (m. nom. sg.), Arjuna.
uvāca (3rd sg. perfect act. √*vac*), he said, he spoke.

1

मदनुग्रहाय परमं
*madanugrahāya paramaṁ**
as a favor to me the highest

गुह्यम् अध्यात्मसंज्ञितम्।
guhyam adhyātmasaṁjñitam
secret, the supreme self known as,

यत् त्वयोक्तं वचस् तेन
yat tvayoktaṁ vacas tena
which by thee spoken the words, by this,

मोहो ऽयं विगतो मम॥
moho 'yam vigato mama
delusion this gone of me.

Arjuna spoke:

As a favor to me, Thou hast spoken
About the highest secret
Known as the Supreme Self.
With this my delusion is gone.

madanugrahāya (m. dat. sg.), as a favor to me, as a kindness to me.
paramam (n. nom. sg.), highest, supreme.
guhyam (n. nom. sg.), secret.
adhyātma (m.), Supreme Self, Supreme Soul.
saṁjñitam (n. nom. sg. denominative p. pass. participle from *saṁjñā*), known as, recognized as.
(*adhyātmasaṁjñitam*, n. nom. sg., known as the Supreme Self.)
yad (n. nom. sg.), which.
tvayā (m. inst. sg.), by thee.
uktam (n. nom. sg. p. pass. participle √*vac*), spoken, uttered.
vacas (n. nom. sg.), word, speech.
tena (m. inst. sg.), by this.
mohas (m. nom. sg.), delusion, confusion.
ayam (m. nom. sg.), this.
vigatas (m. nom. sg. p. pass. participle *vi* √*gam*), gone, departed.
mama (gen. sg.), of me, my.

* The line is one syllable too long, a rarity in the *śloka* stanzas of this poem.

2

भवाप्ययौ हि भूतानां
bhavāpyayāu hi bhūtānāṁ
the origin and dissolution indeed of beings

श्रुतौ विस्तरशो मया ।
śrutāu vistaraśo mayā
they two heard in detail by me

त्वत्तः कमलपत्त्राक्ष
tvattaḥ kamalapattrākṣa
from thee, O Lotus-Petal-Eyed,

माहात्म्यम् अपि चाव्ययम् ॥
māhātmyam api cāvyayam
and majesty also eternal.

bhavāpyayāu (m. nom. dual *bhava api* √*i*), origin and dissolution, origin and going.
hi, indeed.
bhūtānām (m. gen. pl.), of beings, of creatures.
śrutāu (m. nom. dual p. pass. participle √*śru*), heard, they two have been heard.
vistaraśas, in detail.
mayā (m. inst. sg.), by me.
tvattas (m. abl. sg.), from thee.
kamalapattrākṣa (m. voc. sg.), Lotus Petal Eyed, description honorific of Krishna.
māhātmyam (n. nom. sg.), majesty, greatness.
api, also.
ca, and.
avyayam (n. nom. sg.), eternal, imperishable.

The origin and the dissolution of beings,
These two have been heard in detail by me,
From Thee, O Lotus Petal Eyed One,
And also Thine imperishable majesty.

3

एवम् एतद् यथात्थ त्वम्
evam etad yathāttha tvam
thus this (is) as thou sayest, thou

आत्मानं परमेश्वर ।
ātmānaṁ parameśvara
thyself, O Supreme Lord.

द्रष्टुम् इच्छामि ते रूपम्
draṣṭum icchāmi te rūpam
to see I desire of thee the form

ऐश्वरं पुरुषोत्तम ॥
āiśvaram puruṣottama
princely, O Supreme Spirit.

Thus, this is as Thou sayest,
Thou Thyself, O Supreme Lord.
I desire to see Thy princely form
O Supreme Spirit.

evam, thus.
etad (n. nom. sg.), this.
yathā, in which way, as.
āttha (2nd sg. perf. act. √*ah* with present meaning), thou sayest, thou tellest.
tvam (nom. sg.), thou.
ātmānam (m. acc. sg.), thyself, self.
parameśvara (m. voc. sg.), Supreme Lord.
draṣṭum (infinitive √*dṛś*), to see, to behold.
icchāmi (1st sg. pr. indic. act. √*iṣ*), I desire, I wish.
te (gen. sg.), of thee, thy.
rūpam (n. acc. sg.), form, shape, figure.
āiśvaram (n. acc. sg.), lordly, godly, princely.
puruṣottama (m. voc. sg.), Supreme Spirit, Highest of Men.

4

मन्यसे यदि तच्छक्यं
manyase yadi tac chakyaṁ
thou thinkest, if, that possible

मया द्रष्टुम् इति प्रभो ।
mayā draṣṭum iti prabho
by me to see thus O Lord,

योगेश्वर ततो मे त्वं
yogeśvara tato me tvaṁ
Prince of Yoga, then to me thou

दर्शयात्मानम् अव्ययम् ॥
darśayātmānam avyayam
cause to be seen thyself, the imperishable.

manyase (2nd sg. pr. indic. mid. √*man*), thou thinkest, thou considerest.
yadi, if.
tad (n. acc. sg.), that.
śakyam (n. acc. sg.), possible, practicable.
mayā (inst. sg.), by me.
draṣṭum (infinitive √*dṛś*), to see, to behold.
iti, thus.
prabho (m. voc. sg.), O Lord, O God.
yogeśvara (m. voc. sg.), Prince of Yoga.
tatas, then, thence.
me (dat. sg.), to me.
tvam (nom. sg.), thou.
darśaya (2nd sg. causative imperative act. √*dṛś*), cause to be seen! exhibit! allow me to behold!
ātmānam (m. acc. sg.), thyself, self.
avyayam (m. acc. sg.), imperishable, eternal.

If Thou thinkest it possible
For me to see this, O Lord,
Prince of Yoga, then to me
Cause to be seen Thyself, the Imperishable.

श्रीभगवान् उवाच ।
śrībhagavān uvāca
the Blessed Lord spoke:

śrībhagavān (m. nom. sg.), the Blessed Lord, the Blessed One.
uvāca (3rd sg. perfect act. √*vac*), he said, he spoke.

5

पश्य मे पार्थ रूपाणि
paśya me pārtha rūpāṇi
behold of me, Son of Pṛthā, the forms

शतशो ऽथ सहस्रशः ।
śataśo 'tha sahasraśaḥ
a hundred fold, rather, a thousand fold,

नानाविधानि दिव्यानि
nānāvidhāni divyāni
various, divine,

नानावर्णाकृतीनि च ॥
nānāvarṇākṛtīni ca
and of various colors and shapes.

paśya (2nd sg. imperative √*paś*), see! behold!
me (gen. sg.), of me, my.
pārtha (m. voc. sg.), Son of Pṛthā, epithet of Arjuna.
rūpāṇi (n. acc. pl.), forms, shapes, figures.
śataśas, a hundred fold.
atha, rather, or.
sahasraśas, a thousand fold.
nānāvidhāni (n. acc. pl.), various, multiple.
divyāni (n. acc. pl.), divine, heavenly.
nānā, various, multiple.
varṇa (m.), color, caste.
ākṛtīni (n. acc. pl.), shapes, appearances.
(*varṇa-ākṛtīṇi*, n. acc. pl. BV cpd., colors and shapes.)
ca, and.

The Blessed Lord spoke:

Behold, Son of Pṛthā, my forms,
A hundredfold, rather a thousandfold,
Various, divine,
And of various colors and shapes.

6

पश्यादित्यान् वसून् रुद्रान्
paśyādityān vasūn rudrān
behold the Ādityas, the Vasus, the Rudras

अश्विनौ मरुतस् तथा ।
aśvināu marutas tathā
the two Aśvins, the Maruts too

बहून्य् अदृष्टपूर्वाणि
bahūny adṛṣṭapūrvāṇi
many unseen before

पश्याश्चर्याणि भारत ॥
paśyāścaryāṇi bhārata
behold wonders, Descendant of Bharata

Behold the Ādityas,* the Vasus,† the Rudras,‡
The two Aśvins,§ the Maruts|| too;
Many wonders unseen before,
Behold, Descendant of Bharata!

paśya (2nd sg. imperative act. √*paś*), behold! see!
ādityān (m. acc. pl.), the Ādityas.
vasūn (m. acc. pl.), the Vasus.
rudrān (m. acc. pl.), the Rudras.
aśvināu (m. acc. dual), the two Aśvins.
marutas (m. acc. pl.), the Maruts.
tathā, thus, also, too.
bahūni (n. acc. pl.), many.
adṛṣṭa (p. pass. participle *a* √*dṛś*), unseen, not seen.
pūrvāṇi (n. acc. pl.), before, previously.
paśya (2nd sg. imperative act. √*paś*), behold! see!
āścaryāṇi (n. acc. pl.), wonders, marvels.
bhārata (m. voc. sg.), Descendant of Bharata, epithet of Arjuna.

* Ādityas, celestial deities led by the Vedic god Varuṇa.

† Vasus, beneficent gods led by Indra, Agni or Varuna.

‡ Rudras, lit. "roarers," gods who drive away evil.

§ Aśvins, celestial horsemen, always a pair, who herald the dawn and are skilled in healing.

|| Maruts, storm gods, friends of Indra, the thunderbolt hurler and chief god of the Vedas.

7

इहैकस्थं जगत् कृत्स्नं
ihāikastham̐ jagat kṛtsnam̐
here standing together the universe entire

पश्याद्य सचराचरम् ।
paśyādya sacarācaram
behold now with everything moving and not moving

मम देहे गुडाकेश
mama dehe guḍākeśa
of me in the body, Thick Haired One

यच् चान्यद् द्रष्टुम् इच्छसि ॥
yac cānyad draṣṭum icchasi
and whatever else to see thou desirest.

Behold now the entire universe
With everything moving and not moving,
Here standing together in My body, Thick Haired One,
And whatever else thou desirest to see.

iha, here.
ekastham (n. acc. sg.), assembled, standing together, standing as one.
jagat (n. acc. sg.), universe, world.
kṛtsnam (n. acc. sg.), entire, whole.
paśya (2nd sg. imperative act. √*paś*), behold! see!
adya, now, today.
sacarācaram (n. acc. sg.), with everything moving and not moving, with the animate and the inanimate.
mama (gen. sg.), of me, my.
dehe (n. loc. sg.), in the body.
guḍākeśa (m. voc. sg.), Thick Haired One, epithet of Arjuna.
yad (n. acc. sg.), what, whatever.
ca, and.
anyat (n. acc. sg.), other, else.
draṣṭum (infinitive √*dṛś*), to see, to behold.
icchasi (2nd sg. pr. indic. act. √*iṣ*), thou desirest, thou wishest.

8

न तु माम् शक्यसे द्रष्टुम्
na tu mām śakyase draṣṭum
not, but, me thou art able to see

अनेनैव स्वचक्षुषा ।
anenāiva svacakṣuṣā
with this, with own eye;

दिव्यं ददामि ते चक्षुः
divyaṁ dadāmi te cakṣuḥ
divine I give to thee eye

पश्य मे योगम् ऐश्वरम् ।।
paśya me yogam āiśvaram
behold of me the power majestic!

But thou art not able to see Me
With this thine own eye.
I give to thee a divine eye;
Behold My majestic power!

na, not.
tu, but.
mām (acc. sg.), me.
śakyase (2nd sg. pr. indic. pass. √*śak*), thou art able, thou canst.
draṣṭum (infinitive √*dṛś*), to see, to behold.
anena (n. inst. sg.), with this.
eva, indeed (used as a rhythmic filler).
sva, own.
cakṣuṣā (n. inst. sg.), with eye, by eye.
divyam (n. acc. sg.), divine, heavenly.
dadāmi (1st sg. pr. indic. act. √*dā*), I give, I bestow.
te (gen. sg.), to thee, on thee.
cakṣus (n. acc. sg.), eye.
paśya (2nd sg. imperative act. √*paś*), behold! see!
me (gen. sg.), of me, my.
yogam (m. acc. sg.), power, Yoga.
āiśvaram (m. acc. sg.), majestic, princely.

संजय उवाच ।
saṁjaya uvāca
Saṁjaya spoke:

saṁjayas (m. nom. sg.), Saṁjaya, the narrator who is describing the scene to the blind king Dhṛtarāṣṭra.
uvāca (2nd sg. perfect act. √*vac*), he said, he spoke.

9

एवम् उक्त्वा ततो राजन्
evam uktvā tato rājan
thus having spoken then, O King,

महायोगेश्वरो हरिः ।
mahāyogeśvaro hariḥ
the Great Yoga Lord Hari (Vishnu)

दर्शयम् आस पार्थाय
darśayam āsa pārthāya
revealed to the Son of Pṛthā

परमं रूपम् ऐश्वरम् ॥
paramaṁ rūpam āiśvaram
(his) supreme form majestic.

evam, thus.
uktvā (gerund √*vac*), speaking, having spoken.
tatas, then.
rājan (m. voc. sg.), O King (meaning Dhṛtarāṣṭra).
mahāyogeśvaras (m. nom. sg.), the great lord of Yoga, the mighty prince of Yoga.
haris (m. nom. sg.), Hari, epithet of Vishṇu, and hence also of Krishna, his avatār.
darśayam āsa (periphrastic perfect √*dṛś* + √*ās*), he revealed, he showed.
pārthāya (m. dat. sg.), to the Son of Pṛthā, to Arjuna.
paramam (n. acc. sg.), supreme, highest.
rūpam (n. acc. sg.), form, shape, figure.
āiśvaram (n. acc. sg.), majestic, princely.

Saṁjaya spoke:

Thus having spoken, O King,
The Great Lord of Yoga, Hari (Vishnu),
Revealed to the Son of Pṛthā
His majestic supreme form,

10

अनेकवक्त्रनयनम्
anekavaktranayanam
not one mouth and eye

अनेकाद्भुतदर्शनम् ।
anekādbhutadarśanam
not one wondrous aspect

अनेकदिव्याभरणं
anekadivyābharaṇaṁ
not one divine ornament

दिव्यानेकोद्यतायुधम् ॥
divyānekodyatāyudham
divine, not one uplifted, weapon,

Of many mouths and eyes,
Of many wondrous aspects,
Of many divine ornaments,
Of many uplifted divine weapons,

aneka, not one, i.e. many.
vaktra (n.), mouth, "talker."
nayanam (n. acc. sg.), eye, leading organ.
(*anekavaktranayanam,* n. acc. sg. BV cpd., having many mouths and eyes.)
aneka, not one, i.e. many.
adbhuta (n.), wondrous, marvelous.
darśanam (n. acc. sg.), aspect, sight.
(*anekādbhutadarśanam,* n. acc. sg. BV cpd., having many wondrous aspects.)
aneka, not one, i.e. many.
divya (n.), divine, heavenly.
abharaṇam (n. acc. sg.), ornament, decoration.
(*anekadivyābharaṇam,* n. acc sg. BV cpd., having many divine ornaments.)
divya (n.), divine, heavenly.
aneka, not one, i.e. many.
udyata (p. pass. participle *ud* √*yam*), upraised, uplifted, raised.
āyudham (n. acc. sg.), weapon, implement of war.
(*divyānekodyatāyudham,* n. nom. acc. sg. BV cpd., having many uplifted divine weapons.

11

दिव्यमाल्याम्बरधरं
divyamālyāmbaradharaṁ
divine garland and garment wearing,

दिव्यगन्धानुलेपनम् ।
divyagandhānulepanam
divine perfumes and ointments,

सर्वाश्चर्यमयं देवम्
sarvāścaryamayaṁ devam
and all-marvels-made-of, the god

अनन्तं विश्वतोमुखम् ॥
anantaṁ viśvatomukham
infinite, facing in all directions;

divya (n.), divine, heavenly.
mālya (n.), garland, wreath.
ambara (n.), clothing, garment, apparel.
dharam (n. acc. sg.), wearing, supporting, carrying.
(*divya-mālya-ambara-dharam*, n. acc. sg. BV cpd., wearing divine garlands and garments.)
divya (n.), divine, heavenly.
gandha (n.), perfume, scent.
anulepanam (n. acc. sg.), unguent, ointment.
(*divyagandhānulepanam*, n. acc. sg. BV cpd., having divine perfumes and ointments.)
sarvāścarya (n.), all marvel, all wonder.
-mayam (n. acc. sg. suffix), made of.
devam (m. acc. sg.), god.
anantam (n. acc. sg.), endless, infinite.
viśvatomukham (m. acc. sg.), facing in all directions, omniscient.

Wearing divine garlands and garments,
With divine perfumes and ointments,
Made up of all marvels, the god,
Endless, facing in all directions.

12

दिवि सूर्यसहस्रस्य
divi sūryasahasrasya
in the sky of a thousand suns

भवेद् युगपद् उत्थिता ।
bhaved yugapad utthitā
it should be, all at once, risen,

यदि भाः सदृशी सा स्याद्
yadi bhāḥ sadṛśī sā syād
if brightness such it would be

भासस् तस्य महात्मनः ॥
bhāsas tasya mahātmanaḥ
of brightness of this of the Great Self.

If there should be in the sky
A thousand suns risen all at once,
Such splendor would be
Of the splendor of that Great Being.*

divi (m. loc. sg.), in the sky.
sūrya (m.), sun.
sahasras a (m. gen. sg.), of a thousand.
(*sūrya-sahasrasya*, m. gen. sg. TP cpd., a thousand [of] suns.)
bhavet (3rd sg. optative act. √*bhū*), there should be, it might be.
yugapad, at once, all at once.
utthitā (f. nom. sg. p. pass. participle *ud* √*sthā*), risen, rising.
yadi, if.
bhās (f. nom. sg.), brightness, luminescence, brilliance, splendor.
sadṛśī (f. nom. sg.), such.
sā (f. nom. sg.), it, this, she.
syāt (3rd sg. optative act. √*as*), it should be, it would be, it might be.
bhāsas (f. gen. sg.), of brightness, of brilliance, of splendor.
tasya (m. gen. sg.), of it, of this.
mahātmanas (m. gen. sg.), of the Great Self, of the Great Being, (as BV cpd.) of Him whose Self is Great.

* This was the stanza that occurred to the American nuclear physicist Robert Oppenheimer as he witnessed the explosion of the first atom bomb.

13

तत्रैकस्थं जगत् कृत्स्नं
tatrāikasthaṁ jagat kṛtsnaṁ
there standing as one the universe entire

प्रविभक्तम् अनेकधा ।
pravibhaktam anekadhā
divided in not one way

अपश्यद् देवदेवस्य
apaśyad devadevasya
he beheld of the god of gods

शरीरे पाण्डवस् तदा ।।
śarīre pāṇḍavas tadā
in the body the Son of Paṇḍu then.

There the entire universe, standing as one,
Divided in many ways,
The Son of Pāṇḍu then beheld
In the body of the God of Gods.

tatra, there.
ekastham (n. acc. sg.), assembled, standing together.
jagat (n. acc. sg.), universe, world.
kṛtsnam (n. acc. sg.), entire, whole.
pravibhaktam (n. acc. sg. p. pass. participle *pra vi* √*bhaj*), divided, distributed.
anekadhā, in not one way, i.e. in many ways.
apaśyat (3rd sg. imperfect act. √*paś*), he beheld, he saw.
devadevasya (m. gen. sg.), of the god of gods.
śarīre (n. loc. sg.), in the body.
pāṇḍavas (m. nom. sg.), Son of Pāṇḍu, epithet of Arjuna.
tadā, then.

14

ततः स विस्मयाविष्टो
tataḥ sa vismayāviṣṭo
then he, who was possessed by amazement,

हृष्टरोमा धनंजयः ।
hṛṣṭaromā dhanaṁjayaḥ
whose hair was standing on end, Conqueror of Wealth,

प्रणम्य शिरसा देवं
praṇamya śirasā devaṁ
bowing with the head to the god

कृताञ्जलिर् अभाषत ॥
kṛtāñjalir abhāṣata
(with) a reverent gesture he said:

tatas, thereupon, then.
sas (m. nom. sg.), he, the.
vismayāviṣṭas (m. nom. sg.), amazement entered into, possessed by amazement.
hṛṣṭaromā (n. nom. sg. BV cpd.), whose hair was standing on end.
dhanaṁjayas (m. nom. sg.), Conqueror of Wealth, epithet of Arjuna.
praṇamya (gerund *pra* √*nam*), bowing, making obeisance.
śirasā (n. inst. sg.), with the head.
devam (m. acc. sg.), to the god.
kṛtāñjalis (m. nom. sg.), reverent-gesture-making, (as BV cpd.) by whom an *añjali* (reverent gesture) was made.
abhāṣata (3rd sg. imperfect act. √*bhāṣ*), he said, he spoke.

Then he, the Conqueror of Wealth (Arjuna),
Who was possessed by amazement, whose hair was standing on end,
Bowing his head to the God
With a reverent gesture, said:

अर्जुन उवाच ।
arjuna uvāca
Arjuna spoke:

arjunas (m. nom. sg.), Arjuna.
uvāca (3rd sg. perfect act. √*vac*), he said, he spoke.

15

पश्यामि देवांस् तव देव देहे
*paśyāmi devāṅs tava deva dehe**
I see the gods, of thee, O God, in the body

सर्वांस् तथा भूतविशेषसंघान् ।
sarvāṅs tathā bhūtaviśeṣasaṁghān
all, indeed, kinds of beings assembled;

ब्रह्माणम् ईशं कमलासनस्थम्
brahmāṇam īśaṁ kamalāsanastham
Brahmā Lord, lotus seat seated,

ऋषींश्च सर्वान् उरगांश्च दिव्यान् ॥
ṛṣīṅśca sarvān uragāṅśca divyān
and the seers all and the serpents divine;

Arjuna spoke:

I see the gods, O God, in Thy body,
And all kinds of beings assembled;
Lord Brahmā† on his lotus seat
And all the seers and divine serpents;

paśyāmi (1st sg. pr. indic. act. √*paś*), I see, I behold.
devān (m. acc. pl.), gods.
tava (gen. sg.), of thee, thy.
deva (m. voc. sg.), O God.
dehe (m./n. loc. sg.), in the body.
sarvān (m. acc. pl.), all, all of them.
tathā, thus, in this way, and also.
bhūta (n.), being, creature.
viśeṣa, kind, species.
saṁghān (m. acc. pl. from *sam* √*han*), assembled, heaped together, crowded together.
(*bhūta-viśeṣa-saṁghān*, m. acc. pl. KD cpd., kinds of beings assembled.)
brahmāṇam (m. acc. sg.), Brahmā, the Vedic god of creation.
īśam (m. acc. sg.), lord, god.
kamalāsanastham (m. acc. sg.), lotus-seat situated, sitting on the lotus seat (*kamala,* lotus; *āsana,* seat; *stham*, situated).
ṛṣīn (m. acc. pl.), seers.
ca, and.
sarvān (m. acc. pl.), all.
uragān (m. acc. pl.), serpents, "earth-goers."
ca, and.
divyān (m. acc. pl.), divine, heavenly.

* *Triṣṭubh* metre begins as Arjuna commences to describe the Great Manifestation, and continues through most of this book (i.e. until stanza 51).

† Brahmā (masculine), the creator god of the Hindu trinity. Not to be confused with Brahman (neuter), the all-pervading essence.

16

अनेकबाहूदरवक्त्रनेत्रं
anekabāhūdaravaktranetraṁ
not one arm, belly, face, eye;

पश्यामि त्वां सर्वतो ऽनन्तरूपम् ।
paśyāmi tvāṁ sarvato 'nantarūpam
I see thee in every direction, infinite form.

नान्तं न मध्यं न पुनस् तवादिं
nāntaṁ na madhyaṁ na punas tavādiṁ
not end nor middle nor yet, of thee, beginning

पश्यामि विश्वेश्वर विश्वरूप ॥
paśyāmi viśveśvara viśvarūpa
I see, O Lord of All, Whose form is the Universe.

With many arms, bellies, faces, eyes,
I see Thee everywhere, infinite in form;
Not the end, nor the middle, nor yet the beginning of Thee
I see, O Lord of All, Whose Form is the Universe.

aneka, not one, i.e. many.
bāhu (m.), arm.
udara (n.), belly.
vaktra (n.), face, mouth, "talker."
netram (n. acc. sg.), eye.
(*aneka-bāhu-udara-vaktra-netram*, n. acc. sg. BV cpd., having many arms, bellies, faces, and eyes.)
paśyāmi (1st sg. pr. indic. act. √*paś*), I see, I behold.
tvām (acc. sg.), thee.
sarvatas, in every direction, everywhere.
ananta, unending, infinite.
rūpam (n. acc. sg.), form, shape, figure.
na, not.
antam (m. acc. sg.), end.
na, not, nor.
madhyam (n. acc. sg.), middle.
na, not, nor.
punar, again, yet, moreover.
tava (gen. sg.), of thee, thy.
ādim (m. acc. sg.), beginning.
paśyāmi (1st sg. pr. indic. act. √*paś*), I see, I behold.
viśveśvara (m. voc. sg.), O Lord of All (*viśva īśvara*).
viśvarūpa (m. voc. sg.), O Form of All, (as BV cpd.) whose form is the Universe.

17

किरीटिनं गदिनं चक्रिणं च
kirīṭinaṁ gadinaṁ cakriṇaṁ ca
crowned, armed with a club and bearing a discus

तेजोराशिं सर्वतो दीप्तिमन्तम् ।
tejorāśiṁ sarvato dīptimantam
a mass of splendor, on all sides shining,

पश्यामि त्वां दुर्निरीक्ष्यं समन्ताद्
paśyāmi tvāṁ durnirīkṣyaṁ samantād
I see thee who art difficult to behold completely,

दीप्तानलार्कद्युतिम् अप्रमेयम् ।।
dīptānalārkadyutim aprameyam
blazing-fire-sun-radiance immeasurable.

Crowned, armed with a club and bearing a discus,
A mass of splendor, shining on all sides,
With the immeasurable radiance of the sun and blazing fire,
I see Thee, Who art difficult to behold completely.

kirīṭinam (m. acc. sg.), crowned.
gadinam (m. acc. sg.), armed with a club.
cakriṇam (m. acc. sg.), bearing a discus.
ca, and.
tejorāśim (m. acc. sg.), heap of splendor, mass of splendor.
sarvatas, on all sides, in every direction, everywhere.
dīptimantam (m. acc. sg.), shining, full of brilliance.
paśyāmi (1st sg. act. √*paś*), I see, I behold.
tvām (acc. sg.), thee.
durnirīkṣyam (m. acc. sg. gerundive *dus nis* √*īkṣ*), difficult to behold, hard to see.
samantāt (adv.), completely, wholly, on every side.
dīpta (m.), blazing, flaming, shining.
anala (m.), fire.
arka (m.), sun, ray, flame.
dyutim (f. acc. sg.), radiance, brilliance.
(*dīpta-anala-arka-dyutim*, f. acc. sg. KD cpd., blazing-fire-sun-radiance.)
aprameyam (f. acc. sg.), immeasurable, beyond measure.

18

त्वम् ग्रक्षरं परमं वेदितव्यं
tvam akṣaraṁ paramaṁ veditavyaṁ
thou unchanging supreme the to-be-known

त्वम् ग्रस्य विश्वस्य परं निधानम् ।
tvam asya viśvasya paraṁ nidhānam
thou of it, of all, the ultimate resting place

त्वमव्ययः शाश्वतधर्मगोप्ता
tvam avyayaḥ śāśvatadharmagoptā
thou the imperishable, eternal law defender,

सनातनस् त्वं पुरुषो मतो मे ।।
sanātanas tvaṁ puruṣo mato me
primaeval thou spirit understood of me.

Thou art the Unchanging, the Supreme Object of Knowledge;
Thou art the ultimate resting place of all;
Thou art the imperishable defender of the eternal law;
Thou art the primaeval spirit, I believe.

tvam (nom. sg.), thou.
akṣaram (n. nom. sg.), imperishable, unchanging, indestructible.
paramam (n. nom. sg.), supreme.
veditavyam (n. nom. sg. gerundive √*vid*), to-be-known, object of knowledge.
tvam (nom. sg.), thou.
asya (gen. sg.), of it, of this.
viśvasya (m. gen. sg.), of all.
param (n. nom. sg.), the highest, the ultimate, the supreme.
nidhānam (n. nom. sg.), resting place, place for storing up.
tvam (nom. sg.), thou.
avyayas (m. nom. sg.), imperishable, eternal.
śāśvata (m.), eternal, perpetual.
dharma (m.), law, righteousness, virtue.
goptā (m. nom. sg.), defender, protector.
(*śāśvata-dharma-goptā*, m. nom. sg. TP cpd., defender of eternal law.)
sanātanas (m. nom. sg.), primaeval, ancient.
tvam (nom. sg.), thou.
puruṣas (m. nom. sg.), spirit, man.
matas (m. nom. sg. p. pass. participle √*man*), thought, believed, understood.
me (gen. sg.), of me, by me.

19

अनादिमध्यान्तम् अनन्तवीर्यम्
anādimadhyāntam anantavīryam
without beginning, middle or end, infinite power

अनन्तबाहुं शशिसूर्यनेत्रम् ।
anantabāhuṁ śaśisūryanetram
(with) innumerable arms, rabbit-holder*-and-sun-eyed,

पश्यामि त्वां दीप्तहुताशवक्त्रं
paśyāmi tvāṁ dīptahutāśavaktraṁ
I see thee, blazing-oblation-eating mouth,

स्वतेजसा विश्वम् इदं तपन्तम् ॥
svatejasā viśvam idaṁ tapantam
by own splendor all this universe burning.

With infinite power, without beginning, middle or end,
With innumerable arms, moon and sun eyed,
I see Thee, (with) Thy blazing, oblation-eating† mouth,
Burning all this universe with Thine own radiance.

anādimadhyāntam (m. acc. sg.), without beginning, middle or end.
ananta (n.), endless, infinite.
vīryam (n. nom. acc. sg.), power, strength, vigor.
(*anatavīryam,* m. acc. sg. BV cpd., having infinite power.)
ananta (m.), endless, innumerable.
bāhum (m. acc. sg.), arm.
(*anantabāhum,* m. acc. sg. BV cpd., having innumerable arms.)
śaśī (m.), the moon, that which contains the rabbit.
sūrya (m.), sun.
netram (n. acc. sg.), eye.
(*śaśisūryanetram,* m. acc. sg. BV cpd., having the moon and sun as eyes.)
paśyāmi (3rd sg. pr. indic. act. √*paś*), I see, I behold.
tvām (acc. sg.), thee.
dīpta (m.), blazing, fiery.
hutāśa (m.), oblation eating, oblation consuming, oblation fire.
vaktram (n. acc. sg.), mouth, face.
(*dīptahutāśavaktram,* m. acc. sg. BV cpd., with blazing, oblation-eating mouth.)
svatejasā (n. inst. sg.), by own splendor, by own brilliance, by own power.
viśvam idam (n. acc. sg.), all this universe.
tapantam (m. acc. sg. pr. participle √*tap*), burning, consuming, illuminating.

* *śaśin,* that which contains the rabbit. The Hindus saw a rabbit in the moon, and this is a very common term for "moon."

† Most translators avoid *hutāśa* (*huta aśa*), "oblation eating," which refers to the partaking of sacrifice, or render it as "fire," and translate *vaktram* as "face." The present translation, however, coincides with *vaktra,* "mouth," in stanza 23, and *vaktra* means "talker" or organ of speech, as well as "face."

20

द्यावापृथिव्योर् इदम् अन्तरं हि
dyāvāpṛthivyor idam antaraṁ hi
of heaven and earth this between indeed,

व्याप्तं त्वयैकेन दिशश्च सर्वाः ।
vyāptaṁ tvayāikena diśaśca sarvāḥ
pervaded by thee alone and (in) directions all.

दृष्ट्वाद्भुतं रूपम् उग्रं तवेदं
dṛṣṭvādbhutaṁ rūpam ugraṁ tavedaṁ
seeing the marvelous form terrible of thee, this,

लोकत्रयं प्रव्यथितं महात्मन् ॥
lokatrayaṁ pravyathitaṁ mahātman
the three worlds trembling, O Great Self.

This space between heaven and earth,
Is pervaded by Thee alone in all directions.
Seeing this, Thy marvelous and terrible form,
The three worlds tremble, O Great Being.

dyāvāpṛthivyos (f. gen. dual), of heaven and earth.
idam (n. nom. sg.), this.
antaram (n. nom. sg.), between.
hi, indeed, truly.
vyāptam (n. nom. sg. participle *vi* √*āp*), pervaded, filled with, occupied by.
tvayā (m. inst. sg.), by thee.
ekena (m. inst. sg.), alone.
diśas (f. nom. pl.), directions, points, spaces.
ca, and.
sarvās (f. nom. pl.), all.
dṛṣṭvā (gerund √*dṛś*), seeing, having seen, having beheld.
adbhutam (n. acc. sg.), marvelous, wondrous.
rūpam (n. acc. sg.), form, shape, figure.
ugram (n. acc. sg.), terrible, mighty, formidable.
tava (m. gen. sg.), of thee, thy.
idam (n. acc. sg.), this.
lokatrayam (n. nom. sg.), the three worlds (heaven, earth, atmosphere).
pravyathitam (n. nom. p. pass. participle *pra* √*vyath*), trembling, shaking, tremble.
mahātman (m. voc. sg.), O Great Self, O Exalted One, (as BV cpd.) O Thou whose Self is Great.

21

अमी हि त्वां सुरसंघा विशन्ति
amī hi tvāṁ surasaṁghā viśanti
yonder, indeed, thee the throngs of gods they enter,

केचिद् भीताः प्राञ्जलयो गृणन्ति ।
kecid bhītāḥ prāñjalayo gṛṇanti
some, terrified, with reverent gestures they praise

स्वस्तीत्य् उक्त्वा महर्षिसिद्धसंघाः
svastīty uktvā mahārṣisiddhasaṁghāḥ
"hail," thus saying the great-seer-and-perfected-one-throngs,

स्तुवन्ति त्वां स्तुतिभिः पुष्कलाभिः ॥
stuvanti tvāṁ stutibhiḥ puṣkalābhiḥ
they praise thee with praises abundant.

Yonder throngs of gods enter into Thee,
Some, terrified, with reverent gestures they praise;
"Hail" thus saying, the throngs of great seers and perfected ones
Praise Thee with abundant praises.

amī (m. nom. pl.), yonder.
hi, indeed, truly.
tvām (acc. sg.), thee.
surasaṁghās (m. nom. pl.), throngs of gods, assemblages of gods.
viśanti (3rd pl. pr. indic. act. √*viś*), they enter.
kecid (m. nom. pl.), some, some or others.
bhītās (m. nom. pl.), terrified, fearful.
prāñjalayas (m. nom. pl.), reverent gestures, (as BV cpd.) whose *añjalis* (reverent gestures) are proffered.
gṛṇanti (3rd pl. act. √*gṛ*), they praise, they sing praises.
svasti (exclamation), hail! good health!
iti, thus.
uktvā (gerund √*vac*), saying, crying.
mahārṣi (m.), great seer.
siddha (m.), perfected one, successful one.
saṁghās (m. nom. pl. from *sam* √*han*), assemblages, throngs, multitudes, heaps.
(*mahārṣisiddhasaṁghās,* m. nom. pl. TP cpd., the throngs of great seers and perfected ones.)
stuvanti (3rd pl. pr. indic. act. √*stu*), they praise.
tvām (acc. sg.), thee.
stutibhis (f. inst. pl.), with praises.
puṣkalābhis (f. inst. pl.), abundant.

22

रुद्रादित्या वसवो ये च साध्या
rudrādityā vasavo ye ca sādhyā
the Rudras, Adityas, Vasus who and Sādhyas,

विश्वे ऽश्विनौ मरुतश्चोष्मपाश्च ।
viśve 'śvināu marutaścoṣmapāś ca
the Visve devas, the two Asvins, the Maruts and the Steam Drinkers

गन्धर्वयक्षासुरसिद्धसंघा
gandharvayakṣāsurasiddhasaṁghā
the Gandharva-Yaksa-Asura-perfected-one-throngs

वीक्षन्ते त्वां विस्मिताश्चैव सर्वे ॥
vīkṣante tvāṁ vismitāścāiva sarve
they behold thee amazed all.

rudrādityās (m. nom. pl.), the Rudras and Ādityas.
vasavas (m. nom. pl.), Vasus.
ye (m. nom. pl.), who.
ca, and.
sādhyās (m. nom. pl.), Sādhyas.
viśve (m. nom. pl.), Viśve devas.
aśvinau (m. nom. dual), the two Asvins.
marutas (m. nom. pl.), Maruts.
ca, and.
ūṣmapās (m. nom. pl.), Steam Drinkers.
ca, and.
gandharvayakṣāsurasiddhasaṁghās (m. nom. pl. TP cpd.), the throngs of Gandharvas, Yakṣas, Asuras and perfected ones.
vīkṣante (3rd pl. mid. *vi* √*īkṣ*), they behold, they see.
tvām (acc. sg.), thee.
vismitās (m. nom. pl. p. pass. participle *vi* √*smi*), amazed, overcome, astonished.
ca, and.
eva, indeed (often used as a rhythmic filler).
sarve (m. nom. pl.), all.

The Rudras, Ādityas, Vasus,* these and the Sādhyas,†
The Viśve devas,‡ the two Aśvins, the Maruts and the Steam Drinkers,§
The throngs of Gandharvas,|| Yakṣas,¶ Āsuras and Perfected Ones,**
They all behold Thee, amazed.

* Minor gods, see note stanza 6.
† Sādhyas, a group of celestial beings with exquisitely refined natures thought to inhabit the ether.
‡ Viśve devas, a group of twelve minor godlings.
§ Steam Drinkers, a class of ancestors.
|| Gandharvas, celestial musicians.
¶ Yakṣas, a group of supernatural beings, sometimes benelovent, sometimes not.
** Āsuras, a class of demons, enemies of the gods.

23

रूपं महत् ते बहुवक्त्रनेत्रं
rūpaṁ mahat te bahuvaktranetraṁ
form great of thee, many mouthed and eyed

महाबाहो बहुबाहूरुपादम् ।
mahābāho bahubāhūrupādam
O Mighty Armed One, many armed, many thighed and footed

बहूदरं बहुदंष्ट्राकरालं
bahūdaraṁ bahudaṁṣṭrākarālaṁ
many bellied, bearing many tusks

दृष्ट्वा लोकाः प्रव्यथितास् तथा ऽहम् ॥
dṛṣṭvā lokāḥ pravyathitās tathā 'ham
having seen, the worlds trembling, also I.

Having seen Thy great form, which has many mouths and eyes,
Which has many arms, thighs and feet,
Which has many bellies, and the mouths of which gape with many tusks,
O Mighty Armed One,* the worlds tremble, and so do I.

rūpam (n. acc. sg.), form, figure, shape.
mahat (n. acc. sg.), great, mighty.
te (gen. sg.), of thee, thy.
bahuvaktranetram (n. nom. sg.), many mouth and eye, (as BV cpd.) which has many mouths and eyes.
mahābāho (m. voc. sg.), O Great Armed One, epithet of warriors, usually applied to Arjuna, but here to Krishna.
bahu, many.
bāhu (m.), arm.
ūru (m.), thigh, shank.
pādam (m. acc. sg.), foot.
(*bahubāhūrupādam,* m. acc. sg. BV cpd., which has many arms, thighs and feet, having many arms, thighs and feet.)
bahu, many.
udaram (n. nom. sg.), belly.
(*bahūdaram,* n. nom. acc. sg., many bellied.)
bahu, many.
daṁṣṭrā (f.), tusk.
karālam (n. acc. sg.) terrible.
(*bahu-daṁṣṭrā-karālam,* n. acc. sg. BV cpd., having many terrible tusks.)
dṛṣṭvā (gerund √*dṛś*), seeing, having seen.
lokās (m. nom. pl.), worlds.
pravyathitās (m. nom. pl. p. pass. participle *pra* √*vyath*), trembling, quaking, shaking.
tathā, also, thus.
aham (nom. sg.), I.

* Here referring to Krishna.

24

नभःस्पृशं दीप्तम् अनेकवर्णं
nabhaḥspṛśaṁ dīptam anekavarṇaṁ
sky-touching, blazing, not one colored,

व्यात्ताननं दीप्तविशालनेत्रम् ।
vyāttānanaṁ dīptaviśālanetram
gaping-mouthed, blazing, enormous eyed;

दृष्ट्वा हि त्वां प्रव्यथितान्तरात्मा
dṛṣṭvā hi tvāṁ pravyathitāntarātmā
having seen indeed thee, trembling in the inner self,

धृतिं न विन्दामि शमं च विष्णो ॥
dhṛtiṁ na vindāmi śamaṁ ca viṣṇo
courage not I find or tranquility, O Vishnu.

Sky-touching, blazing, many colored,
Gaping-mouthed, with enormous fiery eyes;
Having seen Thee, trembling indeed in my inner self,
I find neither courage nor tranquility, O Vishnu!*

nabhaḥspṛśam (m. acc. sg.), sky touching, touching the sky.
dīptam (m. acc. sg.), blazing, fiery.
anekavarṇam (m. acc. sg.), not one (i.e. many) colored.
vyātta (p. pass. participle *vi ā* √*dā*), opened, gaping.
ānanam (n. acc. sg.), mouth, face, nose.
(*vyattānanam,* n. acc. sg. BV cpd., having a gaping mouth.)
dīpta (n.), blazing, fiery, shining.
viśāla (n.), spacious, extensive.
netram (n. acc. sg.), eye.
(*dīpta-viśāla-netram*, n. acc. sg. KD cpd., fiery-enormous-eyed.)
dṛṣṭvā (gerund √*dṛś*), seeing, having seen.
hi, indeed, truly.
tvām (acc. sg.), thee.
pravyathita (m. p. pass. participle *pra* √*vyath*), trembling, quaking, shaking.
antarātmā (m. nom. sg.), inner self.
(*pravyathita-antarātma*, m. nom. sg. KD cpd., trembling inner self.)
dhṛtim (f. acc. sg.), courage, firmness.
na, not.
vindāmi (1st sg. pr. indic. act. √2 *vid*), I find.
śamam (n. acc. sg.), tranquility, calmness.
ca, and, or.
viṣṇo (m. voc. sg.), O Vishnu.

* Vishnu, the god of whom Krishna is the *avatār*.

25

दंष्ट्राकरालानि च ते मुखानि
daṁṣṭrākarālāni ca te mukhāni
and bearing many tusks of thee the mouths

दृष्ट्वैव कालानलसंनिभानि ।
dṛṣṭvāiva kālānalasaṁnibhāni
having seen time-fire-similar,

दिशो न जाने न लभे च शर्म
diśo na jāne na labhe ca śarma
directions not I know, and not I find comfort.

प्रसीद देवेश जगन्निवास ॥
prasīda deveśa jagannivāsa
have mercy! Lord of Gods, Dwelling of the Universe.

And having seen Thy mouths, bearing many tusks,
Glowing like the fires of universal destruction,
I lose my sense of direction, and I do not find comfort.
Have mercy! Lord of Gods, Dwelling of the Universe!

daṁṣṭrākarālāni (n. acc. pl.), bearing many tusks, gaping with tusks, with terrible tusks.
ca, and.
te (gen. sg.), of thee, thy.
mukhāni (n. acc. pl.), mouths, faces.
dṛṣṭvā (gerund √*dṛś*), seeing, having seen.
eva, indeed (often used as a rhythmic filler).
kālānala (m.), time-fire, fires of time, fires of destruction.
saṁnibhāni (n. acc. pl.), similar, like.
(*kālānala-saṁnibhāni*, n. acc. pl., like the fires of destruction.)
diśas (f. acc. pl.), directions, sense of direction, points of the compass.
na, not.
jāne (1st sg. pr. indic. mid. √*jñā*), I know.
na, not, nor.
labhe (1st sg. pr. indic. mid. √*labh*), I find, I obtain.
ca, and.
śarma (n. acc. sg.), comfort, refuge.
prasīda (2nd sg. imperative act. *pra* √*sad*), have mercy! be merciful!
deveśa (m. voc. sg.), Lord of Gods.
jagat (n.), universe, world.
nivāsa (m. voc. sg. from *ni* √*vas*), dwelling, home.
(*jagat-nivāsa*, m. voc. sg. TP cpd., Dwelling of the Universe.)

26

अमी च त्वां धृतराष्ट्रस्य पुत्राः
amī ca tvāṁ dhṛtarāṣṭrasya putrāḥ
and yonder (into) thee, of Dhṛtarāṣṭra the sons

सर्वे सहैवावनिपालसंघैः ।
sarve sahāivāvanipālasaṁghāiḥ
all indeed along with the earth-ruler (king) throngs,

भीष्मो द्रोणः सूतपुत्रस् तथासौ
bhīṣmo droṇaḥ sūtaputras tathāsāu
Bhīṣma, Droṇa and the son of the charioteer (Karṇa) thus yonder

सहास्मदीयैर् अपि योधमुख्यैः ।।
sahāsmadīyāir api yodhamukhyāiḥ
together with ours also, and with (our) chief warriors

amī (m. nom. pl.), yonder.
ca, and.
tvām (acc. sg.), thee, to thee.
dhṛtarāṣṭrasya (m. gen. sg.), of Dhṛtarāṣṭra.
putrās (m. nom. pl.), sons.
sarve (m. nom. pl.), all.
saha, along with, together with.
eva, indeed (often used as a rhythmic filler).
avanipāla (m.), earth ruler, earth protector, protector of the earth, king.
saṁghāis (m. inst. pl.), with throngs, with assemblages.
(*avanipāla-saṁghais*, m. inst. pl. TP cpd., throngs of kings.)
bhīṣmas (m. nom. sg.), Bhīṣma.
droṇas (m. nom. sg.), Droṇa.
sūtaputras (m. nom. sg.), Son of the Charioteer (i.e. Karṇa).
tathā, thus.
asāu (m. nom. sg.), there, yonder.
saha, together.
asmadīyās (m. inst. pl), with ours.
api, also, even.
yodhamukhyāis (m. inst. pl.), with head warriors, with chief warriors.

And yonder into Thee, all the sons of Dhṛtarāṣṭra,
Along with the throngs of kings,
Bhīṣma, Droṇa and the Son of the Charioteer (Karṇa) thus yonder,
Together with ours, and also with our chief warriors,

27

वक्त्राणि ते त्वरमाणा विशन्ति
vaktrāṇi te tvaramāṇā viśanti
the mouths of thee quickly they enter

दंष्ट्राकरालानि भयानकानि ।
daṁṣṭrākarālāni bhayānakāni
gaping with many tusks, fearful,

केचिद् विलग्ना दशनान्तरेषु
kecid vilagnā daśanāntareṣu
some clinging the teeth in between

संदृश्यन्ते चूर्णितैर् उत्तमाङ्गैः ॥
saṁdṛśyante cūrṇitāir uttamāṅgāiḥ
they are seen with crushed heads.

They quickly enter Thy fearful mouths,
Which gape with many tusks,
Some are seen with crushed heads,
Clinging between Thy teeth.

vaktrāṇi (n. acc. pl.), mouths, faces.
te (gen. sg.), of thee.
tvaramāṇās (adv.), with haste, speedily.
viśanti (3rd pl. pr. indic. act. √*viś*), they enter.
daṁṣṭrākarālāni (n. acc. sg.), gaping with tusks, bearing many tusks.
bhayānakāni (n. acc. pl.), dreadful, fearful, terrible.
kecid (m. nom. pl.), some.
vilagnās (m. nom. pl. p. pass. participle *vi* √*lag*), clinging, attached.
daśana (n.), tooth, bite.
antareṣu (m. loc. pl.), in between.
(*daśana-antareṣu*, m. loc. pl. TP cpd., in between the teeth.)
saṁdṛśyante (3rd pl. pr. passive *sam* √*dṛś*), they are seen, they are observed.
cūrṇitāis (m. inst. pl. pass. participle √*cūrn*), with crushed, with pulverized.
uttamāṅgāis (n. inst. pl.), with heads, lit. "with highest limbs."

28

यथा नदीनां बहवो ऽम्बुवेगाः
yathā nadīnāṁ bahavo 'mbuvegāḥ
as of rivers many water torrents

समुद्रम् एवाभिमुखा द्रवन्ति ।
samudram evābhimukhā dravanti
the ocean toward they flow

तथा तवामी नरलोकवीरा
tathā tavāmī naralokavīrā
so of thee yonder man-world heroes

विशन्ति वक्त्राण्य् अभिविज्वलन्ति ॥
viśanti vaktrāṇy abhivijvalanti
they enter the mouths flaming forth.

As the many torrents of the rivers
Flow toward the ocean,
So yonder heroes of the world of men
Enter Thy mouths as they flame forth.

yathā, as, in which way.
nadīnām (f. gen. pl.), of rivers, of streams.
bahavas (m. nom. pl.), many.
ambuvegās (m. nom. pl.), water torrents, water currents, water floods.
samudram (m. acc. sg.), ocean, sea.
eva, indeed (used as a rhythmic filler).
abhimukhās (m. nom. pl.), toward, facing toward, approaching.
dravanti (3rd pl. pr. indic. act. √*dru*), they flow, they run.
tathā, thus, in this way, so.
tava (gen. sg.), of thee, thy.
amī (m. nom. pl.), yonder.
nara (m.), man.
loka (m.), world.
vīrās (m. nom. pl.), heroes.
(*naralokavīrās,* m. nom. pl. TP cpd., heroes of the world of men.)
viśanti (3rd pl. pr. indic. act. √*viś*), they enter.
vaktrāni (n. acc. pl.), mouths, faces.
abhivijvalanti (n. acc. pl. pr. participle *abhi vi* √*jval*), flaming forth, burning.

29

यथा प्रदीप्तं ज्वलनं पतङ्गा
yathā pradīptaṁ jvalanaṁ pataṅgā
as the blazing flame, moths

विशन्ति नाशाय समृद्धवेगाः ।
viśanti nāśāya saṁṛddhavegāḥ
they enter, to destruction, with great speed,

तथैव नाशाय विशन्ति लोकास्
tathāiva nāśāya viśanti lokās
so thus to destruction they enter, the worlds,

तवापि वक्त्राणि समृद्धवेगाः ॥
tavāpi vaktrāṇi samṛddhavegāḥ
of thee also the mouths with great speed.

As moths enter the blazing flame
To their destruction with great speed,
So also, to their destruction, the worlds
Swiftly enter thy mouths.

yathā, as, in which way.
pradīptam (n. acc. sg. p. pass. participle *pra* √*dīp*), blazing forth, shining forth.
jvalanam (n. acc. sg.), flame, light, fire.
pataṅgās (m./f. nom. pl.), moths, insects.
viśanti (3rd pl. pr. indic. act. √*viś*), they enter.
nāśāya (m. dat. sg. from √*naś*), to destruction, to perishing.
saṁṛddhavegās (m. nom. pl.), having increased flow, having great speed.
tathā, so, in this way.
eva, indeed (often used as a rhythmic filler).
nāśāya (m. dat. sg.), to destruction, to perishing.
viśanti (3rd pl. pr. indic. act. √*viś*), they enter.
lokās (m. nom. pl.), worlds.
tava (gen. sg.), of thee, thy.
api, also, even.
vaktrāṇi (n. acc. pl.), mouths, faces.
samṛddhavegās (m. nom. pl.), with great speed, having increased flow.

30

लेलिह्यसे ग्रसमानः समन्ताल्
lelihyase grasamānaḥ samantāl
thou lickest, swallowing from all sides,

लोकान् समग्रान् वदनैर् ज्वलद्भिः ।
lokān samagrān vadanāir jvaladbhiḥ
the worlds all with mouths flaming.

तेजोभिर् आपूर्य जगत् समग्रं
tejobhir āpūrya jagat samagraṁ
with splendor filling the universe all,

भासस् तवोग्राः प्रतपन्ति विष्णो ।।
bhāsas tavogrāḥ pratapanti viṣṇo
the rays of thee, terrible, they consume it, O Vishnu!

Thou lickest, swallowing from all sides,
All the worlds, with flaming mouths.
Filling all the universe with splendor,
Thy terrible rays consume it, O Vishnu!

lelihyase (2nd sg. intensive √*lih*), thou lickest.
grasamānas (m. nom. sg. pr. participle mid. √*gras*), swallowing, devouring.
samantāt (m. abl. sg.), from all sides, on all sides.
lokān (m. acc. pl.), worlds.
samagrān (m. accl. pl.), all, whole, entire.
vadanāis (n. inst. pl.), with mouths.
jvaladbhis (n. inst. pl. pr. participle act. √*jval*), with flaming, with fiery.
tejobhis (n. inst. pl.), with splendor, with brilliance.
āpūrya (gerund *ā* √*pṛ*), filling.
jagat (n. acc. sg.), universe, world, all that moves.
samagram (n. acc. sg.), all, entire, whole.
bhāsas (f./n. nom. pl.), ray, radiation, radiance.
tava (gen. sg.), of thee, thy.
urgās (f. nom. pl.), terrible, powerful, fierce.
pratapanti (3rd pl. pr. indic. act. *pra* √*tap*), they burn, they consume.
viṣṇo (m. voc. sg.), O Vishnu.

34

ोणं च भीष्मं च जयद्रथं च
roṇaṁ ca bhīṣmaṁ ca jayadrathaṁ ca
Droṇa and Bhīṣma and Jayadratha and

कर्णं तथान्यान् अपि योधवीरान् ।
karṇaṁ tathānyān api yodhavīrān
Karṇa too, others also, warrior heroes

मया हतांस् त्वं जहि मा व्यथिष्ठा
mayā hatāṅs tvaṁ jahi mā vyathiṣṭhā
by me killed, thou kill, do not hesitate!

युध्यस्व जेतासि रणे सपत्नान् ॥
yudhyasva jetāsi raṇe sapatnān
fight! thou shalt conquer in battle the enemies.

Droṇa and Bhīṣma and Jayadratha and
Karṇa too, others also, warrior heroes,
By Me are killed.
Do not hesitate! Kill thou!
Fight! Thou shalt conquer the enemy in battle.

droṇam (m. acc. sg.), Droṇa.
ca, and.
bhīṣmam (m. acc. sg.), Bhīṣma.
ca, and.
jayadratham (m. acc. sg.), Jayadratha.
ca, and.
karṇam (m. acc. sg.), Karṇa.
tathā, also, too, thus.
anyān (m. acc. pl.), others.
api, also, even.
yodhavīrān (m. acc. pl.), warrior heroes, fighter heroes, battle heroes.
mayā (inst. sg.), by me.
hatān (m. acc. pl. p. pass. participle √*han*), killed, slain.
tvam (nom. sg.), thou.
jahi (2nd sg. imperative act. √*han*), kill! slay!
mā (prohibitive), not, never.
vyathiṣṭhās (2nd sg. injunctive √*vyath*), tremble, hesitate.
yudhyasva (2nd sg. imperative mid. √*yudh*), fight!
jetāsi (2nd sg. periphrastic future act. √*ji*), thou shalt conquer.
raṇe (n. loc. sg.), in battle, in joy of battle.
sapatnān (m. acc. pl.), rivals, adversaries.

31

आख्याहि मे को भवान् उग्ररूपो
ākhyāhi me ko bhavān ugrarūpo
tell to me who thou (art, Thou) of terrible form.

नमो ऽस्तु ते देववर प्रसीद ।
namo 'stu te devavara prasīda
homage may it be to thee, O Best of Gods, have mercy!

विज्ञातुम् इच्छामि भवन्तम् आद्यं
vijñātum icchāmi bhavantam ādyaṁ
to understand I wish thee, Primal One,

न हि प्रजानामि तव प्रवृत्तिम् ॥
na hi prajānāmi tava pravṛttim
not indeed I comprehend of thee the working.

Tell me who art Thou, O Thou of Terrible Form?
Homage may it be to Thee, O Best of Gods;
Have mercy! I wish to understand Thee, Primal One;
Indeed, I do not comprehend Thy working.

ākhyāhi (2nd sg. imperative act. *ā* √*khyā*), tell! inform! explain!
me (dat. sg.), to me.
kas (m. nom. sg.), who?
bhavān (m. nom. sg. formal), thou, thy lordship.
ugrarūpas (m. nom. sg.), of terrible form, of mighty form.
namas (n. nom. sg.), honor, homage, reverence.
astu (3rd sg. imperative act. √*as*), may it be! be it!
te (dat. sg.), to thee.
devavara (m. voc. sg.), O Best of Gods, O Chosen of Gods.
prasīda (2nd sg. imperative act. *pra* √*sad*), have mercy! be merciful!
vijñātum (infinitive *vi* √*jñā*), to understand, to comprehend, to know.
icchāmi (1st sg. pr. indic. act. √*iṣ*), I wish, I desire.
bhavantam (m. acc. sg. formal), thee, thy lordship.
ādyam (m. acc. sg.), Primal One, One who has existed from the beginning.
na, not.
hi, indeed, truly.
prajānāmi (1st sg. pr. indic. act. *pra* √*jñā*), I comprehend, I understand.
tava (m. gen. sg.), of thee, thy.
pravṛttim (f. acc. sg.), working, purpose.

श्रीभगवान् उवाच ।
śrībhagavān uvāca
the Blessed Lord spoke:

śrībhagavān (m. nom. sg.), the Blessed Lord, the Blessed One.
uvāca (3rd sg. perf. act. √*vac*), he said, he spoke.

32

कालो ऽस्मि लोकक्षयकृत् प्रवृद्धो
kālo 'smi lokakṣayakṛt pravṛddho
Time I am, world destruction causing, mighty,

लोकान् समाहर्तुम् इह प्रवृत्तः ।
lokān samāhartum iha pravṛttaḥ
the worlds to annihilate here come forth

ऋते ऽपि त्वां न भविष्यन्ति सर्वे
ṛte 'pi tvāṁ na bhaviṣyanti sarve
without even thee, not they shall exist all

ये ऽवस्थिताः प्रत्यनीकेषु योधाः ॥
ye 'vasthitāḥ pratyanīkeṣu yodhāḥ
who arrayed in the opposing ranks, the warriors.

The Blessed Lord spoke:

I am Time, the mighty cause of world destruction,
Here come forth to annihilate the worlds.
Even without any action of thine, all these warriors
Who are arrayed in the opposing ranks, shall cease to exist.

kālas (m. nom. sg.), time.
asmi (1st sg. pr. indic. √*as*), I am.
lokakṣayakṛt (m. nom. sg.), world destruction causing, cause of the perishing of the world.
pravṛddhas (m. nom. sg. p. pass. participle *pra* √*vṛdh*), mighty, powerful.
lokān (m. acc. pl.), worlds.
samāhartum (infinitive *sam ā* √*hṛ*), to destroy, to annihilate.
iha, here, here in the world.
pravṛttas (m. nom. sg.), come forth, arisen.
ṛte, without, excepting, excluding.
api, even, also.
tvām (acc. sg.), thee.
na, not.
bhaviṣyanti (3rd pl. future act. √*bhū*), they shall be, they shall exist.
sarve (m. nom. pl.), all.
ye (m. nom. pl.), who.
avasthitās (m. nom. pl. p. pass. participle *ava* √*sthā*), arrayed, arranged in battle formation.
pratyanīkeṣu (m. loc. pl.), in opposing ranks, in facing armies.
yodhās (m. nom. pl.), warriors, fighters.

33

तस्मात् त्वम् उत्तिष्ठ यशो लभस्व
tasmāt tvam uttiṣṭha yaśo labhasva
therefore thou stand up! glory attain!

जित्वा शत्रून् भुङ्क्ष्व राज्यं समृद्धम् ।
jitvā śatrūn bhuṅkṣva rājyaṁ samṛddham
having conquered foes, enjoy rulership prosperous;

मयैवैते निहताः पूर्वम् एव
mayāivāite nihatāḥ pūrvam eva
by Me these destroyed already;

निमित्तमात्रं भव सव्यसाचिन् ॥
nimittamātraṁ bhava savyasācin
the instrument merely be, O Ambidextrous Archer.

Therefore stand up thou, and attain glory!
Having conquered the foe, enjoy prosperous kingship.
By Me these have already been struck down;
Be the mere instrument, O Ambidextrous Archer.

tasmāt (m. abl. sg.), from this, t
tvam (nom. sg.), thou.
uttiṣṭha (2nd imperative act. *ud* √
up! arise!
yaśas (n. acc. sg.), glory, fame, h
labhasva (2nd sg. imperative mid
attain! obtain!
jitvā (gerund √*ji*), conquering, ha
quered.
śatrūn (m. acc. pl.), enemies, foes.
bhuṅkṣva (2nd sg. imperative mid.
enjoy!
rājyam (m. acc. sg.), kingship, doma
samṛddham (m. acc. sg.), prosperous,
ing.
mayā (m. inst. sg.), by me.
eva, indeed (used as a rhythmic filler).
ete (m. nom. pl.), these.
nihatās (m. nom. pl. p. pass. particip
√*han*), struck down, destroyed.
pūrvam (adv.), already, previously.
eva, indeed (used as a rhythmic filler).
nimitta (n.), instrument, material cause.
mātram (n. acc. sg.), mere, only, to
merely.
(*nimitta-mātram*, n. acc. sg. KD cpd., i
strument-only.)
bhava (2nd sg. imperative act. √*bhū*), be!
savyasācin (m. voc. sg.), O Ambidextrou
Archer.

संजय उवाच ।
saṁjaya uvāca
Saṁjaya spoke:

saṁjayas (m. nom. sg.), Saṁjaya, the narrator who is describing the scene to King Dhṛtarāṣṭra.
uvāca (3rd sg. perfect act. √*vac*), he said, he spoke.

35

एतच् छ्रुत्वा वचनं केशवस्य
etac chrutvā vacanaṁ keśavasya
this having heard, the utterance of the Handsome Haired One

कृताञ्जलिर् वेपमानः किरीटी ।
kṛtāñjalir vepamānaḥ kirīṭī
he who made a reverent gesture, trembling, the Diademed One (Arjuna)

नमस्कृत्वा भूय एवाह कृष्णं
namaskṛtvā bhūya evāha kṛṣṇaṁ
having made obeisance again thus spoke to Krishna

सगद्गदं भीतभीतः प्रणम्य ॥
sagadgadaṁ bhītabhītaḥ praṇamya
falteringly very much frightened, bowing down:

etad (n. acc. sg.), this.
śrutvā (gerund √*śru*), hearing, having heard.
vacanam (m. acc. sg.), utterance, word, speech.
keśavasya (m. gen. sg.), of Keśava of the Handsome Haired One, epithet of Krishna.
kṛtāñjalis (m. nom. sg. BV cpd.), he who made an *añjali*, he who made a reverent gesture.
vepamānas (m. nom. sg. pr. act. participle √*vip*), trembling, quaking.
kirīṭī (m. nom. sg.), the Diademed One, epithet of Arjuna.
namaskṛtvā (gerund *namas* √*kṛ*), making a bow, having made a bow.
bhūyas, again.
eva, thus, indeed (often used as a rhythmic filler).
āha (3rd sg. imperfect act. √*ah*), spoke, bespoke.
kṛṣṇam (m. acc. sg.), Krishna, to Krishna.
sagadgadam (adv.), stammeringly, stutteringly, falteringly.
bhītabhītas (m. nom. sg.), very much frightened.
praṇamya (gerund *pra* √*nam*), bowing low, bowing.

Saṁjaya spoke:

This, the utterance of the Handsome Haired One (Krishna) having heard,
The Diademed One (Arjuna), who made a reverent gesture, trembling,
Making a bow again, very much frightened,
And bowing down, thus spoke falteringly to Krishna:

XI

अर्जुन उवाच ।
arjuna uvāca
Arjuna spoke:

arjunas (m. nom. sg.), Arjuna.
uvāca (3rd sg. perfect act. √*vac*), he said, he spoke.

36

स्थाने हृषीकेश तव प्रकीर्त्या
sthāne hṛṣīkeśa tava prakīrtyā
rightly, Bristling Haired One, of thee by the fame

जगत् प्रहृष्यत्य् अनुरज्यते च ।
jagat prahṛṣyaty anurajyate ca
the universe it rejoices and it is gratified.

रक्षांसि भीतानि दिशो द्रवन्ति
rakṣāṁsi bhītāni diśo dravanti
the demons, terrified, in (all) directions they flee

सर्वे नमस्यन्ति च सिद्धसंघाः ।।
sarve namasyanti ca siddhasaṁghāḥ
and all they shall bow, the throngs of the perfected ones.

sthāne (n. loc. sg.), rightly, justly.
hṛṣīkeśa (m. voc. sg.), Bristling Haired One, epithet of Krishna.
tava (gen. sg.), of thee, thy.
prakīrtyā (f. inst. sg.), by fame, by renown.
jagat (n.nom. sg.), world, universe.
prahṛṣyati (3rd sg. pr. indic. act. *pra* √*hṛṣ*), it rejoices, it is glad, it exults.
anurajyate (3rd sg. pr. indic. *anu* √*rañj*), it is gratified, it is delighted.
ca, and.
rakṣāṁsi (n. nom. pl.), demons.
bhītāni (n. nom. pl.), terrified, frightened.
diśas (f. acc. pl.), directions, points of compass.
dravanti (3rd pl. pr. indic. act. √*dru*), they run, they flee.
sarve (nom. acc. pl.), all.
namasyanti (3rd pl. future act. √*nam*), they shall bow, they shall make reverence.
ca, and.
siddhasaṁghās (m. nom. pl.), the throngs of perfected ones, the assemblages of perfected ones.

Arjuna spoke:

Rightly, O Bristling Haired One (Krishna), the universe
Rejoices and is gratified by Thy fame.
The demons, terrified, flee in all directions,
And all the throngs of the perfected ones shall bow before Thee.

37

कस्माच् च ते न नमेरन् महात्मन्
kasmāc ca te na nameran mahātman
and why to thee not they should bow, O Great One?

गरीयसे ब्रह्मणो ऽप्य् आदिकर्त्रे ।
garīyase brahmaṇo 'py ādikartre
greater than Brahmā even, to the original creator,

अनन्त देवेश जगन्निवास
ananta deveśa jagannivāsa
infinite Lord of Gods, Dwelling of the Universe,

त्वम् अक्षरं सद् असत् तत्परं यत् ॥
tvam akṣaraṁ sad asat tatparaṁ yat
thou the imperishable, the existent, the non-existent, that beyond which.

And why should they not bow to Thee, O Great One?
To the Original Creator, greater even than Brahmā
Infinite Lord of Gods, Dwelling Place of the Universe
Thou, the Imperishable, the Existent, the Non-existent, and that which is beyond both.

kasmāt (abl. sg. interrog.), from what? wherefore? why?
ca, and.
te (dat. sg.), to thee.
na, not.
nameran (3rd pl. optative mid. √*nam*), they should bow, they should make reverence.
mahātman (m. voc. sg.), (as BV cpd.) O Thou whose Self is Great, O Great One, O Great Self.
garīyase (m. dat. sg. comparative of *guru*), greater, heavier, more venerable.
brahmaṇas (n. abl. sg.), than Brahmā.
api, even, also.
ādi (m.), original, beginning, primal.
katre (m. dat. sg.), to the creator, to the maker.
(*ādi-kartre*, m. dat. sg. KD cpd., original creator.)
ananta (m. voc. sg.), unending, infinite.
deveśa (m. voc. sg.), Lord of Gods.
jagat (n.), universe, world.
nivāsa (m. voc. sg.), dwelling place, home.
(*jagat-nivāsa*, m. voc. sg. TP cpd., dwelling place of the universe.)
tvam (nom. sg.), thou.
akṣaram (n. nom. sg.), imperishable, eternal.
sat (n. nom. sg.), true, existing, existent.
asat (n. nom. sg.), untrue, nonexistent.
tatparam yad (n. nom. sg.), which is beyond that.

38

त्वम् आदिदेवः पुरुषः पुराणस्
tvam ādidevaḥ puruṣaḥ purāṇas
thou the Primal God, the spirit of ancient times

त्वम् अस्य विश्वस्य परं निधानम् ।
tvam asya viśvasya paraṁ nidhānam
thou of it, of all the universe the supreme resting place

वेत्तासि वेद्यं च परं च धाम
vettāsi vedyaṁ ca paraṁ ca dhāma
the knower thou art, that which is to be known, and the supreme state,

त्वया ततं विश्वम् अनन्तरूप ॥
tvayā tataṁ viśvam anantarūpa
by thee pervaded all the universe, O Thou of Infinite Form.

Thou the Primal God, the Ancient Spirit,
Thou, the supreme resting place of all the universe;
Thou art the Knower, the Object of Knowledge and the Supreme State.
All the universe is pervaded by Thee, O Thou of Infinite Form.

tvam (nom. sg.), thou.
ādidevas (m. nom. sg.), primal god, original god, god from the beginning.
puruṣas (m. nom. sg.), spirit, man, person.
purāṇas (m. nom. sg.), ancient, prior, from ancient times.
tvam (nom. sg.), thou.
asya (n. gen. sg.), of it, of this.
viśvasya (n. gen. sg.), of all this universe.
param (n. nom. sg.), supreme, highest.
nidhānam (n nom. sg.), resting place, treasure house.
vettā (m. nom. sg.), knower.
asi (2nd sg. pr. indic. √*as*), thou art.
vedyam (n. nom. sg. gerundive √*vid*), the to-be-known, the object of knowledge.
ca, and.
param (n. nom. sg.), supreme, highest.
ca, and.
dhāma (n. nom. sg.), abode, dwelling place, state, condition.
tvayā (m. inst. sg.), by thee.
tatam (n. nom. sg. p. pass. participle √*tan*), pervaded, stretched.
viśvam (n. nom. sg.), all, all this universe.
anantarūpa (m. voc. sg. BV cpd.), O Thou of Infinite Form, O Thou of Unending Form.

39

वायुर् यमो ऽग्निर् वरुण: शशाङ्क:
vāyur yamo 'gnir varuṇaḥ śaśāṅkaḥ
Vāyu, Yama, Agni, Varuṇa, the rabbit-marked,

प्रजापतिस् त्वं प्रपितामहश्च ।
prajāpatis tvaṁ prapitāmahaś ca
Lord of Creatures, thou, original great grandfather,

नमो नमस् ते ऽस्तु सहस्रकृत्व:
namo namas te 'stu sahasrakṛtvaḥ
reverence! reverence! to thee may it be a thousand times made.

पुनश्च भूयो ऽपि नमो नमस् ते ॥
punaśca bhūyo 'pi namo namas te
And further again also reverence! reverence! to thee.

Vāyu,* Yama,† Agni,‡ Varuṇa,* the Moon,||
The Lord of Creatures, Thou art, and the paternal great grandfather.
Reverence! reverence! to Thee may it be made a thousand times,
And further even, reverence! reverence! to Thee!

vāyus (m. nom. sg.), Vāyu, the god of the wind.
yamas (m. nom. sg.), Yama, the god of death.
agnis (m. nom. sg.), Agni, the god of fire.
varuṇas (m. nom. sg.), Varuṇa, the "sustainer" of the Vedic pantheon, later, and here, god of the waters.
śaśāṅkas (m. nom. sg.), the "rabbitmarked," the moon.
prajāpatis (m. nom. sg.), Lord of Creatures, Lord of Reproduction.
tvam (nom. sg.), thou.
prapitāmahas (m. nom. sg.), original paternal great grandfather.
ca, and.
namo namas (n. nom. sg.), reverence! reverence!
te (dat. sg.), to thee.
astu (3rd sg. imperative act. √*as*), may it be! it shall be!
sahasrakṛtvas, a thousand times made.
punar, again, further.
ca, and.
bhūyas, again.
api, even, also.
namo namas (n. nom. sg.), reverence! reverence!
te (dat. sg.), to thee.

* Vāyu, the Vedic wind god.

† Yama, literally "going," the Vedic god of the dead, and punisher of departed spirits.

‡ Agni, god of fire.

§ Varuṇa, Vedic "sustainer of the universe," later, and here, god of the waters.

|| *śaśāṅka*, the moon, literally the "rabbit marked," sometimes simply *śaśin*, "that which contains the rabbit," favorite Hindu designation for the moon, because the Hindu's saw a rabbit instead of a "man" in the moon.

40

नमः पुरस्ताद् अथ पृष्ठतस् ते
namaḥ purastād atha pṛṣṭhatas te
reverence from in front and behind to thee

नमो ऽस्तु ते सर्वत एव सर्व ।
namo 'stu te sarvata eva sarva
reverence may it be to thee on all sides also, O All.

अनन्तवीर्यामितविक्रमस् त्वं
anantavīryāmitavikramas tvaṁ
infinite valor, unmeasured might, thou

सर्वं समाप्नोषि ततो ऽसि सर्वः ॥
sarvaṁ samāpnoṣi tato 'si sarvaḥ
all thou penetratest, therefore thou art all.

Reverence to Thee from in front and behind,
Reverence may it be to Thee on all sides also, O All.
Thou art infinite valor and boundless might.
Thou pentratest all, therefore Thou art All.

namas (n. nom. sg.), reverence, bow.
parastāt (adv.), from in front, from before, from afar.
atha, moreover, and.
pṛṣṭhatas (adv.), from behind.
te (dat. sg.), to thee.
namas (n. nom. sg.), reverence, bow.
astu (3rd sg. imperative act. √*as*), may it be! be it!
te (dat. sg.), to thee.
sarvatas (adv.), on all sides.
eva, indeed, also (used as a rhythmic filler).
sarva (m. voc. sg.), O All.
ananta (m.), unending, infinite.
vīrya (n.), valor, heroism.
amita (m.), unmeasured, boundless.
vikramas (m. nom. sg.), might, force.
(*ananta-vīrya-amita-vikramas*, m. nom. sg. KD cpd., infinite, heroic, boundless might.)
tvam (nom. sg.), thou.
sarvam (m. acc. sg.), all.
samāpnoṣi (2nd sg. pr. indic. act. *sam* √*āp*), thou fulfillest, thou pervadest, thou attainest, thou penetratest.
tatas, from there, therefore.
asi (2nd sg. pr. indic. √*as*), thou art.
sarvas (m. nom. sg.), all.

41

सखेति मत्वा प्रसभं यद् उक्तं
sakheti matvā prasabhaṁ yad uktaṁ
friend thus thinking, impetuously which said,

हे कृष्ण हे यादव हे सखेति ।
he kṛṣṇa he yādava he sakheti
"Oh Krishna, Oh Descendant of Yādu, Oh Comrade," thus,

अजानता महिमानं तवेदं
ajānatā mahimānaṁ tavedaṁ
by not knowing the majesty of thee this

मया प्रमादात् प्रणयेन वापि ॥
mayā pramādāt praṇayena vāpi
by me from negligence or with affection even,

That which has been said impetuously as if in ordinary friendship,
"Oh Krishna, Oh Son of Yādu, Oh Comrade" thus,
In ignorance of this, Thy majesty,
By me through negligence or even through affection,

sakhā (m. nom. sg.), friend, comrade.
iti, thus (often used to close a quotation).
matvā (gerund √*man*), thinking, having thought, imagining.
prasabham (adv.), impetuously, importunately.
yad (n. nom. sg.), which, what.
uktam (acc. p. pass. participle √*vac*), said, uttered, spoken.
he, Oh!, Ho!
kṛṣṇa (m. voc. sg.), Krishna.
he, Oh!, Ho!
yādava (m. voc. sg.), Descendant of Yādu, epithet of Krishna.
he, Oh!, Ho!
sakha (m. voc. sg., *saṁdhi* for *sakhe*), friend, comrade.
iti, thus (often used to close a quotation).
ajānatā (m. inst. sg. pr. act. participle *a* √*jñā*), by ignorant, by ignorance.
mahimānam (m. acc. sg.), majesty, lordliness, power.
tava (gen. sg.), of thee, thy.
idam (n. nom. sg.), this.
mayā (inst. sg.), by me.
pramādāt (m. abl. sg.), from intoxication, from confusion, from negligence.
praṇayena (m. inst. sg.), with love, with affection, with attachment.
vā, or.
api, even, also.

42

यच् चावहासार्थम् असत्कृतो ऽसि
yac cāvahāsārtham asatkṛto 'si
and as if with jesting purpose, disrespectfully treated thou art,

विहारशय्यासनभोजनेषु ।
vihāraśayyāsanabhojaneṣu
in diversion, in bed, while seated or while dining,

एको ऽथवाप्य् अच्युत तत्समक्षं
eko 'thavāpy acyuta tatsamakṣaṁ
alone or even, O Unshaken One, before the eyes of others

तत् क्षामये त्वाम् अहम् अप्रमेयम् ॥
tat kṣāmaye tvām aham aprameyam
(for) that I ask indulgence (of) thee, I, the immeasurable.

And as if, with humorous purpose,
Thou wert disrespectfully treated,
In diversion, in bed, while seated or while dining,
Alone, O Unshakable One, or even before the eyes of others,
For that I ask indulgence of Thee, the Immeasurable.

yac ca (*yad ca*), as if, and as if.
avahāsa (m.), joking, jesting, in jest, laughing.
artham (n. nom. sg.), purpose, aim.
(*avahāsa-artham*, n. nom. sg. TP cpd., purpose of jest.)
asatkṛtas (m. nom. sg.), disrespectfully treated, badly treated.
asi (2nd sg. pr. indic. √*as*), thou art.
vihāra (m.), diversion, play.
śayyā (f.), bed.
āsana (n.), seated, sitting.
bhojaneṣu (n. loc. pl.), in dining.
(*vihāraśayyāsanabhojaneṣu*, n. loc. pl.), in diversion, in bed, while seated and while dining.)
ekas (m. nom. sg.), alone.
athavā, or.
api, even, also.
acyuta (m. voc. sg.), O Unshaken One (Krishna).
tatsamakṣam (adv.), before the eyes, before the eyes of others.
tad (m. acc. sg.), that, this.
kṣāmaye (1st sg. causative mid. √*kṣam*), I ask pardon, I ask indulgence.
tvām (acc. sg.), thee, of thee.
aham (nom. sg.), I.
aprameyam (m. acc. sg.), the Immeasurable One, the Boundless One.

43

पितासि लोकस्य चराचरस्य
pitāsi lokasya carācarasya
father thou art of the world, of the moving and the non-moving

त्वम् अस्य पूज्यश्च गुरुर् गरीयान् ।
tvam asya pūjyaśca gurur garīyān
and thou of it revered guru very venerable

न त्वत्समो ऽस्त्य् अभ्यधिकः कुतो ऽन्यो
na tvatsamo 'sty abhyadhikaḥ kuto 'nyo
not of thee the like there is, greater how other?

लोकत्रये ऽप्य् अप्रतिमप्रभाव ॥
lokatraye 'py apratimaprabhāva
in the three worlds even, O Incomparable Glory!

Thou art the father of the world, of all things moving and motionless,
And Thou art its revered and venerable guru.
There is nothing like Thee in the three worlds even;
How then another greater, O Thou of Incomparable Glory?

pitā (m. nom. sg.), father.
asi (2nd sg. pr. indic. √*as*), thou art.
lokasya (m. gen. sg.), of the world.
carācarasya (n. gen. sg.), of the moving and the not moving, of the animate and the inanimate.
tvam (nom. sg.), thou.
asya (m. gen. sg.), of it, of this.
pūjyas (m. nom. sg. gerundive, √*pūj*), to be revered, to be honored.
ca, and.
gurus (m. nom. sg.), guru, teacher.
garīyān (m. nom. sg. compar.), more venerable, heavier.
na, not.
tvatsamas (m. nom. sg.), of thee the like, like thee, comparable to thee.
asti (3rd sg. pr. indic. √*as*), there is, it is.
abhyadhikas (m. nom. sg.), greater, surpassing.
kutas, how?
anyas (m. nom. sg.), other.
lokatraye (m. loc. sg.), in the three worlds.
api, even, also.
apratimaprabhāva (m. voc. sg. BV cpd.), O Incomparable Being, O Thou of Incomparable Glory.

44

तस्मात् प्रणम्य प्रणिधाय कायं
tasmāt praṇamya praṇidhāya kāyaṁ
therefore making obeisance, prostrating the body,

प्रसादये त्वाम् अहम् ईशम् ईड्यम् ।
prasādaye tvām aham īśam īḍyam
I ask indulgence of thee, I, lord to be praised;

पितेव पुत्रस्य सखेव सख्युः
piteva putrasya sakheva sakhyuḥ
father-like of a son friend-like of a friend

प्रियः प्रियायार्हसि देव सोढुम् ॥
priyaḥ priyāyārhasi deva soḍhum
a lover to a beloved, thou canst, O God, be merciful.

Therefore, making obeisance, prostrating my body,
I ask indulgence of Thee, O Lord to be Praised;
As a father to a son, as a friend to a friend,
A lover to a beloved, please do, O God, be merciful!

tasmāt (m. abl. sg.), from this, therefore.
praṇamya (gerund *pra* √*nam*), making obeisance, bowing with reverence.
praṇidhāya (gerund *pra ni* √*dhā*), prostrating, laying down.
kāyam (m. acc. sg.), body.
prasādaye (1st sg. mid. causative *pra* √*sad*), I ask indulgence, I ask mercy.
tvām (acc. sg.), thee, of thee.
aham (nom. sg.), I.
īśam (m. acc. sg.), lord, prince, ruler.
īḍyam (m. acc. sg. gerundive √*īḍ*), to be praised, to be honored.
pitā (m. nom. sg.), father.
iva, like.
putrasya (m. gen. sg.), of a son, to a son.
sakhā (m. nom. sg.), friend.
iva, like.
sakhyus (m. gen. sg.), of a friend, to a friend.
priyas (m. nom. sg.), dear, a lover.
priyāya (m. dat. sg.), to a beloved, to a lover.
arhasi (2nd sg. pr. indic. act. √*arh*), thou art able, thou canst, please do.
deva (m. voc. sg.), O God.
soḍhum (infinitive √*sah*), to endure, to tolerate, to be merciful, to have patience.

45

अदृष्टपूर्वं हृषितो ऽस्मि दृष्ट्वा
adṛṣṭapūrvaṁ hṛṣito 'smi dṛṣṭvā
the unseen before delighted I am having seen

भयेन च प्रव्यथितं मनो मे ।
bhayena ca pravyathitaṁ mano me
and with fear trembling the mind of me,

तद् एव मे दर्शय देव रूपं
tad eva me darśaya deva rūpaṁ
that to me cause to see, O God, the form (originally seen)

प्रसीद देवेश जगन्निवास ।।
prasīda deveśa jagannivāsa
have mercy Lord of Gods, universe abode.

Having seen that which has never been seen before, I am delighted,
And yet my mind trembles with fear.
Cause me to see that form, O God, in which Thou originally appeared.
Have mercy, Lord of Gods, Dwelling of the Universe.

adṛṣṭa (p. pass. participle *a* √*dṛś*), unseen, not seen.
pūrvam (n. acc. sg.), before, previously.
(*adṛṣṭapūrvam,* n. acc. sg., previously unseen, never before seen.)
hṛṣitas (m. nom. sg. p. pass. participle √*hṛṣ*), excited, delighted.
asmi (1st sg. pr. indic. √*as*), I am.
dṛṣṭvā (gerund √*dṛś*), seeing, having seen.
bhayena (n. inst. sg.), with fear.
ca, and.
pravyathitam (n. nom. p. pass. participle *pra* √*vyath*), trembling, quaking, shaking, shaken.
manas (n. nom. sg.), mind.
me (gen. sg.), of me, my.
tad (n. acc. sg.), that.
eva, indeed (used as a rhythmic filler).
me (dat. sg.), to me.
darśaya (2nd sg. causative imperative), cause to see! cause to behold! show!
deva (m. voc. sg.), O God.
rūpam (n. acc. sg.), form, shape.
prasīda (2nd sg. imperative act. *pra* √*sad*), have mercy! be merciful!
devéśa (m. voc. sg.), Lord of Gods.
jagannivāsa (m. voc. sg.), "universe-abode," abode of the universe, dwelling place of the universe.

46

किरीटिनं गदिनं चक्रहस्तम्
kirīṭinaṁ gadinaṁ cakrahastam
wearing a diadem, armed with a club, discus in hand,

इच्छामि त्वां द्रष्टुम् अहं तथैव ।
icchāmi tvāṁ draṣṭum ahaṁ tathāiva
I desire thee to see, I, thus (i.e. as before),

तेनैव रूपेण चतुर्भुजेन
tenāiva rūpeṇa caturbhujena
with it with the form four armed

सहस्रबाहो भव विश्वमूर्ते ॥
sahasrabāho bhava viśvamūrte
O Thousand Armed One, become, O Embodiment of All.

I desire to see Thee wearing a diadem,
Armed with a club, discus in hand, thus (i.e. as before),
Become that four-armed form
O Thousand Armed One, O Thou Who hast all Forms.

kirīṭinam (m. acc. sg.), wearing a diadem.
gadinam (m. acc. sg.), armed with a club.
cakrahastam (m. acc. sg.), having a discus in hand, holding a discus.
icchāmi (1st sg. pr. indic. act. √*iṣ*), I desire, I wish.
tvām (acc. sg.), thee.
draṣṭum (infinitive √*dṛś*), to see, to behold.
aham (nom. sg.), I.
tathā, thus.
eva, indeed (used as a rhythmic filler.)
tena (n. inst. sg.), with it, with this.
eva, indeed (used as a rhythmic filler).
rūpeṇa (n. inst. sg.), with the form, with the shape.
caturbhujena (n. inst. sg.), with four arms, four-armed.
sahasra, a thousand.
bāho (m. voc. sg.), armed.
(*sahasrabāho*, m. voc. sg. BV cpd., O Thousand Armed One.)
bhava (2nd sg. imperative √*bhū*), be! become!
viśvamūrte (m. voc. sg. BV cpd.), O thou Who hast all Forms.

श्रीभगवान् उवाच ।
śrībhagavān uvāca
the Blessed Lord spoke:

śrībhagavān (m. nom. sg.), the Blessed Lord, the Blessed One.
uvāca (3rd sg. perfect act. √*vac*), he said, he spoke.

47

मया प्रसन्नेन तवार्जुनेदं
mayā prasannena tavārjunedaṁ
by me by grace of thee Arjuna this

रूपं परं दर्शितम् आत्मयोगात् ।
rūpaṁ paraṁ darśitam ātmayogāt
form supreme manifested from my own power

तेजोमयं विश्वम् अनन्तम् आद्यं
tejomayaṁ viśvam anantam ādyaṁ
splendor-made, universal, infinite, primal

यन् मे त्वदन्येन न दृष्टपूर्वम् ॥
yan me tvadanyena na dṛṣṭapūrvam
which of me by other than thee not seen before.

mayā (m. inst. sg.), by me.
prasannena (m. inst. sg.), by being gracious.
tava (gen. sg.), to thee, toward thee.
arjuna (m. voc. sg.), Arjuna.
idam (n. nom. sg.), this.
rūpam (n. nom. sg.), form, shape, figure.
param (n. nom. sg.), highest, supreme.
darśitam (n. nom. sg. p. pass. causative participle √*dṛś*), manifested, shown.
ātmayogāt (m. abl. sg.), from own power, from own Yoga.
tejomayam (n. nom. sg.), made of splendor, made of brilliance.
viśvam (n. nom. sg.), universal, all.
anantam (n. nom. sg.), unending, infinite.
ādyam (n. nom. sg.), primal, original, from the beginning.
yad (n. nom. sg.), which.
me (gen.), of me, my.
tvadanyena (m. inst. sg.), by other than thee.
na, not.
dṛṣṭapūrvam (n. nom. sg.), seen previously, seen before.

The Blessed Lord spoke:

By My grace toward thee, Arjuna, this
Supreme form has been manifested through My own power,
This form made up of splendor, universal, infinite, primal,
Of Mine, which has never before been seen by other than thee.

48

न वेदयज्ञाध्ययनैर् न दानैर्
na vedayajñādhyayanāir na dānāir
not by Veda sacrifice or recitation; not by gifts,

न च क्रियाभिर् न तपोभिर् उग्रैः ।
na ca kriyābhir na tapobhir ugrāiḥ
and not by ritual acts nor by austerities terrible

एवंरूपः शक्य अहं नृलोके
evaṁrūpaḥ śakya ahaṁ nṛloke
(in) such a form can I, in the world of men,

द्रष्टुं त्वदन्येनकुरुप्रवीर ॥
draṣṭuṁ tvadanyena kurupravīra
be seen by other than thee, Kuru Hero.

Not by Vedic sacrifice nor (Vedic) recitation, not by gifts,
And not by ritual acts nor by terrible austerities,
Can I be seen in such a form in the world of men
By other than thee, Hero of the Kurus.

na, not.
veda (m.), Veda.
yajña (m.), sacrifice.
ādhyayana (n.), study, recitation.
(*vedayajñādhyayanāis,* n. inst. pl. TP cpd., by Vedic sacrifice or Vedic recitation.)
na, not.
dānāis (n. inst. pl.), by gifts.
na, not.
ca, and.
kriyābhis (f. inst. pl.), by ritual acts, by ceremonial acts.
na, not, nor.
tapobhis (n. inst. pl.), by austerities.
ugrāis (n. inst. pl.), by terrible, by strenuous.
evam, thus, such.
rūpas (m. nom. sg.), form, shape, figure.
śakye (1st sg. pr. mid. √*śak*), I am able, I can.
aham, I.
nṛloke (m. loc. sg.), in the world of men, in the world of humans.
draṣṭum (infinitive √*dṛś*), to see, to behold.
(*śakya aham draṣṭum,* can I be seen.)
tvadanyena (m. inst. sg.), by other than thee.
kurupravīra (m. voc. sg.), Kuru Hero, Hero of the Kurus.

49

मा ते व्यथा मा च विमूढभावो
mā te vyathā mā ca vimūḍhabhāvo
Do not tremble! and not confused state,

दृष्ट्वा रूपं घोरम् ईदृङ्ममेदम् ।
dṛṣṭvā rūpaṁ ghoram īdṛṅ mamedam
having seen form terrible such of me this

व्यपेतभीः प्रीतमनाः पुनस् त्वं
vyapetabhīḥ prītamanāḥ punas tvaṁ
freed from fear cheered in thought again thou,

तद् एव मे रूपम् इदं प्रपश्य ॥
tad eva me rūpam idaṁ prapaśya
this thus of me the form this behold!

Have no fear or state of confusion,
Having seen this so terrible form of Mine;
Be thou again freed from fear and cheered in heart;
Behold this, My (previous) form!

mā (prohibitive), not, never.
te (gen. sg.), of thee.
vyathās (2nd aorist subjunctive √*vyath*), thou shouldst quake, thou shouldst tremble.
mā (prohibitive), not, never.
ca, and.
vimūḍhabhāvas (m. nom. sg.), confused state, deluded state of being.
dṛṣṭvā (gerund √*dṛś*), having seen, seeing.
rūpam (n. acc. sg.), form, shape, appearance.
ghoram (n. acc. sg.), terrible, frightful, venerable, sublime.
īdṛś, such.
mama (gen. sg.), of me, my.
idam (n. acc. sg.), this.
vyapeta (m. p. pass. participle *vi apa* √*i*), gone away, disappeared, freed from.
bhīs (f. nom. sg.), fear, apprehension, dread.
(*vyapetabhīs*, f. nom. sg. BV cpd., being without fear, whose fear has departed.)
prītamanās (m. nom. sg. BV cpd.), whose mind is cheerful, cheered in heart.
punar, again, once more.
tvam (nom. sg.), thou.
tad (n. acc. sg.), this, that.
eva, indeed (used as a rhythmic filler).
me (gen. sg.), of me.
rūpam (n. acc. sg.), form, appearance.
idam (n. acc. sg.), this.
prapaśya (2nd sg. imperative act. *pra* √*paś*), behold! see!

संजय उवाच ।
saṁjaya uvāca
Saṁjaya spoke:

saṁjaya (m. nom. sg.), Saṁjaya, the original narrator who is describing the scene to the blind King Dhṛtarāṣṭra.
uvāca (3rd sg. perfect act. √*vac*), he said, he spoke.

50

इत्य् अर्जुनं वासुदेवस् तथोक्त्वा
ity arjunaṁ vāsudevas tathoktvā
thus to Arjuna Vāsudeva (Krishna) thus having spoken,

स्वकं रूपं दर्शयाम् आस भूयः ।
svakaṁ rūpaṁ darśayām āsa bhūyaḥ
his own form he revealed again,

आश्वासयाम् आस च भीतम् एनं
āśvāsayām āsa ca bhītam enaṁ
and he calmed frightened one this,

भूत्वा पुनः सौम्यवपुर् महात्मा ।।
bhūtvā punaḥ sāumyavapur mahātmā
having assumed again (his) gentle, wonderful appearance, the Great One.

Saṁjaya spoke:

Having spoken thus to Arjuna, the Son of Vasudeva (Krishna)
Revealed His own (previous) form again
And calmed this fearful one,
The Great One having resumed His gentle, wonderful appearance.

iti, thus.
arjunam (m. acc. sg.), Arjuna, to Arjuna.
vāsudevas (m. nom. sg.), Son of Vasudeva, epithet of Krishna.
tathā, thus.
uktvā (gerund √*vac*), speaking, having spoken.
svakam (n. acc. sg.), own.
rūpam (n. acc. sg.), form, shape, aspect.
darśayām āsa (causative periphrastic perfect 3rd sg. √*dṛś* + √*ās*), he revealed, he caused to be seen.
bhūyas, again, once more.
āśvāsayām āsa (causative periphrastic perfect *ā* √*śvas* + √*ās*), he consoled, he calmed, he caused to take heart, he assuaged.
ca, and.
bhītam (m. acc. sg.), frightened one.
enam (m. acc. sg.), this.
bhūtvā (gerund √*bhū*), becoming, having become.
punar, again, once more.
sāumya (n.), gentle, mild, pleasant.
vapus (m. nom. sg.), handsome appearance, wonderful appearance.
(*sāumya-vapus*, n. acc. sg. KD cpd., gentle, wonderful appearance.)
mahātmā (m. nom. sg.), the Great Self, the Great One, (as BV cpd.) He Whose Self is Great.

अर्जुन उवाच
arjuna uvāca
Arjuna spoke:

arjunas (m. nom. sg.), Arjuna.
uvāca (3rd sg. perfect act. √*vac*), he said, he spoke.

51

दृष्ट्वेदं मानुषं रूपं
*dṛṣṭvedaṁ mānuṣaṁ rūpaṁ**
seeing this human form

तव सौम्यं जनार्दन ।
tava sāumyaṁ janārdana
of thee gentle, O Agitator of Men,

इदानीम् अस्मि संवृत्तः
idānīm asmi saṁvṛttaḥ
now I am composed,

सचेताः प्रकृतिं गतः ॥
sacetāḥ prakṛtiṁ gataḥ
with mind to normal restored.

dṛṣṭvā (gerund √*dṛś*), seeing, having seen, beholding.
idam (n. acc. sg.), this.
mānuṣam (n. acc. sg.), human, manlike.
rūpam (n. acc. sg.), form, aspect.
tava (gen. sg.), of thee, thy.
sāumyam (n. acc. sg.), gentle, mild, pleasant.
janārdana (m. voc. sg.), Agitator of Men, epithet of Krishna.
idānīm, now, at this moment.
asmi (1st sg. pr. indic. √*as*), I am.
saṁvṛttas (m. nom. sg. p. pass. participle *sam* √*vṛt*), fulfilled, composed.
sacetās (f. nom. pl.), with thoughts, with mind, with heart.
prakṛtim (f. acc. sg.), to nature, to natural state, to normal.
gatas (m. nom. sg. p. pass. participle √*gam*), gone, returned, restored.

Arjuna spoke:

Seeing this, Thy gentle
Human form, O Agitator of Men,
Now I am composed,
With mind restored to normal.

* Here *śloka* metre resumes.

श्रीभगवान् उवाच ।
śrībhagavān uvāca
the Blessed Lord spoke:

srībhagavān (m. nom. sg.), the Blessed Lord, the Blessed One.
uvāca (3rd sg. perfect act. √*vac*), he said, he spoke.

52

सुदुर्दर्शम् इदं रूपं
sudurdarśam idaṁ rūpaṁ
difficult to see this form

दृष्टवान् असि यन् मम ।
dṛṣṭavān asi yan mama
beholding thou art which of me

देवा अप्य् अस्य रूपस्य
devā apy asya rūpasya
the gods even of this form

नित्यं दर्शनकाङ्क्षिणः ॥
nityaṁ darśanakāṅkṣiṇaḥ
constantly the sight wishing.

sudurdarśam (n. acc. sg.), hard to discern, difficult to see.
idam (n. acc. sg.), this.
rūpam (n. acc. sg.), form, aspect.
dṛṣṭavān (m. nom. sg. perfect participle √*dṛś*), seeing, having beheld, having seen.
asi (2nd sg. pr. indic. √*as*), thou art.
(*dṛṣṭavān asi*, periphrastic formation, thou hast seen.)
yad (n. acc. sg.), which.
mama (gen. sg.), of me, my.
devās (m. nom. pl.), gods.
api, even, also.
asya (gen. sg.), of it, of this.
rūpasya (n. gen. sg.) of form, of aspect.
nityam (adv.), constantly, eternally.
darśana (n.), sight, beholding, seeing, observing.
kāṅkṣiṇas (m. nom. pl.), desiring, wishing.
(*darśana-kāṅkṣiṇas*, m. nom. pl. TP cpd., wishing for the sight.)

The Blessed Lord spoke:

This form of Mine which thou hast beheld
Is difficult to see;
Even the gods are constantly wishing
To behold the sight of this form.

53

नाहं वेदैर् न तपसा
nāhaṁ vedāir na tapasā
not I by Veda study, not by austerity,

न दानेन न चेज्यया ।
na dānena na cejyayā
not by gift, and not by sacrifice

शक्य एवंविधो द्रष्टुं
śakya evaṁvidho draṣṭuṁ
possible in such a way to be seen

दृष्टवान् असि मां यथा ॥
dṛṣṭavān asi māṁ yathā
seen thou art me in which way.

Not through Veda study, not through austerity,
Not through gifts and not through sacrifice
Can I be seen in such a way
As thou hast beheld Me.

na, not.
aham (nom. sg.), I.
vedāis (m. inst. pl.), by the Vedas, by Veda study.
na, not.
tapasā (n. inst. sg.), by austerity, by discipline.
na, not, nor.
dānena (n. inst. sg.), by gift, by charity.
na, nor, not.
ca, and.
ijyayā (f. inst. sg.), by sacrifice, by ritual.
śakye (1st sg. pr. mid. √*śak*), I am able, I can.
evaṁvidhas (m. nom. sg.), in such a way.
draṣṭum (infinitive √*dṛś*), to see, to be seen.
dṛṣṭavān (m. nom. sg. p. act. participle √*dṛś*), having seen, having beheld.
asi (2nd sg. pr. indic. √*as*), thou art.
(*dṛṣṭavān asi,* periphrastic formation, thou hast seen, thou hast beheld.)
mām (acc. sg.), me.
yathā, as, in which way.

54

भक्त्या त्व् अनन्यया शक्य
bhaktyā tv ananyayā śakya
by devotion alone undistracted, possible

अहम् एवंविधो ऽर्जुन ।
aham evaṁvidho 'rjuna
I in such a way, Arjuna,

ज्ञातुं द्रष्टुं च तत्त्वेन
jñātuṁ draṣṭuṁ ca tattvena
to be known and to be seen, in truth,

प्रवेष्टुं च परंतप ॥
praveṣṭuṁ ca paraṁtapa
and to be entered into, Scorcher of the Foe.

By undistracted devotion alone
Can I in such a way, Arjuna,
Be known,* and be seen, in truth,
And be entered into, Scorcher of the Foe.

bhaktyā (f. inst. sg.), by devotion, by worship, by love.
tu, alone, but, indeed.
ananyayā (f. inst. sg.), not elsewhere directed.
śakye (1st sg. pr. mid. √*śak*), I am able, I can.
aham, I.
evaṁvidhas (m. nom. sg.), in such a way.
arjuna (m. voc. sg.), Arjuna.
jñātum (inifinite √*jñā*), to know.
draṣṭum (infinitive √*dṛś*), to see, to behold.
ca, and.
tattvena (n. inst. sg.), by truth, in truth, truly.
praveṣṭum (infinitive *pra* √*viś*), to enter, into, to reach, to attain.
ca, and.
paraṁtapa (m. voc. sg.), Scorcher of the Foe, epithet of Arjuna and other warriors.

* Sanskrit has no passive infinitive. To form one, the auxiliary √*śak*, is used, as here *śakya draṣṭum*, "I can be seen," *śakya jñātum*, "I can be known."

55

मत्कर्मकृन् मत्परमो
matkarmakṛn matparamo
of me work doing, on me depending,

मद्भक्तः सङ्गवर्जितः ।
madbhaktaḥ sañgavarjitaḥ
to me devoted, attachment abandoned,

निर्वैरः सर्वभूतेषु
nirvāiraḥ sarvabhūteṣu
free from enmity toward all beings,

यः स माम् एति पाण्डव ॥
yaḥ sa mām eti pāṇḍava
who, he to me goes, Son of Pāṇḍu.

He who does My work, depends on Me,
Is devoted to Me, abandons all attachment,
And is free from enmity toward any being,
Goes to Me, Son of Pāṇḍu.

matkarmakṛt (m. nom. sg.), my work doing, performing my action.
matparamas (m. nom. sg.), depending on me, holding me as highest object.
madbhaktas (m. nom. sg.), to me devoted, devoted to me, worshipping me.
sañgavarjitas (m. nom. sg. p. pass. participle *sañga* √*vṛj*), attachment abandoned, renouncing attachment, relinquished clinging.
nirvāiras (m. nom. sg.), free from enmity, free from hostility.
sarvabhūteṣu (n. loc. pl.), in all beings, toward all beings.
yas (m. nom. sg.), who.
sas (m. nom. sg.), he.
mām (acc. sg.), me, to me.
eti (3rd sg. pr. indic. act. √*i*), he goes, he comes.
pāṇḍava (m. voc. sg.), Son of Pāṇḍu, epithet of Arjuna.

End of Book XI

The Yoga of the Vision of Universal Form

BOOK XII

अर्जुन उवाच।
arjuna uvāca
Arjuna spoke:

arjunas (m. nom. sg.), Arjuna.
uvāca (3rd sg. perfect act. √*vac*), he said, he spoke.

1

एवं सततयुक्ता ये
evaṁ satatayuktā ye
thus the constantly steadfast who,

भक्तास् त्वां पर्युपासते।
bhaktās tvāṁ paryupāsate
devoted, thee they worship

ये चाप्य् अक्षरम् अव्यक्तं
ye cāpy akṣaram avyaktaṁ
who and also the eternal unmanifest,

तेषां के योगवित्तमाः॥
teṣāṁ ke yogavittamāḥ
of them which most knowing of Yoga?

Arjuna spoke:

The constantly steadfast
Who worship Thee with devotion,
And those who worship the Eternal Unmanifest;
Which of these has the best knowledge of Yoga?

evam, thus.
satata (adv.), constant, constantly, perpetually.
yuktās (m. nom. pl. p. pass. participle √*yuj*), steadfast, disciplined.
ye (m. nom. pl.), who.
bhaktās (m. nom. pl. p. pass. participle √*bhaj*), devoted.
tvām (acc. sg.), thee,
paryupāsate (3rd pl. mid. *pari upa* √*ās*), they worship, they honor.
ye (m. nom. pl.), who.
ca, and.
api, also, even.
akṣaram (m. acc. sg.), eternal, imperishable.
avyaktam (m. acc. sg. p. pass. participle *a vi* √*añj*), unmanifest, invisible.
teṣām (m. gen. pl.), of them.
ke (m. nom. interrog. pl.), which? which ones?
yogavittamās (m. nom. pl.), most knowing of Yoga, having the best knowledge of Yoga.

XII

श्रीभगवान् उवाच ।
śrībhagavān uvāca
the Blessed Lord spoke:

śrībhagavān (m. nom. sg.), the Blessed Lord, the Blessed One.
uvāca (3rd sg. perfect act. √*vac*), he said, he spoke.

2

मय्यावेश्य मनो ये मां
mayyāveśya mano ye māṁ
on me fixing the mind who me

नित्ययुक्ता उपासते ।
nityayuktā upāsate
those who are eternally steadfast they worship,

श्रद्धया परयोपेतास्
śraddhayā parayopetās
with faith supreme endowed,

ते मे युक्ततमा मताः ।।
te me yuktatamā matāḥ
they to me the most devoted thought to be.

mayi (loc. sg.), in me, on me.
āveśya (causative gerund *ā* √*viś*), delivering, fixing, causing to enter.
manas (n. acc. sg.), mind.
ye (m. nom. pl.), who.
mām (acc. sg.), me.
nitya (adj. or adv.), eternal, eternally, perpetually.
yuktās (m. nom. pl. p. pass. participle √*yuj*), steadfast, disciplined, yoked.
upāsate (3rd pl. mid. *upa* √*ās*), they worship, they honor.
śraddhayā (f. inst. sg.), with faith.
parayā (f. inst. sg.), with highest, with supreme.
upetās (m. nom. pl. p. pass. participle *upa* √*i*), endowed, initiated, fallen to the share of.
te (m. nom. pl.), they.
me (dat. sg.), to me.
yuktatamās (m. nom. pl. superlative), most yoked, most devoted, most disciplined.
matās (m. nom. pl. p. pass. participle √*man*), thought, thought to be, regarded as.

The Blessed Lord spoke:

Those who are eternally steadfast, who worship Me,
Fixing the mind on Me,
Endowed with supreme faith;
Them I consider to be the most devoted to Me.

3

ये त्व् अक्षरम् अनिर्देश्यम्
ye tv akṣaram anirdeśyam
who, but, the imperishable, undefinable,

अव्यक्तं पर्युपासते ।
avyaktaṁ paryupāsate
unmanifest they honor

सर्वत्रगम् अचिन्त्यं च
sarvatragam acintyaṁ ca
the all pervading and unthinkable

कूटस्थम् अचलं ध्रुवम् ॥
kūṭastham acalaṁ dhruvam
the unchanging, immovable, constant,

But those who honor the Imperishable,
The Undefinable, the Unmanifest,
The All-Pervading and Unthinkable,
The Unchanging, the Immovable, the Constant,

ye (m. nom. pl.), who
tu, but, indeed.
akṣaram (m. acc. sg.), imperishable, unchanging.
anirdeśyam (m. acc. sg. gerund *a nir* √*diś*), undefinable, inexplicable, incomparable.
avyaktam (m. acc. sg. p. pass. participle *a vi* √*añj*), unmanifest, unseen.
paryupāsate (3rd pl. mid. *pari upa* √*ās*), they worship, they honor.
sarvatragam (m. acc. sg.), "everywhere going," omnipresent, all pervading.
acintyam (m. acc. sg. gerundive *a* √*cint*), unthinkable, inconceivable, surpassing thought, not to be thought of.
ca, and.
kūṭastham (m. acc. sg.), unchanging, standing on a mountain peak.
acalam (m. acc. sg.), unmoving, immovable.
dhruvam (m. acc. sg.), constant, steady, fixed.

4

संनियम्येन्द्रियग्रामं
saṁniyamyendriyagrāmaṁ
controlling the multitude of the senses,

सर्वत्र समबुद्धयः ।
sarvatra samabuddhayaḥ
on all sides even minded

ते प्राप्नुवन्ति माम् एव
te prāpnuvanti mām eva
they attain to me also

सर्वभूतहिते रताः ॥
sarvabhūtahite ratāḥ
in all creatures welfare rejoicing.

saṁniyamya (gerund *sam ni* √*yam*), controlling, subduing.
indriyagrāmam (m. acc. sg. TP cpd.), the multitude of senses, the aggregate of the senses.
sarvatra, on all sides, everywhere.
samabuddhayas (f. nom. pl.), even minded, impartial, disinterested, dispassionate, indifferent.
te (m. nom. pl.), they.
prāpnuvanti (3rd pl. pr. indic. act. *pra* √*āp*), they attain, they reach.
mām (acc. sg.), me, to me.
eva, also, indeed (often used as a rhythmic filler.)
sarvabhūtahite (n. loc. sg. TP cpd.), in the welfare of all creatures, in the welfare of all beings.
ratās (m. nom. pl. p. pass. participle √*ram*), rejoicing, exulting, made content.

Controlling the multitude of the senses,
Even-minded on all sides,
Rejoicing in the welfare of all creatures,
They also attain to Me.*

* The substance of stanzas 1, 2, 3 and 4 concerns two aspects of the Lord, and this point has been discussed by several native commentators. Those who worship Him as an imaginary form, fixing their minds on Him are considered the most devoted (stanza 2). But those who worship Him as the *ātman*, or *Brahman*, devoid of all attributes and formless (stanzas 3 and 4), also attain to Him.

5

क्लेशो ऽधिकतरस् तेषाम्
kleśo 'dhikataras teṣām
exertion greater of them

अव्यक्तासक्तचेतसाम् ।
avyaktāsaktacetasām
whose minds are attached to the Unmanifest;

अव्यक्ता हि गतिर् दुःखं
avyaktā hi gatir duḥkhaṁ
the unmanifest, indeed, goal (with) difficulty

देहवद्भिर् अवाप्यते ॥
dehavadbhir avāpyate
by embodied (beings) it is attained.

The exertion of those whose minds
Are fixed on the Unmanifest is greater;
The goal of the Unmanifest is attained
With difficulty by embodied beings.

kleśas (m. nom. sg.), exertion, toil, anguish, pain.
adhikataras (m. nom. sg. comparative), greater, surpassing.
teṣām (m. gen. pl.), of them.
avyakta (m.), unmanifest, unseen.
āsakta (m.), attached, clinging.
cetasām (n. gen. pl.), minded, of thoughts, of minds.
(*avyaktāsaktacetasām,* m. gen. pl. BV cpd., of those whose thoughts are fixed on the Unmanifest.)
avyaktā (f. nom. sg.), unmanifest, unseen.
hi, indeed, truly.
gatis (f. nom. sg.), goal, path.
duḥkham (adv.), difficult, with difficulty, hard.
dehavadbhis (m. inst. pl.), by the embodied, by embodied beings.
avāpyate (3rd sg. pr. indic. passive *ava* $\sqrt{}$*āp*), it is attained, it is reached.

6

ये तु सर्वाणि कर्माणि
ye tu sarvāṇi karmāṇi
who, but, all actions

मयि संन्यस्य मत्पराः ।
mayi saṁnyasya matparāḥ
in me renouncing, intent on me as highest,

अनन्येनैव योगेन
ananyenāiva yogena
with undistracted Yoga

मां ध्यायन्त उपासते ॥
māṁ dhyāyanta upāsate
me meditating on, they worship:

ye (m. nom. pl.), who.
tu, but, indeed.
sarvāṇi (n. acc. pl.), all.
karmāṇi (n. acc. pl.), actions, deeds.
mayi (loc. sg.), in me, on me.
saṁnyasya (gerund *sam ni* √2 *as*), renouncing, laying down, abandoning.
matparās (m. nom. pl.), intent on me as highest, holding me as highest object.
ananyena (m. inst. sg.), undistracted, with not going elsewhere.
eva, indeed (used as a rhythmic filler).
yogena (m. inst. sg.), by Yoga, with Yoga.
mām (acc. sg.), me.
dhyāyantas (m. nom. pl. pr. act. participle √*dhyā*), meditating on, thinking of.
upāsate (3rd pl. mid. *upa* √*ās*), they worship, they honor.

But those who, deferring all actions
To Me, intent on Me as the Supreme,
Worship Me, meditating on Me
With undistracted Yoga,*

* Again, the two aspects of the Lord, and the two corresponding methods of worship are discussed. Those who worship the Lord as the *ātman*, or self, or, in a larger sense, *Brahman* (in stanza 5), and those who worship the imaginary image on which the mind is "fixed" or "intent" (in stanzas 6 and 7). The former method is described as the more difficult.

7

तेषाम् अहं समुद्धर्ता
teṣām ahaṁ samuddhartā
of them I the deliverer

मृत्युसंसारसागरात् ।
mṛtyusaṁsārasāgarāt
from the death-transmigration-ocean,

भवामि नचिरात् पार्थ
bhavāmi nacirāt pārtha
I am, before long, Son of Pṛthā,

मय्यावेशितचेतसाम् ॥
mayyāveśitacetasām.
whose thoughts have entered into me.

Of them, of those whose thoughts have entered into Me,
I am soon the deliverer, Son of Pṛthā,
From the ocean
Of death and transmigration.

teṣām (m. gen. pl.), of them.
aham (nom. sg), I.
samuddhartā (m. nom. sg.), deliverer, lifter up, extricator.
mṛtyu (m.), death.
saṁsāra (m.), transmigration, reincarnation.
sāgarāt (m. abl. sg.), from the ocean.
(*mṛtyusaṁsārasāgarāt,* m. abl. sg. TP cpd., from the ocean of death and reincarnation.)
bhavāmi (1st sg. pr. indic. act. √*bhū*), I am.
nacirāt (adv.), before long, presently, soon.
pārtha (m. voc. sg.), Son of Pṛthā, epithet of Arjuna.
mayi (loc. sg.), in me.
āveśita (causative participle *ā* √*viś*), entered, abiding in.
cetasām (n. gen. pl.), of thoughts, in thoughts.
(*āveśitacetasām*, n. gen. pl. BV cpd., of those whose thoughts have entered, of those whose consciousness has entered.)

8

मय्य् एव मन आधत्स्व
mayy eva mana ādhatsva
on me alone the mind keep.

मयि बुद्धिं निवेशय ।
mayi buddhiṁ niveśaya
into me the intelligence cause to enter.

निवसिष्यसि मय्येव
nivasiṣyasi mayyeva
thou shalt dwell in me

अत ऊर्ध्वं न संशयः ॥
ata ūrdhvaṁ na saṁśayaḥ
thenceforward, not doubt (of this).

Keep thy mind on Me alone.
Cause thine intelligence to enter into Me.
Thus thou shalt dwell in Me thenceforward.
There is no doubt of this.

mayi (loc. sg.), in me, on me.
eva, alone, indeed (often used as a rhythmic filler).
manas (n. acc. sg.), mind, thought.
ādhatsva (2nd sg. imperative mid. *ā* √*dhā*), keep! place!
mayi (loc. sg.), in me, on me.
buddhim (f. acc. sg.), intelligence, understanding.
niveśaya (2nd sg. causative act. imperative *ni* √*viś*), cause to enter! cause to approach!
nivasiṣyasi (2nd sg. future act. *ni* √*vas*), thou shalt dwell, thou shalt abide.
mayi (loc. sg.), in me.
eva, indeed (used as a rhythmic filler).
ata ūrdhvam (adv.), henceforth, thence-forward.
na, not.
saṁśayas (m. nom. sg.), doubt, question.

9

अथ चित्तं समाधातुं
atha cittaṁ samādhātuṁ
or if thought to keep

न शक्नोषि मयि स्थिरम् ।
na śaknoṣi mayi sthiram
not thou art able on me, steadily,

अभ्यासयोगेन ततो
abhyāsayogena tato
by Yoga practice, then,

माम् इच्छाप्तुं धनंजय ॥
mām icchāptuṁ dhanaṁjaya
me seek to attain, Conqueror of Wealth.

Or if thou art not able
To keep thy thought on Me steadily,
Then seek to attain Me
By the practice of Yoga, Conqueror of Wealth.

atha, or if.
cittam (n. acc. sg.), thought, concentration.
samādhātum (infinitive *sam ā* √*dhā*), to keep, to place.
na, not.
śaknoṣi (2nd sg. pr. indic. act. √*śak*), thou art able, thou canst.
mayi (loc. sg.), on me, in me.
sthiram (adv.), steadily, fixedly.
abhyāsa (m.), practice, continued effort.
yogena (m. inst. sg.), by Yoga.
(*abhyāsayogena,* m. inst. sg. TP, by Yoga practice, by the practice of Yoga.)
tatas, then, from there.
mām (acc. sg.), me.
iccha (2nd sg. imperative, act. √*iṣ*), seek! wish!
āptum (infinitive √*āp*), to attain, to reach.
dhanaṁjaya (m. voc. sg.), Conqueror of Wealth, epithet of Arjuna.

10

अभ्यासे ऽप्य् असमर्थो ऽसि
abhyāse 'py asamartho 'si
(if) in practice even incapable thou art,

मत्कर्मपरमो भव ।
matkarmaparamo bhava
my work intent-on be;

मदर्थम् अपि कर्माणि
madartham api karmāṇi
for my sake even, actions

कुर्वन् सिद्धिम् अवाप्स्यसि ॥
kurvan siddhim avāpsyasi
performing, perfection thou shalt attain.

abhyāse (m. loc. sg.), in practice, in continued effort.
api, even, also.
asamarthas (n. nom. sg.), incapable, unable.
asi (2nd sg. pr. indic. √*as*), thou art.
matkarma (n.), my work, work of me.
paramas (m. nom. sg.), intent on, holding as highest object.
(*matkarma-paramas*, m. nom. sg. TP cpd., intent on my work.)
bhava (2nd sg. imperative act. √*bhū*), be!
madartham (m. acc. sg.), for the sake of me, for my sake.
api, even, also.
karmāṇi (n. acc. pl.), actions.
kurvan (m. nom. sg. pr. participle act. √*kṛ*), performing, doing, making.
siddhim (f. acc. sg.), perfection, success.
avāpsyasi (2nd sg. future act. *ava* √*āp*), thou shalt attain, thou shalt reach.

If thou art incapable even of practice,
Be intent on My work;
Even performing actions for My sake,
Thou shalt attain perfection.

11

अथैतद् अप्य् अशक्तो ऽसि
athāitad apy aśakto 'si
or if this even unable thou art

कर्तुं मद्योगम् आश्रितः।
kartuṁ madyogam āśritaḥ
to do, my power resorting to,

सर्वकर्मफलत्यागं
sarvakarmaphalatyāgaṁ
all action fruit abandoning,

ततः कुरु यतात्मवान्॥
tataḥ kuru yatātmavān
then act, self-restrained.

But if thou art unable even to do this,
Then, resorting to My power,
Abandoning all the fruits of action,
Act, with self restraint.

atha, or if.
etad (n. acc. sg.), this.
api, even, also.
aśaktas (m. nom. sg. p. pass. participle *a* √*śak*), unable, incapable.
asi (2nd sg. pr. indic. √*as*), thou art.
kartum (infinitive √*kṛ*), to do, to perform, to make.
madyogam (m. acc. sg.), of-me-Yoga, my Yoga, my power.
āśritas (nom. sg. p. pass. participle *ā* √*śri*), resorting to, depending on, adhering to, resting on.
sarvakarmaphala (n.), all action fruit, all fruit of action.
tyāgam (m. acc. sg. from √*tyaj*), abandonment, abandoning, relinquishing.
(*sarva-karma-phala-tyāgam*, m. acc. sg. TP cpd., abandoning all fruits of action.)
tatas, then, thereupon, from there.
kuru (2nd sg. imperative act. √*kṛ*), act! do! perform!
yatātmavān (m. nom. sg.) with controlled self, self-restrained, with self restraint.

12

श्रेयो हि ज्ञानम् अभ्यासाज्
śreyo hi jñānam abhyāsāj
better indeed knowledge than practice;

ज्ञानाद् ध्यानं विशिष्यते ।
jñānād dhyānaṁ viśiṣyate
than knowledge, meditation is superior;

ध्यानात् कर्मफलत्यागस्
dhyānāt karmaphalatyāgas
than meditation, action-fruit abandonment;

त्यागाच् छान्तिर् अनन्तरम् ॥
tyāgāc chāntir anantaram
from abandonment, peace immediately.

śreyas (n. nom. sg.), better, more fortunate, more valuable.
hi, indeed, truly.
jñānam (n. nom. sg.), knowledge.
abhyāsāt (m. abl. sg.), from practice, than practice.
jñānāt (n. abl. sg.), from knowledge, than knowledge.
dhyānam (n. nom. sg.), meditation.
viśiṣyate (3rd sg. passive *vi* √*śiṣ*), it is preferred, it is superior.
dhyānāt (n. abl. sg.), from meditation, than meditation.
karmaphalatyāgas (m. nom. sg.), abandonment of the fruit of action.
tyāgāt (m. abl. sg.), from abandonment.
śāntis (f. nom. sg.), peace, tranquility.
anantaram (adv.), immediately, soon.

Knowledge is indeed better than practice;
Meditation is superior to knowledge;
Abandonment of the fruit of action is better than meditation;
From abandonment, peace immediately follows.

13

अद्वेष्टा सर्वभूतानां
adveṣṭā sarvabhūtānāṁ
a non-hater of all beings,

मैत्रः करुण एव च ।
māitraḥ karuṇa eva ca
friendly and compassionate,

निर्ममो निरहंकारः
nirmamo nirahaṁkārah
free from "mine," free from "I" making,

समदुःखसुखः क्षमी ॥
samaduḥkhasukhaḥ kṣamī
indifferent to pain and pleasure, patient,

adveṣṭā (m. nom. sg.), non-hater.
sarvabhūtānām (n. gen. pl.), of all beings, of all creatures.
māitras (m. nom. sg.), friendly, a friend.
karuṇas (m. nom. sg.), compassionate.
eva, indeed (used as a rhythmic filler).
ca, and.
nirmamas (m. nom. sg.), free from "mine," free from attachment to possessions.
nirahaṁkāras (m. nom. sg.), free from "I" making, free from egotism.
samaduḥkhasukhas (m. nom. sg.), indifferent to pain and pleasure, the same in pain and pleasure.
kṣamī (m. nom. sg.), patient, enduring.

A non-hater of any being,
Friendly and compassionate,
Free from attachment to possessions, free from egotism,
Indifferent to pain and pleasure, patient,

14

संतुष्टः सततं योगी
saṁtuṣṭaḥ satataṁ yogī
contented always, the yogin,

यतात्मा दृढनिश्चयः ।
yatātmā dṛḍhaniścayaḥ
of controlled self and firm resolve,

मय्य् अर्पितमनोबुद्धिर्
mayy arpitamanobuddhir
on me, whose mind and intelligence are fixed,

यो मद्भक्तः स मे प्रियः ॥
yo madbhaktaḥ sa me priyaḥ
who of me devoted, he to me dear.

The yogin who is always contented,
Whose self is controlled and whose resolve is firm,
Whose mind and intelligence are fixed on Me,
Who is devoted to Me, is dear to Me.

saṁtuṣṭas (m. nom. sg. p. pass. participle *sam* √*tuṣ*), contented, satisfied, delighted.
satatam (adv.), constantly, always, perpetually.
yogī (m. nom. sg.), yogin.
yatātmā (m. nom. sg. KD cpd.), of controlled self, of subdued self.
dṛḍhaniścayas (m. nom. sg. BV cpd.), being of firm resolve, being of fixed resolve.
mayi (loc. sg.), on me, in me.
arpita (causative participle √*ṛ*), fixed, entrusted.
manas (n.), mind, thought.
buddhis (f. nom. sg.), intelligence, understanding.
(*arpitamanobuddhis,* f. nom. sg. with mind and intelligence fixed.)
yas (m. nom. sg.), who.
madbhaktas (m. nom. sg.), of me devoted, devoted to me.
sas (m. nom. sg.), he.
me (gen. sg.), of me, to me.
priyas (m. nom. sg.), dear, beloved.

15

यस्मान् नोद्विजते लोको
yasmān nodvijate loko
from whom not it shrinks, the world,

लोकान् नोद्विजते च यः ।
lokān nodvijate ca yaḥ
and from the world not he shrinks, who;

हर्षामर्षभयोद्वेगैर्
harṣāmarṣabhayodvegāir
from joy, impatience, fear, distress,

मुक्तो यः स च मे प्रियः ॥
mukto yaḥ sa ca me priyaḥ
released who, he also to me dear.

He from whom the world does not shrink,
And who does not shrink from the world,
Who is released from joy, impatience, fear and distress,
Is also dear to Me.*

yasmāt (m. abl. sg.), from whom.
na, not.
udvijate (3rd sg. pr. indic. mid. *ud* √*vij*), it shrinks, it trembles, it shudders.
lokas (m. nom. sg.), world.
lokāt (m. abl. sg.), from the world.
na, not.
udvijate (3rd sg. pr. indic. mid. *ud* √*vij*), he shrinks, he trembles, he shudders.
ca, and.
yas (m. nom. sg.), who.
harṣa (m.), joy, pleasure, happiness.
āmarṣa (m.), impatience, indignation.
bhaya (n.), fear.
udvegais (m. instr. pl.), distress, trembling, anxiety.
(*harṣāmarṣabhayodvegāis,* m. inst. pl., by pleasure, impatience, fear and distress.)
muktas (m. nom. sg. p. pass. participle √*muc*), released, freed, liberated.
yas (m. nom. sg.), who.
sas (m. nom. sg.), he.
ca, and, also.
me (gen. sg.), of me, to me.
priyas (m. nom. sg.), dear, beloved.

* "A devotee who, through...*karmayoga* (the Yoga of action), practices *bhaktiyoga* (the Yoga of devotion or love) is beloved of God. So is the *karmayogin* (practitioner of the Yoga of action) who does nothing to vex the world, who is not vexed by the world because he is not interested in it and who therefore is not joyous, intolerant, fearful and irascible." – Rāmānuja.

16

अनपेक्षः शुचिर् दक्ष
anapekṣaḥ śucir dakṣa
indifferent, pure, capable,

उदासीनो गतव्यथः ।
udāsīno gatavyathaḥ
disinterested, free from anxiety,

सर्वारम्भपरित्यागी
sarvārambhaparityāgī
all undertakings abandoning,

यो मद्भक्तः स मे प्रियः ।।
yo madbhaktaḥ sa me priyaḥ
who, to me devoted, he to me dear.

He who is indifferent, pure, capable,
Disinterested, free from anxiety,
Who has abandoned all undertakings
And is devoted to Me, is dear to Me.

anapekṣas (m. nom. sg.), indifferent, impartial, disinterested.
śucis (m. nom. sg.), pure, holy, bright.
dakṣas (m. nom. sg.), capable, dextrous, able.
udāsīnas (m. nom. sg.), indifferent, "sitting apart," unprejudiced.
gatavyathas (m. nom. sg.), free from anxiety, free from trembling, (as BV cpd.) whose anxiety is gone.
sarva, all.
ārambha (m.), undertaking, beginning, commencement.
parityāgī (m. nom. sg. from √*tyaj*), abandoning, relinquishing.
(*sarvārambhaparityāgī*, m. nom. sg. TP cpd., who has abandoned all undertakings.)
yas (m. nom. sg.), who.
madbhaktas (m. nom. sg.), devoted to me.
sas (m. nom. sg.), he.
me (gen. sg.), of me, to me.
priyas (m. nom. sg.), dear, beloved.

17

यो न हृष्यति न द्वेष्टि
yo na hṛṣyati na dveṣṭi
who not he rejoices, not he hates,

न शोचति न काङ्क्षति ।
na śocati na kāñkṣati
not he mourns, not he desires,

शुभाशुभपरित्यागी
śubhāśubhaparityāgī
agreeable and disagreeable abandoning,

भक्तिमान् यः स मे प्रियः ॥
bhaktimān yaḥ sa me priyaḥ
full of devotion, who, he to me dear.

He who neither rejoices nor hates,
Nor mourns nor desires,
Has abandoned the agreeable and the disagreeable,
And is full of devotion, is dear to Me.

yas (m. nom. sg.), who.
na, not.
hṛṣyati (3rd sg. pr. indic. act. √*hṛṣ*), he rejoices, he is happy.
na, not.
dveṣṭi (3rd sg. pr. indic. √*dviṣ*), he hates, he loathes.
na, not.
śocati (3rd sg. pr. indic. act. √*śuc*), he mourns, he sorrows.
na, not.
kāñkṣati (3rd sg. pr. indic. √*kāñkṣ*), he desires, he lusts after.
śubhāśubha (n.), agreeable and disagreeable, pleasant and unpleasant.
parityāgī (m. nom. sg.), abandoning, relinquishing, renouncing.
(*śubha-aśubha-parityāgī*, m. nom. sg. TP cpd., abandoning the agreeable and the disagreeable.)
bhaktimān (m. nom. sg.), full of devotion, filled with devotion, devoted.
yas (m. nom. sg.), who.
sas (m. nom. sg.), he.
me (gen. sg.), of me, to me.
priyas (m. nom. sg.), dear, beloved.

18

समः शत्रौ च मित्रे च
samaḥ śatrāu ca mitre ca
alike toward enemy and toward friend,

तथा मानापमानयोः ।
tathā mānāpamānayoḥ
the same in honor and disgrace,

शीतोष्णसुखदुःखेषु
śītoṣṇasukhaduḥkheṣu
in cold and heat, pleasure and pain,

समः सङ्गविवर्जितः ॥
samaḥ saṅgavivarjitaḥ
alike, attachment freed from,

Alike toward enemy and friend,
The same in honor and disgrace,
Alike in cold and heat, pleasure and pain,
Freed from attachment,

samas (m. nom. sg.), alike, the same.
śatrāu (m. loc. sg.), in enemy, toward enemy.
ca, and.
mitre (m. loc. sg.), in friend, toward friend.
ca, and.
tathā, thus, in this way, the same.
mānāpamānayos (m. loc. dual), in honor and disgrace, in good name and bad.
śīta (n.), cold.
uṣṇa (m. n.), heat.
sukha (n.), pleasure, happiness.
duḥkheṣu (n. loc. pl.), pain, misery.
(*śītoṣṇasukhaduḥkheṣu,* n. loc. pl., in cold, heat, pleasure and pain.)
samas (m. nom. sg.), alike, the same, indifferent, unchanged.
saṅga (m.), attachment, clinging.
vivarjitas (m. nom. sg. p. pass. participle *vi* √*vṛj*), twisted, freed from.
(*saṅga-vivarjitas*, m. nom. sg. TP cpd., freed from attachment.)

19

तुल्यनिन्दास्तुतिर् मौनी
tulyanindāstutir māunī
similar in blame or praise, taciturn,

संतुष्टो येन केनचित् ।
saṁtuṣṭo yena kenacit
content with anything whatever,

अनिकेतः स्थिरमतिर्
aniketaḥ sthiramatir
homeless, steady minded,

भक्तिमान् मे प्रियो नरः ॥
bhaktimān me priyo naraḥ
full of devotion to me dear (this) man.

Indifferent to blame or praise, taciturn,
Content with anything whatever,
Homeless, steady minded,
Full of devotion; this man is dear to Me.

tulya, similar, comparable.
nindā (f.), blame, censure.
stutis (f. nom. sg.), praise.
(*tulya-nindā-stutis*, f. nom. sg. KD cpd., alike in blame or praise.)
māunī (m. nom. sg.), taciturn, silent.
saṁtuṣṭas (m. nom. sg. p. pass. participle *sam* √*tuṣ*), content, satisfied.
yena (m. inst. sg.), with what.
kenacid, with anything.
(*yena kenacid,* with anything whatever).
aniketas (m. nom. sg.), homeless, without a house.
sthira (adj.), steady, firm.
matis (f. nom. sg.), mind, judgement, sense.
(*sthira-matis*, f. nom. sg. KD cpd., steady minded.)
bhaktimān (m. nom. sg.), full of devotion, devoted.
me (gen. sg.), of me, to me.
priyas (m. nom. sg.), dear, beloved.
naras (m. nom. sg.), man.

20

ये तु धर्म्यामृतम् इदं
ye tu dharmyāmṛtam idaṁ
who indeed wisdom nectar this

यथोक्तं पर्युपासते ।
yathoktaṁ paryupāsate
above declared, they honor,

श्रद्दधाना मत्परमा
śraddadhānā matparamā
faith holding, me as Supreme intent on,

भक्तास् ते ऽतीव मे प्रियाः ॥
bhaktās te 'tīva me priyāḥ
devoted, they exceedingly to me dear.

Those who honor this above-declared
Nectar of wisdom,* holding faith, devoted
And intent on Me as the Supreme;
They are exceedingly dear to Me.

ye (m. nom. pl.), who.
tu, but, indeed.
dharmya (n.), righteousness, virtue, duty, wisdom.
amṛtam (n. acc. sg.), nectar, immortality.
(*dharmyāmṛtam,* n. acc. sg., has been translated both "nectar of duty" and "immortal law.")
idam (n. acc. sg.), this.
yathā, in which way, as, above, previously.
uktam (n. acc. sg. p. pass. participle √*vac*), declared, said, propounded.
paryupāsate (3rd pl. pr. indic. mid. *pari upa* √*ās*), they worship, they honor.
śraddadhānās (m. nom. pl.), faith holding, giving faith.
matparamās (m. nom. pl.), intent on me as supreme object, holding me as highest object.
bhaktās (m. nom. pl.), devoted.
te (m. nom. pl.), they.
atīva (adv.), exceedingly, surpassingly.
me (gen. sg.), of me, to me.
priyās (m. nom. pl.), dear, beloved.

End of Book XII

The Yoga of Devotion

* Some translators have rendered *dharmyāmṛtam idam* as "this means of attaining immortality." Either translation may be correct. The confusion arises because "*amṛta*" means both "nectar" and "immortality."

BOOK XIII

अर्जुन उवाच ।
arjuna uvāca
Arjuna spoke:

arjunas (m. nom. sg.), Arjuna.
uvāca (3rd sg. perfect act. √*vac*), he said, he spoke.

*

प्रकृतिं पुरुषं चैव
prakṛtiṁ puruṣaṁ cāiva
material nature and spirit,

क्षेत्रं क्षेत्रज्ञम् एव च ।
kṣetraṁ kṣetrajñam eva ca
the field and the field knower,

एतद् वेदितुम् इच्छामि
etad veditum icchāmi
this to know I wish

ज्ञानं ज्ञेयं च केशव ॥
jñānaṁ jñeyaṁ ca keśava
knowledge and the to-be-known, O Handsome Haired One.

prakṛtim (f. acc. sg.), material nature.
puruṣam (m. acc. sg.), spirit, person, man.
ca, and.
eva, indeed (used as a rhythmic filler).
kṣetram (n. acc. sg.), field.
kṣetrajñam (m. acc. sg.), field knower, knower of the field.
eva, indeed (used as a rhythmic filler).
ca, and.
etad (n. acc. sg.), this.
veditum (infinitive √*vid*), to know.
icchāmi (1st sg. act. √*iṣ*), I wish, I desire.
jñānam (n. acc. sg.), knowledge, wisdom.
jñeyam (n. acc. sg. gerundive √*jñā*), the to-be-known, the object of knowledge.
ca, and.
keśava (m. voc. sg.), O Handsome Haired One, epithet of Krishna.

Arjuna spoke:

Material nature and spirit,
The field and the knower of the field,
Knowledge and the object of knowledge,
Concerning these I wish to know, Handsome Haired One.

* This first unnumbered stanza does not occur in all versions. It may have been deleted in order to make the total number of verses an even seven hundred.

XIII

श्रीभगवान् उवाच ।
śrībhagavān uvāca
the Blessed Lord spoke:

śrībhagavān (m. nom. sg.), the Blessed Lord, the Blessed One.
uvāca (3rd sg. perfect act. √*vac*), he said, he spoke.

1

इदं शरीरं कौन्तेय
idaṁ śarīraṁ kāunteya
this body, Son of Kuntī,

क्षेत्रम् इत्य् अभिधीयते ।
kṣetram ity abhidhīyate
the field, thus it is explained.

एतद् यो वेत्ति तं प्राहुः
etad yo vetti taṁ prāhuḥ
this who knows, him they declare

क्षेत्रज्ञ इति तद्विदः ॥
kṣetrajña iti tadvidaḥ
the field knower, thus the knowers of that.

idam (n. nom. sg.), this.
śarīram (n. nom. sg.), body, bodily, frame.
kāunteya (m. voc. sg.), O Son of Kuntī, epithet of Arjuna.
kṣetram (n. nom. sg.), field.
iti, thus.
abhidhīyate (3rd sg. pr. indic. passive *abhi* √*dhā*), it is called, it is explained.
etad (n. acc. sg.), this.
yas (m. nom. sg.), who.
vetti (3rd sg. pr. indic. act. √*vid*), he knows.
tam (m. acc. sg.), him, it, this.
prāhus (3rd pl. perf. act. *pra* √*ah* with present meaning), they declare, they say, they call.
kṣetrajñas (m. nom. sg.), field knower, knower of the field, knowing the field.
iti, thus.
tadvidas (m. nom. pl.), the knowers of that, the knowers of this.

The Blessed Lord spoke:
This body, Son of Kuntī,
Is said to be the field;
Him who knows this, those who are wise in such things
Declare to be the knower of the field.*

* "Sages who possess exact knowledge of the body call it the experiencing-*ātman's* field of experience. A person who knows this body and, because of this very knowledge, must be different from his body which is the object of his knowledge, is called a *kṣetrajña* (knower of the field) by these sages." – Rāmānuja.

2

क्षेत्रज्ञं चापि मां विद्धि
kṣetrajñaṁ cāpi māṁ viddhi
and the field knower also me, know!

सर्वक्षेत्रेषु भारत ।
sarvakṣetreṣu bhārata
in all fields, Descendant of Bharata

क्षेत्रक्षेत्रज्ञयोर् ज्ञानं
kṣetrakṣetrajñayor jñānaṁ
of the field and the field knower, the knowledge

यत् तज् ज्ञानं मतं मम ॥
yat taj jñānaṁ mataṁ mama
which that (true) knowledge considered by me.

Know also that I am the knower of the field,
In all fields, Descendant of Bharata;
Knowledge of the field and of the field-knower;
That is considered by Me to be true knowledge.

kṣetrajñam (m. acc. sg.), field knower, knower of the field.
ca, and.
api, also, even.
mām (acc. sg.), me.
viddhi (2nd sg. imperative act. √*vid*), know! learn!
sarvakṣetreṣu (n. loc. pl.), in all fields.
bhārata (m. voc. sg.), Descendant of Bharata, epithet of Arjuna.
kṣetrakṣetrajñayor (m. gen. dual), of the field and the knower of the field.
jñānam (n. nom. sg.), knowledge.
yad (n. nom. sg.), which.
tad (n. acc. sg.), this, that.
jñānam (n. acc. sg.), knowledge.
matam (m. acc. sg. p. pass. participle √*man*), thought, considered, deemed.
mama (gen. sg.), of me, by me.

3

तत् क्षेत्रं यच् च यादृक् च
tat kṣetraṁ yac ca yādṛk ca
this field what (it is) and what kind

यद्विकारि यतश्च यत् ।
yadvikāri yataśca yat
what (its) modifications, whence which (i.e. the modifications),

स च यो यत्प्रभावश्च
sa ca yo yatprabhāvaśca
and he who, and what (his) powers

तत् समासेन मे शृणु ॥
tat samāsena me śṛṇu
that, briefly, of me hear!

This field, what it is, and of what kind,
What its modifications and whence they come,
And who he (the knower of the field) is, and what his powers,
That, in brief, hear from Me:

tad (n. nom. sg.), this, that.
kṣetram (n. nom. sg.), field.
yad (n. nom. sg.), which, what.
ca, and.
yādṛś, what kind, what like, of what nature.
ca, and.
yad (n. nom. sg.), what, which.
vikāri (n. nom. sg.), having modifications, transformations, liability to change.
yatas, whence, from where.
ca, and.
yad (n. nom. sg.), which, what.
sas (m. nom. sg.), he, this.
ca, and.
yas (m. nom. sg.), who.
yad (n. nom. sg.), what, which.
prabhāvas (m. nom. sg.), power, might.
ca, and.
tad (n. acc. sg.), that.
samāsena (adv.), with briefness, in brief, briefly.
me (gen. sg.), of me, from me.
śṛṇu (2nd sg. imperative act. √*śru*), hear! learn!

4

ऋषिभिर् बहुधा गीतं
ṛṣibhir bahudhā gītaṁ
by the seers many times chanted

छन्दोभिर् विविधैः पृथक् ।
chandobhir vividhāiḥ pṛthak
with sacred (Vedic) hymns various, distinctly,

ब्रह्मसूत्रपदैश्चैव
brahmasūtrapadāiścāiva
and with Brāhman aphroisms,*

हेतुमद्भिर् विनिश्चितैः ॥
hetumadbhir viniścitāiḥ
provided with reasons, and definite,

Chanted many times, distinctly, by the seers,
In various sacred (Vedic) hymns,
And with quotations concerning Brahman,
Provided with definite reasons,

ṛṣbhis (m. inst. pl.), by the seers.
bahudhā, many times, in many ways.
gītam (m. acc. sg. p. pass. participle √*gāi*), sung, chanted.
chandobhis (n. inst. pl.), with sacred hymns, with Vedic hymns.
vividhāis (n. inst. pl.), of many kinds, various.
pṛthak (adv.), distinctly, separately, singly.
brahmasūtrapadāis (n. inst. pl. TP cpd.), with Brāhman aphorisms, with lines sacred to the Brāhmans.
ca, and.
eva, indeed (used as a rhythmic filler).
hetumadbhis (m./n. inst. pl.), with full reasons, provided with reasons.
viniścitāis (m./n. inst. pl.), with definite, with undeniable, with unquestionable.

* Edgerton has pointed out that Bādarāyaṇa's Brahma Sūtra (200 A.D.) probably did not exist at the time the Gītā was written, and that the meaning of "*brāhma sūtra padāis*" here is probably therefore more general.

5

महाभूतान्य् अहंकारो
mahābhūtāny ahamkāro
the great elements, the consciourness of "I,"

बुद्धिर् अव्यक्तम् एव च ।
buddhir avyaktam eva ca
the intelligence and the unmanifest,

इन्द्रियाणि दशैकं च
indriyāṇi daśāikaṁ ca
the senses ten and one,

पञ्च चेन्द्रियगोचराः ॥
pañca cendriyagocarāḥ
and the five fields of action of the senses,

The great elements,* the consciousness of "I,"
The intelligence and the unmanifest,
The senses, ten† and one,‡
And the five fields of action of the senses,§

mahābhūtāni (n. nom. pl.), great elements, gross elements.
ahaṁkāras (m. nom. sg.), consciousness of "I," consciousness of self.
buddhis (f. nom. sg.), intelligence.
avyaktam (n. nom. sg.), unmanifest.
eva, indeed (used as a rhythmic filler).
ca, and.
indriyāṇi (n. nom. pl.), senses, sensations.
daśa, ten.
ekam (n. nom. sg.), one.
(*daśāikam,* acc., ten and one, i.e. eleven.)
ca, and.
pañca, five.
ca, and.
indriyogocarās (m. nom. pl. TP cpd.), fields of action of the senses, fields perceptible to the senses.

* I.e. ether, air, fire, water and earth.

† Eye, ear, skin, tongue, nose and the five organs of action, viz. hand, foot, mouth, anus, genital organ.

‡ The mind.

§ Sound, touch, color, taste and smell. N.B. These are all *Sāṁkhya* concepts, as are the *guṇas*.

6

इच्छा द्वेषः सुखं दुःखं
icchā dveṣaḥ sukhaṁ duḥkhaṁ
desire, aversion, pleasure, pain,

संघातश्चेतना धृतिः ।
saṁghātaścetanā dhṛtiḥ
the organic whole, consciousness, steadfastness,

एतत् क्षेत्रं समासेन
etat kṣetraṁ samāsena
this the field, briefly

सविकारम् उदाहृतम् ॥
savikāram udāhṛtam
with modifications, described.

icchā (f. nom. sg.), desire, inclination, wish.
dveṣas (m. nom. sg.), aversion, hatred, dislike.
sukham (n. nom. sg.), pleasure, comfort.
duḥkham (n. nom. sg.), pain, misery, misfortune.
saṁghātas (m. nom. sg.), multitude, aggregation, whole, organism, organic whole.
cetanā (f. nom. sg.), consciousness, intelligence, mind.
dhṛtis (f. nom. sg.), steadfastness, courage, firmness.
etad (n. nom. sg.), this.
kṣetram (n. nom. sg.), field.
samāsena (m. inst. sg.), briefly, in brief.
savikāram (n. acc. sg.), with modifications, with transformations, with capacity for change.
udāhṛtam (n. nom. sg. p. pass. participle *ud ā* √*hṛ*), described, explained, illustrated, announced.

Desire, aversion, pleasure, pain,
The organic whole,* consciousness, steadfastness,
This briefly is described as the field
With its modifications.

* The physical body.

7

अमानित्वम् अदम्भित्वम्
amānitvam adambhitvam
absence of pride, freedom from hypocrisy,

अहिंसा क्षान्तिर् आर्जवम् ।
ahiṁsā kṣāntir ārjavam
non-violence, patience, rectitude,

आचार्योपासनं शौचं
ācāryopāsanaṁ śāucaṁ
teacher attendance upon, purity,

स्थैर्यम् आत्मविनिग्रहः ॥
sthāiryam ātmavinigrahaḥ
stability, self restraint,

Absence of pride, freedom from hypocrisy,
Non-violence, patience, rectitude,
Attendance on a teacher, purity,
Constancy, self restraint,

amānitvam (n. nom. sg.), absence of pride, absence of arrogance.
adambhitvam (n. nom. sg.), freedom from hypocrisy, absence of deceit.
ahiṁsā (f. nom. sg.), non-violence, harmlessness.
kṣāntis (f. nom. sg.), patience, fortitude.
ārjavam (n. nom. sg.), rectitude, virtue, honesty.
ācāryopāsanam (n. nom. sg.), attendance on a teacher, sitting beside a teacher.
śāucam (n. nom. sg.), purity, integrity.
sthāiryam (n. nom. sg.), stability, firmness, constancy.
ātmavinigrahas (m. nom. sg.), self restraint, self control.

8

इन्द्रियार्थेषु वैराग्यम्
indriyārtheṣu vāirāgyam
toward the objects of the senses, aversion,

अनहंकार एव च ।
anahaṁkāra eva ca
and absence of egotism,

जन्ममृत्युजराव्याधि-
janmamṛtyujarāvyādhi-
birth-death-old age-disease-

दुःखदोषानुदर्शनम् ॥
duḥkhadoṣānudarśanam
pain-evil keeping in view,

Aversion toward the objects of sense,
And absence of egotism;
Keeping in view the evils of birth, death,
Old age, disease and pain;

indriyārtheṣu (m. loc. pl.), in the objects of sense, toward the objects of sense.
vāirāgyam (n. nom. sg.), aversion, hatred.
anahaṁkāras (m. nom. sg.), absence of egotism, absense of the sense of "I," lit. "not I making."
eva, indeed (used as a rhythmic filler).
ca, and.
janma (n.), birth.
mṛtyu (m.), death.
jarā (f.), becoming old, old age, decrepitude.
vyādhi (m.), disease, ailment, sickness.
duḥkha (n.), plain, misery, unhappiness.
doṣa (m.), wrong, evil.
anudarśanam (n. nom. sg.), keeping in view, keeping in mind.
(*janmamṛtyujarāvyādhiduḥkhadoṣānudarśanam,* n. nom. sg. TP cpd., keeping in view the evils of birth, death, old age, disease and pain.)

9

असक्तिर् अनभिष्वङ्ग
asaktir anabhiṣvaṅga
non-attachment, absence of clinging

पुत्रदारगृहादिषु ।
putradāragṛhādiṣu
to son, wife, home beginning with,

नित्यं च समचित्तत्वम्
nityaṁ ca samacittatvam
and constantly even mindedness

इष्टानिष्टोपपत्तिषु ॥
iṣṭāniṣṭopapattiṣu
toward desired and undesired events,

Non-attachment, absence of clinging
To son, wife, home, et cetera,
And constant even-mindedness
Toward desired and undesired events;

asaktis (f. nom. sg.), non-attachment, absence of clinging.
anabhiṣvaṅgas (m. nom. sg.), absence of clinging, non-attachment.
putra (m.), son.
dāra (m.), wife.
gṛha (m.), home, house.
ādi (m. loc. pl.), beginning with, et cetera.
(*putradāragṛhādiṣu,* m. loc. pl. TP cpd., to son, wife, home, et cetera.)
nityam (adv.), constant, perpetual, as adv. perpetually.
ca, and.
samacittatvam (n. nom. sg.), evenness of mind, steadiness of thought.
iṣṭa (p. pass. participle √*iṣ*), desired.
aniṣṭa, undesired.
upapattiṣu (f. loc. pl.), in happenings, in events.
(*iṣṭāniṣṭopapattiṣu,* f. loc. pl. KD cpd., toward desired and undesired events.)

10

मयि चानन्ययोगेन
mayi cānanyayogena
and in me with not other Yoga

भक्तिर् अव्यभिचारिणी ।
bhaktir avyabhicāriṇī
devotion not going astray

विविक्तदेशसेवित्वम्
viviktadeśasevitvam
a secluded place frequenting

अरतिर् जनसंसदि ॥
aratir janasaṁsadi
having dislike of men-crowd,

mayi (m. loc. sg.), in me.
ca, and.
ananyayogena (m. inst. sg.), with Yoga exclusively, with not other discipline.
bhaktis (f. nom. sg.), devotion, love.
avyabhicāriṇi (f. nom. sg. from *a vi abhi* √*car*), not going astray, not wandering away.
vivikta (m. p. pass. participle *vi* √*vic*), secluded, solitary, lonely, separated.
deśa (m.), place.
sevitvam (n. nom. sg.), frequenting, inhabiting, resorting to.
(*vivikta-deśa-sevitvam*, n. nom. sg. TP cpd., frequenting a secluded place.)
aratis (f. nom. sg.), having dislike, having discontent, having dissatisfaction.
janasaṁsadi (f. loc. sg. TP cpd.), in man-crowd, in meeting crowds of men, in the society of men.

And unswerving devotion to Me
With single minded Yoga,
Frequenting a secluded place,
Disliking the society of men,

11

अध्यात्मज्ञाननित्यत्वं
adhyātmajñānanityatvaṁ
Supreme-Spirit-knowledge-constancy,

तत्त्वज्ञानार्थदर्शनम् ।
tattvajñānārthadarśanam
truth-knowledge-goal-observing,

एतज् ज्ञानम् इति प्रोक्तम्
etaj jñānam iti proktam
this knowledge thus, declared to be.

अज्ञानं यद् अतो ऽन्यथा ॥
ajñānaṁ yad ato 'nyathā
ignorance which to this contrary.

Constancy in knowledge of the Supreme Spirit,
Observing the goal of knowledge of the truth;
This is declared to be true knowledge.
Ignorance is what is contrary to this.

adhyātmajñāna (n.), knowledge of the Supreme Spirit, knowledge of the Supreme Self.
nityatvam (n. nom. sg.), constancy, continualness, perpetualness.
(*adhyātmajñānanityatvam,* n. nom. sg. TP cpd., constancy in knowledge of the Supreme Spirit.)
tattva (n.), "thatness," truth.
jñāna (n.), knowledge, wisdom.
artha (m./n.), goal, object, purpose.
darśanam (n. nom. sg. pr. participle √*dṛś*), observing, seeing, keeping in sight.
(*tattvajñānārthadarśanam,* n. nom. sg. TP cpd., observing the goal of knowledge of the truth.)
etad (n. nom. sg.), this.
jñānam (n. nom. sg.), knowledge.
iti, thus, so.
proktam (n. nom. sg. p. pass. participle *pra* √*vac*), said to be, called, declared to be.
ajñānam (n. nom. sg.), ignorance, absence of knowledge.
yad (n. nom. sg.), which, what.
atas, from this, to this.
anyathā, contrary, not in which way, otherwise.

12

ज्ञेयं यत् तत् प्रवक्ष्यामि
jñeyaṁ yat tat pravakṣyāmi
the to-be-known, which, that I shall declare,

यज् ज्ञात्वा ऽमृतम् अश्नुते ।
yaj jñātvā 'mṛtam aśnute
which knowing, immortality one attains;

अनादिमत् परं ब्रह्म
anādimat paraṁ brahma
the beginningless supreme Brahman

न सत् तन् नासद् उच्यते ॥
na sat tan nāsad ucyate
not being, this, not *not* being, it is said.

That which is the object of knowledge, I shall declare,
Knowing which, one attains immortality;
It is the beginningless supreme Brahman
Which is said to be neither existent nor non-existent.

jñeyam (n. acc. sg. gerundive √*jñā*), to-be-known, the object of knowledge.
yad (n. acc. sg.), what, which.
tad (n. acc. sg.), that.
pravakṣyāmi (1st future act. *pra* √*vac*), I shall declare, I shall explain.
yad (n. acc. sg.), which.
jñātvā (gerund √*jñā*), knowing, having known.
amṛtam (n. acc. sg.), immortality.
aśnute (3rd sg. pr. indic. mid. √*aś*), one attains, he attains, he reaches.
anādimat (n. nom. sg.), beginningless, without beginning.
param (n. nom. sg.), supreme, highest.
brahma (n. nom. sg.), Brahman.
na, not.
sat (n. nom. sg.), being, existing.
tad (n. nom. sg.), this, that.
na, not.
asat (n. nom. sg.), not being, not existing.
ucyate (3rd sg. pr. indic. passive √*vac*), it is said.

13

सर्वतःपाणिपादं तत्
sarvataḥpāṇipādaṁ tat
everywhere hand and foot, this,

सर्वतो ऽक्षिशिरोमुखम् ।
sarvato 'kṣiśiromukham
everywhere eye, head and face,

सर्वतःश्रुतिमल् लोके
sarvataḥśrutimal loke
everywhere having hearing in the world,

सर्वम् आवृत्य तिष्ठति ॥
sarvam āvṛtya tiṣṭhati
all enveloping it stands;

Having hands and feet everywhere,
Everywhere eyes, a head and a face,
Having hearing everywhere in the world,
It stands, enveloping all;

sarvatas (adv.), everywhere.
paṇi (m.), hand.
pādam (n. nom. acc. sg.), foot.
(*pāṇipādam,* n. nom. sg. BV cp., having a hand and foot.)
tad (n. nom. sg.), this, that.
sarvatas (adv.), everywhere.
akṣi (n.), eye.
śiras (n.), head, skull.
mukham (n. nom. acc. sg.), face, mouth.
(*akṣiśiromukham,* n. nom. sg. BV cpd., having an eye, head and face.)
sarvatas (adv.), everywhere.
śrutimat (n. nom. sg.), having ears, having hearing.
loke (m. loc. sg.), in the world, on earth.
sarvam (n. acc. sg.), all.
āvṛtya (gerund *ā* √*vṛ*), enveloping, covering, spreading, pervading.
tiṣṭhati (3rd sg. pr. indic. act. √*sthā*), it stands, it is present, it remains.

14

सर्वेन्द्रियगुणाभासं
sarvendriyaguṇābhāsaṁ
all sense guṇa appearance,

सर्वेन्द्रियविवर्जितम् ।
sarvendriyavivarjitam
all sense freed from,

असक्तं सर्वभृच् चैव
asaktaṁ sarvabhṛc cāiva
unattached and all maintaining thus,

निर्गुणं गुणभोक्तृ च ॥
nirguṇaṁ guṇabhoktṛ ca
free from the guṇas and experiencing the guṇas;

Having the appearance of all guṇas of the senses,
Yet freed from all the senses,
Unattached yet maintaining all,
Free from the guṇas yet experiencing the guṇas;

sarva (m.), all.
indriya (m.), sense, power.
guṇa (m.), guṇa.
ābhāsam (n. nom. sg.), appearance, color, semblance.
(*sarvendriyaguṇābhāsam,* n. nom. sg. BV cpd., having the appearance of all the guṇas of the senses.)
sarva (m.), all.
indriya (m.), sense, power.
vivarjitam (n. nom. sg. p. pass. participle *vi* √*vṛj*), freed from, twisted away from.
(*sarvendriyavivarjitam,* n. nom. sg. TP cpd., freed from all the senses.)
asaktam (n. nom. sg. p. pass. participle *a* √*sañj*), unattached, not clinging.
sarvabhṛt (n. nom. sg.), all-maintaining, maintaining all.
ca, and.
eva, indeed (used as a rhythmic filler).
nirguṇam (n. nom. sg.), free from the guṇas.
guṇabhoktṛ (n. nom. sg.), enjoyer of the guṇas, experiencer of the guṇas, experiencing the guṇas.
ca, and.

15

बहिर् अन्तश्च भूतानाम्
bahir antaś ca bhūtānām
outside and inside of beings

अचरं चरम् एव च ।
acaraṁ caram eva ca
the unmoving and the moving

सूक्ष्मत्वात् तद् अविज्ञेयं
sūkṣmatvāt tad avijñeyaṁ
because of subtlety this not to be comprehended

दूरस्थं चान्तिके च तत् ॥
dūrasthaṁ cāntike ca tat
remote situated and near, this.

Outside and inside beings,
Those that are moving and not moving,
Because of its subtlety this is not to be comprehended.
This is remote and also near.

bahis (adv.), outside.
antas (adv.), inside.
ca, and.
bhūtānām (m. gen. pl.), of beings, of creatures.
acaram (n. nom. sg.), unmoving, inanimate.
caram (n. nom. sg.), moving, animate.
eva, indeed (used as a rhythmic filler).
ca, and.
sūkṣmatvāt (n. abl. sg.), from subtlety, because of fineness, because of subtlety.
tad (n. nom. sg.), this, that.
avijñeyam (n. nom. sg. gerundive *a vi* √*jñā*), not to be known, not to be understood, not to be comprehended.
dūrastham (n. nom. sg.), remotely situated, situated far off.
ca, and.
antike (n. loc. sg.), in the vicinity, near, proximate.
ca, and.
tad (n. nom. sg.), this, that.

16

अविभक्तं च भूतेषु
avibhaktaṁ ca bhūteṣu
undivided in beings

विभक्तम् इव च स्थितम् ।
vibhaktam iva ca sthitam
(yet) divided-as-if remaining,

भूतभर्तृ च तज् ज्ञेयं
bhūtabhartṛ ca taj jñeyaṁ
and being-maintainer, this, the to-be-known,

ग्रसिष्णु प्रभविष्णु च ॥
grasiṣṇu prabhaviṣṇu ca
devourer and creator.

Undivided yet remaining as if divided
In all beings,
And the sustainer of beings, this is the object of knowledge,
Their devourer and creator.*

avibhaktam (n. nom. sg. p. pass. participle *a vi* √*bhaj*), undivided, unshared, undistributed.
ca, and.
bhūteṣu (m. loc. pl.), in beings, among beings.
vibhaktam (n. nom. sg. p. pass. participle *vi* √*bhaj*), divided, distributed, shared.
iva, like, as if.
ca, and.
sthitam (n. nom. sg. p. pass participle √*sthā*), remaining, standing, existing.
bhūtabhartṛ (n. nom. sg. nomen agentis), being-supporter, supporter of beings.
ca, and.
tad (n. nom. sg.), this, that.
jñeyam (n. nom. sg. gerundive √*jñā*), the to-be-known, the object of knowledge.
grasiṣṇu (n. nom. sg.), accustomed to absorb, devourer, accustomed to devour.
prabhaviṣṇu (n. nom. sg.), creator, lord of creation.
ca, and.

* This and stanzas 13, 14 and 15 are, of course, a description of *Brahman* and the *ātman*.

17

ज्योतिषां अपि तज् ज्योतिस्
jyotiṣāṁ api taj jyotis
of lights also this the light

तमसः परम् उच्यते ।
tamasaḥ param ucyate
of darkness beyond, it is said,

ज्ञानं ज्ञेयं ज्ञानगम्यं
jñānaṁ jñeyaṁ jñānagamyaṁ
knowledge, the to-be-known, the goal of knowledge,

हृदि सर्वस्य विष्ठितम् ॥
hṛdi sarvasya viṣṭhitam
in the heart of all seated.

jyotiṣām (n. gen. pl.), of lights, of stars.
api, also, even.
tad (n. nom. sg.), this, that.
jyotis (n. nom. sg.), light.
tamasas (n. gen. sg.), of darkness.
param (n. nom. sg.), beyond.
ucyate (3rd sg. pr. indic. passive √*vac*), it is said.
jñānam (n. nom. sg.), knowledge, wisdom.
jñeyam (n. nom. sg. gerundive √*jñā*), the to-be-known, the object of knowledge.
jñānagamyam (n. nom. sg.), goal of knowledge, the attainable through knowledge.
hṛdi (n. loc. sg.), in the heart.
sarvasya (m. gen. sg.), of all.
viṣṭhitam (n. nom. sg. p. pass. participle *vi* √*sthā*), seated, situated.

Also this is said to be the light of lights
That is beyond darkness;*
It is knowledge, the object of knowledge and that which is to be attained through knowledge.
It is seated in the hearts of all.

* "Knowledge, the light of the *ātman*, illuminates even luminaries – such as the sun, a lamp, etc. – which dispel only that darkness which hinders the contacts of the senses with objects. It is beyond *prakṛti* (material nature)." – Rāmānuja.

18

इति क्षेत्रं तथा ज्ञानं
iti kṣetraṁ tathā jñānaṁ
thus the field, thus knowledge

ज्ञेयं चोक्तं समासतः ।
jñeyaṁ coktaṁ samāsataḥ
and the to-be-known, described briefly.

मद्भक्त एतद् विज्ञाय
madbhakta etad vijñāya
my devotee, this understanding,

मद्भावायोपपद्यते ॥
madbhāvāyopapadyate
to my state of being approaches.

Thus the field and thus knowledge
And the object of knowledge, briefly described.
My devotee, understanding this,
Approaches My state of being.

iti, thus.
kṣetram (n. nom. sg.), field.
tathā, thus.
jñānam (n. nom. sg.), knowledge, wisdom.
jñeyam (n. nom. sg. gerundive √*jñā*), the to-be-known, the object of knowledge.
ca, and.
uktam (n. nom. sg. p. pass. participle √*vac*), said, described, explained.
samāsatas, with briefness, briefly, in brief.
madbhaktas (m. nom. sg.), devotee of me, my devotee, my worshipper.
etad (n. acc. sg.), this.
vijñāya (gerund *vi* √*jñā*), understanding, comprehending.
madbhāvāya (m. dat. sg.), to my state of being.
upapadyate (3rd sg. pr. indic. mid. *upa* √*pad*), he approaches, he enters, he arrives at.

19

प्रकृतिं पुरुषं चैव
prakṛtiṁ puruṣaṁ cāiva
material nature and spirit

विद्ध्य् अनादी उभाव् अपि ।
viddhy anādī ubhāv api
know to be beginningless both also,

विकारांस् च गुणांस् चैव
vikārāṇś ca guṇāṅś cāiva
and the modifications and the guṇas

विद्धि प्रकृतिसंभवान् ॥
viddhi prakṛtisaṁbhavān
know to be those which spring from material nature

Know that material nature and spirit
Are both also beginningless,
And know also that the modifications of the field,
And the guṇas too, arise from material nature.

prakṛtim (f. acc. sg.), material nature.
puruṣam (m. acc. sg.), spirit.
ca, and.
eva, indeed (used as a rhythmic filler).
viddhi (2nd sg. act. imperative √*vid*), know! learn!
anādī (n. acc. dual), beginningless, not having a beginning.
ubhāu (n. acc. dual), both.
api, also, even.
vikārān (m. acc. pl.), modifications, changes, transformations, capacities for modifcation.
ca, and.
guṇān (m. acc. pl.), guṇas.
ca, and.
eva, indeed (used as a rhythmic filler).
viddhi (2nd sg. imperative √*vid*), know! learn!
prakṛti (f.), material nature.
saṁbhavān (m. acc. pl.), origins.
(*prakṛtisaṁbhavān,* m. acc. pl. BV cpd., which spring from material nature.)

20

कार्यकारणकर्तृत्वे
kāryakāraṇakartṛtve
as to the to-be-done, the instrument and the doer,

हेतुः प्रकृतिर् उच्यते ।
hetuḥ prakṛtir ucyate
the cause: material nature, it is said.

पुरुषः सुखदुःखानां
puruṣaḥ sukhaduḥkhānāṁ
the spirit, of pleasure and pain

भोक्तृत्वे हेतुर् उच्यते ॥
bhoktṛtve hetur ucyate
in the experiencing, the cause it is said.

Material nature is said to be the cause
Where the object of action, the instrument and the agent are concerned.
The spirit is said to be the cause
In the experiencing of pleasure and pain.*

kārya (gerundive √*kṛ*), to to-be-done, the to-be-performed.
karaṇa (n.), instrument.
kartṛtve (n. loc. sg.), in the matter of the agent.
(*kārykaraṇakartṛtve*, n. loc. sg. DV cpd., in the matter of the to-be-done, the instrument and the doer, where the object of action, the instrument and the agent are concerned.)
hetus (m. nom. sg.), cause, reason.
prakṛtis (f. nom. sg.), material nature.
ucyate (3rd sg. pr. indic. passive √*vac*), it is said.
puruṣas (m. nom. sg.), spirit.
sukhaduḥkhānām (n. gen. pl.), of pleasures and pains, of happinesses and unhappinesses.
bhoktṛtve (n. loc. sg.), in the experiencing, in the enjoying, in the state of being an enjoyer.
hetus (m. nom. sg.), cause, reason.
ucyate (3rd sg. pr. indic. passive √*vac*), it is said.

* "The activity of body and organs – which are activities in experiencing – depend on the *prakṛti* (material nature) developed into *kṣetra* (field or body). This *prakṛti* is subservient to the person or *puruṣa* who is the agent, as stated in the Sūtras. This agency of the *puruṣa* means that the *puruṣa* is the cause and initiator of all activities to which the subservient *prakṛti* is instrumental. So all experience of happiness and unhappiness depends on the *puruṣa* conjoined with *prakṛti*. The *puruṣa* itself finds no happiness except in self-experience. When, however, the *puruṣa* is conjoined with *prakṛti*, it has experiences of happiness, unhappiness, etc., which are conditioned by its conjunction with *prakṛti* and effectuated by *guṇas*, *sattva*, etc." – Rāmānuja.

21

पुरुषः प्रकृतिस्थो हि
puruṣaḥ prakṛtistho hi
spirit (in) material nature abiding indeed,

भुङ्क्ते प्रकृतिजान् गुणान् ।
bhuṅkte prakṛtijān guṇān
it experiences the born-of-material-nature guṇas.

कारणं गुणसङ्गो ऽस्य
kāraṇaṁ guṇasaṅgo 'sya
the source, guṇa-attachment, of it,

सदसद्योनिजन्मसु ॥
sadasadyonijanmasu
in good-and-evil-wombs birth.

puruṣas (m. nom. sg.), spirit.
prakṛtisthas (m. nom. sg.), abiding in material nature, situated in material nature.
hi, indeed, truly.
bhuṅkte (3rd sg. pr. indic. mid. $\sqrt{bhuj}$), it enjoys, it experiences.
prakṛtijān (m. acc. pl.), born of material nature, originating, in material nature.
guṇān (m. acc. pl.), guṇas.
kāraṇam (n. nom. sg.), cause, reason, instrument, origin, source.
guṇasaṅgas (m. nom. sg.), guṇa attachment, clinging to the guṇas.
asya (m. gen. sg.), of it, of this.
sat (n.), good.
asat (n.), evil, not good.
yoni (f.), womb.
janman (n.), birth.
(*sadasadyonijanmasu,* m. loc. pl. TP cpd., births in good and evil wombs.)

For the spirit, abiding in material nature,
Experiences the guṇas born of material nature.
Attachment to the guṇas
Is the source of its birth in good and evil wombs.*

* "The *puruṣa* (spirit of the individual), existing in a particular shape and nature – divine, human etc. – which is a result of previous developments of *prakṛti,* is attached to happiness, etc. which consist of the *guṇas* and are proper to that particular nature, and is active in performing the good and evil acts leading to that happiness, etc. In order to experience the results of his acts he is born in a certain nature, good or evil; this new existence induces him again to be active and consequently to be born again in *saṁsāra* (reincarnation), until he cultivates the qualities of humility, etc. by which he may attain the *ātman.*" – Rāmānuja.

22

उपद्रष्टानुमन्ता च
upadraṣṭānumantā ca
the witness and the consenter

भर्ता भोक्ता महेश्वरः ।
bhartā bhoktā maheśvaraḥ
the supporter, the experiencer, the Great Lord

परमात्मेति चाप्य् उक्तो
paramātmeti cāpy ukto
and the Supreme Self thus also is called

देहे ऽस्मिन् पुरुषः परः ॥
dehe 'smin puruṣaḥ paraḥ
in the body, this, the spirit highest.

upadraṣṭā (m. nom. sg.), witness, observer.
anumantā (m. nom. sg.), consenter, permitter, approver.
ca, and.
bhartā (m. nom. sg.), supporter, bearer.
bhoktā (m. nom. sg.), experiencer, enjoyer.
maheśvaras (m. nom. sg.), great lord.
paramātmā (m. nom. sg.), Supreme Self.
iti, thus.
ca, and.
api, also, even.
uktas (m. nom. sg. p. pass. participle √*vac*), called, said to be.
dehe (m. loc. sg.), in the body.
asmin (m. loc. sg.), in this.
puruṣas (m. nom. sg.), spirit.
paras (m. nom. sg.), highest.

The highest spirit in this body
Is called the witness, the consenter,
The supporter, the experiencer, the Great Lord
And also the Supreme Spirit.*

* "The *puruṣa* (spirit of the individual), when existing in such a body and conniving at its activities, looks on and consents; therefore it is the lord of the body. In the same way it experiences the happiness and unhappiness resulting from the body's activities. So because it rules, supports and exceeds the body, it is a sovereign lord as compared to its body, senses and mind. Likewise it is called the body's sovereign *ātman* – sovereign as compared to the body – and a most sublime *puruṣa*, i.e. a *puruṣa* whose knowledge and power are not to be circumscribed by the body. . . . Nevertheless, so long as it is attached to *guṇas*, the *puruṣa* is sovereign only as compared with the servile body." – Rāmānuja.

23

य एवं वेत्ति पुरुषं
ya evaṁ vetti puruṣaṁ
who thus he knows the spirit

प्रकृतिं च गुणैः सह ।
prakṛtiṁ ca guṇāiḥ saha
and material nature with the guṇas together,

सर्वथा वर्तमानो ऽपि
sarvathā vartamāno 'pi
in whatever (stage of transmigration) existing even,

न स भूयो ऽभिजायते ॥
na sa bhūyo 'bhijāyate
not be again is born.

yas (m. nom. sg.), who, which.
evam, thus.
vetti (3rd sg. pr. indic. act. √*vid*), he knows.
puruṣam (m. acc. sg.), spirit.
prakṛtim (f. acc. sg.), material nature.
ca, and.
guṇāis (m. inst. pl.), with the guṇas.
saha, together.
sarvathā, however, in whatever way, in whatever stage of transmigration.
vartamānas (m. nom. sg. pr. mid. participle √*vṛt*), existing, moving, living.
api, even, also.
na, not.
sas (m. nom. sg.), he, this.
bhūyas, again.
abhijāyate (3rd sg. pr. indic. passive *abhi* √*jan*), he is born.

He who in this way knows spirit
And material nature, along with the guṇas,
In no matter what stage of transmigration he exists,
Is not born again.*

* "He who knows that the *puruṣa* and the *prakṛti* have the aforesaid natures and who knows the nature of the *guṇas* – which is still left to explain – he knows discriminatingly. He will not be reborn conjointly with *prakṛti* but attain the purified *ātman* characterized by non-circumscribable knowledge, as soon as he dies." – Rāmānuja.

24

ध्यानेनात्मनि पश्यन्ति
dhyānenātmani paśyanti
by meditation in the self they perceive,

केचिद् आत्मानम् आत्मना ।
kecid ātmānam ātmanā
some, the self by the self;

अन्ये सांख्येन योगेन
anye sāṁkhyena yogena
others by Sāṁkhya discipline

कर्मयोगेन चापरे ॥
karmayogena cāpare
and by action-Yoga still others.

dhyānena (n. inst. sg.), by meditation, through meditation.
ātmani (m. loc. sg.), in the self.
paśyanti (3rd pl. pr. indic. act. √paś), they perceive, they see, they discern.
kecid, some, whoever.
ātmānam (m. acc. sg.), self.
ātmanā (m. inst. sg.), by the self, with the self.
anye (m. nom. pl.), others, some.
sāṁkhyena (n. inst. sg.), by the Sāṁkhya doctrine.
yogena (m. inst. sg.), by the discipline, by the power, by the Yoga.
karmayogena (m. inst. sg.), by the discipline of action, by the Yoga of action.
ca, and.
apare (m. nom. pl.), others.

Some perceive the self in the self
By the self through meditation;
Others by the discipline of Sāṁkhya*
And still others by the Yoga of action.

* *Sāṁkhya*, one of the earliest systems of Hindu philosophy, rational, non-theistic, dualistic, regarding *prakṛti* and *puruṣa* as the ultimate realities of existence, and believing that nothing new is ever created, all things being manifestations of what already exists. See note, II 39.

25

अन्ये त्व् एवम् अजानन्तः
anye tv evam ajānantaḥ
some, however, thus not knowing,

श्रुत्वान्येभ्य उपासते ।
śrutvānyebhya upāsate
hearing from others, they worship,

ते ऽपि चातितरन्त्य् एव
te 'pi cātitaranty eva
they also cross beyond

मृत्युं श्रुतिपरायणाः ॥
mṛtyuṁ śrutiparāyaṇāḥ
death (what they) hear devoted to.

Some, however, not knowing this,
But hearing it from others,
Worship, and they also cross beyond death,*
Devoted to what they hear.

anye (m. nom. pl.), some, others.
tu, but, however.
evam, thus.
ajānantas (m. nom. pl. pr. act. participle *a* √*jñā*), not knowing, ignorant.
śrutvā (gerund √*śru*), hearing.
anyebhyas (m. abl. pl.), from others.
upāsate (3rd pl. pr. indic. mid. *upa* √*ās*), they worship, they honor.
te (m. nom. pl.), they.
api, also, even.
ca, and.
atitaranti (3rd pl. pr. indic. act. *ati* √*tṛ*), they cross beyond, they transcend.
eva, indeed (often used as a rhythmic filler).
mṛtyum (m. acc. sg.), death.
śruti (f.), hearing.
parāyaṇās (n. nom. pl.), devoted to, holding as highest object.
(*śruti-parāyaṇas*, n. nom. pl. TP cpd., devoted to what they hear.)

* Death, i.e. the kind of death that eventuates in rebirth.

26

यावत् संजायते किंचित्
yāvat saṁjāyate kiṁcit
inasmuch as it is born, any whatever

सत्त्वं स्थावरजङ्गमम् ।
sattvaṁ sthāvarajaṅgamam
being, standing still or moving,

क्षेत्रक्षेत्रज्ञसंयोगात्
kṣetrakṣetrajñasaṁyogāt
from the field and the field-knower union,

तद् विद्धि भरतर्षभ ॥
tad viddhi bharatarṣabha
that know! Bull of the Bharatas.

Know, Bull of the Bharatas, that
Any being whatever, standing or moving,
Inasmuch as it is born,
Arises from the union of the field and the field-knower.*

yāvat, so much, as much, inasmuch, as.
saṁjāyate (3rd sg. pr. indic. passive *sam* √*jan*), it is born.
kiṁcid, any whatever, any.
sattvam (n. nom. sg.), being, existence.
sthāvara (n.), standing still, not moving, inanimate.
jaṅgamam (n. nom. sg.), moving, animate, living.
(*sthāvarjaṅgamam,* n. nom. sg. DV cpd., standing and moving, standing or moving.)
kṣetra (n.), field.
kṣetrajña (m.), field knower.
saṁyogāt (m. abl. sg.), from the union.
(*kṣetrakṣetrajñasaṁyogāt,* m. abl. sg. TP cpd., from the union of the field and the field-knower.
tad (n. acc. sg.), this, that.
viddhi (2nd sg. imperative act. √*vid*), know! learn!
bharatarṣabha (m. voc. sg.), Bull of the Bharatas, epithet of Arjunas.

* I.e. the union of body (field) and spirit (*puruṣa*).

27

समं सर्वेषु भूतेषु
samaṁ sarveṣu bhūteṣu
alike in all beings

तिष्ठन्तं परमेश्वरम् ।
tiṣṭhantaṁ parameśvaram
existing the Supreme Lord

विनश्यत्स्व् अविनश्यन्तं
vinaśyatsv avinaśyantaṁ
in (their) perishings not perishing,

यः पश्यति स पश्यति ॥
yaḥ paśyati sa paśyati
who sees, he (truly) sees.

samam (m. acc. sg.), alike, similar, the same.
sarveṣu (m. loc. pl.), in all.
bhūteṣu (m. loc. pl.), in beings, in creatures.
tiṣṭhantam (m. acc. sg. pr. act. participle √*sthā*), existing, standing, situated.
parameśvaram (m. acc. sg.), the Supreme Lord, the Highest Lord.
vinaśyatsu (m. loc. pl. gerund *vi* √*naś*), in perishings, in losings, in deaths.
avinaśyantam (m. acc. sg. pr. act. participle *a vi* √*naś*), not perishing, not lost, not dying.
yas (m. nom. sg.), who, what.
paśyati (3rd sg. pr. indic. act. √*paś*), he sees, he perceives.
sas (m. nom. sg.), he, this.
paśyati (3rd sg. pr. indic. act. √*paś*), he perceives, he sees.

He who sees the Supreme Lord,
Existing alike in all beings,
Not perishing when they perish,
Truly sees.

28

समं पश्यन् हि सर्वत्र
samaṁ paśyan hi sarvatra
the same seeing indeed everywhere

समवस्थितम् ईश्वरम् ।
samavasthitam īśvaram
established the Lord

न हिनस्त्य् आत्मना ऽत्मानं
na hinasty ātmanā 'tmānaṁ
not he injures, by the self, the self.

ततो याति परां गतिम् ॥
tato yāti parāṁ gatim
then he goes to the supreme goal.

samam (m. acc. sg.), same, equal, similar.
paśyan (m. nom. sg. pr. participle act. √*paś*), seeing, beholding, discerning.
hi, indeed, truly.
sarvatra, everywhere, on all sides.
samavasthitam (m. acc. sg. p. pass. participle *sam ava* √*sthā*), established, existing.
īśvaram (m. acc. sg.), lord, prince, ruler.
na, not.
hinasti (3rd sg. pr. indic. act. √*hiṅs*), he injures, he hurts.
ātmanā (m. inst. sg.), by the self.
ātmānam (m. acc. sg.), the self.
tatas, then, from there.
yāti (3rd sg. √*yā*), he goes.
parām (f. acc. sg.), supreme, highest.
gatim (f. acc. sg.), goal, path.

Seeing indeed the same Lord
Established everywhere,
He does not injure the self by the self.*
Thereupon he goes to the Supreme Goal.

* Since the self (*ātman*) of others is identical with one's own self, the line means that in injuring the self of others, one injures one's own self.

29

प्रकृत्यैव च कर्माणि
prakṛtyāiva ca karmāṇi
and by material nature actions

क्रियमाणानि सर्वशः ।
kriyamāṇāni sarvaśaḥ
performed exclusively

यः पश्यति तथात्मानम्
yaḥ paśyati tathātmānam
who he sees, thus himself

अकर्तारं स पश्यति ॥
akartāraṁ sa paśyati
not the doer, he (truly) sees.

And he who sees all actions
Performed exclusively by material nature,
And thus himself not the doer,
Truly sees.*

prakṛtyā (f. inst. sg.), by material nature.
eva, indeed (used as a rhythmic filler).
ca, and.
karmāṇi (n. acc. pl.), actions, deeds.
kriyamāṇāni (n. acc. pl. pr. pass. participle √*kṛ*), performed, done, made.
sarvaśas, wholly, completely, exclusively.
yas (m. nom. sg.), who.
paśyati (3rd sg. pr. indic. act. √*paś*), he sees, he perceives.
tathā, thus.
ātmānam (m. acc. sg.), himself, self.
akartāram (m. acc. sg.), non-doer, non-maker.
sas (m. nom. sg.), he, this.
paśyati (3rd sg. pr. indic. act. √*paś*), he sees, he perceives.

* "When a person perceives that all acts are performed by the *prakṛti* (material nature), that therefore the *ātman* (self) is non-agent, and that the *ātman* has the form of knowledge, then he perceives that the *ātman*'s conjunction with *prakṛti* (material nature), its (the *ātman*'s) directing capacity and its experience of happiness or unhappiness all result from ignorance – effected by *karman* (action) –, and then he has an exact perception of the *ātman*." – Rāmānuja.

30

यदा भूतपृथग्भावम्
yadā bhūtapṛthagbhāvam
when being-various-states

एकस्थम् अनुपश्यति ।
ekastham anupaśyati
resting in one he perceives,

तत एव च विस्तारं
tata eva ca vistāraṁ
and from that alone spreading out

ब्रह्म संपद्यते तदा ॥
brahma saṁpadyate tadā
Brahman he attains then.

When the various states of being
He perceives as resting in one,
And from that alone spreading out,
Then he attains Brahman.*

yadā, when.
bhūtapṛthagbhāvam (m. acc. sg.), various states of being, multiple states of being.
ekastham (m. acc. sg.), resting in one, abiding in one.
anupaśyati (3rd sg. pr. indic. act. *anu* √*paś*), he perceives, he discerns, he sees.
tatas, from there, from that.
eva, alone, indeed (often used as a rhythmic filler).
ca, and.
vistāram (m. acc sg.), spreading out, extent.
brahma (n. acc. sg.), Brahman.
saṁpadyate (3rd sg. pr. indic. mid. *sam* √*pad*), he goes to, he attains, he arrives at.
tadā, then.

* "When a person perceives that all different modes of existence of all beings depend on one principle, *prakṛti* (material nature), and not on the *ātman*, and that the varieties of new beings issuing from these beings again arise from *prakṛti*, then he will attain the *ātman* in its purest form" – Rāmānuja.

31

अनादित्वान् निर्गुणत्वात्
anāditvān nirguṇatvāt
from having no beginning and from absence of guṇas

परमात्मायम् अव्ययः ।
paramātmāyam avyayaḥ
Supreme Self this, imperishable,

शरीरस्थो ऽपि कौन्तेय
śarīrastho 'pi kāunteya
in the body situated even, Son of Kuntī,

न करोति न लिप्यते ॥
na karoti na lipyate
not it acts, not it is befouled.

Because this imperishable Supreme Self
Is beginningless and without guṇas,
Even though situated in the body, Son of Kuntī,
It does not act, and is not befouled.

anāditvāt (n. abl. sg.), from having no beginning, from beginninglessness.
nirguṇatvāt (n. abl. sg.), from absence of guṇas, from guṇaslessness.
paramātmā (m. nom. sg.), Supreme Self.
ayam (m. nom. sg.), this.
avyayas (m. nom. sg.), imperishable, eternal.
śarīrasthas (m. nom. sg.), situated in the body, abiding in the body.
api, even, also.
kāunteya (m. voc. sg.), Son of Kuntī, epithet of Arjuna.
na, not.
karoti (3rd sg. pr. indic. act. √*kṛ*), he acts, it acts.
na not.
lipyate (3rd sg. pr. indic. passive √*lip*), it is smeared, it is stained, it is polluted, it is befouled.

32

यथा सर्वगतं सौक्ष्म्याद्
yathā sarvagataṁ sāukṣmyād
as the all pervading, from subtlety,

आकाशं नोपलिप्यते ।
ākāśaṁ nopalipyate
the ether not it is befouled,

सर्वत्रावस्थितो देहे
sarvatrāvasthito dehe
in all cases seated in the body,

तथात्मा नोपलिप्यते ॥
tathātmā nopalipyate
so the self not it is befouled.

yathā, in which way, as.
sarvagatam (n. nom. sg.), all pervading, omnipresent.
sāukṣmyāt (n. abl. sg.), from subtlety, because of subtlety.
ākāśam (n. nom. sg.), space, ether.
nā, not.
upalipyate (3rd sg. pr. indic. passive *upa* √*lip*), it is smeared, it is polluted, it is befouled.
sarvatra, in all cases, everywhere.
avasthitas (m. nom. sg. p. pass. participle *ava* √*sthā*), seated, situated, abiding.
dehe (m./n. loc. sg.), in the body.
tathā, in this way, thus, so.
ātmā (m. nom. sg.), self.
na, not.
upalipyate (3rd sg. pr. indic. passive *upa* √*lip*), it is smeared, it is stained, it is befouled.

As the all-pervading ether, because of its subtlety,
Is not befouled,
So the self, seated in the body,
Is not befouled in any case.

33

यथा प्रकाशयत्य् एकः
yathā prakāśayaty ekaḥ
as it illumines alone

कृत्स्नं लोकम् इमं रविः ।
kṛtsnaṁ lokam imaṁ raviḥ
entire world this, the sun,

क्षेत्रं क्षेत्री तथा कृत्स्नं
kṣetraṁ kṣetrī tathā kṛtsnaṁ
the field, the lord of the field, so the entire

प्रकाशयति भारत ॥
prakāśayati bhārata
he illumines, Descendant of Bharata.

As the sun alone illumines
This entire world,
So the Lord of the Field illumines
The entire field, Descendant of Bharata.

yathā, in which way, as.
prakāśayati (3rd sg. pr. indic. causative *pra* √*kāś*), it illumines, it causes to appear.
ekas (m. nom. sg.), one, alone, singly.
kṛtsnam (n. acc. sg.), entire, whole.
lokam (m. acc. sg.), world, universe.
imam (m. acc. sg.), this.
ravis (m. nom. sg.), sun.
kṣetram (n. acc. sg.), field.
kṣetrī (m. nom. sg.), lord of the field, owner of the field.
tathā, in this way, thus, so.
kṛtsnam (n. acc. sg.), entire, whole.
prakāśayati (3rd sg. pr. indic. causative act. *pra* √*kāś*), he illumines, he causes to appear.
bhārata (m. voc. sg.), Descendant of Bharata.

34

क्षेत्रक्षेत्रज्ञयोर् एवम्
kṣetrakṣetrajñayor evam
of the field and the field-knower thus

अन्तरं ज्ञानचक्षुषा ।
antaraṁ jñānacakṣuṣā
the distinction by the knowledge-eye

भूतप्रकृतिमोक्षं च
bhūtaprakṛtimokṣaṁ ca
and being-from-material-nature-liberation

ये विदुर् यान्ति ते परम् ॥
ye vidur yānti te param
who they know, they go, they, to the Supreme.

kṣetrakṣetrajñayos (m. gen. dual DV cpd.), of the field and the knower of the field.
evam, thus.
antaram (n. acc. sg.), distinction, difference, relation.
jñānacakṣuṣā (n. inst. sg. TP cpd.), by the knowledge-eye, by the eye of knowledge, by the eye of wisdom.
bhūta (m.), being.
prakṛti (f.), material nature.
mokṣam (m. acc. sg.), liberation, release.
(*bhūtaprakṛtimokṣam,* m. acc. sg., liberation of being from material nature.)
ca, and.
ye (m. nom. pl.), who.
vidus (3rd pl. perfect √*vid* with present meaning), they know.
yānti (3rd pl. √*yā*), they go.
te (m. nom. pl.), they.
param (m. acc. sg.), the Supreme, the highest, to the Supreme.

They who know, through the eye of knowledge,
The distinction between the field and the knower of the field,
As well as the liberation of beings from material nature,
Go to the Supreme.

End of Book XIII

The Yoga of Distinction between the Field-Knower and the Field

BOOK XIV

श्रीभगवान् उवाच ।
śrībhagavān uvāca
the Blessed Lord spoke:

śrībhagavān (m. nom. sg.), the Blessed Lord, the Blessed One.
uvāca (3rd sg. perfect act. √*vac*), he said, he spoke.

1

परं भूयः प्रवक्ष्यामि
paraṁ bhūyaḥ pravakṣyāmi
the highest further I shall declare

ज्ञानानां ज्ञानम् उत्तमम् ।
jñānānāṁ jñānam uttamam
of knowledges, the knowledge best

यज् ज्ञात्वा मुनयः सर्वे
yaj jñātvā munayaḥ sarve
which, having known, the sages all

परां सिद्धिम् इतो गताः ॥
parāṁ siddhim ito gatāḥ
to supreme perfection from here gone.

The Blessed Lord spoke:

I shall declare, further, the highest
Knowledge – of knowledges the best –
Which, having known, all the sages
Have gone from here to supreme perfection.

param (m. acc. sg.), highest, supreme.
bhūyas, again, further.
pravakṣyāmi (1st sg. future act. *pra* √*vac*), I shall declare, I shall explain.
jñānānām (n. gen. pl.), of knowledges, of wisdoms.
jñānam (n. acc. sg.), knowledge.
uttamam (n. acc. sg.) highest, best.
yad (n. acc. sg.), which.
jñātvā (gerund √*jñā*), knowing, having known.
munayas (m. nom. pl.), sages, wise men.
sarve (m. nom. pl.), all.
parām (f. acc. sg.), supreme, highest.
siddhim (f. acc. sg.), perfection, success.
itas (adv.), from here.
gatās (m. nom. pl.), gone.

2

इदं ज्ञानम् उपाश्रित्य
idaṁ jñānam upāśritya
this knowledge resorting to,

मम साधर्म्यम् आगताः ।
mama sādharmyam āgatāḥ
of me state of identity arrived at,

सर्गे ऽपि नोपजायन्ते
sarge 'pi nopajāyante
at creation (of the world) even, not they are born,

प्रलये न व्यथन्ति च ॥
pralaye na vyathanti ca
and at the dissolution (of the world), not they tremble.

idam (n. acc. sg.), this.
jñānam (n. acc. sg.), knowledge, wisdom.
upāśritya (gerund *upa ā* √*śri*), resorting to, depending on.
mama (gen. sg.), of me, my.
sādharmyam (n. acc. sg.), state of identity of nature.
āgatās (m. nom. pl.), arrived at, come to.
sarge (m. loc. sg.), at creation, at letting go.
api, even, also.
na, not.
upajāyante (3rd pl. pr. indic. passive *upa* √*jan*), they are born.
pralaye (m. loc. sg.), at dissolution, at the dissolution.
na, not.
vyathanti (3rd pl. pr. indic. act. √*vyath*), they tremble, they quake.
ca, and.

Resorting to this knowledge,
And arriving at a state of identity with Me,
Even at the creation of the world they are not born,*
Nor do they tremble at its dissolution.

* In reading stanzas like this, one must remember that, in the Hindu view, to be born is a misfortune. The ideal is to escape birth, or rebirth, and go on to *nirvāṇa*, or divine non-existence. Also, in this instance, "beings" are assumed to be born at the creation of the universe and to be constantly reborn thereafter until the dissolution of this particular universe.

3

मम योनिर् महद् ब्रह्म
mama yonir mahad brahma
for me the womb (is) great Brahman;

तस्मिन् गर्भं दधाम्य् अहम् ।
tasmin garbhaṁ dadhāmy aham
in this the seed I place, I,

संभवः सर्वभूतानां
saṁbhavaḥ sarvabhūtānāṁ
the origin of all beings

ततो भवति भारत ॥
tato bhavati bhārata
from that it exists, Descendant of Bharata.

mama (gen. sg.), of me, for me, my.
yonis (f. nom. sg.), womb.
mahat (n. nom. sg.), great.
brahma (n. nom. sg.), Brahman.
tasmin (n. loc. sg.), in it, in this.
grabham (m. acc. sg.), foetus, egg, seed.
dadhāmi (1st. sg. pr. indic. act. √*dhā*), I place, I put.
aham (nom. sg.), I.
saṁbhavas (m. nom. sg.), origin, coming to be.
sarvabhūtānām (m. gen. pl.), of all beings, of all creatures.
tatas, from there, from that.
bhavati (3rd sg. pr. indic. act. √*bhū*), it exists, it comes to be.
bhārata (m. voc. sg.), Descendant of Bharata, epithet of Arjuna.

For Me great Brahman is the womb.
In it I place the seed.
The origin of all beings
Exists from that, Descendant of Bharata.

4

सर्वयोनिषु कौन्तेय
sarvayoniṣu kāunteya
in all wombs, Son of Kuntī,

मूर्तयः संभवन्ति याः ।
mūrtayaḥ saṁbhavanti yāḥ
forms come to be which

तासां ब्रह्म महद् योनिर्
tāsāṁ brahma mahad yonir
of them Brahman the great womb.

अहं बीजप्रदः पिता ॥
ahaṁ bījapradaḥ pitā
I the seed-sowing father.

sarvayoniṣu (f. loc. pl.), in all wombs.
kāunteya (m. voc. sg.), Son of Kuntī, epithet of Arjuna.
mūrtayas (f. nom. pl.), forms, images.
saṁbhavanti (3rd pl. pr. indic. act. *sam* √*bhū*), they arise, they come to be.
yās (f. nom. pl.), which.
tāsām (f. gen. pl.), of them.
brahma (n. nom. sg.), Brahman.
mahat (n. nom. sg.), great.
yonis (f. nom. sg.), womb.
aham (nom. sg.), I.
bījapradas (m. nom. sg.), seed giving, seed sowing.
pitā (m. nom. sg.), father.

In all wombs, Son of Kunti,
Forms come to be of which
Brahman is the great womb.
I am the seed-sowing father.

5

सत्त्वं रजस् तम इति
sattvaṁ rajas tama iti
sattva, rajas, tamas, thus

गुणाः प्रकृतिसंभवाः ।
guṇāḥ prakṛtisambhavāḥ
the guṇas material-nature-born-of,

निबध्नन्ति महाबाहो
nibadhnanti mahābāho
they bind down, O Mighty Armed One,

देहे देहिनम् अव्ययम् ॥
dehe dehinam avyayam
in the body the embodied one, imperishable.

Sattva, rajas, tamas, thus,
The guṇas born of material nature,
Bind down in the body, O Mighty Armed,
The Imperishable Embodied One (the *ātman*).

sattvam (n. nom. sg.), sattva, truth, virtue.
rajas (n. nom. sg.), rajas, passion, emotion.
tamas (n. nom. sg.), tamas, darkness, sloth.
iti, thus.
guṇās (m. nom. pl.), guṇas.
prakṛti (f.), nature, material nature.
saṁbhavās (m. nom. pl.), born of, originating in, springing from.
(*prakṛtisambhavās*, m. nom. pl. BV cpd., whose origins are in material nature.)
nibadhnanti (3rd pl. pr. indic. act. *ni* √*badh*), they bind, they bind down, they fetter.
mahābāho (m. voc. sg.), O Great Armed One, epithet of Arjuna and other warriors.
dehe (m./n. loc. sg.), in the body.
dehinam (m. acc. sg.), the embodied, the embodied one, the *ātman*, the self.
avyayam (m. acc. sg.), imperishable, eternal.

6

तत्र सत्त्वं निर्मलत्वात्
tatra sattvaṁ nirmalatvāt
there sattva free from impurity,

प्रकाशकम् अनामयम् ।
prakāśakam anāmayam
illuminating, free from disease,

सुखसङ्गेन बध्नाति
sukhasañgena badhnāti
by virtue attachment it binds

ज्ञानसङ्गेन चानघ ॥
jñānasañgena cānagha
and by knowledge attachment, Sinless One.

Of these, sattva, free from impurity,
Illuminating, free from disease,
Binds by attachment to virtue
And by attachment to knowledge, Sinless One.

tatra, there, in regard to these.
sattvam (n. nom. sg.), sattva, truth, virtue.
nirmalatvāt (n. abl. sg.), free from impurity, free from dirtiness.
prakāśakam (n. nom. sg.), illuminating, shining.
anāmayam (n. nom. sg.), free from disease, healthy, salubrious.
sukhasañgena (m. inst. sg.), by attachment to virtue, by attachment to the good.
hadhnāti (3rd sg. pr. indic. act. √*badh*), it binds, in connects.
jñānasañgena (m. inst. sg. TP cpd.), by attachment to knowledge, by attachment to wisdom.
ca, and.
anagha (m. voc. sg.), Sinless One, epithet of Arjuna.

7

रजो रागात्मकं विद्धि
rajo rāgātmakaṁ viddhi
rajas passion characterized by, know,

तृष्णासङ्गसमुद्भवम् ।
tṛṣṇāsaṅgasamudbhavam
thirst-attachment-arising-from,

तन् निबध्नाति कौन्तेय
tan nibadhnāti kāunteya
this it binds down, Son of Kuntī,

कर्मसङ्गेन देहिनम् ॥
karmasaṅgena dehinam
by action-attachment the embodied one.

rajas (n. acc. sg.), rajas, passion, emotion.
rāgātmakam (n. acc. sg.), of the nature of passion, characterized by passion.
viddhi (2nd sg. imperative act. √*vid*), know! learn!
tṛṣṇā (f.), thirst, desire.
saṅga (m.), attachment.
samudbhavam (m. acc. sg. ifc.), born of, originating in, arising from.
(*tṛṣṇā-saṅga-samudbhavam*, m. acc. sg. TP cpd., arising from thirst and attachment.)
tad (n. nom. sg.), this, that.
nibadhnāti (3rd sg. pr. indic. act. *ni* √*badh*), it binds down, it fetters.
kāunteya (m. voc. sg.), Son of Kuntī, epithet of Arjuna.
karmasaṅgena (m. inst. sg. TP cpd.), by attachment to action.
dehinam (m. acc. sg.), the embodied, the embodied one, the *ātman*, the self.

Know that rajas is characterized by passion
Arising from thirst and attachment.
This binds down the embodied one, Son of Kuntī,
By attachment to action.

8

तमस् त्व् अज्ञानजं विद्धि
tamas tv ajñānajaṁ viddhi
tamas, indeed, ignorance-born, know,

मोहनं सर्वदेहिनाम् ।
mohanaṁ sarvadehinām
the confusion of all embodied ones.

प्रमादालस्यनिद्राभिस्
pramādālasyanidrābhis
by distraction, indolence and sleepiness

तन् निबध्नाति भारत ॥
tan nibadhnāti bhārata
this it binds down Descendant of Bharata.

Know indeed that tamas is born of ignorance,
Which confuses all embodied ones.
This binds down, Descendant of Bharata,
With negligence, indolence and sleepiness.

tamas (n. acc. sg.), tamas, darkness, sloth.
tu, but, indeed.
ajñānajam (n. acc. sg.), born of ignorance, arising from ignorance.
viddhi (2nd sg. imperative √*vid*), know! learn!
mohanam (n. acc. sg.), confusing, deluding, delusion.
sarvadehinām (m. gen. pl.), of all embodied ones, of all *ātmans*.
pramāda (m.), distraction, confusion, negligence.
ālasya (n.), indolence, laziness.
nidrābhis (f. instr. pl.), sleep, drowsiness.
(*pramādālasyanidrābhis*, f. inst. pl. DV cpd., by distraction, laziness and sleepiness.)
tad (n. nom. sg.), this, that.
nibadhnāti (3rd sg. pr. indic. act. *ni* √*badh*), it binds down, it fetters down, it ties down.
bhārata (m. voc. sg.), Descendant of Bharata, epithet of Arjuna.

9

सत्त्वं सुखे सञ्जयति
sattvaṁ sukhe sañjayati
sattva to happiness it causes attachment,

रजः कर्मणि भारत ।
rajaḥ karmaṇi bhārata
rajas to action, Descendant of Bharata,

ज्ञानम् आवृत्य तु तमः
jñānam āvṛtya tu tamaḥ
knowledge-obscuring indeed tamas,

प्रमादे सञ्जयत्य् उत ॥
pramāde sañjayaty uta
to negligence it causes attachment even.

Sattva causes attachment to happiness
Rajas to action, Descendant of Bharata;
Tamas, obscuring knowledge,
Causes attachment to negligence.

sattvam (n. nom. sg.), sattva, truth, goodness, reality.
sukhe (m. n. loc. sg.), in happiness, to happiness.
sañjayati (3rd sg. pr. indic. causative act. √*sañj*), it causes attachment.
rajas (n. nom. sg.), rajas, passion, emotion.
karmaṇi (n. loc. sg.), to action, in action.
bhārata (m. voc. sg.), Descendant of Bharata.
jñānam (n. acc. sg.), knowledge, wisdom.
āvṛtya (gerund *ā* √*vṛ*), obscuring, veiling, enveloping.
tu, but, indeed.
tamas (n. nom. sg.), tamas, darkness, sloth.
pramāde (m. loc. sg.), to confusion, to delusion, to negligence, in delusion.
sañjayati (3rd sg. pr. indic. causative act. √*sañj*), it causes attachment.
uta, even, indeed.

10

रजस् तमश्चाभिभूय
rajas tamaścābhibhūya,
rajas-and-tamas-prevailing over,

सत्त्वं भवति भारत ।
sattvaṁ bhavati bhārata
sattva it arises, Descendant of Bharata,

रजः सत्त्वं तमश्चैव
rajaḥ sattvaṁ tamaścāiva
rajas (prevailing over) sattve and tamas (similarly),

तमः सत्त्वं रजस् तथा ॥
tamaḥ sattvaṁ rajas tathā
tamas (prevailing over) sattva and rajas likewise.

rajas (n. acc. sg.), rajas, emotion, passion.
tamas (n. acc. sg.), tamas, darkness, sloth.
ca, and.
abhibhūya (gerund *abhi* √*bhū*), over-powering, predominating, prevailing.
sattvam (n. nom. sg.), sattva, truth, goodness.
bhavati (3rd sg. pr. indic. act. √*bhū*), it arises, it comes to be.
bhārata (m. voc. sg.), Descendant of Bharata, epithet of Arjuna.
rajas (n. nom. sg.), rajas, passion, emotion.
sattvam (n. acc. sg.), sattva, truth, purity.
tamas (n. acc. sg.), tamas, darkness, sloth.
ca, and.
eva, indeed (used as a rhythmic filler).
tamas (n. nom. sg.), tamas, darkness, sloth.
sattvam (n. acc. sg.), sattva, truth, purity, reality.
rajas (n. acc. sg.), rajas, passion, emotion.
tathā, likewise, thus.

When prevailing over rajas and tamas
Sattva arises, Descendant of Bharata;
Rajas prevailing over sattva and tamas also comes to be;
Tamas prevailing over sattva and rajas likewise.*

---

* Three different relationships between, or proportions of, the three *guṇas*, representing three types of personality, or three phases of behavior, are intended here. The distinction is in the relative proportion of one *guṇa* to the others in a given personality. The idea is continued in the next three stanzas.

11

सर्वद्वारेषु देहे ऽस्मिन्
sarvadvāreṣu dehe 'smin
in all the gates of the body in this,

प्रकाश उपजायते ।
prakāśa upajāyate
a light is born

ज्ञानं यदा तदा विद्याद्
jñānaṁ yadā tadā vidyād
knowledge, when, then it should be known

विवृद्धं सत्त्वम् इत्य् उत ॥
vivṛddhaṁ sattvam ity uta
dominant sattva thus indeed.

When the light of knowledge is born
Within all the gates of this body,
Then it should be known that
Sattva is dominant, thus indeed.

sarvadvāreṣu (n. loc. pl.), in all the gates, in all the doors.
dehe (m./n. loc. sg.), in the body, of the body.
asmin (m. loc. sg.), in this.
prakāśas (m. nom. sg.), light, splendor, shine.
upajāyate (3rd sg. pr. indic. mid. *upa* √*jan*), it is born.
jñānam (n. nom. sg.), knowledge, wisdom.
yadā, when.
tadā, then.
vidyāt (3rd sg. optative act. √*vid*), it should be known, may it be known.
vivṛddham (n. nom. sg. participle *vi* √*vṛdh*), grown powerful, mighty, dominant.
sattvam (n. nom. sg.), sattva, truth, goodness.
iti, thus, so.
uta, even, indeed.

12

लोभः प्रवृत्तिर् आरम्भः
lobhaḥ pravṛttir ārambhaḥ
avarice, activity the undertaking

कर्मणाम् अशमः स्पृहा ।
karmaṇām aśamaḥ spṛhā
of actions, disquietude, desire;

रजस्य् एतानि जायन्ते
rajasy etāni jāyante
in rajas these are born,

विवृद्धे भरतर्षभ ॥
vivṛddhe bharatarṣabha
when dominant, Bull of the Bharatas.

lobhas (m. nom. sg.), greed, avarice.
pravṛttis (f. nom. sg.), activity, exertion, progress.
ārambhas (m. nom. sg.), undertaking, setting out, commencing.
karmaṇām (n. gen. pl.), of actions, of deeds.
aśamas (m. nom. sg.), lack of calmness, disquietude, restlessness.
spṛhā (f. nom. sg.), desire, lust.
rajasi (n. loc. sg.), in rajas, in the guṇa of passion.
etāni (n. nom. pl), these.
jāyante (3rd pl. pr. indic. mid. √*jan*), they are born, they arise.
vivṛddhe (n. loc. sg.), in the dominance, when dominant.
bharatarṣabha (m. voc. sg.), Bull of the Bharatas, epithet of Arjuna.

Avarice, activity and the undertaking
Of actions, disquietude, desire;
These are born when rajas
Is dominant, Bull of the Bharatas.

13

अप्रकाशो ऽप्रवृत्तिश्च
aprakāśo 'pravṛttiśca
unenlightenment and inertness,

प्रमादो मोह एव च ।
pramādo moha eva ca
heedlessness and confusion, thus,

तमस्य् एतानि जायन्ते
tamasy etāni jāyante
in tamas these are born

विवृद्धे कुरुनन्दन ॥
vivṛddhe kurunandana
when dominant, Descendant of Kuru.

aprakāśas (m. nom. sg.), unenlightenment, absence of illumination.
apravṛttis (f. nom. sg.), lack of exertion, inertness.
ca, and.
pramādas (m. nom. sg.), heedlessness, negligence.
mohas (m. nom. sg.), delusion, confusion.
eva, indeed (used as a rhythmic filler).
ca, and.
tamasi (n. loc. sg.), in tamas, in the guṇa of tamas, in darkness.
etāni (n. nom. pl.), these.
jāyante (3rd pl. pr. indic. mid. √*jan*), they are born, they are produced.
vivṛddhe (n. loc. sg.), in the dominance, when dominant.
kurunandana (m. voc. sg.), Descendant of Kuru, Joy of Kuru, epithet of Arjuna.

Unenlightenment and inertness,
Heedlessness and confusion;
These are born when tamas
Is dominant, Descendant of Kuru.

14

यदा सत्त्वे प्रवृद्धे तु
yadā sattve pravṛddhe tu
when in sattva in the dominance, indeed,

प्रलयं याति देहभृत् ।
pralayaṁ yāti dehabhṛt
to dissolution he goes, the embodied one,

तदोत्तमविदां लोकान्
tadottamavidāṁ lokān
then to the highest-knowing worlds,

अमलान् प्रतिपद्यते ॥
amalān pratipadyate
stainless, he arrives at.

yadā, when.
sattve (n. loc. sg.), in sattva, in truth, in virtue.
pravṛddhe (n. loc. sg.), in the dominance, when dominant.
tu, but, indeed.
pralayam (m. acc. sg.), dissolution, death, to dissolution.
yāti (3rd sg. pr. indic. act. √*yā*), he goes.
dehabhṛt (m. nom. sg.), the embodied one, the body-borne, the *ātman*.
tadā, then.
uttamavidām (m. gen. pl.), of those who know the highest.
lokān (m. acc. pl.), worlds.
amalān (m. acc. pl.), stainless, pure, shining.
pratipadyate (3rd sg. pr. indic. mid. *prati* √*pad*), he arrives at, he enters, he attains.

When the embodied one goes to dissolution (death)
Under the dominance of sattva,
Then he attains the stainless worlds
Of those who know the highest.

15

रजसि प्रलयं गत्वा
rajasi pralayaṁ gatvā
in rajas to dissolution having gone

कर्मसङ्गिषु जायते ।
karmasaṅgiṣu jāyate
among the action-attached he is born;

तथा प्रलीनस् तमसि
tathā pralīnas tamasi
likewise dissolving in tamas

मूढयोनिषु जायते ॥
mūḍhayoniṣu jāyate
in deluded wombs he is born.

He who goes to dissolution (death) when rajas is dominant,
Is reborn among those attached to action;
Likewise, dissolved (dying) when tamas is dominant,
He is reborn from the wombs of the deluded.

rajasi (n. loc. sg.), in rajas, in passion, in emotion.
pralayam (m. acc. sg.), dissolution, to death, to dissolution.
gatvā (gerund √*gam*), going, having gone.
karmasaṅgiṣu (m. loc. pl.), in the action attached, among those attached to action.
jāyate (3rd sg. pr. indic. mid. √*jan*), he is born.
tathā, thus, likewise.
pralīnas (m. nom. sg. from *pra* √*lī*), dissolving, dying.
tamasi (n. loc. sg.), in tamas, in darkness, in sloth.
mūḍhayoniṣu (f. loc. pl.), in deluded wombs, in wombs of the deluded.
jāyate (3rd sg. pr. indic. mid. √*jan*), he is born.

16

कर्मणः सुकृतस्याहुः
karmaṇaḥ sukṛtasyāhuḥ
of action well done they say

सात्त्विकं निर्मलं फलम् ।
sāttvikaṁ nirmalaṁ phalam
sattvic, without impurity, the fruit;

रजसस् तु फलं दुःखम्
rajasas tu phalaṁ duḥkham
of rajas but the fruit pain;

अज्ञानं तमसः फलम् ॥
ajñānaṁ tamasaḥ phalam
ignorance of tamas the fruit.

karmaṇas (n. gen. sg.), of action.
sukṛtasya (n. gen. sg.), of well performed, of well done.
āhus (3rd pl. perfect act. √*ah* with present meaning), they say.
sāttvikam (n. nom. sg.), sattvic, pertaining to the guṇa of sattva.
nirmalam (n. nom. sg.), without impurity, without stain.
phalam (n. nom. sg.), fruit.
rajasas (n. gen. sg.), of rajas, of the guṇa of rajas.
tu, but.
phalam (n. nom. sg.), fruit.
duḥkham (n. nom. sg.), pain, misery.
ajñānam (n. nom. sg.), ignorance, lack of knowledge.
tamasas (n. gen. sg.), of tamas, of the guṇa of tamas.
phalam (n. nom. sg.), fruit.

Of action well done, they say,
The fruit is sattvic and without impurity,
But the fruit of rajasic action is pain
And the fruit of tamasic action is ignorance.

17

सत्त्वात् संजायते ज्ञानं
sattvāt saṁjāyate jñānaṁ
from sattva is born knowledge

रजसो लोभ एव च ।
rajaso lobha eva ca
and from rajas desire,

प्रमादमोहौ तमसो
pramādamohau tamaso
negligence and delusion from tamas

भवतोऽज्ञानम् एव च ॥
bhavato 'jñānam eva ca
arise and ignorance also.

From sattva knowledge is born,
And from rajas desire;
Negligence and delusion arise
From tamas, and ignorance too.

sattvāt (n. abl. sg.), from sattva, from truth, from purity.
saṁjāyate (3rd sg. pr. indic. mid. *sam* √*jan*), it is born.
jñānam (n. nom. sg.), knowledge, wisdom.
rajasas (n. abl. sg.), from rajas, from desire, from passion.
lobhas (m. nom. sg.), greed, avarice, desire.
eva, indeed (used as a rhythmic filler).
ca, and.
pramādamohāu (n. nom. dual), distraction and delusion, heedlessness and confusion.
tamasas (n. abl. sg.), from tamas, from darkness.
bhavatas (3rd dual pr. indic. act. √*bhū*), they two arise, they two come to be.
ajñānam (n. nom. sg.), ignorance, lack of knowledge.
eva ca, and also.

18

ऊर्ध्वं गच्छन्ति सत्त्वस्था
ūrdhvaṁ gacchanti sattvasthā
upward they go, the sattva-established

मध्ये तिष्ठन्ति राजसाः ।
madhye tiṣṭhanti rājasāḥ
in the middle they stay, the rajasic

जघन्यगुणवृत्तिस्था
jaghanyaguṇavṛttisthā
lowest guṇa condition established

अधो गच्छन्ति तामसाः ॥
adho gacchanti tāmasāḥ
below they go, the tamasic.

Those established in sattva go upward,
The rajasic stay in the middle,
Established in the lowest guṇa condition,
The tamasic go below.

ūrdhvam (adv.), upward, rising.
gacchanti (3rd pl. pr. indic. act. √*gam*), they go.
sattvasthās (m. nom. pl.), the sattva-established, those established in sattva.
madhye (m. loc. sg.), in the middle.
tiṣṭhanti (3rd pl. pr. indic. act. √*sthā*), they stay, they remain, they stand.
rājasās (m. nom. pl.), the rajasic, those attached to rajas.
jaghanya (m.), lowest, hindmost, last.
guṇavṛttisthās (m. nom. pl.), established in guṇa condition, remaining in guṇa condition.
(*jaghanya-guṇa-vṛtti-sthās*, m. nom. pl. TP cpd., established in the lowest guṇa condition.)
adhas, below, downward.
gacchanti (3rd pl. pr. indic. act. √*gam*), they go.
tāmasās (m. nom. pl.), the tamasic, those who are ruled by tamas.

19

नान्यं गुणेभ्यः कर्तारं
nānyaṁ guṇebhyaḥ kartāraṁ
not other than the guṇas, the doer

यदा द्रष्टानुपश्यति ।
yadā draṣṭānupaśyati
when the beholder perceives,

गुणेभ्यश्च परं वेत्ति
guṇebhyaśca paraṁ vetti
and than the guṇas higher he knows

मद्भावं सो ऽधिगच्छति ॥
madbhāvaṁ so 'dhigacchati
my being he attains.

When the beholder perceives
No doer other than the guṇas,
And knows that which is higher than the guṇas,
He attains to My being.

na, not.
anyam (n. acc. sg.), other, else.
guṇebhyas (m. abl. pl.), than the guṇas, from the guṇas.
kartāram (m. acc. sg.), doer, maker.
yadā, when.
draṣṭā (m. nom. sg.), beholder, observer.
anupaśyati (3rd sg. pr. indic. act. *anu* √*paś*), he perceives, he sees.
guṇebhyas (m. abl. pl.), than the guṇas, from the guṇas.
ca, and.
param (n. acc. sg.), higher, highest.
vetti (3rd sg. pr. indic. act. √*vid*), he knows.
madbhāvam (m. acc. sg.), my being, me, my state of being.
sas (m. nom. sg.), he.
adhigacchati (3rd sg. pr. indic. act. *adhi* √*gam*), he atains, he goes to.

20

गुणान् एतान् अतीत्य त्रीन्
guṇān etān atītya trīn
guṇas these transcending, three,

देही देहसमुद्भवान् ।
dehī dehasamudbhavān
the embodied one, the body originating in,

जन्ममृत्युजरादुःखैर्
janmamṛtyujarāduḥkhāir
from birth, death, age and pain

विमुक्तो ऽमृतम् अश्नुते ॥
vimukto 'mṛtam aśnute
released, immortality he attains.*

guṇān (m. acc. pl.), guṇas.
etān (m. acc. pl.), these.
atītya (gerund *ati* √*i*), going beyond, transcending.
trīn (m. acc. pl.), three.
dehī (m. nom. sg.), the embodied, the embodied one, the *ātman*.
dehasamudbhavān (m. acc. pl. TP cpd.), originating in the body, coming to be in the body.
janma (n.), birth.
mṛtyu (m.), death.
jarā (f.), old age.
duḥkha (n.), pain, misery, misfortune.
(*janmamṛtyujarāduḥkhāis*, n. inst. pl. DV cpd., by birth, death, old age and pain.)
vimuktas (m. nom. sg. p. pass. participle *vi* √*muc*), liberated, released, freed.
amṛtam (n. acc. sg.), immortality.
aśnute (3rd sg. pr. indic. mid. √*aś*), he attains.

When the embodied one transcends
These three guṇas, which originate in the body,
Released from birth, death, old age and pain,
He attains immortality.*

* This would appear on the surface to be one of the Gītā's slight contradictions. Since the *ātman* of every being is already considered to be "immortal" the attainment of immortality through transcendence of the *guṇas* would seem to be redundant. Rāmānuja suggests that *amṛtam*, immortality, means the opposite of what it means to us, that is, absorption in Brahman, *nirvāṇa*, or divine non-existence. The stanza makes sense if one considers that Brahman is "immortal," "unchanging" and "permanent."

XIV

अर्जुन उवाच ।
arjuna uvāca
Arjuna spoke:

arjunas (m. nom. sg.), Arjuna.
uvāca (3rd sg. perfect act. √*vac*), be said, he spoke.

21

कैर् लिङ्गैस् त्रीन् गुणान् एतान्
kāir liṅgāis trīn guṇān etān
by what marks, three guṇas these

अतीतो भवति प्रभो ।
atīto bhavati prabho
transcending, he is (recognized), O Majestic One?

किमाचारः कथं चैतांस्
kimācāraḥ kathaṁ cāitāṅs
what conduct? and how these

त्रीन् गुणान् अतिवर्तते ॥
trīn guṇān ativartate
three guṇas he goes beyond?

Arjuna spoke:

By what marks is he recognized
Who has transcended these three guṇas, O Majestic One?
What is his conduct? and how
Does he go beyond these three guṇas?

kāis (n. inst. pl.), by what?
liṅgāis (n. inst. pl.), by marks, by characteristics.
trīn (m. acc. pl.), three.
guṇān (m. acc. pl.), guṇas.
etān (m. acc. pl.), these.
atītas (m. nom. sg. p. pass. participle *ati* √*i*), going beyond, transcending.
bhavati (3rd sg. pr. indic. act. √*bhū*), he is, he comes to be.
prabho (m. voc. sg.), O Majestic One, epithet of Krishna.
kim, what?
ācāras (m. nom. sg.), conduct, behaviour, practice.
(*kimācāras*, m. nom. sg. BV cpd., of what behavior? of what conduct?)
katham, how?
ca, and.
etān (m. acc. pl.), these.
trīn (m. acc. pl.), three.
guṇān (m. acc. pl.), guṇas.
ativartate (3rd sg. pr. indic. mid. *ati* √*vṛt*), he moves beyond, he transcends.

XIV

श्रीभगवान् उवाच ।
śrībhagavān uvāca
the Blessed Lord spoke:

śrībhagavān (m. nom. sg.), the Blessed Lord, the Blessed One.
uvāca (3rd sg. perfect act. √*vac*), he said, he spoke.

22

प्रकाशं च प्रवृत्तिं च
prakāśaṁ ca pravṛttiṁ ca
illumination or activity

मोहम् एव च पाण्डव ।
moham eva ca pāṇḍava
or delusion, Son of Paṇḍu,

न द्वेष्टि संप्रवृत्तानि
na dveṣṭi saṁpravṛttāni
not he hates the presences

न निवृत्तानि काङ्क्षति ॥
na nivṛttāni kāṅkṣati
nor the absences he desires.

The Blessed Lord spoke:

He neither hates nor desires
The presence or the absence
Of illumination* or activity*
Or delusion,* Son of Paṇḍu.

prakāśam (m. acc. sg.), illumination, brightness, splendor.
ca, and, or.
pravṛttim (f. acc. sg.), activity, advance, progress.
ca, and, or.
moham (m. acc. sg.), delusion, confusion.
eva, indeed (used as a rhythmic filler).
ca, and, or.
pāṇḍava (m. voc. sg.), Son of Pāṇḍu, epithet of Arjuna.
na, not.
na, not.
dveṣṭi (3rd sg. pr. indic. act. √*dviṣ*), he hates, he loathes.
saṁpravṛttāni (n. acc. pl.), presences, occurrings, comings forth, occurrences.
na, not, nor.
nivṛttāni (n. acc. pl.), non-occurrings, non-occurrences.
kāṅkṣati (3rd sg. pr. indic. act. √*kāṅkṣ*), he desires, he wishes for.

* The characteristic attributes of *sattva*, *rajas* and *tamas*.

23

उदासीनवद् आसीनो
udāsīnavad āsīno
as if seated apart seated

गुणैर् यो न विचाल्यते ।
guṇāir yo na vicālyate
by the guṇas who not he is disturbed,

गुणा वर्तन्त इत्य् एव
guṇā vartanta ity eva
"the gunas working" (only), thus

यो ऽवतिष्ठति नेङ्गते ॥
yo 'vatiṣṭhati neñgate
who he stands firm, not he wavers,

He who is seated as if seated apart (i.e. impartially, indifferently),
Who is not disturbed by the guṇas,
Thinking "the guṇas only are operating",
And who stands firm and does not waver,

udāsīnavat (adv.), as if seated apart, impartially, indifferently, disinterestedly, dispassionately.
āsīnas (m. nom. sg. pr. participle √*ās*), seated, sitting.
guṇāis (m. inst. pl.), by the guṇas.
yas (m. nom. sg.), who.
na, not.
vicālyate (3rd sg. pr. indic. causative passive *vi* √*cal*), he is disturbed, he is shaken.
guṇās (m. nom. pl.), guṇas.
vartanta (saṁdhi for *vartante*, 3rd pl. pr. indic. mid. √*vṛt*), they move, they roll, they operate, they work, they exist.
iti, thus (often used to close a quotation).
eva, indeed (used as a rhythmic filler).
yas (m. nom. sg.), who.
avastiṣṭhati (3rd sg. pr. indic. act. *ava* √*sthā*), he stands firm, he remains standing, he takes his stand.
na, not.
iñgate (3rd sg. pr. indic. mid. √*iñg*), he wavers, he stirs.

24

समदुःखसुखः स्वस्थः
samaduḥkhasukhaḥ svasthaḥ
(to whom are) the same pain and pleasure, self contained,

समलोष्टाश्मकाञ्चनः ।
samaloṣṭāśmakāñcanaḥ
(to whom are) the same a clod, a stone and gold

तुल्यप्रियाप्रियो धीरस्
tulyapriyāpriyo dhīras
(to whom are) equal the loved and the unloved, steadfast,

तुल्यनिन्दात्मसंस्तुतिः ॥
tulyanindātmasaṁstutiḥ
(to whom are) equal blame of himself and praise,

To whom pain and pleasure are equal, who is self contained,
To whom a clod, a stone and gold are the same,
To whom the loved and the unloved are equivalent, who is steadfast,
To whom blame and praise of himself are alike,

samaduḥkhasukhas (m. nom. sg.), being the same in pain and pleasure, being equal in pain and pleasure, (as BV cpd.) he who is indifferent to pain and pleasure.
svasthas (m. nom. sg.), self contained, depending on the self.
sama (m.), same, equal.
loṣṭa (m./n.), clod, lump of earth.
aśma (m.), stone, a stone.
kāñcana (n.), gold.
(*samaloṣṭāśmakāñcanas,* m. nom. sg. BV cpd., for whom a clod, a stone and gold are the same.)
tulya (m./n.), equal.
priyāpriyas (m. nom. sg.), the loved and the unloved, the dear and the undear, the pleasant and the unpleasant.
(*tulyapriyāpriyas,* m. nom. sg. BV cpd., to whom the pleasant and the unpleasant are equal.)
dhīras (m. nom. sg.), steadfast, constant, firm.
tulya (m./n.), equal.
nindātmasaṁstutis (f. nom. sg.), blame of himself or praise (*nindā* = blame, *ātma* = self, *saṁstuti* = praise).
(*tulyanindātmasaṁstutis,* m. nom. sg. BV cpd., to whom blame and praise of himself are alike.)

25

मानापमानयोस् तुल्यस्
mānāpamānayos tulyas
in honor and dishonor equal,

तुल्यो मित्रारिपक्षयोः ।
tulyo mitrāripakṣayoḥ
impartial toward friend or enemy sides

सर्वारम्भपरित्यागी
sarvārambhaparityāgī
all undertakings renouncing,

गुणातीतः स उच्यते ॥
guṇātītaḥ sa ucyate
transcending the guṇas, he, it is said.

To whom honor and dishonor are equal;
Dispassionate toward the side of friend or foe,
Renouncing all undertakings,
He is said to transcend the guṇas.

mānāpamānayos (m. loc. dual DV cpd.), in honor and dishonor, in esteem and disesteem.
tulyas (m. nom. sg.), equal, indifferent.
tulyas (m. nom. sg.), equal, impartial, disinterested.
mitrāripakṣayos (m. loc. dual TP cpd.), toward friend or enemy sides, toward the party or faction of friend or enemy (*mitra* = friend, *ari* = enemy, *pakṣa* = wing, side, faction).
sarva (m.), all.
ārambha (m.), undertaking, commencement.
parityāgī (m. nom. sg.), renouncing, abandoning.
(*sarva-ārambha-parityāgī*, m. nom. sg. TP cpd., renouncing all undertakings.)
guṇātītas (m. nom. sg. TP cpd. *guṇa* + p. pass. participle *ati* √*i*), going beyond the guṇas, transcending the guṇas.
sas (m. nom. sg.), he, this.
ucyate (3rd sg. pr. indic. passive √*vac*), it is said, he is said to be.

26

मां च यो ऽव्यभिचारेण
māṁ ca yo 'vyabhicāreṇa
and me who with unswerving

भक्तियोगेन सेवते ।
bhaktiyogena sevate
devotion Yoga he serves

स गुणान् समतीत्यैतान्
sa guṇān samatītyāitān
he the guṇas transcending, these,

ब्रह्मभूयाय कल्पते ॥
brahmabhūyāya kalpate
for absorption in Brahman he is ready.

mām (acc. sg.), me.
ca, and.
yas (m. nom. sg.), who.
avyabhicāreṇa (m. inst. sg.), with unswerving, with unwavering, with constant.
bhaktiyogena (m. inst. sg.), with devotion-Yoga, with the Yoga of devotion, with the power of devotion.
sevate (3rd sg. mid. √*sev*), he serves, he waits upon, he honors, he obeys.
sas (m. nom. sg.), he, this.
guṇān (m. acc. pl.), the guṇas.
samatītya (gerund *sam ati* √*i*), passed through, passed beyond, transcending.
etān (m. acc. pl.), these.
brahmabhūyāya (m. dat. sg.), to absorption in Brahman, for absorption in Brahman.
kalpate (3rd sg. pr. indic. mid. √*klp*), he is adapted, he is suited, he is ready.

And he who serves Me
With the Yoga of unswerving devotion,
Transcending these guṇas,
Is ready for absorption in Brahman.

27

ब्रह्मणो हि प्रतिष्ठाहम्
brahmaṇo hi pratiṣṭhāham
of Brahman indeed the foundation I,

अमृतस्याव्ययस्य च ।
amṛtasyāvyayasya ca
of the immortal and imperishable

शाश्वतस्य च धर्मस्य
śāśvatasya ca dharmasya
and of everlasting virtue

सुखस्यैकान्तिकस्य च ॥
sukhasyāikāntikasya ca
and of bliss absolute.

brahmaṇas (n. gen. sg.), of Brahman.
hi, indeed, truly.
pratiṣṭhā (f. nom. sg.), foundation, support, basis.
aham (nom. sg.), I.
amṛtasya (n. gen. sg.), of the immortal.
avyayasya (n. gen. sg.), of the imperishable, of the eternal.
ca, and.
śāśvatasya (n. gen. sg.), of the everlasting, of the perpetual.
ca, and.
dharmasya (m. gen. sg.), of the law, of righteousness.
sukhasya (m./n. gen. sg.), of bliss, of happiness.
ekāntikasya (n. gen. sg.), of absolute, of singular, of unique, of the one and only.
ca, and.

For I am the foundation of Brahman,
Of the Immortal and the Imperishable,
And of everlasting virtue,
And of absolute bliss.

End of Book XIV

The Yoga of Distinction between the
Three Guṇas

BOOK XV

श्रीभगवान् उवाच ।
śrībhagavān uvāca
the Blessed Lord spoke:

śrībhagavān (m. nom. sg.), the Blessed Lord, the Blessed One.
uvāca (3rd sg. perf. act. √*vac*), he said, he spoke.

1

ऊर्ध्वमूलम् अधःशाखम्
ūrdhvamūlam adhahśākham
high the root, below the bough,

अश्वत्थं प्राहुर् अव्ययम् ।
aśvattham prāhur avyayam
the aśvattha tree,* they say, eternal

छन्दांसि यस्य पर्णानि
chandāmsi yasya parṇāni
the (Vedic) hymns, of which the leaves

यस् तं वेद स वेदवित् ।।
yas tam veda sa vedavit
who it knows, he Veda knowing.

The Blessed Lord spoke:

**High the root, below the branch,
The eternal aśvattha tree,* they say,
Of which the leaves are the (Vedic) hymns.
He who knows this is a knower of the Vedas.**

ūrdhva, high, above.
mūlam (n. acc. sg.), root.
adhas, below, low.
śākham, (n. acc. sg.), branch, bough, limb.
(*adhahśākham*, m. acc. sg. BV cpd., whose branches stretch forth below.)
aśvattham (m. acc. sg.), the *aśvattha* tree.
prāhus (3rd pl. per. act. *pra* √*ah* with present meaning), they say.
avyayam (m. acc. sg.), eternal, imperishable.
chandāmsi (n. acc. pl.), Vedic hymns, sacred hymns.
yasya (gen. sg.), of which.
parṇāni (n. acc. pl.), leaves.
yas (m. nom. sg.), who.
tam (m. acc. sg.), this, it, him.
veda (3rd sg. perf. act. √*vid.*, with present meaning), he knows.
sas (m. nom. sg.), he, this.
vedavit (m. nom. sg.), Veda-knowing, wise in the Veda, knower of the Veda.

* The *aśvattha* (derived by some from *aśva stha* meaning "where the horse remains" or "where the horse is tied"), is mentioned in the Vedas, but not in this fanciful upside down form, which appears, however, in the later Kaṭha Upanishad (6, 1). It is a sacred tree whose wood, along with that of the parṇa tree, was used to kindle sacrifices. It belongs to the fig family. The symbol refers to the Supreme Spirit branching downward into the

2.

अधश्चोर्ध्वं प्रसृतास् तस्य शाखा
*adhaścordhvaṁ prasṛtās tasya śākhā**
below and above wide spreading of it the branches

गुणप्रवृद्धा विषयप्रवालाः।
guṇapravṛddhā viṣayapravālāḥ
guṇa nourished, sense-object sprouts,

अधश्च मूलान्य् अनुसंततानि
adhaśca mūlāny anusaṁtatāni
and below roots stretched forth,

कर्मानुबन्धीनि मनुष्यलोके ॥
karmānubandhīni manuṣyaloke
action-engendering in the world of men.

Below and above its branches spread,
Nourished by the guṇas, with objects of the senses as sprouts;
And below its roots stretch forth
Engendering action in the world of men.

adhas, low, below.
ca, and.
ūrdhvam, high, above.
prasṛtās (nom. pl. p. pass. participle *pra* √*sṛ*), wide spreading, widely flowing.
tasya (m. gen. sg.), of it, of this.
śākhās (f. nom. pl.), branches, boughs, limbs.
guṇapravṛddhās (m. nom. pl. TP cpd. pass. particle *pra* √*vṛdh*), guṇa nourished, fostered by the guṇas.
viṣaya (m.), sense object, object of the senses, realm of the senses.
pravālās (m. nom. pl.), young shoots, sprouts.
(*viṣaya-pravālās*, m. nom. pl. TP cpd., sprouts composed of sense objects.)
adhas, below, low.
ca, and.
mūlāni (n. nom. pl.), roots.
anusaṁtatāni (n. nom. pl. p. pass. participle *anu sam* √*tan*), stretched forth, stretched out.
karmānubhandīni (n. nom. pl. TP cpd. *karma anubandhīni*), action engendering, followed by action, promoting action.
manuṣyaloke (m. loc. sg.), in the human world, in the world of men.

---

earthly realm. The following stanza seems to blur the symbolism somewhat by speaking of the "roots stretched forth below," but the *aśvattha* tree, like the banyan to which it is related, strikes roots from its branches. Both trees are considered sacred in India.

* *Triṣṭubh* metre begins again.

3

न रूपम् अस्येह तथोपलभ्यते
*na rūpam asyeha tathopalabhyate**
not the form of it here in the world thus it is perceptible

नान्तो न चादिर् न च संप्रतिष्ठा ।
nānto na cādir na ca saṁpratiṣṭhā
not the end and not the beginning and not the staying.

अश्वत्थम् एनं सुविरूढमूलम्
aśvattham enaṁ suvirūḍhamūlam
aśvattha tree this well grown root

असङ्गशस्त्रेण दृढेन छित्त्वा ॥
asaṅgaśastreṇa dṛḍhena chittvā
non-attachment axe strong cutting.

Its form is not perceptible here in the world,
Not its end, nor its beginning nor its staying.
This aśvattha tree, with its well grown root,
Cutting by the strong axe of non-attachment,†

na, not.
rūpam (n. nom. sg.), form, shape, figure.
asya (m. gen. sg.), of it, of this.
iha, here, here in the world, here on earth.
tathā, thus, in this way.
upalabhyate (3rd sg. pr. passive *upa* √*labh*), it is perceptible, it is attainable.
na, not.
antas (m. nom. sg.), end, termination.
na, not, nor.
ca, and.
ādis (m. nom. sg.), beginning.
na, not.
ca, and.
saṁpratiṣṭhā (f. nom. sg.), maintenance, continuance, basis, staying, existence.
aśvattham (m. acc. sg.), aśvattha tree.
enam (m. acc. sg.), this.
suvirūḍha (p. pass. participle *su vi* √*ruh*), fully developed, fully grown, fully ascended.
mūlam (n. acc. sg.), root.
(*suviruḍhamūlam,* n. acc. sg. BV cpd., whose roots are fully grown.)
asaṅga (m.), non-attachment.
śastreṇa (m. inst. sg.), by the axe, by the knife, by the weapon.
(*asaṅga-śastreṇa,* m. instr. sg. TP cpd., by the axe of non-attachment.)
dṛḍhena (m. inst. sg.), by the strong.
chittvā (gerund √*chid*), cutting, severing, chopping.

* Line 1 of stanza 3 (*triṣṭubh* metre) has an extra syllable.

† Cutting the supernatural *aśvattha* tree is a symbol for destroying the process of rebirth, and stanza 4 indicates that after the tree of life, or of rebirth, is cut, one seeks the place (*nirvāṇa*) from which there is no return to rebirth, and seeks refuge in the primal spirit whence activity streamed forth (see following stanza), that is to say *Brahman.* The cutting of the tree involves doing away with earthly desires (the branches – or roots of stanza 2), and leaving only the spiritual part which exists "above." The metaphor is rather confused by the lower "roots" of stanza 2, line 3.

4

ततः पदं तत् परिमार्गितव्यं
tataḥ padaṁ tat parimārgitavyaṁ
then place that to be sought

यस्मिन् गता न निवर्तन्ति भूयः ।
yasmin gatā na nivartanti bhūyaḥ
to which, gone, not they return again,

तम् एव चाद्यं पुरुषं प्रपद्ये
tam eva cādyaṁ puruṣaṁ prapadye
and "in that very primal spirit I take refuge

यतः प्रवृत्तिः प्रसृता पुराणी ।।
yataḥ pravṛttiḥ prasṛtā purāṇī
whence activity streamed forth anciently."

Then that place is to be sought
From which, having gone they do not return,
Thinking "In that very primal spirit I take refuge,
Whence primaeval activity anciently streamed forth."

tatas, then, from there.
padam (n. nom. sg.), place, abode, site, footing.
tad (n. nom. sg.), this, that.
parimārgitavyam (n. acc. sg. gerundive *pari* √*mārg*), to be sought, to be run after.
yasmin (n. loc. sg.), in which, to which.
gatās (m. nom. pl. p. pass. participle √*gam*), gone.
na, not.
nivartanti (3rd pl. pr. indic. act. *ni* √*vṛt*), they return, they turn back.
bhūyas, again, once more.
tam (m. acc. sg.), that, to that, him.
eva, indeed (often used as a rhythmic filler, but here intensifying *tam*).
ca, and.
ādyam (m. acc. sg.), beginning, primal, in the primal, to the primal, to the original.
puruṣam (m. acc. sg.), spirit, being.
prapadye (1st sg. pr. indic. mid. *pra* √*pad*), I take refuge, I resort to.
yatas, whence, from where.
pravṛttis (f. nom. sg.), activity, progress.
prasṛtā (f. nom. sg. p. pass. participle *pra* √*sṛ*), streamed forth, flowed.
purāṇī (f. nom. sg.), anciently, in former times, primaeval, ancient.

5

निर्मानमोहा जितसङ्गदोषा
*nirmānamohā jitasaṅgadoṣā**
without arrogance or delusion, conquered attachment-evils,

अध्यात्मनित्या विनिवृत्तकामाः ।
adhyātmanityā vinivṛttakāmāḥ
(in the) Supreme Self constantly (dwelling), turned away desires,

द्वन्द्वैर् विमुक्ताः सुखदुःखसंज्ञैर्
dvandvāir vimuktāḥ sukhaduḥkhasaṁjñāir
by the dualities released, pleasure-pain-known-as,

गच्छन्त्य् अमूढाः पदम् अव्ययं तत् ॥
gacchanty amūḍhāḥ padam avyayaṁ tat
they go undeluded to place imperishable that.

Without arrogance or delusion, with the evils of attachment conquered,
Dwelling constantly in the Supreme Self, with desires turned away,
Released by the dualities known as pleasure and pain,
The undeluded go to that Imperishable Place.†

nirmāna (m.), without pride, without arrogance.
mohās (m. nom. pl.), confusions, delusions.
(*nirmāna-mohās*, m. nom. pl. DV cpd., without pride or delusions.)
jita (p. pass. participle √*ji*), conquered.
saṅga (m.), attachment, clinging.
doṣās (m. n. nom. pl.), evils, wrongs.
(*jitasaṅgadoṣās*, m. nom. pl., conquered attachment-evils, with the evils of attachment conquered; as BV cpd., whose attachment-evils are conquered.)
adhyātma (m.), Supreme Self.
nityās (m. nom. pl.), constantly, perpetually, eternally.
(*adhyātma-nityās*, m. nom. pl. TP cpd., eternally in the supreme self.)
vinivṛtta (p. pass. participle *vi ni* √*vṛt*), turned away, twisted away.
kāmās (m. nom. pl.), desires, lusts.
(*vinivṛttakāmās*, m. nom. pl. BV cpd., whose desires have been turned away.)
dvandvāis (n. inst. pl.), by the dualities, by the pairs of opposites.
vimuktās (m. nom. pl. p. pass. participle *vi* √*muc*), released, freed.
sukhaduḥkha, pleasure and pain, happiness, and misery.
saṁjñāis (m. inst. pl.), by known as, recognized as.
(*sukha-duḥkha-saṁjñāis*, m. instr. pl. BV cpd., known as pleasure and pain.)
gacchanti (3rd pl. pr. indic. act. √*gam*), they go.
amūḍhās (m. nom. pl.), unconfused, undeluded.
padam (n. acc. sg.), place, site, abode, to place, to abode.
avyayam (n. acc. sg.), imperishable, eternal.
tad (n. acc. sg.), this, that.

* *Triṣṭubh* metre continues.
† I.e. Brahman.

6

न तद् भासयते सूर्यो
*na tad bhāsayate sūryo**
not that (place) it illumines, the sun,

न शशाङ्को न पावकः ।
na śaśāṅko na pāvakaḥ
nor the rabbit-marked, nor fire,

यद् गत्वा न निवर्तन्ते
yad gatvā na nivartante
to which, having gone, not they return,

तद् धाम परमं मम ॥
tad dhāma paramaṁ mama
that abode supreme of me.

na, not.
tad (n. acc. sg.), that, this.
bhāsayate (3rd sg. causative √*bhās*), it causes to shine, it illumines.
sūryas (m. nom. sg.), sun, the sun.
na, not, nor.
śaśāṅkas (m. nom. sg.), the "rabbit-marked," the moon.
na, not, nor.
pāvakas (m. nom. sg.), fire, flame.
yad (n. acc. sg.), which, to which.
gatvā (gerund √*gam*), going, having gone.
na, not.
nivartante (3rd pl. pr. indic. mid. *ni* √*vṛt*), they return, they turn back.
tad (n. nom. sg.), this, that.
dhāma (n. nom. sg.), abode, home.
paramam (n. nom. sg.), highest, supreme.
mama (gen. sg.), of me, my.

The sun does not illumine,
Nor the moon, nor fire, that place
To which, having gone, they do not return;
That is My supreme abode.

* *Śloka* metre resumes.

7

ममैवांशो जीवलोके
mamāivāṁśo jīvaloke
of me merely a fragment in the world of the living,

जीवभूत: सनातन: ।
jīvabhūtaḥ sanātanaḥ
a soul becoming, eternal,

मन:षष्ठानीन्द्रियाणि
manaḥ ṣaṣṭhānīndriyāṇi
mind, the sixth, and the (other) senses,

प्रकृतिस्थानि कर्षति ॥
prakṛtisthāni karṣati
material-nature-existing, it draws to itself.

Merely a fragment of Myself in the world of the living.
Becoming an eternal (individual) self,
Draws to itself the senses, of which the sixth is the mind,*
That exist in material nature.

mama (gen. sg.), of me, my.
eva, indeed, merely (often used as a rhythmic filler).
aṁśas (m. nom. sg.), fragment, part, share.
jīvaloke (m. loc. sg.), in the world of the living.
jīvabhūtas (m. nom. sg.), being, becoming alive, becoming a self.
sanātanas (m. nom. sg.), ancient, primaeval, eternal.
manas (n. acc. sg.), mind.
ṣaṣṭhāni (n. acc. pl.), sixth, as the sixth.
indriyāṇi (n. acc. pl.), senses.
prakṛtisthāni (n. acc. pl.), abiding in material nature, existing in material nature.
karṣati (3rd sg. pr. indic. act. √*kṛṣ*), it draws to itself, it draws (as in plowing).

---

* Mind, in Gītā psychology, is regarded as the sixth sense.

8

शरीरं यद् अवाप्नोति
śarīraṁ yad avāpnoti
a body when he acquires

यच् चाप्य् उत्क्रामतीश्वरः ।
yac cāpy utkrāmatīśvaraḥ
and when also he departs from, the Lord,

गृहीत्वैतानि संयाति
gṛhītvāitāni saṁyāti
taking these along, he goes,

वायुर् गन्धान् इवाशयात् ॥
vāyur gandhān ivāśayāt
the wind-perfumes-like from (their) source.

śarīram (n. acc. sg.), body, bodily frame.
yad (n. acc. sg.), when, which.
avāpnoti (3rd sg. pr. indic. act. *ava* √*āp*), he attains, he obtains, he acquires.
yad (n. acc. sg.), when, which.
ca, and.
api, also, even.
utkrāmati (3rd sg. pr. indic. act. *ud* √*kram*), he departs from, he steps out of.
īśvaras (m. nom. sg.), the Lord.
gṛhītvā (gerund √*grah*), taking, grasping, taking along.
etāni (n. acc. pl.), these, them.
saṁyāti (3rd sg. pr. indic. act. *sam* √*yā*), he goes.
vāyus (m. nom. sg.), wind, the wind.
gandhān (m. acc. pl.), perfumes, scents.
iva, like, as if.
āśayāt (m. abl. sg.), from resting place, from source, from seat.

When the Lord acquires a body,
And also when He departs from it,
He goes, taking them* along,
Like the wind blowing perfumes from their source.†

* The mind and other senses, to be used in connection with another acquired body.

† "Whatever body the *ātman* enters and from whatever body it departs, it will always retain those senses with the subtle elements and roam with them *as* the breeze roams with odors which it has carried from their original abodes." – Rāmānuja. Thus, apparently, the *ātman* is not totally devoid of characteristics between one incarnation and another.

9

श्रोत्रं चक्षुः स्पर्शनं च
śrotraṁ cakṣuḥ sparśanaṁ ca
hearing, sight and touch

रसनं घ्राणम् एव च ।
rasanaṁ ghrāṇam eva ca
taste and smell

अधिष्ठाय मनश्चायं
adhiṣṭhāya manaścāyaṁ
presiding over, and the mind, this one

विषयान् उपसेवते ॥
viṣayān upasevate
the objects of sense he enjoys.

Presiding over hearing, sight and touch,
Taste and smell, as well as mind,
This one (i.e. the fragment of the Lord incarnated as the individual self)
Enjoys the objects of the senses.

śrotram (n. acc. sg.), hearing, sense of hearing.
cakṣus (n. acc. sg.), sight, eye, sense of sight.
sparśanam (n. acc. sg.), touch, sense of touch.
ca, and.
rasanam (n. acc. sg.), taste, flavor, sense of taste.
ghrāṇam (n. acc. sg.), smell, sense of smell.
eva, indeed (used as a rhythmic filler).
ca, and.
adhiṣṭhāya (gerund *adhi* √*sthā*), presiding over, commanding, ruling.
manas (n. acc. sg.), mind.
ca, and.
ayam (m. nom. sg.), this, this one.
viṣayān (m. acc. pl.), objects of the senses, territory of the senses.
upasevate (3rd sg. pr. indic. mid. *upa* √*sev*), he enjoys, he is addicted to, he abides in.

10

उत्क्रामन्तं स्थितं वापि
utkrāmantaṁ sthitaṁ vāpi
departing, remaining, whether,

भुञ्जानं वा गुणान्वितम् ।
bhuñjānaṁ vā guṇānvitam
enjoying or, guṇa-accompanied,

विमूढा नानुपश्यन्ति
vimūḍhā nānupaśyanti
the deluded, not they perceive (him).

पश्यन्ति ज्ञानचक्षुषः ॥
paśyanti jñānacakṣuṣaḥ
they see (him), the knowledge-eyed.

When He departs, remains,
Or enjoys (sense objects) while accompanied by the guṇas,
The deluded do not perceive Him.
Those with the eye of knowledge see Him.*

utkrāmantam (m. acc. sg. pr. participle *ud* √*kram*), departing, stepping away.
sthitam (m. acc. sg. p. pass. participle √*sthā*), staying, remaining.
vāpi (*vā api*), whether.
bhuñjānam (m. acc. sg. pr. participle √*bhuj*), enjoying.
vā, or.
guṇānvitam (m. acc. sg. p. pass. participle *guṇa anu* √*i*), guṇa-accompanied, accompanied by the guṇas.
vimūḍhās (m. nom. pl.), the deluded, those who are confused.
na, not.
anupaśyanti (3rd pl. pr. indic. act. *anu* √*paś*), they perceive, they see.
paśyanti (3rd pl. pr. indic. act. √*paś*), they perceive, they see, they behold.
jñānacakṣuṣas (m. nom. pl.), the knowledge-eyed, those with the eye of knowledge, (as BV cpd.) those who have the eye of knowledge.

* "Those who are perplexed by ignorance do not perceive that the *ātman*-with-*guṇas* is conjoined, forms a whole, with human nature etc., which are particular developments of *prakṛti* consisting of *guṇas*, nor do they perceive that this *ātman* is either departing from a certain mass of *prakṛti*, or existing in it and experiencing the objects (of the senses), and that (this) *ātman* might at some time be different from such a mass – human nature etc. – and have only one form, knowledge. They are unable to perceive this, for they have the misconception that the *ātman* is akin to that mass to which it is conjoined. Those, however, who know the difference between mass and *ātman* and so perceive that the *ātman*, albeit present in all conditions, is different from whatever mass it is conjoined with, have a clear vision of the truth." – Rāmānuja.

11

यतन्तो योगिनश्चैनं
yatanto yoginaścāinaṁ
striving, the yogins this one

पश्यन्त्य् आत्मन्य् अवस्थितम् ।
paśyanty ātmany avasthitam
they see in the self situated

यतन्तो ऽप्य् अकृतात्मानो
yatanto 'py akṛtātmāno
(but) striving even, unperfected selves

नैनं पश्यन्त्य् अचेतसः ॥
nāinaṁ paśyanty acetasaḥ
not this one they see, the unthinking.

The yogins, striving, see this one (the embodied fraction of the Lord)
Situated in the self,
But the unthinking, those of unperfected selves,
Do not see him.

yatantas (m. nom. pl. pr. act. particple √*yat*), striving, stretching.
yoginas (m. nom. pl.), yogins.
ca, and.
enam (m. acc. sg.), this, this one.
paśyanti (3rd pl. pr. indic. act. √*paś*), they see, they perceive.
ātmani (m. loc. sg.), in the self.
avasthitam (m. acc. sg. p. pass. participle *ava* √*sthā*), situated, existing, abiding.
yatantas (m. nom. pl. pr. act. participle √*yat*), striving, stretching.
api, even, also.
akṛtātmānas (m. nom. pl. from *akṛta ātmanas*), unperfected selves, of unprepared selves, (as BV cpd.) those whose selves are unperfected.
na, not.
enam (m. acc. sg.), this, this one, him.
paśyanti (3rd pl. pr. indic. act. √*paś*), they see, they perceive.
acetasas (m. nom. pl.), the unthinking, the thoughtless ones, the fools.

12

यद् आदित्यगतं तेजो
yad ādityagataṁ tejo
which sun-proceeding splendor

जगद् भासयते ऽखिलम् ।
jagad bhāsayate 'khilam
the universe it illumines, without a gap,

यच् चन्द्रमसि यच् चाग्नौ
yac candramasi yac cāgnau
which in the moon and which in fire

तत् तेजो विद्धि मामकम् ॥
tat tejo viddhi māmakam
that splendor know to be mine.

That brilliance which resides in the sun,
Which illumines the entire universe,
Which is in the moon and which is in fire,
That brilliance know to be Mine.

yad (n. nom. sg.), which, what.
ādityagatam (n. nom. sg.), proceeding from the sun, sun-proceeding.
tejas (n. nom. sg.), splendor, brightness, brilliance.
jagat (n. acc. sg.), universe, world, all that moves.
bhāsayate (3rd sg. causative mid. √*bhās*), it illumines, it causes to shine.
akhilam (adv.), without a gap, completely.
yad (n. nom. sg.), which, what.
candramasi (m. loc. sg.), in the moon.
yad (n. nom. sg.), which, what.
ca, and.
agnāu (m. loc. sg.), in fire.
tad (n. acc. sg.), that, this.
tejas (n. acc. sg.), splendor, brightness, brilliance.
viddhi (2nd sg. imperative act. √*vid*), know! be aware!
māmakam (m. acc. sg.), belonging to me, mine.

XV

13

गाम् आविश्य च भूतानि
gām āviśya ca bhūtāni
and the earth entering, all beings

धारयाम्य् अहम् ओजसा ।
dhārayāmy aham ojasā
I support, I, by energy,

पुष्णामि चौषधीः सर्वाः
puṣṇāmi cāuṣadhīḥ sarvāḥ
and I cause to thrive the plants all

सोमो भूत्वा रसात्मकः ॥
somo bhūtvā rasātmakaḥ
the Soma having become, juicy-selved.

**And entering the earth, I support
All beings with energy,
And I cause all the plants to thrive,
Having become the juicy-selved Soma.***

gām (f. acc. sg.), the earth, that on which one goes (√*gā*).
āviśya (gerund *ā* √*viś*), entering, approaching, settling on.
ca, and.
bhūtāni (n. acc. pl.), beings, creatures.
dhārayāmi (1st sg. pr. indic. causative act. √*dhṛ*), I support, I maintain, I preserve.
aham (nom. sg.), I.
ojasā (n. inst. sg.), by energy, with power, with strength.
puṣṇāmi (1st sg. pr. indic. act. √*puṣ*), I cause to thrive, I cause to prosper, lit. I cause to flower.
ca, and.
āuṣadhīs (f. acc. pl.), plants, herbs.
sarvās (f. acc. pl.), all.
somas (m. nom. sg.), soma, Vedic drink of the gods.
bhūtvā (gerund √*bhū*), becoming, having become.
rasātmakas (m. nom. sg.), juicy-selved, flavor-selved, liquid-selved, having the nature of flavor or juice.

* There has been much speculation among scholars as to the identity of Soma, the drink of the gods – the juice of a plant with inebriating properties that was drunk by the priests, the laity and the gods during sacrifices described in the Vedas. As the Vedic Aryans moved into India, the knowledge of the Soma plant seems to have disappeared, and, even from late Vedic times, substitutes for it were used – mostly plants of the milkweed family whose juice is not inebriating. Recently R. Gordon Wasson, a mycologist acquainted with the Vedas in translation, has advanced a persuasive but still controversial hypothesis – that the Soma plant was, in fact, a hallucinogenic mushroom (the *amanita muscaria*) which grew in the Aryans' original homeland in western Asia, and in Southern Asia only in the highest mountains. This circumstance, Wasson thinks, would explain the loss of the Soma as the Aryans migrated southward. It would also explain the rapturous descriptions of the effects of Soma drinking recorded in the Ṛg Veda. (See "Soma the Divine Mushroom," published by the Stamperia Valdonega, Verona.)

14

अहं वैश्वानरो भूत्वा
ahaṁ vāiśvānaro bhūtvā
I, the digestive fire of all men becoming,

प्राणिनां देहम् आश्रितः ।
prāṇināṁ deham āśritaḥ
of breathing beings the body entering,

प्राणापानसमायुक्तः
prāṇāpānasamāyuktaḥ
the vital breath and the abdominal breath joined with,

पचाम्य् अन्नं चतुर्विधम् ॥
pacāmy annaṁ caturvidham
I cook (digest) four kinds of food.

Becoming the digestive fire of all men,
Entering the body of all breathing beings,
Joining with the vital and the abdominal breaths,
I cook (digest) four kinds of food.

aham (nom. sg.), I.
vāiśvānaras (m. nom. sg.), belonging to all men, the digestive fire of all men.
bhūtvā (gerund √*bhū*), becoming, having become.
prāṇinām (m. gen. pl.), of the breathing, of breathing beings.
deham (m./n. acc. sg.), body, bodily frame.
āśritas (m. nom. sg. p. pass. participle *ā* √*śri*), entering, joining, inhabiting.
prāṇāpāna (m.), inhalation and exhalation, vital and abdominal breaths.
samāyuktas (m. nom. sg. p. pass. participle *sam ā* √*yuj*), joined with, united with.
(*prāṇāpāna-samāyuktas*, m. nom. sg. TP cpd., joined with the vital and abdominal breaths.)
pacāmi (1st sg. pr. indic. act. √*pac*), I cook, I digest.
annam (n. acc. sg.), food (esp. grain).
caturvidham (n. acc. sg.), of four kinds, fourfold.

15

सर्वस्य चाहं हृदि संनिविष्टो
*sarvasya cāhaṁ hṛdi saṁniviṣṭo**
and of all I in the heart entered,

मत्तः स्मृतिर् ज्ञानम् अपोहनं च ।
mattaḥ smṛtir jñānam apohanaṁ ca
from me memory, knowledge and reasoning

वेदैश्च सर्वैर् अहम् एव वेद्यो
vedāiśca sarvāir aham eva vedyo
and by the Vedas all I alone to be known,

वेदान्तकृद् वेदविद् एव चाहम् ॥
vedāntakṛd vedavid eva cāham
Vedānta making and Veda knowing, I.

And I have entered into the heart of all beings,
From Me come memory, knowledge and reasoning;
I alone am that which is to be known in all the Vedas;
I am the maker of the Vedānta† and the knower of the Vedas.

sarvasya (m. gen. sg.), of all.
ca, and.
aham (nom. sg.), I.
hṛdi (n. loc. sg.), in the heart.
saṁniviṣṭas (m. nom. sg. p. pass. participle *sam ni* √*viś*), entered, seated.
mattas (m. abl. sg.), from me.
smṛtis (f. nom. sg.), memory, knowledge.
jñānam (n. nom. sg.), wisdom, knowledge.
apohanam (n. nom. sg.), reasoning, objection, denial.
ca, and.
vedāis (m. inst. pl.), by the Vedas.
ca, and.
sarvāis (m. inst. pl.), by all, with all.
aham (nom. sg.), I.
eva, alone, indeed (often used as a rhythmic filler).
vedyas (m. nom. sg. gerundive √*vid*), to be known, to be recognized.
vedāntakṛt (m. nom. sg.), Vedānta making, Vedānta maker.
vedavit (m. nom. sg.), Veda knowing.
eva, indeed (used as a rhythmic filler).
ca, and.
aham (nom. sg.), I.

* *Triṣṭubh* metre.

† Vedānta, literally "the end (in the sense of conclusion) of the Veda," the predominant system of religious thought in India, expressed in the *Brahma sūtra* of Bādarāyaṇa and the Upanishads, as well as in the present poem. Its formulation dates from approximately 500 B.C. and it has many points of difference from the Vedas of the original Aryans who invaded India *circa* 1600 B.C. Vedānta means primarily the thought expressed in the Upanishads, and secondarily, a system of philosophy based on it.

16

द्वाव् इमौ पुरुषौ लोके
*dvāv imāu puruṣāu loke**
two, these spirits in the world,

क्षरश्चाक्षर एव च ।
kṣaraścākṣara eva ca
the perishable and the imperishable;

क्षर: सर्वाणि भूतानि
kṣaraḥ sarvāṇi bhūtāni
perishable all beings

कूटस्थो ऽक्षर उच्यते ॥
kūṭastho 'kṣara ucyate
the unchanging, imperishable it is called.

dvāu (m. nom. dual), two.
imāu (m. nom. dual), these two.
puruṣāu (m. nom. dual), two spirits, two entities.
loke (m. loc. sg.), in the world.
kṣaras (m. nom. sg.), perishable, destructible.
ca, and.
akṣaras (m.nom. sg.), imperishable, eternal.
eva, indeed (used as a rhythmic filler).
ca, and.
kṣaras (m. nom. sg.), perishable, destructible.
sarvāṇi (n. nom. pl.), all.
bhūtāni (n. nom. sg.), beings, creatures.
kūṭasthas (m. nom. sg.), unchanging, immovable.
akṣaras (m. nom. sg.), imperishable, eternal.
ucyate (3rd sg. pr. indic. passive √*vac*), it is called, it is said, it is said to be.

There are these two spirits in the world –
The perishable and the imperishable.
Perishable are all beings;
The unchanging is called the imperishable.

* *Śloka* metre resumes.

17

उत्तमः पुरुषस् त्व् अन्यः
uttamaḥ puruṣas tv anyaḥ
the highest spirit, but, other

परमात्मेत्य् उदाहृतः ।
paramātmety udāhṛtaḥ
the Supreme Self thus called

यो लोकत्रयम् आविश्य
yo lokatrayam āviśya
who, the three worlds entering,

बिभर्त्य् अव्यय ईश्वरः ॥
bibharty avyaya īśvaraḥ
he supports, the Eternal Lord.

But the highest spirit is another,
Called the Supreme Self,
Who, entering the three worlds as the Eternal Lord,
Supports them.

uttamas (m. nom. sg.), highest, higher.
puruṣas (m. nom. sg.), spirit, man, being.
tu, but.
anyas (m. nom. sg.), other.
paramātmā (m. nom. sg.), Supreme Self, Supreme Being.
iti, thus.
udāhṛtas (m. nom. sg. p. pass. participle *ud ā* √*hṛ*), called, named.
yas (m. nom. sg.), who, which.
lokatrayam (m. acc. sg.), the three worlds.
āviśya (gerund *ā* √*viś*), entering, approaching, taking possession of.
bibharti (3rd sg. pr. indic. act. √*bhṛ*), he supports, he bears.
avyayas (m. nom. sg.), eternal, imperishable.
īśvaras (m. nom. sg.), Lord, God.

18

यस्मात् क्षरम् अतीतो ऽहम्
yasmāt kṣaram atīto 'ham
since the perishable transcending I,

अक्षराद् अपि चोत्तमः ।
akṣarād api cottamaḥ
and than the imperishable also higher,

अतो ऽस्मि लोके वेदे च
ato 'smi loke vede ca
therefore I am, in the world and in the Veda,

प्रथितः पुरुषोत्तमः ॥
prathitaḥ puruṣottamaḥ
celebrated as the Supreme Spirit.

Since I transcend the perishable
And am higher than the imperishable,
Therefore I am, in the world, and in the Veda,
Celebrated as the Supreme Spirit.

yasmāt (m. abl. sg.), from which, inasmuch, as, since.
kṣaram (m. acc. sg.), perishable, destructible.
atītas (m. nom. sg. p. pass. participle *ati* √*i*), going beyond, gone beyond, transcending, transcended.
aham (nom. sg.), I.
akṣarāt (m. abl. sg.), than the imperishable, than the eternal.
api, even, also.
ca, and.
uttamas (m. nom. sg.), higher, highest.
atas, from this, therefore.
asmi (1st sg. pr. √*as*), I am.
loke (m. loc. sg.), in the world.
vede (m. loc. sg.), in the Veda.
ca, and.
prathitas (m. nom. sg. p. pass. participle √*prath*), celebrated as, known as.
puruṣa (m.), spirit.
uttamas (m. nom. sg.), highest, supreme.
(*puruṣottamas,* m. nom. sg., Supreme Spirit.)

19

यो माम् एवम् असंमूढो
yo mām evam asaṁmūḍho
who me thus undeluded

जानाति पुरुषोत्तमम् ।
jānāti puruṣottamam
he knows (as) the Supreme Spirit,

स सर्वविद् भजति मां
sa sarvavid bhajati māṁ
he, all knowing, worships me

सर्वभावेन भारत ॥
sarvabhāvena bhārata
with whole being, Descendant of Bharata.

yas (m. nom. sg.), who, which.
mām (acc. sg.), me.
evam, thus.
asaṁmūḍhas (m. nom. sg. p. pass. participle *a sam* √*muh*), undeluded, unconfused.
jānāti (3rd sg. pr. indic. act. √*jñā*), he knows.
puruṣottamam (m. acc. sg.), Supreme Spirit.
sas (m. nom. sg.), he, this.
sarvavit (m. nom. sg.), all-knowing, omniscient, omni cognizant.
bhajati (3rd sg. pr. indic. act. √*bhaj*), he worships, he loves.
mām (acc. sg.), me.
sarvabhāvena (m. inst. sg.), with all being, with whole being, with entire being.
bhārata (m. voc. sg.), O Descendant of Bharata, epithet of Arjuna.

He who, thus undeluded, knows Me
As the Supreme Spirit,
He, all-knowing, worships Me
With his whole being, Descendant of Bharata.

20

इति गुह्यतमं शास्त्रम्
iti guhyatamaṁ śāstram
thus most secret doctrine

इदम् उक्तं मया ऽनघ ।
idam uktaṁ mayā 'nagha
this declared by me, O Blameless One,

एतद् बद्ध्वा बुद्धिमान् स्यात्
etad buddhvā buddhimān syāt
(to) this having awakened, enlightened one should be,

कृतकृत्यश्च भारत ॥
kṛtakṛtyaśca bhārata
and fulfilled all duties, Descendant of Bharata.

iti, thus, so.
guhyatamam (n. nom. sg. superl.), most secret.
śāstram (n. nom. sg.), doctrine, teaching, treatise.
idam (n. nom. sg.), this.
uktam (n. nom. sg. p. pass. participle √*vac*), declared, proclaimed, explained.
mayā (inst. sg.), by me.
anagha (m. voc. sg.), O Blameless One, epithet of Arjuna.
etad (n. acc. sg.), this.
buddhvā (gerund √*budh*), knowing, having known, awakened, having awakened.
buddhimān (m. nom. sg.), wise, enlightened.
syāt (3rd sg. optative act. √*as*), he should be, one should be.
kṛtakṛtyas (m. nom. sg.), with all duties fulfilled.
ca, and.
bhārata (m. voc. sg.), Descendant of Bharata, epithet of Arjuna.

Thus this most secret doctrine
Is declared by Me, O Blameless One;
Having awakened to this, one should be enlightened,
With all duties fulfilled, Descendant of Bharata.

End of Book XV

The Yoga of the Supreme Spirit

BOOK XVI

श्रीभगवान् उवाच ।
śrībhagavān uvāca
the Blessed Lord spoke:

śrībhagavān (m. nom. sg.), the Blessed Lord, the Blessed One.
uvāca (3rd sg. perfect act. √*vac*), he said, he spoke.

1

अभयं सत्त्वसंशुद्धिर्
abhayaṁ sattvasaṁśuddhir
fearlessness, purity of being,

ज्ञानयोगव्यवस्थितिः ।
jñānayogavyavasthitiḥ
knowledge-Yoga persevering in,

दानं दमश्च यज्ञश्च
dānaṁ damaśca yajñaśca
giving and self restraint and sacrifice,

स्वाध्यायस् तप आर्जवम् ॥
svādhyāyas tapa ārjavam
reciting sacred texts to oneself, austerity, rectitude,

The Blessed Lord spoke:

Fearlessness, purity of being,
Perseverence in the Yoga of knowledge,
Giving, self-restraint and sacrifice,
Reciting sacred texts to oneself, austerity, rectitude,

abhayam (n. nom. sg.), fearlessness, absence of fear.
sattvasaṁśuddhis (f. nom. sg.), purity of being, purity of heart.
jñānayoga (m.), knowledge-Yoga, the Yoga of knowledge.
vyavasthitis (f. nom. sg. from *vi ava* √*sthā*), persevering in, directed towards, staying with, abiding in.
(*jñāna-yoga-vyavasthitis*, f. nom. sg. TP cpd., abiding in jñāna-yoga.)
dānam (n. nom. sg.), giving, charity.
damas (m. nom. sg.), self-control, restraint, taming, domination.
ca, and.
yajñas (m. nom. sg.), sacrifice, worship.
ca, and.
svādhyāyas (m. nom. sg.), repeating to oneself, reciting sacred texts to oneself, Vedic recitation.
tapas (n. nom. sg.), austerity, self-denial, heat.
ārjavam (n. nom. sg.), rectitude, righteousness.

2

अहिंसा सत्यम् अक्रोधस्
ahiṁsā satyam akrodhas
non-violence, veracity, absence of anger,

त्यागः शान्तिर् अपैशुनम् ।
tyāgaḥ śāntir apāiśunam
renunciation, serenity, non-calumny,

दया भूतेषु अलोलुप्त्वं
dayā bhūteṣv aloluptvaṁ
compassion for beings, freedom from desire,

मार्दवं ह्रीर् अचापलम् ॥
mārdavaṁ hrīr acāpalam
gentleness, modesty, absence of fickleness,

Non-violence, veracity, absence of anger,
Renunciation, serenity, absence of calumny,
Compassion for all beings, freedom from desire,
Gentleness, modesty, absence of fickleness,

ahiṁsā (f. nom. sg.), non-violence, harmlessness.
satyam (n. nom. sg.), veracity, truth telling.
akrodhas (m. nom. sg.), absence of anger, absence of wrath.
tyāgas (m. nom. sg.), renunciation, abandonment.
śāntis (f. nom. sg.), peace, serenity, tranquility.
apāiśunam (n. nom. sg.), absence of calumny, non-slanderousness.
dayā, (f. nom. sg.), compassion, pity.
bhūteṣu (n. loc. pl.), in beings, for beings, for creatures.
aloluptvam (n. nom. sg.), freedom from desire, freedom from lust.
mārdavam (n. nom. sg.), gentleness, kindness.
hrīs (f. nom. sg.), modesty, timidity, shyness.
acāpalam (n. nom. sg.), discretion, absence of fickleness, steadiness

3

तेजः क्षमा धृतिः शौचम्
tejaḥ kṣamā dhṛtiḥ śāucam
vigor, patience, fortitude, purity,

अद्रोहो नातिमानिता ।
adroho nātimānitā
freedom from malice, not excessive pride,

भवन्ति संपदं दैवीम्
bhavanti saṁpadaṁ dāivīm
they are the endowment to the divine destiny

अभिजातस्य भारत ॥
abhijātasya bhārata
of the born, Descendant of Bharata.

tejas (n. nom. sg.), vigor, splendor, power.
kṣamā (f. nom. sg.), patience, forbearance.
dhṛtis (f. nom. sg.), fortitude, courage, strength.
śāucam (n. nom. sg.), purity, cleanliness of mind and body.
adrohas (m. nom. sg.), freedom from malice, absence of hatred.
na, not.
atimānitā (f. nom. sg.), excessive pride, high honor.
bhavanti (3rd pl. pr. indic. act. √*bhū*), they are.
saṁpadam (f. acc. sg.), endowment, acquisition, requisite, condition, destiny.
dāivīm (f. acc. sg.), divine, to the divine.
abhijātasya (n. gen. sg.), of the born.
bhārata (m. voc. sg.), Descendant of Bharata, epithet of Arjuna.

Vigor, patience, fortitude, purity,
Freedom from malice, freedom from excessive pride;
They are the endowment of those
Born to the divine destiny, Descendant of Bharata.

4

दम्भो दर्पो ऽभिमानश्च
dambho darpo 'bhimānaśca
hypocrisy, arrogance, and conceit,

क्रोधः पारुष्यम् एव च ।
krodhaḥ pāruṣyam eva ca
anger and harshness (of language) too,

अज्ञानं चाभिजातस्य
ajñānaṁ cābhijātasya
and ignorance of the born,

पार्थ संपदम् आसुरीम् ॥
pārtha saṁpadam āsurīm
Son of Pṛthā, endowment, to the demonic destiny.

dambhas (m. nom. sg.), hypocrisy, fraud.
darpas (m. nom. sg.), arrogance, insolence.
abhimānas (m. nom. sg.), conceit, haughtiness, hostility.
ca, and.
krodhas (m. nom. sg.), anger, wrath.
pāruṣyam (n. nom. sg.), harshness, roughness (esp. of language).
eva, indeed (used as a rhythmic filler).
ca, and.
ajñānam (n. nom. sg.), ignorance, lack of knowledge.
ca, and.
abhijātasya (n. gen. sg.), of the well-born, of the born.
pārtha (m. voc. sg.), Son of Pṛthā, epithet of Arjuna.
saṁpadam (f. acc. sg.), endowment, condition, quality, destiny.
āsurīm (f. acc. sg.), the demonic, to the demonic.

Hypocrisy, arrogance, excessive pride,
Anger and harshness of language too,
And ignorance, are the endowment of those born
To the demonic destiny, Son of Pṛthā.

5

दैवी संपद् विमोक्षाय
dāivī sampad vimokṣāya
the divine destiny (leads) to liberation;

निबन्धायासुरी मता ।
nibandhāyāsurī matā
to bondage the demonic thought to be.

मा शुचः संपदं दैवीम्
mā śucaḥ sampadam dāivīm
do not grieve! to the endowment divine

अभिजातो ऽसि पाण्डव ॥
abhijāto 'si pāṇḍava
born thou art, Son of Pāṇḍu.

The divine destiny leads to liberation;
To bondage the demonic, it is thought.
Do not grieve! To the divine destiny
Thou art born, Son of Pāṇḍu.

dāivī (f. nom. sg.), divine, heavenly.
sampad (f. nom. sg.), endowment, characteristic, quality, destiny.
vimokṣāya (m. dat. sg.), to liberation, to release.
nibandhāya (m. dat. sg.), to bondage.
āsurī (f. nom. sg.), demonic, pertaining to demons.
matā (f. nom. sg. p. pass. participle √*man*), thought, thought to be, it is thought.
mā, do not, never.
śucas (2nd sg. aorist subjunctive √*śuc*), grieve, thou grievest, thou sorrowest.
(*mā śucas*, 2nd sg. aorist subjunctive √*śuc*, do not grieve, do not sorrow.)
sampadam (f. acc. sg.), endowment, characteristic, quality.
dāivīm (f. acc. sg.), divine, heavenly.
abhijātas (n. nom. sg. p. pass. participle *abhi* √*jan*), born, well-born.
asi (2nd sg. √*as*), thou art.
pāṇḍava (m. voc. sg.), Son of Pāṇḍu, epithet of Arjuna.

6

द्वौ भूतसर्गौ लोकेऽस्मिन्
dvāu bhūtasargāu loke 'smin
two being-creations in world this

दैव आसुर एव च ।
dāiva āsura eva ca
the divine and the demonic.

दैवो विस्तरशः प्रोक्त
dāivo vistaraśaḥ prokta
the divine at length (has already been) explained.

आसुरं पार्थ मे शृणु ॥
āsuraṁ pārtha me śṛṇu
the demonic, Son of Pṛthā, from me hear.

dvāu (m. nom. dual.), two.
bhūtasargāu (m. nom. dual), two being-creations, two classes of created being.
loke (m. loc. sg.), in the world.
asmin (m. loc. sg.), in this.
dāivas (m. nom. sg.), divine, heavenly.
āsuras (m. nom. sg.), demonic, pertaining, to demons.
eva, indeed (used as a rhythmic filler).
ca, and.
dāivas (m. nom. sg.), divine, heavenly.
vistaraśas (adv.), at length, in detail.
proktas (m. nom. sg. p. pass. participle *pra* √*vac*), declared, explained.
āsuram (m. acc. sg.), demonic, pertaining to demons.
pārtha (m. voc. sg.), Son of Pṛthā, epithet of Arjuna.
me (gen. sg.), of me, from me.
śṛṇu (2nd imperative act. √*śru*), hear!

There are two classes of created beings in this world –
The divine and the demonic.
The divine has been explained at length;
Now hear from Me, Son of Pṛthā, about the demonic.

7

प्रवृत्तिं च निवृत्तिं च
pravṛttiṁ ca nivṛttiṁ ca
activity and inactivity

जना न विदुर् आसुराः ।
janā na vidur āsurāḥ
men not they know the demonic,

न शौचं नापि चाचारो
na śāucaṁ nāpi cācāro
nor purity nor even good conduct.

न सत्यं तेषु विद्यते ॥
na satyaṁ teṣu vidyate
not truth in them it is found.

When to act and when to refrain from action
Demonic men do not understand,
Nor do they understand purity, or even good conduct.
Truth is not found in them.

pravṛttim (f. acc. sg.), activity, progress.
ca, and.
nivṛttim (f. acc. sg.), inactivity, cessation, leaving off.
ca, and.
janās (m. nom. pl.), men.
na, not.
vidus (3rd pl. perfect act. √*vid* with present meaning), they know, they understand.
āsurās (nom. pl.), the demonic.
na, not, nor.
śāucam (n. nom. sg.), purity, cleanliness of mind and body.
na, not.
api, even.
ca, and.
ācāras (m. nom. sg.), good conduct, good behavior.
na, not.
satyam (n. nom. sg.), truth.
teṣu (m. loc. pl.), in them.
vidyate (3rd sg. pr. passive √2 *vid*), it is found.

8

असत्यम् अप्रतिष्ठं ते
asatyam apratiṣṭhaṁ te
without truth, unstable, they

जगद् आहुर् अनीश्वरम् ।
jagad āhur anīśvaram
"the universe," they say (is) "without a God.

अपरस्परसंभूतं
aparasparasaṁbhūtaṁ
not one by the other (cause) brought into being.

किम् अन्यत् कामहैतुकम् ॥
kim anyat kāmahāitukam
what else? desire-caused."

They are without truth and unstable.
"The universe," they say, "is without a God;
It is not brought into being by a succession of causes.*
How else? It is caused by desire alone."

asatyam (n. nom. sg.), non-truth, untruth, without truth.
apratiṣṭham (n. nom. sg. from *a prati* √*sthā*), unstable, having no solid ground.
te (m. nom. pl.), they.
jagat (n. acc. sg.), universe, world, all that moves.
āhus (3rd pl. perfect act. √*ah* with present meaning), they say, they declare, they maintain.
anīśvaram (m. acc. sg.), without a god, godless.
aparaspara, not one by the other, not by a succession.
saṁbhūtam (m./n. acc. sg.), brought into being, originated, created.
kim anyat, what else? how other?
kāma (m.), desire, lust.
hāitukam (m. acc. sg.), caused, motivated.
(*kāmahāitukam,* m. acc. sg. TP cpd., caused by desire.)

---

* *aparasparasaṁbhūtam* is somethines translated as "brought about by mutual union of man and woman," i.e. by sex, an interpretation favored by some native translators which does explain the fourth line better than the common translation. However, if one accepts this version of the line, the last line becomes redundant. The idea that sexual passion was the cause of all beings was held by the *lokāyatikas*, followers of a *nāstika*, or atheist and anti-orthodox school of philosophy which may be the object of this denunciation.

9

एतां दृष्टिम् अवष्टभ्य
etāṁ dṛṣṭim avaṣṭabhya
this view holding,

नष्टात्मानो ऽल्पबुद्धयः ।
naṣṭātmāno 'lpabuddhayaḥ
(men of) lost selves and (of) small intelligence,

प्रभवन्त्य् उग्रकर्माणः
prabhavanty ugrakarmāṇaḥ
they come forth, cruel actions,

क्षयाय जगतो ऽहिताः ।।
kṣayāya jagato 'hitāḥ
to destruction of the world, enemies.

Holding this view,
Men of lost selves, of small intelligence
And of cruel actions, come forth as enemies,
For the destruction of the world.

etām (f. acc. sg.), this.
dṛṣṭim (f. acc. sg.), view, point of view.
avaṣṭabhya (gerund *ava* √*stabh*), holding, supporting.
naṣṭātmanas (m. nom. pl. BV cpd.), they of lost selves, they who have lost their selves.
alpabuddhayas (m. nom. pl. BV cpd.), of small intelligence, those whose intelligence is small.
prabhavanti (3rd pl. pr. indic. act. *pra* √*bhū*), they come forth, they arise, they come into being.
ugrakarmāṇas (m. nom. pl.), of evil actions, of cruel actions (as BV cpd.), those whose actions are evil.
kṣayāya (m. dat. sg.), to destruction, for destruction.
jagatas (n. gen. sg.), of the world, of the universe, of all that moves.
ahitās (m. nom. pl.), enemies, foes.

10

कामम् आश्रित्य दुष्पूरं
kāmam āśritya duṣpūraṁ
desire attached to, insatiable,

दम्भमानमदान्विताः ।
dambhamānamadānvitāḥ
hypocrisy, arrogance, lust attended by,

मोहाद् गृहीत्वा ऽसद्ग्राहान्
mohād gṛhītvā 'sadgrāhān
from delusion having accepted false notions,

प्रवर्तन्ते ऽशुचिव्रताः ॥
pravartante 'śucivratāḥ
they proceed (with) unclean purposes,

Attached to insatiable desire,
Attended by hypocrisy, arrogance and lust,
Having accepted false notions through delusion,
They proceed with unclean vows,

kāmam (m. acc. sg.), desire, lust.
āśritya (gerund *ā* √*śri*), attaching to, adhering to, attached to, depending on.
duṣpūram (m. acc. sg.), "difficult to fill," insatiable, voracious.
dambha (m.), hypocrisy, fraud.
māna (m.), arrogance, pride.
mada (m.), lust, intoxication, hilarity, drunkenness.
anvitas (m. nom. pl. p. pass. participle *anu* √*i*), attended by, accompanying.
(*dambhamānamadānvitās*, m. nom. pl. TP cpd., attended by hypocrisy, arrogance and lust.)
mohāt (m. abl. sg.), from delusion, from confusion.
gṛhītvā (gerund √*grah*), accepting, having accepted, grasping, having grasped.
asat (pr. participle *a* √*as*), untrue, unreal, false.
grāhān (m. acc. pl.), conceptions, ideas, notions.
(*asat-grāhān*, m. acc. pl. KD cpd., false notions.)
pravartante (3rd pl. pr. indic. mid. *pra* √*vṛt*), they proceed, they act.
aśuci (m.), unclean, impure.
vratās (n./m. nom. pl.), vows, purposes, rules, customs.
(*aśuci-vratās*, m. nom. pl. KD cpd., unclean vows.)

11

चिन्ताम् अपरिमेयां च
cintām aparimeyāṁ ca
and of anxiety immeasurable

प्रलयान्ताम् उपाश्रिताः ।
pralayāntām upāśritāḥ
in death ending clinging,

कामोपभोगपरमा
kāmopabhogaparamā
desire gratification highest aim,

एतावद् इति निश्चिताः ॥
etāvad iti niścitāḥ
so much, thus convinced;

And clinging to immeasurable
Anxiety, ending only in death,
With gratification of desire as their highest aim,
Convinced that this is all;

cintām (f. acc. sg.), thought, care, anxiety.
aparimeyām (f. acc. sg.), beyond measure, immeasurable.
ca, and.
pralayāntām (f. acc. sg. noun from *pra* √*lī* + *antām*), ending in death, dissolution and death, dissolution and end.
upāśritās (m. nom. pl. p. pass. participle *upa ā* √*śri*), clinging, adhering to.
kāma (m.), desire, lust.
upabhoga (m.), gratification, enjoyment.
paramās (m. nom. pl.), highest aim, holding as highest object.
(*kāmopabhogaparamās,* m. nom. pl. BV cpd., holding gratification of desire as highest aim [pl. refers to "those of lost selves," stanza 9].)
etāvat, so much.
iti, thus.
niścitās (m. nom. pl.), convinced, having no doubt.

12

आशापाशशतैर् बद्धाः
āśāpāśaśatāir baddhāḥ
by hope-snare a hundred bound

कामक्रोधपरायणाः ।
kāmakrodhaparāyaṇāḥ
desire and anger devoted to,

ईहन्ते कामभोगार्थम्
īhante kāmabhogārtham
they seek, desire-gratification-aim,

अन्यायेनार्थसंचयान् ॥
anyāyenārthasaṁcayān
by unjust means, hoards (of wealth).

Bound by a hundred snares of hope,
Devoted to desire and anger,
They seek, by unjust means,
Hoards of wealth for the gratification of their desires.

āśāpāśa (m.), hope-snare, trap of hope.
śatāis (m. inst. pl.), by a hundred.
(*āśāpāśa-śatāis*, m. instr. pl. TP cpd., a hundred (of) hope-snares.)
baddhās (m. nom. pl. p. pass. participle √*bandh*), bound, fettered.
kāma (m.), desire, lust.
krodha (m.), anger, wrath.
parāyaṇās (m. nom. pl. ifc.), devoted to, holding as highest aim.
(*kāmakrodhaparāyaṇās,* m. nom. pl. BV cpd., devoted to desire and anger.)
īhante (3rd pl. pr. indic. mid. √*īh*), they seek, they wish for.
kāmabhogārtham (m. acc. sg.), aim of the gratification of desire, desire-gratification goal.
anyāyena (m. inst. sg.), by other than proper, by unjust, by erroneous.
artha (m.), means, method, aim, object, wealth.
saṁcayān (m. acc. pl.), hoards, accumulations, quantities.
(*artha-saṁcayān*, m. acc. pl. TP cpd., hoards of wealth.)

13

इदम् अद्य मया लब्धम्
idam adya mayā labdham
"this today by me obtained,

इदं प्राप्स्ये मनोरथम् ।
idaṁ prāpsye manoratham
this I shall attain wish,

इदम् अस्तीदम् अपि मे
idam astīdam api me
this it is, this also mine

भविष्यति पुनर् धनम् ॥
bhaviṣyati punar dhanam
it shall be, again, wealth;

**"This has been obtained by me today;
This wish I shall attain;
This is, and this wealth also,
Shall be mine;**

idam (n. nom. sg.), this.
adya, today.
mayā (inst. sg.), by me.
labdham (n. nom. sg. p. pass. participle √*labh*), obtained, acquired.
imam (m. acc. sg.), this.
prāpsye (1st sg. mid. fut. *pra* √*āp*), I shall get, I shall obtain, I shall attain.
manoratham (m. acc. sg.), lit. "chariot of the mind," wish, desire.
idam (n. nom. sg.), this.
asti (3rd sg. pr. indic. √*as*), it is.
idam (n. nom. sg.), this.
api, also, even.
me (gen. sg.), of me, mine, my.
bhaviṣyati (3rd sg. fut. act. √*bhū*), it shall be, it shall become.
punar, again, also.
dhanam (n. nom. sg.), wealth, property, booty.

14

असौ मया हतः शत्रुर्
asāu mayā hataḥ śatrur
"that by me slain enemy

हनिष्ये चापरान् अपि ।
haniṣye cāparān api
and I shall slay others also,

ईश्वरो ऽहम् अहं भोगी
īśvaro 'ham ahaṁ bhogī
the Lord I, I the enjoyer,

सिद्धो ऽहं बलवान् सुखी ॥
siddho 'haṁ balavān sukhī
successful I, powerful, happy,

"That enemy has been slain by me,
And I shall slay others too;
I am the Lord, I am the enjoyer,
I am successful, powerful, happy,

asāu (m. nom. sg.), that, yonder.
mayā (m. inst. sg.), by me.
hatas (m. nom. sg. p. pass. participle √*han*), slain, killed.
śatrus (m. nom. sg.), enemy, foe.
haniṣye (1st sg. fut. mid. √*han*), I shall slay, I shall kill.
ca, and.
aparān (m. acc. pl.), others.
api, also, even.
īśvaras (m. nom. sg.), lord, God.
aham (nom. sg.), I.
aham (nom. sg.), I.
bhogī (m. nom. sg.), enjoyer, eater.
siddhas (m. nom. sg.), successful, accomplished, fulfilled.
aham (nom. sg.), I.
balavān (m. nom. sg.), powerful, mighty.
suhkī (m. nom. sg.), happy, blissful.

15

आढ्यो ऽभिजनवान् अस्मि
āḍhyo 'bhijanavān asmi
"wealthy, high-born I am.

को ऽन्यो ऽस्ति सदृशो मया ।
ko 'nyo 'sti sadṛśo mayā
what other there is such as me?

यक्ष्ये दास्यामि मोदिष्य
yakṣye dāsyāmi modiṣya
I shall sacrifice, I shall give, I shall rejoice."

इत्य् अज्ञानविमोहिताः ॥
ity ajñānavimohitāḥ
thus those who are deluded by ignorance.

"I am wealthy, high born.
What other is there such as me?
I shall sacrifice, I shall give, I shall rejoice."
Thus, those who are deluded by ignorance.

āḍhyas (m. nom. sg.), wealthy, opulent.
abhijanavān (m. nom. sg.), high born, aristocratic.
asmi (1st sg. pr. indic. √*as*), I am.
kas (m. nom. sg.), what? who?
anyas (m. nom. sg.), other.
asti (3rd sg. pr. indic. √*as*), there is, he is, it is.
sadṛśas (m. nom. sg.), like, resembling, such as.
mayā (m. inst. sg.), me, by me.
yakṣye (1st. sg. mid. fut. √*yaj*), I shall sacrifice, I shall worship.
dāsyāmi (1st sg. act. fut. √*dā*), I shall give, I shall be charitable.
modiṣya (*saṁdhi* for *modiṣye*, 1st sg. mid. fut. √*mud*), I shall rejoice, I shall be merry.
iti, thus (often used to close a quotation).
ajñāna (n.), ignorance.
vimohitās (m. nom. pl. p. pass. participle *vi* √*muh*), the deluded, those who are deluded.
(*ajñānavimohitās*, m. nom. pl. TP cpd., those who are deluded by ignorance.)

16

अनेकचित्तविभ्रान्ता
anekacittavibhrāntā
not one imagining led astray

मोहजालसमावृताः।
mohajālasamāvṛtāḥ
delusion net enveloped,

प्रसक्ताः कामभोगेषु
prasaktāḥ kāmabhogeṣu
attached to desire gratifications,

पतन्ति नरके ऽशुचौ ॥
patanti narake 'śucāu
they fall into hell, unclean.

Led astray by many imaginings,
Enveloped in a net of delusion,
Attached to the gratification of desires,
They fall into an unclean hell.

aneka, not one, i.e. many.
citta (n.), thought, imagining.
vibhrāntās (m. nom. pl. p. pass. participle *vi* √*bhram*), led astray, carried away, wandering away.
(*anekacittavibhrāntās*, m. nom. pl. TP cpd., led astray by many imaginings.)
mohajāla (n.), net of delusion, trap of delusion.
samāvṛtās (m. nom. pl. p. pass. participle *sam ā* √*vṛ*), enveloped, covered.
(*mohajālasamāvṛtās*, m. nom. pl. TP cpd., enveloped in a net of delusion.)
prasaktās (m. nom. pl. p. pass. participle *pra* √*sañj*), attached, clinging.
kāmabhogeṣu (m. loc. pl.), in desire-gratifications, to the gratification of desire.
patanti (3rd sg. pr. indic. act. √*pat*), they fall.
narake (m. loc. sg.), into hell.
aśucāu (m. loc. sg.), unclean, impure.

17

आत्मसंभाविताः स्तब्धा
ātmasaṁbhāvitāḥ stabdhā
self conceited, stubborn,

धनमानमदान्विताः ।
dhanamānamadānvitāḥ
wealth-pride-arrogance accompanied by,

यजन्ते नामयज्ञैस् ते
yajante nāmayajñāis te
they sacrifice with only-in-name sacrifice, they,

दम्भेनाविधिपूर्वकम् ॥
dambhenāvidhipūrvakam
with hypocrisy, not according to (Vedic) injunction.

Self-conceited, stubborn,
Accompanied by the pride and arrogance of wealth,
They sacrifice with sacrifices that are sacrifices only in name,
With hypocrisy, and not according to Vedic injunction.

ātmasaṁbhāvitās (m. nom. pl. p. pass. participle *ātma sam* √*bhū*), self conceited, self-centered.

stabdhās (m. nom. pl. p. pass. participle √*stambh*), stubborn, obstinate, immovable.

dhana (n.), wealth, booty.

māna (m. n.), pride, conceit.

mada (m.), intoxication, lust, arrogance.

anvitās (m. nom. pl. p. pass. participle *anu* √*i*), accompanied by, attended by.

(*dhanamānamadānvitas,* m. nom. pl. TP cpd., accompanied by the pride and arrogance of wealth.)

yajante (3rd pl. pr. indic. mid. √*yaj*), they sacrifice, they worship.

nāmayajñāis (m. inst. pl.), with sacrifices only in name, with nominal sacrifices.

te (m. nom. pl.), they.

dambhena (m. inst. sg.), with hypocrisy, with fraud.

avidhipūrvakam (adv.), not according to rule, not according to Vedic injunction.

18

अहंकारं बलं दर्पं
ahaṁkāraṁ balaṁ darpaṁ
egotism, force, insolence,

कामं क्रोधं च संश्रिताः ।
kāmaṁ krodhaṁ ca saṁśritāḥ
desire and anger clinging to

माम् आत्मपरदेहेषु
mām ātmaparadeheṣu
me in (their) own and others' bodies

प्रद्विषन्तो ऽभ्यसूयकाः ॥
pradviṣanto 'bhyasūyakāḥ
hating, the envious ones.

Clinging to egotism, force, insolence,
Desire and anger,
Those who are envious hate Me
In their own and others' bodies.

ahaṁkāram (m. acc. sg.), egotism "I making."
balam (n. acc. sg.), force, might.
darpam (m. acc. sg.), insolence, haughtiness, arrogance.
kāmam (m. acc. sg.), desire, lust.
krodham (m. acc. sg.), anger, wrath.
ca, and.
saṁśritās (m. nom. pl. p. pass. participle *sam* √*śri*) clinging to, attached to.
mām (acc. sg.), me.
ātmaparadeheṣu (m./n. loc. pl.), in own and others' bodies.
pradviṣantas (m. nom. pl. pr. participle act. *pra* √*dviṣ*), hating, loathing.
abhyasūyakās (m. nom. pl.), the envious, the indignant, those who are envious, those who grumble.

19

तान् अहं द्विषतः क्रूरान्
tān aham̐ dviṣataḥ krūrān
them I the hating, the cruel,

संसारेषु नराधमान् ।
sam̐sāreṣu narādhamān
in the cycles of rebirth, men vile,

क्षिपाम्य् अजस्रम् अशुभान्
kṣipāmy ajasram aśubhān
I hurl constantly, the vicious,

आसुरीष्व् एव योनिषु ॥
āsurīṣv eva yoniṣu
into demonic wombs.

tān (m. acc. pl.), them.
aham (nom. sg.), I.
dviṣatas (m. acc. pl. pr. participle act. √*dviṣ*), the hating, those who hate.
krūrān (m. acc. pl.), the ferocious, those who are cruel.
samsāreṣu (m. loc. pl.), in the cycles of rebirth, into the cycles of reincarnation.
narādhamān (m. acc. pl.), vile men, wretches.
kṣipāmi (1st. sg. pr. indic. act. √*kṣip*), I hurl, I throw.
ajasram (adv.), perpetually, always.
aśubhān (m. acc. pl.), the vicious, the unclean, the unpurified.
āsurīṣu (f. loc. pl.), into demonic.
eva, indeed (used as a rhythmic filler).
yoniṣu (f. loc. pl.), into wombs, in wombs.
(*āsuriṣu yoniṣu*, f. loc. pl., into demonic wombs, into the wombs of demons.)

Them, the hating, the cruel, the vile
And vicious men, I constantly hurl
In the cycles of rebirth,
Into the wombs of demons.

20

आसुरीं योनिम् आपन्ना
āsurīṁ yonim āpannā
demonic womb entering

मूढा जन्मनि जन्मनि ।
mūḍhā janmani janmani
the deluded in birth in birth

माम् अप्राप्यैव कौन्तेय
mām aprāpyāiva kāunteya
me not attaining, Son of Kuntī,

ततो यान्त्य् अधमां गतिम् ॥
tato yānty adhamāṁ gatim
from there they go to the lowest goal.

āsurīm (f. acc. sg.), demonic pertaining to demons.
yonim (f. acc. sg.), womb.
āpannās (m. nom. pl. p. pass. participle *ā* √*pad*), entering, approaching.
mūḍhās (m. nom. pl. p. pass. participle √*muh*), the deluded, those who are deluded.
janmani janmani (n. loc. sg.), in birth after birth.
mām (acc. sg.), me.
aprāpya (gerund *a pra* √*āp*), not attaining, not reaching to.
eva, indeed (used as a rhythmic filler).
kāunteya (m. voc. sg.), Son of Kuntī, epithet of Arjuna.
tatas, then, from there.
yānti (3rd pl. pr. indic. act. √*yā*), they go.
adhāmam (f. acc. sg. superl.), lowest, worst.
gatim (f. acc. sg.), goal, path.

Having entered the wombs of demons,
Those who are deluded, not attaining Me
In birth after birth, Son of Kuntī,
From there go to the lowest goal.

21

त्रिविधं नरकस्येदं
trividhaṁ narakasyedaṁ
threefold of hell this

द्वारं नाशनम् आत्मनः ।
dvāraṁ nāśanam ātmanaḥ
the gate, destructive of the self,

कामः क्रोधस् तथा लोभस्
kāmaḥ krodhas tathā lobhas
desire, anger and also greed,

तस्माद् एतत् त्रयं त्यजेत् ॥
tasmād etat trayaṁ tyajet
therefore this triad one should abandon.

**This is the threefold gate of hell,
Destructive of the self:
Desire, anger and greed.
Therefore one should abandon this triad.**

trividham (n. nom. sg.), threefold, of three kinds.
narakasya (m. gen. sg.), of hell.
idam (n. nom. sg.), this.
dvāram (n. nom. sg.), gate, door.
nāśanam (n. nom. sg.), destructive, destroying.
ātmanas (m. gen. sg.), of the self.
kāmas (m. nom. sg.), desire, greed, love.
krodhas (m. nom. sg.), anger, wrath.
tathā, thus, also.
lobhas (m. nom. sg.), greed, covetousness, cupidity.
tasmāt (m. abl. sg.), from this, therefore.
etad (n. acc. sg.), this.
trayam (n. acc. sg.), triad, group of three.
tyajet (3rd sg. opt. act. √*tyaj*), one should abandon, he should renounce.

22

एतैर् विमुक्तः कौन्तेय
etāir vimuktaḥ kāunteya
by these released, Son of Kuntī,

तमोद्वारैस् त्रिभिर् नरः ।
tamodvārāis tribhir naraḥ
by tamas gates three, a man

आचरत्य् आत्मनः श्रेयस्
ācaraty ātmanaḥ śreyas
does for the self best

ततो याति परां गतिम् ॥
tato yāti parāṁ gatim
then he goes to the highest goal.

etāis (m. inst. pl.), by these.
vimuktas (m. nom. sg. p. pass. participle *vi* √*muc*), released, liberated.
kāunteya (m. voc. sg.), Son of Kuntī, epithet of Arjuna.
tamodvārāis (n. inst. pl.), by tamas gates, by doors of tamas.
tribhis (n. inst. pl.), by three.
naras (m. nom. sg.), man, a man.
ācarati (3rd sg. pr. indic. act. *ā* √*car*), he does, he moves, he behaves.
ātmanas (m. gen. sg.), of the self, for the self.
śreyas (m. nom. sg. superl.), best.
tatas, then, from there, thereupon.
yāti (3rd sg. pr. indic. act. √*yā*), he goes, he proceeds.
parām (f. acc. sg.), highest, supreme.
gatim (f. acc. sg.), goal, path.

Released from these three gates of tamas,
Son of Kuntī,
A man does what is best for himself.
Then he goes to the highest goal.

23

य: शास्त्रविधिम् उत्सृज्य
yaḥ śāstravidhim utsṛjya
who, scripture injunction casting aside,

वर्तते कामकारत: ।
vartate kāmakārataḥ
he follows (his own) inclinations

न स सिद्धिम् अवाप्नोति
na sa siddhim avāpnoti
not he to perfection attains

न सुखं न परां गतिम् ।।
na sukhaṁ na parāṁ gatim
nor to happiness nor to the highest goal.

He who follows his own inclinations,
Casting aside the injunctions of scripture,
Does not attain to perfection
Nor to happiness nor to the highest goal.

yas (m. nom. sg.), who.
śāstravidhim (m. acc. sg.), scripture knowledge, scripture injunction.
utsṛjya (gerund *ud* √*sṛj*), casting aside, letting go, ignoring.
vartate (3rd sg. pr. indic. mid. √*vṛt*), he follows, he turns.
kāmakāratas (m. abl. sg.), according to inclination, "from desire-making," according to own desire.
na, not.
sas (m. nom. sg.), he, this one.
siddhim (f. acc. sg.), perfection, to perfection, to success.
avāpnoti (3rd sg. pr. indic. act. *ava* √*āp*), he attains, he reaches.
na, nor, not.
sukham (n. acc. sg.), happiness, bliss, to happiness.
na, not, nor.
parām (f. acc. sg.), highest, supreme.
gatim (f. acc. sg.), goal, path.

24

तस्माच् छास्त्रं प्रमाणं ते
tasmāc chāstraṁ pramāṇaṁ te
therefore scripture standard of thee

कार्याकार्यव्यवस्थितौ ।
kāryākāryavyavasthitāu
the to-be-done and the not-to-be-done determining,

ज्ञात्वा शास्त्रविधानोक्तं
jñātvā śāstravidhānoktaṁ
knowing the scripture injunction prescribed,

कर्म कर्तुम् इहार्हसि ॥
karma kartum ihārhasi
action to perform here in this world thou shouldst.

Therefore, determining thy standard by scripture,
As to what is and what is not to be done,
Knowing the scripture injunction prescribed,
Thou shouldst perform action here in this world.

tasmāt (m. abl. sg.), from this, therefore.
śāstram (n. nom. sg.), scripture, sacred writing.
pramāṇam (n. nom. sg.), standard, measure.
te (gen. sg.), of thee.
kārya (gerundive √*kṛ*), to be done, duty.
akārya (gerundive *a* √*kṛ*), not to be done.
vyavasthitāu (m. acc. dual p. pass. participle *vi ava* √*sthā*), determining, adhering to, established, settled, establishing.
(*kārya-akārya-vyavasthitau*, m. acc. dual. TP cpd., the 2 determinations of what is to be done and what is not to be done.)
jñātvā (gerund √*jñā*), knowing, having known.
śāstravidhāna (n.), scripture knowledge, scripture injunction.
uktam (n. acc. sg. p. pass. participle √*vac*), said, declared, prescribed.
(*śāstra-vidhāna-uktam*, n. acc. sg. TP cpd., declared by scriptural injunction.)
karma (n. acc. sg.), action, work.
kartum (infinitive √*kṛ*), to do, to perform, to make.
iha, here, here in the world.
arhasi (2nd sg. pr. indic. act. √*arh*), thou shouldst, thou art obliged, thou deservest, thou art able.

End of Book XVI

The Yoga of the Distinction between
the Divine and the Demonic Destinies

BOOK XVII

अर्जुन उवाच।
arjuna uvāca
Arjuna spoke:

arjunas (m. nom. sg.), Arjuna.
uvāca (3rd sg. perf. act. √*vac*), he said, he spoke.

1

ये शास्त्रविधिम् उत्सृज्य
ye śāstravidhim utsṛjya
who, scripture injunction casting aside,

यजन्ते श्रद्धयान्विताः।
yajante śraddhayānvitāḥ
they sacrifice, faith filled with,

तेषां निष्ठा तु का कृष्ण
teṣāṁ niṣṭhā tu kā kṛṣṇa
of them the standing, indeed, what Krishna?

सत्त्वम् आहो रजस् तमः॥
sattvam āho rajas tamaḥ
sattva, which? rajas, tamas?

Arjuna spoke:

Those who sacrifice
Casting the injunctions of scripture aside, but filled with faith,
What is their standing, Krishna?
Is it sattva, rajas or tamas?

ye (m. nom. pl.), who, they who.
śāstravidhim (m. acc. sg.), scripture injunction, rule of Vedic scripture.
utsṛjya (gerund *ud* √*sṛj*), casting aside, throwing away.
yajante (3rd pl. pr. indic. mid. √*yaj*), they sacrifice, they worship.
śraddhayānvitās (m. nom. pl.), full of faith, accompanied by faith.
teṣām (m. gen. pl.), of these, of them.
niṣṭhā (f. nom. sg.), standing, position.
tu, indeed, but.
kā (f. nom. sg. interrog.), what?
kṛṣṇa (m. voc. sg.), Krishna.
sattvam (n. nom. sg.), sattva, truth, virtue.
āho (interrog. particle), is it so?
rajas (n. nom. sg.), rajas, passion, emotion.
tamas (n. nom sg.), tamas, darkness, sloth.

XVII

श्रीभगवान् उवाच ।
śrībhagavān uvāca
the Blessed Lord spoke:

śrībhagavān (m. nom. sg.), The Blessed Lord, the Blessed One.
uvāca (3rd sg. perf. act. √*vac*), he said, he spoke.

2

त्रिविधा भवति श्रद्धा
trividhā bhavati śraddhā
three kinds is faith

देहिनां सा स्वभावजा ।
dehināṁ sā svabhāvajā
of the embodied, it, innate-nature-born,

सात्त्विकी राजसी चैव
sāttvikī rājasī cāiva
sattvic and rajasic

तामसी चेति तां शृणु ॥
tāmasī ceti tāṁ śṛṇu
and tamasic thus; (of) this hear!

trividhā (f. nom. sg.), triple, of three kinds.
bhavati (3rd sg. pr. indic. √*bhū*), is, it is.
śraddhā (f. nom. sg.), faith.
dehinām (m. gen. pl.), of the embodied, of embodied beings, of embodied ones.
sā (f. nom. sg.), it, this, she.
svabhāvajā (f. nom. sg.), born of own nature, born of innate nature.
sāttvikī (f. nom. sg.), sattvic, pertaining to the guṇa of sattva.
rājasī (f. nom. sg.), rajasic, pertaining to the guṇa of rajas.
ca, and.
eva, indeed (used as a rhythmic filler).
tāmasī (f. nom. sg.), tamasic, pertaining to the guṇa of tamas.
ca, and.
iti, thus, so.
tām (f. acc. sg.), this, of this.
śṛṇu (2nd sg. imperative √*śru*), hear!

The Blessed Lord spoke:
The faith of the embodied is of three kinds;
Born of innate nature,
It is sattvic, rajasic
And tamasic, thus; of this now hear.

3

सत्त्वानुरूपा सर्वस्य
sattvānurūpā sarvasya
the truth in accordance with of each,

श्रद्धा भवति भारत ।
śraddhā bhavati bhārata
faith it is, Descendant of Bharata.

श्रद्धामयो ऽयं पुरुषो
śraddhāmayo 'yaṁ puruṣo
made of faith this man

यो यच्छ्रद्धः स एव सः ॥
yo yacchraddhaḥ sa eva saḥ
who which faith he, thus he.

Faith is in accordance
With the truth (nature) of each, Descendant of Bharata.
Man is made of faith.
Whatever faith he has, thus he is.

sattva (n.), truth, essential nature.
anurūpā (f. nom. sg.), following the form, corresponding, like, in accordance with.
(*sattva-anurūpā*, f. nom. sg. TP cpd., following truth.)
sarvasya (m. gen. sg.), of all, of each.
śraddhā (f. nom. sg.), faith.
bhavati (3rd sg. pr. indic. √*bhū*), it is.
bhārata (m. voc. sg.), Descendant of Bharata, epithet of Arjuna.
śraddhāmayas (m. nom. sg.), "faith-made," made of faith.
ayam (m. nom. sg.), this.
puruṣas (m. nom. sg.), man, spirit.
yas (m. nom. sg.), who.
yad (n. nom. sg.), which.
śraddhas (m. nom. sg.), faith.
sas (m. nom. sg.), he, this.
eva, thus, indeed (often used as a rhythmic filler).
sas (m. nom. sg.), he, this one.

4

यजन्ते सात्त्विका देवान्
yajante sāttvikā devān
they sacrifice, the sattvic, to the gods

यक्षरक्षांसि राजसाः ।
yakṣarakṣāṁsi rājasāḥ
to the spirits and demons the rajasic

प्रेतान् भूतगणांश्चान्ये
pretān bhūtagaṇāṅścānye
to the departed and the hordes of ghosts, the others,

यजन्ते तामसा जनाः ॥
yajante tāmasā janāḥ
they sacrifice, the tamasic men.

yajante (3rd pl. pr. indic. mid. √*yaj*), they sacrifice, they worship.
sāttvikās (m. nom. pl.), the sattvic, those who are characterized by sattva.
devān (m. acc. pl.), the gods, to the gods.
yakṣarakṣāmsi (n. acc. pl.), spirits and demons, to the yakṣas, and rakṣas, to the spirits and demons.
rājasās (m. nom. pl.), the rajasic, those who are characterized by the guṇa of rajas.
pretān (m. acc. pl. p. pass. participle *pra* √*i*), to the departed, to the dead.
bhūtagaṇān (m. acc. pl.), to the hordes of ghosts, to the multitudes of spirits.
ca, and.
anye (m. nom. pl.), others.
yajante (3rd pl. pr. indic. mid. √*yaj*), they sacrifice, they worship.
tāmasās (m. nom. pl.), the tamasic, those characterized by the guṇa of tamas.
janās (m. nom. pl.), men.

The sattvic sacrifice to the gods,
To the spirits and demons the rajasic;
The others, the tamasic men, sacrifice
To the departed and to the hordes of ghosts.

5

अशास्त्रविहितं घोरं
aśāstravihitaṁ ghoraṁ
not scripture enjoined, terrible,

तप्यन्ते ये तपो जनाः ।
tapyante ye tapo janāḥ
they undergo, who, austerities men

दम्भाहंकारसंयुक्ताः
dambhāhaṁkārasaṁyuktāḥ
hypocrisy and egotism joined with,

कामरागबलान्विताः ॥
kāmarāgabalānvitāḥ
desire, passion and force along with,

Men who undergo terrible austerities,
Not enjoined by the scriptures,
Accompanied by hypocrisy and egotism,
Along with desire, passion and force,

aśāstravihitam (n. acc. sg. p. pass. participle *a śāstra vi* √*dhā*), not ordained by scripture, not prescribed by scripture.
ghoram (n. acc. sg.), terrible, awful.
tapyante (3rd pl. pr. mid. √*tap*), they undergo, they suffer.
ye (m. nom. pl.), who, they who.
tapas (n. acc. sg.), austerity, heat.
janās (m. nom. pl.), men.
dambha (m.), fraud, deceit, hypocrisy.
ahaṁkāra (m.), "I making," egotism.
saṁyuktās (m. nom. pl. p. pass. participle *sam* √*yuj*), united with, joined with.
(*dambhāhaṁkārasaṁyuktās,* m. nom. pl. TP cpd., joined with hypocrisy and egotism, yoked to hypocrisy and egotism.)
kāma (m.), desire, lust, love.
rāga (m.), anger, rage, passion.
bala (n.), force, strength, might.
anvitās (m. nom. pl. p. pass. participle *anu* √*i*), accompanied by, along with.
(*kāmarāgabalānvitās,* m. nom. pl. TP cpd., accompanied by desire, anger and force.)

6

कर्षयन्तः शरीरस्थं
karṣayantaḥ śarīrastham̐
torturing in the body

भूतग्रामम् अचेतसः ।
bhūtagrāmam acetasaḥ
the aggregate of elements, unthinking,

मां चैवान्तः शरीरस्थं
mām̐ cāivāntaḥ śarīrastham̐
and me thus within the body

तान्विद्ध्य् आसुरनिश्चयान् ॥
tān viddhy āsuraniścayān
them know, demonic resolved.

The unthinking, torturing within the body
The aggregate of elements,
And also torturing Me thus within the body,
Them know to be demonic resolved.*

karṣayantas (m. nom. pl. causative pr. participle act. √*kṛṣ*), torturing, causing to plow up, causing to injure.
śarīrastham (m. acc. sg.), within the body, existing in the body.
bhūtagrāmam (m. acc. sg.), aggregate of elements, multitude of elements.
acetasas (m. nom. pl.), unthinking, mindless.
mām (acc. sg.), me.
ca, and.
eva, thus, indeed (often used as a rhythmic filler).
antar, within, inside.
śarīrastham (m. acc. sg.), within the body, existing within the body.
tān (m. acc. pl.), them.
viddhi (2nd sg. imperative act. √*vid*), know! learn!
āsura, demonic.
niścayān (m. acc. pl.), resolved, determined, fixed in intention.
(*āsuraniścayān,* m. acc. pl., BV cpd., those who are demonic-resolved.)

* This and the preceding stanzas constitute one of several injunctions in the Bhagavad Gītā against exaggerated austerities, or mortifications of the flesh. These injunctions are interesting because they show that such abuses were common enough to arouse denunciation.

7

आहारस् त्व् अपि सर्वस्य
āhāras tv api sarvasya
food but also of all

त्रिविधो भवति प्रियः ।
trividho bhavati priyaḥ
three kinds it is preferred

यज्ञस् तपस् तथा दानं
yajñas tapas tathā dānaṁ
sacrifice austerity also gift

तेषां भेदम् इमं शृणु ॥
teṣāṁ bhedam imaṁ śṛṇu.
of them the distinction, this hear.

But also the food preferred by all
Is of three kinds,
As are their sacrifices, austerities and gifts.
Hear now the distinction between them.

āhāras (m. nom. sg.), food.
tu, but.
api, also, even.
sarvasya (m. gen. sg.), of all.
trividhas (m. nom. sg.), triple, of three kinds.
bhavati (3rd sg. pr. indic. √*bhū*), it is, it comes to be.
priyas (m. nom. sg.), dear, preferred.
yajñas (m. nom. sg.), sacrifice, worship.
tapas (n. nom. sg.), austerity, heat.
tathā, also, thus.
dānam (n. nom. sg.), gift, charity.
teṣām (m. gen. pl.), of them.
bhedam (m. acc. sg.), distinction, difference, "splitting."
imam (m. acc. sg.), this.
śṛṇu (2nd sg. imperative act. √*śru*), hear!

8

आयुः सत्त्वबलारोग्य-
āyuḥsattvabalārogya-
life, virtue, strength, health,

सुखप्रीतिविवर्धनाः ।
sukhaprītivivardhanāḥ
happiness, satisfaction promoting,

रस्याः स्निग्धाः स्थिरा हृद्या
rasyāḥ snigdhāḥ sthirā hṛdyā
savory, smooth, firm, pleasant to the stomach;

आहाराः सात्त्विकप्रियाः ॥
āhārāḥ sāttvikapriyāḥ
foods the sattvic dear to.

Promoting life, virtue, strength, health,
Happiness and satisfaction,
Savory, smooth, firm and pleasant to the stomach;
Such foods are dear to the sattvic.

āyus (n.), living, moving life, duration of life.
sattva (n.), truth, virtue.
bala (m.), strength, force, might.
ārogya (n.), health, freedom from disease.
sukha (n.), happiness, good fortune, joy.
prīti (f.), satisfaction, pleasure.
vivardhanās (m. nom. pl. pr. pr. participle *vi* √*vṛdh*), promoting, increasing, augmenting.
(*ayuḥsattvabalārogyasukhaprītivivardhanās,* m. nom pl. TP cpd., promoting life, virtue, strength, health, happiness and satisfaction.)
rasyās (m. nom. pl.), savory, flavorful, pleasant tasting.
snigdhās (m. nom. pl.), smooth, glutinous, sticky.
sthirās (m. nom. pl.), firm, solid.
hṛdyās (m. nom. pl.), "hearty," pleasant, dainty, pleasant to the stomach.
āhārās (m. nom. pl.), foods.
sāttvikapriyās (m. nom. pl.), dear to the sattvic, preferred by those characterized by the guṇa of sattva.

9

कट्वम्ललवणात्युष्ण-
kaṭvamlalavaṇātyuṣṇa-
pungent, sour, salty, excessively hot,

तीक्ष्णरूक्षविदाहिनः ।
tīkṣṇarūkṣavidāhinaḥ
harsh, astringent, scorching

आहारा राजसस्येष्टा
āhārā rājasasyeṣṭā
foods by the rajasic desired,

दुःखशोकामयप्रदाः ॥
duḥkhaśokāmayapradāḥ
pain, misery, sickness causing.

**Causing pain, misery and sickness,
Pungent, sour, salty, excessively hot,
Harsh, astringent, scorching;
Such foods are desired by the rajasic.**

kaṭu, pungent, acrid, sharp.
amla, sour, acid, vinegary.
lavaṇa, salty, briny, saline.
atyuṣṇa, excessively hot.
tīkṣṇa, harsh, fiery, acid.
rūkṣa, astringent, rough, dry.
vidāhinas (m. nom. pl.), burning, scorching (the plural serves for all the preceding adjectives).
(*kaṭvamlalavaṇātyuṣṇatīkṣṇarūkṣavidāhinas,* m. nom. pl. dvandva cpd., pungent, sour, salty, excessively hot, harsh, astringent and scorching.)
āhārās (m. nom. pl.), foods.
rājasasya (m. gen. sg.), of the rajasic, of him who is characterized by the guṇa of rajas.
iṣṭās (m. nom. pl. p. pass. participle √*iṣ*), desired, wished for.
duḥkha (n.), pain, misery.
śoka (m.), sorrow, grief.
āmaya (m.), sickness, disease.
pradās (m. nom. pl.), causing, yielding.
(*duḥkhaśokāmayapradās,* m. nom. pl. TP cpd., causing pain, sorrow and sickness.)

10

यातयामं गतरसं
yātayāmaṁ gatarasaṁ
stale, tasteless

पूति पर्युषितं च यत् ।
pūti paryuṣitaṁ ca yat
putrid and left-over which

उच्छिष्टम् अपि चामेध्यं
ucchiṣṭam api cāmedhyaṁ
rejected and also foul

भोजनं तामसप्रियम् ॥
bhojanaṁ tāmasapriyam
food the tamasic dear to.

yātayāmam (n. nom. sg.), used, spoiled, stale.
gatarasam (n. nom. sg.), tasteless, flavorless.
pūti (n. nom. sg.), putrid, stinking, fetid.
paryuṣitam (n. nom. sg. p. pass. participle *pari* √*vas*), left over, stale.
ca, and.
yad (n. nom. sg.), which.
ucchiṣṭam (n. nom. sg. p. pass. participle *ud* √*śiṣ*), rejected, left remaining.
api, also, even.
ca, and.
amedhyam (n. nom. sg.), impure, foul, not fit for sacrifice.
bhojanam (n. nom. sg.), food, feeding.
tāmasapriyam (n. nom. sg.), dear to the tamasic, preferred by those characterized by the guṇa of tamas.

**Stale, tasteless, putrid, left-over,
And the rejected as well as
The foul, is the food which
Is dear to the tamasic.***

* It is not difficult to detect in this and the preceding two stanzas the hand of the brāhman caste, insisting on its superiority to an extent that is almost comic. It has been pointed out by historians that, though the Mahābhārata is primarily an epic of the *kṣatriya*, or warrior, caste, the Bhagavad Gītā, along with some other interpolations of a moral or religious character, was probably inserted into the poem later by the priestly caste of brāhmans.

11

अफलाकाङ्क्षिभिर् यज्ञो
aphalākāṅkṣibhir yajño
by the non-fruit-desiring, sacrifice,

विधिदृष्टो य इज्यते ।
vidhidṛṣṭo ya ijyate
scripture observing, which it is offered,

यष्टव्यम् एवेति मनः
yaṣṭavyam eveti manaḥ
"to be sacrificed" only thus the mind

समाधाय स सात्त्विकः ॥
samādhāya sa sāttvikaḥ
concentrating, that sattvic.

Sacrifice which is offered, observing the scriptures,
By those who do not desire fruit,
Concentrating the mind only on the thought "this is to be sacrificed;"
That sacrifice is sattvic.

aphalākāṅkṣibhis (m. inst. pl.), by the non-fruit-desiring (as TP cpd.) by those who do not desire fruit.
yajñas (m. nom. sg.), sacrifice, worship.
vidhidṛṣṭas (m. nom. sg. p. pass. participle *vidhi* √*dṛś*), scripture observing.
yas (m. nom. sg.), who, which.
ijyate (3rd sg. pr. passive √*yaj*), it is offered, it is sacrificed.
yaṣṭavyam (n. acc. sg. gerundive √*yaj*), to be offered, to be sacrificed.
eva, only, indeed (often used as a rhythmic filler).
iti, thus.
manas (n. nom. sg.), mind.
samādhāya (gerund *sam ā* √*dhā*), concentrating, composing, fixing.
sas (m. nom. sg.), this, he.
sāttvikas (m. nom. sg.), sattvic, pertaining to him who is characterized by the guṇa of sattva.

12

अभिसंधाय तु फलं
abhisaṁdhāya tu phalaṁ
having in view, but, the fruit,

दम्भार्थम् अपि चैव यत् ।
dambhārtham api cāiva yat
and hypocritical purpose also which

इज्यते भरतश्रेष्ठ
ijyate bharataśreṣṭha
it is offered, Best of the Bharatas,

तं यज्ञं विद्धि राजसम् ॥
taṁ yajñaṁ viddhi rājasam
this sacrifice know to be rajasic.

But sacrifice which is offered
With a view to the fruit, Best of the Bharatas,
And also for the purpose of hypocrisy;
That know to be rajasic.

abhisaṁdhāya (gerund *abhi sam* √*dhā*), having in view, having in mind, seeking.
tu, but.
phalam (n. acc. sg.), fruit.
dambhārtham (m. acc. sg.), fraudulent aim, (as TP cpd.) for the purpose of hypocrisy, with hypocritical aim.
api also, even.
ca, and.
eva, indeed (used as a rhythmic filler).
yad (n. nom. sg.), which.
ijyate (3rd sg. pr. indic. passive √*yaj*), it is offered, it is sacrificed.
bharataśreṣṭha (m. voc. sg.), Best of the Bharatas, epithet of Arjuna.
tam (m. acc. sg.), this, him.
yajñam (m. acc. sg.), sacrifice, offering.
viddhi (2nd imperative act. √*vid*), know! learn!
rājasam (m. acc. sg.), rajasic, pertaining to him who is characterized by the guṇa of rajas.

13

विधिहीनम् असृष्टान्नं
vidhihīnam asṛṣṭānnaṁ
scripture discarded, not offered food,

मन्त्रहीनम् अदक्षिणम् ।
mantrahīnam adakṣiṇam
sacred text discarded, without fee,

श्रद्धाविरहितं यज्ञं
śraddhāvirahitaṁ yajñam
faith-devoid sacrifice

तामसं परिचक्षते ॥
tāmasaṁ paricakṣate
tamasic they regard as.

Sacrifice devoid of faith
With scripture discarded, no food offered,
With sacred text lacking and without fee (to the presiding priest),
They regard as tamasic.

vidhihīnam (n. acc. sg.), scripture discarded, scripture lacking.
asṛṣṭa (p. pass. participle *a* √*sṛj*), not offered, not let go.
annam (n. nom. acc. sg.), grain, food.
(*asṛṣṭa-ānnam*, n. acc. sg. KD cpd., unoffered food.)
mantrahīnam (n. acc. sg.), sacred formula discarded, sacred formula lacking.
adakṣiṇam (n. acc. sg.), without fee, fee not being paid.
śraddhāvirahitam (n. acc. sg. p. pass. participle *śraddhā vi* √*rah*), devoid of faith, faith deserted.
yajñam (m. acc. sg.), sacrifice, worship.
tāmasam (m. acc. sg.), tamasic, pertaining to him who is characterized by the guṇa of tamas.
paricakṣate (3rd pl. mid. *pari* √*cakṣ*), they regard as, they see as.

14

देवद्विजगुरुप्राज्ञ-
devadvijaguruprājña-
gods, the twice born, teachers and wise men

पूजनं शौचम् आर्जवम् ।
pūjanaṁ śāucam ārjavam
reverencing; purity, rectitude,

ब्रह्मचर्यम् अहिंसा च
brahmacaryam ahiṁsā ca
continence non-violence

शारीरं तप उच्यते ॥
śārīraṁ tapa ucyate
bodily austerity, it is called.

Reverencing of the gods, the twice-born, teachers
And wise men, purity, rectitude,
Continence and non-violence;
This is called austerity of the body.

deva (m.), god.
dvija (m.), twice-born, member of one of the three highest castes.
guru (m.), teacher, elder, master.
prājña (m.), wise man, man of wisdom.
pūjanam (n. nom. sg. from √*pūj*), revering, reverencing.
(*devadvijagurruprājñapūjanam,* n. nom. sg. TP cpd., revering the gods, the twice-born, the teacher and the man of wisdom.)
śāucam (n. nom. sg.), purity, cleanliness of mind and body.
ārjavam (n. nom. sg.), rectitude, virtue.
brahmacaryam (n. nom. sg.), continence, chastity, keeping the vow of the brahmacārin.
ahiṁsā (f. nom. sg.), non-violence, harmlessness.
ca, and.
śarīram (adv.), bodily, of the body.
tapas (n. nom. sg.), austerity, heat.
ucyate (3rd sg. pr. indic. passive √*vac*), it is said to be, it is called.

15

अनुद्वेगकरं वाक्यं
anudvegakaraṁ vākyaṁ
not-causing-distress speech

सत्यं प्रियहितं च यत् ।
satyaṁ priyahitaṁ ca yat
truthful, agreeable and salutary, which

स्वाध्यायाभ्यसनं चैव
svādhyāyābhyasanaṁ cāiva
and recitation-of-sacred-texts practice

वाङ्मयं तप उच्यते ॥
vāṅmayaṁ tapa ucyate
speech formed austerity it is called.

Words that do not cause distress,
Truthful, agreeable and salutary;
And practice in the recitation of sacred texts;
This is called the austerity of speech.

anudvegakaram (n. nom. sg.), not causing distress, not overawing, not causing apprehension.
vākyam (n. nom. sg.), word, speech.
satyam (n. nom. sg.), true, truthful.
priya (m.), agreeable, pleasant.
hitam (n. nom. sg. p. pass. participle √*dhā*), salutary, beneficial, wholesome.
(*priya-hitam*, n. nom. sg. DV cpd., agreeable and salutary.)
ca, and.
yad (n. nom. sg.), which.
svādhyāya (m.), speaking sacred texts to oneself, reciting sacred texts.
abhyasanam (n. nom. sg.), practice, exercise.
(*svādhyāya-abhyasanam*, n. nom. sg. DV cpd., recitation and practice.)
ca, and.
eva, indeed (used as a rhythmic filler).
vāṅmayam (*vāc mayam*, n. nom. sg.), speech-formed, speech-made.
tapas (n. nom. sg.), austerity, heat.
ucyate (3rd sg. pr. indic. passive √*vac*), it is called, it is said to be.

16

मनःप्रसादः सौम्यत्वं
manaḥprasādaḥ sāumyatvaṁ
mind-peace, gentleness,

मौनम् आत्मविनिग्रहः ।
māunam ātmavinigrahaḥ
silence, self restraint,

भावसंशुद्धिर् इत्य् एतत्
bhāvasaṁśuddhir ity etat
being-purity thus, this

तपो मानसम् उच्यते ॥
tapo mānasam ucyate
austerity mental it is called.

Peace of mind, gentleness,
Taciturnity, self restraint,
Purity of being; this
Is called austerity of the mind.

manas (n. nom. sg.), mind.
prasādas (m. nom. sg.), peace, clarity, calmness, kindness.
sāumyatvam (n. nom. sg.), gentleness, benevolence. mildness.
māunam (n. nom. sg.), silence, taciturnity.
ātmavinigrahas (m. nom. sg.), self-restraint, self-control.
bhāvasaṁśuddhis (f. nom. sg.), purity of being, cleanliness of being.
iti, thus.
etad (n. nom. sg.), this.
tapas (n. nom. sg.), austerity, heat.
mānasam (n. nom. sg.), mental, of the mind.
ucyate (3rd sg. pr. indic. passive √*vac*), it is called, it is said to be.

17

श्रद्धया परया तप्तं
śraddhayā parayā taptaṁ
with faith the highest undergone

तपस् तत् त्रिविधं नरैः ।
tapas tat trividhaṁ narāiḥ
austerity this threefold by men,

अफलाकाङ्क्षिभिर् युक्तैः
aphalākāṅkṣibhir yuktāiḥ
by the non-fruit-desiring, by the steadfast,

सात्त्विकं परिचक्षते ॥
sāttvikaṁ paricakṣate
sattvic they regard as.

śraddhayā (f. inst. sg.), by faith, with faith.
parayā (f. inst. sg.), by the highest, with the highest.
taptam (n. nom. sg. p. pass. participle √*tap*), practiced, undergone.
tapas (n. nom. sg.), austerity, heat.
tad (n. nom. sg.), this, that.
trividham (n. nom. acc. sg.), threefold, of three kinds, triple.
narāis (m. inst. pl.), by men.
aphalākāṅkṣibhis (m. inst. pl.), by the non-desirous of fruit, by those who do not desire fruit.
yuktāis (m. inst. pl.), by the steadfast, by the disciplined, by those who are disciplined in Yoga.
sāttvikam (m. acc. sg.), sattvic, pertaining to him who is characterized by the guṇa of sattva.
paricakṣate (3rd pl. pr. indic. mid. *pari* √*cakṣ*), they regard as, they see as.

This threefold austerity
Undergone with the highest faith by men,
Who are not desirious of fruits and are steadfast,
They regard as sattvic.

18

सत्कारमानपूजार्थं
satkāramānapūjārtham
honor, respect, reverence for the sake of

तपो दम्भेन चैव यत् ।
tapo dambhena cāiva yat
and austerity with hypocrisy which

क्रियते तद् इह प्रोक्तं
kriyate tad iha proktam
it is performed, that here in the world declared to be

राजसं चलम् अध्रुवम् ॥
rājasaṁ calam adhruvam
rajasic, unsteady, impermanent.

Austerity which is undergone with hypocrisy
For the sake of honor, respect and reverence;
That, here in the world, is declared to be
Rajasic, unsteady and impermanent.

satkāra (n.), honor, reverence, favor, hospitality; lit. "good-doing."
māna (m.), honor, respect.
pūjā (f.), reverence.
artha (n.), aim, for the sake of.
(*satkāramānapūjārtham,* (n. nom. sg. TP cpd., for the sake of honor, respect and reverence.)
tapas (n. nom. sg.), austerity, heat.
dambhena (m. inst. sg.), by fraud, with fraud, with hypocrisy.
ca, and.
eva, indeed (used as a rhythmic filler).
yad (n. nom. sg.), which.
kriyate (3rd sg. pr. passive √*kṛ*), it is performed, it is done, it is made.
tad (n. acc. sg.), this, that.
iha, here, here on earth.
proktam (m. acc. sg. p. pass. participle *pra* √*vac*), declared, said to be.
rājasam (m. acc. sg.), rajasic, pertaining to one who is characterized by the guṇa of rajas.
calam (m. acc. sg.), unsteady, wavering.
adhruvam (m. acc. sg.), impermanent, infirm, unfixed.

19

मूढग्राहेणात्मनो यत्
mūḍhagrāheṇātmano yat
with deluded notion of the self, which,

पीडया क्रियते तपः ।
pīḍayā kriyate tapaḥ
with torture, it is performed, austerity,

परस्योत्सादनार्थं वा
parasyotsādanārthaṁ vā
of another destroying aim or

तत् तामसम् उदाहृतम् ॥
tat tāmasam udāhṛtam
that tamasic declared to be.

Austerity which is performed
With deluded notions and with torture of the self,
Or with the aim of destroying another,
Is declared to be tamasic.

mūḍha (p. pass. participle √*muh*), deluded, confused.
grāheṇa (m. inst. sg.), by notion, by grasp, with notion.
(*mūḍhagrāheṇa,* m. inst. sg., with deluded notion.)
ātmanas (m. gen. sg.), of the self.
yad (n. nom. sg.), which.
pāḍayā (f. inst. sg.), with torture, with torment.
kriyate (3rd sg. pr. indic. pass. √*kṛ*), it is performed, it is done, it is made.
tapas (n. nom. sg.), austerity, heat, self-denial.
parasya (m. gen. sg.), of another.
utsādana (pr. participle *ut* √*sad*), destroying, overturning.
artham (n. nom. sg.), aim, purpose.
(*parasyotsādanārtham,* (n. nom. sg., TP cpd., with the purpose of destroying another.)
vā, or.
tad, that, this.
tāmasam (n. acc. sg.), tamasic, pertaining to the guṇa of tamas.
udāhṛtam (n. acc. sg. p. pass. participle *ud ā* √*hṛ*), declared to be, said to be.

20

दातव्यम् इति यद् दानं
dātavyam iti yad dānaṁ
"to be given" thus which gift

दीयते ऽनुपकारिणे।
dīyate 'nupakāriṇe
is given to one who has done no prior favor,

देशे काले च पात्रे च
deśe kāle ca pātre ca
in (proper) place and time and to a worthy person

तद् दानं सात्त्विकं स्मृतम्॥
tad dānaṁ sāttvikaṁ smṛtam
that gift sattvic remembered as.

The gift which is given only with the thought "to be given,"
To a worthy person who has done no prior favor,
At the proper place and time;
That gift is held to be sattvic.

dātavyam (n. nom. sg. gerundive √*dā*), to be given.
iti, thus (often used to close a quotation).
yad (n. nom. sg.), which.
dānam (n. nom. sg.), gift.
dīyate (3rd sg. pr. indic. passive √*dā*), it is given, it is bestowed.
anupakāriṇe (m. dat. sg.), to him who has not done a friendly service, to him who has performed no prior favor.
deśe (m. loc. sg.), in a place, in a proper place.
kāle (m. loc. sg.), in time, at a proper time.
ca, and.
pātre (n. loc. sg.), to a worthy person, to a competent person.
ca, and.
tad (n. nom. sg.), this, that.
dānam (n. nom. sg.), gift.
sāttvikam (n. nom. sg.), sattvic, pertaining to the guṇa of sattva.
smṛtam (n. nom. sg. p. pass. participle √*smṛ*), known as, recorded as, remembered as, held to be.

21

यत् तु प्रत्युपकारार्थं
yat tu pratyupakārārthaṁ
which but with recompense aim

फलम् उद्दिश्य वा पुनः ।
phalam uddiśya vā punaḥ
fruit with regard to, or again,

दीयते च परिक्लिष्टं
dīyate ca parikliṣṭaṁ
and is given grudgingly,

तद् दानं राजसं स्मृतम् ॥
tad dānaṁ rājasaṁ smṛtam
that gift rajasic recorded as.

But that gift which is given grudgingly,
With the aim of recompense,
Or, again, with regard to fruit,
Is recorded as rajasic.

yad (n. nom. sg.), which.
tu, but.
pratyupakārārtham (m. acc. sg.), with the aim of recompense, with the purpose of gaining reward.
phalam (n. acc. sg.), fruit, result.
uddiśya (gerund *ud* √*diś*), pointing to, with regard to.
vā, or.
punar, again.
dīyate (3rd sg. pr. indic. passive √*dā*), it is given, it is bestowed.
ca, and.
parikliṣṭam (n. nom. sg. p. pass. participle *pari* √*kliś*), unwillingly, grudgingly.
tad (n. nom. sg.), that, this.
dānam (n. nom. sg.), gift, charity.
rājasam (n. nom. sg.), rajasic, pertaining to the guṇa of rajas.
smṛtam (n. nom. sg. p. pass. participle √*smṛ*), remembered as, recorded as, thought to be.

22

अदेशकाले यद् दानम्
adeśakāle yad dānam
at wrong place and time which gift,

अपात्रेभ्यश्च दीयते ।
apātrebhyaśca dīyate
and to the unworthy, is given,

असत्कृतम् अवज्ञातं
asatkṛtam avajñātaṁ
without paying respect, with contempt,

तत् तामसम् उदाहृतम् ॥
tat tāmasam udāhṛtam
that tamasic declared to be.

adeśakāle (m. loc. sg.), in wrong place and time.
yad (n. acc. sg.), which.
dānam (n. acc. sg.), gift, charity.
apātrebhyas (n. dat. pl.), to the unworthy, to unworthy persons.
ca, and.
dīyate (3rd sg. pr. indic. passive √*dā*), it is given.
asatkṛtam (adv.), without paying respect.
avajñātam (n. nom. sg. p. pass. participle *ava* √*jñā*), with contempt, without wisdom, with disrespect.
tad (n. nom. sg.), that, this.
tāmasam (n. nom. sg.), tamasic, pertaining to the guṇa of tamas.
udāhṛtam (n. nom. sg. p. pass. participle *ud ā* √*hṛ*), declared, said to be.

That gift which is given at the wrong place and time
To the unworthy,
Without paying respect, and with contempt,
Is declared to be tamasic.

23

ओं तत् सद् इति निर्देशो
oṁ tat sad iti nirdeśo
"*om tat sat*" – thus the designation

ब्रह्मणस् त्रिविधः स्मृतः ।
brahmaṇas trividhaḥ smṛtaḥ
of Brahman threefold remembered.

ब्राह्मणास् तेन वेदाश्च
brāhmaṇās tena vedāśca
the Brāhmans by this and the Vedas

यज्ञाश्च विहिताः पुरा ॥
yajñāśca vihitāḥ purā
and the sacrifices ordained anciently.

"Oṁ tat sat"* – this is recorded as
The threefold designation of Brahman.
By this the brāhmans, the Vedas
And the sacrifices were anciently ordained.

oṁ, the sacred syllable or one-syllable mantra.
tad (n. nom. sg.), that, this.
sat (n. nom. sg.), true, real, good.
iti, thus, so.
nirdeśas (m. nom. sg.), designation, command, order, instruction.
brahmaṇas (n. g. sg.), of Brahman.
trividhas (m. nom. sg.), threefold, of three kinds.
smṛtas (m. nom. sg. p. pass. participle √*smṛ*), remembered, known, called to mind.
brāhmaṇās (m. nom. pl.), the Brāhmans.
tena (m. inst. sg.), by this, with this.
vedās (m. nom. pl.), the Vedas.
ca, and.
yajñās (m. nom. pl.), sacrifices, religious ceremonies.
ca, and.
vihitās (nom. pl. p. pass. participle *vi* √*dhā*), ordained, apportioned, arranged, determined.
purā (adv.), anciently, ancient, in olden times, prior.

* *oṁ tat sat* ("oṁ that [is] real") is a common *mantra*, or sacred utterance, among Hindus. It begins with the sacred syllable "*oṁ*" which is made up of three sounds – a, u, m – representing the three Vedas, the "three worlds" (heaven, atmosphere, earth), the three principal deities (Brahmā, Vishnu and Śiva) and the beginning, middle and ending of all things. The rest of the *mantra* is an affirmation of the existence of Brahman, for which "*oṁ*" is a designation, but see commentary on "tat sat" in stanzas 25 and 26. "*Sat*" in Sanskrit has the meanings of "real" or "true" and that of "good."

24

तस्मादो इत्य् उदाहृत्य
tasmād om ity udāhṛtya
therefore "om" thus uttering,

यज्ञदानतप:क्रिया: ।
yajñadānatapaḥkriyāḥ
sacrifice, gift and austerity acts

प्रवर्तन्ते विधानोक्ता:
pravartante vidhānoktāḥ
they are begun prescribed in the (Vedic) scriptures,

सततं ब्रह्मवादिनाम् ॥
satatam̐ brahmavādinām
always by the expounders of Brahman.

Therefore, acts of sacrifice, giving and austerity
Are always begun uttering the syllable "Om̐"
By the expounders of Brahman,
As prescribed in the Vedic injunctions.

tasmāt (m. abl. sg.), from this, therefore.
om, the sacred syllable or one-syllable mantra.
iti, thus, so, in this way.
udāhṛtya (gerund *ud ā* √*hṛ*), uttering, illustrating, bringing forward.
yajña (m.), sacrifice, worship.
dāna (n.), charity, gift.
tapas (n.), austerity, heat, self-denial.
kriyās (m. nom. pl.), acts, religious acts.
(*yajñadānatapaḥkriyās,* m. nom. pl., acts of sacrifice, gifts and austerities.)
pravartante (3rd pl. pr. indic. mid. *pra* √*vṛt*), they begin, they are begun, they commence, they are commenced.
vidhāna (from *vi* √*dhā*), prescription, precept.
uktās (m. nom. pl. p. pass. participle √*vac*), said, proclaimed.
(*vidhāna-uktās,* m. nom. pl. TP cpd., proclaimed in the precepts.)
satatam (adv.), perpetually, always.
brahma (n.), Brahman.
vādinām (m. gen. pl.), of the speakers, of the explainers, of the expounders.
(*brahma-vādinām,* m. gen. pl. TP cpd., of the expounders of Brahman.)

25

तद् इत्य् अनभिसंधाय
tad ity anabhisaṁdhāya
"tat" thus without aiming at

फलं यज्ञतपःक्रियाः ।
phalaṁ yajñatapaḥkriyāḥ
fruit; sacrifice austerity acts

दानक्रियाश्च विविधाः
dānakriyāśca vividhāḥ
and giving acts of various sorts

क्रियन्ते मोक्षकाङ्क्षिभिः ॥
kriyante mokṣakāṅkṣibhiḥ
they are performed by the desirous of release.

With "tat" and without aiming at
Fruits, acts of sacrifice and austerity,
And acts of giving of various sorts
Are performed by those who are desirous of release.

tad (n. nom. sg.), this, that, here simply "tat."

iti, thus, so.

anabhisaṁdhāya (gerund *an abhi sam* √*dhā*), not aiming at, without interest in.

phalam (n. acc. sg.), fruit, result.

yajña (m.), sacrifice, worship.

tapas (n.), austerity, self-denial.

kriyās (m. nom. pl.), actions, acts, religious actions.

(*yajñatapaḥkriyās*, m. nom. pl. TP cpd., acts of sacrifice and austerity.)

dānakriyās (m. nom. pl.), acts of giving, acts of charity.

ca, and.

vividhās (m. nom. pl.), of various kinds, varied, of many sorts.

kriyante (3rd pl. pr. indic. passive √*kṛ*), they are done, they are performed, they are made.

mokṣa (m.), release, liberation.

kāṅkṣibhis (inst. pl.), by the desirous, by those who are desirous.

(*mokṣakāṅkṣibhis,* m. inst. pl. TP cpd., by those who desire release, by those who desire liberation from the cycles of re-birth.)

26

सद्भावे साधुभावे च
sadbhāve sādhubhāve ca
in "reality" meaning and in "goodness" meaning,

सद् इत्य् एतत् प्रयुज्यते ।
sad ity etat prayujyate
"sat" thus, this is used.

प्रशस्ते कर्मणि तथा
praśaste karmaṇi tathā
for a praiseworthy act also

सच्छब्दः पार्थ युज्यते ॥
sacchabdaḥ pārtha yujyate
the "sat" sound, Son of Pṛthā, is used.

In its meaning of "reality" and in its meaning of "goodness"
"Sat" is used.
Also for a praiseworthy act
The word "sat," Son of Pṛthā, is used.

sat (n.), truth, reality, goodness.
bhāve (m. loc. sg.), in meaning, in intention.
(*sat-bhāve*, m. loc. sg. TP cpd., in the meaning of "reality.")
sādhu (n.), straight, right, good, goodness.
bhāve (m. loc. sg.), in being, in intention, in meaning.
(*sādhu bhāve*, m. loc. sg. TP cpd., in the meaning of "goodness.")
ca, and.
sat (n. nom. sg.), reality, truth, goodness (here simply "sat").
iti, thus, so, in this way.
etad (n. nom. sg.), that, this.
prayujyate (3rd sg. pr. indic. passive *pra* √*yuj*), it is used, it is employed.
praśaste (n. loc. sg. p. pass. participle *pra* √*śaṁs*), in praiseworthy, in laudable.
karmaṇi (n. loc. sg.), in action, in act.
tathā, thus, also, even.
sat (n.), truth, reality, goodness (here simply "sat").
śabdas (m. nom. sg.), sound, word.
(*sat-śabdas*, m. nom. sg. TP cpd., sound of "sat").
pārtha (m. voc. sg.), Son of Pṛthā, epithet of Arjuna.
yujyate (3rd sg. pr. indic. passive √*yuj*), it is used, it is employed, it is pronounced.

27

यज्ञे तपसि दाने च
yajñe tapasi dāne ca
in sacrifice, in austerity and in giving

स्थितिः सद् इति चोच्यते ।
sthitiḥ sad iti cocyate
steadfastness "sat" thus also it is called,

कर्म चैव तदर्थीयं
karma cāiva tadarthīyaṁ
and action relating to this purpose,

सद् इत्य् एवाभिधीयते ॥
sad ity evābhidhīyate
"sat" thus likewise it is designated.

In sacrifice, austerity and giving
Steadfastness is also called "sat,"
And action relating to this
Is likewise designated as "sat."

yajñe (m. loc. sg.), in sacrifice, in worship.
tapasi (n. loc. sg.), in austerity, in self-denial.
dāne (n. loc. sg.), in giving, in charity.
ca, and.
sthitis (f. nom. sg.), steadfastness, dependability.
sat (n. nom. sg.), truth, reality, goodness (here simply "sat").
iti, thus, in this way (often used to close a quotation).
ca, and.
ucyate (3rd sg. pr. indic. passive √*vac*), it is called, it is said to be.
karma (n. nom. sg.), action.
ca, and.
eva, indeed, likewise (often used as a rhythmic filler).
tadarthīyam (n. nom. sg.), relating to that, serving the purpose of that.
sat (n. nom. sg.), truth, reality, goodness (here simply "sat").
iti, thus, in this way (often used to close a quotation).
eva, indeed, likewise (often used as a rhythmic filler).
adhidhīyate (3rd sg. pr. indic. passive *abhi* √*dhā*), it is designated, it is proclaimed.

28

अश्रद्धया हुतं दत्तं
aśraddhayā hutaṁ dattaṁ
with lack of faith oblation offered,

तपस् तप्तं कृतं च यत् ।
tapas taptaṁ kṛtaṁ ca yat
austerity performance done, which

असद् इत्य् उच्यते पार्थ
asad ity ucyate pārtha
"asat" thus it is called, Son of Pṛthā,

न च तत् प्रेत्य नो इह ॥
na ca tat pretya no iha
and not that (is anything) to us hereafter, nor here in the world.

An oblation offered or an austerity undergone
Which is without faith
Is called "asat," Son of Pṛthā,
And is nothing to us in the hereafter or here in the world.

aśraddhayā (f. inst. sg.), by lack of faith, with absence of faith.
hutam (n. nom. sg.), oblation, pouring into the sacrificial fire.
dattam (n. nom. sg. p. pass. participle √*dā*), given, offered, presented.
tapas (n. nom. sg.), austerity, heat.
taptam (n. nom. sg. p. pass. participle √*tap*), undergone, practiced, performed.
kṛtam (n. nom. sg. p. pass. participle √*kṛ*), done, made.
ca, and.
yad (n. nom. sg.), which.
asat (n. nom. sg. *a* + pr. participle √*as*), untruth, unreality, not good, lacking in virtue (here simply "asat").
iti, thus, in this way (often used to close a quotation.)
ucyate (3rd sg. pr. passive √*vac*), it is called, it is said, it is said to be.
pārtha (m. voc. sg.), Son of Pṛthā, epithet of Arjuna.
na, not.
ca, and.
tad (n. nom. sg.), that, this.
pretya (gerund *pra* √*i*), having died, after death, having gone, hereafter.
nas (dat. sg.), of us, to us.
iha, here, here in the world.

End of Book XVII

The Yoga of the Distinction of the Three Kinds of Faith

BOOK XVIII

अर्जुन उवाच ।
arjuna uvaca
Arjuna spoke:

arjunas (m. nom. sg.), Arjuna.
uvāca (3rd sg. perf. act. √*vac*), he said, he spoke.

1

संन्यासस्य महाबाहो
saṁnyāsasya mahābāho
of renunciation, O Mighty Armed One,

तत्त्वम् इच्छामि वेदितुम् ।
tattvam icchāmi veditum
the truth I wish to know

त्यागस्य च हृषीकेश
tyāgasya ca hṛṣīkeśa
and of abandonment, Bristling Haired One,

पृथक् केशिनिषूदन ॥
pṛthak keśiniṣūdana
separately, Slayer of Keśin.

saṁnyāsasya (m. gen. sg.), of renunciation, of relinquishment, lit. "of throwing aside."
mahābāho (m. voc. sg.), O mighty Armed One, epithet of various warriors, here applied to Krishna.
tattvam (n. acc. sg.), truth, "thatness."
icchāmi (1st sg. pr. indic. act. √*iṣ*), I wish, I desire.
veditum (infinitive √*vid*), to know, to learn.
tyāgasya (m. gen. sg.), of abandonment, of leaving behind.
ca, and.
hṛṣīkeśa (m. voc. sg.), Bristling Haired One, epithet of Krishna.
pṛthak (adv.), separately, singly, one by one.
keśiniṣūdana (m. voc. sg.), Slayer of Keśin, epithet of Krishna.

Arjuna spoke:

I wish to know the truth
Of renunciation, O Mighty Armed One,*
And of abandonment, Bristling Haired One,
And the difference between them, Slayer of Keśin.†

---

* *mahābāho*, "O Mighty Armed One," usually an epithet of Arjuna, is here applied to Krishna. It is a general epithet of distinguished warriors.

† The āsura Keśin was slain by Vishnu (Krishna) in another part of the Mahābhārata. (See chapter on "The Setting of the Bhagavād Gītā".)

श्रीभगवान् उवाच।
śrībhagavān uvāca
the Blessed Lord spoke:

śrībhagavān (m. nom. sg.), the Blessed Lord the Blessed one.
uvāca (3rd sg. perf. act. √*vac*), he said, he spoke.

2

काम्यानां कर्मणां न्यासं
kāmyānāṁ karmaṇāṁ nyāsaṁ
of rites undertaken to achieve desires, the relinquishment,

संन्यासं कवयो विदुः।
saṁnyāsaṁ kavayo viduḥ
renunciation the poets understand;

सर्वकर्मफलत्यागं
sarvakarmaphalatyāgaṁ
all action-fruit abandonment

प्राहुस् त्यागं विचक्षणाः॥
prāhus tyāgaṁ vicakṣaṇāḥ
they declare (to be) abandonment, the clear sighted.

The Blessed Lord spoke:

The relinquishment of actions prompted by desire
The chroniclers understand as renunciation;
The relinquishment of the fruit of all action
Those who are clear sighted declare to be abandonment.*

kāmyānām (n. gen. pl.), of desiderative, of springing from desire.
karmaṇām (n. gen. pl.), of actions, of acts.
nyāsam (m. acc. sg. from *ni* √2 *as*), renunciation, throwing down, relinquishment.
saṁnyāsam (m. acc. sg. from *sam ni* √2 *as*), renunciation, relinquishment, lit. "throwing down."
kavayas (m. nom. pl.), the poets, the chroniclers, the seers.
vidus (3rd pl. perf. act. √*vid* with present meaning), they understand, they know.
sarva, all.
karma (n.), action.
phala (n.), fruit, result.
tyāgam (m. acc. sg.), abandonment desertion, giving up.
(*sarvakarmaphalatyāgam,* m. acc. sg. TP cpd., abandonment of all fruit of action.)
prāhus (3rd pl. perf. act. *pra* √*ah* with present meaning), they say, they declare.
tyāgam (m. acc. sg.), abandonment, desertion, leaving behind.
vicakṣaṇās (m. nom. pl.), the clear-eyed, the clear-sighted, the sagacious.

* The words are clear enough, but, to avoid any misunderstanding, what is said is that renunciation (*saṁnyāsa*) is the relinquishment of all action which is aimed at a desired result; abandonment (*tyāga*) is the relinquishment of the *results* of action, and thus does not imply non-action as renunciation does.

3

त्याज्यं दोषवद् इत्य् एके
tyājyaṁ doṣavad ity eke
to be abandoned, full of evil thus some

कर्म प्राहुर् मनीषिणः ।
karma prāhur manīṣiṇaḥ
action, they declare, men of wisdom,

यज्ञदानतपःकर्म
yajñadānatapaḥkarma
and sacrifice-giving-austerity action

न त्याज्यम् इति चापरे ॥
na tyājyam iti cāpare
not to be abandoned thus others.

Some men of wisdom declare
That action is to be abandoned and is full of evil,
And others that acts of sacrifice, giving and austerity
Are not to be abandoned.

tyājyam (n. acc. sg. gerundive √*tyaj*), to be abandoned, to be relinquished.
doṣavat (n. acc. sg.), full of evil, evil, wrong.
iti, thus, in this way.
eke (m. nom. pl. of *eka*, "one"), some.
karma (n. acc. sg.), action, work.
prāhus (3rd pl. perf. act. *pra* √*ah* with present meaning), they say, they declare.
manīṣiṇas (m. nom. pl.), the thoughtful, the wise ones, the men of wisdom.
yajña (m.), sacrifice, worship.
dāna (n.), giving, charity.
tapas (n.), austerity, heat.
karma (n. acc. sg.), action, work.
(*yajñadānatapaḥkarma,* n. nom. sg. TP cpd., action by sacrifice, gifts and austerity.)
na, not.
tyājyam (n. acc. sg. gerundive √*tyaj*), to be abandoned, to be given up, to be deserted.
iti, thus, in this way, so.
ca, and.
apare (m. nom. pl.), others.

4

निश्चयं शृणु मे तत्र
niścayaṁ śṛṇu me tatra
the conclusion hear of me there

त्यागे भरतसत्तम ।
tyāge bharatasattama
concerning abandonment, Best of the Bharatas,

त्यागो हि पुरुषव्याघ्र
tyāgo hi puruṣavyāghra
abandonment indeed, Man-Tiger,

त्रिविधः संप्रकीर्तितः ॥
trividhaḥ saṁprakīrtitaḥ
threefold designated.

Hear My conclusion in this matter
Concerning abandonment, Best of the Bharatas.
Abandonment indeed, Tiger among Men,
Is designated as threefold:

niścayam (m. acc. sg.), conclusion, conviction, ascertainment.
śṛṇu (2nd sg. imperative act. √*śru*), hear! learn!
me (gen. sg.), of me, my.
tatra, there, in this case.
tyāge (m. loc. sg.), in abandonment, concerning abandonment.
bharatasattama (m. voc. sg.), O Best of the Bharatas, epithet of Arjuna.
tyāgas (m. nom. sg.), abandonment, desertion, giving up.
hi, indeed, truly.
puruṣavyāghra (m. voc. sg.), Man-Tiger, Tiger among Men, epithet of Arjuna.
trividhas (m. nom. sg.), threefold, of three kinds.
saṁprakīrtitas (m. nom. sg.p. pass. participle *sam pra* √*kīrt*), designated, enumerated.

5

यज्ञदानतपःकर्म
yajñadānatapaḥkarma
sacrifice-giving-austerity action

न त्याज्यं कार्यम् एव तत् ।
na tyājyaṁ kāryam eva tat
not to be abandoned, to be performed rather that;

यज्ञो दानं तपश्चैव
yajño dānaṁ tapaścāiva
sacrifice, giving and austerity

पावनानि मनीषिणाम् ॥
pāvanāni manīṣiṇām
purifiers of those who are wise.

Acts of sacrifice, giving and austerity
Are not to be abandoned, but rather to be performed.
Sacrifice, giving and austerity
Are purifiers of those who are wise.

yajña (m.), sacrifice, worship.
dāna (n.), giving, charity.
tapas (n.), austerity, heat.
karma (n. nom. acc. sg.), action.
(*yajñadānatapaḥkarma*, n. nom. sg. TP cpd., actions of sacrifice, giving and austerity, sacrifice-giving-austerity-action).
na, not.
tyājyam (n. nom. sg. gerundive √*tyaj*), to be abandoned, to be left behind.
kāryam (n. nom. sg. gerundive √*kṛ*), to be done, to be made, to be performed.
eva, indeed, rather (often used as a rhythmic filler).
tad (n. nom. sg.), this, that.
yajñas (m. nom. sg.), sacrifice, worship.
dānam (n. nom. sg.), giving, charity.
tapas (n. nom. sg.), austerity, heat.
ca, and.
eva, indeed (used as a rhythmic filler).
pāvanāni (n. nom. pl.), purifiers, cleansers.
manīṣiṇām (m. gen. pl.), of the wise, of the thoughtful, of those who are wise.

6

एतान्य् अपि तु कर्माणि
etāny api tu karmāṇi
these, however, indeed, actions

सङ्गं त्यक्त्वा फलानि च ।
saṅgaṁ tyaktvā phalāni ca
attachment and abandoning fruits,

कर्तव्यानीति मे पार्थ
kartavyānīti me pārtha
to be performed, thus of me, Son of Pṛthā,

निश्चितं मतम् उत्तमम् ॥
niścitaṁ matam uttamam
without doubt belief highest.

These actions, however, are to be performed
With abandonment of attachment to the fruits.
This, Son of Pṛthā,
Is My definite and highest belief.

etāni (n. nom. pl.), these.
api, but, however.
tu, indeed.
karmāṇi (n. nom. pl.), actions, deeds.
saṅgam (m. acc. sg.), attachment, coming together.
tyaktvā (gerund √*tyaj*), abandoning, having abandoned, having left behind.
phalāni (n. acc. pl.), fruits, results.
ca, and.
kartavyāni (n. nom. pl. gerundive √*kṛ*), to be done, to be made, to be performed.
iti, thus, in this way.
me (gen. sg.), of me, my.
pārtha (m. voc. sg.), Son of Pṛthā, epithet of Arjuna.
niścitam (adv.), without doubt, surely, definite.
matam (n. nom. sg.), thought, belief.
uttamam (n. nom. sg.), highest, supreme.

7

नियतस्य तु संन्यासः
niyatasya tu saṁnyāsaḥ
of obligatory, but, renunciation

कर्मणो नोपपद्यते ।
karmaṇo nopapadyate
of action not it is proper;

मोहात् तस्य परित्यागस्
mohāt tasya parityāgas
from delusion, of it, abandonment

तामसः परिकीर्तितः ॥
tāmasaḥ parikīrtitaḥ
tamasic proclaimed to be.

But renunciation of obligatory action
Is not proper;
The abandonment of it through delusion
Is proclaimed to be tamasic.

niyatasya (n. gen. sg.), of obligatory, of mandatory, of prescribed.
tu, but, indeed.
saṁnyāsas (m. nom. sg.), renunciation, throwing aside.
karmaṇas (n. gen. sg.), of action.
na, not.
upapadyate (3rd sg. pr. indic. mid. *upa* √*pad*), it takes place, it is fitting, it is proper, it happens.
mohāt (m. abl. sg.), from delusion, from confusion.
tasya (n. gen. sg.), of this, of it.
parityāgas (m. nom. sg. from *pari* √*tyaj*), abandonment.
tāmasas (n. nom. sg.), tamasic, pertaining to the guṇa of tamas.
parikīrtitas (m. nom. sg. p. pass. participle *pari* √*kīrt*), declared, proclaimed, said.

8

दुःखम् इत्येव यत् कर्म
duḥkham ityeva yat karma
difficult thus merely, which action,

कायक्लेशभयात् त्यजेत् ।
kāyakleśabhayāt tyajet
from bodily-suffering = fear he should abandon,

स कृत्वा राजसं त्यागं
sa kṛtvā rājasaṁ tyāgaṁ
he, having performed rajasic abandonment,

नैव त्यागफलं लभेत् ॥
nāiva tyāgaphalaṁ labhet
not abandonment-fruit he should obtain.

He who abandons action merely because it is difficult,
Or because of fear of bodily suffering,
Performs rajasic abandonment.
He should not obtain the fruit of that abandonment.

duḥkham (n. acc. sg.), difficult, evil, sorrowful.
iti, thus, in this way.
eva, indeed, merely (often used as a rhythmic filler).
yad (n. acc. sg.), what, which.
karma (n. acc. sg.), action.
kāya (m.), body, bodily.
kleśa (m.), suffering, pain.
bhayāt (n. abl. sg.), from fear, from apprehension, from dread.
(*kāyakleśabhayāt,* n. abl. sg., from fear of bodily suffering.)
tyajet (3rd sg. optative act. √*tyaj*), he should abandon, one should abandon.
sas (m. nom. sg.), he, this.
kṛtvā (gerund √*kṛ*), performing, having performed, having made, having done.
rājasam (n. acc. sg.), rajasic, pertaining to the guṇa of rajas.
tyāgam (m. acc. sg.), abandonment.
na, not.
eva, indeed (used as a rhythmic filler).
tyāgaphalam (n. acc. sg.), fruit of abandonment, fruit of giving up.
labhet (3rd sg. optative act. √*labh*), he should obtain, he should attain, he should get.

9

कार्यम् इत्येव यत् कर्म
kāryam ityeva yat karma
to-be-done* which action,

नियतं क्रियते ऽर्जुन ।
niyatam̐ kriyate 'rjuna
disciplined, it is done, Arjuna,

सङ्गं त्यक्त्वा फलं चैव
sañgam̐ tyaktvā phalam̐ cāiva
with attachment having abandoned fruit

स त्यागः सात्त्विको मतः ॥
sa tyāgaḥ sāttviko mataḥ
this abandonment sattvic thought to be.

When action is done because it is a duty,*
In a disciplined manner, Arjuna,
And with abandonment of attachment to fruit;
Such abandonment is thought to be sattvic.

kāryam (n. nom. sg. gerundive √*kṛ*), to be done, to be performed, a duty.
iti, thus, in this way.
eva, indeed (used as a rhythmic filler).
yad (n. nom. sg.), what, which.
karma (n. nom. sg.), action.
niyatam (n. nom. sg.), disciplined, controlled.
kriyate (3rd sg. pr. indic. passive √*kṛ*), it is done, it is made, it is performed.
arjuna (m. voc. sg.), Arjuna.
sañgam (m. acc. sg.), attachment, clinging.
tyaktvā (gerund √*tyaj*), abandoning, having abandoned.
phalam (n. acc. sg.), fruit, result.
ca, and.
eva, indeed (used as a rhythmic filler).
sas (m. nom. sg.), he, this.
tyāgas (m. nom. sg.), abandonment, giving up.
sāttvikas (m. nom. sg.), sattvic, pertaining to the guṇa of sattva.
matas (m. nom. sg. p. pass. participle √*man*), thought, thought to be, considered.

* Action "to be done," i.e. religiously prescribed action such as sacrifice, purification, giving, austerity.

10

न द्वेष्ट्य् अकुशलं कर्म
na dveṣṭy akuśalaṁ karma
not he hates disagreeable action,

कुशले नानुषज्जते ।
kuśale nānuṣajjate
in agreeable not he is attached,

त्यागी सत्त्वसमाविष्टो
tyāgī sattvasamāviṣṭo
the abandoner, goodness filled with,

मेधावी छिन्नसंशयः ॥
medhāvī chinnasaṁśayaḥ
the wise man, cut away doubt.

The abandoner, the wise man
Whose doubt is cut away, filled with goodness,
Does not hate disagreeable action,
Nor is he attached in agreeable action.

na, not.
dveṣṭi (3rd sg. act. √*dviṣ*), he hates, he dislikes.
akuśalam (n. acc. sg.), disagreeable, inauspicious.
karma (n. acc. sg.), action.
kuśale (n. loc. sg.), in agreeable, in auspicious.
na, not.
anuṣajjate (3rd sg. pr. indic. mid. *anu* √*sañj*), he is attached, he clings.
tyāgī (m. nom. sg.), abandoner, giver up.
sattva (n.), goodness, truth, reality.
samāviṣṭas (m. nom. sg. p. pass. participle *sam ā* √*viś*), filled with, entered into.
(*sattva-samāviṣṭas*, m. nom. sg. TP cpd., filled with goodness.)
medhāvī (m. nom. sg.), wise man, learned man, paṇḍit.
chinna (p. pass. participle √*chid*), cut away, abolished, eliminated, chopped.
saṁśayas (m. nom. sg.), doubt, irresolution.
(*chinnasaṁśayas*, m. nom. sg. BV cpd., whose doubt has been cut away.)

11

न हि देहभृता शक्यं
na hi dehabhṛtā śakyaṁ
not indeed by the body-borne able

त्यक्तुं कर्माण्य् अशेषतः ।
tyaktuṁ karmāṇy aśeṣataḥ
to abandon actions without remainder;

यस् तु कर्मफलत्यागी
yas tu karmaphalatyāgī
who then the action-fruit abandoner,

स त्यागीत्य् अभिधीयते ॥
sa tyāgīty abhidhīyate
he "abandoner" thus is called.

Indeed body-borne beings are not able
To abandon actions entirely;
He, then, who is an abandoner of the fruit of action,
Is called "abandoner."

na, not.
hi, indeed, truly.
dehabhṛtā (n. instr. sg.), by body-borne beings, by the body borne, by those inhabiting the body, by creatures.
śakyam (n. acc. sg.), able, capable, possible.
tyaktum (infinitive √*tyaj*), to abandon, to give up.
karmāṇi (n. acc. pl.), actions.
aśeṣatas (adv.), without remainder, entirely.
yas (m. nom. sg.), who.
tu, indeed, then, but.
karma (n.), action.
phala (n.), fruit, result.
tyāgī (m. nom. sg.), abandoner, giver up.
(*karmaphalatyāgī,* m. nom. sg. TP cpd., abandoner of the fruit of action.)
sas (m. nom. sg.), he, this.
tyāgī (m. nom. sg.), abandoner, giver up.
iti, thus, in this way.
abhidhīyate (3rd sg. pr. passive *abhi* √*dhā*), he is called, he is said to be, he is designated as.

12

अनिष्टम् इष्टं मिश्रं च
aniṣṭam iṣṭaṁ miśraṁ ca
undesired, desired and mixed

त्रिविधं कर्मणः फलम् ।
trividhaṁ karmaṇaḥ phalam
threefold of action the fruit

भवत्य् अत्यागिनां प्रेत्य
bhavaty atyāgināṁ pretya
it is for the non-abandoners, departing;

न तु संन्यासिनां क्वचित् ॥
na tu saṁnyāsināṁ kvacit
not, but, for the renouncers any (fruit) whatever.

The fruit of action for the non-abandoners
When they depart (die) is threefold:
Undesired, desired and mixed;
But for the renouncers there is none whatever.

aniṣṭam (n. nom sg.), undesired, unwished for.
iṣṭam (n. nom. sg.), desired, wished for.
miśram (n. nom. sg.), mixed.
ca, and.
trividham (n. nom. sg.), threefold, of three kinds.
karmaṇas (n. gen. sg.), of action.
phalam (n. nom. sg.), fruit, result.
bhavati (3rd sg. pr. indic. act. √*bhū*), it is, it comes to be.
atyāginām (m. gen. pl.), of the non-abandoners, of those who do not abandon.
pretya (gerund *pra* √*i*), departing, dying.
na, not.
tu, indeed, but, however.
saṁnyāsinām (m. gen. pl.), of the renouncers, of the throwers aside.
kvacit, any whatever.

13

पञ्चैतानि महाबाहो
pañcāitāni mahābāho
five these, O Mighty Armed One,

कारणानि निबोध मे ।
kāraṇāni nibodha me
factors learn from me

सांख्ये कृतान्ते प्रोक्तानि
sāṁkhye kṛtānte proktāni
in the Sāṁkhya doctrine declared

सिद्धये सर्वकर्मणाम् ॥
siddhaye sarvakarmaṇām
for the accomplishment of all actions.

pañca, five.
etāni (n. acc. pl.), these.
mahābāho (m. voc. sg.), Mighty Armed One.
kāraṇāni (n. acc. pl.), factors, causes, motives.
nibodha (2nd sg. imperative act. *ni* √*budh*), learn! be enlightened as to!
me (gen. sg.), of me, from me.
sāṁkhye (m. loc. sg.), in Sāṁkhya, in the Sāṁkhya Doctrine.
kṛtānte (m. loc. sg. from *kṛta anta*), in making an end, in making a conclusion, in doctrine, in dogma.
proktāni (n. acc. pl. p. pass. participle *pra* √*vac*), declared, proclaimed, maintained.
siddhaye (f. dat. sg.), to the accomplishment, for the success.
sarvakarmaṇām (n. gen. pl.), of all actions.

Learn from Me, O Mighty Armed One,
These five factors,
Declared in the Sāṁkhya* doctrine
For the accomplishment of all actions:

* See note to stanza 39, Book II, for explanation of the Sāṁkhya system.

14

अधिष्ठानं तथा कर्ता
adhiṣṭhānaṁ tathā kartā
the body also the agent

करणं च पृथग्विधम् ।
karaṇaṁ ca pṛthagvidham
and the instrument of various kinds,

विविधाश्च पृथक्चेष्टा
vividhāśca pṛthakceṣṭā
and the various separate activities

दैवं चैवात्र पञ्चमम् ॥
daivaṁ cāivātra pañcamam
and divine providence, in this matter, the fifth.

adhiṣṭhānam (n. nom. sg.), seat, basis, abode, body.
tathā, also, thus, so.
kartā (m. nom. sg.), maker, doer, agent.
karaṇam (n. nom. sg.), means, instrument.
ca, and.
pṛthagvidham (n. nom. sg.), various kinds, separate sorts.
vividhās (f. nom pl.), various, manifold.
ca, and.
pṛthak, separate, distinct.
ceṣṭās (f. nom. pl.), activities, gestures, motions.
dāivam (n. nom. sg.), belonging to the gods, divine, divine providence, fate.
ca, and.
eva, indeed.
atra, here, in this case.
(*evātra,* in this case, in this matter.)
pañcamam (n. nom. sg.), the fifth.

The seat of action,* the agent,†
The instrument, of various kinds,
And the various separate activities
With divine providence as the fifth;

* *adhiṣṭhāna* (seat of action) is interpreted by most commentators as the physical body.

† The word "agent" is used here and elsewhere in this book in the meaning of "one who acts," an actor or doer.

15

शरीरवाङ्मनोभिर् यत्
śarīravāñmanobhir yat
with body, speech, mind, whatever

कर्म प्रारभते नरः ।
karma prārabhate naraḥ
action he undertakes, a man,

न्याय्यं वा विपरीतं वा
nyāyyaṁ vā viparītaṁ vā
either right or wrong

पञ्चैते तस्य हेतवः ॥
pañcāite tasya hetavaḥ
five these of it the factors.

Whatever action a man undertakes
With body, speech or mind,*
Either right or wrong,
These are its five factors.

śarīra (n.), bodily frame.
vāc (f.), speech, language.
manas (n.), mind, thought.
(*śarīravāñmanobhis,* n. inst. sg. DV cpd., by body, speech and mind, with body, speech and mind.)
yad (n. acc. sg.), whatever, which.
karma (n. acc. sg.), action.
prārabhate (3rd sg. pr. indic. mid. *pra ā* √*rabh*), he undertakes, he commences, he begins.
naras (m. nom. sg.), man, a man.
nyāyyam (n. acc. sg.), right, regular, customary.
vā-vā, either-or.
viparītam (n. acc. sg. p. pass. participle *vi pari* √*i*), contrary, perverse, wrong.
pañca, five.
ete (m. nom. pl.), these.
tasya (n. gen. sg.), of it, of this.
hetavas (m. nom. pl.), factors, causes, origins.

* Again, in Gītā psychology the mind acts, and so does speech.

16

तत्रैवं सति कर्तारम्
tatrāivaṁ sati kartāram
this case thus being, the agent

आत्मानं केवलं तु यः ।
ātmānaṁ kevalaṁ tu yaḥ
himself sole, indeed, who

पश्यत्य् अकृतबुद्धित्वान्
paśyaty akṛtabuddhitvān
he sees from unperfected understanding,

न स पश्यति दुर्मतिः ॥
na sa paśyati durmatiḥ
not he sees, the blockhead.

This being so, he who sees himself
As sole agent does not really see,
Because of the fact that he is one
Who has not perfected his understanding, the fool!

tatra, there, in this case.
evam, thus, in this way.
sati (n. loc. sg. pr. act. participle √*as*), in being, in reality, in truth.
kartāram (m. acc. sg.), agent, one who acts.
ātmānam (m. acc. sg.), himself, self.
kevalam (m. acc. sg.), sole, only, exclusive.
tu, but, indeed.
yas (m. nom. sg.), who.
paśyati (3rd sg. pr. indic. act. √*paś*), he sees, he perceives.
akṛta (n.), incomplete, undone, unmade, imperfect, unperfected.
buddhitvāt (n. abl. sg.), from understanding.
(*akṛtabuddhitvāt,* n. abl. sg. BV cpd., because he has not perfected his understanding, from not having a perfected understanding.)
na, not.
sas (m. nom. sg.), he, this.
paśyati (3rd sg. pr. indic. act. √*paś*), he sees, he perceives.
durmatis (m. nom. sg.), blockhead, fool.

17

यस्य नाहंकृतो भावो
yasya nāhaṁkṛto bhāvo
of whom not egoistic state (of mind),

बुद्धिर् यस्य न लिप्यते ।
buddhir yasya na lipyate
the intelligence of whom not it is befouled,

हत्वापि स इमाँल् लोकान्
hatvāpi sa imāṁl lokān
slaying even he these people

न हन्ति न निबध्यते ॥
na hanti na nibadhyate
not he slays not he is bound.

**He whose state of mind is not egoistic,
Whose intelligence is not befouled,
Even though he slays these people,
Does not slay, and is not bound (by his actions).**

yasya (m. gen. sg.), of whom.
na, not.
ahaṁkṛtas (m. nom. sg.), egoistic, haughty.
bhāvas (m. nom. sg.), state, condition.
buddhis (f. nom. sg.), intelligence, discernment, intuition.
yasya (m. gen. sg.), of whom.
na, not.
lipyate (3rd sg. pr. indic. passive √*lip*), he is befouled, it is smeared, it is defiled.
hatvā (gerund √*han*), slaying, having slain, having killed.
api, even.
sas (m. nom. sg.), he, this.
imān (m. acc. pl.), these.
lokān (m. acc. pl.), worlds, people.
na, not.
hanti (3rd sg. pr. indic. act. √*han*), he slays, he kills.
na, not.
nibadhyate (3rd sg. pr. indic. passive *ni* √*bandh*), he is bound, he is bound down, he is fettered.

18

ज्ञानं ज्ञेयं परिज्ञाता
jñānaṁ jñeyaṁ parijñātā
knowledge, the-to-be-known, the knower

त्रिविधा कर्मचोदना ।
trividhā karmacodanā
threefold propulsions to action

करणं कर्म कर्तेति
karaṇaṁ karma karteti
the instrument, the act, the agent, thus

त्रिविधः कर्मसंग्रहः ॥
trividhaḥ karmasaṁgrahaḥ
the threefold action-constituents.

Knowledge, that which is to be known, and the knower,
Are the threefold propulsions to action;
The instrument, the act and the agent
Are the threefold constituents of action.

jñānam (n. nom. sg.), knowledge, wisdom.
jñeyam (n. nom. sg. gerundive √*jñā*), the to-be-known, the object of knowledge.
parijñātā (m. nom. sg.), knower.
trividhā (f. nom. sg.), threefold, of three kinds.
karmacodanā (f. nom. sg.), propulsion to action, inspiration to action.
karaṇam (n. nom. sg.), instrument, means.
karma (n. nom. sg.), act, action.
kartā (m. nom. sg.), agent, doer, performer.
iti, thus, so, in this way.
trividhas (m. nom. sg.), threefold, of three kinds.
karmasaṁgrahas (m. nom. sg.), assemblage of factors involved in action, constituents of action.

19

ज्ञानं कर्म च कर्ता च
jñānaṁ karma ca kartā ca
knowledge and action and the agent,

त्रिधैव गुणभेदतः ।
tridhāiva guṇabhedataḥ
three kinds guṇa distinguished,

प्रोच्यते गुणसंख्याने
procyate guṇasaṁkhyāne
it is declared in guṇa theory;

यथावच् छृणु तान्य् अपि ॥
yathāvac chṛṇu tāny api
duly hear these also:

jñānam (n. nom. sg.), knowledge, wisdom.
karma (n. nom. sg.), action.
ca, and.
kartā (m. nom. sg.), agent, doer.
ca, and.
tridhā (f. nom. sg.), threefold, of three kinds.
eva, indeed (used as a rhythmic filler).
guṇabhedatas (m. abl. sg.), guṇa-distinguished, determined by the guṇas, split up according to the guṇas.
procyate (3rd sg. pr. indic. pass. *pra* √*vac*), it is said, it is declared.
guṇasaṁkhyāne (n. loc. sg.), in guṇa doctrine, in guṇa reckoning.
yathāvat (adv.), duly, properly, rightly.
śṛṇu (2nd sg. imperative act. √*śru*), hear! learn!
tāni (n. acc. pl.), these.
api, also, even.

It is declared in guṇa theory that
Knowledge, action and the agent
Are of three kinds, distinguished according to the guṇas.
Hear duly about these also:

20

सर्वभूतेषु येनैकं
sarvabhūteṣu yenāikaṁ
in all beings by which one

भावम् अव्ययम् ईक्षते ।
bhāvam avyayam īkṣate
being imperishable one sees,

अविभक्तं विभक्तेषु
avibhaktaṁ vibhakteṣu
undivided in the divided;

तज् ज्ञानं विद्धि सात्त्विकम् ॥
taj jñānaṁ viddhi sāttvikam
that knowledge know to be sattvic.

That knowledge by which one sees
One imperishable being in all beings,
Undivided in the divided;
Know that knowledge to be sattvic.

sarvabhūteṣu (n. loc. pl.), in all beings, in all creatures.
yena (m. inst. sg.), by which, with which.
ekam (m. acc. sg.), one.
bhāvam (m. acc. sg.), being, creature.
avyayam (m. acc. sg.), imperishable, eternal.
īkṣate (3rd sg. pr. indic. mid. √*īkṣ*), he sees, one sees.
avibhaktam (m. acc. sg.), undivided, undistributed.
vibhakteṣu (m. loc. pl.), in the divided, in the multiple.
tad (n. acc. sg.), that, this.
jñānam (n. acc. sg.), knowledge, wisdom.
viddhi (2nd imperative act. √*vid*), know! learn!
sāttvikam (n. acc. sg.), sattvic, pertaining to the guṇa of sattva.

21

पृथक्त्वेन तु यज् ज्ञानं
pṛthaktvena tu yaj jñānaṁ
as separate but which knowledge

नानाभावान् पृथग्विधान् ।
nānābhāvān pṛthagvidhān
different beings (of) various kinds

वेत्ति सर्वेषु भूतेषु
vetti sarveṣu bhūteṣu
it knows in all beings;

तज् ज्ञानं विद्धि राजसम् ॥
taj jñānaṁ viddhi rājasam
that knowledge know to be rajasic.

But that knowledge which knows as separate
Different beings of various kinds
Among all beings;
Know that knowledge to be rajasic.

pṛthaktvena (n. inst. sg.), as separate, with one by one.
tu, but, indeed.
yad (n. nom. sg.), which.
jñānam (n. nom. sg.), knowledge, wisdom.
nānā, various, different, distinct.
bhāvān (m. acc. pl.), beings, existences.
pṛthagvidhān (m. acc. pl.), of various kinds, of separate kinds.
vetti (3rd sg. pr. indic. act. √*vid*), he knows, it knows.
sarveṣu (m. loc. pl.), in all.
bhūteṣu (m. loc. pl.), in beings, in creatures, in existences.
tad (n. acc. sg.), that, this.
jñānam (n. acc. sg.), knowledge, wisdom.
viddhi (2nd sg. imperative act. √*vid*), know! learn! know to be!
rājasam (n. acc. sg.), rajasic, pertaining to the guṇa of rajas.

22

यत् तु कृत्स्नवद् एकस्मिन्
yat tu kṛtsnavad ekasmin
which but as if it were all, in one

कार्ये सक्तम् अहैतुकम् ।
kārye saktam ahāitukam
in the to-be-done attached, without concern for cause,

अतत्त्वार्थवद् अल्पं च
atattvārthavad alpaṁ ca
without real purpose and small (in value or significance)

तत् तामसम् उदाहृतम् ॥
tat tāmasam udāhṛtam
that tamasic declared to be.

yad (n. nom. sg.), which.
tu, but, indeed.
kṛtsnavat (n. nom. sg.), as if it were all, as if it were the whole.
ekasmin (loc. sg.), in one.
kārye (n. loc. sg.), in the to-be-done, in the order of action.
saktam (n. nom. sg.), attached, clinging.
ahāitukam (n. nom. sg.), without motive, without concern for cause.
atattvārthavat (n. nom. sg.), without true purpose, without real aim.
alpam (n. nom. sg.), small, piddling, slight.
ca, and.
tad (n. nom. sg.), that, this.
tāmasam (n. nom. sg.), tamasic, pertaining to the guṇa of tamas.
udāhṛtam (n. nom. sg. p. pass. participle *ud ā* √*hṛ*), declared, proclaimed, said to be.

That (knowledge), however, which is attached to one object of action
As if it were all, and without concern for cause,
Without a real purpose and small in significance,
Is declared to be tamasic.

23

नियतं सङ्गरहितम्
niyataṁ saṅgarahitam
controlled, attachment free from,

अरागद्वेषतः कृतम् ।
arāgadveṣataḥ kṛtam
without desire or hatred performed,

अफलप्रेप्सुना कर्म
aphalaprepsunā karma
without fruit desiring to obtain, action,

यत् तत् सात्त्विकम् उच्यते ॥
yat tat sāttvikam ucyate
which, that sattvic said to be

That action which is controlled and free from attachment,
Performed without desire or hate,
With no wish to obtain fruit,
Is said to be sattvic.

niyatam (n. nom. sg.), controlled, subdued.
saṅga (m.), attachment, clinging.
rahitam (n. nom. sg. p. pass. participle √*rah*), freed from, quitted, forsaken, separated from.
(*saṅga-rahitam*, n. nom. sg. TP cpd., freed from clinging.)
arāgadveṣatas (adv.), without desire or hatred, neither liking nor disliking.
kṛtam (n. nom. sg.), done, performed.
aphala (n.), without fruit, non-fruit.
prepsunā (m. inst. desiderative adj. from *pra* √*āp*), desiring to obtain, wishing to acquire.
karma (n. nom. sg.), action.
yad (n. nom. sg.), which.
tad (n. acc. sg.), that, this.
sāttvikam (n. acc. sg.), sattvic, pertaining to the guṇa of sattva.
ucyate (3rd sg. pr. indic. passive √*vac*), it is said, it is called, it is said to be.

24

यत् तु कामेप्सुना कर्म
yat tu kāmepsunā karma
which, but, with desire wishing to obtain, action,

साहंकारेण वा पुनः ।
sāhaṁkāreṇa vā punaḥ
with selfishness, or again,

क्रियते बहुलायासं
kriyate bahulāyāsaṁ
it is performed (with) much effort;

तद् राजसम् उदाहृतम् ॥
tad rājasam udāhṛtam
that rajasic declared to be

yad (n. nom. sg.), which.
tu, but, however, indeed.
kāma (m.), desire, lust.
īpsunā (m. inst. sg. desiderative adj. from √*āp*), wishing to obtain, desiring to get.
karma (n. nom. sg.), action.
sāhaṁkāreṇa (m. inst. sg.), by selfishness, with egotism with self-centeredness.
vā, or.
punar, again, further.
kriyate (3rd sg. pr. indic. passive √*kṛ*), it is done, it is performed.
bahula (m.), much, many.
āyāsam (m. acc. sg.), effort, exertion, toil.
(*bahula-āyāsam*, m. acc. sg. KD cpd., much effort.)
tad (n. nom. sg.), that, this.
rājasam (n. nom. sg.), rajasic, pertaining to the guṇa of rajas.
udāhṛtam (n. nom. sg. p. pass. participle *ud ā* √*hṛ*), declared, said to be.

But that action which is performed with a wish to obtain desires,
With selfishness, or, again,
With much effort,
Is declared to be rajasic.

25

अनुबन्धं क्षयं हिंसाम्
anubandhaṁ kṣayaṁ hiṁsām
consequence, loss, injury (to others)

अनपेक्ष्य च पौरुषम् ।
anapekṣya ca pāuruṣam
disregarding, and (one's own) strength,

मोहाद् आरभ्यते कर्म
mohād ārabhyate karma
from delusion it is undertaken, action

यत् तत् तामसम् उच्यते ॥
yat tat tāmasam ucyate
which, that tamasic said to be.

anubandham (m. acc. sg.), consequence, inevitable result.
kṣayam (m. acc. sg.), loss, destruction.
hiṁsām (f. acc. sg.), injury, violence.
anapekṣya (gerund *an apa* √*ikṣ*), disregarding, regardless, careless.
ca, and.
pāuruṣam (n. acc. sg.), strength, might, virility.
mohāt (m. abl. sg.), from delusion, from confusion.
ārabhyate (3rd sg. pr. indic. passive *ā* √*rabh*), it is undertaken, it is commenced.
karma (n. nom. sg.), action.
yad (n. nom. sg.), which.
tad (n. nom. sg.), that, this.
tāmasam (n. nom. sg.), tamasic, pertaining to the guṇa of tamas.
ucyate (3rd sg. pr. indic. passive √*vac*), it is said, it is said to be.

That action which is undertaken because of delusion,
Disregarding consequences, loss or injury to others,
As well as one's own strength,
Is said to be tamasic.

26

मुक्तसङ्गो ऽनहंवादी
muktasaṅgo 'nahaṁvādī
released from attachment, free from self-speaking,

धृत्युत्साहसमन्वितः ।
dhṛtyutsāhasamanvitaḥ
steadfastness and resolution accompanied by

सिद्ध्यसिद्ध्योर् निर्विकारः
siddhyasiddhyor nirvikāraḥ
in success or failure unperturbed;

कर्ता सात्त्विक उच्यते ॥
kartā sāttvika ucyate
agent sattvic said to be.

Released from attachment, free from talk of self,
Accompanied by steadfastness and resolution,
Unperturbed in success or failure;
Such an agent is said to be sattvic.

mukta (p. pass. participle √*muc*), released, freed from.
saṅgas (m. nom. sg.), attachment, clinging.
(*mukta-saṅgas*, m. nom. sg. KD cpd., freed from attachment.)
anahaṁvādī (m. nom. sg.), free from talk of self, free from self-speaking.
dhṛti (f.), courage, steadfastness.
utsāha (m.), resolution, effort, power, perseverance.
samanvitas (m. nom. sg. p. pass. participle *sam anu* √*i*), accompanied by, going along with.
(*dhṛtyutsāhasamanvitas*, m. nom. sg., accompanied by steadfastness and resolution.)
siddhi (f.), success, accomplishment.
asiddhi (f.), failure, non-success.
(*siddhyasiddhyos*, f. loc. dual DV cpd., in success and failure, in attainment and non-attainment.)
nirvikāras (m. nom. sg.), unperturbed, unchanged, unmodified.
kartā (m. nom. sg.), agent, doer.
sāttvikas (m. nom. sg.), sattvic, pertaining to the guṇa of sattva.
ucyate (3rd sg. pr. indic. passive √*vac*), it is said, it is said to be.

27

रागी कर्मफलप्रेप्सुर्
rāgī karmaphalaprepsur
passionate action, fruit desiring to obtain,

लुब्धो हिंसात्मको ऽशुचिः ।
lubdho hiṁsātmako 'śuciḥ
greedy, violent natured, impure,

हर्षशोकान्वितः कर्ता
harṣaśokānvitaḥ kartā
joy and sorrow filled with, agent,

राजसः परिकीर्तितः ॥
rājasaḥ parikīrtitaḥ
rajasic proclaimed to be.

Passionate, desiring the fruits of action,
Greedy, violent-natured, impure,
Filled with joy or sorrow;
Such an agent is proclaimed to be rajasic.

rāgī (n. nom. sg.), passionate, head-long.
karma (n.), action.
phala (n.), fruit.
prepsus (m. nom. sg. desiderative adj. from *pra* √*āp*), desiring to obtain, wishing to get.
(*karmaphalaprepsus,* m. nom. sg., TP cpd. desiring to obtain the fruit of action.)
lubdhas (m. nom. sg.), greedy, desirous, avaricious.
hiṁsātmakas (m. nom. sg.), violent natured, bent on injury.
aśucis (m. nom. sg.), impure, polluted.
harṣa (m.), joy, happiness, bliss.
śoka (m.), sorrow, mourning, pain.
anvitas (m. nom. sg. p. pass. participle *anu* √*i*), accompanied by.
(*harṣaśokānvitas,* m. nom. sg. TP cpd., accompanied by joy and sorrow, filled with joy and sorrow.)
kartā (m. nom. sg.), agent, doer.
rājasas (m. nom. sg.), rajasic, pertaining to the guṇa of rajas.
parikīrtitas (m. nom. sg. p. pass. participle *pari* √*kīrt*), proclaimed to be, declared to be, celebrated as.

28

अयुक्तः प्राकृतः स्तब्धः
ayuktaḥ prākṛtaḥ stabdhaḥ
undisciplined, vulgar, obstinate,

शठो नैकृतिको ऽलसः ।
śaṭho nāikṛtiko 'lasaḥ
wicked, deceitful, lazy,

विषादी दीर्घसूत्री च
viṣādī dīrghasūtrī ca
despondent and dilatory;

कर्ता तामस उच्यते ॥
kartā tāmasa ucyate
agent tamasic said to be.

ayuktas (m. nom. sg. p. pass. participle *a* √*yuj*), undisciplined, unyoked.
prākṛtas (m. nom. sg.), vulgar, ostentatious, vain.
stabdhas (m. nom. sg.), obstinate, stubborn.
śaṭhas (m. nom. sg.), wicked, false, deceitful.
nāikṛtikas (m. nom. sg.), dishonest, vile.
alasas (m. nom. sg.), idle, indolent, lazy.
viṣādī (m. nom. sg.), despondent, desperate, depressed.
dīrghasūtrī (m. nom. sg.), dilatory, procrastinating.
ca, and.
kartā (m. nom. sg.), agent, doer.
tāmasas (m. nom. sg.), tamasic, pertaining to the guṇa of tamas.
ucyate (3rd sg. pr. indic. passive √*vac*), it is said, he is said to be, he is called.

Undisciplined, vulgar, obstinate,
Wicked, deceitful, lazy,
Despondent and dilatory;
Such an agent is said to be tamasic.

29

बुद्धेर् भेदं धृतेश्चैव
buddher bhedaṁ dhṛteścāiva
understanding the distinction, and also of firmness

गुणतस् त्रिविधं शृणु।
guṇatas trividhaṁ śṛṇu
according to the guṇas, threefold, hear,

प्रोच्यमानम् अशेषेण
procyamānam aśeṣeṇa
set forth without remainder

पृथक्त्वेन धनंजय ॥
pṛthaktvena dhanaṁjaya
separately, Conqueror of Wealth.

The threefold distinctions of understanding
And also of firmness, according to the guṇas, now hear,
Set forth completely
And separately, Conqueror of Wealth:

buddhes (f. gen. sg.), of intelligence, of discrimination, of understanding.
bhedam (m. acc. sg.), distinction, splitting, difference.
dhṛtes (f. gen. sg.), of steadfastness, of courage, of firmness.
ca, and.
eva, also, indeed (often used as a rhythmic filler).
guṇatas (adv.), according to the guṇas, in reference to the guṇas.
trividham (m. acc. sg.), threefold, of three kinds.
śṛṇu (2nd sg. imperative √*śru,*), hear! learn!
procyamānam (m. acc. sg. pass. pr. participle *pra* √*vac*), set forth, proclaimed, explained.
aśeṣeṇa (m. inst. sg.), without remainder, wholly, completely.
pṛthaktvena (m. inst. sg.), separately, distinctly.
dhanaṁjaya (m. voc. sg.), Conqueror of Wealth, epithet of Arjuna.

30

प्रवृत्तिं च निवृत्तिं च
pravṛttiṁ ca nivṛttiṁ ca
activity and inactivity

कार्याकार्ये भयाभये ।
kāryākārye bhayābhaye
the to-be-done and the not-to-be-done, the to-be-feared and the not-to-be-feared,

बन्धं मोक्षं च या वेत्ति
bandhaṁ mokṣaṁ ca yā vetti
bondage and liberation, which it knows

बुद्धिः सा पार्थ सात्त्विकी ॥
buddhiḥ sā pārtha sāttvikī
the understanding that, Son of Pṛthā, (is) sattvic.

That understanding which knows when to act and when not to act,
What is to be done and what is not to be done,
And what is to be feared and what is not to be feared,
Along with the knowledge of bondage and liberation, Son of Pṛthā, is sattvic.

pravṛttim (f. acc. sg.), activity, progress, exertion.
ca, and.
nivṛttim (f. acc. sg.), inactivity, non-exertion.
ca, and.
kārya (gerundive √*kṛ*), the to-be-done, the object of action.
akārya (gerundive *a* √*kṛ*), the not-to-be-done, not to be performed.
(*kāryākārye,* n. acc. dual gerundive DV cpd. √*kṛ*, the to-be-done and the not-to-be-done, what is to be done and what is not to be done.)
bhayābhaye (n. acc. dual DV cpd.) the to-be-feared and the not-to-be-feared, what is to be feared and what is not to be feared.
bandham (m. acc. sg.), bondage.
mokṣam (m. acc. sg.), liberation, freedom.
ca, and.
yā (f. nom. sg.), which.
vetti (3rd sg. pr. indic. act. √*vid*), it knows, it perceives.
buddhis (f. nom. sg.), intelligence, discrimination, understanding.
sā (f. nom. sg.), it, this, she.
pārtha (m. voc. sg.), Son of Pṛthā, epithet of Arjuna.
sāttvikī (f. nom. sg.), sattvic, pertaining to the guṇa of sattva.

31

यया धर्मम् अधर्मं च
yayā dharmam adharmaṁ ca
by which the right and the wrong

कार्यं चाकार्यम् एव च ।
kāryaṁ cākāryam eva ca
the to-be-done and the not-to-be-done,

अयथावत् प्रजानाति
ayathāvat prajānāti
incorrectly it distinguishes,

बुद्धिः सा पार्थ राजसी ॥
buddhiḥ sā pārtha rājasī
understanding, that, Son of Pṛthā, (is) rajasic.

That understanding which distinguishes incorrectly
Between the right and the wrong,
And between that which is to be done and that which is not to be done,
Is rajasic, Son of Pṛthā.

yayā (f. inst. sg.), by which, with which.
dharmam (m. acc. sg.), right, righteousness, law.
adharmam (m. acc. sg.), wrong, unlawful, unrighteousness.
ca, and.
kāryam (n. nom. sg. gerundive √*kṛ*), to-be-done, to-be-performed, duty.
ca, and.
akāryam (n. nom. sg. gerundive *a* √*kṛ*), not-to-be-done, not-to-be-performed.
eva, indeed (used as a rhythmic filler.)
ca, and.
ayathāvat (adv.), incorrectly, mistakenly.
prajānāti (3rd sg. pr. indic. act. *pra* √*jñā*), it distinguishes, it discriminates.
buddhis (f. nom. sg.), intelligence, discrimination, understanding.
sā (f. nom. sg.), this, she.
pārtha (m. voc. sg.), Son of Pṛthā, epithet of Arjuna.
rājasī (f. nom. sg.), rajasic, pertaining to the guṇa of rajas.

32

अधर्मं धर्मम् इति या
adharmaṁ dharmam iti yā
the wrong right thus which

मन्यते तमसावृता ।
manyate tamasāvṛtā
it imagines, darkness-enveloped,

सर्वार्थान् विपरीतांश्च
sarvārthān viparītāṁśca
and all things perverted

बुद्धिः सा पार्थ तामसी ॥
buddhiḥ sā pārtha tāmasī
understanding, that, Son of Pṛthā, (is) tamasic.

That understanding which, enveloped in darkness,
Imagines wrong to be right,
And all things to be perverted,
Is tamasic, Son of Pṛthā.

adharmam (m. acc. sg.), wrong, unlawful, contrary to usage.
dharmam (m. acc. sg.), right, righteous, lawful.
iti, thus, in this way.
yā (f. nom. sg.), which.
manyate (3rd sg. pr. indic. mid. √*man*), it thinks, it imagines.
tamasā (n. inst. sg.), by darkness.
āvṛtā (f. nom. sg. p. pass. participle *ā* √*vṛ*), enveloped.
sarvārthān (m. acc. pl.), all things, all aims.
viparītān (n. acc. pl. p. pass. participle *vi pari* √*i*), perverted, turned backward.
ca, and.
buddhis (f. nom. sg.), intelligence, discrimination, understanding.
sā (f. nom. sg.), this, she, it.
pārtha (m. voc. sg.), Son of Pṛthā, epithet of Arjuna.
tāmasī (f. nom. sg.), tamasic, pertaining to the guṇa of tamas.

33

धृत्या यया धारयते
dhṛtyā yayā dhārayate
by firmness by which one holds

मनःप्राणेन्द्रियक्रियाः
manaḥprāṇendriyakriyāḥ
mind, vital breath and sense functions

योगेनाव्यभिचारिण्या
yogenāvyabhicāriṇyā
by yoga unswerving

धृतिः सा पार्थ सात्त्विकी ।।
dhṛtiḥ sā pārtha sāttvikī
firmness that, Son of Pṛthā, (is) sattvic.

The firmness by which one holds
The functions of the mind, vital breath and senses
With unswerving Yoga;
That firmness, Son of Pṛthā, is sattvic.

dhṛtyā (f. inst. sg.), by firmness, by steadfastness.
yayā (f. inst. sg.), by which.
dhārayate (3rd sg. causative √*dhṛ*), he holds, one bears, one maintains.
manas (n.), mind, thought.
prāṇa (m.), vital breath.
indiryakriyās (f. nom. pl.), sense functions, functions of the senses.
(*manaḥprāṇendriyakriyās,* f. nom. pl., DV cpd. functions of the mind, the vital breath and the senses.)
yogena (m. inst. sg.), by Yoga, with Yoga.
avyabhicāriṇyā (f. inst. sg.), by not going astray, by unswerving.
dhṛtis (f. nom. sg.), firmness, steadfastness, courage.
sā (f. nom. sg.), this, that, she.
pārtha (m. voc. sg.), Son of Pṛthā, epithet of Arjuna.
sāttvikī (f. nom. sg.), sattvic, pertaining to the guṇa of sattva.

34

यया तु धर्मकामार्थान्
yayā tu dharmakāmārthān
by which, but, duty, desire, wealth

धृत्या धारयते ऽर्जुन ।
dhṛtyā dhārayate 'rjuna
with firmness one holds to, Arjuna,

प्रसङ्गेन फलाकाङ्क्षी
prasaṅgena phalākāṅkṣī
with attachment, fruit desiring,

धृतिः सा पार्थ राजसी ॥
dhṛtiḥ sā pārtha rājasī
firmness that, Son of Pṛthā, (is) rajasic.

But the firmness by which one holds to
Duty, desire and wealth,
With attachment and desire for the fruits of action;
That firmness, Son of Pṛthā, is rajasic.

yayā (f. inst. sg.), by which.
tu, but, however, indeed.
dharma (m.), duty, law, righteousness.
kāma (m.), desire.
arthān (m. acc. pl.), wealth, objects of desire, booty.
(*dharmakāmārthān,* m. acc. pl., duty, desire and wealth.)
dhṛtyā (f. inst. sg.), with firmness, by steadfastness.
dhārayate (3rd sg. pr. indic. causative mid. √*dhṛ*), he holds to, one holds to, one bears, one maintains.
arjuna (m. voc. sg.), Arjuna.
prasaṅgena (m. inst. sg.), with attachment, by clinging.
phalākāṅkṣī (m. nom. sg. from *phala ā kāṅkṣin*), fruit desiring, desiring results.
dhṛtis (f. nom.sg.), firmness, steadfastness.
sā (f. nom. sg.), that, this, she, it.
pārtha (m. voc. sg.), Son of Pṛthā, epithet of Arjuna.
rājasī (f. nom. sg.), rajasic, pertaining to the guṇa of rajas.

35

यया स्वप्नं भयं शोकं
yayā svapnaṁ bhayaṁ śokaṁ
by which sleep, fear, grief,

विषादं मदम् एव च ।
viṣādaṁ madam eva ca
depression and conceit

न विमुञ्चति दुर्मेधा
na vimuñcati durmedhā
not be abandons, the dull witted (man)

धृतिः सा पार्थ तामसी ॥
dhṛtiḥ sā pārtha tāmasī
firmness that, Son of Pṛthā, (is) tamasic.

That firmness by which one, whose wit is dull,
Does not abandon sleep, fear, grief,
Depression and conceit,
Is tamasic, Son of Pṛthā.

yayā (f. inst. sg.), by which, with which.
svapnam (m. acc. sg.), sleep.
bhayam (n. acc. sg.), fear.
śokam (m. acc. sg.), sorrow, grief.
viṣādam (m.acc. sg.), depression, lassitude.
madam (m. acc. sg.), pride, conceit, intoxication.
eva, indeed (used as a rhythmic filler).
ca, and.
na, not.
vimuñcati (3rd sg. act. *vi* √*muc*), he abandons, he relinquishes.
durmedhā (m. nom. sg.), the dull witted, the stupid man, one whose wit is dull.
dhṛtis (f. nom. sg.), firmness, steadfastness, courage.
sā (f. nom. sg.), this, it, she, that.
pārtha (m. voc. sg.), Son of Pṛthā, epithet of Arjuna.
tāmasī (f. nom. sg.), tamasic, pertaining to the guṇa of tamas.

36

सुखं त्व् इदानीं त्रिविधं
sukhaṁ tv idānīṁ trividhaṁ
happiness but now threefold

शृणु मे भरतर्षभ ।
śṛṇu me bharatarṣabha
hear from me, Bull of the Bharatas,

अभ्यासाद् रमते यत्र
abhyāsād ramate yatra
from practice one enjoys, where

दुःखान्तं च निगच्छति ॥
duḥkhāntaṁ ca nigacchati
and suffering-end one come to.

But now, hear from Me, Bull of the Bharatas,
The threefold happiness
That one enjoys through practice,
And in which one comes to the end of suffering.

sukham (n. nom. sg.), happiness, joy.
tu, but, indeed.
idānīm, now.
trividham (m. acc. sg.), threefold, of three kinds.
śṛṇu (2nd sg. imperative act. √*śru,*), hear! learn!
me (abl. sg.), from me, of me.
bharatarṣabha (m. voc. sg.), Bull of the Bharatas, epithet of Arjuna.
abhyāsāt (m. abl. sg.), from practice, from exercise, from repetition.
ramate (3rd sg. pr. indic. mid. √*ram*), he enjoys, one enjoys.
yatra, where, whither, in which.
duḥkha (n.), suffering, pain.
antam (m. acc. sg.), end, termination.
(*duḥkhāntam,* m. acc. sg., end of suffering, termination of pain.)
ca, and.
nigacchati (3rd sg. pr. indic. act. *ni* √*gam*), he goes to, he comes to, one comes to.

37

यत् तद् अग्रे विषम् इव
yat tad agre viṣam iva
which that in the beginning poison-like

परिणामे ऽमृतोपमम् ।
pariṇāme 'mṛtopamam
when transformed, nectar semblance;

तत् सुखं सात्त्विकं प्रोक्तम्
tat sukhaṁ sāttvikaṁ proktam
that happiness satvic declared to be

आत्मबुद्धिप्रसादजम् ॥
ātmabuddhiprasādajam
own spirit (and) tranquility born.

That which in the beginning is like poison
And whose semblance in transformation is nectar;
That happiness, born from the tranquility of the spirit of oneself,
Is declared to be sattvic.

yad (n. nom. sg.), which, what.
tad (n. nom. sg.), that, this.
agre (n. loc. sg.), in the beginning, at the start.
viṣam (n. nom. sg.), poison, venom.
iva, like.
pariṇāme (m. loc. sg.), in transformation, when transformed, in development.
amṛta (n.), nectar, immortality.
upamam (n. nom. sg.), comparison, resemblance, semblance.
(*amṛtopamam,* n. nom. sg. BV cpd., whose resemblance is nectar.)
tad (n. nom. sg.), that, this.
sukham (n. nom. sg.), happiness, joy.
sāttvikam (n. nom. sg.), sattvic, pertaining to the guṇa of sattva.
proktam (n. nom. sg. p. pass. participle *pra* √*vac*), declared, said to be.
ātmabuddhi (f.), own intelligence, own spirit.
prasāda (m.), purity, clarity, brightness, tranquility.
-jam (suffix), born, originating in.
(*ātmabuddhiprasādajam,* n. nom. sg. TP cpd., born from the tranquility of the spirit of oneself.)

38

विषयेन्द्रियसंयोगाद्
viṣayendriyasaṁyogād
from sense-object sense contact

यत् तद् अग्रे ऽमृतोपमम् ।
yat tad agre 'mṛtopamam
which that in the beginning resembles nectar,

परिणामे विषम् इव
pariṇāme viṣam iva
when transformed, poison-like;

तत् सुखं राजसं स्मृतम् ॥
tat sukhaṁ rājasaṁ smṛtam
that happiness rajasic recorded as.

That which in the beginning, through contact
Between the objects of the senses and the senses, resembles nectar,
And whose semblance in transformation is poison-like;
That happiness is recorded as rajasic.

viṣaya (m.), sense-object, object of the senses, sphere of activity.
indriya (n.), sense (as in the five senses).
saṁyogāt (m. abl. sg.), from joining together, from contact.
(*viṣayendriyasaṁyogāt,* m. abl. sg., TP cpd., from contact between the sense and the sense-object.)
yad (n. nom. sg.), which.
tad (n. nom. sg.), that, this.
agre (n. loc. sg.), in the beginning, at the start.
amṛta (n.), nectar, immortality.
upamam (n. nom. sg.), resemblance, likeness, semblance.
(*amṛtopamam,* n. nom. sg. BV cpd., whose resemblance is nectar.)
pariṇāme (m. loc. sg.), in transformation, when transformed.
viṣam (n. nom. sg.), poison, venom.
iva, like.
tad (n. nom. sg.), that, this.
sukham (n. nom. sg.), happiness, delight, joy.
rājasam (n. nom. sg.), rajasic, pertaining to the guṇa of rajas.
smṛtam (n. nom. sg. p. pass. participle √*smṛ*), remembered as, recorded as, known as.

39

यद् अग्रे चानुबन्धे च
yad agre cānubandhe ca
and which in the beginning and in (its) consequence,

सुखं मोहनम् आत्मनः ।
sukhaṁ mohanam ātmanaḥ
happiness, deluding of the self,

निद्रालस्यप्रमादोत्थं
nidrālasyapramādotthaṁ
sleep, indolence, negligence arising from,

तत् तामसम् उदाहृतम् ॥
tat tāmasam udāhṛtam
that tamasic declared to be.

That happiness which both in the beginning
And in its consequence, deludes the self,
Arising from sleep, indolence and negligence,
Is declared to be tamasic.

yad (n. nom. sg.), which.
agre (n. loc. sg.), in the beginning, at the start.
ca, and.
anubandhe (m. loc. sg.), in consequence, in result.
ca, and.
sukham (n. nom. sg.), happiness, joy, delight.
mohanam (n. nom. sg.), deluding, confusing.
ātmanas (m. gen. sg.), of the self.
nidrā (f.), sleep, sleepiness, slumber.
ālasya (n.), idleness, sloth, indolence, laziness.
pramāda (m.), negligence, confusion.
uttham (n. nom. sg. from *ud* √*sthā*), arising from, originating in.
(*nidrālasyapramādottham,* m. acc. sg. TP cpd., arising from sleepiness, indolence and negligence.)
tad (n. nom. sg.), that, this.
tāmasam (n. nom. sg.), tamasic, pertaining to the guṇa of tamas.
udāhṛtam (n. nom. sg. p. pass. participle *ud ā* √*hṛ*), declared, said to be.

40

न तद् अस्ति पृथिव्यां वा
na tad asti pṛthivyāṁ vā
not that there is either on earth

दिवि देवेषु वा पुनः ।
divi deveṣu vā punaḥ
or in heaven among the gods yet,

सत्त्वं प्रकृतिजैर् मुक्तं
sattvaṁ prakṛtijāir muktaṁ
a being, from material nature born, free,

यद् एभिः स्यात् त्रिभिर् गुणैः ॥
yad ebhiḥ syāt tribhir guṇāiḥ
which from these it may exist by the three guṇas.

There is no thing, either on earth
Or yet in heaven among the gods,
No being, which can exist
Free from these three guṇas born of material nature.

na, not.
tad (n. nom. sg.), that, this.
asti (3rd sg. pr. indic. √*as*), it is, there is.
pṛthivyām (f. loc. sg.), on earth.
vā-vā, either-or.
divi (m. loc. sg.), in heaven.
deveṣu (m. loc. pl.), among the gods.
punar, yet, even, again.
sattvam (n. nom. sg.), being, existence.
prakṛtijāis (m. inst. sg.), by material nature produced, born of material nature.
muktam (n. nom. sg. p. pass. participle √*muc*), free, freed, liberated.
yad (n. nom. sg.), which.
ebhis (m. inst. pl.), by these, from these.
syāt (3rd sg. optative act. √*as*), it may be, it can be, it may exist.
tribhis (m. inst. pl.), by three, from three.
guṇāis (m. inst. pl.), by the guṇas, from the guṇas.

41

ब्राह्मणक्षत्रियविशां
brāhmaṇakṣatriyaviśāṁ
of the brāhmans, the kṣatriyas and the vāiśyas

शूद्राणां च परंतप ।
śūdrāṇāṁ ca paraṁtapa
and the śūdras, Scorcher of the Foe,

कर्माणि प्रविभक्तानि
karmāṇi pravibhaktāni
the actions (are) distributed

स्वभावप्रभवैर् गुनैः ॥
svabhāvaprabhavāir guṇāiḥ
by the innate-nature-arising guṇas.

The actions of the brāhmans, the kṣatriyas, the vāiśyas
And of the śūdras, Scorcher of the Foe,
Are distributed according to
The guṇas which arise from innate nature.

brāhmaṇa (m.), brāhman, member of the brāhman caste.
kṣatriya (m.), ksatriya, member of the warrior caste.
viś (m.), vaiśya, member of the merchant or farmer caste.
(*brāhmaṇakṣatryaviśām,* m. gen. pl., of the brāhmans, kṣatriyas and vāiśyas.)
śūdrāṇām (m. gen. pl.), of the śūdras, of the members of the fourth or servant caste.
ca, and.
paraṁtapa (m. voc. sg.), Scorcher of the Foe, epithet of Arjuna.
karmāṇi (n. nom. pl.), actions.
pravibhaktāni (n. nom. pl. p. pass. participle *pra vi* √*bhaj*), distributed, apportioned.
svabhāva, (m.), own nature, innate nature.
prabhavāis (m. inst. pl.), by arising, by existing.
(*svabhāvaprabhavāis,* m. inst. pl., TP cpd., by innate-nature-arising, by arising from innate nature.)
guṇāis (m. inst. pl.), by the guṇas.

42

शमो दमस् तपः शौचं
śamo damas tapaḥ śāucaṁ
tranquility, restraint, austerity, purity,

क्षान्तिर् आर्जवम् एव च ।
kṣāntir ārjavam eva ca
patience and uprightness,

ज्ञानं विज्ञानम् आस्तिक्यं
jñānaṁ vijñānam āstikyaṁ
knowledge, discrimination, religious faith,

ब्रह्मकर्म स्वभावजम् ॥
brahmakarma svabhāvajam
brāhman action, innate nature born.

Tranquility, restraint, austerity, purity,
Patience and uprightness,
Knowledge, discrimination and religious faith
Are brāhman action,* born of innate nature.

śamas (m. nom. sg.), tranquility, calmness.
damas (m. nom. sg.), restraint, taming, subduing, control.
tapas (n. nom. sg.), austerity, heat.
śāucam (n. nom. sg.), purity, cleanliness of mind and body.
kṣāntis (f. nom. sg.), patience.
ārjavam (n. nom. sg.), uprightness, honesty, sincerity.
eva, indeed (used as a rhythmic filler).
ca, and.
jñānam (n. nom. sg.), knowledge, wisdom.
vijñānam (n. nom. sg.), discrimination, discernment.
āstikyam (n. nom. sg.), piety, belief in God.
brahmakarma (n. nom. sg.), brāhman action, action of the brāhman caste.
svabhāva (m.), innate nature, own nature.
-jam (n. nom. sg. suffix), born, arising from.
(*svabhāvajam,* n. nom. sg., born of innate nature, arising from innate nature.)

* Thus states of mind, in Gītā psychology, also constitute action.

43

शौर्यं तेजो धृतिर् दाक्ष्यं
śauryaṁ tejo dhṛtir dākṣyaṁ
heroism, majesty, firmness, skill

युद्धे चाप्य् अपलायनम् ।
yuddhe cāpy apalāyanam
and in battle also not fleeing,

दानम् ईश्वरभावश्च
dānam īśvarabhāvaśca
generosity and lordly spirit,

क्षात्रं कर्म स्वभावजम् ॥
kṣātraṁ karma svabhāvajam
kṣatriya action innate nature born.

Heroism, majesty, firmness, skill,
Not fleeing in battle,
Generosity and lordly spirit
Are kṣatriya action, born of innate nature.

śauryam (n. nom. sg.), heroism, valor, might.
tejas (n. nom. sg.), splendor, majesty.
dhṛtis (f. nom. sg.), courage, steadfastness, firmness.
dākṣyam (n. nom. sg.), skill, virtuosity, dexterity.
yuddhe (n. loc. sg.), in battle, in fighting.
ca, and.
api, also, even.
apalāyanam (n. nom. sg.), not fleeing, not disappearing from the battlefield.
dānam (n. nom. sg.), generosity, charity, giving.
īśvarabhāvas (m. nom. sg.), lordly being, lordly spirit.
ca, and.
kṣātram (n. nom. sg.), related to the kṣatriya or warrior caste.
karma (n. nom. sg.), action.
svabhāvajam (n. nom. sg.), born of innate nature, produced by innate nature.

44

कृषिगौरक्ष्यवाणिज्यं
kṛṣigāurakṣyavāṇijyaṁ
plowing, cow-herding, trade,

वैश्यकर्म स्वभावजम् ।
vāiśyakarma svabhāvajam
vāiśya action, innate nature born;

परिचर्यात्मकम् कर्म
paricaryātmakam karma
service-type action,

शूद्रस्यापि स्वभावजम्
śūdrasyāpi svabhāvajam
of the śūdra, innate nature born.

Plowing, cow-herding and trade
Are vāiśya actions, born of innate nature.
Service-type action
Is born of the śūdra's innate nature.

kṛṣi (f.), plowing, cultivation, agriculture.
gāurakṣya (n.), cow-herding, cow protecting.
vāṇijyam (n. nom. sg.), trade, commerce.
(*kṛṣigāurakṣyavāṇijyam,* n. nom. sg., DV cpd. plowing, cow-herding and trade.)
vāiśya (m.), vāiśya, pertaining to the third, or merchant-farmer caste.
karma (n. nom. sg.), action.
(*vāiśyakarma,* n. nom. sg., TP cpd. vāisya action.)
svabhāvajam (n. nom. sg.), born of innate nature.
paricaryā (f. determinative noun from *pari* √*car*), service, doing service.
ātmakam (n. nom. sg. ifc.), type, of the nature of, consisting of.
(*paricaryātmakam,* n. nom. sg., TP cpd. consisting of service, "service-selved.")
karma (n. nom. sg.), action.
śūdrasya (m. gen. sg.), of the śūdra, of the members of the fourth or lowest caste, of the servant caste.
api, also, even.
svabhāvajam (n. nom. sg.), born of innate nature, arising from innate nature.

45

स्वे स्वे कर्मण्य् अभिरतः
sve sve karmaṇy abhirataḥ
in own repeated action content,

संसिद्धिं लभते नरः ।
saṁsiddhiṁ labhate naraḥ
perfection he attains, a man,

स्वकर्मनिरतः सिद्धिं
svakarmanirataḥ siddhiṁ
own action contented with, perfection

यथा विन्दति तच् छृणु ॥
yathā vindati tac chṛṇu
how he finds, that hear!

Content in his own repeated kind of action,
A man attains perfection.
Hear then how one who is content in his own action
Finds perfection:

sve sve (m. loc. sg.), in own repeated.
karmaṇi (n. loc. sg.), in action.
abhiratas (m. nom. sg. p. pass. participle *abhi* √*ram*), contented, satisfied, pleased.
saṁsiddhim (f. acc. sg.), perfection, success, fulfillment.
labhate (3rd sg. pr. indic. mid. √*labh*), he attains, he obtains.
naras (m. nom. sg.), man, a man.
svakarma (n.), own action, own deeds.
niratas (m. nom. sg.), content, satisfied, pleased.
(*svakarma-niratas*, m. nom. sg. TP cpd., content in own action.)
siddhim (f. acc. sg.), perfection, success, fulfillment.
yathā, how, in which way.
vindati (3rd sg. pr. indic. act. √2 *vid*), he finds.
tad (n. acc. sg.), that, this.
śṛṇu (2nd sg. imperative act. √*śru*), hear! learn!

46

यतः प्रवृत्तिर् भूतानां
yataḥ pravṛttir bhūtānāṁ
from whom the origin of beings,

येन सर्वम् इदं ततम् ।
yena sarvam idaṁ tatam
by whom all this universe pervaded,

स्वकर्मणा तम् अभ्यर्च्य
svakarmaṇā tam abhyarcya
by one's own action him worshipping,

सिद्धिं विन्दति मानवः ॥
siddhiṁ vindati mānavaḥ
perfection he finds, man.

By worshipping with his own proper action
Him from Whom beings have their origin,
Him by Whom all this universe is pervaded,
Man finds perfection.

yatas (m. abl. sg.), from whom.
pravṛttis (f. nom. sg.), origin, coming forth.
bhūtānām (n. gen. pl.), of beings, of creatures.
yena (m. inst. sg.), by whom.
sarvam idam (n. nom. sg.), all this, all this universe.
tatam (n. nom. sg. p. pass. participle √*tan*), pervaded, stretched, diffused.
svakarmaṇā (n. inst. sg.), by own action.
tam (m. acc. sg.), him, it.
abhyarcya (gerund *abhi* √*ṛc* √*arc*), worshipping, praising.
siddhim (f. acc. sg.), perfection, success, fulfillment.
vindati (3rd sg. pr. indic. act. √2 *vid*), he finds.
mānavas (m. nom. sg.), man, a man, a human being, a descendant of Manu, the primal patriarch.

47

श्रेयान् स्वधर्मो विगुणः
śreyān svadharmo viguṇaḥ
better own duty imperfect

परधर्मात् स्वनुष्ठितात् ।
paradharmāt svanuṣṭhitāt
than another's duty well performed;

स्वभावनियतं कर्म
svabhāvaniyataṁ karma
own-nature-prescribed action

कुर्वन् नाप्नोति किल्बिषम् ॥
kurvan nāpnoti kilbiṣam
performing, not one incurs guilt.

Better one's own duty,* though imperfect,
Than the duty of another well performed;
Performing action prescribed by one's own nature,
One does not incur evil.

śreyān (m. nom. sg. comparative), better, superior, preferable.
svadharmas (m. nom. sg.), own duty, own caste duty.
viguṇas (m. nom. sg.), imperfect, lacking, wanting.
paradharmāt (m. abl. sg.), than another's duty, than the duty of another caste.
svanuṣṭhitāt (m. abl. sg. *su anuṣṭhitāt*), well done, well performed, well executed.
svabhāva (m.), own nature, own being.
niyatam (n. acc. sg.), prescribed, controlled, subdued.
(*svabhāva-niyatam*, n. nom. sg. TP cpd., prescribed by one's own nature.)
karma (n. acc. sg.), action.
kurvan (n. nom. sg. pr. act. participle √*kṛ*), performing, doing.
na, not.
āpnoti (3rd sg. pr. indic. act. √*āp*), he incurs, one obtains, he attains.
kilbiṣam (n. acc. sg.), guilt, fault, sin, evil.

* Caste duty is meant here.

48

सहजं कर्म कौन्तेय
sahajaṁ karma kāunteya
together-born action, Son of Kuntī,

सदोषम् अपि न त्यजेत् ।
sadoṣam api na tyajet
with deficiency even, not one should abandon.

सर्वारम्भा हि दोषेण
sarvārambhā hi doṣeṇa
all undertakings indeed with deficiency

धूमेनाग्निर् इवावृताः ॥
dhūmenāgnir ivāvṛtāḥ
with smoke fire-like, enveloped.

One should not abandon one's inborn action
Even though it be deficient, Son of Kuntī.
Indeed, all undertakings are enveloped in deficiency
As fire is in smoke.

sahajam (n. acc. sg.), together-born, inborn.
karma (n. acc. sg.), action.
kāunteya (m. voc. sg.), Son of Kuntī, epithet of Arjuna.
sadoṣam (n. acc. sg.), with deficiency, with fault.
api, even, also.
na, not.
tyajet (3rd sg. optative act. √*tyaj*), one should abandon, he should abandon.
sarvārambhās (m. nom. pl. from *sarva ā* √*rambh*), all undertakings, all beginnings, all commencements.
hi, indeed.
doṣeṇa (n. inst. sg.), with deficiency, with fault, with error.
dhūmena (m. inst. sg.), with smoke, by smoke.
agnis (m. nom. sg.), fire, god of fire.
iva, like, similar.
āvṛtās (m. nom. pl. p. pass. participle *ā* √*vṛ*), enveloped, veiled, hidden.

49

असक्तबुद्धिः सर्वत्र
asaktabuddhiḥ sarvatra
unattached intelligence everywhere,

जितात्मा विगतस्पृहः।
jitātmā vigataspṛhaḥ
conquered self, disappeared desire,

नैष्कर्म्यसिद्धिं परमां
nāiṣkarmyasiddhiṁ paramāṁ
actionlessness perfection supreme

संन्यासेनाधिगच्छति ॥
saṁnyāsenādhigacchati
by renunciation, one attains.

With intelligence unattached at all times,
With conquered self, free from desire,
By recunciation, one attains
The supreme perfection of actionlessness.

asakta (p. pass. participle *a* √*sañj*), unattached, not clinging.
buddhis (f. nom. sg.), intelligence, discrimination, understanding.
(*asaktabuddhis*, m. nom. sg. BV cpd., whose intelligence is unattached.)
sarvatra, everywhere, on all sides, at all times.
jita (p. pass. participle √*ji*), conquered, subdued.
ātmā (m. nom. sg.), self.
(*jitātmā*, m. nom. sg. BV cpd., whose self is conquered).
vigata (p. pass. participle *vi* √*gam*), gone away, disappeared.
spṛhas (m. nom. sg.), deep desire, longing, envy.
(*vigataspṛhas*, m. nom. sg. BV cpd., whose desire has disappeared.)
nāiṣkarmya (n.), actionlessness, inactivity.
siddhim (f. acc. sg.), success, perfection, fulfillment.
(*nāiṣkarmya-siddhim*, f. acc. sg. TP cpd., perfection of actionlessness.)
paramām (f. acc. sg.), supreme.
saṁnyāsena (m. inst. sg.), by renunciation, through renunciation, by throwing down.
adhigacchati (3rd sg. pr. indic. act. *adhi* √*gam*), one goes to, one attains, he attains.

50

सिद्धिं प्राप्तो यथा ब्रह्म
siddhiṁ prāpto yathā brahma
perfection attained, how brahman

तथाप्नोति निबोध मे ।
tathāpnoti nibodha me
also one attains, learn from me,

समासेनैव कौन्तेय
samāsenāiva kāunteya
briefly, Son of Kuntī,

निष्ठा ज्ञानस्य या परा ॥
niṣṭhā jñānasya yā parā
state of knowledge which highest.

Learn from Me briefly, Son of Kuntī,
How one who has attained perfection
Also attains Brahman
Which is the highest state of knowledge.

siddhim (f. acc. sg.), perfection, success, fulfillment.
prāptas (m. nom. sg. p. pass. participle *pra* √*āp*), having attained, obtained.
yathā, how, in what way, in which way.
brahma (n. acc. sg.), Brahman.
tathā, thus, also.
āpnoti (3rd sg. pr. indic. act. √*āp*), he attains, one attains.
nibodha (2nd sg. imperative act. *ni* √*budh*), learn!
me (gen. abl. sg.), of me, from me.
samāsena (adv.), briefly, in brief.
eva, indeed (used as a rhythmic filler).
kāunteya (m. voc. sg.), Son of Kuntī, epithet of Arjuna.
niṣṭhā (f. nom. sg.), state, condition, position.
jñānasya (n. gen. sg.), of knowledge, of wisdom.
yā (f. nom. sg.), which.
parā (f. nom. sg.), highest, supreme.

51

बुद्ध्या विशुद्धया युक्तो
buddhyā viśuddhayā yukto
with intelligence pure yoked

धृत्यात्मानं नियम्य च ।
dhṛtyātmānaṁ niyamya ca
and with firmness self controlling

शब्दादीन् विषयांस् त्यक्त्वा
śabdādīn viṣayāṅs tyaktvā
sound beginning with, objects abandoning,

रागद्वेषौ व्युदस्य च ॥
rāgadveṣāu vyudasya ca
passion and hatred casting off,

Yoked with pure intelligence,
Controlling the self with firmness,
Abandoning sound and the other objects* of sense,
Casting off passion and hatred,

buddhyā (f. inst. sg.), by intelligence, with discrimination, with intuition.
viśuddhayā (f. inst. sg.), with pure, with cleansed, with purified.
yuktas (m. nom. sg. p. pass. participle √*yuj*), joined, disciplined in Yoga, yoked.
dhṛtyā (f. inst. sg.) with firmness, with steadfastness.
ātmānam (m. acc. sg.), self.
niyamya (gerund *ni* √*yam*), controlling, subduing.
ca, and.
śabda (m.), sound.
ādīn (m. acc. pl. ifc.), beginning with, and so forth, lit. "whose first was," etcetera.
(*śabda-ādīn*, m. acc. pl. TP cpd., beginning with sound.)
viṣayān (m. acc. pl.), objects of the senses, spheres of the senses.
tyaktvā (gerund √*tyaj*), abandoning, having abandoned.
rāga (m.), passion, vehement desire.
dveṣa (m.), hatred.
(*rāgadveṣāu*, m. acc. dual, DV cpd. desire and hatred, liking and disliking.)
vyudasya (gerund *vi ud* √2 *as*), rejecting, casting aside, abandoning.
ca, and.

---

* There are five objects, or "provinces" (*viṣayās*), of the senses (*indriyāṇi*):

1. *śabda* or *śruti viṣaya* (sound) for the ear.
2. *sparśa viṣaya* (tangibility) for the touch.
3. *rūpa viṣaya* (form) for the eye.
4. *rasa viṣaya* (flavor) for the tongue.
5. *gandha viṣaya* (smell) for the nose. And these are often referred to as the *guṇas* respectively of: (1) ether; (2) air; (3) fire; (4) water; (5) earth.

52

विविक्तसेवी लघ्वाशी
viviktasevī laghvāśī
solitary dwelling, lightly eating,

यतवाक्कायमानसः ।
yatavākkāyamānasaḥ
controlled speech, body (and) mind,

ध्यानयोगपरो नित्यं
dhyānayogaparo nityaṁ
meditation Yoga devoted-to constantly,

वैराग्यं समुपाश्रितः ॥
vāirāgyaṁ samupāśritaḥ
dispassion taking refuge in,

Dwelling in solitude, eating lightly,
Controlling speech, body and mind,
Constantly devoted to Yoga meditation,
Taking refuge in dispassion,

vivikta (p. pass. participle *vi* √*vic*), separated, isolated, solitary.
sevī (m. nom. sg. ifc.), inhabiting, dwelling, frequenting.
(*vivikta-sevī*, m. nom. sg. TP cpd., dwelling in solitude.)
laghu (m.), light, lightly, easily digested.
āśī (m. nom. sg. ifc.), eating, consuming.
(*laghu-āśī*, m. nom. sg. TP cpd., eating little.)
yata (p. pass. participle √*yam*), controlled, subdued.
vāc (f.), speech, talk.
kāya (m.), body, bodily frame.
mānasas (n. nom. sg. ifc.), belonging to the mind, thought.
(*yatavākkāyamānasas*, m. nom. sg. BV cpd., whose speech, body and mind are controlled.)
dhyāna (n.), meditation.
yoga (m.), Yoga.
paras (m. nom. sg. ifc.), devoted to, holding as highest object.
(*dhyānayogaparas*, m. nom. sg., TP cpd. devoted to meditation-Yoga, devoted to the Yoga of meditation.)
nityam (adv.), eternally, constantly, perpetually.
vāirāgyam (n. acc. sg.), dispassion, disinterest, impartiality.
samupāśritas (m. nom. sg. p. pass. participle *sam upa ā* √*śri*), taking refuge in, being supported by.

53

अहंकारं बलं दर्पं
ahaṁkāraṁ balaṁ darpaṁ
egotism, force, arrogance,

कामं क्रोधं परिग्रहम् ।
kāmaṁ krodhaṁ parigraham
desire, anger (and) possession

विमुच्य निर्ममः शान्तो
vimucya nirmamaḥ śānto
relinquishing; unselfish, tranquil,

ब्रह्मभूयाय कल्पते ॥
brahmabhūyāya kalpate
for oneness with Brahman one is fit.

Relinquishing egotism, force, arrogance,
Desire, anger and possession of property;
Unselfish, tranquil,
One is fit for oneness with Brahman.

ahaṁkāram (m. acc. sg.), egotism, "I making," ego-consciousness.
balam (n. acc. sg.), force, might, strength.
darpam (m. acc. sg.), arrogance, pride.
kāmam (m. acc. sg.), desire, longing.
krodham (m. acc. sg.), anger, fury, wrath.
parigraham (m. acc. sg.), grasping, laying hold of, possessing, possession of property.
vimucya (gerund *vi* √*muc*), relinquishing, abandoning.
nirmamas (m. nom. sg.), unselfish, "not mine," not acquisitive.
śāntas (m. nom. sg.), tranquil, calm, at peace.
brahma (n.), Brahman.
bhūyāya (n. dat. sg.), to oneness with.
(*brahmabhūyāya,* n. dat. sg., to oneness with Brahman, for Brahman's being.)
kalpate (3rd pr. indic. mid. sg. √*klp*), he is fit, he is adapted, one is fit.

54

ब्रह्मभूतः प्रसन्नात्मा
brahmabhūtaḥ prasannātmā
Brahman absorbed, the serene self

न शोचति न काङ्क्षति ।
na śocati na kāṅkṣati
not he mourns, not he desires,

समः सर्वेषु भूतेषु
samaḥ sarveṣu bhūteṣu
impartial among all beings

मद्भक्तिं लभते पराम् ॥
madbhaktiṁ labhate parām
me devotion to, he attains, supreme.

Absorbed in Brahman, he whose self is serene
Does not mourn, nor does he desire;
Impartial among all beings*
He attains supreme devotion to Me.

brahmabhūtas (m. nom. sg.), absorbed in Brahman, at one with Brahman.
prasanna (p. pass. participle *pra* √*sad*), serene, tranquil, soothed, kindly.
ātmā (m. nom. sg.), self.
(*prasannātmā*, m. nom. sg. BV cpd., whose self is serene.)
na, not.
śocati (3rd sg. pr. indic. act. √*śuc*), he grieves, he mourns.
na, not.
kāṅkṣati (3rd sg. pr. indic. act. √*kāṅkṣ*), he desires, he longs for, he hankers after.
samas (m. nom. sg.), the same, impartial, dispassionate.
sarveṣu (m./n. loc. pl.), in all, among all.
bhūteṣu (m./n. loc. pl.), in beings, among beings, among creatures.
madbhaktim (f. acc. sg.), devotion to me, love for me.
labhate (3rd sg. pr. indic. mid. √*labh*), he attains, he reaches.
parām (f. acc. sg.), supreme, highest.

* Impartial, lit. "the same," i.e. regarding his own *ātman* (self) as identical with the *ātmans* of all beings.

55

भक्त्या माम् अभिजानाति
bhaktyā mām abhijānāti
by devotion to me he comes to know

यावान् यश्चास्मि तत्त्वतः।
yāvān yaścāsmi tattvataḥ
how great and who I am in reality,

ततो मां तत्त्वतो ज्ञात्वा
tato māṁ tattvato jñātvā
then me in reality having known

विशते तदनन्तरम्॥
viśate tadanantaram
he enters (me) immediately.

bhakyā (f. inst. sg.), by devotion, by love, with devotion.
mām (acc. sg.), me, to me.
abhijānāti (3rd sg. pr. indic. act. *abhi* √*jñā*), he comes to know, one comes to realize.
yāvān (m. nom. sg.), how great, how much.
yas (m. nom. sg.), who.
ca, and.
asmi (1st sg. pr. indic. √*as*), I am.
tattvatas (n. abl. sg.), in truth, in reality.
tatas, then, from there.
mām (acc. sg.), me.
tattvatas (n. abl. sg.), in truth, in reality.
jñātvā (gerund √*jñā*), having known, knowing.
viśate (3rd sg. pr. indic. mid. √*viś*), he enters, one enters.
tadanantaram (adv.), immediately, thereupon.

By devotion to Me he comes to know
How great and who I am in truth,
Then having known Me in truth
He enters Me immediately.

56

सर्वकर्माण्य् अपि सदा
sarvakarmāṇy api sadā
all actions, moreover, always

कुर्वाणो मद्व्यपाश्रयः ।
kurvāṇo madvyapāśrayaḥ
performing, me trusting in,

मत्प्रसादाद् अवाप्नोति
matprasādād avāpnoti
from my grace he attains

शाश्वतं पदम् अव्ययम् ॥
śāśvataṁ padam avyayam
the eternal abode, imperishable.

Performing all actions,
He whose reliance is always on Me,
Attains, by My grace,
The eternal, imperishable abode.

sarvakarmāṇi (n. acc. pl.), all actions.
api, moreover, also, even.
sadā, always, perpetually, forever.
kurvāṇas (m. nom. sg. pr. participle mid. √*kṛ*), doing, performing.
madvyapāśrayas (m. nom. sg. from *mat vi apa ā* √*śri*), trusting in me, taking refuge in me.
matprasādāt (m. abl. sg.), from my grace, from my kindness, from my favor.
avāpnoti (3rd sg. pr. indic. act. *ava* √*āp*), he attains, one attains, one obtains.
śāśvatam (n. acc. sg.), eternal, perpetual.
padam (n. acc. sg.), home, abode.
avyayam (n. acc. sg.), imperishable, unchanging.

57

चेतसा सर्वकर्माणि
cetasā sarvakarmāṇi
by thought all actions

मयि संन्यस्य मत्परः ।
mayi saṁnyasya matparaḥ
on me renouncing, me devoted-to as supreme,

बुद्धियोगम् उपाश्रित्य
buddhiyogam upāśritya
intelligence-Yoga taking refuge in,

मच्चित्तः सततं भव ॥
maccittaḥ satataṁ bhava
me thinking (of) constantly be!

Relinquishing by thought
All actions to Me, devoted to Me as Supreme,
Taking refuge in intuitive determination,
Constantly be thinking of Me.

cetasā (n. inst. sg.), by thought, by mind.
sarvakarmāṇi (n. acc. pl.), all actions.
mayi (loc. sg.), on me, in me.
saṁnyasya (gerund *sam ni* √2 *as*), renouncing, relinquishing, throwing down.
matparas (m. nom. sg.), devoted to me, holding me as highest object, holding me as supreme.
buddhiyogam (m. acc. sg. TP cpd.), intelligence-Yoga, the Yoga of intelligence, the Yoga of understanding, intuitive determination, trained intuition.
upāśritya (gerund *upa ā* √*śri*), taking refuge in, depending upon.
maccittas (m. nom. sg.), thinking of me, with mind on me.
satatam (adv.), perpetually, constantly.
bhava (2nd sg. imperative act. √*bhū*), be! become!

58

मच्चित्तः सर्वदुर्गाणि
maccittaḥ sarvadurgāṇi
of me thinking, all difficulties

मत्प्रसादात् तरिष्यसि ।
matprasādāt tariṣyasi
from my grace thou shalt pass over;

अथ चेत् त्वम् अहंकारान्
atha cet tvam ahaṁkārān
but if thou from egotism

न श्रोष्यसि विनङ्क्ष्यसि ॥
na śroṣyasi vinaṅkṣyasi
not thou shalt listen, thou shalt perish.

Thinking of Me, thou shalt pass over
All difficulties, through My grace;
But if, through egotism, thou wilt not listen,
Then thou shalt perish.

maccitas (m. nom. sg.), thinking of me, with mind on me.
sarva, all.
durgāṇi (n. acc. pl.), difficulties, "hard goings," obstacles.
matprasādāt (m. abl. sg.), from my grace, from my favor.
tariṣyasi (2nd sg. act. future act. √*tṛ*), thou shalt pass over, thou shalt transcend.
atha, but, however.
ced, if.
tvam (nom. sg.), thou.
ahaṁkārāt (m. abl. sg.), from egotism, from "I making."
na, not.
śroṣyasi (2nd sg. future act. √*śru*), thou shalt hear, thou shalt listen, thou wilt listen.
vinaṅkṣyasi (2nd sg. future act. *vi* √*naś*), thou shalt be lost, thou shalt perish.

59

यद् अहंकारम् आश्रित्य
yad ahaṁkāram āśritya
when egotism taking refuge in

न योत्स्य इति मन्यसे ।
na yotsya iti manyase
"not I shall fight" thus thou thinkest,

मिथ्यैष व्यवसायस् ते
mithyāiṣa vyavasāyas te
vain this resolve of thee;

प्रकृतिस् त्वां नियोक्ष्यति ॥
prakṛtis tvāṁ niyokṣyati
(thine own) material nature, thee, it will command.

yad (n. acc. sg.), which, when.
ahaṁkāram (m. acc. sg.), egotism, "I making."
āśritya (gerund *ā* √*śri*), taking refuge in, depending on.
na, not.
yotsya (*saṁdhi* for *yotsye* 1st sg. mid. future √*yudh*), I shall fight, I may fight.
iti, thus (often used to close a quotation).
manyase (2nd sg. pr. indic. mid. √*man*), thou thinkest, thou imaginest.
mithyā (adv.), vain, untrue, hopeless.
eṣas (m. nom. sg.), this.
vyavasāyas (m. nom. sg.), resolve, determination.
te (gen. sg.), of thee, thy.
prakṛtis (f. nom. sg.), nature, material nature.
tvām (acc. sg.), thee.
niyokṣyati (3rd sg. act. future *ni* √*yuj*), it will enjoin, it will command.

If, taking refuge in egotism,
Thou thinkest "I shall not fight," thus,
Vain will be this, thy resolve.
Thine own material nature will command thee.

60

स्वभावजेन कौन्तेय
svabhāvajena kāunteya
by born of own nature, Son of Kuntī,

निबद्धः स्वेन कर्मणा ।
nibaddhaḥ svena karmaṇā
bound by own karma

कर्तुं नेच्छसि यन् मोहात्
kartuṁ necchasi yan mohāt
to do not thou wishest, what, from delusion

करिष्यस्य् अवशो ऽपि तत् ॥
kariṣyasy avaśo 'pi tat
thou shalt do, against will, even that.

What thou wishest not to do, through delusion,
Thou shalt do even that
Against thy will, Son of Kuntī,
Bound by thine own karma,* born of thine own material nature.

svabhāvajena (n. inst. sg.), by own nature born, by originating in own nature.
kāunteya (m. voc. sg.), Son of Kuntī, epithet of Arjuna.
nibaddhas (m. nom. sg. p. pass. participle *ni* √*bandh*), bound, bound down.
svena (inst. sg.), by own, by one's own, by thine own.
karmaṇā (n. inst. sg.), by action, by karma.
kartum (infinitive √*kṛ*), to do, to make.
na, not.
icchasi (2nd sg. pr. indic. √*iṣ*), thou desirest, thou wishest.
yad (n. nom. sg.), what, which.
mohāt (m. abl. sg.), from delusion, from confusion.
kariṣyasi (2nd sg. act. future √*kṛ*), thou shalt do, thou shalt perform, thou shalt make.
avaśas (m. nom. sg.), without will, against will, willy-nilly.
api, even, also.
tad (n. acc. sg.), that, this.

* I have left the word "*karma*" untranslated here, as it refers in this case, not to action in general, but to fate resulting from action in a previous incarnation. Arjuna is foredoomed to certain actions by the laws governing his "material nature" as a kṣatriya, or member of the warrior caste.

61

ईश्वरः सर्वभूतानां
īśvaraḥ sarvabhūtānāṁ
the Lord of all beings

हृद्देशे ऽर्जुन तिष्ठति ।
hṛddeśe 'rjuna tiṣṭhati
in the heart region, Arjuna, he abides,

भ्रामयन् सर्वभूतानि
bhrāmayan sarvabhūtāni
causing to move all beings

यन्त्रारूढानि मायया ॥
yantrārūḍhāni māyayā
on a machine fixed by power of illusion.

The Lord abides in the heart
Of all beings, Arjuna,
Causing all beings to move
By the power of illusion, as if fixed on a machine.*

īśvaras (m. nom. sg.), Lord, The Lord.
sarvabhūtānām (n. gen. pl.), of all beings, of all creatures.
hṛd (n.), heart.
deśe (m. loc. sg.), in the region, in the place, in the direction.
(*hṛd-deśe*, m. loc. sg. TP cpd., in the region of the heart.)
arjuna (m. voc. sg.), Arjuna.
tiṣṭhati (3rd sg. pr. indic. act. √*sthā*), he stands, he abides, he exists.
bhrāmayan (m. nom. sg. causative pr. participle), causing to move, causing to wander.
sarvabhūtāni (n. acc. pl.), all beings, all creatures.
yantra (n.), machine, mechanism.
ārūḍhāni (n. acc. pl. p. pass. participle *ā* √*ruh*), fixed to, attached to, mounted on.
(*yantrārūḍhāni*, n. acc. pl. TP cpd., fixed to a mechanism, attached to a machine, mounted on a machine.)
māyayā (f. inst. sg.), by power of illusion, by magic.

* Like puppets fixed to a merry-go-round, an interpretation made by Śaṁkara (*circa* 800 A.D.).

62

तम् एव शरणं गच्छ
tam eva śaraṇaṁ gaccha
to him alone, the refuge, go!

सर्वभावेन भारत।
sarvabhāvena bhārata
with (thy) whole being, Descendant of Bharata,

तत्प्रसादात् परां शान्तिं
tatprasādāt parāṁ śāntiṁ
from that grace supreme peace

स्थानं प्राप्स्यसि शाश्वतम्॥
sthānaṁ prāpsyasi śāśvatam
abode thou shalt attain, eternal.

tam (m. acc. sg.), to him, him, it.
eva, indeed, alone (often used as a rhythmic filler).
śaraṇam (n. acc. sg.), refuge, shelter, place of rest.
gaccha (2nd sg. imperative act. √*gam*), go!
sarvabhāvena (m. inst. sg.), with whole being, with all being.
bhārata (m. voc. sg.), Descendant of Bharata, epithet of Arjuna.
tatprasādāt (m. abl. sg.), from that grace, from this favor.
parām (f. acc. sg.), supreme, highest.
śāntim (f. acc. sg.), peace, tranquility.
sthānam (n. acc. sg.), home, abode.
prāpsyasi (2nd sg. future, act. *pra* √*āp*), thou shalt attain, thou shalt reach.
śāśvatam (n. acc. sg.), eternal, imperishable.

Go to Him alone for refuge
With thy whole being, Descendant of Bharata.
From that grace, thou shalt attain
Supreme peace and the eternal abode.

63

इति ते ज्ञानम् आख्यातं
iti te jñānam ākhyātaṁ
thus to thee knowledge expounded

गुह्याद् गुह्यतरं मया ।
guhyād guhyataraṁ mayā
than the secret more secret by me.

विमृश्यैतद् अशेषेण
vimṛśyāitad aśeṣeṇa
reflecting on this without remainder,

यथेच्छसि तथा कुरु ॥
yathecchasi tathā kuru
as thou desirest, thus do!

Thus to thee by Me has been expounded
The knowledge that is more secret than the secret.
Having reflected on this fully,
Do as thou desirest.

iti, thus, in this way, so.
te (dat. sg.), to thee.
jñānam (n. nom. sg.), knowledge, wisdom.
ākhyātam (n. nom. sg. p. pass. participle *ā* √*khya*), told, explained, expounded.
guhyāt (m. abl. sg.), than secret, than the secret.
guhyataram (m. acc. sg. comparative), more secret.
mayā (inst. sg.), by me.
vimṛśya (gerund *vi* √*mṛś*), reflecting on, having considered, having felt.
etad (n. acc. sg.), this.
aśeṣeṇa (m./n. inst. sg.), without remainder, wholly, in toto, entirely.
yathā, how, as, in which way.
icchasi (2nd sg. pr. indic. act. √*iṣ*), thou desirest, thou wishest.
tathā, thus, in this way, so.
kuru (2nd sg. imperative act. √*kṛ*), do! make! perform!

64

सर्वगुह्यतमं भूयः
sarvaguhyatamaṁ bhūyaḥ
of all most secret again,

शृणु मे परमं वचः।
śṛṇu me paramaṁ vacaḥ
hear of me the supreme word;

इष्टो ऽसि मे दृढम् इति
iṣṭo 'si me dṛḍham iti
loved thou art of me surely;

ततो वक्ष्यामि ते हितम्॥
tato vakṣyāmi te hitam
therefore I shall speak (for) thy good.

Hear again My supreme word,
Most secret of all.
Thou art surely loved by Me;
Therefore, I shall speak for thy good.

sarvaguhyatamam (n. acc. sg. superl.), of all most secret, most secret of all.
bhūyas, again, further.
śṛṇu (2nd sg. imperative act. √*śru*), hear! learn!
me (gen. sg.), of me, my.
paramam (n. acc. sg. superl.), highest, supreme.
vacas (n. acc. sg.), word, discourse, doctrine.
iṣṭas (m. nom. sg. p. pass. participle √*iṣ*), loved, desired.
asi (2nd sg. pr. indic. √*as*), thou art.
me (gen. sg.), of me, by me.
dṛḍham (adv.), surely, firmly, closely.
iti, thus, so.
tatas, from there, therefore.
vakṣyāmi (1st sg. future act. √*vac*), I shall speak, I shall disclose.
te (gen. sg.), of thee, thy.
hitam (m. acc. sg. p. pass. participle √*dhā*), advantage, benefit, good.

65

मन्मना भव मद्भक्तो
manmanā bhava madbhakto
me devoted be, me worshipping,

मद्याजी मां नमस्कुरु ।
madyājī māṁ namaskuru
to me sacrificing, to me make reverence,

माम् एवैष्यसि सत्यं ते
mām evāiṣyasi satyaṁ te
to me in this way thou shalt go truly; to thee

प्रतिजाने प्रियो ऽसि मे ॥
pratijāne priyo 'si me
I promise, dear thou art to me.

Fix thy mind on Me, worshipping Me,
Sacrificing to Me, make reverence to Me;
In this way thou shalt go truly to Me,
I promise, for thou art dear to Me.

manmanās (m. nom. sg.), with zeal for me, me-minded, (as BV cpd.) whose mind is fixed on me.
bhava (2nd sg. imperative act. √*bhū*), be! become!
madbhaktas (m. nom. sg. p. pass. participle *mat* √*bhaj*), me-worshipping, devoted to me.
madyājī (m. nom. sg.), to me sacrificing, sacrificing to me.
mām (acc. sg.), me, to me.
namaskuru (2nd sg. imperative act. *namas* √*kṛ*), make reverence! bow to!
mām (acc. sg.), me, to me.
eva, thus, in this way (often used as a rhythmic filler).
eṣyasi (2nd sg. future act. √*i*), thou shalt come, thou shalt go.
satyam (adv.), truly, in reality.
te (dat. sg.), to thee.
pratijāne (1st sg. pr. indic. mid. prati √*jñā*), I promise, I acknowledge.
priyas (m. nom. sg.), dear, favored.
asi (2nd sg. pr. indic. √*as*), thou art.
me (gen. sg.), of me, to me.

66

सर्वधर्मान् परित्यज्य
sarvadharmān parityajya
all duties abandoning,

माम् एकं शरणं व्रज ।
mām ekaṁ śaraṇaṁ vraja
(in) me alone refuge take.

अहं त्वा सर्वपापेभ्यो
ahaṁ tvā sarvapāpebhyo
I thee from all evils

मोक्षयिष्यामि मा शुचः ॥
mokṣayiṣyāmi mā śucaḥ
I shall cause to be released, do not grieve.

Abandoning all duties,
Take refuge in Me alone.
I shall cause thee to be released
From all evils; do not grieve.

sarvadharmān (m. acc. pl.), all duties, all usages.
parityajya (gerund *pari* √*tyaj*), abandoning, relinquishing.
mām (acc. sg.), me, to me, in me.
ekam (n. acc. sg.), alone, one.
śaraṇam (n. acc. sg.), refuge, place of rest.
vraja (2nd sg. imperative act. √*vraj*), take! vow!
aham (nom. sg.), I.
tvā (acc. sg.), thee.
sarvapāpebhyas (m. abl. pl.), from all evils, from all wrongs.
mokṣayiṣyāmi (1st sg. causative future act. √*muc*), I shall release, I shall cause to be released.
mā (prohibitive), do not, never.
śucas (2nd sg. aorist subjunctive √*śuc*), thou shouldst grieve.
(*mā śucas,* do not grieve.)

67

इदं ते नातपस्काय
idaṁ te nātapaskāya
this from thee not to one without austerity

नाभक्ताय कदाचन।
nābhaktāya kadācana
not to one who neglects worship, at any time,

न चाशुश्रूषवे वाच्यं
na cāśuśrūṣave vācyaṁ
and not to one who does not desire to hear what is to be said

न च मां यो ऽभ्यसूयति ॥
na ca māṁ yo 'bhyasūyati
and not (to one) me who speaks evil of.

This shall not be spoken of by thee to one who is without austerity,
Nor to one who neglects worship at any time,
Nor to one who does not desire to hear what is to be said,
Nor to one who speaks evil of Me.

idam (n. nom. sg.), this.
te (gen. sg.), of thee, from thee.
na, not.
atapaskāya (m. dat. sg.), to one who neglects austerity, to one who fails to perform austerities.
na, not.
abhaktāya (m. dat. sg.), to one who neglects worship, to one who is not devoted.
kadācana, at any time, at any time whatever.
na, not.
ca, and.
aśuśrūṣave (m. dat. sg. from desiderative √*śru*), to one who does not desire to hear, to one who wishes not to listen, to the non-obedient.
vācyam (n. nom. sg. gerundive √*vac*), to be said, what is to be said.
na, not.
ca, and.
mām (acc. sg.), me.
yas (m. nom. sg.), who.
abhyasūyati (3rd sg. pr. indic. act. verb derived from *abhi* √*asūya*), he speaks evil of, he shows indignation toward, he sneers at.

68

य इदं परमं गुह्यं
ya idaṁ paramaṁ guhyaṁ
who this supreme secret

मद्भक्तेष्व् अभिधास्यति ।
madbhakteṣv abhidhāsyati
to my worshippers he shall set forth,

भक्तिं मयि परां कृत्वा
bhaktiṁ mayi parāṁ kṛtvā
devotion to me highest having made,

माम् एवैष्यत्य् असंशयः ॥
mām evāiṣyaty asaṁśayaḥ
to me he shall go without doubt.

yas (m. nom. sg.), who.
idam (n. acc. sg.), this.
paramam (n. acc. sg.), supreme, highest.
guhyam (n. acc. sg.), secret.
madbhakteṣu (m. loc. pl.), in my worshippers, to my devotees.
abhidhāsyati (3rd sg. act. future *abhi* √*dhā*), he shall set forth, he shall explain.
bhaktim (f. acc. sg.), devotion, love.
mayi (loc. sg.), in me, to me.
parām (f. acc. sg.), highest, supreme.
kṛtvā (gerund √*kṛ*), having made, performing.
mām (acc. sg.), me, to me.
eva, indeed (used as a rhythmic filler).
eṣyati (3rd sg. future act. √*i*), he shall go, he shall come.
asaṁśayas (adv.), surely, without doubt.

He who shall set forth this Supreme Secret to My worshippers,
Having performed the highest devotion to Me,
Shall go to Me, without doubt.

69

न च तस्मान् मनुष्येषु
na ca tasmān manuṣyeṣu
and not than he among men

कश्चिन् मे प्रियकृत्तमः ।
kaścin me priyakṛttamaḥ
anyone to me more pleasing doing

भविता न च मे तस्माद्
bhavitā na ca me tasmād
shall be, and not to me than he

अन्यः प्रियतरो भुवि ॥
anyaḥ priyataro bhuvi
another dearer on earth.

na, not.
ca, and.
tasmāt (m. abl. sg.), than he, than this one.
manuṣyeṣu (m. loc. pl.), in men, among men, among mankind.
kaścid, anyone, anyone whoever.
me (dat. sg.), to me.
priyakṛttamas (m. nom. sg. compar.), more pleasing doing, more dear making, giving more pleasure.
bhavitā (3rd sg. periphrastic future act. √*bhū*), he shall be, he will be.
na, not.
ca, and.
me (dat. sg.), to me (or gen. sg.), of me.
tasmāt (m. abl. sg.), than he, than this one.
anyas (m. nom. sg.), other, another.
priyataras (m. nom. sg. compar.), dearer, more pleasing.
bhuvi (f. loc. sg.), on earth.

And no one among men shall
Do more pleasing service to Me than he,
And no other on earth
Shall be dearer to Me.

XVIII

70

अध्येष्यते च य इमं
adhyeṣyate ca ya imaṁ
and he shall study, who, this

धर्म्यं संवादम् आवयोः ।
dharmyaṁ saṁvādam āvayoḥ
sacred dialogue of ours

ज्ञानयज्ञेन तेनाहम्
jñānayajñena tenāham
with the knowledge sacrifice by him, I

इष्टः स्याम् इति मे मतिः ॥
iṣṭaḥ syām iti me matiḥ
loved should be, thus of me the thought.

And he who shall study this
Sacred dialogue of ours,
By him I should be loved
With the knowledge sacrifice; such is
My thought.

adhyeṣyate (3rd sg. future mid. *adhi* √*i*), he shall study, he shall recite.
ca, and.
yas (m. nom. sg.), who.
imam (m. acc. sg.), this.
dharmyam (m. acc. sg.), sacred, lawful, righteous.
saṁvādam (m. acc. sg.), dialogue, "together speaking," conversation.
āvayos (gen. dual), of us two, of ours.
jñānayajñena (m. inst. sg.), by the knowledge sacrifice, with the knowledge sacrifice.
tena (m. inst. sg.), by him, by this one.
aham (nom. sg.), I.
iṣṭas (m. nom. sg. p. pass. participle √*iṣ*), desired, loved.
syām (1st sg. optative act. √*as*), I should be, might I be.
iti, thus, in this way, so.
me (gen. sg.), of me, my.
matis (f. nom. sg.), thought, belief, opinion, mind.

71

श्रद्धावान् अनसूयश्च
śraddhāvān anasūyaśca
full of faith, not scoffing,

शृणुयाद् अपि यो नरः ।
śṛṇuyād api yo naraḥ
he should hear even who, the man,

सो ऽपि मुक्तः शुभाँल् लोकान्
so 'pi muktaḥ śubhāṅl lokān
he also, liberated, happy worlds

प्राप्नुयात् पुण्यकर्मणाम् ॥
prāpnuyāt puṇyakarmaṇām
he should attain of those of pure actions.

Even the man who hears it
With faith, not scoffing,
He also, liberated, should attain
The happy worlds of those whose actions are pure.

śraddhāvān (m. nom. sg.), full of faith.
anasūyas (m. nom. sg.), not scoffing, not sneering, not speaking evil.
ca, and.
śṛṇuyāt (3rd sg. optative act. √*śru*), he should hear, he should listen.
api, even, also.
yas (m. nom. sg.), who.
naras (m. nom. sg.), man, the man.
sas (m. nom. sg.), he, this one.
api, also, even.
muktas (m. nom. sg. p. pass. participle √*muc*), liberated, released.
śubhān (m. acc. pl.), happy, joyful.
lokān (m. acc. pl.), worlds.
prāpnuyāt (3rd sg. optative *act. pra* √*āp*), he should attain, he should reach.
puṇya (n.), pure, cleansed, purified.
karmaṇām (n. gen. pl.), of actions.
(*puṇyakarmaṇām*, n. gen. pl. BV cpd., of those of pure actions, of those whose actions are pure.)

72

कच्चिद् एतच् छ्रुतं पार्थ
kaccid etac chrutaṁ pārtha
has this been heard, Son of Pṛthā,

त्वयैकाग्रेण चेतसा ।
tvayāikāgreṇa cetasā
by thee with concentrated thought?

कच्चिद् अज्ञानसंमोहः
kaccid ajñānasaṁmohaḥ
have ignorance and delusion

प्रणष्टस् ते धनंजय ॥
praṇaṣṭas te dhanaṁjaya
been destroyed of thee, Conqueror of Wealth?

Has this been heard by thee, Son of Pṛthā,
With concentrated mind?
Have thine ignorance and delusion
Been destroyed, Conqueror of Wealth?

kaccid (n. nom. sg. interrog.), has it?
etad (n. nom. sg.), this.
śrutam (n. nom. sg. p. pass. participle √*śru*), heard, been heard.
pārtha (m. voc. sg.), Son of Pṛthā, epithet of Arjuna.
tvayā (inst. sg.), by thee.
ekāgreṇa (n. inst. sg.), with concentration, concentrated on one point.
cetasā (n. instr. sg.), with thought, with mind.
kaccid (n. nom. sg. interrog.), has it? have they?
ajñāna (n.), ignorance.
saṁmohas (m. nom. sg.), delusion, confusion.
(*ajñāna-saṁmohas*, m. nom. sg. TP cpd., delusion of ignorance.)
praṇaṣṭas (m. nom. sg. p. pass. participle *pra* √*naś*), destroyed, lost.
te (gen. sg.), of thee, thy.
dhanaṁjaya (m. voc. sg.), Conqueror of Wealth, epithet of Arjuna.

अर्जुन उवाच ।
arjuna uvāca
Arjuna spoke:

arjunas (m. nom. sg.), Arjuna.
uvāca (3rd sg. perf. act. √*vac*), he said, he spoke.

73

नष्टो मोहः स्मृतिर् लब्धा
naṣṭo mohaḥ smṛtir labdhā
lost delusion, wisdom gained

त्वत्प्रसादान् मयाच्युत ।
tvatprasādān mayācyuta
from thy grace by me, Unchanging One;

स्थितो ऽस्मि गतसंदेहः
sthito 'smi gatasaṁdehaḥ
standing I am (with) dispelled doubt.

करिष्ये वचनं तव ॥
kariṣye vacanaṁ tava
I shall do command of thee.

naṣṭas (m. nom. sg. p. pass. participle √*naś*), lost, destroyed.
mohas (m. nom. sg.), delusion, confusion.
smṛtis (f. nom. sg.), memory, wisdom.
labdhā (f. nom. sg. p. pass. participle √*labh*), obtained, gained.
tvat (abl. sg.), of thee, of thy.
prasādāt (m. abl. sg.), from grace, from kindness, from favor.
mayā (m. inst. sg.), by me.
acyuta (m. voc. sg.), Unchanging One, epithet of Krishna.
sthitas (m. nom. sg.), standing, existing.
asmi (1st sg. √*as*), I am.
gatasaṁdehas (m. nom. sg.), gone doubt, dispelled doubt.
kariṣye (1st sg. future mid. √*kṛ*), I shall do, I shall perform.
vacanam (n. acc. sg.), command, injunction.
tava (gen. sg.), of thee, thy.

Arjuna spoke:

Delusion is lost and wisdom gained,
Through Thy grace, by me, Unchanging One.
I stand with doubt dispelled.
I shall do Thy command.

XVIII

संजय उवाच ।
saṁjaya uvāca
Saṁjaya spoke:

saṁjayas (m. nom. sg.), Saṁjaya, the minister of King Dhṛtarāṣṭra, who has narrated the poem.
uvāca (3rd sg. perfect act. √*vac*), he said, he spoke.

74

इत्य् अहं वासुदेवस्य
ity ahaṁ vāsudevasya
thus, I of the Son of Vasudeva

पार्थस्य च महात्मनः ।
pārthasya ca mahātmanaḥ
and of the Son of Pṛthā great selved

संवादम् इमम् अश्रौषम्
saṁvādam imam aśrāuṣam
dialogue this I have heard,

अद्भुतं रोमहर्षणम् ॥
adbhutaṁ romaharṣaṇam
marvelous, causing the hair to stand on end.

iti, thus, in this way.
aham (nom. sg.), I.
vāsudevasya (m. gen. sg.), of the son of Vasudeva, i.e. of Krishna.
pārthasya (m. gen. sg.), of the Son of Pṛthā, i.e. of Arjuna.
ca, and.
mahātmanas (m. gen. sg. BV cpd.), him whose soul is great, him whose self is great.
saṁvādam (m. acc. sg.), dialogue, conversation, "together speaking."
imam (m. acc. sg.), this.
aśrāuṣam (1st sg. aorist act. √*śru*), I have heard.
adbhutam (m. acc. sg.), marvellous, miraculous, wondrous.
romaharṣaṇam (m. acc. sg.), causing the hair to stand on end, causing the hair to bristle.

Saṁjaya spoke:

Thus I have heard from the Son of Vasudeva
And the great-selved Son of Pṛthā,
This wondrous dialogue
Which causes the hair to stand on end.

75

व्यासप्रसादाच् छ्रुतवान्
vyāsaprasādāc chrutavān
by Vyāsa's grace one who has heard

एतद् गुह्यम् अहं परम् ।
etad guhyam ahaṁ param
this secret I supreme

योगं योगेश्वरात् कृष्णात्
yogaṁ yogeśvarāt kṛṣṇāt
Yoga from the Lord of Yoga, from Krishna,

साक्षात् कथयतः स्वयम् ॥
sākṣāt kathayataḥ svayam
before the eyes, speaking Himself.

By the grace of Vyāsa* I am one who has heard
This supreme and holy secret Yoga
Which Krishna, the Lord of Yoga, has divulged,
Before the eyes, speaking himself.

vyāsa (m.), Vyāsa, legendary sage, who is supposed to have compiled the Vedas as well as the Mahābhārata, and who is the natural grandfather of the Pāṇḍava princes.
prasādāt (m. abl. sg.), from grace, from the grace, from the favor.
(*vyāsaprasādāt,* m. abl. sg. TP cpd., by the grace of Vyāsa.)
śrutavān (m. nom. sg.), hearing, one who has heard.
etad (n. acc. sg.), this.
guhyam (n. acc. sg.), secret.
aham (nom. sg.), I.
param (n. acc. sg.), supreme.
yogam (m. acc. sg.), Yoga.
yoga (m.), Yoga.
īśvarāt (m. abl. sg.), from the Lord.
(*yogeśvarāt,* m. abl. sg., TP cpd. from the Lord of Yoga.)
kṛṣṇāt (m. abl. sg.), from Krishna.
sākṣāt (adv.), before the eyes.
kathayatas (m. abl. sg. pr. participle √*kath*), speaking, narrating, relating.
svayam (m. acc. sg.), himself, own.

* Vyāsa, legendary sage, compiler of the Vedas; also, according to legend, the natural father of Pāṇḍu and Dhṛtarāṣṭra, thus the grandfather of Arjuna, as well as of the Pāṇḍava princes along with the hundred sons of Dhṛtarāṣṭra. Vyāsa is also said to have compiled the Mahābhārata including the Gītā, though he must have existed before most of the events recounted in these works.

76

राजन् संस्मृत्य संस्मृत्य
rājan saṁsmṛtya saṁsmṛtya
O King, recollecting again and again

संवादम् इमम् अद्भुतम् ।
saṁvādam imam adbhutam
dialogue this marvelous

केशवार्जुनयोः पुण्यं
keśavārjunayoḥ puṇyaṁ
of the Handsome Haired One and Arjuna, holy,

हृष्यामि च मुहुर् मुहुः ॥
hṛṣyāmi ca muhur muhuḥ
and I rejoice again and again.

O King, recollecting again and again
This marvelous and holy dialogue
Of the Handsome Haired One and Arjuna,
I rejoice again and again.

rājan (m. voc. sg.), O King (refers to King Dhṛtarāṣṭra, to whom the poem has been narrated).
saṁsmṛtya (gerund *sam* √*smṛ*), recollecting, remembering.
(*saṁsmṛtya saṁsmṛtya,* recollecting again and again.)
saṁvādam (m. acc. sg.), dialogue, conversation, "together speaking."
imam (m. acc. sg.), this.
adbhutam (m. acc. sg.), marvellous, miraculous.
keśava, The Handsome Haired One, epithet of Krishna.
arjuna, Arjuna.
(*keśavārjunayos,* m. gen. dual, DV cpd. of the Handsome Haired One and Arjuna.)
puṇyam (m. acc. sg.), pure, sacred, holy.
hṛṣyāmi (1st sg. pr. indic. act. √*hṛṣ*), I rejoice, I am excited.
ca, and.
muhur muhur, again and again, constantly, at every moment.

77

तच् च संस्मृत्य संस्मृत्य
tac ca saṁsmṛtya saṁsmṛtya
and that recollecting again and again

रूपम् अत्यद्भुतं हरेः ।
rūpam atyadbhutaṁ hareḥ
the form marvelous of Hari (Krishna),

विस्मयो मे महान् राजन्
vismayo me mahān rājan
the amazement of me (is) great, O King,

हृष्यामि च पुनः पुनः ॥
hṛṣyāmi ca punaḥ punaḥ
and I rejoice again and again.

tad (n. acc. sg.), this, that.
ca, and.
saṁsmṛtya saṁsmṛtya (gerund *sam* √*smṛ*), recollecting again and again.
rūpam (n. acc. sg.), form, appearance.
atyadbhutam (n. acc. sg.), more than marvellous, extremely marvellous.
hares (m. gen. sg.), of Hari, epithet of both Krishna and Vishnu, of whom Krishna is the earthly avatār.
vismayas (m. nom. sg.), amazement, astonishment.
me (gen. sg.), of me, my.
mahān (m. nom. sg.), great.
rājan (m. voc. sg.), O King (referring to King Dhṛtarāṣṭra).
hṛṣyāmi (1st sg. pr. indic. act. √*hṛṣ*), I rejoice, I am excited.
ca, and.
punar punar, again and again.

And recollecting again and again
That marvelous form of Hari (Krishna)
My amazement is great, O King,
And I rejoice again and again.

78

यत्र योगेश्वरः कृष्णो
yatra yogeśvaraḥ kṛṣṇo
wherever the Lord of Yoga, Krishna,

यत्र पार्थो धनुर्धरः।
yatra pārtho dhanurdharaḥ
wherever the Son of Pṛthā, the archer,

तत्र श्रीर् विजयो भूतिर्
tatra śrīr vijayo bhūtir
there splendor, victory, wealth

ध्रुवा नीतिर् मतिर् मम ॥
dhruvā nītir matir mama
surely (and) righteousness, the thought of me.

yatra, where, wherever.
yogeśvaras (m. nom. sg.), the Lord of Yoga.
kṛṣnas (m. nom. sg.), Krishna.
yatra, where, wherever.
pārthas (m. nom. sg.), the Son of Pṛthā, epithet of Arjuna.
dhanus (n.), bow.
dharas (m. nom. sg.), holder.
(*dhanurdharas*, m. nom. sg., TP cpd. archer, bowman.)
tatra, there.
śrīs (f. nom. sg.), splendor, radiance.
vijayas (m. nom. sg.), victory.
bhūtis (f. nom. sg.), wealth, well-being, riches.
dhruvā (f. nom. sg.), sure, eternal.
nītis (f. nom. sg.), prudence, moral conduct, righteousness.
matis (f. nom. sg.), thought, opinion, mind.
mama (gen. sg.), of me, my.

Wherever there is Krishna, Lord of Yoga,
Wherever there is the Son of Pṛthā, the archer,
There, there will surely be
Splendor, victory, wealth and righteousness; this is my thought.

End of Book XVIII

The Yoga of Renunciation

Here ends the Bhagavadgītā Upanishad